MVS TSO/ISPF

J. Ranade IBM Series

MVS TSO/ISPF

A Guide for Users and Developers

Kurt Bosler

Boston, Massachusetts   Burr Ridge, Illinois
Debuque, Iowa   Madison, Wisconsin   New York, New York
San Francisco, California   St. Louis, Missouri

Library of Congress Cataloging-in-Publication Data

Bosler, Kurt.
    MVS TSO/ISPF : a guide for users and developers / by Kurt Bosler.

        p.   cm.
    Includes index.
    ISBN 0-07-006565-9
    1. Time-sharing computer systems. 2. IBM MVS. 3. ISPF dialog
manager. I. Title.
    QA76.53.B67   1993
    005.2'25—dc20   92-45745
                                                       CIP

McGraw-Hill

A Division of The McGraw·Hill Companies

   6 7 8 9 10 11 12 13 14 BKMBKM 9 9 8 7

ISBN 0-07-006565-9

*The editors for this book were Gerald T. Papke and Sally Anne Glover, and the
production supervisor was Katherine G. Brown. This book was set in Century Schoolbook.
It was composed by TAB Books.*

*For more information about other McGraw-Hill materials,
call 1-800-2-MCGRAW in the United States. In other
countries, call your nearest McGraw-Hill office.*

Contents

Part 2   Selecting and Viewing Data Sets

Part 3. The ISPF Editor

Part 4. ISPF Utilities

Part 8 Programmer Utilities

Preface

Time Sharing Option Extensions (*TSO*) and Interactive System Productivity Facility (*ISPF/PDF*) are among the most used and most valuable tools for accessing a mainframe computer. The products are very similar in function but very dissimilar in appearance. Together they provide basic functions for creating, viewing, modifying, and printing data. They support running tasks in the foreground, including the execution of CLIST and REXX EXEC code. Background execution is also supported, providing the means for job submission, tracking, control, and display. In addition, TSO and ISPF/PDF support program development. This includes source code conversion and program execution as well as ISPF dialog management testing and table maintenance.

Considering that many individuals spend several hours a day using TSO and ISPF, learning how to best use the products is a good investment. Using the products can eventually become second nature, but initially learning how to use them is not easy. Many of the subtle nuances can easily be overlooked. The products are so complex that they can be used for years without revealing some of the many helpful features and shortcuts that are available. This book will show you everything you need to know about TSO and ISPF to immediately become a productive user.

Intended for all levels of computer users, this book contains information for both programmers and computer end-users. Programming topics are separated from topics of universal interest and are placed at the end of the book. Chapter 41, which covers the execution of CLIST and REXX EXEC code, precedes the programming section, but this chapter might only be of interest to advanced users. Relevant data processing concepts are presented to allow those less familiar with data processing to benefit fully. Chapter 27, for example, discusses underlying data management concepts that are essential to data processing. The first part of chapter 42 discusses program development and explains what's involved with compile and link edit processing. Appendix A covers *JCL* (Job Control Language) jobcard parameters. These topics are not specific to TSO and ISPF, and you can skip them if they don't present information that's new or beneficial to you.

I cover a given topic in proportion to its expected use and importance. The very complex ISPF editor, for example, is featured in the largest of the eight parts. Where possible, the features discussed are graphically illustrated in more than 630 figures. This will make it easier for you to apply what you learn to actual use, since ISPF panel formats will already be very familiar.

The material in this book is typically presented in several separate courses. Comprehensive coverage of this sort is necessary to bring together the many elements encountered in the data processing environment and to provide exposure to the tools that are available. Knowing what can be done will help you choose the most appropriate function to apply in a given situation.

The book is divided into eight parts, with the most fundamental information in the earlier parts. The chapters within a part are also organized starting with the more basic information. The following is a summary of the eight parts.

Part 1 gives an overview of TSO and ISPF and tells how each product is accessed. This includes logon and logoff processing as well as starting and terminating ISPF.

Part 2 provides information on how to specify data set and member names and how to use the browse function to view data sets. Information here provides the background for data set and member selection in all other areas discussed.

Part 3 discusses the ISPF editor. Its many features are detailed in 17 chapters. The chapters cover the basic edit function, line commands, primary commands, data storage commands, data movement commands, special text editing features, and edit profiles. This part ends with a discussion of how to change certain fundamental characteristics of an edit session.

Part 4 discusses basic ISPF utilities. These are functions that all ISPF users should know and are likely to use. This part starts with a complete chapter that discusses general data management concepts. The chapter is followed by a discussion of the main ISPF utility for creating and deleting data sets. Utilities that provide for library member maintenance and copying data are also presented. The important topic of printing is covered in this part, as well as the popular data set list utility that allows ISPF users to perform various functions from a list of data sets, rather than use several different utilities.

Part 5 discusses more advanced utilities. These utilities are very useful but not necessarily crucial to basic ISPF functioning. The exception is chapter 34, which is very important to those who must view and exercise control over their background jobstreams. This chapter includes a discussion of the optional product SDSF. This part also includes the compare and search utilities as well as the ISPF tutorial.

Part 6 discusses various ways to customize the ISPF environment. This includes certain efficiency measures as well as making adjustments to the many ISPF settings. This is the last part on ISPF that would be of interest to all users.

Part 7 steps away from ISPF to describe the commands that are available to native TSO mode. CLIST and REXX EXEC processing are also discussed. These are subjects that might appeal only to programmers and the more advanced general user.

Part 8 incorporates the ISPF functions that are used to program in various third-generation languages. A small FORTRAN program is actually compiled, link edited, and run through the interactive debug facility. The dialog test option is also covered to describe how it can be used to aid in the development of ISPF dialog management applications.

The appendices briefly cover related subject material. Appendix A discusses job-card parameters. These are a part of the Job Control Language that's better known as JCL. The parameters are included because they can be seen on many ISPF screens that create and submit JCL for background execution. Appendix B briefly discusses edit macros, which are implemented by a separate element of ISPF but are used within the ISPF editor as if they were standard primary commands.

Text examples are highlighted to bring attention to a particular part of the screen. ISPF has its own, significantly different highlighting and use of color to signify input fields and draw attention to significant text. User-supplied data is generally represented in the book as lowercase characters to cause it to stand out from field labels, which are generally uppercase. In most instances, field data entered in lowercase characters is automatically translated to uppercase.

Wherever ISPF commands are mentioned, consider what PF keys can be used to invoke the command. This is especially true of the commands that are defined to PF keys by default. The END command, for example, would be easy to invoke because it's such a short command. Using PF key 3 or 15 makes the command easier to invoke and almost instinctive after using the key dozens of times during a typical ISPF session.

System Access

Software Overview

The software products TSO/E (Time Sharing Option Extensions) and ISPF (Interactive System Productivity Facility) can enhance computer access and greatly simplify working with the computer. Both TSO/E and ISPF run under *MVS* (Multiple Virtual Storage). MVS is a type of operating system and is used here to represent a range or evolution of operating system versions. Those operating systems provide fundamental services such as data management, scheduling, and resource control. They also support program execution including TSO/E, which, as its name implies, allows multiple users to use the system at one time. TSO/E supports foreground or real-time processing through its many commands. It also facilitates background or deferred processing using JCL (Job Control Language). TSO/E has a help function that lists and describes the syntax of its many commands. The commands that are available with TSO/E and the two languages (CLIST and REXX) that it supports are provided to satisfy the needs of computer system users. Users need not be programmers to need or make use of these services.

The ISPF/PDF (Program Development Facility) product was introduced to make TSO users more productive. Functionally equivalent to TSO/E services, ISPF features formatted screens, parameter validation, and a superior help facility that cause it to be used almost to the exclusion of the native TSO environment. By far the most useful function of the ISPF product is its editor. This is where most TSO/ISPF users spend most of their time, and the editor will dominate our discussions as well. In fact, all of ISPF/PDF will be featured over the equivalent TSO/E functions. Certain TSO/E functions will be highlighted, however, where they add significant value to the data processing environment.

There's another component of ISPF known as the *dialog manager*, which allows programmers to create their own screen applications that function much as the ISPF/PDF functions do. Discussion of the dialog manager component will be limited to the discussion of the dialog test option of PDF. Subsequent reference to ISPF will imply the ISPF/PDF facilities. The facilities available with TSO/E will be referred to simply as TSO.

Features of ISPF

ISPF is such a widely accepted product that it serves as the standard for much of the third-party software that's produced. By following ISPF standards, software vendors realize that their products will be easier to use and better accepted. Standard screen formats across ISPF options and across products that run under ISPF make tasks easier to perform. ISPF verifies many user-supplied parameters before a given task is executed. This expedites feedback to the user about the information they have supplied. It also saves computer time since tasks are not executed until needed information is correctly supplied.

Many execution parameters (field values) are saved not only during ISPF sessions, but also between sessions, making functions easier to invoke. ISPF also gives greater visibility to the requirements for task execution since all fields are labeled and often accompanied by comments. Help screens and tutorials further document function requirements, and help text is also context sensitive to facilitate its use. Movement to fields themselves is made easier with attribute bytes that can be quickly reached using tab keys. In some cases, the completion of one field will automatically cause the cursor to be placed in the next field.

Most installations customize ISPF in some way to suit their own needs. This might cause a different product look from what's presented here. Some installations might even try to limit the computer users' view of ISPF. If a particular installation doesn't present the basic features that are presented here, the TSO administrator should be approached for access to the standard ISPF product. ISPF also serves as the presentation platform for additional software products that your installation has acquired. Some installations even add their own ISPF-based functions. How and where these are installed might also change the way the ISPF product looks.

Types of ISPF Screens

ISPF is made up of four types of screens or panels. These are selection menus, data entry panels, table display screens, and tutorial panels. The selection menus are the basis for a hierarchy of functions. A function and/or subfunction is entered by selecting from listed screen options. Entering the number or letter that corresponds to a function tells the computer to move down into the hierarchy to invoke that function. The function in turn could be another selection menu pointing to other functions lower in the hierarchy. The network of selection menus also makes it possible to move laterally in the hierarchy. This is known as the *jump function*.

The lowest-level functions are represented by data entry or table display panels. Data entry panels serve to communicate information to a particular function. It assists the user in supplying the information by labeling what the information is. Data entry screens also typically contain validation routines that verify the data before it's passed to the function. The screens are designed to collect required information before invoking a given function. This feature, and checks made for data types and values, increase the user's chances of successfully executing the function. The ISPF user is often assisted by default information written to the screen before it's displayed, as well as default values that will be supplied if the user leaves a particular field blank. Users are also assisted by field values that are retained either within or between ISPF sessions.

To increase productivity, the entire ISPF hierarchy can be attached to a TSO session twice using the split screen function. This is especially useful when it's impossible or undesirable to leave the current function. Provision is also made for switching from one screen to the other using the swap function. When both screens are visible, the active screen is determined by the cursor position, making it very easy to activate one screen or the other.

Table display screens are often used when the ISPF user is called upon to select or work with certain pieces of data from a list. Screen displays and scrolling are automatically adjusted for the terminal type and the current screen split. The lists are scrollable to allow the user to work with more data than will fit on a single screen. A prominent example of this is the member list that can be used in several different options.

Tutorial and information panels are used to display information about ISPF itself. They're chained together in a hierarchy of their own, but can also be accessed from an index. They're also accessible from a context sensitive help function. The help function will sense which option is being executed and display help screens that are germane to that function. The help function can also be used after an ISPF error message to display more information about the error. A second request for help will display the tutorial screens that relate to the error situation.

Basic Screen Layout

There are common elements that appear in most ISPF screens. These elements are demonstrated in the next two figures. Figure 1.1 shows what the element is and where it typically appears. Figure 1.2 shows the application of those screen elements to an actual ISPF panel.

The first line of an ISPF screen contains the title line. The title line describes the active function, whether it's from a selection menu, data entry panel, or tutorial. The right extreme of the line is used to display short messages. This is a feedback area that's generally used to describe errors and warnings as well as messages indicating normal or successful completion.

The command or option line supports several types of input information. This includes option selections, ISPF commands, TSO commands, and temporary scroll amounts. This field is labeled as an option field when the screen has options that can be specified there. It's labeled as a command area when such options don't exist. Where selection options don't exist, the field can still be used for entering ISPF and TSO commands.

The scroll area doesn't exist on all panels. Screens that have a scroll field support movement of the screen up and down if not also left and right. Conceptually, scrolling "moves" the screen over the data to make other data visible. Recent en-

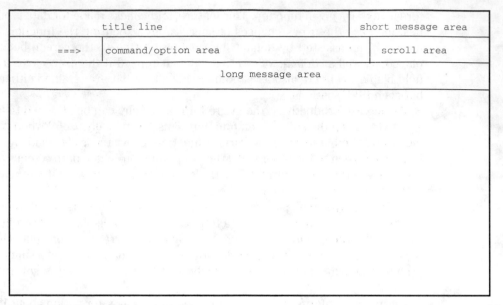

title line	short message area
===> command/option area	scroll area
long message area	

Figure 1.1 Basic screen elements.

```
EDIT ---- TSO1234.SAMPLE.DATA - 01.01 ---------------------- COLUMNS 001 072
COMMAND ===>                                                 SCROLL ===> CSR
****** **************************** TOP OF DATA ****************************
000001
000002
000003
000004
000005
000006
000007
000008
000009
000010
000011
000012
000013
000014
000015
000016
000017
000018
000019
000020
****** **************************** BOTTOM OF DATA ****************************
```

Figure 1.2 Application of basic screen elements.

hancements to ISPF allow scrolling to also reveal otherwise fixed panel fields. Several predefined scroll values are supported to define how much the screen will move when a scroll command is issued, or, a numeric value can be specified to represent the number of rows or columns that each scroll will encompass.

The long message area is located just below the line that contains the command and scroll areas. It complements the short message area with further text. This text is invoked using the HELP command after a short message is issued.

The particular screen that was used to demonstrate the screen areas is taken from the edit function. It has two distinct areas that are not available on all screens. These two areas are the line command and data areas. The line command area is to the extreme left of the screen displayed in Figure 1.2. In the edit function, the line command area is used to enter commands to modify data in the data portion of the screen, which is just to the right of the line command area.

2

Terminal Information

Display Characteristics

The terminal display characteristics can be adjusted to suit the individual. The manner in which the characteristics are changed varies by terminal type and should be documented in material supplied with the terminal, if not obvious from the labels on the keyboard and CRT. The terminal intensity on an IBM 3279 terminal, for example, is controlled by a dimmer switch on the CRT. On a 3180, the same characteristic is controlled by repeating a particular key sequence.

Certain characteristics take on additional significance based on how they're used by ISPF. One of these is the contrast, which determines the display intensity difference between information that's highlighted and information that's not. This is even more important when using a monochrome display because the ISPF product highlights pertinent information.

Another terminal characteristic that can be set is whether letters are displayed in uppercase or both uppercase and lowercase. On some terminals, this display characteristic is easily set with a toggle switch. In many cases, the case setting is not important because data can be automatically translated to uppercase, or either case can be accommodated by the application using it. There are times, however, when the case is important, and setting the terminal to display both uppercase and lowercase characters will avoid problems in these situations. This is primarily a consideration for using the ISPF editor on a source language that can't use lowercase, or conversely when creating text that should use lowercase. The editor has commands that convert to uppercase or lowercase, but using them might not be as convenient as creating the data with the proper case in the first place.

Special Keys

Before discussing any particular keys, it should be noted that many keyboards support an alternate key function. This allows key functions shown on the front of the key to be accessed by pressing the ALT key at the same time that the other key is pressed. Some terminals support a setup key that allows the terminal characteristics to be altered. This again is accomplished in combination with other keys once the setup environment has been established. The other keys to be discussed include those that control cursor movement, those that provide special functions throughout the TSO environment, and those that provide special functions only through ISPF or some other special program.

Cursor Control Keys

The space bar can be used to move the cursor from left to right. It removes data in its path. Other keys move the cursor without erasing data. These are known as the *cursor control keys*. These keys are normally identified by arrows that show the direction of cursor movement. Some keyboards support accelerated movement using these keys by pressing the ALT key at the same time. While it's generally safer to use these keys to position the cursor, there are times when their use will not produce the desired result. Specifically, in edit with nulls on or in most ISPF screen fields, use of the cursor control keys will not maintain proper spacing. After pressing the ENTER key, the data might collapse to the left. The space bar should be used to enter spaces and prevent this from happening.

Tab and New Line Keys

Cursor movement on ISPF screens is greatly facilitated using tab keys. That's because attribute bytes have been established on the screens to create fields. Use of the tab keys automatically positions the cursor behind the attribute byte. Information can then be entered in the screen field. The new line key works in a way similar to the forward tab key to position the cursor in the next field. This key is often represented by an arrow that points down and to the left. It's like the carriage return on a typewriter. It will locate the next left-most field and is especially suited for selecting items from lists (like member lists) and for getting to the next line in edit. A TSO session is efficient when using keys like this because they're controlled by a terminal controller. Such a device sits between the terminal and the CPU and controls low-level functions. Pressing the *ENTER* key or any program function key uses CPU time and is usually noticeably slower.

General Function Keys

Keys are available to support the insertion and deletion of characters. This is a hardware function that also takes place in the terminal control unit. Pressing the *INSERT* key places the terminal in insert mode. A caret is displayed in the operator information area to signify that insert mode is active. Information that's typed while in insert mode might "push" subsequent data ahead of it. At times, it might also be necessary to delete existing information at the end of a line or field to make room to insert. The *RESET* key is used to terminate the insert mode so that data can again be overwritten. The opposite function is performed by the *DELETE* character key, which will remove characters from the current cursor position. As characters are removed, the subsequent portion of the line or field data will collapse to the left. Because data can be moved when either key is used, they can be the basis of crude data shifting in addition to allowing data to be inserted or deleted.

Three keys are particularly important in the interrupt sequence. These keys are labeled *PA1, ATTN,* and *SYS REQ* and should be used in that order to interrupt processing. When a function is started, the terminal will become input inhibited. This normal condition is usually indicated in some fashion in the operator information area at the bottom of the screen. Usually, a clock is displayed indicating the time is required to process the request. The terminal operator can't enter new information while the terminal is input inhibited. Whether a command is entered in error or the terminal operator merely wishes to switch to a new function, it might be necessary to interrupt the current processing. The PA1 (Program Attention 1) key is the first key to use to interrupt processing. This key is normally effective against TSO commands and CLIST execution. If the PA1 key doesn't stop the currently executing function, the ATTN key should be used. The attention key seems to be especially effective in an ISPF screen environment, but its effect is typically more disruptive than that of the PA1 key. The most disruptive of all is SYS REQ. This key will force the start of a logoff sequence, and is therefore used when all else fails. When the screen clears, enter the *LOGOFF* command and wait for the VTAM message to again appear before attempting to logon to the system.

In the case of a system failure, all terminal functionality could be lost. If it's necessary to clear the information from the display when none of the previously mentioned keys are functional, switch the terminal to *test mode* and then back again. In test mode, character patterns are displayed over the entire usable display. In switching back, those characters are removed. Avoid turning the terminal power off. This will, of course, clear the display, but also carries a slight risk that the terminal will not power on properly. If forced to turn the power off, wait at least a minute before turning the power back on.

The RESET key is used to remove a keyboard lock. The keyboard could lock (just like a typewriter with separate strike bars) when multiple keys are pressed simultaneously. It's even more likely to lock when trying to insert where no space is available or typing on part of an ISPF screen that's not defined as an input field. It's not possible to type during a keyboard lock. When the lock is removed, it might be necessary to erase information before more can be added or to use the cursor control keys to establish the proper position on an ISPF screen.

The key labeled *ERASE EOF* (ERASE End Of Field) can be used to provide additional room to insert. It can be especially useful in the formatted fields of an ISPF screen or in the ISPF editor. As mentioned before, data or even spaces at the end of a field can prevent new data from being inserted. The ERASE EOF key can remove either. It can also be used to remove information that's no longer required in the same two instances as well as in the native TSO mode following the READY prompt.

The PA2 key has a redisplay function. There are times when the display contents have been erased. This might have been caused by pressing a wrong key like the one marked *CLEAR*. That key will clear the entire screen content. That situation should not be confused with one in which the terminal clears the display. The latter is a normal response for some terminal types. It was designed to prolong the life of the CRT by removing the display contents if the terminal appeared to be inactive. In this latter instance, when a key is pressed, the display contents will be redisplayed. If the PA2 key doesn't cause the previous display contents to be shown, it might be necessary to re-execute the function that was active.

ISPF Program Function Keys

While some number of PF (Program Function) keys are standard, their function can vary by the context in which they're used. Stated another way, PF keys are given function by the program that's being executed. While in regular TSO line mode, the PF keys have no special function. Using such a key in that environment produces the same effect as using the ENTER key. Within ISPF, however, different functions are assigned to the keys. Different programs running under ISPF are also able to assign functions to the keys or maintain separate key functions. The latter is important because in most cases the terminal user can modify or reassign the key functions. More will be said about the functions attached to PF keys as they're applied to other ISPF functions. Standard PF key settings and customizing PF keys are also detailed in Chapter 36.

Typematic Keys

Typematic keys are those that repeat the key function as the key is held. The alternative is to discretely press a particular key each time the function is invoked. Which keys are typematic depends on the keyboard and might even vary for terminals of the same type since keyboard options can be ordered separately. Learning which keys are typematic can make certain tasks (like the deletion of multiple characters) much easier.

3

Accessing TSO

Until fairly recently, computer access meant using the LOGON command to start the sign-on process. The LOGON command might still be used, but more and more installations have personalized the process by substituting other commands or have found it necessary to create replacement commands to identify which of several processors should be accessed. Other network or session manager software might also intervene just to confuse the issue. This means it might be necessary to see an installation's TSO or security administrator to see which command or application-id to use. The administrator will typically supply a user-id and an initial password for computer access.

The logon process requires computer users to identify themselves with a specific user-id and password combination. The user-id is usually entered with the appropriate application-id or in response to system prompts that result from having entered the application-id. Many installations use a standard screen provided for logon information. Such a screen is displayed in Figure 3.1.

Logon Parameters

Once the user-id has been entered, information peculiar to that user-id can be used for screen fields (in addition to the user-id already supplied). With this convenience, it's not necessary to remember or type logon field values unless they must be changed. The values are typically stored from one TSO session to the next and, therefore, should not be deleted indiscriminately. Prominent logon fields are discussed in the following.

USERID   This information is carried forward from an earlier response to a prompt. If it's incorrect, the other information on the screen will either be incorrect as well, or missing. If the user-id is incorrectly supplied, it would be best to abort the logon

```
--------------------------- TSO/E LOGON ---------------------------------
PF1/PF13 ==> Help   PF3/PF15 ==> Logoff   PA1 ==> Attention   PA2 ==> Reshow
You may request specific HELP information by entering a ? in any entry field
   ENTER LOGON PARAMETERS BELOW:              RACF LOGON PARAMETERS:

   USERID    ===> TSO1234               SECLABEL     ===>

   PASSWORD  ===>                       NEW PASSWORD ===>

   PROCEDURE ===> TSOUSER               GROUP IDENT  ===>

   ACCT NMBR ===> TSO12349999

   SIZE      ===> 2048

   PERFORM   ===>

   COMMAND   ===> EX (STARTUP)


   ENTER AN 'S' BEFORE EACH OPTION DESIRED BELOW:

        -NOMAIL          -NONOTICE        -RECONNECT        -OIDCARD
```

Figure 3.1 Logon information screen.

process and start over. Follow the instructions on the screen to abort logon and restart the process with the proper user-id.

PASSWORD This is a non-display field. As the password is typed, the cursor moves to the right, but the one-to-eight-character password is not shown. This feature makes it more difficult for someone else to sense the password and use another's access to the computer. The password is made up of the letters A through Z, the numbers 0 through 9, and the special characters @, #, and $. Any installation can impose more restrictive rules for forming a password, generally to make it even more difficult to discern.

NEW PASSWORD A field also exists to enter a new password. This, of course, is only possible when the existing password is matched. The new password field can be used when (or even before) the old password expires. Most installations also require that a new password be established at the first logon since the initial password was created by the TSO or security administrator. Many installations cause passwords to expire periodically, and some prohibit the use of recently used passwords. These too are designed to make an individual's password more difficult to discern.

PROCEDURE This field makes reference to the TSO procedure that's to be used as a TSO session is started. The procedure points to resources that should be allocated to an individual's session as they logon to the system. These resources might include software and data that the user will want to access later in the session as well as the default amount of computer memory. In most cases, the procedure name value will already be entered. If not, it might be necessary to obtain this information from the TSO or security administrator. It's important not to type over this information in error, as it could hamper the ability to properly logon to the system.

ACCT NMBR Many installations require that account information be entered. The account information might then be used in a charge-back system for the computer services used during the TSO session. If an installation requires an account number, whether for charge-back or not, it will be necessary to find out the unique format for that information at that installation. Many installations have validation routines that will not allow logon to the system with invalid account information.

SIZE This parameter can be used to override the default amount of computer memory that the session will use. A numeric value is specified (usually in multiples of four). The memory value is in terms of K, which itself is 1024 bytes. A value of 2048 would therefore be 2048 × 1024 bytes of memory. Multiples of four are typically used because that's the size of a page frame in memory.

Values that are not a multiple of four will be rounded up, and so this is not an important concern. An assumption can be made that the system default memory is adequate until proven otherwise by "insufficient storage" messages or abend codes like 106, 878, or 80A. On the other hand, an abend code of 822 indicates that more memory was requested than was available on the system. (Here, memory is also known as *region*.)

COMMAND This parameter is a sort of autoexec feature that's available on many computers and software products alike. The command, CLIST, and REXX EXEC references here are retained between sessions and therefore take effect at every logon. Because it's a convenient way to execute such functions, the command field entries are often used to tailor the TSO/ISPF environment.

Multiple commands can generally be stacked here and in other places in TSO and ISPF that support command invocation. The commands are separated by a semicolon to represent the field mark character. The following example shows commands to execute a CLIST and then invoke ISPF:

```
COMMAND ===> EX (STARTUP);ISPF
```

The CLIST could contain other commands (such as those needed to access key system files) to prepare the environment for further processing. The command ISPF would follow and initiate the ISPF/PDF program. Consideration should be given to the order in which commands are specified. The LOGOFF command could even be added to the end of the other commands. It would not be executed until ISPF was terminated.

```
COMMAND ===> EX (STARTUP);ISPF;LOGOFF
```

Selection Options

Other parameters at the bottom of the screen can be selected by placing an "S" in front of the option. These options include:

NOMAIL This parameter indicates that the TSO user doesn't wish to see messages directed specifically to them as they begin to access the system. The default is to have personal messages displayed.

NONOTICE   This parameter indicates that the TSO user doesn't wish to see system messages as they begin to access the system. The default is to have system messages displayed. It's not advisable to turn system messages off just in case they contain important information.

RECONNECT   This parameter is selected when logging on to the system after the prior session has been interrupted. This can, at times, be an essential element in re-accessing the system.

OIDCARD   This parameter specifies that a prompt be issued for operator identification card information during logon processing. This information is only used on systems with RACF security installed, and even then it's seldom required.

Logon Panel Help

Use the help facility (PF keys 1 or 13) as documented on the panel to view a description of the fields just mentioned as well as other fields that might be required at a particular installation. Note that a computer installation can also alter the panel to show only particular fields or add fields that are not standard. It's also possible that such a screen will not be presented in favor of traditional prompts. The same kind of information would be supplied to each prompt in turn. The LOGON command itself has many optional parameters that can be used to specify logon information.

Initial TSO Access

During the logon process, data sets are allocated to the session by the TSO procedure mentioned above. These data sets can provide access to TSO functions and products like ISPF as well as other vendor-supplied products that might have been added to the standard TSO/ISPF environment. Some go further to add private or specialized software. Problems with the TSO procedure can cause the logon process to fail. Even a single missing data set then becomes crucial to allowing access to the system. Problems of this sort should be reported to the system programmer.

Once the TSO proc has successfully completed, the system broadcast message is displayed (unless the option NONOTICE has been selected), as in Figure 3.2. Any personal messages sent and held until next logon are also displayed (unless the option NOMAIL has been selected). Finally, any commands or CLISTs that have been specified in the COMMAND field of the logon screen are executed.

The TSO READY Prompt

The TSO READY prompt is a signal that all of the initial processing is finished. The TSO command prompter issues the READY prompt to show that it's able to accept a command. The READY prompt would not be shown (or displayed only briefly) when going straight into ISPF (or some other product) either through some device specified in the TSO proc or by what's specified in the COMMAND field of the logon information screen.

The cursor will be positioned on the line below the READY prompt. A command can be entered right at the cursor position and can, if necessary, be continued onto

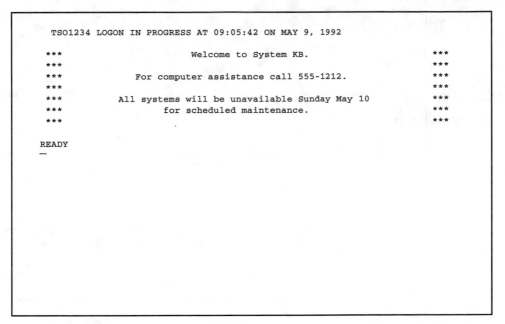

```
   TSO1234 LOGON IN PROGRESS AT 09:05:42 ON MAY 9, 1992

***                     Welcome to System KB.                    ***
***                                                              ***
***          For computer assistance call 555-1212.             ***
***                                                              ***
***      All systems will be unavailable Sunday May 10          ***
***                 for scheduled maintenance.                  ***
***                              .                               ***


READY
—
```

Figure 3.2 System broadcast message and READY prompt.

subsequent lines. To continue a command, merely keep typing even though the command or its parameters seems to be interrupted in the middle of a word. Command continuation is shown in Figure 3.3, where the SEND command is used to send a message to another TSO user.

The TSO command prompter issues the READY prompt at the conclusion of each command to show that it's able to accept another command. That's the only noticeable result of having executed the SEND command (Figure 3.4). The SEND command only responds with a message to the sender if the command fails. For some commands, the fact that no message is issued means that they were successful. For other commands, no message would be a sign that they have failed. This is a function of what type of output a command is designed to produce. Knowledge of what type of output to expect can only be developed over time.

Many TSO users fail to realize that a previously issued command can be used to issue another command. In Figure 3.4 the previous command is used to send a similar message to a different TSO user. The cursor was moved up to type over the text that's already on the screen. The portion of the command that was changed is highlighted.

The second message that was sent says that Tricia already knows about the canceled meeting, but unless she is logged on or will logon before the meeting, she will not get the message in time. The second consecutive READY prompt indicates that the second message has also been sent, and that the system is no longer input inhibited (Figure 3.5).

Following the last READY prompt, a TSO command has been added to list the system catalog for all personal data sets. The command LISTC (short for LISTCAT)

```
    TSO1234 LOGON IN PROGRESS AT 09:05:42 ON MAY 9, 1992

    ***                      Welcome to System KB.                  ***
    ***                                                             ***
    ***          For computer assistance call 555-1212.            ***
    ***                                                             ***
    ***       All systems will be unavailable Sunday May 10        ***
    ***                 for scheduled maintenance.                 ***
    ***                                                             ***

     READY
     send 'Tricia, the meeting scheduled for tomorrow has been cancelled. Please t
     ell the others in your group.' u(tso2345) logon _
```

Figure 3.3 Continued TSO command.

```
    TSO1234 LOGON IN PROGRESS AT 09:05:42 ON MAY 9, 1992

    ***                      Welcome to System KB.                  ***
    ***                                                             ***
    ***          For computer assistance call 555-1212.            ***
    ***                                                             ***
    ***       All systems will be unavailable Sunday May 10        ***
    ***                 for scheduled maintenance.                 ***
    ***                                                             ***

     READY
     send 'Kathy,  the meeting scheduled for tomorrow has been cancelled. Tricia a
     lready knows.  5/9/92       ' u(tso1906) logon
      READY
```

Figure 3.4 Typing over a previous command.

without additional parameters will list the name of each cataloged data set under the current TSO prefix.

Part of the LISTCAT command output is shown at the bottom of Figure 3.6. The very last line of the display contains three asterisks. These indicate that the end of the logical screen has been reached. Pressing the ENTER key (or any PF key since they have no set meaning to TSO) will page through the command output.

After the ENTER key is pressed, the remainder of LISTCAT command output is written on the next screen (Figure 3.7). The content of the previous screen is no longer accessible. The READY prompt is again the signal that command execution is finished and that another command can be entered.

Another trick that can be used to save typing is to type over computer-generated output. In Figure 3.8 the cursor has been moved over the last line of computer output. The DELETE command has been typed there to scratch one of the data sets listed by the LISTCAT command. In this particular instance, the fact that TSO can accept shortened data set names is also taken advantage of.

The result of the DELETE command is shown in Figure 3.9. The data set TSO1234.TEMP.DATA has been deleted from the system. The one drawback to typing over computer-generated output is that the result can't be larger than what was placed there to begin with. In this case, information typed over previous output would have been restricted to positions 4 through 20 of the line used.

Many other commands can be executed from the READY prompt. These include commands to allocate data sets, run programs, and submit, track, and control back-

```
        TSO1234 LOGON IN PROGRESS AT 09:05:42 ON MAY 9, 1992

    ***                        Welcome to System KB.                    ***
    ***                                                                  ***
    ***              For computer assistance call 555-1212.             ***
    ***                                                                  ***
    ***           All systems will be unavailable Sunday May 10         ***
    ***                     for scheduled maintenance.                   ^^^
    ***                                                                  ***

  READY
 send 'Kathy,  the meeting scheduled for tomorrow has been cancelled. Tricia a
 lready knows.   5/9/92        ' u(tso1906) logon
  READY

  READY
 listc_
```

Figure 3.5 LISTCAT command.

```
    TSO1234 LOGON IN PROGRESS AT 09:05:42 ON MAY 9, 1992

  ***                      Welcome to System KB.                 ***
  ***                                                            ***
  ***            For computer assistance call 555-1212.          ***
  ***                                                            ***
  ***         All systems will be unavailable Sunday May 10      ***
  ***                   for scheduled maintenance.               ***
  ***                                                            ***

 READY
send 'Kathy,  the meeting scheduled for tomorrow has been cancelled. Tricia a
lready knows.  5/9/92        ' u(tso1906) logon
 READY

 READY
listc
 IN CATALOG CATALOG.MASTCAT

 TSO1234.CLIST
 TSO1234.CNTL
 TSO1234.COBOL
 ***
```

Figure 3.6 Start of LISTCAT command output.

```
 TSO1234.EXAMPLE.DATA
 TSO1234.FINANCE.REPORT
 TSO1234.FORT
 TSO1234.ISPPROF
 TSO1234.LOAD
 TSO1234.TEMP.DATA

 READY
 _
```

Figure 3.7 Remainder of LISTCAT command output.

```
TSO1234.EXAMPLE.DATA
TSO1234.FINANCE.REPORT
TSO1234.FORT
TSO1234.ISPPROF
TSO1234.LOAD
del     TEMP.DATA
        _


READY
```

Figure 3.8 Typing over computer-generated output.

```
TSO1234.EXAMPLE.DATA
TSO1234.FINANCE.REPORT
TSO1234.FORT
TSO1234.ISPPROF
TSO1234.LOAD
del     TEMP.DATA

READY

ENTRY (A)  TSO1234.TEMP.DATA DELETED
READY
_
```

Figure 3.9 Result of TSO DELETE command.

ground jobs. More is mentioned about TSO commands starting in Chapter 39. CLIST and REXX EXEC code can also be executed from the READY prompt, and, of course, ISPF can be invoked at this point to create a vastly different processing environment.

The Logoff Process

It's also from this point (the READY prompt) that the TSO session is terminated. If ISPF has been invoked, it must be terminated to cause return to the READY prompt before being able to terminate the session. The session is terminated with the TSO command LOGOFF. When the LOGOFF command is executed, all files connected to the session are freed as the session is ended. This includes the files and data sets connected to the session while logging on, as well as to any that were added as a result of subsequent processing.

The command LOGON will also terminate the current TSO session as it starts the next session. The next session will, however, be confined to the same TSO system as the one just terminated, and will therefore allow no choice to be made.

4

Accessing ISPF

ISPF can be started from TSO using the command ISPF. Two other standard commands are typically provided for the same purpose; they're PDF and SPF. Any of the commands can be entered from the READY prompt to cause the ISPF primary option menu to display. The primary option menu (shown in Figure 4.1) is the starting point of the ISPF program. The figure lists a hierarchy of functions that will be detailed in subsequent chapters.

Installations might provide other commands that can be used to invoke ISPF. These commands might be combined with other functions like allocating the profile data set. The profile data set must be connected to the TSO session before ISPF can be invoked. If it's not, ISPF will fail to start and will issue the error message: THE FOLLOWING FILE WAS NOT PRE-ALLOCATED ISPPROF. Additional information about the ISPF profile is given at the end of this chapter, under the heading ISPF Profile Allocation.

The ISPF Hierarchy

The primary option menu is the first of many selection menus. One of the offered subfunctions is selected from the menu by typing the option number or letter into the OPTION field and pressing the ENTER key. In Figure 4.2, the utility option is selected by entering the number 3.

Subfunctions might, in turn, be selection menus that offer other subfunctions. These connections between any option and its suboptions is what creates the ISPF hierarchy. The utility option shown in Figure 4.3 shows 14 suboptions that can be selected. Suboption 1 is selected to invoke the library utility.

Figure 4.4 shows the screen that represents the library utility. From that screen, one of several options can be selected to apply a particular utility function against a

```
--------------------- ISPF/PDF V3 PRIMARY OPTION MENU ---------------------
OPTION  ===>_
                                                    USERID   - TSO1234
    0 ISPF PARMS    - Specify terminal and user parameters   TIME     - 11:03
    1 BROWSE        - Display source data or output listings DATE     - 92/11/13
    2 EDIT          - Create or change source data           JUL DATE - 92.317
    3 UTILITIES     - Perform utility functions              TERMINAL - 3278
    4 FOREGROUND    - Invoke foreground language processors   PF KEYS  - 24
    5 BATCH         - Submit job for language processing
    6 COMMAND       - Enter TSO command, CLIST, or REXX exec
    7 DIALOG TEST   - Perform dialog testing
    8 LM UTILITIES  - Perform library administrator utility functions
    9 IBM PRODUCTS  - Additional IBM program development products
   10 SCLM          - Software configuration and library manager
    C CHANGES       - Display summary of changes for this release
    T TUTORIAL      - Display information about ISPF/PDF
    X EXIT          - Terminate ISPF using log and list defaults

 Enter END command to terminate ISPF.
```

Figure 4.1 Primary option menu.

```
--------------------- ISPF/PDF V3 PRIMARY OPTION MENU ---------------------
OPTION  ===> 3_
                                                    USERID   - TSO1234
    0 ISPF PARMS    - Specify terminal and user parameters   TIME     - 11:07
    1 BROWSE        - Display source data or output listings DATE     - 92/11/13
    2 EDIT          - Create or change source data           JUL DATE - 92.317
    3 UTILITIES     - Perform utility functions              TERMINAL - 3278
    4 FOREGROUND    - Invoke foreground language processors   PF KEYS  - 24
    5 BATCH         - Submit job for language processing
    6 COMMAND       - Enter TSO command, CLIST, or REXX exec
    7 DIALOG TEST   - Perform dialog testing
    8 LM UTILITIES  - Perform library administrator utility functions
    9 IBM PRODUCTS  - Additional IBM program development products
   10 SCLM          - Software configuration and library manager
    C CHANGES       - Display summary of changes for this release
    T TUTORIAL      - Display information about ISPF/PDF
    X EXIT          - Terminate ISPF using log and list defaults

 Enter END command to terminate ISPF.
```

Figure 4.2 Selecting an option.

```
------------------------  UTILITY SELECTION MENU  ------------------------
OPTION  ===> 1_

    1   LIBRARY    - Compress or print data set.  Print index listing
                       Print, rename, delete, or browse members
    2   DATASET    - Allocate, rename, delete, catalog, uncatalog, or
                       display information of an entire data set
    3   MOVE/COPY  - Move, copy, or promote members or data sets
    4   DSLIST     - Print or display (to process) list of data set names
                       Print or display VTOC information
    5   RESET      - Reset statistics for members of ISPF library
    6   HARDCOPY   - Initiate hardcopy output
    8   OUTLIST    - Display, delete, or print held job output
    9   COMMANDS   - Create/change an application command table
   10   CONVERT    - Convert old format menus/messages to new format
   11   FORMAT     - Format definition for formatted data Edit/Browse
   12   SUPERC     - Compare data sets                     (Standard dialog)
   13   SUPERCE    - Compare data sets and Search-For strings (Extended dialog)
   14   SEARCH-FOR - Search data sets for strings of data   (Standard dialog)
```

Figure 4.3 Utility selection menu.

```
-------------------------  LIBRARY UTILITY  -----------------------------
OPTION  ===>_

   blank - Display member list        B - Browse member
   C - Compress data set              P - Print member
   X - Print index listing            R - Rename member
   L - Print entire data set          D - Delete member
   I - Data set information           S - Data set information (short)

ISPF LIBRARY:
   PROJECT ===>
   GROUP   ===>           ===>           ===>           ===>
   TYPE    ===>
   MEMBER  ===>                (If "P", "R", "D", "B", or blank selected)
   NEWNAME ===>                (If "R" selected)

OTHER PARTITIONED OR SEQUENTIAL DATA SET:
   DATA SET NAME  ===> CNTL(JOB)
   VOLUME SERIAL  ===>         (If not cataloged)

DATA SET PASSWORD ===>         (If password protected)
```

Figure 4.4 Library utility.

named library. The END command is used to return from an option. This command is assigned to PF keys 3 and 15 by default to make the command easier to invoke. Return from an option typically takes as many steps as were required to get there. While at the utility menu, other utility options can be selected by entering an option number and pressing ENTER. Pressing the END PF key from the library utility will cause the utility selection menu to display (Figure 4.5).

Pressing the END PF key from the utility selection menu will cause the primary option menu to again display (Figure 4.6). Once at the primary option menu, other options can be selected. In Figure 4.6, the same option is selected. The difference here's that both the option and the suboption are specified at the same time. The option and its suboption are separated by a period.

Once the ENTER key is pressed, the suboption is directly displayed (Figure 4.7). In this mode, the intermediate screen (the utility menu) is not displayed. Since only a single step was used to get to the library utility, issuing the END command would return back to the primary option menu in a single step.

RETURN Command

The RETURN command is also used to move up in the ISPF hierarchy. The RETURN command, however, will always return to the primary option menu in one step, no matter how many steps were required to get to a particular point in the hierarchy. This is possible because the primary option menu is defined as an anchor point or parent menu. The RETURN command is the default setting for PF keys 4 and 16.

Direct Option Entry

It's also possible to specify the option or option and suboption(s) as ISPF is invoked. The command ISPF 3.1 issued from the TSO READY prompt would start ISPF and invoke the library utility directly without displaying either the primary option menu or the utility selection screen. Any other ISPF option could be directly invoked in similar fashion. Moving up in the hierarchy will still stop at the entry point of ISPF, the primary option menu.

The Jump Function

The jump function allows for lateral movement throughout the ISPF hierarchy. It provides a way to go directly to an option without having to go up to the primary option menu and then back down again. The jump function is used by preceding the option number with an equals sign and pressing the ENTER key. Suboptions can be specified with option numbers in the normal fashion (separated by a period). The jump function can be used in any field that's marked with three equal signs followed by a greater than sign (===>). In Figure 4.8 the jump function is used on an edit screen field to go directly to the library utility. Note that at least one space was left after the jump option number and that the text in the GROUP field will ultimately be restored to its value before the jump function was typed there.

```
--------------------------- UTILITY SELECTION MENU --------------------------
OPTION  ===>

     1  LIBRARY    - Compress or print data set.  Print index listing
                         Print, rename, delete, or browse members
     2  DATASET    - Allocate, rename, delete, catalog, uncatalog, or
                         display information of an entire data set
     3  MOVE/COPY  - Move, copy, or promote members or data sets
     4  DSLIST     - Print or display (to process) list of data set names
                         Print or display VTOC information
     5  RESET      - Reset statistics for members of ISPF library
     6  HARDCOPY   - Initiate hardcopy output
     8  OUTLIST    - Display, delete, or print held job output
     9  COMMANDS   - Create/change an application command table
    10  CONVERT    - Convert old format menus/messages to new format
    11  FORMAT     - Format definition for formatted data Edit/Browse
    12  SUPERC     - Compare data sets                      (Standard dialog)
    13  SUPERCE    - Compare data sets and Search-For strings (Extended dialog)
    14  SEARCH-FOR - Search data sets for strings of data    (Standard dialog)
```

Figure 4.5 Return to the utility menu.

```
---------------------- ISPF/PDF V3 PRIMARY OPTION MENU ---------------------
OPTION  ===> 3.1
                                                  USERID   - TSO1234
     0  ISPF PARMS   - Specify terminal and user parameters  TIME     - 11:15
     1  BROWSE       - Display source data or output listings DATE     - 92/11/13
     2  EDIT         - Create or change source data           JUL DATE - 92.317
     3  UTILITIES    - Perform utility functions              TERMINAL - 3278
     4  FOREGROUND   - Invoke foreground language processors  PF KEYS  - 24
     5  BATCH        - Submit job for language processing
     6  COMMAND      - Enter TSO command, CLIST, or REXX exec
     7  DIALOG TEST  - Perform dialog testing
     8  LM UTILITIES - Perform library administrator utility functions
     9  IBM PRODUCTS - Additional IBM program development products
    10  SCLM         - Software configuration and library manager
     C  CHANGES      - Display summary of changes for this release
     T  TUTORIAL     - Display information about ISPF/PDF
     X  EXIT         - Terminate ISPF using log and list defaults

Enter END command to terminate ISPF.
```

Figure 4.6 Specifying both option and suboption.

```
--------------------------- LIBRARY UTILITY -----------------------------
OPTION   ===> _

   blank - Display member list        B - Browse member
   C - Compress data set              P - Print member
   X - Print index listing            R - Rename member
   L - Print entire data set          D - Delete member
   I - Data set information           S - Data set information (short)

ISPF LIBRARY:
   PROJECT ===>
   GROUP   ===>          ===>          ===>          ===>
   TYPE    ===>
   MEMBER  ===>                   (If "P", "R", "D", "B", or blank selected)
   NEWNAME ===>                   (If "R" selected)

OTHER PARTITIONED OR SEQUENTIAL DATA SET:
   DATA SET NAME  ===>
   VOLUME SERIAL  ===>            (If not cataloged)

DATA SET PASSWORD ===>            (If password protected)


```

Figure 4.7 Result of selecting both option and suboption.

```
------------------------- EDIT - ENTRY PANEL -----------------------------
COMMAND ===>

ISPF LIBRARY:
   PROJECT ===> TSO1234
   GROUP   ===> =3.1 LE ===>          ===>          ===>
   TYPE    ===> DATA
   MEMBER  ===>                   (Blank or pattern for member selection list)

OTHER PARTITIONED OR SEQUENTIAL DATA SET:
   DATA SET NAME  ===>
   VOLUME SERIAL  ===>            (If not cataloged)

DATA SET PASSWORD ===>            (If password protected)

PROFILE NAME      ===>            (Blank defaults to data set type)

INITIAL MACRO     ===>            LMF LOCK   ===> YES    (YES, NO or NEVER)

FORMAT NAME       ===>            MIXED MODE ===> NO     (YES or NO)


```

Figure 4.8 Specifying the jump function.

Figure 4.9 shows that using the jump function has invoked the library utility in one step without going through the primary option menu. This becomes a common mode of switching options for those who already know the option number or letter that they want without selecting it from a menu.

Split Screen Processing

The entire ISPF hierarchy can be attached twice. The SPLIT function is used to obtain the second screen, which will initially display the primary option menu. The SPLIT function is defined to default PF keys 2 and 14. The size of the resulting two screens is determined by the cursor position when the SPLIT function is invoked. The example in Figure 4.10 shows an edit menu before the split function is invoked. Note that the cursor is currently positioned in the field labeled MEMBER.

Figure 4.11 shows the result of using the SPLIT function. The presence of a second screen is denoted by a line of dots. This will signal the presence of a second screen even when each screen is a full screen. This later type of split is effected when the cursor is placed at the absolute top or bottom before the SPLIT function is invoked. It allows the maximum size possible for each screen and therefore ensures that all panel fields are accessible.

No matter how the screens are split, only one screen is active at a time. The active screen is determined by the position of the cursor when the ENTER key or a PF key is pressed. When both screens are visible, the cursor control or tab keys can be used to move the cursor to the other screen.

```
-------------------------- LIBRARY UTILITY ----------------------------
OPTION  ===> _

   blank - Display member list        B - Browse member
   C - Compress data set              P - Print member
   X - Print index listing            R - Rename member
   L - Print entire data set          D - Delete member
   I - Data set information           S - Data set information (short)

ISPF LIBRARY:
   PROJECT ===>
   GROUP   ===>         ===>          ===>          ===>
   TYPE    ===>
   MEMBER  ===>              (If "P", "R", "D", "B", or blank selected)
   NEWNAME ===>              (If "R" selected)

OTHER PARTITIONED OR SEQUENTIAL DATA SET:
   DATA SET NAME   ===>
   VOLUME SERIAL   ===>      (If not cataloged)

DATA SET PASSWORD ===>       (If password protected)
```

Figure 4.9 Result of the jump function.

```
-------------------------- EDIT - ENTRY PANEL  --------------------------
COMMAND ===>

ISPF LIBRARY:
   PROJECT ===> TSO1234
   GROUP   ===> JCL        ===>           ===>           ===>
   TYPE    ===> CNTL
   MEMBER  ===> _                 (Blank or pattern for member selection list)

OTHER PARTITIONED OR SEQUENTIAL DATA SET:
   DATA SET NAME  ===>
   VOLUME SERIAL  ===>           (If not cataloged)

DATA SET PASSWORD ===>           (If password protected)

PROFILE NAME      ===>           (Blank defaults to data set type)

INITIAL MACRO     ===>           LMF LOCK   ===> YES    (YES, NO or NEVER)

FORMAT NAME       ===>           MIXED MODE ===> NO     (YES or NO)
```

Figure 4.10 Cursor on edit screen before split.

```
-------------------------- EDIT - ENTRY PANEL  --------------------------
COMMAND ===>

ISPF LIBRARY:
   PROJECT ===> TSO1234
   GROUP   ===> JCL        ===>           ===>           ===>
   TYPE    ===> CNTL
. . . . .     . . . . .         . . . . .         . . . . . . .
-------------------- ISPF/PDF V3 PRIMARY OPTION MENU --------------------
OPTION ===> _
                                               USERID   - TSO1234
   0 ISPF PARMS  - Specify terminal and user parameters  TIME     - 11:32
   1 BROWSE      - Display source data or output listings DATE     - 92/11/13
   2 EDIT        - Create or change source data           JUL DATE - 92.317
   3 UTILITIES   - Perform utility functions              TERMINAL - 3278
   4 FOREGROUND  - Invoke foreground language processors  PF KEYS  - 24
   5 BATCH       - Submit job for language processing
   6 COMMAND     - Enter TSO Command, CLIST, or REXX exec
   7 DIALOG TEST - Perform dialog testing
   8 LM UTILITIES - Perform library administrator utility functions
   9 IBM PRODUCTS - Additional IBM program development products
  10 SCLM        - Software Configuration and Library Manager
   C CHANGES     - Display summary of changes for this release
   T TUTORIAL    - Display information about ISPF/PDF
```

Figure 4.11 Result of screen split.

When a full screen split is used, the SWAP function can be used to display the screen that's not currently visible. The default PF key setting for the SWAP function is 9 or 21. As its name implies, its function is merely to swap from one screen to the other. This might entail an apparent change in screen size as one screen is made prominent at the expense of the other. With full screen swaps, the hidden screen will be displayed while the dotted line is the only indication that the previous screen still exists. Either type of movement from one screen to another can only be accomplished when the terminal is not input inhibited.

Changing the Screen Size

One reason to split the screen is to facilitate viewing information from two sources at the same time. In this case, it might be more convenient to ready the information on each screen and then resplit them. The size of the screens can easily be changed by moving the cursor and again invoking the SPLIT function. Since split screen mode has already been invoked, this will merely change the size of the existing screens. Because each screen accesses the complete ISPF hierarchy, each must be exited separately when leaving ISPF.

ISPF Commands

Four ISPF commands have already been mentioned in this chapter. The first two mentioned were END and RETURN. They're important because they terminate ISPF functions and move up in the ISPF hierarchy. The other two commands were SPLIT and SWAP, which both concern screen control. It was also mentioned that these commands are assigned to default Program Function (PF) keys. Many more ISPF commands are available, and many of these too are assigned to PF keys. The commands assigned to PF keys by default are shown in Figure 4.12 with the actual command name highlighted. Obviously, a command can be entered in the command or option field of any ISPF panel (the upper-left field). When a command is assigned to a PF key, it also allows the command to be invoked by pressing the corresponding PF key.

Two ISPF commands relate specifically to the execution of other commands. These commands are RETRIEVE and CRETRIEV. Both will retrieve the last command statement (from the command field) so that it can be invoked again or altered before it's executed. Both commands will work backward through commands previously entered in the ISPF session to provide access to earlier command statements. CRETRIEV is different in that it also acts like the CURSOR command, which moves the cursor to the command field. When the cursor is already in the command field, CRETRIEV acts like RETRIEVE to iteratively bring back past commands. When the cursor is not already in the command field, CRETRIEV merely places it there like the CURSOR command. Other ISPF commands will be discussed in the context in which they're used.

A primary command can also be preceded by an ampersand to cause it to remain in the command field. From there, it too can be executed again, or altered before it's again invoked. The command field can be used to execute a TSO command when the

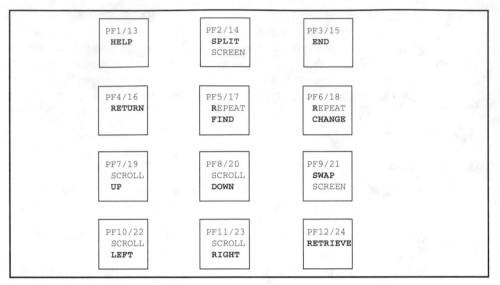

Figure 4.12 Standard PF keys.

command is preceded by the word TSO. The word TSO sets up a special environment for the command to be executed in, much like ISPF Option 6, which was designed specifically for TSO command execution.

Exiting ISPF

The END function can be used to move up the ISPF hierarchy to the primary option menu. When the END function is used from the primary option menu, ISPF is terminated. If the log and list data sets have not been used, the next display should be the TSO READY prompt. If one or both of the ISPF data sets have been used, it will be necessary to specify their disposition before leaving ISPF. In this case, the screen in Figure 4.13 will be displayed.

When option X is used to terminate ISPF, it directs ISPF to use the existing or default log and list data set processing options. These options can be supplied in option 0.2. When exiting ISPF with the X option, the log and list data sets are automatically processed according to the specified defaults and the extra screen is never displayed. The screen will still be displayed, however, if the X option is used and acceptable defaults have not been supplied.

Log and List Data Set Processing

The left half of the screen in Figure 4.13 represents the log data set. It's a log of events during the ISPF session. The right half of the screen represents the list data set. It contains material printed from one of several ISPF sources (see Chapter 38 for details of the log and list data set contents and setting defaults).

Each of the data sets is treated separately since they might need to be printed differently or not at all. If one of the data sets has not been used, its information will not be displayed while exiting ISPF. The processing option for each data set is used to determine what happens to that data set. Each can be deleted, kept (and added to during the next ISPF session), kept (but not reused), or printed. Additional fields are used to specify the print class and jobcard. These fields are not used when the data set is kept or deleted.

The print class is generally a letter or number designation that an installation uses to specify one or more print characteristics. Features like where and when something prints as well as the print device can all be controlled by the print class. Specifying a letter or number causes the print output to print with those corresponding characteristics. It's important to find the proper print class at any given installation before sending data to print.

When one or both data sets are printed, the jobcard information at the bottom of the screen must be complete and correct. The jobcard will be added to JCL (Job Control Language) created by ISPF to print the data as a background job. The jobcard itself is JCL and must conform to the syntax rules of that language. It's also dependent on installation standards and so should be derived from the installation standards or provided by the TSO administrator.

Jobcards are used in several ISPF functions. They're usually shared within but not typically across options. Once a working jobcard is created, it can be used as a model for the jobcard in a different ISPF function. Once created, jobcards are stored in the profile data set and retained for future use so they're not a daily concern. Appendix

```
-------------- SPECIFY DISPOSITION OF LOG AND LIST DATA SETS --------------
COMMAND ===>

LOG OPTIONS FOR THIS SESSION           LIST OPTIONS FOR THIS SESSION
---------------------------            ---------------------------
Process option   ===> D                Process option   ===> D
SYSOUT class     ===> A                SYSOUT class     ===> A
Local printer ID ===>                  Local printer ID ===>

VALID PROCESS OPTIONS:
    PD - Print data set and delete
    D  - Delete data set without printing
    K  - Keep data set (allocate same data set in next session)
    KN - Keep data set and allocate new data set in next session

  Press ENTER key to complete ISPF termination.
  Enter END command to return to the primary option menu.

JOB STATEMENT INFORMATION:  (Required for system printer)
  ===> //TSO1234A  JOB ,'SAMPLE JOB',CLASS=A,
  ===> //   MSGCLASS=A,NOTIFY=TSO1234
  ===> /*ROUTE  PRINT  R27
  ===> //*
```

Figure 4.13 Processing log and list data sets.

A contains a sample jobcard with a brief explanation of what the more common parameters are.

When the information contained on the screen properly reflects how the log and list data sets should be processed, the ENTER key is used to terminate the ISPF session. Using the END function from this screen will instead return to the primary option menu. This is an important change to note to keep from looping between the log/list processing options and the primary option menu.

Terminating Split Screen Mode

When exiting from split screen mode, each set of screens must be exited separately. The RETURN function can be used to expedite the process since it will return to the primary option menu no matter how many intermediate screens there might be. The exit process can also be expedited by using the X option from both primary option menus. When used on the first of two primary option menus, it merely ends split screen mode so there's only a single screen. When used from the last primary option menu, X indicates that the defaults for the log and list data sets should be used. The data sets are processed according to the defaults set in Option 0.2, and control is returned to TSO as evidenced by the READY prompt. It should be noted again that if appropriate defaults have not already been assigned to the log and list data sets, the screen for their disposition will be displayed anyway. Upon return to TSO, a message is issued describing the processing of the data sets. It will indicate that they have been kept or deleted, or will name the batch job that will print them.

Exiting ISPF and TSO

Once TSO processing is finished, the TSO session can be terminated using the LOG-OFF command as described in the previous chapter. It's also possible to exit from ISPF and TSO at the same time. This is accomplished by chaining the LOGOFF command to the exit function while still in ISPF. These can be executed together from most ISPF screens while in single screen mode. The LOGOFF command is chained to the ISPF exit function using the fieldmark character (generally ";" unless it has been reassigned). Other commands or CLISTs can also be combined before or in place of the LOGOFF command. Figure 4.14 shows the LOGOFF command chained to the exit option value from the primary option menu. When the ENTER key is pressed, ISPF will be terminated. The LOGOFF command will be passed to TSO causing the TSO session to terminate as well.

It's not necessary to be at the primary option menu to exit from both ISPF and TSO at the same time. Using the jump function that was discussed earlier in this chapter, it's possible to terminate the session from any single screen (but not while in split screen mode). The jump function is demonstrated from the edit menu in Figure 4.15. Notice in Figure 4.15 that the combined functions could have been invoked from any field marked with the special characters ===>. A field was chosen, however, that was long enough to support the number of characters needed.

```
---------------------- ISPF/PDF V3 PRIMARY OPTION MENU ---------------------
OPTION ===> x;logoff
                                                      USERID   - TSO1234
     0  ISPF PARMS   - Specify terminal and user parameters  TIME     - 11:57
     1  BROWSE       - Display source data or output listings DATE     - 92/11/13
     2  EDIT         - Create or change source data           JUL DATE - 92.317
     3  UTILITIES    - Perform utility functions              TERMINAL - 3278
     4  FOREGROUND   - Invoke foreground language processors  PF KEYS  - 24
     5  BATCH        - Submit job for language processing
     6  COMMAND      - Enter TSO command, CLIST, or REXX exec
     7  DIALOG TEST  - Perform dialog testing
     8  LM UTILITIES - Perform library administrator utility functions
     9  IBM PRODUCTS - Additional IBM program development products
    10  SCLM         - Software configuration and library manager
     C  CHANGES      - Display summary of changes for this release
     T  TUTORIAL     - Display information about ISPF/PDF
     X  EXIT         - Terminate ISPF using log and list defaults

Enter END command to terminate ISPF.
```

Figure 4.14 Exiting ISPF and TSO.

```
------------------------- EDIT - ENTRY PANEL ------------------------------
COMMAND ===>

ISPF LIBRARY:
   PROJECT ===> TSO1234
   GROUP   ===> EXAMPLE  ===>             ===>            --->
   TYPE    ===> DATA
   MEMBER  ===>                (Blank or pattern for member selection list)

OTHER PARTITIONED OR SEQUENTIAL DATA SET:
   DATA SET NAME  ===> =x;logoff
   VOLUME SERIAL  ===>            (If not cataloged)

DATA SET PASSWORD ===>           (If password protected)

PROFILE NAME     ===>            (Blank defaults to data set type)

INITIAL MACRO    ===>      LMF LOCK   ===>      (YES, NO or NEVER)

FORMAT NAME      ===>      MIXED MODE ===>      (YES or NO)
```

Figure 4.15 Using the jump function to exit ISPF and TSO.

ISPF Profile Data Set

A special data set must be allocated to each TSO session before it's possible to enter ISPF. The data set is known as the ISPF profile and is used to store information from most of the ISPF options. The information it contains comes largely from screen variables that can be carried over to subsequent ISPF sessions. It also contains settings from the edit profile that describe how to treat each class of data set. It presents a significant benefit since it will not be necessary to remember the information that it stores, nor will the information have to be recreated. ISPF will automatically create the member that contains the profile, but the data set that it uses must already exist and must be connected to the TSO session before entering ISPF. The remainder of the chapter details the mechanics involved in creating or allocating the data set to the TSO session and might be of interest to only those who are having problems in this area. As described earlier in the chapter, the symptom that this is a problem is the error message THE FOLLOWING FILE WAS NOT PRE-ALLOCATED ISPPROF.

ISPF Profile Allocation

Most installations provide a mechanism to automatically create and allocate the profile data set. Other installations provide a command to do the same thing. If an installation doesn't provide these conveniences, it will first be necessary to create the data set. The following command (entered from the READY prompt) does that as well as connecting the data set to the proper ISPF file, ISPPROF.

```
ALLOC F(ISPPROF) DA(ISPF.PROFILE) CAT SPACE(3 2) TRACK DIR(10)
```

In most cases, the operating system will determine the best placement of the data set being created. If this is not true at a particular installation, UNIT and VOLUME information might need to be added (see Chapter 40 regarding ALLOCATE command parameters).

It should only be necessary to create the data set once. For every subsequent session, it's necessary to connect the data set to the file name ISPPROF. The process of connecting the data set to its special ISPF file will have to be done during every TSO session that makes use of ISPF. In most cases, it should only be necessary to connect the data set once during a TSO session. The command to connect the data set is very similar to the one before. A REUSE parameter has been added to allow the command to work even if the file ISPPROF is already allocated to the session.

```
ALLOC F(ISPPROF) DA(ISPF.PROFILE) SHR REUSE
```

If necessary, this second ALLOCATE command can be included on the "COMMAND" line of the logon panel that the password is entered on. In that way, it will be executed at the beginning of every session automatically. It's also common to place the ALLOCATE command (and perhaps other commands too) in a CLIST to make it easier to invoke.

Selecting and Viewing Data Sets

5

Specifying
Data Set Names

The basic unit of a data set name is referred to as a *simple name*. Simple names are also used for file names and member names. Data set names are formed by joining simple names together with periods. The fully qualified data set name cannot exceed 44 characters. This includes the periods that are used to join the simple names or qualifiers. Simple names in turn have rules for how they're formed. One of those rules limits the simple name to eight characters or less. A simple name is formed using letters, numbers, and the characters @, #, $, -, and {, although simple names cannot start with a number or the characters - and {. It's also not advisable to use the characters - and { ,even though they're available and otherwise valid.

ISPF panels generally accept data set names in two formats. Figure 5.1 shows a typical ISPF screen (the edit menu),which shows both data set name formats. In one format, the data set name qualifiers are each placed in a separate field on the formatted screen. Because they're in separate fields, periods are not included. ISPF automatically combines the separate qualifiers into a fully qualified data set name. The advantage to using this format is that the name will be retained across screens and between ISPF sessions. A field is also added to accommodate a member name where appropriate.

Another advantage to using this particular format is that several partitioned data sets can be specified. This is a process known as *data set concatenation*. All listed data sets (up to four) will be searched for the member specified. Figure 5.2 shows the fields as they appear on the edit menu. Again, this format is common to most ISPF screens where data set names are specified.

A drawback to this particular format of data set name is that all referenced data sets must be three qualifiers. Many have found it convenient to use this format for a

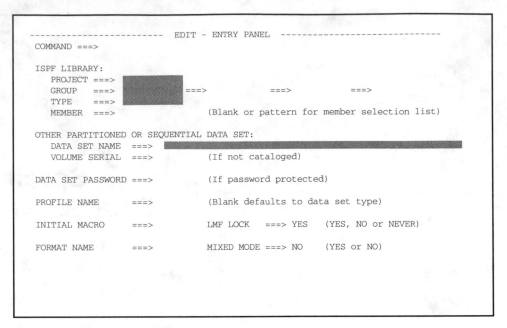

```
------------------------ EDIT - ENTRY PANEL ----------------------------
COMMAND ===>

ISPF LIBRARY:
    PROJECT ===>
    GROUP   ===>                 ===>             ===>          ===>
    TYPE    ===>
    MEMBER  ===>                      (Blank or pattern for member selection list)

OTHER PARTITIONED OR SEQUENTIAL DATA SET:
    DATA SET NAME  ===>
    VOLUME SERIAL  ===>              (If not cataloged)

DATA SET PASSWORD ===>              (If password protected)

PROFILE NAME      ===>              (Blank defaults to data set type)

INITIAL MACRO     ===>              LMF LOCK   ===> YES    (YES, NO or NEVER)

FORMAT NAME       ===>              MIXED MODE ===> NO     (YES or NO)
```

Figure 5.1 Fields used to specify data-set names.

```
------------------------ EDIT - ENTRY PANEL ----------------------------
COMMAND ===>

ISPF LIBRARY:
    PROJECT ===> tso1234
    GROUP   ===> example ===>             ===>          ===>
    TYPE    ===> data
    MEMBER  ===>                      (Blank or pattern for member selection list)

OTHER PARTITIONED OR SEQUENTIAL DATA SET:
    DATA SET NAME  ===>
    VOLUME SERIAL  ===>              (If not cataloged)

DATA SET PASSWORD ===>              (If password protected)

PROFILE NAME      ===>              (Blank defaults to data set type)

INITIAL MACRO     ===>              LMF LOCK   ===> YES    (YES, NO or NEVER)

FORMAT NAME       ===>              MIXED MODE ===> NO     (YES or NO)
```

Figure 5.2 Use of project, group, and type fields.

few of their most frequently used data sets while using the other format for all others. Most ISPF screens also accommodate data set names that are in TSO format. In fields of this type, all data set name qualifiers are joined by periods, and the full data set name is enclosed in single quotes. Figure 5.3 shows the same data set name specified in the alternate format. Member names, when used, are enclosed in parentheses and added to the end of the data set name.

When this alternate form of data set name is used, it preempts whatever is specified in the fields PROJECT, GROUP, and TYPE. It's therefore not necessary and actually counterproductive to erase the values of the PROJECT, GROUP, and TYPE fields. On the other hand, it would be necessary to erase any information from the DATA SET NAME field before being able to use what's in the PROJECT, GROUP, and TYPE fields.

TSO makes an assumption when it's given a data set name that doesn't contain single quotes. The assumption is that an owned data set is being referenced and that the terminal operator's user-id should be used as the data set high-level qualifier. This is a convenience to save the terminal operator from having to type the entire data set name. The second form of data set name on this and many other ISPF screens accepts the data set name in TSO format. For that reason, it's often possible to omit the quotes surrounding the data set name as well as the first simple name of the data set. The data set name specified in Figure 5.4 is equivalent to the others demonstrated previously. ISPF will add the current user's prefix to the data set name before it's processed.

```
------------------------- EDIT - ENTRY PANEL -----------------------------
COMMAND ===>

ISPF LIBRARY:
   PROJECT ===>
   GROUP   ===>          ===>           ===>            ===>
   TYPE    ===>
   MEMBER  ===>                  (Blank or pattern for member selection list)

OTHER PARTITIONED OR SEQUENTIAL DATA SET:
   DATA SET NAME   ===> 'tso1234.example.data'
   VOLUME SERIAL   ===>          (If not cataloged)

DATA SET PASSWORD ===>           (If password protected)

PROFILE NAME      ===>           (Blank defaults to data set type)

INITIAL MACRO     ===>           LMF LOCK   ===> YES    (YES, NO or NEVER)

FORMAT NAME       ===>           MIXED MODE ===> NO     (YES or NO)
```

Figure 5.3 Use of the dataset name field.

```
------------------------ EDIT - ENTRY PANEL ----------------------------
COMMAND ===>

ISPF LIBRARY:
   PROJECT ===>
   GROUP   ===>          ===>             ===>            ===>
   TYPE    ===>
   MEMBER  ===>                    (Blank or pattern for member selection list)

OTHER PARTITIONED OR SEQUENTIAL DATA SET:
   DATA SET NAME  ===> example.data
   VOLUME SERIAL  ===>             (If not cataloged)

DATA SET PASSWORD ===>             (If password protected)

PROFILE NAME     ===>              (Blank defaults to data set type)

INITIAL MACRO    ===>         LMF LOCK    ===> YES    (YES, NO or NEVER)

FORMAT NAME      ===>         MIXED MODE ===> NO      (YES or NO)
```

Figure 5.4 Use of a partially qualified data-set name.

Data Set Validation

ISPF will check the syntax of the data set name entered. If the syntax is incorrect, it will stop processing and issue an error message. If the syntax is correct, ISPF will search for the data set to be sure that it's available. This saves time and valuable processor resources that should not be expended if the data set to be processed is not available. The search for a data set normally starts with the system catalog. This is somewhat analogous to a phone book. Instead of people, though, the catalog keeps track of data sets and where they reside. Once a data set's volume residence is obtained from the catalog, the disk volume is checked to be sure that the data set is indeed there. If the data set is not cataloged or is not on the volume pointed to by the catalog, ISPF will issue an error message and stop processing.

In some rare instances, a data set might exist but not be cataloged. In this case the data set can still be referenced by supplying the disk volume serial number in the field labeled VOLUME SERIAL. It's not advisable to maintain uncataloged data sets since it's necessary to remember where they are and to specify a volume serial number to get to them. It's even less advisable to password protect a data set. Most installations don't even support this feature, preferring to rely on security packages that are either profile or rules driven. If the data set is password protected, the password will have to be specified before it can be used in an ISPF application. The PASSWORD field is a no echo field. Information typed in the field will not display on the screen to protect the integrity of the password.

TSO Data Set Names

Data set names are specified to TSO commands in the same way they're specified in the DATA SET NAME field of an ISPF screen. When a member name is specified, it's enclosed in single quotes and appended to the end of the data set name.

`'TSO1234.EXAMPLE.DATA(MEMNAME)'` or `EXAMPLE.DATA(MEMNAME)`

Certain TSO commands can also make assumptions about the member name in the proper context. Under those circumstances, the member name TEMPNAME is usually assumed when the member name is omitted. Omitting the member name on most ISPF screens will cause a member list to be displayed. The desired member(s) can then be selected from the list. This will be covered in more detail in the next chapter.

The leftmost qualifier of a data set name is called the *high-level qualifier*. The rightmost qualifier is called the *low level* or *descriptive qualifier*. Certain descriptive qualifiers have a special significance to TSO and ISPF and in other data processing contexts. This is especially true of the ISPF edit function, which maintains unique edit profiles for the different descriptive qualifiers. Certain low-level qualifiers are automatically tailored for the kind of data they're expected to contain.

The TSO PROFILE command allows the terminal operator to change the data set prefix that's appended. That would make it easier to process data sets that have a different high-level qualifier. The same command can be used to specify that no such prefix be appended. TSO assumptions can also be made about the data set name low-level qualifier based upon the context of its use. Table 5.1 contains common descriptive qualifiers that have special meaning within certain TSO functions.

TABLE 5.1 Special Descriptive Qualifiers

Descriptive qualifier	Normal use
ASM	Assembler source statements (assembler input)
CLIST	Command List (CLIST) statements
CNTL	Job Control Language (JCL) statements
COBOL	COBOL source statements (compiler input)
DATA	Uppercase data
EXEC	REXX statements
FORT	FORTRAN source statements (compiler input)
LINKLIST	Message output from linkage editor
LOAD	Executable load code (linkage editor output)
LOADLIST	Message output from loader
OBJ	Object code (compiler output and linkage editor input)
OUTLIST	Batch execution listing (converted by TSO OUTPUT command)
PASCAL	PASCAL source statements (compiler input)
PLI	PL/I source statements (compiler input)

TABLE 5.1 Special Descriptive Qualifiers (Continued)

Descriptive qualifier	Normal use
TESTLIST	Output listing from the TEST command
TEXT	Data stored in both uppercase and lowercase
VSBASIC	BASIC source statements

Specifying Generation Data Set Names

A special form of data set name supported by both TSO and ISPF is the generation data set. Each generation data set is part of a generation data group (GDG), which is defined to the system catalog to allow a special grouping of data sets. It's usually defined with cyclic processing in mind. Data sets within the GDG can then be referenced using either of two forms of data set name. The first form is known as the *absolute generation number*. It looks like data set names discussed earlier, except that the last qualifier is always a set pattern.

```
PAYROLL.DAILY.TRANS.G0211V00
```

The last qualifier in the data set name above makes reference to a generation number. The G____ portion of the qualifier represents the generation number. That number is constant and uniquely identifies a particular generation data set. Each time a new generation data set is created, its generation number is one greater than the previous generation. The V__ portion of the qualifier represents the version number. This version number is almost always zero, but is present to allow multiple versions of a particular generation.

If a full generation data set name is three qualifiers, it can be specified in the PROJECT, GROUP, and TYPE fields. The other form of generation data set name must always be specified in the DATA SET NAME field. In this format, the absolute generation number is replaced by a relative generation number. That number changes for any given data set every time a new generation is created. The last generation is always generation zero.

```
PAYROLL.DAILY.TRANS(0)
```

In this format, the generation number looks more like a member name. The value within parentheses is, however, always numeric. Previous generations are counted back from the current generation. The previous generation would be –1. The one before that would be –2, and so on. This method of specifying a generation data set name makes it unnecessary to keep track of the absolute generation number.

6

Member List Processing

Partitioned data sets are designed to maintain separate sequential data sets that are called *members*. Part of the partitioned data set (or PDS) is set aside as a directory to keep track of the members it contains. ISPF supports the processing of PDS members directly or through scrollable member lists. The edit menu in Figure 6.1 shows a PDS name specified in the PROJECT, GROUP, and TYPE fields in the upper left of the screen. When specified (in the three fields or in the field labeled DATA SET NAME) without a member name, a member list is displayed.

Member List Scrolling

The member list shown in Figure 6.2 is in alphanumeric order by member name. The short message area indicates that the first of 44 members in the PDS is displayed at the top of the list. The list is scrollable using the commands UP and DOWN and the PF keys with those assigned values. UP is assigned by default to PF keys 7 and 19, while DOWN is assigned by default to PF keys 8 and 20. This makes scrolling as easy as pressing a single key. The amount of the scroll depends on the value in the SCROLL field. The current scroll value is set at CSR, which is short for CURSOR. The values CUR or C can also be entered to have the same effect. In fact, any of the scroll values that will be discussed can be designated using the first letter of the scroll amount. ISPF will automatically fill in the rest of the value even if the old scroll value fills the rest of the scroll amount field.

   The scroll amount CSR will scroll one page at a time when the cursor is above the member list. When the cursor is in the member list itself, scrolling will bring the cursor to the edge of the member display. Other scroll values include PAGE and HALF,

```
-------------------------- EDIT - ENTRY PANEL --------------------------
COMMAND ===>

ISPF LIBRARY:
   PROJECT ===> TSO1234
   GROUP   ===> EXAMPLE   ===>          ===>          ===>
   TYPE    ===> DATA
   MEMBER  ===> _              (Blank or pattern for member selection list)

OTHER PARTITIONED OR SEQUENTIAL DATA SET:
   DATA SET NAME   ===>
   VOLUME SERIAL   ===>        (If not cataloged)

DATA SET PASSWORD ===>         (If password protected)

PROFILE NAME      ===>         (Blank defaults to data set type)

INITIAL MACRO     ===>         LMF LOCK   ===> YES   (YES, NO or NEVER)

FORMAT NAME       ===>         MIXED MODE ===> NO    (YES or NO)
```

Figure 6.1 Displaying a member list.

```
EDIT --- TSO1234.EXAMPLE.DATA --------------------------- ROW 00001 OF 00044
COMMAND ===> _                                          SCROLL ===> CSR
  NAME          VV.MM  CREATED    CHANGED      SIZE  INIT  MOD  ID
  ALLOC         01.01 92/12/04 92/12/11 17:04   270   270    0 TSO1234
  ALTLIB        01.01 92/12/04 92/12/11 17:10   329   327    0 TSO1234
  ATTRIB        01.00 92/12/04 92/12/04 17:48   102   102    0 TSO1234
  CALL          01.01 92/12/04 92/12/11 17:05    31    31    0 TSO1234
  CANCEL        01.00 92/12/04 92/12/04 17:49    20    20    0 TSO1234
  CLIST         01.01 92/12/11 92/12/11 17:16   639   655    0 TSO1234
  COPY          01.00 92/12/04 92/12/04 17:50    68    68    0 TSO1234
  DEFINE        01.00 92/12/04 92/12/04 17:51   545   545    0 TSO1234
  DELETE        01.03 92/12/04 92/12/11 17:06   123   123    0 TSO1234
  EDIT          01.00 92/12/04 92/12/04 17:52   106   106    0 TSO1234
  EXEC          01.00 92/12/04 92/12/04 17:53    48    48    0 TSO1234
  FORMAT        01.00 92/12/04 92/12/04 17:54    60    60    0 TSO1234
  FREE          01.00 92/12/04 92/12/04 17:44    55    55    0 TSO1234
  LINK          01.00 92/12/04 92/12/04 17:55   116   116    0 TSO1234
  LIST          01.00 92/12/04 92/12/04 17:56    38    38    0 TSO1234
  LISTALC       01.00 92/12/04 92/12/04 17:56    22    22    0 TSO1234
  LISTBC        01.00 92/12/04 92/12/04 17:57    27    27    0 TSO1234
  LISTCAT       01.00 92/12/04 92/12/04 17:57   104   104    0 TSO1234
  LISTDS        01.00 92/12/04 92/12/04 17:58    29    29    0 TSO1234
  LOADGO        01.00 92/12/04 92/12/04 17:59    68    68    0 TSO1234
  LOGOFF        01.00 92/12/04 92/12/04 17:59    16    16    0 TSO1234
```

Figure 6.2 Initial member list display.

which scroll a complete page and a half-page respectively. A numeric value can also be used as the scroll amount. Scrolling would then adjust the member list up or down by that many lines (in this case members). Finally, the scroll value of MAX can be used to scroll a maximum distance and thus reveal the top or bottom of the member list.

Any scroll value specified in the primary command area of the member list becomes a one-time scroll amount. The value is used to determine the extent of scrolling and then is removed from the primary command area. When MAX is used in either the scroll field or the primary command area, it's also considered to be a temporary value.

The direction of the scroll is dependent on the scroll command or PF key used at the time. Since the scroll value is CSR and the cursor is off the member list, scrolling down a page positions the list starting with the twenty-second member, as shown in Figure 6.3. The 21 members displayed on the previous screen are now above the current position in the member list and can be revealed by scrolling up. Additional members are listed below the current screen position and could be revealed by scrolling down again. The number of lines scrolled with PAGE or HALF values is automatically adjusted to the current screen size.

Additional scrolling functions can be used on the member list. The commands FORWARD and BACKWARD provide the same scrolling direction as DOWN and UP respectively. The commands TOP and BOTTOM expose the top and bottom of the member list doing the same thing as a maximum scroll up or down.

```
 EDIT --- TSO1234.EXAMPLE.DATA ------------------------- ROW 00022 OF 00044
 COMMAND ===> _                                         SCROLL ===> CSR
   NAME           VV.MM  CREATED    CHANGED       SIZE  INIT   MOD    ID
   MERGE          01.00  92/12/04  92/12/04 18:00   68    68     0  TSO1234
   NAME           01.00  92/12/10  92/12/10 19:13   31    31     0  TSO1234
   OUTDES         01.00  92/12/04  92/12/04 18:00  329   329     0  TSO1234
   OUTPUT         01.00  92/12/04  92/12/04 18:01   99    99     0  TSO1234
   PRINT          01.00  92/12/04  92/12/04 18:01  113   113     0  TSO1234
   PRINTDS        01.00  92/12/04  92/12/04 17:42  434   434     0  TSO1234
   PROTECT        01.00  92/12/04  92/12/04 18:02   56    56     0  TSO1234
   RECEIVE        01.00  92/12/10  92/12/10 19:13  371   371     0  TSO1234
   RENAME         01.00  92/12/04  92/12/04 18:03   15    15     0  TSO1234
   REPRO          01.00  92/12/10  92/12/10 19:13  294   294     0  TSO1234
   RUN            01.00  92/12/10  92/12/10 19:13    7     7     0  TSO1234
   SEND           01.00  92/12/10  92/12/10 19:13   49    49     0  TSO1234
   SHIFT          01.00  92/12/11  92/12/11 17:10   30    30     0  TSO1234
   STATUS         01.00  92/12/10  92/12/10 19:13   20    20     0  TSO1234
   SUBMIT         01.00  92/12/10  92/12/10 19:13  105   105     0  TSO1234
   TERMINAL       01.00  92/12/10  92/12/10 19:13   94    94     0  TSO1234
   TEST           01.00  92/12/10  92/12/10 19:13   99    99     0  TSO1234
   TIME           01.00  92/12/10  92/12/10 19:13   13    13     0  TSO1234
   TRANSMIT       01.00  92/12/10  92/12/10 19:13  557   557     0  TSO1234
   TSOEXEC        01.00  92/12/10  92/12/10 19:13   16    16     0  TSO1234
   UNALLOC        01.00  92/12/10  92/12/10 19:13   55    55     0  TSO1234
```

Figure 6.3 Scroll down result.

Member Statistics

The member list usually contains statistics about the members. The statistics are usually generated by the ISPF editor and include the following columns of information:

VV   The version number (generally 1 unless explicitly set to some other value).

MM   The modification level (this number is automatically updated by the ISPF editor, indicating how many times the member has been updated. Note that none of the members in the current PDS have been updated, and so the modification number is 0 for each member).

CREATED   The date that the member was first created (or the date that the member's statistics were created/reset).

CHANGED   The date and time that the member was last updated/saved.

SIZE   The current size of the member (in number of lines).

INIT   The initial size of the member (in number of lines).

MOD   The number of lines modified from the initial member to the current version.

ID   The TSO user-id of the individual who last updated the member.

The absence of member statistics doesn't indicate a problem. Member statistics are optional, and those members without statistics might have been generated outside of the ISPF editor or saved while the edit profile was set for STATS OFF. Different statistics exist for executable program code known also as *load modules*. Load module statistics are created by the linkage editor. They include the size of the load module (a base 16 value for the number of bytes) as well as the load module attributes (like overlay, re-entrant, and reusable). A column of the member statistics is also used to indicate if an alias is assigned.

Member List Line Commands

Some member lists, like those for the browse and edit functions, support processing of one member at a time. On those member lists, only one member at a time can be selected. Other member lists, like those for the library utility and the move/copy utility, support multiple line commands entered at one time. In the latter instance, no scrolling takes place after the commands are entered and control is returned to the member list. With the former, however, the last selected member is always scrolled to the top in anticipation of processing subsequent members in the order they're listed. A later topic in this chapter will discuss how to change the order of the member list.

The line commands that can be used from a member list vary by the function that the member list is used in. The edit function member list, shown in Figure 6.4, supports only the line command S to select a member to be edited. When the ENTER key is pressed, the contents of the selected member PRINTDS will be displayed by the ISPF editor, allowing its data to be modified.

```
EDIT --- TSO1234.EXAMPLE.DATA -------------------------- ROW 00022 OF 00044
COMMAND ===>                                              SCROLL ===> CSR
    NAME          VV.MM  CREATED      CHANGED       SIZE  INIT  MOD   ID
    MERGE         01.00  92/12/04  92/12/04 18:00     68    68    0 TSO1234
    NAME          01.00  92/12/10  92/12/10 19:13     31    31    0 TSO1234
    OUTDES        01.00  92/12/04  92/12/04 18:00    329   329    0 TSO1234
    OUTPUT        01.00  92/12/04  92/12/04 18:01     99    99    0 TSO1234
    PRINT         01.00  92/12/04  92/12/04 18:01    113   113    0 TSO1234
 S_PRINTDS        01.00  92/12/04  92/12/04 17:42    434   434    0 TSO1234
    PROTECT       01.00  92/12/04  92/12/04 18:02     56    56    0 TSO1234
    RECEIVE       01.00  92/12/10  92/12/10 19:13    371   371    0 TSO1234
    RENAME        01.00  92/12/04  92/12/04 18:03     15    15    0 TSO1234
    REPRO         01.00  92/12/10  92/12/10 19:13    294   294    0 TSO1234
    RUN           01.00  92/12/10  92/12/10 19:13      7     7    0 TSO1234
    SEND          01.00  92/12/10  92/12/10 19:13     49    49    0 TSO1234
    SHIFT         01.00  92/12/11  92/12/11 17:10     30    30    0 TSO1234
    STATUS        01.00  92/12/10  92/12/10 19:13     20    20    0 TSO1234
    SUBMIT        01.00  92/12/10  92/12/10 19:13    105   105    0 TSO1234
    TERMINAL      01.00  92/12/10  92/12/10 19:13     94    94    0 TSO1234
    TEST          01.00  92/12/10  92/12/10 19:13     99    99    0 TSO1234
    TIME          01.00  92/12/10  92/12/10 19:13     13    13    0 TSO1234
    TRANSMIT      01.00  92/12/10  92/12/10 19:13    557   557    0 TSO1234
    TSOEXEC       01.00  92/12/10  92/12/10 19:13     16    16    0 TSO1234
    UNALLOC       01.00  92/12/10  92/12/10 19:13     55    55    0 TSO1234
```

Figure 6.4 Select line command.

Member List Primary Commands

SELECT primary command

Returning from the edit function to the member list (Figure 6.5) would display the last selected member at the top of the member list. The same screen shows how the SELECT primary command can be used to select members, whether they're on the currently displayed portion of the member list or not. SELECT as a primary command can be abbreviated SEL or S and is used here to select a member that's listed above those on the current screen. The SELECT primary command can, in certain utilities, also be used to select a group or pattern of members. This is discussed within the various utility topics that support that format.

RESET command

The RESET command (abbreviated RES) is used on member lists much like it's used in other functions to reset line commands that have already been typed. In addition to setting the line command area of each member to blank, RESET will blank out most of the communication fields (fields used to display command status information). Figure 6.6 shows the RESET command used within the library utility (Option 3.1). The screen shows three pending line commands as well as status information (in the RENAME column) from the execution of previous line commands.

```
EDIT --- TSO1234.EXAMPLE.DATA ---------------------------- ROW 00027 OF 00044
COMMAND ===> s alloc_                                     SCROLL ===> CSR
   NAME          VV.MM  CREATED     CHANGED       SIZE  INIT  MOD   ID
   PRINTDS       01.00 92/12/04 92/12/04 17:42    434   434   0 TSO1234
   PROTECT       01.00 92/12/04 92/12/04 18:02     56    56   0 TSO1234
   RECEIVE       01.00 92/12/10 92/12/10 19:13    371   371   0 TSO1234
   RENAME        01.00 92/12/04 92/12/04 18:03     15    15   0 TSO1234
   REPRO         01.00 92/12/10 92/12/10 19:13    294   294   0 TSO1234
   RUN           01.00 92/12/10 92/12/10 19:13      7     7   0 TSO1234
   SEND          01.00 92/12/10 92/12/10 19:13     49    49   0 TSO1234
   SHIFT         01.00 92/12/11 92/12/11 17:10     30    30   0 TSO1234
   STATUS        01.00 92/12/10 92/12/10 19:13     20    20   0 TSO1234
   SUBMIT        01.00 92/12/10 92/12/10 19:13    105   105   0 TSO1234
   TERMINAL      01.00 92/12/10 92/12/10 19:13     94    94   0 TSO1234
   TEST          01.00 92/12/10 92/12/10 19:13     99    99   0 TSO1234
   TIME          01.00 92/12/10 92/12/10 19:13     13    13   0 TSO1234
   TRANSMIT      01.00 92/12/10 92/12/10 19:13    557   557   0 TSO1234
   TSOEXEC       01.00 92/12/10 92/12/10 19:13     16    16   0 TSO1234
   UNALLOC       01.00 92/12/10 92/12/10 19:13     55    55   0 TSO1234
   VERIFY        01.00 92/12/10 92/12/10 19:13     31    31   0 TSO1234
   WHEN          01.00 92/12/10 92/12/10 19:13     25    25   0 TSO1234
   **END**
```

Figure 6.5 SELECT primary command.

```
LIBRARY - TSO1234.PROD.DATA ------------------------------ ROW 00001 OF 00053
COMMAND ===> reset_                                       SCROLL ===> CSR
   NAME     RENAME     VV.MM  CREATED     CHANGED       SIZE  INIT  MOD   ID
   ALLOC    *PRINTED   01.01 92/12/04 92/12/11 17:04    270   270   0 TSO1234
   ALTLIB   *PRINTED   01.01 92/12/04 92/12/11 17:10    329   327   0 TSO1234
   ATTRIB   *PRINTED   01.00 92/12/04 92/12/04 17:48    102   102   0 TSO1234
 d BLKSIZE             01.05 92/12/11 92/12/21 23:15     23    18   0 TSO1234
   BLKSIZE2 *DELETED
   BLKSIZE3 *DELETED
   BLKSIZE4 *DELETED
   CALL                01.01 92/12/04 92/12/11 17:05     31    31   0 TSO1234
 r CANCEL   can        01.00 92/12/04 92/12/04 17:49     20    20   0 TSO1234
 p CLIST               01.01 92/12/11 92/12/11 17:16    639   655   0 TSO1234
   COPY                01.00 92/12/04 92/12/04 17:50     68    68   0 TSO1234
   C1       *DELETED
   C2       *DELETED
   C3       *DELETED
   C4       *DELETED
   C5       *DELETED
   DEFINE              01.00 92/12/04 92/12/04 17:51    545   545   0 TSO1234
   DELETE              01.03 92/12/04 92/12/11 17:06    123   123   0 TSO1234
   EDIT                01.00 92/12/04 92/12/04 17:52    106   106   0 TSO1234
   EXEC                01.00 92/12/04 92/12/04 17:53     48    48   0 TSO1234
   FORMAT              01.00 92/12/04 92/12/04 17:54     60    60   0 TSO1234
```

Figure 6.6 RESET primary command.

After the RESET command is issued, the pending line commands and status information is removed from the screen (Figure 6.7). In this instance, this could be misleading since deleted members still appear on the member list. Deleted members will not appear on the member list when it's re-created.

LOCATE command

The LOCATE command provides another way to move through the member list. The command can be abbreviated LOC or simply L. Its only parameter is a member name or member name prefix. The object of the command is to bring that member to the top of the member list when there's an exact match on the member name specified. When there's not an exact match on the member name (either because it doesn't exist or because a member name prefix was specified) the member name just prior to the match (or position in the list where such a member would be) is brought to the top of the list. In Figure 6.8 the LOCATE command is used to locate the first member starting with the letter P.

Figure 6.9 shows the result of the LOCATE command. The member PRINT is the first member that meets the specified criteria. The member list has been scrolled to bring the member just prior to it to the top of the list.

If no members match the member name or prefix specified with the LOCATE command, the member list is still scrolled in the same way to reveal where such a member would be if it did exist. If the member list has been sorted in an order other than by member name, the string specified with the locate command is used to search that column.

```
LIBRARY - TSO1234.PROD.DATA ----------------------------- ROW 00001 OF 00053
COMMAND ===> _                                             SCROLL ===> CSR
     NAME     RENAME      VV.MM  CREATED      CHANGED      SIZE  INIT  MOD   ID
     ALLOC                01.01 92/12/04 92/12/11 17:04    270   270    0 TSO1234
     ALTLIB               01.01 92/12/04 92/12/11 17:10    329   327    0 TSO1234
     ATTRIB               01.00 92/12/04 92/12/04 17:48    102   102    0 TSO1234
     BLKSIZE              01.05 92/12/11 92/12/21 23:15     23    18    0 TSO1234
     BLKSIZE2
     BLKSIZE3
     BLKSIZE4
     CALL                 01.01 92/12/04 92/12/11 17:05     31    31    0 TSO1234
     CANCEL               01.00 92/12/04 92/12/04 17:49     20    20    0 TSO1234
     CLIST                01.01 92/12/11 92/12/11 17:16    639   655    0 TSO1234
     COPY                 01.00 92/12/04 92/12/04 17:50     68    68    0 TSO1234
     C1
     C2
     C3
     C4
     C5
     DEFINE               01.00 92/12/04 92/12/04 17:51    545   545    0 TSO1234
     DELETE               01.03 92/12/04 92/12/11 17:06    123   123    0 TSO1234
     EDIT                 01.00 92/12/04 92/12/04 17:52    106   106    0 TSO1234
     EXEC                 01.00 92/12/04 92/12/04 17:53     48    48    0 TSO1234
     FORMAT               01.00 92/12/04 92/12/04 17:54     60    60    0 TSO1234
```

Figure 6.7 Result of the RESET command.

```
EDIT --- TSO1234.EXAMPLE.DATA -------------------------- ROW 00001 OF 00044
COMMAND ===> l p_                                        SCROLL ===> CSR
  NAME        VV.MM  CREATED     CHANGED       SIZE  INIT  MOD   ID
  ALLOC       01.01  92/12/04 92/12/11 17:04   270   270   0 TSO1234
  ALTLIB      01.01  92/12/04 92/12/11 17:10   329   327   0 TSO1234
  ATTRIB      01.00  92/12/04 92/12/04 17:48   102   102   0 TSO1234
  CALL        01.01  92/12/04 92/12/11 17:05    31    31   0 TSO1234
  CANCEL      01.00  92/12/04 92/12/04 17:49    20    20   0 TSO1234
  CLIST       01.01  92/12/11 92/12/11 17:16   639   655   0 TSO1234
  COPY        01.00  92/12/04 92/12/04 17:50    68    68   0 TSO1234
  DEFINE      01.00  92/12/04 92/12/04 17:51   545   545   0 TSO1234
  DELETE      01.03  92/12/04 92/12/11 17:06   123   123   0 TSO1234
  EDIT        01.00  92/12/04 92/12/04 17:52   106   106   0 TSO1234
  EXEC        01.00  92/12/04 92/12/04 17:53    48    48   0 TSO1234
  FORMAT      01.00  92/12/04 92/12/04 17:54    60    60   0 TSO1234
  FREE        01.00  92/12/04 92/12/04 17:44    55    55   0 TSO1234
  LINK        01.00  92/12/04 92/12/04 17:55   116   116   0 TSO1234
  LIST        01.00  92/12/04 92/12/04 17:56    38    38   0 TSO1234
  LISTALC     01.00  92/12/04 92/12/04 17:56    22    22   0 TSO1234
  LISTBC      01.00  92/12/04 92/12/04 17:57    27    27   0 TSO1234
  LISTCAT     01.00  92/12/04 92/12/04 17:57   104   104   0 TSO1234
  LISTDS      01.00  92/12/04 92/12/04 17:58    29    29   0 TSO1234
  LOADGO      01.00  92/12/04 92/12/04 17:59    68    68   0 TSO1234
  LOGOFF      01.00  92/12/04 92/12/04 17:59    16    16   0 TSO1234
```

Figure 6.8 LOCATE primary command.

```
EDIT --- TSO1234.EXAMPLE.DATA -------------------------- ROW 00025 OF 00044
COMMAND ===> _                                           SCROLL ===> CSR
  NAME        VV.MM  CREATED     CHANGED       SIZE  INIT  MOD   ID
  OUTPUT      01.00  92/12/04 92/12/04 18:01    99    99   0 TSO1234
  PRINT       01.00  92/12/04 92/12/04 18:01   113   113   0 TSO1234
  PRINTDS     01.00  92/12/04 92/12/04 17:42   434   434   0 TSO1234
  PROTECT     01.00  92/12/04 92/12/04 18:02    56    56   0 TSO1234
  RECEIVE     01.00  92/12/10 92/12/10 18:13   371   371   0 TSO1234
  RENAME      01.00  92/12/04 92/12/04 18:03    15    15   0 TSO1234
  REPRO       01.00  92/12/10 92/12/10 19:13   294   294   0 TSO1234
  RUN         01.00  92/12/10 92/12/10 19:13     7     7   0 TSO1234
  SEND        01.00  92/12/10 92/12/10 19:13    49    49   0 TSO1234
  SHIFT       01.00  92/12/11 92/12/11 17:10    30    30   0 TSO1234
  STATUS      01.00  92/12/10 92/12/10 19:13    20    20   0 TSO1234
  SUBMIT      01.00  92/12/10 92/12/10 19:13   105   105   0 TSO1234
  TERMINAL    01.00  92/12/10 92/12/10 19:13    94    94   0 TSO1234
  TEST        01.00  92/12/10 92/12/10 19:13    99    99   0 TSO1234
  TIME        01.00  92/12/10 92/12/10 19:13    13    13   0 TSO1234
  TRANSMIT    01.00  92/12/10 92/12/10 19:13   557   557   0 TSO1234
  TSOEXEC     01.00  92/12/10 92/12/10 19:13    16    16   0 TSO1234
  UNALLOC     01.00  92/12/10 92/12/10 19:13    55    55   0 TSO1234
  VERIFY      01.00  92/12/10 92/12/10 19:13    31    31   0 TSO1234
  WHEN        01.00  92/12/10 92/12/10 19:13    25    25   0 TSO1234
  **END**
```

Figure 6.9 Located member name prefix.

Pattern member lists

In some instances it's desirable to filter the member list to include only the members that contain a certain member pattern. This is especially helpful with otherwise long member lists. It can reduce the amount of scrolling and help to make selecting members easier. Member patterns are developed using the wild card characters % or *. The special character % is used to represent any value in a single position. It can be used multiply to indicate any value in exactly that number of positions. The special character * represents one or more positions in the member name instead of the exact position reference that % provides.

Figure 6.10 shows the edit menu with a member pattern of LIST* specified in the MEMBER field. This will cause only the members starting with LIST to display on the member list. Member patterns can also be used when the PDS is specified in the DATA SET NAME field. The equivalent name in that field would be specified:

```
'TSO1234.EXAMPLE.DATA(LIST*)'
```

or

```
EXAMPLE.DATA(LIST*)
```

The result of specifying a member pattern is a filtered list like that shown in Figure 6.11. Only the members starting with LIST are displayed in the list. Other members can still be selected using the primary form of the SELECT command, even though they don't appear on the current list.

```
---------------------------- EDIT - ENTRY PANEL ----------------------------
COMMAND ===>

ISPF LIBRARY:
    PROJECT ===> TSO1234
    GROUP   ===> EXAMPLE   ===>             ===>           ===>
    TYPE    ===> DATA
    MEMBER  ===> LIST*_           (Blank or pattern for member selection list)

OTHER PARTITIONED OR SEQUENTIAL DATA SET:
    DATA SET NAME   ===>
    VOLUME SERIAL   ===>         (If not cataloged)

DATA SET PASSWORD ===>           (If password protected)

PROFILE NAME      ===>           (Blank defaults to data set type)

INITIAL MACRO     ===>           LMF LOCK   ===> YES    (YES, NO or NEVER)

FORMAT NAME       ===>           MIXED MODE ===> NO     (YES or NO)
```

Figure 6.10 Specifying a member pattern.

```
EDIT --- TSO1234.EXAMPLE.DATA ------------------------- ROW 00001 OF 00005
COMMAND ===> _                                             SCROLL ===> CSR
   NAME          VV.MM  CREATED      CHANGED      SIZE   INIT   MOD    ID
   LIST          01.00  92/12/04  92/12/04 17:56    38     38     0 TSO1234
   LISTALC       01.00  92/12/04  92/12/04 17:56    22     22     0 TSO1234
   LISTBC        01.00  92/12/04  92/12/04 17:57    27     27     0 TSO1234
   LISTCAT       01.00  92/12/04  92/12/04 17:57   104    104     0 TSO1234
   LISTDS        01.00  92/12/04  92/12/04 17:58    29     29     0 TSO1234
   **END**
```

Figure 6.11 Filtered member list.

Wild-card characters need not be restricted to the end of the member name. They can also be specified at the beginning or middle of the member name. The wild-card characters can also be specified more than once in developing a member pattern.

Sorting the member list

The member list is initially in alphanumeric order by member name. It's possible to sort the member list by any of the column headings or their abbreviations. Columns that contain dates or numbers of lines are sorted in descending order. All other columns are sorted in ascending sequence. Figure 6.12 shows the SORT command used to sort on the CHANGED column. It uses the abbreviation CHA for CHANGED (CRE can be used when sorting the CREATED column).

After the sort, the member list (Figure 6.13) is now in order by date and time changed. The order is from most recently changed working backward, and so the member list displays the last changed member at the top of the list. This particular sequence is very helpful for those who need help to remember what they were last working on. The member list can be resequenced any number of times. In Figure 6.14, the SORT command is issued to sort the member list by the values in the SIZE column.

Figure 6.15 shows the new member list order. The members are now listed from largest to smallest in terms of the current number of lines. Sorting by ID can be very useful to isolate the members updated by particular individuals since all members last updated by an individual would be displayed together.

The LOCATE command works against whatever member list column is sorted. Values that are appropriate for that particular column should be used when the member list is no longer in member name order. A numeric value, for example, would be used while the member list is in order by the SIZE column values. A user-id or user-id prefix would be used if the member list were sorted by the ID column and so on.

```
EDIT --- TSO1234.EXAMPLE.DATA -------------------------- ROW 00001 OF 00044
COMMAND ===> sort cha_                                   SCROLL ===> CSR
   NAME         VV.MM  CREATED    CHANGED        SIZE  INIT  MOD   ID
   ALLOC        01.01  92/12/04  92/12/11 17:04   270   270    0 TSO1234
   ALTLIB       01.01  92/12/04  92/12/11 17:10   329   327    0 TSO1234
   ATTRIB       01.00  92/12/04  92/12/04 17:48   102   102    0 TSO1234
   CALL         01.01  92/12/04  92/12/11 17:05    31    31    0 TSO1234
   CANCEL       01.00  92/12/04  92/12/04 17:49    20    20    0 TSO1234
   CLIST        01.01  92/12/11  92/12/11 17:16   639   655    0 TSO1234
   COPY         01.00  92/12/04  92/12/04 17:50    68    68    0 TSO1234
   DEFINE       01.00  92/12/04  92/12/04 17:51   545   545    0 TSO1234
   DELETE       01.03  92/12/04  92/12/11 17:06   123   123    0 TSO1234
   EDIT         01.00  92/12/04  92/12/04 17:52   106   106    0 TSO1234
   EXEC         01.00  92/12/04  92/12/04 17:53    48    48    0 TSO1234
   FORMAT       01.00  92/12/04  92/12/04 17:54    60    60    0 TSO1234
   FREE         01.00  92/12/04  92/12/04 17:44    55    55    0 TSO1234
   LINK         01.00  92/12/04  92/12/04 17:55   116   116    0 TSO1234
   LIST         01.00  92/12/04  92/12/04 17:56    38    38    0 TSO1234
   LISTALC      01.00  92/12/04  92/12/04 17:56    22    22    0 TSO1234
   LISTBC       01.00  92/12/04  92/12/04 17:57    27    27    0 TSO1234
   LISTCAT      01.00  92/12/04  92/12/04 17:57   104   104    0 TSO1234
   LISTDS       01.00  92/12/04  92/12/04 17:58    29    29    0 TSO1234
   LOADGO       01.00  92/12/04  92/12/04 17:59    68    68    0 TSO1234
   LOGOFF       01.00  92/12/04  92/12/04 17:59    16    16    0 TSO1234
```

Figure 6.12 SORT primary command.

```
EDIT --- TSO1234.EXAMPLE.DATA -------------------------- ROW 00001 OF 00044
COMMAND ===> _                                           SCROLL ===> CSR
   NAME         VV.MM  CREATED    CHANGED        SIZE  INIT  MOD   ID
   CLIST        01.01  92/12/11  92/12/11 17:16   639   655    0 TSO1234
   ALTLIB       01.01  92/12/04  92/12/11 17:10   329   327    0 TSO1234
   SHIFT        01.00  92/12/11  92/12/11 17:10    30    30    0 TSO1234
   DELETE       01.03  92/12/04  92/12/11 17:06   123   123    0 TSO1234
   CALL         01.01  92/12/04  92/12/11 17:05    31    31    0 TSO1234
   ALLOC        01.01  92/12/04  92/12/11 17:04   270   270    0 TSO1234
   NAME         01.00  92/12/10  92/12/10 19:13    31    31    0 TSO1234
   RECEIVE      01.00  92/12/10  92/12/10 19:13   371   371    0 TSO1234
   REPRO        01.00  92/12/10  92/12/10 19:13   294   294    0 TSO1234
   RUN          01.00  92/12/10  92/12/10 19:13     7     7    0 TSO1234
   SEND         01.00  92/12/10  92/12/10 19:13    49    49    0 TSO1234
   STATUS       01.00  92/12/10  92/12/10 19:13    20    20    0 TSO1234
   SUBMIT       01.00  92/12/10  92/12/10 19:13   105   105    0 TSO1234
   TERMINAL     01.00  92/12/10  92/12/10 19:13    94    94    0 TSO1234
   TEST         01.00  92/12/10  92/12/10 19:13    99    99    0 TSO1234
   TIME         01.00  92/12/10  92/12/10 19:13    13    13    0 TSO1234
   TRANSMIT     01.00  92/12/10  92/12/10 19:13   557   557    0 TSO1234
   TSOEXEC      01.00  92/12/10  92/12/10 19:13    16    16    0 TSO1234
   UNALLOC      01.00  92/12/10  92/12/10 19:13    55    55    0 TSO1234
   VERIFY       01.00  92/12/10  92/12/10 19:13    31    31    0 TSO1234
   WHEN         01.00  92/12/10  92/12/10 19:13    25    25    0 TSO1234
```

Figure 6.13 Member list sorted by change field.

```
EDIT --- TSO1234.EXAMPLE.DATA ---------------------------- ROW 00001 OF 00044
COMMAND ===> sort size_                                    SCROLL ===> CSR
   NAME              VV.MM  CREATED    CHANGED      SIZE  INIT  MOD  ID
   CLIST             01.01 92/12/11 92/12/11 17:16   639   655    0 TSO1234
   ALTLIB            01.01 92/12/04 92/12/11 17:10   329   327    0 TSO1234
   SHIFT             01.00 92/12/11 92/12/11 17:10    30    30    0 TSO1234
   DELETE            01.03 92/12/04 92/12/11 17:06   123   123    0 TSO1234
   CALL              01.01 92/12/04 92/12/11 17:05    31    31    0 TSO1234
   ALLOC             01.01 92/12/04 92/12/11 17:04   270   270    0 TSO1234
   TRANSMIT          01.00 92/12/10 92/12/10 19:13   557   557    0 TSO1234
   RECEIVE           01.00 92/12/10 92/12/10 19:13   371   371    0 TSO1234
   REPRO             01.00 92/12/10 92/12/10 19:13   294   294    0 TSO1234
   SUBMIT            01.00 92/12/10 92/12/10 19:13   105   105    0 TSO1234
   TEST              01.00 92/12/10 92/12/10 19:13    99    99    0 TSO1234
   TERMINAL          01.00 92/12/10 92/12/10 19:13    94    94    0 TSO1234
   UNALLOC           01.00 92/12/10 92/12/10 19:13    55    55    0 TSO1234
   SEND              01.00 92/12/10 92/12/10 19:13    49    49    0 TSO1234
   NAME              01.00 92/12/10 92/12/10 19:13    31    31    0 TSO1234
   VERIFY            01.00 92/12/10 92/12/10 19:13    31    31    0 TSO1234
   WHEN              01.00 92/12/10 92/12/10 19:13    25    25    0 TSO1234
   STATUS            01.00 92/12/10 92/12/10 19:13    20    20    0 TSO1234
   TSOEXEC           01.00 92/12/10 92/12/10 19:13    16    16    0 TSO1234
   TIME              01.00 92/12/10 92/12/10 19:13    13    13    0 TSO1234
   RUN               01.00 92/12/10 92/12/10 19:13     7     7    0 TSO1234
```

Figure 6.14 Sorting the size field.

```
EDIT --- TSO1234.EXAMPLE.DATA ---------------------------- ROW 00001 OF 00044
COMMAND ===> _                                             SCROLL ===> CSR
   NAME              VV.MM  CREATED    CHANGED      SIZE  INIT  MOD  ID
   CLIST             01.01 92/12/11 92/12/11 17:16   639   655    0 TSO1234
   TRANSMIT          01.00 92/12/10 92/12/10 19:13   557   557    0 TSO1234
   DEFINE            01.00 92/12/04 92/12/04 17:51   545   545    0 TSO1234
   PRTNTDS           01.00 92/12/04 92/12/04 17:42   434   434    0 TSO1234
   RECEIVE           01.00 92/12/10 92/12/10 19:13   371   371    0 TSO1234
   ALTLIB            01.01 92/12/04 92/12/11 17:10   329   327    0 TSO1234
   OUTDES            01.00 92/12/04 92/12/04 18:00   329   329    0 TSO1234
   REPRO             01.00 92/12/10 92/12/10 19:13   294   294    0 TSO1234
   ALLOC             01.01 92/12/04 92/12/11 17:04   270   270    0 TSO1234
   DELETE            01.03 92/12/04 92/12/11 17:06   123   123    0 TSO1234
   LINK              01.00 92/12/04 92/12/04 17:55   116   116    0 TSO1234
   PRINT             01.00 92/12/04 92/12/04 18:01   113   113    0 TSO1234
   EDIT              01.00 92/12/04 92/12/04 17:52   106   106    0 TSO1234
   SUBMIT            01.00 92/12/10 92/12/10 19:13   105   105    0 TSO1234
   LISTCAT           01.00 92/12/04 92/12/04 17:57   104   104    0 TSO1234
   ATTRIB            01.00 92/12/04 92/12/04 17:48   102   102    0 TSO1234
   TEST              01.00 92/12/10 92/12/10 19:13    99    99    0 TSO1234
   OUTPUT            01.00 92/12/04 92/12/04 18:01    99    99    0 TSO1234
   TERMINAL          01.00 92/12/10 92/12/10 19:13    94    94    0 TSO1234
   MERGE             01.00 92/12/04 92/12/04 18:00    68    68    0 TSO1234
   LOADGO            01.00 92/12/04 92/12/04 17:59    68    68    0 TSO1234
```

Figure 6.15 Member list sorted by size field.

Two sort fields can be specified while sorting. The result would be to sort by the second field specified within the primary field (first) specified.

SAVE command

The SAVE primary command is used to print or write the current member list. When used by itself, the SAVE command will print the member list to the list data set. The list data set must then be processed to see any result of that processing. The SAVE command followed by a one- to eight-character name will write the current member list to a data set. The name specified will become the middle qualifier of the data set name that the member list is written to. The first qualifier will be the user-id or prefix of the terminal operator, and the last qualifier will be the word MEMBERS. The command SAVE TEMP would write the member list to a data set called TSO1234.TEMP.MEMBERS.

Concatenated Member Lists

Using the fields PROJECT, GROUP, and TYPE, partitioned data sets can be concatenated. A concatenation is accomplished by including additional GROUP field references. That means, of course, that the data sets that are concatenated must have the same PROJECT and TYPE values. Stated another way, data sets concatenated on ISPF screens must share the same first and third qualifiers. Up to four different groups (second qualifiers) can be specified. All specified data sets (identified by combining the PROJECT, GROUP, and TYPE qualifiers in data set names) will be searched until the requested member is found. In Figure 6.16 two libraries are concatenated on the edit menu.

```
-------------------------- EDIT - ENTRY PANEL --------------------------
COMMAND ===>

ISPF LIBRARY:
   PROJECT ===> TSO1234
   GROUP   ===> JCL        ===> TEST      ===>          ===>
   TYPE    ===> CNTL
   MEMBER  ===>                  (Blank or pattern for member selection list)

OTHER PARTITIONED OR SEQUENTIAL DATA SET:
   DATA SET NAME  ===> _
   VOLUME SERIAL  ===>              (If not cataloged)

DATA SET PASSWORD ===>              (If password protected)

PROFILE NAME      ===>              (Blank defaults to data set type)

INITIAL MACRO     ===>          LMF LOCK    ===> YES     (YES, NO or NEVER)

FORMAT NAME       ===>          MIXED MODE ===> NO      (YES or NO)
```

Figure 6.16 Specifying concatenated libraries.

```
EDIT --- TSO1234.JCL.CNTL ------------------------------ ROW 00001 OF 00010
COMMAND ===> _                                               SCROLL ===> CSR
  NAME          LIB VV.MM  CREATED      CHANGED      SIZE  INIT   MOD   ID
  COMPILE         1 01.03 92/10/16 92/10/16 17:58     17     4    16 TSO1234
  COMPILE2        1 01.00 92/10/16 92/10/16 17:50     17    17     0 TSO1234
  COMPONLY        2 01.02 92/12/10 92/12/10 20:33      9    17     8 TSO1234
  COMPRESS        1 01.00 92/11/13 92/11/13 17:44      8     8     0 TSO1234
  COMPRES2        1 01.00 92/12/10 92/12/10 19:25      8     8     0 TSO1234
  COMP2           2 01.00 92/10/16 92/10/16 17:50     17    17     0 TSO1234
  JOB             2 01.00 92/10/09 92/10/09 21:47      4     4     0 TSO1234
  LINK            1 01.00 92/12/10 92/12/10 19:20     11    11     0 TSO1234
  PROB3           2 01.00 92/10/30 92/10/30 18:17     27    27     0 TSO1234
  SORT            1 01.02 92/10/09 92/10/30 18:01     14     9     7 TSO1234
  **END**
```

Figure 6.17 Concatenated library member list.

Because the member name is omitted, a member list is displayed. This member list, however, must also identify which library provided any given member. This is accomplished in an extra column (see Figure 6.17) immediately following the member name. The column labeled LIB contains a number from one to four to reflect which of up to four libraries the member came from. The members can otherwise be selected in the same fashion as before. Duplicate member names are not supported. Only the first member encountered with a given name is accessible from concatenated libraries. The same member name might exist in subsequent libraries in the concatenation, but they will not be visible here. Those other members should be accessed without concatenating libraries.

The ability to concatenate libraries is a feature of many ISPF functions. Most feature the same fields that were just illustrated. Some of the language processing utilities feature a different form of data set concatenation that must support a greater variance in data set name. This accounts for the need to concatenate libraries that are not typically controlled by the individual and which will be described as they're encountered.

Chapter

7

The Browse Function

The browse function is used to display PDS members or sequential data sets. It presents a read-only view of the data, so there's no chance that the data will inadvertently be modified. When it's not necessary to change the data being viewed, the browse function has other advantages over the edit function. Because it's not necessary to establish a change mechanism, browse will operate in a more expedient fashion than edit. Browse will also display data records up to 32,760 bytes in length, while edit's limited to 255 bytes for fixed-length records and 259 bytes for variable-length records. The browse function will also make more of the data visible on any given screen because it has no line command area. In a typical browse session, that would mean that 80 columns of data can be viewed as opposed to 72 columns of data in edit.

Browse is Option 1 from the primary option menu. The first screen displayed (the browse menu) is shown in Figure 7.1. The data set name is the only required field and is subject to the checks described in Chapter 5. This is the first of many applications that requires that a data set name be specified. As stated in Chapter 5, the data set name can be specified in one of two places. These fields are present on the browse menu and therefore allow names that conform to the ISPF standard as well as those that don't.

Assuming that a data set with a three-qualifier name is to be viewed, it's convenient to use the PROJECT, GROUP, and TYPE fields, as was done in Figure 7.1. Again, the advantage to using these fields is that the data set name typed here will remain during and between ISPF sessions.

Scrolling

When a browse session is first started, the screen will be positioned at the upper left portion of the data set. Additional data might exist that can't be seen from this initial

```
--------------------------  BROWSE - ENTRY PANEL  -----------------------------
COMMAND ===>

ISPF LIBRARY:
   PROJECT ===> TSO1234
   GROUP   ===> EXAMPLE   ===>              ===>             ===>
   TYPE    ===> DATA
   MEMBER  ===> CLIST_          (Blank or pattern for member selection list)

OTHER PARTITIONED OR SEQUENTIAL DATA SET:
   DATA SET NAME   ===>
   VOLUME SERIAL   ===>          (If not cataloged)

DATA SET PASSWORD ===>          (If password protected)

MIXED MODE          ===>        (Specify YES or NO)

FORMAT NAME         ===>
```

Figure 7.1 The browse menu.

position. The data displayed in the browse function can be scrolled. Think of scrolling as moving the screen over the data to display what's not currently visible. Obviously, the screen doesn't really move, but thinking of it this way helps to choose the proper scroll key. If the data extends below the screen, use the scroll down key to view it. That would be PF key 8 or 20. If data is to the right of the current screen (for most terminals beyond position 80 of the data record), use the scroll right key. That would be PF key 11 or 23. PF keys 7 or 19 would be used to scroll up in the data set, while PF keys 10 or 22 would be used to scroll to the left.

Figure 7.2 shows the initial browse positioning within a data set. Notice that the short message area (upper right corner) displays the line number of the first data line displayed. The current position is at line zero because of the marker that has been placed there marking the top of the data. This was placed there by ISPF and is not really part of the data itself. The short message area also indicates that columns 1 through 80 are displayed.

The default scroll amount (displayed just below the short message area) for the browse function is a page. The value for PAGE is variable and is dependent upon both the terminal type (since different terminal types have different display capabilities) and the size of the current logical screen (when in split screen mode). From the current screen, scrolling down would move down 22 lines. Scrolling to the right would move the screen eighty columns to the right, but only if the data contained at least 160 columns of data. If the data set were between 81 and 159 columns, scrolling would be to the physical right boundary of the data set. The current data set TSO1234.EXAMPLE.DATA is only 80 columns wide, and therefore left and right scrolling would have no effect on the screen positioning.

Pressing the scroll down key (PF8 or 20) would cause a completely new page of data to be displayed, as in Figure 7.3. The scroll amount is displayed in a modifiable field at the upper right corner of the screen. The short message area now displays

```
BROWSE -- TSO1234.EXAMPLE.DATA(CLIST) - 01.01 ---- LINE 00000000 COL 001 080
COMMAND ===> _                                          SCROLL ===> PAGE
****************************** TOP OF DATA  *********************************

                            CLIST Execution


                       Modes Of CLIST Execution

There are four modes of CLIST execution, explicit, modified explicit,
implicit, and modified implicit. CLIST execution is made possible by
the TSO command, EXEC. That command can also be abbreviated as EX.
Because the command is explicitly stated in the first two modes, they
are known as explicit modes. The implicit modes do not contain EX or
EXEC as part of the command syntax. They also differ in their reliance
upon a special file to identify which CLIST code to execute.

CLISTS are invoked at the TSO prompter or an interface to it. For
those who have ISPF installed, this could also be OPTION 6 as well as
most Productivity Development Facility (PDF) panels that have a
command line. When a CLIST (or TSO command for that matter) is entered
from a PDF panel it should be preceded by the word TSO. This is not
required from PDF Option 6 because it was designed to accept TSO
commands and CLISTS.
```

Figure 7.2 Initial browse positioning.

```
BROWSE -- TSO1234.EXAMPLE.DATA(CLIST) - 01.01 ---- LINE 00000022 COL 001 080
COMMAND ===>                                            SCROLL ===> HAGE _

The modes of CLIST execution will now be covered in more detail. The
next few examples, used to demonstrate that execution, will assume
that there is a partitioned data set, TSO1234.SAMPLE.CLIST, that
contains several executable CLISTS.



                            Explicit Mode

The first execution mode uses the TSO command EXEC followed by the
complete name of the data set that contains the CLIST. That can
optionally be followed by two types of parameter information that will
be discussed later. The TSO EXEC command can also be abbreviated EX, and
has the following syntax:

  EXEC clist-name 'positional-parameters(s) keyword-parameter(s)'

Using our sample CLIST library, the explicit mode of the EXEC command
followed by the CLIST name might look like the following:

  EX 'TSO1234.SAMPLE.CLIST(HARDCOPY)'
```

Figure 7.3 Changing the browse scroll amount.

the new line number of the line at the top of the display. The scroll amount can be changed to a value of HALF to scroll half a page or logical screen at a time. Notice that it was only necessary to specify the first letter of the new scroll amount. Each scroll amount (PAGE, HALF, DATA, CURsor, CSR, and MAXimum) can be abbreviated with the first letter of the scroll amount. ISPF will automatically convert the abbreviation into the standard value in the scroll amount field. Any numeric value can also be used in place of the scroll values just discussed. These too will be retained after they're used to determine the extent of scrolling.

Scrolling down a page moved down 22 lines. Scrolling down half a page additionally moved down 11 lines (half the page value) to leave the data positioned at line 33 (Figure 7.4). Notice too that the scroll value was automatically changed to the word HALF. The command field can also be used to specify a scroll amount. When this field is used, it overrides the normal scroll field. It should also be noted that a scroll value used in the command field is always considered to be temporary and is therefore not retained. In Figure 7.4, a one-time scroll value of 200 is specified.

When the scroll down function is used again, the current position in the data set is changed by 200 lines (the value specified as a temporary scroll value). The scroll amount is not retained in either the scroll field or the primary command area. The change in line number again is noted in the short message area. If the 200 had been specified in the normal scroll field, it would be retained there until replaced with some other value. The scroll amount is again changed in Figure 7.5. This scroll amount, CUR or CSR has the advantage of operating in a page fashion except when the cursor itself is in the data portion. At that point, the scroll value acts to bring the cursor to the edge of the data area.

When the scroll left key is used, the cursor is brought to the right extreme of the data area. Conversely, when the scroll right key is used, the cursor is brought to the left extreme of the data area. When the scroll up key is used, the cursor is taken to the bottom of the data area, and finally, when the scroll down key is used (as in Figure 7.5), the cursor is brought to the top of the data area.

The CSR scroll value is very practical in both browse and edit modes since it allows the current cursor position to be used as the end boundary for scrolling. It's a convenient way of bringing data to the edge of the screen (where it might well be easier to view) without having to count how many lines or columns would have to be scrolled to do so. In Figure 7.6, the CSR scroll value was used to bring the line with "The PROC Statement" to the top of the screen.

The scroll amount MAX can be used to scroll to the physical end of the data, whether that be the top, bottom, left, or right boundary. Pressing the scroll down key with a scroll value of MAX would cause the last page of the data to be displayed. MAX is considered to be a temporary scroll amount, so while other scroll amounts will be retained in the scroll amount field, MAX will be removed in favor of the last previous scroll value.

Figure 7.7 shows the result of having scrolled the maximum distance up. Notice the top-of-data indicator as well as the line number in the short message area. A final scroll value DATA is much like PAGE. DATA can be abbreviated D and causes a scroll just one line or column short of the current page. In that way, one line or col-

```
 BROWSE -- TSO1234.EXAMPLE.DATA(CLIST) - 01.01 ---- LINE 00000033 COL 001 080
 COMMAND ===> 200_                                         SCROLL ===> HALF
optionally be followed by two types of parameter information that will
be discussed later. The TSO EXEC command can also be abbreviated EX, and
has the following syntax:

  EXEC clist-name 'positional-parameters(s) keyword-parameter(s)'

Using our sample CLIST library, the explicit mode of the EXEC command
followed by the CLIST name might look like the following:

  EX 'TSO1234.SAMPLE.CLIST(HARDCOPY)'

This mode of execution might also be considered explicit because it
pinpoints the name of the CLIST being executed. The same syntax will
work for a CLIST contained in a sequential data set except, of course,
that no member name is specified. You may be pleased to know that, as
we progress, the syntax for CLIST execution becomes shorter.


                         TSO Naming Conventions

Before proceeding to the second execution mode, it is necessary to
discuss how TSO handles data set names. When data set names are not
```

Figure 7.4 Using a temporary scroll amount.

```
 BROWSE -- TSO1234.EXAMPLE.DATA(CLIST) - 01.01 ---- LINE 00000233 COL 001 080
 COMMAND ===>                                             SCROLL ===> CALF
show how their values can be set as the CLIST is invoked. Those familiar
with JCL will see that this is very much like the symbolic variable
substitution that can occur when executing a cataloged procedure. The
variables in either language give the process flexibility.

In our first CLIST example, the HARDCOPY CLIST, we will see how
variables can give the CLIST user the flexibility of printing a
different data set each time the CLIST is executed. This flexibility
can extend to other information that may change over time, like the
number of copies that are required and where the print output is to be
routed. The statement that facilitates the communication of variable
information in both CLISTS and JCL procedures is called the PROC
statement. This is just the first of many similarities that will be
pointed out between the two languages.


                         The PROC Statement

The CLIST PROC statement is used to establish and communicate variable
information to a CLIST as it is invoked. It is also used to establish
which variables are required for execution and which are optional.
Required variables are defined as positional parameters and those that
```

Figure 7.5 The cursor scroll value.

```
BROWSE -- TSO1234.EXAMPLE.DATA(CLIST) - 01.01 ---- LINE 00000249 COL 001 080
COMMAND ===> m_                                       SCROLL ===> CSR
                          The PROC Statement

The CLIST PROC statement is used to establish and communicate variable
information to a CLIST as it is invoked. It is also used to establish
which variables are required for execution and which are optional.
Required variables are defined as positional parameters and those that
are optional are defined as keyword parameters. When discussing
keyword parameters, we will also see how the PROC statement can be
used to define defaults for optional variables.


                        Positional Parameters

Positional parameters are, as their name implies, sensitive to the
position they hold on the CLIST PROC statement. That means that these
parameters must be specified in the same order that they occur on the
PROC statement when the CLIST is executed. Positional parameters are
provided for the CLIST writer to be able to specify information deemed
critical to the CLIST execution. With that in mind, it should be noted
that a CLIST will not execute until its positional parameter
information has been specified. If the positional parameters are not
specified when the CLIST is executed, the user will be prompted to
```

Figure 7.6 Scrolling to the extremes of the data set.

```
BROWSE -- TSO1234.EXAMPLE.DATA(CLIST) - 01.01 ---- LINE 00000000 COL 001 080
COMMAND ===> _                                        SCROLL ===> CSR
***************************** TOP OF DATA ********************************

                          CLIST Execution


                      Modes Of CLIST Execution

There are four modes of CLIST execution, explicit, modified explicit,
implicit, and modified implicit. CLIST execution is made possible by
the TSO command, EXEC. That command can also be abbreviated as EX.
Because the command is explicitly stated in the first two modes, they
are known as explicit modes. The implicit modes do not contain EX or
EXEC as part of the command syntax. They also differ in their reliance
upon a special file to identify which CLIST code to execute.

CLISTS are invoked at the TSO prompter or an interface to it. For
those who have ISPF installed, this could also be OPTION 6 as well as
most Productivity Development Facility (PDF) panels that have a
command line. When a CLIST (or TSO command for that matter) is entered
from a PDF panel it should be preceded by the word TSO. This is not
required from PDF Option 6 because it was designed to accept TSO
commands and CLISTS.
```

Figure 7.7 The result of maximum scroll up.

umn from the previous view of the data will still be visible after scrolling. This is helpful to provide a meaningful context to the new data being viewed.

Certain primary commands have been created to facilitate scrolling. They represent aliases for common scroll amounts and directions. Included in the commands are TOP to correspond to a maximum up scroll and BOTTOM for a maximum scroll down. While the commands TOP and BOTTOM can be used to scroll to the extremes of the data set, the commands UP, DOWN, FORWARD, BACKWARD, LEFT, and RIGHT can be used in place of PF keys to give direction to scrolling. The commands that provide direction to scrolling can also be used with a numeric value. DOWN 20, for example, would cause the data to be scrolled down 20 lines. Any of the commands can be assigned to a PF key to make them more convenient to use. The same scrolling facilities are available in the edit function.

Terminating the Browse Function

The browse function can be terminated using either the END or RETURN commands. These are easily invoked using the PF keys with those assigned values. By default, PF keys 3 and 15 are set to END, and keys 4 and 16 are set to RETURN. As discussed previously, END moves back one screen in the hierarchy. RETURN will return to an anchor point like the primary option menu. Either function will terminate the currently active browse session. Figure 7.8 shows the result of having used the END PF key. It caused a return to the browse menu. Notice that the member name has been automatically removed in anticipation of entering a new member name.

Selecting from the Member List

By leaving the member name blank as in Figure 7.8, it will be possible to process members from the member list. Because the member name is omitted, a member list is generated like that in Figure 7.9. Any given member can be selected from either the primary command area or by placing an S in front of the member to be selected. When the desired member is not on the current screen, it's possible to scroll up or down until the member name is exposed. Figure 7.9 shows how the member CLIST can be selected from the list.

The advantage of selecting members from the member list is that it's only necessary to recognize the member name from those listed. Processing additional members is also made easy since the last selected member will appear at the top of the list in anticipation of processing them in order (by member name). When selecting a member from the primary command area, it's necessary to type the letter S (or SEL or SELECT) followed by the member name. This might be more convenient than scrolling when the member name is known but not on the current screen.

LOCATE Command

The LOCATE command can be used to locate either a particular line number or an assigned label. Just like scrolling, LOCATE can be used to move the data to display a particular portion of the data set. The LOCATE command is specified in the primary

```
----------------------- BROWSE - ENTRY PANEL -----------------------------
COMMAND ===>

ISPF LIBRARY:
   PROJECT ===> TSO1234
   GROUP   ===> EXAMPLE  ===>            ===>            ===>
   TYPE    ===> DATA
   MEMBER  ===> _              (Blank or pattern for member selection list)

OTHER PARTITIONED OR SEQUENTIAL DATA SET:
   DATA SET NAME  ===>
   VOLUME SERIAL  ===>          (If not cataloged)

DATA SET PASSWORD ===>          (If password protected)

MIXED MODE        ===>          (Specify YES or NO)

FORMAT NAME       ===>
```

Figure 7.8 Return to the browse menu.

```
  BROWSE - TSO1234.EXAMPLE.DATA -------------------------- ROW 00001 OF 00054
  COMMAND ===>                                            SCROLL ===> CSR
     NAME            VV.MM  CREATED      CHANGED       SIZE  INIT  MOD   ID
     ALLOC           01.01 92/12/04 92/12/11 17:04     270   270    0 TSO1234
     ALTLIB          01.01 92/12/04 92/12/11 17:10     329   327    0 TSO1234
     ATTRIB          01.00 92/12/04 92/12/04 17:48     102   102    0 TSO1234
     BLKSIZE         01.05 92/12/11 92/12/21 23:15      23    18    0 TSO1234
     BLKSIZE2        01.00 92/12/14 92/12/14 14:22      19    19    0 TSO1234
     BLKSIZE3        01.00 92/12/14 92/12/14 15:32      22    22    0 TSO1234
     BLKSIZE4        01.02 92/12/19 92/12/19 17:53      17    19    0 TSO1234
     CALL            01.01 92/12/04 92/12/11 17:05      31    31    0 TSO1234
     CANCEL          01.00 92/12/04 92/12/04 17:49      20    20    0 TSO1234
  S_ CLIST           01.01 92/12/11 92/12/11 17:16     639   655    0 TSO1234
     COPY            01.00 92/12/04 92/12/04 17:50      68    68    0 TSO1234
     C1              01.00 92/12/21 92/12/21 23:08      11    11    0 TSO1234
     C2              01.00 92/12/21 92/12/21 23:17      10    10    0 TSO1234
     C3              01.01 92/12/21 92/12/21 23:32      11    11    0 TSO1234
     C4              01.00 92/12/21 92/12/21 23:31      11    11    0 TSO1234
     C5              01.00 92/12/21 92/12/21 23:39       6     6    0 TSO1234
     DEFINE          01.00 92/12/04 92/12/04 17:51     545   545    0 TSO1234
     DELETE          01.03 92/12/04 92/12/11 17:06     123   123    0 TSO1234
     EDIT            01.00 92/12/04 92/12/04 17:52     106   106    0 TSO1234
     EXEC            01.00 92/12/04 92/12/04 17:53      48    48    0 TSO1234
     FORMAT          01.00 92/12/04 92/12/04 17:54      60    60    0 TSO1234
```

Figure 7.9 Selecting a member from the member list.

command area. The command can also be abbreviated LOC or simply L. It's always followed by a line number or a label that was assigned during that particular browse session.

Locating Line Numbers

A line number used with the LOCATE command is simply the number of a particular line relative to the start of the data set. In the browse function, line numbers can be noted from the short message area. It's common practice to scroll to a particular place in the data and note the line number from the short message area. Returning to that place in the data set later in the browse session would be as easy as specifying the LO-CATE command and the line number. When specified in that way, the data line corresponding to the line number used will be positioned at the top of the data display.

The LOCATE command has an advantage over normal scrolling since the current position within the data set is not important in getting to any other point in the data set. For example, to scroll to line 256 from line 93, it would first be necessary to calculate the difference between the two line numbers and specify that as a scroll amount. With the LOCATE command, it would merely be necessary to specify L 256 in the primary command area.

Label Assignment

It's not always easy to remember line numbers. For that reason, it might be more convenient to attach a label to a particular portion of the browse data set to later be referenced using the LOCATE command. The underlying idea is that the label (especially if it's meaningful) will be easier to remember than a line number. Labels are one to seven characters in length, and they're preceded by a period. The period must be specified to help differentiate labels from ISPF commands since both are specified in the primary command area. When a label is created, it's assigned to the line that's currently at the top of the browse display.

Label assignments only exist for the duration of the current browse session. During that time, it's possible to assign more than one label to a particular line (the line at the top of the display). Any of those labels will then cause the same data set positioning when used. It's also possible to reuse a particular label. When a particular label is reused, it retains only the positioning information for its last use. When the label is reassigned, the short message will indicate that it's being reassigned rather than assigned.

Locating Labels

Locating a label is as simple as specifying the label name after the LOCATE command in the primary command area. When it follows the LOCATE command, the label need not start with a period unless that label starts with a numeric. The line associated with that label will be placed at the top of the data display. If a label is referenced that has not been defined, that will be indicated in the short message area and the current position in the data set will be retained. Remember, only the labels assigned during the current browse session can be referenced with the LOCATE command. Following is a short example of locating both line numbers and labels. In Figure 7.10, the LOCATE command is used to position line 29 at the top of the display.

In Figure 7.11, line 29 has been located (brought to the top of the display). The label .EX is then assigned to that line to make it easier to return to that point. The short message in Figure 7.12 indicates that the label .EX was assigned to the line at the top of the display. On the same screen, another LOCATE command is issued to bring line 149 to the top of the display. In Figure 7.13 line 149 has been located. A label associating it with .IM is created. Following the creation of the second label, a LOCATE command is issued to locate the first label (Figure 7.14).

Figure 7.15 shows that the first label was located. The message in the short message area also reflects this. It didn't matter that the label was associated with a line above the current data set position. From that screen, a LOCATE command is issued to locate the second label. Figure 7.16 shows the data set contents repositioned to bring the second label (.IM) to the top of the data display.

Ending the browse session will return to the member list shown in Figure 7.17 since that's where member selection took place. All label assignments made during the session are now erased. The last selected member (CLIST) is now at the top of the list. Any member can now be selected from the member list to start a new browse session, or the END function can be used to return to the browse menu.

```
BROWSE -- TSO1234.EXAMPLE.DATA(CLIST) ------------ LINE 00000000 COL 001 080
COMMAND ===> 1 29_                                          SCROLL ===> CSR
****************************** TOP OF DATA *********************************

                        CLIST Execution


                   Modes Of CLIST Execution

There are four modes of CLIST execution, explicit, modified explicit,
implicit, and modified implicit. CLIST execution is made possible by
the TSO command, EXEC. That command can also be abbreviated as EX.
Because the command is explicitly stated in the first two modes, they
are known as explicit modes. The implicit modes do not contain EX or
EXEC as part of the command syntax. They also differ in their reliance
upon a special file to identify which CLIST code to execute.

CLISTS are invoked at the TSO prompter or an interface to it. For
those who have ISPF installed, this could also be OPTION 6 as well as
most Productivity Development Facility (PDF) panels that have a
command line. When a CLIST (or TSO command for that matter) is entered
from a PDF panel it should be preceded by the word TSO. This is not
required from PDF Option 6 because it was designed to accept TSO
commands and CLISTS.
```

Figure 7.10 Locating a line number.

```
 BROWSE -- TSO1234.EXAMPLE.DATA(CLIST) ------------ LINE 00000029 COL 001 080
 COMMAND ===> .ex_                                   SCROLL ===> CSR
                        Explicit Mode

 The first execution mode uses the TSO command EXEC followed by the
 complete name of the data set that contains the CLIST. That can
 optionally be followed by two types of parameter information that will
 be discussed later in this chapter. The TSO EXEC command can also be
 abbreviated EX, and has the following syntax:

   EXEC clist-name 'positional-parameters(s) keyword-parameter(s)'

 Using our sample CLIST library, the explicit mode of the EXEC command
 followed by the CLIST name might look like the following:

   EX 'TSO1234.SAMPLE.CLIST(HARDCOPY)'

 This mode of execution might also be considered explicit because it
 pinpoints the name of the CLIST being executed. The same syntax will
 work for a CLIST contained in a sequential data set except, of course,
 that no member name is specified. You may be pleased to know that, as
 we progress, the syntax for CLIST execution becomes shorter.
```

Figure 7.11   Assigning a browse label.

```
 BROWSE -- TSO1234.EXAMPLE.DATA(CLIST) ----------------- LABEL '.EX' ASSIGNED
 COMMAND ===> 1 149                                   SCROLL ===> CSR
                        Explicit Mode

 The first execution mode uses the TSO command EXEC followed by the
 complete name of the data set that contains the CLIST. That can
 optionally be followed by two types of parameter information that will
 be discussed later in this chapter. The TSO EXEC command can also be
 abbreviated EX, and has the following syntax:

   EXEC clist-name 'positional-parameters(s) keyword-parameter(s)'

 Using our sample CLIST library, the explicit mode of the EXEC command
 followed by the CLIST name might look like the following:

   EX 'TSO1234.SAMPLE.CLIST(HARDCOPY)'

 This mode of execution might also be considered explicit because it
 pinpoints the name of the CLIST being executed. The same syntax will
 work for a CLIST contained in a sequential data set except, of course,
 that no member name is specified. You may be pleased to know that, as
 we progress, the syntax for CLIST execution becomes shorter.
```

Figure 7.12   Using the locate command to reposition browse data.

```
BROWSE -- TSO1234.EXAMPLE.DATA(CLIST) ------------ LINE 00000149 COL 001 080
COMMAND ===> .im_                                           SCROLL ===> CSR
                              Implicit Mode

Implicit execution of a CLIST is made possible by connecting a CLIST
library or libraries to the SYSPROC file. The process of allocating
CLIST libraries was described in the previous chapter, and is well
worth the effort. Subsequent CLIST execution is very much simplified
and is as easy as specifying the member name followed by any
parameters. The libraries allocated to the SYSPROC file are searched
in the order they were allocated until a member name matching the one
specified is found. If there is no match, TSO stops and returns the
message "COMMAND NOT FOUND".

Conversely, the same member name may exist in more than one CLIST
library in the SYSPROC file. The contents of the like named members
could vary widely, but only the first member found with the specified
name will be executed. If you save your CLIST code and execute it in
this fashion, only to find yourself in a totally different process,
check the other CLIST libraries for a member of the same name. This
problem does not occur with either of the explicit modes of execution
because you are directing TSO to look at a single, specific data set.

In the implicit mode of execution, CLISTS look and act just like TSO
```

Figure 7.13 A second label assignment.

```
BROWSE -- TSO1234.EXAMPLE.DATA(CLIST) ----------------- LABEL '.IM' ASSIGNED
COMMAND ===> l .ex_                                         SCROLL ===> CSR
                              Implicit Mode

Implicit execution of a CLIST is made possible by connecting a CLIST
library or libraries to the SYSPROC file. The process of allocating
CLIST libraries was described in the previous chapter, and is well
worth the effort. Subsequent CLIST execution is very much simplified
and is as easy as specifying the member name followed by any
parameters. The libraries allocated to the SYSPROC file are searched
in the order they were allocated until a member name matching the one
specified is found. If there is no match, TSO stops and returns the
message "COMMAND NOT FOUND".

Conversely, the same member name may exist in more than one CLIST
library in the SYSPROC file. The contents of the like named members
could vary widely, but only the first member found with the specified
name will be executed. If you save your CLIST code and execute it in
this fashion, only to find yourself in a totally different process,
check the other CLIST libraries for a member of the same name. This
problem does not occur with either of the explicit modes of execution
because you are directing TSO to look at a single, specific data set.

In the implicit mode of execution, CLISTS look and act just like TSO
```

Figure 7.14 Locating a label.

```
BROWSE -- TSO1234.EXAMPLE.DATA(CLIST) ----------------- LABEL '.EX' LOCATED
COMMAND ===> l .im_                                      SCROLL ===> CSR
                          Explicit Mode

The first execution mode uses the TSO command EXEC followed by the
complete name of the data set that contains the CLIST. That can
optionally be followed by two types of parameter information that will
be discussed later in this chapter. The TSO EXEC command can also be
abbreviated EX, and has the following syntax:

  EXEC clist-name 'positional-parameters(s) keyword-parameter(s)'

Using our sample CLIST library, the explicit mode of the EXEC command
followed by the CLIST name might look like the following:

  EX 'TSO1234.SAMPLE.CLIST(HARDCOPY)'

This mode of execution might also be considered explicit because it
pinpoints the name of the CLIST being executed. The same syntax will
work for a CLIST contained in a sequential data set except, of course,
that no member name is specified. You may be pleased to know that, as
we progress, the syntax for CLIST execution becomes shorter.
```

Figure 7.15 Locating another label.

```
BROWSE -- TSO1234.EXAMPLE.DATA(CLIST) --------------- LABEL '.IM' LOCATED
COMMAND ===> _                                          SCROLL ===> CSR
                          Implicit Mode

Implicit execution of a CLIST is made possible by connecting a CLIST
library or libraries to the SYSPROC file. The process of allocating
CLIST libraries was described in the previous chapter, and is well
worth the effort. Subsequent CLIST execution is very much simplified
and is as easy as specifying the member name followed by any
parameters. The libraries allocated to the SYSPROC file are searched
in the order they were allocated until a member name matching the one
specified is found. If there is no match, TSO stops and returns the
message "COMMAND NOT FOUND".

Conversely, the same member name may exist in more than one CLIST
library in the SYSPROC file. The contents of the like named members
could vary widely, but only the first member found with the specified
name will be executed. If you save your CLIST code and execute it in
this fashion, only to find yourself in a totally different process,
check the other CLIST libraries for a member of the same name. This
problem does not occur with either of the explicit modes of execution
because you are directing TSO to look at a single, specific data set.

In the implicit mode of execution, CLISTS look and act just like TSO
```

Figure 7.16 Locating the second label.

```
BROWSE - TSO1234.EXAMPLE.DATA --------------------------- ROW 00010 OF 00054
COMMAND ===> _                                          SCROLL ===> CSR
  NAME              VV.MM  CREATED     CHANGED      SIZE  INIT  MOD    ID
  CLIST             01.01  92/12/11  92/12/11 17:16  639   655    0  TSO1234
  COPY              01.00  92/12/04  92/12/04 17:50   68    68    0  TSO1234
  C1                01.00  92/12/21  92/12/21 23:08   11    11    0  TSO1234
  C2                01.00  92/12/21  92/12/21 23:17   10    10    0  TSO1234
  C3                01.01  92/12/21  92/12/21 23:32   11    11    0  TSO1234
  C4                01.00  92/12/21  92/12/21 23:31   11    11    0  TSO1234
  C5                01.00  92/12/21  92/12/21 23:39    6     6    0  TSO1234
  DEFINE            01.00  92/12/04  92/12/04 17:51  545   545    0  TSO1234
  DELETE            01.03  92/12/04  92/12/11 17:06  123   123    0  TSO1234
  EDIT              01.00  92/12/04  92/12/04 17:52  106   106    0  TSO1234
  EXEC              01.00  92/12/04  92/12/04 17:53   48    48    0  TSO1234
  FORMAT            01.00  92/12/04  92/12/04 17:54   60    60    0  TSO1234
  FREE              01.00  92/12/04  92/12/04 17:44   55    55    0  TSO1234
  LINK              01.00  92/12/04  92/12/04 17:55  116   116    0  TSO1234
  LIST              01.00  92/12/04  92/12/04 17:56   38    38    0  TSO1234
  LISTALC           01.00  92/12/04  92/12/04 17:56   22    22    0  TSO1234
  LISTBC            01.00  92/12/04  92/12/04 17:57   27    27    0  TSO1234
  LISTCAT           01.00  92/12/04  92/12/04 17:57  104   104    0  TSO1234
  LISTDS            01.00  92/12/04  92/12/04 17:58   29    29    0  TSO1234
  LOADGO            01.00  92/12/04  92/12/04 17:59   68    68    0  TSO1234
  LOGOFF            01.00  92/12/04  92/12/04 17:59   16    16    0  TSO1234
```

Figure 7.17 Return to the browse member list.

Data Set Concatenation

Using the fields PROJECT, GROUP, and TYPE, partitioned data sets can be concatenated. A concatenation is accomplished by including additional GROUP field references. Up to four groups can be specified. All specified data sets (identified by combining the PROJECT, GROUP, and TYPE qualifiers in data set names) will be searched until the requested member is found. Figure 7.18 shows a concatenation of three data sets with second qualifiers DEVL, TEST, and PROD respectively.

Again, when the member name is omitted, a member list is displayed. This member list, however, has an extra column (Figure 7.19) immediately following the member name. The column labeled LIB contains a number from one to four to reflect which of up to four libraries the member came from. The member list displayed shows members from all three of the concatenated libraries specified on the browse menu. The data set name at the top of the member list screen is the first of the concatenated data sets, while the member selected is from the third library. When the member contents are displayed, the name of the data set (contained on the title line) is changed to reflect the actual source library (Figure 7.20).

```
----------------------- BROWSE - ENTRY PANEL ----------------------------
COMMAND ===>

ISPF LIBRARY:
   PROJECT ===> TSO1234
   GROUP   ===> DEVL      ===> TEST      ===> PROD      ===>
   TYPE    ===> DATA
   MEMBER  ===> _               (Blank or pattern for member selection list)

OTHER PARTITIONED OR SEQUENTIAL DATA SET:
   DATA SET NAME  ===>
   VOLUME SERIAL  ===>          (If not cataloged)

DATA SET PASSWORD ===>          (If password protected)

MIXED MODE        ===> NO       (Specify YES or NO)

FORMAT NAME       ===>
```

Figure 7.18 Specifying a browse concatenation.

```
BROWSE - TSO1234.DEVL.DATA ------------------------------ ROW 00001 OF 00053
COMMAND ===>                                              SCROLL ===> CSR
   NAME        LIB VV.MM  CREATED     CHANGED      SIZE  INIT  MOD   ID
s_ALLOC         3  01.01 92/12/04 92/12/11 17:04   270   270    0 TSO1234
  ALTLIB        2  01.01 92/12/04 92/12/11 17:10   329   327    0 TSO1234
  ATTRIB        2  01.00 92/12/04 92/12/04 17:48   102   102    0 TSO1234
  BLKSIZE       3  01.05 92/12/11 92/12/21 23:15    23    18    0 TSO1234
  BLKSIZE2      1  01.00 92/12/14 92/12/14 14:22    19    19    0 TSO1234
  BLKSIZE3      1  01.00 92/12/14 92/12/14 15:32    22    22    0 TSO1234
  BLKSIZE4      1  01.02 92/12/19 92/12/19 17:53    17    19    0 TSO1234
  CALL          3  01.01 92/12/04 92/12/11 17:05    31    31    0 TSO1234
  CANCEL        3  01.00 92/12/04 92/12/04 17:49    20    20    0 TSO1234
  CLIST         2  01.01 92/12/11 92/12/11 17:16   639   655    0 TSO1234
  COPY          3  01.00 92/12/04 92/12/04 17:50    68    68    0 TSO1234
  C1            1  01.00 92/12/21 92/12/21 23:08    11    11    0 TSO1234
  C2            1  01.00 92/12/21 92/12/21 23:17    10    10    0 TSO1234
  C3            1  01.01 92/12/21 92/12/21 23:32    11    11    0 TSO1234
  C4            1  01.00 92/12/21 92/12/21 23:31    11    11    0 TSO1234
  C5            1  01.00 92/12/21 92/12/21 23:39     6     6    0 TSO1234
  DEFINE        3  01.00 92/12/04 92/12/04 17:51   545   545    0 TSO1234
  DELETE        2  01.03 92/12/04 92/12/11 17:06   123   123    0 TSO1234
  EDIT          2  01.00 92/12/04 92/12/04 17:52   106   106    0 TSO1234
  EXEC          3  01.00 92/12/04 92/12/04 17:53    48    48    0 TSO1234
  FORMAT        3  01.00 92/12/04 92/12/04 17:54    60    60    0 TSO1234
```

Figure 7.19 Concatenated browse member list.

```
BROWSE -- TSO1234.PROD.DATA(ALLOC) - 01.01 -------- LINE 00000000 COL 001 080
COMMAND ===> _                                              SCROLL ===> CSR
***************************** TOP OF DATA  ********************************

FUNCTION  -
     THE ALLOCATE COMMAND PERFORMS THE FOLLOWING FUNCTIONS:
               - DYNAMICALLY DEFINES AND ALLOCATES A DATA SET WITH OR
                 WITHOUT AN ATTRIBUTE LIST OF DCB PARAMETERS.
               - ALLOCATES A NEW DATASET WITH ATTRIBUTES COPIED FROM AN
                 EXISTING DATA SET.
               - CONCATENATES A LIST OF DATA SETS.

SYNTAX  -
          ALLOCATE    DATASET('DSNAME'/'LIST OF DSNAMES'/*)
                          OR
                      DUMMY
                      FILE('DDNAME') ALTFILE('DDNAME')
                      DEST('DESTINATION' OR 'NODE.USERID')
                      NEW/OLD/MOD/SHR/SYSOUT('CLASS')
                      VOLUME('SERIAL'/SERIAL LIST)/MSVGP('IDENTIFIER')
                      SPACE('QUANTITY','INCREMENT') DIR('INTEGER')
                      BLOCK('VALUE')/AVBLOCK('VALUE')/TRACKS/CYLINDERS
                      USING('ATTR-LIST-NAME')
                          OR
```

Figure 7.20 Contents of member from library number three.

8

Browse Commands

All browse commands are issued from the primary command area (upper left of the screen), although the commands can also be assigned to PF keys. The commands can be entered anywhere within the primary command area; they need not be left justified in the command field. Primary commands can be entered in either uppercase or lowercase characters. Command parameters can generally be specified in any order, with multiple parameters separated by blanks or commas.

COLUMNS and RESET Commands

The COLUMNS command is used to display column indicators at the top of the screen. These are used to help determine the column positions of data in the browse session. The command can also be abbreviated COLS or COL. Figure 8.1 shows the COLUMNS command invoked in a browse session.

As a result of the command, a single line of column indicators is displayed (Figure 8.2). The line will always remain at the top of the display, even while scrolling up or down within the data set. Every 10 positions is represented by a numeric value of the column number. Every five columns contains a plus sign (+) to make the display easier to interpret.

Scrolling to the left or right also affects the column indicators as they adjust to reflect the actual columns currently viewed. Column indicators should be used, in longer data sets, with the start and end column message in the short message area. The message helps to establish the range of columns displayed, since column indicator values are always a single digit. That's true whether the first display column is 1 or 1001.

Also in Figure 8.2 is the RESET command to turn the column indicators off. The RESET command, which should not be confused with the RESET key to unlock the

```
 BROWSE -- TSO1234.EXAMPLE.DATA(CLIST) - 01.01 ---- LINE 00000000 COL 001 080
 COMMAND ===> cols_                                        SCROLL ===> CSR
****************************** TOP OF DATA  ********************************

                            CLIST Execution


                      Modes Of CLIST Execution

There are four modes of CLIST execution, explicit, modified explicit,
implicit, and modified implicit. CLIST execution is made possible by
the TSO command, EXEC. That command can also be abbreviated as EX.
Because the command is explicitly stated in the first two modes, they
are known as explicit modes. The implicit modes do not contain EX or
EXEC as part of the command syntax. They also differ in their reliance
upon a special file to identify which CLIST code to execute.

CLISTS are invoked at the TSO prompter or an interface to it. For
those who have ISPF installed, this could also be OPTION 6 as well as
most Productivity Development Facility (PDF) panels that have a
command line. When a CLIST (or TSO command for that matter) is entered
from a PDF panel it should be preceded by the word TSO. This is not
required from PDF Option 6 because it was designed to accept TSO
commands and CLISTS.
```

Figure 8.1 COLUMNS command.

```
 BROWSE -- TSO1234.EXAMPLE.DATA(CLIST) - 01.01 ---- LINE 00000000 COL 001 080
 COMMAND ===> reset_                                       SCROLL ===> CSR
----+----1----+----2----+----3----+----4----+----5----+----6----+----7----+--
****************************** TOP OF DATA  ********************************

                            CLIST Execution


                      Modes Of CLIST Execution

There are four modes of CLIST execution, explicit, modified explicit,
implicit, and modified implicit. CLIST execution is made possible by
the TSO command, EXEC. That command can also be abbreviated as EX.
Because the command is explicitly stated in the first two modes, they
are known as explicit modes. The implicit modes do not contain EX or
EXEC as part of the command syntax. They also differ in their reliance
upon a special file to identify which CLIST code to execute.

CLISTS are invoked at the TSO prompter or an interface to it. For
those who have ISPF installed, this could also be OPTION 6 as well as
most Productivity Development Facility (PDF) panels that have a
command line. When a CLIST (or TSO command for that matter) is entered
from a PDF panel it should be preceded by the word TSO. This is not
required from PDF Option 6 because it was designed to accept TSO
```

Figure 8.2 Column indicators and the RESET command.

keyboard, can also be abbreviated RES. Column indicators can also be turned off by issuing the primary command COLS OFF. If not turned off, column indicators will be active any time browse is used during a given ISPF session. Upon entering the next ISPF session, the column indicators will initially be turned off.

DISPLAY Command

The DISPLAY command is used to alter what's viewed in browse. Specifically, the DISPLAY command deals with the display of carriage control characters and non-display characters. Carriage control characters are used to specify printer line spacing. When used, they occupy the first column of the data set and are not normally displayed in a browse session. To cause the carriage control characters to display with the rest of the data, the DISPLAY command can be used with the CC (Carriage Control) option, as in Figure 8.3.

The DISPLAY command can be abbreviated DISPL, DISP, or DIS. Figure 8.4 shows the same data with the carriage control characters displayed. The display of carriage control characters can be turned off using the command DISPLAY NOCC.

In some instances data values exist that have no corresponding terminal display character. The DISPLAY command can also be used to describe how these non-display characters should be represented. The default is to display them as periods, as is done in most memory dumps. They can be shown as any normal display character by using that character after the DISPLAY command. DISPLAY @, for example, would cause the character @ to be displayed in place of each non-display character.

```
 BROWSE -- TSO1234.PRINT.TEXT --------------------- LINE 00000000 COL 001 080
 COMMAND ===> display cc_                                   SCROLL ===> CSR
 ****************************** TOP OF DATA ********************************
                              CLIST Execution
                          Modes Of CLIST Execution
    There are four modes of CLIST execution, explicit, modified explicit,
    implicit, and modified implicit. CLIST execution is made possible by
    the TSO command, EXEC. That command can also be abbreviated as EX.
    Because the command is explicitly stated in the first two modes, they
    are known as explicit modes. The implicit modes do not contain EX or
    EXEC as part of the command syntax. They also differ in their reliance
    upon a special file to identify which CLIST code to execute.
    CLISTS are invoked at the TSO prompter or an interface to it. For
    those who have ISPF installed, this could also be OPTION 6 as well as
    most Productivity Development Facility (PDF) panels that have a
    command line. When a CLIST (or TSO command for that matter) is entered
    from a PDF panel it should be preceded by the word TSO. This is not
    required from PDF Option 6 because it was designed to accept TSO
    commands and CLISTS.
    The modes of CLIST execution will now be covered in more detail. The
    next few examples, used to demonstrate that execution, will assume
    that there is a partitioned data set, TSO1234.SAMPLE.CLIST, that
    contains several executable CLISTS.
```

Figure 8.3 DISPLAY command.

```
 BROWSE -- TSO1234.PRINT.TEXT -------------------- LINE 00000000 COL 001 080
 COMMAND ===> _                                          SCROLL ===> CSR
****************************** TOP OF DATA  ********************************
1
0                            CLIST Execution
-                          Modes Of CLIST Execution
0  There are four modes of CLIST execution, explicit, modified explicit,
   implicit, and modified implicit. CLIST execution is made possible by
   the TSO command, EXEC. That command can also be abbreviated as EX.
   Because the command is explicitly stated in the first two modes, they
   are known as explicit modes. The implicit modes do not contain EX or
   EXEC as part of the command syntax. They also differ in their reliance
   upon a special file to identify which CLIST code to execute.
0  CLISTS are invoked at the TSO prompter or an interface to it. For
   those who have ISPF installed, this could also be OPTION 6 as well as
   most Productivity Development Facility (PDF) panels that have a
   command line. When a CLIST (or TSO command for that matter) is entered
   from a PDF panel it should be preceded by the word TSO. This is not
   required from PDF Option 6 because it was designed to accept TSO
   commands and CLISTS.
0  The modes of CLIST execution will now be covered in more detail. The
   next few examples, used to demonstrate that execution, will assume
   that there is a partitioned data set, TSO1234.SAMPLE.CLIST, that
   contains several executable CLISTS.
```

Figure 8.4 Display of carriage control characters.

DISPLAY "or DISPLAY " could be used to cause each non-display character to display as a blank. This setting, as well as that for displaying carriage control characters, is retained in the profile (even between ISPF sessions) and is therefore active in any browse sessions until changed again.

HEX Command

The HEX command is used to cause the hexadecimal representation of the data to be displayed along with the character display. Often that display mode is used when the data set contains data that can't readily be displayed. In many instances the information is numeric data stored in binary or packed format. Binary data is stored as base 16, using the digits 0 through 9 as well as the letters A through F to represent the numbers 10 through 15 respectively (base 16 only uses the numbers 0 through 15 the way base 10 only uses the numbers 0 through 9). This alone doesn't make the data difficult to display. The difficulty comes from the compressed form of numeric values stored in binary format where each column actually contains two values. The same is true for packed data, even though its format is different (base 10 ending with a letter to represent the sign). Figure 8.5 shows the HEX command to turn on the hexadecimal representation of data.

Figure 8.6 shows the same data display with the hexadecimal representation turned on. Each line of data is now represented by three lines on the display. Each group of three lines is separated from every other group by a dashed line. With the expanded nature of the display, much less of the data set can actually be displayed

```
 BROWSE -- TSO1234.JCL.CNTL(SORT2) - 01.01 -------- LINE 00000000 COL 001 080
 COMMAND ===> hex on_                                    SCROLL ===> CSR
****************************** TOP OF DATA  ********************************
//TSO1234S JOB 'HEX EXAMPLE',                                       00010
//   MSGLEVEL=(1,1),                                                00011
//   CLASS=A,MSGCLASS=H,NOTIFY=TSO1234                              00012
//STEP1   EXEC PGM=SYNCSORT                                         00012
//SYSPRINT DD SYSOUT=*                                              00012
//SYSOUT   DD SYSOUT=*                                              00012
//SORTIN   DD DSN=TSO1234.TEST.DATA,DISP=SHR                        00012
//SORTOUT  DD DSN=TSO1234.TEST.DATA,DISP=OLD                        00012
//SORTWK01 DD UNIT=SYSDA,SPACE=(CYL,(5,1))                          00012
//SORTWK02 DD UNIT=SYSDA,SPACE=(CYL,(5,1))                          00012
//SORTWK03 DD UNIT=SYSDA,SPACE=(CYL,(5,1))                          00012
//SYSIN DD *                                                        00013
   SORT FIELDS=(1,12,CH,A)                                          00014
***************************** BOTTOM OF DATA ******************************
```

Figure 8.5 HEX command.

```
 BROWSE - TSO1234.JCL.CNTL(SORT2) - 01.01 ----- LINE 00000000 COL 001 080
 COMMAND ===> _                                          SCROLL ===> CSR
****************************** TOP OF DATA  ********************************



   _____
//TSO1234S JOB 'HEX EXAMPLE'-+
```

Figure 8.6 Hexadecimal display of data.

on a given screen. The first of the three lines is the same as before the hex mode was turned on. The next two lines show the hexadecimal equivalent of the first line. In the first line of data, for example, the hex value 61 represents the special character / while the hex value E3 represents the capital letter T. The hex value 40 is used to represent a space and can be seen over a large part of the data display.

The hexadecimal representation is given in a vertical display by default. It can also be explicitly stated or changed to display vertically with the command HEX ON VERT. The hexadecimal portion of the display can also be changed to display horizontally using the command HEX ON DATA. When the hexadecimal display is turned on, it remains on during a given ISPF session. The next ISPF session will start with the hexadecimal display turned off. The command HEX OFF can also be used to return to a normal character display.

Recursive Browse

Recursive browse entails leaving the current browse session for another. The first browse session remains suspended until returned to using the END function. Any number of additional browse sessions can be started (within computer memory constraints). Each one is ended as if it were the only browse session, causing return to the one established before it. The BROWSE command is shown in Figure 8.7 with the optional member name parameter. In this format, the BROWSE command will start another browse session with the member specified. That member must already exist and, using this format, must be in the same PDS as the member it was invoked from.

```
 BROWSE -- TSO1234.JCL.CNTL(SORT2) - 01.01 -------- LINE 00000000 COL 001 080
 COMMAND ===> browse compress_                          SCROLL ===> CSR
****************************** TOP OF DATA  ********************************
//TSO1234S JOB 'HEX EXAMPLE',                                       00010
//   MSGLEVEL=(1,1),                                                00011
//   CLASS=A,MSGCLASS=H,NOTIFY=TSO1234                              00012
//STEP1    EXEC PGM=SYNCSORT                                        00012
//SYSPRINT DD SYSOUT=*                                              00012
//SYSOUT   DD SYSOUT=*                                              00012
//SORTIN   DD DSN=TSO1234.TEST.DATA,DISP=SHR                        00012
//SORTOUT  DD DSN=TSO1234.TEST.DATA,DISP=OLD                        00012
//SORTWK01 DD UNIT=SYSDA,SPACE=(CYL,(5,1))                          00012
//SORTWK02 DD UNIT=SYSDA,SPACE=(CYL,(5,1))                          00012
//SORTWK03 DD UNIT=SYSDA,SPACE=(CYL,(5,1))                          00012
//SYSIN DD *                                                        00013
   SORT FIELDS=(1,12,CH,A)                                          00014
***************************** BOTTOM OF DATA ******************************
```

Figure 8.7 Recursive BROWSE command.

```
 BROWSE -- TSO1234.JCL.CNTL(COMPRESS) - 01.01 ----- LINE 00000000 COL 001 080
 COMMAND ===> browse_                                       SCROLL ===> CSR
****************************** TOP OF DATA *********************************
//TSO1234A JOB 'COMPRESS  ',                                           00010
//  CLASS=A,MSGCLASS=T,NOTIFY=TSO1234                                  00012
//COMPRESS  EXEC PGM=IEBCOPY                                           00013
//SYSPRINT DD SYSOUT=*                                                 00014
//SYSUT1   DD UNIT=3380,SPACE=(TRK,(5,5))                              00015
//PDS      DD DSN=TSO1234.CLIST,DISP=OLD                               00016
//SYSIN    DD *                                                        00016
  COPY INDD=PDS,OUTDD=PDS                                              00016
^^^^************************** BOTTOM OF DATA ******************************
```

Figure 8.8 Second browse session.

```
      ------------------------- BROWSE COMMAND PANEL --------------------------
      COMMAND ===>

      ISPF LIBRARY:
         PROJECT ===>
         GROUP   ===>            ===>            ===>            ===>
         TYPE    ===>
         MEMBER  ===>                 (Blank or pattern for member selection list)

      OTHER PARTITIONED OR SEQUENTIAL DATA SET:
         DATA SET NAME  ===> EXAMPLE.DATA(ALLOC)_
         VOLUME SERIAL  ===>            (If not cataloged)

      DATA SET PASSWORD ===>           (If password protected)

      MIXED MODE        ===> NO        (Specify YES or NO)

      FORMAT NAME       ===>
```

Figure 8.9 BROWSE command panel.

Figure 8.8 shows the second browse session, a member called COMPRESS. From this second session, the BROWSE command is issued again to start yet another browse session. In this particular instance, the command is entered without a member name.

When the member name is omitted, the browse command panel is displayed. This screen, just like the original browse menu, allows any data set to be specified. This screen, therefore, allows other data sets to be accessed and can be used to browse sequential data sets as well as partitioned data sets. The name of a different PDS (and member name) is specified in Figure 8.9. Omitting the member name on this screen would force the PDS member list to display just as it would from the browse menu. Members could then be selected from the member list.

Figure 8.10 shows the third browse session. Notice the different data set and member name in the title line at the top. The previous two browse sessions are suspended and will be displayed when returned to using the END function.

The only other browse command to discuss is the FIND command. It's one of the most complex commands available in terms of optional parameters and will be the topic of the entire next chapter.

```
   BROWSE -- TSO1234.EXAMPLE.DATA(ALLOC) - 01.01 ---- LINE 00000000 COL 001 080
   COMMAND ===> _                                            SCROLL ===> CSR
   ****************************** TOP OF DATA  ********************************

   FUNCTION  -
     THE ALLOCATE COMMAND PERFORMS THE FOLLOWING FUNCTIONS:
           - DYNAMICALLY DEFINES AND ALLOCATES A DATA SET WITH OR
             WITHOUT AN ATTRIBUTE LIST OF DCB PARAMETERS.
           - ALLOCATES A NEW DATASET WITH ATTRIBUTES COPIED FROM AN
             EXISTING DATA SET.
           - CONCATENATES A LIST OF DATA SETS.

   SYNTAX  -
           ALLOCATE    DATASET('DSNAME'/'LIST OF DSNAMES'/*)
                            OR
                       DUMMY
                       FILE('DDNAME') ALTFILE('DDNAME')
                       DEST('DESTINATION' OR 'NODE.USERID')
                       NEW/OLD/MOD/SHR/SYSOUT('CLASS')
                       VOLUME('SERIAL'/'SERIAL LIST)/MSVGP('IDENTIFIER')
                       SPACE('QUANTITY','INCREMENT') DIR('INTEGER')
                       BLOCK('VALUE')/AVBLOCK('VALUE')/TRACKS/CYLINDERS
                       USING('ATTR-LIST-NAME')
                            OR
```

Figure 8.10 Third browse session.

9

The Browse FIND Command

The FIND command is used to find character strings. It can be used in both the browse and edit functions and is closely tied to the edit CHANGE command in function and syntax. The command can be spelled out, or it can be abbreviated with the letter F. The only required parameter is the string to be searched for. The string should be enclosed in single or double quotes under the circumstances shown in Table 9.1.

TABLE 9.1 Quoted Strings

When the string contains embedded blanks	F 'the end'
When the string contains single or double quotes	F "value '99'"
When the string coincides with a FIND command parameter	F 'next' PREV
When the string is numeric and columns are specified	F '05' 12 72

The quotes serve to avoid misinterpretation. If there's a chance of this happening, ISPF will issue a short message requesting that quotes be specified rather than attempting to execute the FIND command. When the string itself contains single or double quotes, it can easily be specified using the other type of quote:

```
FIND '"yes"'
```

or

```
FIND "parm='update'"
```

Repeat Find

The search will start at the current cursor position on the current screen (not at the top of the data) and work toward the bottom of the data. If the string is not found, a message will be issued to indicate that. Once a string has been found, however, the cursor is positioned at the start of the character string. The screen contents will be scrolled when necessary to show the context of the string within the data set. The FIND command can be repeated using the RFIND command. This will locate the next occurrence of the string and reposition the cursor at the start of that string. If the repeat find function reaches the bottom of the data before it finds the string, a message will be issued indicating that the bottom of the data has been reached. If the repeat find function is used after reaching the bottom of the data, the search continues from the top of the data.

Implementing the repeat find function is made easier when RFIND is assigned to a PF key. That allows the current cursor position to be retained and each subsequent search to be started with a single keystroke. RFIND is the default function assigned to PF keys 5 and 17. The search direction and any other parameters specified with the initial FIND command are retained with the repeat find function. As an alternative, the previous FIND command could again be listed using the RETRIEVE or CRETRIEV functions and entered again. Because this is not as efficient, it should not be used unless it's necessary to alter the string or the command parameters in some way.

ISPF retention of the FIND string allows the repeat find function to operate. It also allows the string to be specified in shorthand form. The last FIND string can be represented in another FIND command as an asterisk. This makes it easy to add parameters (which will be discussed shortly) to the previous string:

```
FIND * 8 72 PREV
```

When it's necessary to find an asterisk rather than use it to designate the previous string, the asterisk should be enclosed in single or double quotes:

```
FIND '*' 8 72 PREV
```

Additional FIND command parameters are generally used to limit the scope of the string search. When they're specified, they can be listed in any order and are separated by blanks or commas.

Case-Sensitive Search

The FIND command is not normally sensitive to case. It will find a string in uppercase or lowercase. The string could in fact be a mixture of both and still be found. This default mode is called the text string:

```
FIND T'EiThEr CaSe Is Ok'
```

Because it's the default, it's not necessary to specify a text string, and the letter T can be omitted:

```
FIND 'EiThEr CaSe Is Ok'
```

When it's necessary to obtain an exact match on uppercase and lowercase characters for a particular string, the character string feature can be specified. This merely requires the letter C in front of the string itself. The string might then need to be enclosed in quotes to separate it from the parameter:

```
FIND C'UPPER Also lower'
```

Specifying the Search Direction

The default is to search for the next occurrence of a string. Since NEXT is the default search direction, it's never required as a parameter. To reverse the normal search direction, PREV can be specified. The current cursor position on the current screen is still used as the starting position, but the search is conducted up toward the top of the data. If the repeat find function is used after reaching the top of the data, the search will restart at the bottom of the data.

Two other parameters, FIRST and LAST, also determine the direction of a search. FIRST, for example, will start at the top of the data to search for the string specified. This is true no matter what the current position is in the data set. Using the parameter FIRST, it's not necessary to first scroll to the top of the data. The implied direction for the repeat find function is NEXT or down. Conversely, LAST will start at the bottom of the data to search for the last occurrence of a string. With LAST, the implied direction for the repeat find function is PREV or up.

Another parameter, ALL, has much the same effect as FIRST since it will find the first occurrence no matter where in the data it's invoked. Like FIRST, the implied direction for the repeat find function is to search down into the data from the first string found. An added benefit from using ALL is that the number of strings found throughout all the data is displayed in the short message area. In Chapter 16, the FIND command is used in the editor with excluded lines to highlight particular elements of the data. The discussion of X and NX parameters (to deal with excluded and non-excluded lines) is saved for that chapter since they're an exclusive feature of the edit function.

Specifying the String Context

Additional FIND command parameters can be used to specify the string context. They help to limit the search to strings used as a word prefix (PREFIX or PRE), a word suffix (SUFFIX or SUF), or the entire word (WORD). The default CHARS will find the string no matter what the context is. It includes all three, as well as strings that are embedded within a word. It should be noted that word in this context merely means characters grouped together with spaces on both sides. Most special characters (except @, #, and $) have the same effect as spaces in this context. No check is made to ensure that a particular group of characters is part of the English language. The group could in fact contain numbers or special characters and still qualify as a word. Table 9.2 illustrates the effect of the context parameters.

TABLE 9.2   BROWSE Command Context Parameters

F ant PRE (PREFIX)	F ant SUF (SUFFIX)	F ant WORD (WORD)	F ant (CHARS)
anterior	anterior	anterior	**ant**erior
significant	signific**ant**	signific**ant**	signific**ant**
ant	ant	**ant**	**ant**
planted	planted	planted	pl**ant**ed

Limiting Columns Searched

Limiting the columns searched for a particular string can make the search more efficient. It can also help to differentiate or isolate one use of a particular string from another. This is especially true of some programming languages that are column specific. Both a starting column number and an ending column number can be specified. When only one column value is specified, it's interpreted as the start column. In this case, the string will only be found if it starts in that particular column. When two columns are specified, the second column number represents the end column. The entire string must then fall within the column range created by the two values before it will be found.

A COBOL programmer might, for example, need to find the line that contains the string "PROCEDURE DIVISION." The following FIND command can be used since that statement must start in column 8:

```
FIND PROC 8
```

In addition to being more efficient to execute, the command in this format requires less typing than to type the entire character string. The following form of the command could be used to find any other form of the string PROC since it defines the entire range of the indented coding area in COBOL:

```
FIND PROC 12 72
```

Finding Hexadecimal Strings

It's not always possible to identify data with a combination of keyboard characters. In some cases, the data represents symbols not on the keyboard. In other cases, significant data was not meant to display. This might include binary and packed data formats. The data can still be referenced in a FIND command using its hexadecimal representation. The following FIND commands are used to search for hex zeros (known as low values):

```
FIND X'00'
```

and a packed field containing the value +357:

```
FIND X'357C'
```

The letter X immediately preceding or following the character string identifies it as a hexadecimal value. Such values must be specified in pairs. To specify an odd number of values or values other than 0 through 9 and A through F would constitute an error.

Finding Picture Strings

A picture string is a special designation just like a hex or character string. The picture string supports a number of special characters that are used to represent a class of characters rather than a specific character itself. This allows a search to be conducted for that particular class. For example, the character # is used in a picture string to represent any single numeric value:

```
FIND P'#'
```

The FIND command example would find the next numeric value. The special characters that are used to represent a type of character can also be used with actual alphabetic and numeric characters. This helps to further restrict the search for certain character strings by further defining the context.

```
FIND P'page ##'
```

This FIND command example would find the next instance of the string page followed by a space and two numeric values. Other instances of the string page would not be obtained, even when the string page was followed by a blank and a single numeric value. Table 9.3 details the use of the special characters that can be used within the picture string context.

TABLE 9.3 Picture String Symbols

String symbol	Use within a picture string
=	Any character
¬	Any non-blank character
#	Any numeric character
–	Any non-numeric character
@	Any alphabetic character
$	Any special character
>	Any uppercase alphabetic character
<	Any lowercase alphabetic character
•	Any non-display character

The following command could be used to check that data was not inadvertently entered in a particular area:

```
FIND P'┬' 73 80
```

It checks for any non-blank characters between columns 73 through 80, inclusive. A slight variation of the same command (using a hyphen) can be made to find any non-numeric character since that column range is often used for sequence numbers. That's illustrated in the following example.

```
FIND P'-' 73 80
```

FIND Command Syntax Summary

Table 9.4 shows the FIND command syntax for browse. Brackets indicate optional parameters. Underscored parameters are defaults and need not be specified. Another set of parameters distinguishes between excluded and non-excluded lines in edit mode as well as a range of lines to search. Those parameters are discussed in Chapter 16.

TABLE 9.4 FIND Command Syntax Summary

FIND	string	NEXT	CHARS	[start-col]	[end-col]	X	label-
F	*	PREV	PREFIX			NX	range
		FIRST	SUFFIX				
		LAST	WORD				
		ALL					

Using FIND Command Parameters

Figure 9.1 shows the FIND command in the context of an actual browse session. In this particular instance, the command is used to find the character string "PROC."

In Figure 9.2 the specified string has been found and the cursor has been placed under the start of the string to show its location. Scrolling has automatically been conducted to show the string on the second line of the current display (the first line happens to be blank), so the previous line will serve to provide some context. The short message also indicates that the string has been found and even reflects the case of the particular string found.

The RFIND command can be used to find additional instances of the string. A PF key with the RFIND command assigned to it (the default for PF keys 5 and 17) was used to get to the second occurrence of the string (shown in Figure 9.3). Use of the PF key allowed the cursor to remain on the first string and therefore start the next search from that position. As an alternative, the RFIND command can be typed in the primary command area and the cursor moved into the data portion beyond the first string before pressing the ENTER key. That too will ensure that ISPF doesn't merely keep finding the first instance of the string.

```
BROWSE -- TSO1234.EXAMPLE.DATA(CLIST) - 01.01 ---- LINE 00000000 COL 001 080
COMMAND ===> f proc_                                    SCROLL ===> CSR
****************************** TOP OF DATA ********************************

                          CLIST Execution


                     Modes Of CLIST Execution

There are four modes of CLIST execution, explicit, modified explicit,
implicit, and modified implicit. CLIST execution is made possible by
the TSO command, EXEC. That command can also be abbreviated as EX.
Because the command is explicitly stated in the first two modes, they
are known as explicit modes. The implicit modes do not contain EX or
EXEC as part of the command syntax. They also differ in their reliance
upon a special file to identify which CLIST code to execute.

CLISTS are invoked at the TSO prompter or an interface to it. For
those who have ISPF installed, this could also be OPTION 6 as well as
most Productivity Development Facility (PDF) panels that have a
command line. When a CLIST (or TSO command for that matter) is entered
from a PDF panel it should be preceded by the word TSO. This is not
required from PDF Option 6 because it was designed to accept TSO
commands and CLISTS.
```

Figure 9.1 Browse FIND command.

```
BROWSE -- TSO1234.EXAMPLE.DATA(CLIST) - 01.01 ----------- CHARS 'proc' FOUND
COMMAND ===>                                            SCROLL ===> CSR

Before proceeding to the second execution mode, it is necessary to
discuss how TSO handles data set names. When data set names are not
literally specified (enclosed in single quotes), TSO will append a
prefix in front of the data set name. This prefix is usually the
individual's user-id, but can be changed by any TSO user, by using the
TSO PROFILE command. Based upon the context in which it is used, TSO
can also detect special data set types and attach an appropriate
suffix. This too will only occur when the data set name is not
literally specified. This suffix would become the last data set
qualifier. This last qualifier (which precedes the member name, if
any) is also known as the descriptive qualifier. Two such descriptive
qualifiers that pertain especially to CLIST execution are .CLIST for
CLIST data sets and .LOAD for load module libraries. The former is the
basis for the modified explicit execution mode, while the latter will
be discussed  later with the resource controlling aspects of CLISTS.
Finally, if a CLIST library is specified but the member name is
omitted, TSO will assume that a member name of TEMPNAME is to be
applied.



                        Modified Explicit Mode
```

Figure 9.2 Result of FIND command.

```
BROWSE -- TSO1234.EXAMPLE.DATA(CLIST) - 01.01 ----------- CHARS 'PROC' FOUND
COMMAND ===>                                              SCROLL ===> CSR
Implicit execution of a CLIST is made possible by connecting a CLIST
library or libraries to the SYSPROC file. The process of allocating
CLIST libraries was described previously, and is well worth the effort.
Subsequent CLIST execution is very much simplified and is as easy as
specifying the member name followed by any parameters. The libraries
allocated to the SYSPROC file are searched in the order they were
allocated until a member name matching the one specified is found. If
there is no match, TSO stops and returns the message "COMMAND NOT
FOUND".

Conversely, the same member name may exist in more than one CLIST
library in the SYSPROC file. The contents of the like named members
could vary widely, but only the first member found with the specified
name will be executed. If you save your CLIST code and execute it in
this fashion, only to find yourself in a totally different process,
check the other CLIST libraries for a member of the same name. This
problem does not occur with either of the explicit modes of execution
because you are directing TSO to look at a single, specific data set.

In the implicit mode of execution, CLISTS look and act just like TSO
commands. When invoking your CLIST, you might also run into like named
TSO commands. When an implicitly invoked CLIST has the same name as a
```

Figure 9.3 Result of RFIND command.

With the second instance of the string, the short message has changed slightly to reflect that this instance of the string is in capital letters. Again, the line containing the string was brought up to be the second line of the display. That allows the preceding line to be viewed too without scrolling. The PF key could be used again to find the next occurrence of the string. That string happens to be four lines below the current cursor position. Because it's on the currently visible screen, no scrolling would take place. The cursor would merely move to align itself below the start of the string.

Rather than continue the search down into the data set, the FIND command shown in Figure 9.4 reverses the direction of the search. The use of the asterisk takes advantage of the fact that last used string is "remembered." It will, therefore, continue to search for the string "PROC."

It's not surprising that the search from the current cursor position up into the data set has found the same string that was found on the way down (Figure 9.5). When the RFIND key is used here, the search for additional previous strings will continue upward since that's now the established direction.

The short message area in Figure 9.6 indicates that the top of the data set was reached before another occurrence of the string was located. No scrolling occurred either since there was no new string to display. If the RFIND key is used again, the search will resume from the bottom of the data set. The search direction would still be up or PREV.

Figure 9.7 shows the FIND command used at the top of the data set to find the same character string "proc." This time, however, the string context has been limited

```
BROWSE -- TSO1234.EXAMPLE.DATA(CLIST) - 01.01 ----------- CHARS 'PROC' FOUND
COMMAND ===> f * prev_                                          SCROLL ===> CSR
Implicit execution of a CLIST is made possible by connecting a CLIST
library or libraries to the SYSPROC file. The process of allocating
CLIST libraries was described previously, and is well worth the effort.
Subsequent CLIST execution is very much simplified and is as easy as
specifying the member name followed by any parameters. The libraries
allocated to the SYSPROC file are searched in the order they were
allocated until a member name matching the one specified is found. If
there is no match, TSO stops and returns the message "COMMAND NOT
FOUND".

Conversely, the same member name may exist in more than one CLIST
library in the SYSPROC file. The contents of the like named members
could vary widely, but only the first member found with the specified
name will be executed. If you save your CLIST code and execute it in
this fashion, only to find yourself in a totally different process,
check the other CLIST libraries for a member of the same name. This
problem does not occur with either of the explicit modes of execution
because you are directing TSO to look at a single, specific data set.

In the implicit mode of execution, CLISTS look and act just like TSO
commands. When invoking your CLIST, you might also run into like named
TSO commands. When an implicitly invoked CLIST has the same name as a
```

Figure 9.4 FIND PREV command.

```
BROWSE -- TSO1234.EXAMPLE.DATA(CLIST) - 01.01 ----------- CHARS 'proc' FOUND
COMMAND ===>                                                   SCROLL ===> CSR

Before proceeding to the second execution mode, it is necessary to
discuss how TSO handles data set names. When data set names are not
literally specified (enclosed in single quotes), TSO will append a
prefix in front of the data set name. This prefix is usually the
individual's user-id, but can be changed by any TSO user, by using the
TSO PROFILE command. Based upon the context in which it is used, TSO
can also detect special data set types and attach an appropriate
suffix. This too will only occur when the data set name is not
literally specified. This suffix would become the last data set
qualifier. This last qualifier (which precedes the member name, if
any) is also known as the descriptive qualifier. Two such descriptive
qualifiers that pertain especially to CLIST execution are .CLIST for
CLIST data sets and .LOAD for load module libraries. The former is the
basis for the modified explicit execution mode, while the latter will
be discussed later with the resource controlling aspects of CLISTS.
Finally, if a CLIST library is specified but the member name is
omitted, TSO will assume that a member name of TEMPNAME is to be
applied.



                       Modified Explicit Mode
```

Figure 9.5 Result of FIND PREV command.

```
 BROWSE -- TSO1234.EXAMPLE.DATA(CLIST) - 01.01 ------ * TOP OF DATA REACHED *
 COMMAND ===> _                                           SCROLL ===> CSR

Before proceeding to the second execution mode, it is necessary to
discuss how TSO handles data set names. When data set names are not
literally specified (enclosed in single quotes), TSO will append a
prefix in front of the data set name. This prefix is usually the
individual's user-id, but can be changed by any TSO user, by using the
TSO PROFILE command. Based upon the context in which it is used, TSO
can also detect special data set types and attach an appropriate
suffix. This too will only occur when the data set name is not
literally specified. This suffix would become the last data set
qualifier. This last qualifier (which precedes the member name, if
any) is also known as the descriptive qualifier. Two such descriptive
qualifiers that pertain especially to CLIST execution are .CLIST for
CLIST data sets and .LOAD for load module libraries. The former is the
basis for the modified explicit execution mode, while the latter will
be discussed  later with the resource controlling aspects of CLISTS.
Finally, if a CLIST library is specified but the member name is
omitted, TSO will assume that a member name of TEMPNAME is to be
applied.



                       Modified Explicit Mode
```

Figure 9.6   Result of RFIND PREV command.

```
 BROWSE -- TSO1234.EXAMPLE.DATA(CLIST) - 01.01 ---- LINE 00000000 COL 001 080
 COMMAND ===> f proc word_                                SCROLL ===> CSR
 ****************************** TOP OF DATA ********************************

                          CLIST Execution


                       Modes Of CLIST Execution

There are four modes of CLIST execution, explicit, modified explicit,
implicit, and modified implicit. CLIST execution is made possible by
the TSO command, EXEC. That command can also be abbreviated as EX.
Because the command is explicitly stated in the first two modes, they
are known as explicit modes. The implicit modes do not contain EX or
EXEC as part of the command syntax. They also differ in their reliance
upon a special file to identify which CLIST code to execute.

CLISTS are invoked at the TSO prompter or an interface to it. For
those who have ISPF installed, this could also be OPTION 6 as well as
most Productivity Development Facility (PDF) panels that have a
command line. When a CLIST (or TSO command for that matter) is entered
from a PDF panel it should be preceded by the word TSO. This is not
required from PDF Option 6 because it was designed to accept TSO
commands and CLISTS.
```

Figure 9.7   FIND WORD command.

to only those instances that constitute a word. Figure 9.8 shows the character string found. Notice that instances found in previous examples were bypassed because they didn't constitute a word. Notice too that the format of the short message has changed slightly to indicate that the WORD parameter was used rather than the default CHARS. In this case, too, the command could have been entered FIND ' proc ' since the string was not likely to be surrounded by special characters.

Starting from the top of the data set again, the parameter is added to search for the same string, but only where it appears as a suffix (Figure 9.9). The cursor is placed at the start of the string (Figure 9.10) and again the format of the short message has changed slightly to indicate that the SUFFIX parameter was used rather than the default CHARS.

Figure 9.11 shows the use of the character string feature to make the FIND command sensitive to the case of the text entered. In this instance the character string "exec" should be found, but only where it contains all uppercase characters.

Although the string "exec" could be found on any of the first five non-blank lines, the first four were skipped because there was not an exact match on the case of the string entered. The string was found on the fifth non-blank line, where it contains all uppercase characters (Figure 9.12).

Figure 9.13 shows the FIND command parameters (start and end column numbers) that will limit the columns searched. In this variation of the data used previously, the intent is to find the number zero when it occurs in the normal text as opposed to column one, where it serves as a carriage control character.

In this instance (Figure 9.14) the FIND command didn't work. A request is made in the short message area that the string be placed in quotes. In that way, the string

```
BROWSE -- TSO1234.EXAMPLE.DATA(CLIST) - 01.01 ------------ WORD 'PROC' FOUND
COMMAND ===>                                               SCROLL ===> CSR
into them. At present, we will confine our discussion to the
parameters that are found on the CLIST PROC statement. This includes
the use of positional and keyword parameters to pass variable
information to the CLIST. The additional communication components will
be discussed later.



                         CLIST Variables

A CLIST variable is a named area of storage used to hold data. It is
called a variable because the data it contains is allowed to vary in
value. Most programming languages have a similar facility, typically
called a data element or field. Like some other programming languages,
CLIST variables can be used virtually anywhere without having to be
previously defined. Unlike most programming languages, however, CLIST
variables are free to contain numeric and/or character data without
having to commit to one or the other. CLIST variables are also dynamic
in the amount of information they are able to hold. You do not have to
define the length of a CLIST variable. Our first look at variables will
show how their values can be set as the CLIST is invoked. Those familiar
with JCL will see that this is very much like the symbolic variable
substitution that can occur when executing a cataloged procedure. The
```

Figure 9.8 Result of FIND WORD command.

```
BROWSE -- TSO1234.EXAMPLE.DATA(CLIST) - 01.01 ---- LINE 00000000 COL 001 080
COMMAND ===> f proc suf_                                      SCROLL ===> CSR
****************************** TOP OF DATA ********************************

                          CLIST Execution


                       Modes Of CLIST Execution

There are four modes of CLIST execution, explicit, modified explicit,
implicit, and modified implicit. CLIST execution is made possible by
the TSO command, EXEC. That command can also be abbreviated as EX.
Because the command is explicitly stated in the first two modes, they
are known as explicit modes. The implicit modes do not contain EX or
EXEC as part of the command syntax. They also differ in their reliance
upon a special file to identify which CLIST code to execute.

CLISTS are invoked at the TSO prompter or an interface to it. For
those who have ISPF installed, this could also be OPTION 6 as well as
most Productivity Development Facility (PDF) panels that have a
command line. When a CLIST (or TSO command for that matter) is entered
from a PDF panel it should be preceded by the word TSO. This is not
required from PDF Option 6 because it was designed to accept TSO
commands and CLISTS.
```

Figure 9.9 FIND SUFFIX command.

```
BROWSE -- TSO1234.EXAMPLE.DATA(CLIST) - 01.01 ---------- SUFFIX 'PROC' FOUND
COMMAND ===>                                                  SCROLL ===> CSR
Implicit execution of a CLIST is made possible by connecting a CLIST
library or libraries to the SYSPROC file. The process of allocating
CLIST libraries was described previously, and is well worth the effort.
Subsequent CLIST execution is very much simplified and is as easy as
specifying the member name followed by any parameters. The libraries
allocated to the SYSPROC file are searched in the order they were
allocated until a member name matching the one specified is found. If
there is no match, TSO stops and returns the message "COMMAND NOT
FOUND".

Conversely, the same member name may exist in more than one CLIST
library in the SYSPROC file. The contents of the like named members
could vary widely, but only the first member found with the specified
name will be executed. If you save your CLIST code and execute it in
this fashion, only to find yourself in a totally different process,
check the other CLIST libraries for a member of the same name. This
problem does not occur with either of the explicit modes of execution
because you are directing TSO to look at a single, specific data set.

In the implicit mode of execution, CLISTS look and act just like TSO
commands. When invoking your CLIST, you might also run into like named
TSO commands. When an implicitly invoked CLIST has the same name as a
```

Figure 9.10 Result of FIND SUFFIX command.

```
BROWSE -- TSO1234.EXAMPLE.DATA(CLIST) - 01.01 ---- LINE 00000000 COL 001 080
COMMAND ===> f c'EXEC'_                                      SCROLL ===> CSR
****************************** TOP OF DATA ******************************

                              CLIST Execution


                          Modes Of CLIST Execution

There are four modes of CLIST execution, explicit, modified explicit,
implicit, and modified implicit. CLIST execution is made possible by
the TSO command, EXEC. That command can also be abbreviated as EX.
Because the command is explicitly stated in the first two modes, they
are known as explicit modes. The implicit modes do not contain EX or
EXEC as part of the command syntax. They also differ in their reliance
upon a special file to identify which CLIST code to execute.

CLISTS are invoked at the TSO prompter or an interface to it. For
those who have ISPF installed, this could also be OPTION 6 as well as
most Productivity Development Facility (PDF) panels that have a
command line. When a CLIST (or TSO command for that matter) is entered
from a PDF panel it should be preceded by the word TSO. This is not
required from PDF Option 6 because it was designed to accept TSO
commands and CLISTS.
```

Figure 9.11 FIND character string command.

```
BROWSE -- TSO1234.EXAMPLE.DATA(CLIST) - 01.01 ----------- CHARS 'EXEC' FOUND
COMMAND ===>                                                SCROLL ===> CSR
****************************** TOP OF DATA ******************************

                              CLIST Execution


                          Modes Of CLIST Execution

There are four modes of CLIST execution, explicit, modified explicit,
implicit, and modified implicit. CLIST execution is made possible by
the TSO command, EXEC. That command can also be abbreviated as EX.
Because the command is explicitly stated in the first two modes, they
are known as explicit modes. The implicit modes do not contain EX or
EXEC as part of the command syntax. They also differ in their reliance
upon a special file to identify which CLIST code to execute.

CLISTS are invoked at the TSO prompter or an interface to it. For
those who have ISPF installed, this could also be OPTION 6 as well as
most Productivity Development Facility (PDF) panels that have a
command line. When a CLIST (or TSO command for that matter) is entered
from a PDF panel it should be preceded by the word TSO. This is not
required from PDF Option 6 because it was designed to accept TSO
commands and CLISTS.
```

Figure 9.12 Result of FIND character string command.

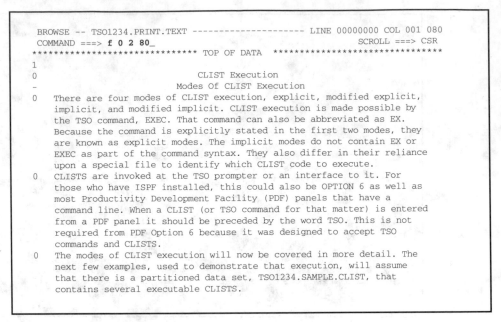

```
 BROWSE -- TSO1234.PRINT.TEXT -------------------- LINE 00000000 COL 001 080
 COMMAND ===> f 0 2 80_                                SCROLL ===> CSR
****************************** TOP OF DATA  *******************************
1
0                           CLIST Execution
-                       Modes Of CLIST Execution
0   There are four modes of CLIST execution, explicit, modified explicit,
    implicit, and modified implicit. CLIST execution is made possible by
    the TSO command, EXEC. That command can also be abbreviated as EX.
    Because the command is explicitly stated in the first two modes, they
    are known as explicit modes. The implicit modes do not contain EX or
    EXEC as part of the command syntax. They also differ in their reliance
    upon a special file to identify which CLIST code to execute.
0   CLISTS are invoked at the TSO prompter or an interface to it. For
    those who have ISPF installed, this could also be OPTION 6 as well as
    most Productivity Development Facility (PDF) panels that have a
    command line. When a CLIST (or TSO command for that matter) is entered
    from a PDF panel it should be preceded by the word TSO. This is not
    required from PDF Option 6 because it was designed to accept TSO
    commands and CLISTS.
0   The modes of CLIST execution will now be covered in more detail. The
    next few examples, used to demonstrate that execution, will assume
    that there is a partitioned data set, TSO1234.SAMPLE.CLIST, that
    contains several executable CLISTS.
```

Figure 9.13 Conflicting FIND command parameters.

```
 BROWSE -- TSO1234.PRINT.TEXT ------------------------- PUT STRING IN QUOTES
 COMMAND ===> f '0'_2 80                                SCROLL ===> CSR
****************************** TOP OF DATA  *******************************
1
0                           CLIST Execution
-                       Modes Of CLIST Execution
0   There are four modes of CLIST execution, explicit, modified explicit,
    implicit, and modified implicit. CLIST execution is made possible by
    the TSO command, EXEC. That command can also be abbreviated as EX.
    Because the command is explicitly stated in the first two modes, they
    are known as explicit modes. The implicit modes do not contain EX or
    EXEC as part of the command syntax. They also differ in their reliance
    upon a special file to identify which CLIST code to execute.
0   CLISTS are invoked at the TSO prompter or an interface to it. For
    those who have ISPF installed, this could also be OPTION 6 as well as
    most Productivity Development Facility (PDF) panels that have a
    command line. When a CLIST (or TSO command for that matter) is entered
    from a PDF panel it should be preceded by the word TSO. This is not
    required from PDF Option 6 because it was designed to accept TSO
    commands and CLISTS.
0   The modes of CLIST execution will now be covered in more detail. The
    next few examples, used to demonstrate that execution, will assume
    that there is a partitioned data set, TSO1234.SAMPLE.CLIST, that
    contains several executable CLISTS.
```

Figure 9.14 Find within columns.

```
BROWSE -- TSO1234.PRINT.TEXT ----------------------------- CHARS '0' FOUND
COMMAND ===>                                              SCROLL ===> CSR
         keywords. The statement would then be coded
0          PROC 1 PRINTDSNAME CLASS(A) COPIES(1) DEST(RMT0) _
0        Notice that the position specification parameter has been changed from
         4 to 1 to reflect the number of positional parameters now on the PROC
         statement. The name of the data set to be printed was retained as a
         positional parameter because it is the one piece of required
         information. It is hard to imagine a value which would be a suitable
         default for this parameter. Another obvious difference is the use of
         parentheses after the keyword variable name. This is the standard
         format for keyword parameters that you will see carried over to
         parameters in other CLIST statements. Think of the parentheses as a
         way to equate two things. In fact, if this were a JCL jobstream, you
         would see the COPIES variable coded as COPIES=1. Here, the variable
         &COPIES is equated to the number one.
0        If the HARDCOPY CLIST, containing the PROC statement above, were
         executed specifying no parameters, the only prompt would be for
         PRINTDSNAME. The other variables, &CLASS, &COPIES, and &DEST, would
         take their values from what is coded on the PROC statement. Those
         values, then, constitute default values that can be overridden when
         the CLIST is executed. Because there is no prompting for keyword
         parameter information, keywords must be specified on the statement
         that is used to invoke the CLIST. Because all positional parameters
```

Figure 9.15 Result of find within columns.

```
BROWSE -- TSO1234.PRINT.TEXT -------------------- LINE 00000000 COL 001 080
COMMAND ===> f p'~' 75 80                                SCROLL ===> CSR
****************************** TOP OF DATA *********************************
1
0                            CLIST Execution
-                         Modes Of CLIST Execution
0        There are four modes of CLIST execution, explicit, modified explicit,
         implicit, and modified implicit. CLIST execution is made possible by
         the TSO command, EXEC. That command can also be abbreviated as EX.
         Because the command is explicitly stated in the first two modes, they
         are known as explicit modes. The implicit modes do not contain EX or
         EXEC as part of the command syntax. They also differ in their reliance
         upon a special CLIST file to identify which CLIST code to execute.
0        CLISTS are invoked at the TSO prompter or an interface to it. For
         those who have ISPF installed, this could also be OPTION 6 as well as
         most Productivity Development Facility (PDF) panels that have a
         command line. When a CLIST (or TSO command for that matter) is entered
         from a PDF panel it should be preceded by the word TSO. This is not
         required from PDF Option 6 because it was designed to accept TSO
         commands and CLISTS.
0        The modes of CLIST execution will now be covered in more detail. The
         next few examples, used to demonstrate that execution, will assume
         that there is a partitioned data set, TSO1234.SAMPLE.CLIST, that
```

Figure 9.16 Find picture string.

can't be confused with the column values specified. The command is corrected by placing the string in single quotes before again pressing the ENTER key. Double quotes could also have been used.

Figure 9.15 shows how the browse function bypassed the zeros in column one to find the first other instance of the number 0. Figure 9.16 shows the FIND command issued from the top of the data set to find a non-blank character. The picture string is used since non-blank is a class of character rather than a specific character. A column range is also specified here to limit the search to the last six columns of this data set. A non-blank character is found in the range specified and is indicated by the cursor position (Figure 9.17). The short message in this case reflects the actual character value found rather than the class of data that was specified in the original FIND command.

```
BROWSE -- TSO1234.PRINT.TEXT ------------------------------ CHARS 'n' FOUND
COMMAND ===>                                                SCROLL ===> CSR
      optionally be followed by two types of parameter information that will
      be discussed later. The TSO EXEC command can also be abbreviated EX, and _
      has the following syntax:
 0      EXEC clist-name 'positional-parameters(s) keyword-parameter(s)'
 0    Using our sample CLIST library, the explicit mode of the EXEC command
      followed by the CLIST name might look like the following:
 0      EX 'TSO1234.SAMPLE.CLIST(HARDCOPY)'
 0    This mode of execution might also be considered explicit because it
      pinpoints the name of the CLIST being executed. The same syntax will
      work for a CLIST contained in a sequential data set except, of course,
      that no member name is specified. You may be pleased to know that, as
      we progress, the syntax for CLIST execution becomes shorter.
 -                    TSO Naming Conventions
 0    Before proceeding to the second execution mode, it is necessary to
      discuss how TSO handles data set names. When data set names are not
      literally specified (enclosed in single quotes), TSO will append a
      prefix in front of the data set name. This prefix is usually the
      individual's user-id, but can be changed by any TSO user, by using the
      TSO PROFILE command. Based upon the context in which it is used, TSO
      can also detect special data set types and attach an appropriate
      suffix. This too will only occur when the data set name is not
      literally specified. This suffix would become the last data set
```

Figure 9.17 Result of find picture string.

The ISPF Editor

The Edit Function

The edit function provides a way to enter new data or modify existing data. It's the most heavily used of all ISPF functions and is used to create or maintain raw data, source language code, and various texts. Edit can be used for sequential data sets or members of a PDS. Edit works with fixed-length records from 10 to 255 bytes and variable-length records from 14 to 259 bytes. Edit provides visibility to the process of creating and modifying data. It also provides primary and line commands to facilitate global and specific changes as well as movement and reformatting of data.

Edit is option two from the primary option menu. The first screen displayed (the edit menu) is shown in Figure 10.1. It looks very similar to the browse menu and, like many other screens, allows the data set name to be entered in standard TSO format or in three separate fields labeled PROJECT, GROUP, and TYPE. The data set name is the only required information on the edit menu.

One of the significant additions to the edit menu is a field that can be used to specify an edit profile name. An edit profile contains settings for edit session characteristics. Profiles are maintained (and named) by the data set descriptive qualifier. This is the last or low-level qualifier of the data set name. All data sets with the same descriptive qualifier share the same default profile, which the editor will create automatically. It's only necessary to specify a profile name on the edit menu when a profile name other than the default profile should be used. It's also possible to switch to other edit profiles after an edit session is started (described in chapter 25).

Edit menu fields also allow an initial edit macro name to be specified. *Edit macros* are commands that can be used to orchestrate or automate edit functions. The use of an initial edit macro could, for example, allow edit profile information to be changed prior to the start of the edit session. An initial edit macro can also allow edit data to be manipulated automatically before the data is displayed.

```
--------------------------- EDIT - ENTRY PANEL ---------------------------------
COMMAND ===>

ISPF LIBRARY:
    PROJECT ===> TSO1234
    GROUP   ===> BLKSIZE ===>              ===>              ===>
    TYPE    ===> TEXT _
    MEMBER  ===>                   (Blank or pattern for member selection list)

OTHER PARTITIONED OR SEQUENTIAL DATA SET:
    DATA SET NAME   ===>
    VOLUME SERIAL   ===>          (If not cataloged)

DATA SET PASSWORD ===>            (If password protected)

PROFILE NAME      ===>            (Blank defaults to data set type)

INITIAL MACRO     ===>           LMF LOCK   ===> YES   (YES, NO or NEVER)

FORMAT NAME       ===>           MIXED MODE ===> NO    (YES or NO)
```

Figure 10.1 The edit menu.

The Edit Entry Screen

A data set, whether sequential or partitioned, must already exist before it can be used in the edit function. Chapter 28 details how to create a data set. When an existing data set name is specified, edit will display a screen like that in Figure 10.2. Edit supports the use of primary commands, just as the browse function does. These commands will be used largely to change edit profile characteristics and to support movement of other data to and from the current edit session.

Edit also provides an area for entering line commands. These commands will largely support the manipulation of data in the current edit session and, in some cases, line commands will work in conjunction with other line commands or primary commands. Both primary and line commands will be detailed in subsequent chapters. The line command area (highlighted in Figure 10.2) is to the left of the data display. Its presence in an edit session leaves only 72 columns of data visible on a standard screen. The line command area is not part of the data itself; it's merely a mechanism to allow line commands to be entered.

Line Command Format

Line commands can be entered in uppercase or lowercase characters. Line commands need not start in the first position of the line command area. It's also not necessary to enter a space or use the ERASE EOF key after the line command, although this will be common in the examples to provide greater visibility to the commands entered. To remove a line command that's not needed, merely space over or erase the command itself. There's a permanent tab stop that allows the ERASE EOF key to be used in the line command area without erasing information in the data portion of the display. It's not necessary to replace line numbers in the line command area since they're maintained automatically by the editor. The primary command RESET is also available to remove all existing line commands.

Most line commands have a consistent format. The format includes the first letter of the function to be performed. A D would be used, for example, to delete a line from the edit session. The letter D would be placed somewhere in the line command area to the left of the line to be deleted. The line would be deleted when the ENTER (or any PF) key is pressed. A second format for line commands includes the letter code followed by a number. That will cause the function invoked (like delete) to be performed over the number of lines specified. D20 would delete 20 lines of data starting with the line it was included on. A third format for line commands is to mark a block of lines with a double letter code. To delete a block of lines, for example, DD would be placed on the first line to be deleted as well as on the last line. After pressing the ENTER key, those lines and all lines between them will be deleted.

Certain line command sequences can be started on one screen and finished on another. It might, for example, be desirable to delete a block of lines up to a point in the data set that's not currently visible. The block delete command can be started on one screen and be pending during scroll operations to locate the end of the block of lines. Once the end of the block is visible, the delete command can be completed.

It's also possible to enter multiple line commands as long as the commands don't create a conflict. Conflicts are caused when the scope of line commands overlap or make it difficult to interpret the commands. If two sets of block delete commands

```
π EDIT ---- TSO1234.BLKSIZE.TEXT - 01.01 ---------------------- COLUMNS 001 072
  COMMAND ===> _                                           SCROLL ===> HALF
  ****** *************************** TOP OF DATA ***********************
  000001
  000002
  000003  ┌──────────────────────────────────────────────────────┐
  000004  │              DASD PHYSICAL RECORD CHART               │
  000005  │ ───────────────────────────────────────────────────  │
  000006  │      3380          Device            3390            │
  000007  │ ───────────────────────────────────────────────────  │
  000008  │                   Blocks                             │
  000009  │  Min.      Max.   Per Track   Min.       Max.        │
  000010  │                                                      │
  000011  │  23477    47476      1       27999      56664        │
  000012  │  15477    23476      2       18453      27998        │
  000013  │  11477    15476      3       13683      18452        │
  000014  │   9077    11476      4       10797      13682        │
  000015  │   7477     9076      5        8907      10796        │
  000016  │   6357     7476      6        7549       8906        │
  000017  │   5493     6356      7        6519       7548        │
  000018  │   4821     5492      8        5727       6518        │
  000019  │   4277     4820      9        5065       5726        │
  000020  │   3861     4276     10        4567       5064        │
  000021  │   3477     3860     11        4137       4566        │
          └──────────────────────────────────────────────────────┘
```

Figure 10.2 The edit screen.

were issued, for example, it might not be possible to link any two of the four lines tagged with the DD command. Under such a circumstance, the editor would issue a warning about the command conflict rather than execute the commands. Multiple line commands that don't create a conflict are executed from the top to the bottom of the edit session.

Entering Data

Entering data is as easy as typing. Merely place the cursor on the line and column where the data should start and begin typing. Cursor placement using the cursor control keys (indicated by arrows) avoids altering existing data. Use of the space bar (and on some keyboards, the backspace key) will remove data. Data can also be deleted using the delete character key. In this instance, however, the current cursor position is maintained, and the subsequent portion of the data line collapses to the left to fill the void just created by removing characters or spaces. Removing spaces at the beginning of a line can, therefore, also be used as a means of shifting data on that line to the left.

Use of the insert key allows information to be entered in front of the current cursor position. Pressing the insert key places the terminal in insert mode. It remains in insert mode until the RESET key is used. Inserting information, however, is not always a straightforward matter. In many cases it will be necessary to remove data at the end of a line of data before inserting additional data. This is because spaces are also considered to be significant characters. The spaces at the end of a line can be removed by positioning the cursor after the visible data and pressing the ERASE EOF key. That will turn the spaces, which have a hexadecimal value of 40, into nulls that have a hex value of 00. At that point it will be possible to insert additional data until existing data runs into the end of the edit screen. Null characters can also be created using the delete character key. That key creates one null position at a time. It would, therefore, be necessary to strike the key at the end of the line as many times as there are characters to be inserted. When insert can't push data to the right, the keyboard will lock and provide an indication of that in the operator information area at the bottom of the terminal. The RESET key should be used to unlock the keyboard, and characters should be removed at the end of the line before attempting to insert additional information.

It should also be noted that when the ENTER key is pressed, nulls might be converted into spaces. Those spaces would again have to be erased before inserting characters into a data line. The use of PF keys will have the same effect as the ENTER key in converting nulls to spaces. It therefore will not be possible to scroll in the middle of insert processing. The screen should be optimally positioned before erasing existing data or end-of-line spaces.

Null characters at the end of the line can be permanently established using the NULLS primary command. This would make insert processing much easier at the expense of data positioning. The latter problem is noted when data is placed in a particular column only to come crashing to the left when the ENTER key is pressed. When nulls are turned on, spaces don't exist at the end of a line, and this helps to maintain proper column positioning. The solution would be to use the primary command NULLS OFF or to use the space bar to establish proper column position on a line. Using the space bar will place a space in each column up to the point that other data is entered, even when nulls are turned on.

Inserting spaces before existing data can obviously be used to shift line contents to the right. The following examples illustrate basic data shifting techniques based on terminal insert and delete character functions. In Figure 10.3 the cursor has been brought to the end of a line and the ERASE EOF key has been pressed. That turns the spaces at the end of the line into nulls. Take care not to erase useful data.

In Figure 10.4, the cursor has been moved to the front of the same line of data to prepare to shift the line contents to the right. After pressing the insert character key, the space bar is pressed eight times (Figure 10.5). Each time the space bar is pressed, the significant data on the line moves one position to the right.

Figure 10.6 shows the cursor positioned on the next line of data to prepare to shift the remaining portion of that line to the left. Figure 10.7 shows the result of having used the delete character key eight times. Each time the key is pressed, one column of data is removed and the rest of the line collapses to the left to fill the void.

Pressing the delete character key again would start to delete significant data (the "2") from the line. As before, the rest of the line would shift to the left, but data would be destroyed in the process. The ISPF editor also provides two line commands that support more sophisticated data shifting techniques. These line commands are discussed in Chapter 14.

```
EDIT ---- TSO1234.EXAMPLE.DATA(BLKSIZE) - 01.02 ------------- COLUMNS 001 072
COMMAND ===>                                               SCROLL ===> CSR
****** ***********************AA TOP OF DATA ****************************
000001                         Block Size Chart
000002
000003          3380             Device              3390
000004                         Blocks Per
000005     Min.      Max.        Track          Min.      Max.
000006
000007    23477     47476          1            27999     56664_
000008    15477     23476          2            18453     27998
000009    11477     15476          3            13683     18452
000010     9077     11476          4            10797     13682
000011     7477      9076          5             8907     10796
000012     6357      7476          6             7549      8906
000013     5493      6356          7             6519      7548
000014     4821      5492          8             5727      6518
000015     4277      4820          9             5065      5726
000016     3861      4276         10
000017     3477
000018
000019
****** ************************ BOTTOM OF DATA ****************************
```

Figure 10.3 Erasing spaces at the end of a line.

```
EDIT ---- TSO1234.EXAMPLE.DATA(BLKSIZE) - 01.02 ------------- COLUMNS 001 072
COMMAND ===>                                              SCROLL ===> CSR
****** ************************** TOP OF DATA ***************************
000001                     Block Size Chart
000002
000003        3380              Device            3390
000004                         Blocks Per
000005    Min.      Max.        Track        Min.      Max.
000006
000007  _23477    47476           1          27999    56664
000008   15477    23476           2          18453    27998
000009   11477    15476           3          13683    18452
000010    9077    11476           4          10797    13682
000011    7477     9076           5           8907    10796
000012    6357     7476           6           7549     8906
000013    5493     6356           7           6519     7548
000014    4821     5492           8           5727     6518
000015    4277     4820           9           5065     5726
000016    3861     4276          10
000017    3477
000018
000019
****** ************************** BOTTOM OF DATA ***************************
```

Figure 10.4 Cursor positioned at front of data line.

```
EDIT ---- TSO1234.EXAMPLE.DATA(BLKSIZE) - 01.02 ------------- COLUMNS 001 072
COMMAND ===>                                              SCROLL ===> CSR
****** ************************** TOP OF DATA ***************************
000001                     Block Size Chart
000002
000003        3380              Device            3390
000004                         Blocks Per
000005    Min.      Max.        Track        Min.      Max.
000006
000007            _23477    47476              1          27999    56664
000008   15477    23476           2          18453    27998
000009   11477    15476           3          13683    18452
000010    9077    11476           4          10797    13682
000011    7477     9076           5           8907    10796
000012    6357     7476           6           7549     8906
000013    5493     6356           7           6519     7548
000014    4821     5492           8           5727     6518
000015    4277     4820           9           5065     5726
000016    3861     4276          10
000017    3477
000018
000019
****** ************************** BOTTOM OF DATA ***************************
```

Figure 10.5 Shifting data to the right.

```
EDIT ---- TSO1234.EXAMPLE.DATA(BLKSIZE) - 01.02 ------------- COLUMNS 001 072
COMMAND ===>                                               SCROLL ===> CSR
****** ************************** TOP OF DATA ****************************
000001                       Block Size Chart
000002
000003        3380               Device              3390
000004                         Blocks Per
000005    Min.      Max.         Track          Min.      Max.
000006
000007          23477     47476          1            27999    56664
000008  15477   23476           _      2     18453    27998
0U0009  11477   15476                  3     13683    18452
000010   9077   11476                  4     10797    13682
000011   7477    9076                  5      8907    10796
000012   6357    7476                  6      7549     8906
000013   5493    6356                  7      6519     7548
000014   4821    5492                  8      5727     6518
0U0015   4277    4820                  9      5065     5726
000016   3861    4276                 10
000017   3477
000018
000019
****** ************************** BOTTOM OF DATA *************************
```

Figure 10.6 Preparing to shift data to the left.

```
EDIT ---- TSO1234.EXAMPLE.DATA(BLKSIZE) - 01.02 ------------ COLUMNS 001 072
COMMAND ===>                                               SCROLL ===> CSR
****** ************************** TOP OF DATA ****************************
000001                       Block Size Chart
000002
000003        3380               Device              3390
000004                         Blocks Per
000005    Min.      Max.         Track          Min.      Max.
000006
000007          23477     47476          1            27999    56664
000008  15477   23476          2        18453   27998
000009  11477   15476                  3     13683    18452
000010   9077   11476                  4     10797    13682
000011   7477    9076                  5      8907    10796
000012   6357    7476                  6      7549     8906
000013   5493    6356                  7      6519     7548
000014   4821    5492                  8      5727     6518
000015   4277    4820                  9      5065     5726
000016   3861    4276                 10
000017   3477
000018
000019
****** ************************** BOTTOM OF DATA *************************
```

Figure 10.7 Result of using the delete character key.

Creating a New Member

When a new member or empty sequential data set is specified, edit will display a blank screen like that in Figure 10.8. Whether empty or not, the data set to contain the member must already exist before it can be edited. That points out a significant advantage to using a partitioned data set. Such a PDS need be created only once, and any number of members can easily be added to it. In this case, a new member name was specified on the edit menu. It could have also been selected from the primary command area of the member list.

On the initial display, the line command area displays as a series of apostrophes. These will turn to line numbers after the ENTER key is used. The data lines displayed for a new data set (or member) are the same type of lines that are created by the insert line command. Lines of this type have nulls turned off automatically despite the current profile setting. That, of course, will affect character insertion. Another unique feature of this line type is that only the lines that have actually been used are retained. In Figure 10.9, four of the lines have been used.

After the ENTER key is pressed, the lines not used are removed from the display. This is shown in Figure 10.10. Even a single space typed on a given line is enough to ensure that it will be retained. Notice too that lowercase characters were converted to uppercase. This is a default for many profile types and can be changed with the CAPS primary command. The command CAPS OFF, for example, will ensure that typed data is not converted to uppercase characters. The apostrophes in the line command area have been converted to line sequence numbers, which signify permanent data lines.

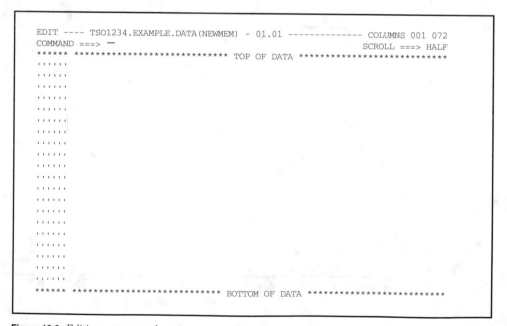

Figure 10.8 Editing a new member.

```
EDIT ---- TSO1234.EXAMPLE.DATA(NEWMEM) - 01.01 -------------- COLUMNS 001 072
COMMAND ===>                                                  SCROLL ===> HALF
****** *************************** TOP OF DATA ***************************
'''''''
'''''''
'''''''          any line that is
'''''''
'''''''
'''''''              not used,
'''''''
'''''''
'''''''          will not be retained
'''''''
'''''''
'''''''
'''''''
'''''''
'''''''
'''''''
'''''''
'''''''          once the enter key is used  _
****** *************************** BOTTOM OF DATA ***************************
```

Figure 10.9 Using insert lines.

```
EDIT --- TSO1234.EXAMPLE.DATA(NEWMEM) - 01.01 -------------- COLUMNS 001 072
COMMAND ===>                                                  SCROLL ===> HALF
****** *************************** TOP OF DATA ***************************
000001     ANY LINE THAT IS
000002        NOT USED,
000003     WILL NOT BE RETAINED
000004     ONCE THE ENTER KEY IS USED   _
****** *************************** BOTTOM OF DATA ***************************
```

Figure 10.10 Inserted data lines.

New or modified edit data can be saved using the SAVE primary command. The command causes the edit contents to be written to disk. The END command or the END PF key (PF3 or PF15) can also be used to save the data and return to the previous screen. Data is saved because the default profile setting is to have the autosave function turned on. Upon returning to the edit menu (Figure 10.11), a message is issued in the short message area to confirm that the member has been saved. The member name, if any, is also removed from the MEMBER field so another member name can be typed there.

Modifying an Existing Member

When the member name is omitted from the edit menu (as in Figure 10.11), a member list is displayed (Figure 10.12). The new line key can be used to efficiently move the cursor down the left side of the member list to the member to be selected. An existing member can be selected from the member list using the letter S in front of the desired member, or the SELECT primary command can be used.

The member list can be scrolled up and down to expose other members. The scroll down key was used to position the member list in Figure 10.13. That member list now starts with the twenty-second member in the PDS. The letter S is used here to select member PRINTDS.

When selected, the current member content is displayed (Figure 10.14). The data content can be changed by typing over what's already there or by using edit line and primary commands. The edit display can be scrolled just as in the browse function. Note that the default scroll amount in edit is half a page at a time. This is based on the assumption that you would want to move more slowly through an edit session. The scroll amount can be changed (as was done here), and one-time scroll amounts can also be used just as in browse.

```
------------------------- EDIT - ENTRY PANEL ----------- MEMBER NEWMEM SAVED
COMMAND ===>

ISPF LIBRARY:
   PROJECT ===> TSO1234
   GROUP   ===> EXAMPLE  ===>           ===>           ===>
   TYPE    ===> DATA
   MEMBER  ===> _              (Blank or pattern for member selection list)

OTHER PARTITIONED OR SEQUENTIAL DATA SET:
   DATA SET NAME  ===>
   VOLUME SERIAL  ===>         (If not cataloged)

DATA SET PASSWORD ===>         (If password protected)

PROFILE NAME      ===>         (Blank defaults to data set type)

INITIAL MACRO     ===>         LMF LOCK  ===>        (YES, NO or NEVER)

FORMAT NAME       ===>         MIXED MODE ===>       (YES or NO)
```

Figure 10.11 Return to edit menu.

```
EDIT ---- TSO1234.EXAMPLE.DATA -------------------------- ROW 00001 OF 00044
COMMAND ===> _                                          SCROLL ===> CSR
   NAME          VV.MM  CREATED    CHANGED      SIZE  INIT  MOD   ID
   ALLOC         01.01 92/12/04 92/12/11 17:04   270   270    0 TSO1234
   ALTLIB        01.01 92/12/04 92/12/11 17:10   329   327    0 TSO1234
   ATTRIB        01.00 92/12/04 92/12/04 17:48   102   102    0 TSO1234
   CALL          01.01 92/12/04 92/12/11 17:05    31    31    0 TSO1234
   CANCEL        01.00 92/12/04 92/12/04 17:49    20    20    0 TSO1234
   CLIST         01.01 92/12/11 92/12/11 17:16   639   655    0 TSO1234
   COPY          01.00 92/12/04 92/12/04 17:50    68    68    0 TSO1234
   DEFINE        01.00 92/12/04 92/12/04 17:51   545   545    0 TSO1234
   DELETE        01.03 92/12/04 92/12/11 17:06   123   123    0 TSO1234
   EDIT          01.00 92/12/04 92/12/04 17:52   106   106    0 TSO1234
   EXEC          01.00 92/12/04 92/12/04 17:53    48    48    0 TSO1234
   FORMAT        01.00 92/12/04 92/12/04 17:54    60    60    0 TSO1234
   FREE          01.00 92/12/04 92/12/04 17:44    55    55    0 TSO1234
   LINK          01.00 92/12/04 92/12/04 17:55   116   116    0 TSO1234
   LIST          01.00 92/12/04 92/12/04 17:56    38    38    0 TSO1234
   LISTALC       01.00 92/12/04 92/12/04 17:56    22    22    0 TSO1234
   LISTBC        01.00 92/12/04 92/12/04 17:57    27    27    0 TSO1234
   LISTCAT       01.00 92/12/04 92/12/04 17:57   104   104    0 TSO1234
   LISTDS        01.00 92/12/04 92/12/04 17:58    29    29    0 TSO1234
   LOADGO        01.00 92/12/04 92/12/04 17:59    68    68    0 TSO1234
   LOGOFF        01.00 92/12/04 92/12/04 17:59    16    16    0 TSO1234
```

Figure 10.12 Member list display.

```
EDIT ---- TSO1234.EXAMPLE.DATA -------------------------- ROW 00022 OF 00044
COMMAND ===>                                            SCROLL ===> CSR
   NAME          VV.MM  CREATED    CHANGED      SIZE  INIT  MOD   ID
   MERGE         01.00 92/12/04 92/12/04 18:00    68    68    0 TSO1234
   NAME          01.00 92/12/10 92/12/10 19:13    31    31    0 TSO1234
   OUTDES        01.00 92/12/04 92/12/04 18:00   329   329    0 TSO1234
   OUTPUT        01.00 92/12/04 92/12/04 18:01    99    99    0 TSO1234
   PRINT         01.00 92/12/04 92/12/04 18:01   113   113    0 TSO1234
s_ PRINTDS       01.00 92/12/04 92/12/04 17:42   434   434    0 TSO1234
   PROTECT       01.00 92/12/04 92/12/04 18:02    56    56    0 TSO1234
   RECEIVE       01.00 92/12/10 92/12/10 19:13   371   371    0 TSO1234
   RENAME        01.00 92/12/04 92/12/04 18:03    15    15    0 TSO1234
   REPRO         01.00 92/12/10 92/12/10 19:13   294   294    0 TSO1234
   RUN           01.00 92/12/10 92/12/10 19:13     7     7    0 TSO1234
   SEND          01.00 92/12/10 92/12/10 19:13    49    49    0 TSO1234
   SHIFT         01.00 92/12/11 92/12/11 17:10    30    30    0 TSO1234
   STATUS        01.00 92/12/10 92/12/10 19:13    20    20    0 TSO1234
   SUBMIT        01.00 92/12/10 92/12/10 19:13   105   105    0 TSO1234
   TERMINAL      01.00 92/12/10 92/12/10 19:13    94    94    0 TSO1234
   TEST          01.00 92/12/10 92/12/10 19:13    99    99    0 TSO1234
   TIME          01.00 92/12/10 92/12/10 19:13    13    13    0 TSO1234
   TRANSMIT      01.00 92/12/10 92/12/10 19:13   557   557    0 TSO1234
   TSOEXEC       01.00 92/12/10 92/12/10 19:13    16    16    0 TSO1234
   UNALLOC       01.00 92/12/10 92/12/10 19:13    55    55    0 TSO1234
```

Figure 10.13 Individual member selection.

Because the edit session was started from the member list, normal end of the session returns to the list (Figure 10.15). The short message area gives no indication that the member was saved. Indeed, the member contents were not written back to disk at the end of the edit session since no changes were made. The last member edited is now at the top of the member list. Other members can be selected from the current screen or other members exposed by scrolling up or down. The SELECT primary command (abbreviated SEL or S) can also be used to specify a member name, as illustrated. Either an existing member name or a new member name (the name of a member to be created) can be selected. In the latter case, the SELECT primary command must be used since the member name will not already be in the member list to pick from. A new member will initially display insert lines as discussed earlier in the chapter.

Concatenated Data Sets

Using the fields PROJECT, GROUP, and TYPE, partitioned data sets can be concatenated. Just as in the browse function, all specified data sets will be searched until the requested member is found. This form of concatenation has a different twist, however, from that seen in the browse function. In edit, no matter which of the four data sets a member comes from, if saved, a member is always stored back into the first of the specified data sets. This is true whether the member is specified from the edit menu or from the member list, and even if the member name didn't previously exist in the first PDS. This typifies a data processing standard where input can be concatenated, but output can't.

```
EDIT ---- TSO1234.EXAMPLE.DATA(PRINTDS) - 01.00 ------------- COLUMNS 001 072
COMMAND ===> _                                            SCROLL ===> CSR
****** ************************** TOP OF DATA ******************************
000001
000002 FUNCTION -
000003    THE PRINTDS COMMAND CAN BE USED TO OBTAIN HARDCOPY OF DATA SET(S)
000004    OR A FILE THROUGH FOREGROUND COPYING
000005          - TO SYSOUT OR
000006          - TO A SPECIFIED OUTPUT DATA SET (TODATASET/TODSNAME).
000007
000008    THE COMMAND PRINTS AN INPUT DATA SET OR AN INPUT FILE WHICH IS
000009          - SEQUENTIAL OR
000010          - PARTITIONED,
000011          - BLOCKED OR
000012          - UNBLOCKED,
000013      AND HAS
000014          - A FIXED RECORD FORMAT OR
000015          - A VARIABLE RECORD FORMAT.
000016
000017
000018
000019 SYNTAX -
000020    PRINTDS/PR    DATASET(DSNAME-LIST)/DSNAME(DSNAME-LIST)/
000021                  FILE(FILE-NAME)/DDNAME(FILE-NAME)
```

Figure 10.14 Existing member edit.

```
EDIT ---- TSO1234.EXAMPLE.DATA ------------------------- ROW 00027 OF 00044
COMMAND ===> s nextmem_                                    SCROLL ===> CSR
   NAME             VV.MM  CREATED    CHANGED       SIZE  INIT  MOD   ID
   PRINTDS          01.00 92/12/04 92/12/04 17:42    434   434    0 TSO1234
   PROTECT          01.00 92/12/04 92/12/04 18:02     56    56    0 TSO1234
   RECEIVE          01.00 92/12/10 92/12/10 19:13    371   371    0 TSO1234
   RENAME           01.00 92/12/04 92/12/04 18:03     15    15    0 TSO1234
   REPRO            01.00 92/12/10 92/12/10 19:13    294   294    0 TSO1234
   RUN              01.00 92/12/10 92/12/10 19:13      7     7    0 TSO1234
   SEND             01.00 92/12/10 92/12/10 19:13     49    49    0 TSO1234
   SHIFT            01.00 92/12/11 92/12/11 17:10     30    30    0 TSO1234
   STATUS           01.00 92/12/10 92/12/10 19:13     20    20    0 TSO1234
   SUBMIT           01.00 92/12/10 92/12/10 19:13    105   105    0 TSO1234
   TERMINAL         01.00 92/12/10 92/12/10 19:13     94    94    0 TSO1234
   TEST             01.00 92/12/10 92/12/10 19:13     99    99    0 TSO1234
   TIME             01.00 92/12/10 92/12/10 19:13     13    13    0 TSO1234
   TRANSMIT         01.00 92/12/10 92/12/10 19:13    557   557    0 TSO1234
   TSOEXEC          01.00 92/12/10 92/12/10 19:13     16    16    0 TSO1234
   UNALLOC          01.00 92/12/10 92/12/10 19:13     55    55    0 TSO1234
   VERIFY           01.00 92/12/10 92/12/10 19:13     31    31    0 TSO1234
   WHEN             01.00 92/12/10 92/12/10 19:13     25    25    0 TSO1234
   **END**
```

Figure 10.15 Primary command to select a member.

Basic
Edit Line Commands:
Section 1

Line Command Format

Line commands provide the basic mechanism for manipulating data in an edit session. Line commands are very easy to use. In general, the first letter of the function to be applied is entered in the line command area. The basic line commands include Insert, Delete, Repeat, Copy, Move, Before, and After. The letter I represents the insert function, while D is used to delete, and so on.

Most commands have three formats. The first format, a single letter command, affects the line the command was entered on. The second format, the letter command followed by a number, affects that many lines, starting with the line the command was entered on. The third format is known as the block format. It's designated by double letter pairs. Using the block format, the command letter is typed twice on the first line to be affected and on the last contiguous line. The block command affects those two lines and all lines between them. A block command can be started on a line that's currently visible and finished (after scrolling) on a subsequent screen. While scrolling, a message is issued to warn that a command sequence has not been completed.

Entering Line Commands

The ENTER key is used to activate a line command or commands. Most PF keys will also cause line commands to be executed. The line commands will only be executed, however, when the command is complete. That's why it's possible to scroll after a block command has been started. As mentioned in the previous chapter, a line command doesn't need to start in the first position of the line command area. The examples also show the remaining portion of the line command area erased. This is done to further highlight the commands being entered and is by no means necessary to execute a line command.

There are several ways to negate a pending line command. If the line command is on the current screen, merely type over the command or erase it using the space bar or ERASE EOF key. It's not necessary to replace the numeric values in the line command area since they only provide a place to enter line commands. The ISPF editor will automatically fill in missing numbers in the line command area after the ENTER key is used. It will also adjust line numbers to account for lines that are added, moved, or deleted during the edit session.

The RESET primary command will also negate pending line commands whether they're on the current screen or not. The command will also affect temporary line displays (COLS, TABS, BNDS, etc.) within the edit session and the status of excluded lines. The command should, therefore, not be used when it will have a disruptive effect on other edit session features.

Insert Line Command

The insert line command is used to add lines to the edit session. The lines added are the same type of line as those in an empty data set or member. The content of inserted lines can be changed, however, with the Mask function. In simplest form the insert sequence is started by entering the I line command as in Figure 11.1. The insert line will appear on the line immediately after the one it was entered on. The insert line is marked by apostrophes in the line command area to distinguish it from other edit lines (Figure 11.2).

Data can then be entered on the insert line (Figure 11.3). The line automatically has nulls turned off. That would make it necessary to delete or erase characters on the line before using the insert character function despite the current profile setting.

A feature that's unique to insert is that lines continue to be inserted each time the ENTER key is used. Figure 11.4 shows the addition of another insert line just below the previous one (which now has the normal line command numbers). Notice that the cursor is automatically positioned under the first character of the previous line.

The insert process is ended by moving the cursor off the last insert line before using the ENTER key. If data has not been typed onto the insert line, it's not necessary to move the cursor off the line. In Figure 11.5, the cursor has been placed on the line after the insert line. Pressing the ENTER key to terminate the insert sequence also removes the last insert line, in this case, since no data was entered on the line (Figure 11.6).

Insert doesn't support a block form of the line command. Instead, a specified number of lines can be inserted. Figure 11.7 shows (on line 8) the line command to insert twelve lines.

Just like the temporary lines of a new data set, any lines that are not used are not retained after the ENTER key is pressed. To retain even a blank line, at least a space must be typed on the line. In Figure 11.8, data is typed on nine of the twelve inserted lines.

```
EDIT ---- TSO1234.EXAMPLE.DATA(BLKSIZE) - 01.02 ------------- COLUMNS 001 072
COMMAND ===>                                                SCROLL ===> CSR
****** ************************** TOP OF DATA ****************************
000001                        Block Size Chart
i_
000003          3380              Device                 3390
000004                          Blocks Per
000005     Min.      Max.          Track         Min.        Max.
000006
000007    23477     47476           1            27999       56664
000008    15477     23476           2            18453       27998
000009    11477     15476           3            13683       18452
000010     9077     11476           4            10797       13682
000011     7477      9076           5             8907       10796
000012     6357      7476           6             7549        8906
000013     5493      6356           7             6519        7548
000014     4821      5492           8             5727        6518
000015     4277      4820           9             5065        5726
000016     3861      4276          10
000017     3477
000018
000019
****** ************************** BOTTOM OF DATA *************************
```

Figure 11.1 Single insert line command.

```
EDIT ---- TSO1234.EXAMPLE.DATA(BLKSIZE) - 01.02 ------------- COLUMNS 001 072
COMMAND ===>                                                SCROLL ===> CSR
****** ************************** TOP OF DATA ****************************
000001                        Block Size Chart
000002
''''''          _
000003          3380              Device                 3390
000004                          Blocks Per
000005     Min.      Max.          Track         Min.        Max.
000006
000007    23477     47476           1            27999       56664
000008    15477     23476           2            18453       27998
000009    11477     15476           3            13683       18452
000010     9077     11476           4            10797       13682
000011     7477      9076           5             8907       10796
000012     6357      7476           6             7549        8906
000013     5493      6356           7             6519        7548
000014     4821      5492           8             5727        6518
000015     4277      4820           9             5065        5726
000016     3861      4276          10
000017     3477
000018
000019
****** ************************** BOTTOM OF DATA *************************
```

Figure 11.2 Line insertion screen one.

```
EDIT ---- TSO1234.EXAMPLE.DATA(BLKSIZE) - 01.02 ------------- COLUMNS 001 072
COMMAND ===>                                                  SCROLL ===> CSR
****** *************************** TOP OF DATA *****************************
000001                     Block Size Chart
000002
''''''  -------------------------------------------------------------_
000003          3380              Device              3390
000004                           Blocks Per
000005     Min.      Max.          Track         Min.       Max.
000006
000007   23477     47476            1           27999      56664
000008   15477     23476            2           18453      27998
000009   11477     15476            3           13683      18452
000010    9077     11476            4           10797      13682
000011    7477      9076            5            8907      10796
000012    6357      7476            6            7549       8906
000013    5493      6356            7            6519       7548
000014    4821      5492            8            5727       6518
000015    4277      4820            9            5065       5726
000016    3861      4276           10
000017    3477
000018
000019
****** *************************** BOTTOM OF DATA *****************************
```

Figure 11.3 Line insertion screen two.

```
EDIT ---- TSO1234.EXAMPLE.DATA(BLKSIZE) - 01.03 ------------- COLUMNS 001 072
COMMAND ===>                                                  SCROLL ===> CSR
****** *************************** TOP OF DATA *****************************
000001                     Block Size Chart
000002
000003  -------------------------------------------------------------
''''''   _
000004          3380              Device              3390
000005                           Blocks Per
000006     Min.      Max.          Track         Min.       Max.
000007
000008   23477     47476            1           27999      56664
000009   15477     23476            2           18453      27998
000010   11477     15476            3           13683      18452
000011    9077     11476            4           10797      13682
000012    7477      9076            5            8907      10796
000013    6357      7476            6            7549       8906
000014    5493      6356            7            6519       7548
000015    4821      5492            8            5727       6518
000016    4277      4820            9            5065       5726
000017    3861      4276           10
000018    3477
000019
000020
```

Figure 11.4 Line insertion screen three.

```
EDIT ---- TSO1234.EXAMPLE.DATA(BLKSIZE) - 01.03 ------------- COLUMNS 001 072
COMMAND ===>                                                  SCROLL ===> CSR
****** ************************** TOP OF DATA ****************************
000001                        Block Size Chart
000002
000003  ------------------------------------------------------------------
''''''
000004      _    3380             Device              3390
000005                         Blocks Per
000006    Min.     Max.          Track          Min.      Max.
000007
000008  23477    47476            1            27999     56664
000009  15477    23476            2            18453     27998
000010  11477    15476            3            13683     18452
000011   9077    11476            4            10797     13682
000012   7477     9076            5             8907     10796
000013   6357     7476            6             7549      8906
000014   5493     6356            7             6519      7548
000015   4821     5492            8             5727      6518
000016   4277     4820            9             5065      5726
000017   3861     4276           10
000018   3477
000019
000020
```

Figure 11.5 Line insertion screen four.

```
EDIT ---- TSO1234.EXAMPLE.DATA(BLKSIZE) - 01.03 ------------- COLUMNS 001 072
COMMAND ===>                                                  SCROLL ===> CSR
****** ************************** TOP OF DATA ****************************
000001                        Block Size Chart
000002
000003  ------------------------------------------------------------------
000004           3380            Device              3390
000005                         Blocks Per
000006    Min.     Max.          Track          Min.      Max.
000007
000008  23477    47476            1            27999     56664
000009  15477    23476            2            18453     27998
000010  11477    15476            3            13683     18452
000011   9077    11476            4            10797     13682
000012   7477     9076            5             8907     10796
000013   6357     7476            6             7549      8906
000014   5493     6356            7             6519      7548
000015   4821     5492            8             5727      6518
000016   4277     4820            9             5065      5726
000017   3861     4276           10
000018   3477
000019
000020
****** ************************** BOTTOM OF DATA ****************************
```

Figure 11.6 End of line insert sequence.

```
EDIT ---- TSO1234.EXAMPLE.DATA(BLKSIZE) - 01.03 ------------- COLUMNS 001 072
COMMAND ===>                                               SCROLL ===> CSR
****** ************************** TOP OF DATA ******************************
000001                    Block Size Chart
000002
000003   -----------------------------------------------------------------
000004        3380              Device              3390
000005                        Blocks Per
000006     Min.      Max.       Track       Min.       Max.
000007
i12_      23477     47476         1         27999      56664
000009    15477     23476         2         18453      27998
000010    11477     15476         3         13683      18452
000011     9077     11476         4         10797      13682
000012     7477      9076         5          8907      10796
000013     6357      7476         6          7549       8906
000014     5493      6356         7          6519       7548
000015     4821      5492         8          5727       6518
000016     4277      4820         9          5065       5726
000017     3861      4276        10
000018     3477
000019
000020
****** ************************** BOTTOM OF DATA ***************************
```

Figure 11.7 Multiple line insertion screen one.

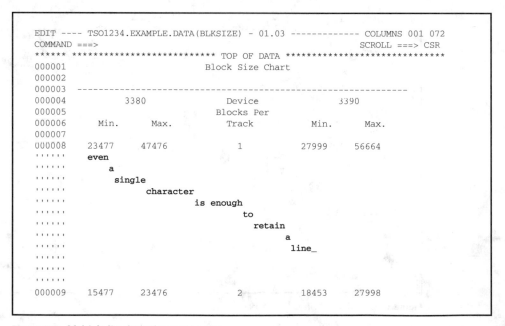

```
EDIT ---- TSO1234.EXAMPLE.DATA(BLKSIZE) - 01.03 ------------- COLUMNS 001 072
COMMAND ===>                                               SCROLL ===> CSR
****** ************************** TOP OF DATA ******************************
000001                    Block Size Chart
000002
000003   -----------------------------------------------------------------
000004        3380              Device              3390
000005                        Blocks Per
000006     Min.      Max.       Track       Min.       Max.
000007
000008    23477     47476         1         27999      56664
''''''     even
''''''          a
''''''             single
''''''                 character
''''''                        is enough
''''''                              to
''''''                                 retain
''''''                                     a
''''''                                     line_
''''''
''''''
''''''
000009    15477     23476         2         18453      27998
```

Figure 11.8 Multiple line insertion screen two.

After the ENTER key is used, the three insert lines not used are removed from the display (Figure 11.9). Notice that an insert mode is still active (indicated by apostrophes on line 17) since the cursor was within the range of insert lines when the ENTER key was pressed.

Delete Line Command

The delete line command is used to remove lines from the edit session. All three line command modes are supported, making it possible to delete a single line, a specified number of lines, or a block of lines. The delete line command is used in Figure 11.10 to remove the first of the lines that were inserted earlier. The command is implemented using a single letter D on line 9.

In Figure 11.11, line 9 has been deleted using the single form of the command. The line sequence area has been renumbered so it's not obvious that the line has been removed. The next form of the command will use a number value to delete several lines at once. That command is placed on line 13 and, with a value of 4, will delete the line it's coded on as well as the next three lines.

Figure 11.12 shows the result of deleting four lines from the data set. The same effect could have been obtained by using the single form of the command on each of the four lines, but that would not be as convenient to use. On the same screen, the block form of the delete line command is used to remove the last of the lines that were inserted earlier. The block form identifies the first and last lines to be affected by the command. Those two lines and all lines between them will be deleted.

```
EDIT ---- TSO1234.EXAMPLE.DATA(BLKSIZE) - 01.03 ------------- COLUMNS 001 072
COMMAND ===>                                                  SCROLL ===> CSR
****** ************************** TOP OF DATA ******************************
000001                      Block Size Chart
000002
000003 --------------------------------------------------------------
000004          3380               Device               3390
000005                            Blocks Per
000006     Min.       Max.          Track          Min.       Max.
000007
000008   23477      47476             1           27999      56664
000009   even
000010      a
000011        single
000012           character
000013              is enough
000014                 to
000015                    retain
000016                       a
''''''                          line         -
000018   15477      23476             2           18453      27998
000019   11477      15476             3           13683      18452
000020    9077      11476             4           10797      13682
000021    7477       9076             5            8907      10796
```

Figure 11.9 End of multiple line insertion.

```
EDIT ----- TSO1234.EXAMPLE.DATA(BLKSIZE) - 01.03 ------------- COLUMNS 001 072
COMMAND ===>                                                   SCROLL ===> CSR
****** ************************** TOP OF DATA ******************************
000001                        Block Size Chart
000002
000003  -------------------------------------------------------------
000004        3380            Device            3390
000005                        Blocks Per
000006      Min.      Max.      Track        Min.      Max.
000007
000008    23477     47476         1          27999     56664
d_        even
000010        a
000011      single
000012          character
000013              is enough
000014                  to
000015                  retain
000016                        a
''''''                        line
000018    15477     23476         2          18453     27998
000019    11477     15476         3          13683     18452
000020     9077     11476         4          10797     13682
000021     7477      9076         5           8907     10796
```

Figure 11.10 Single delete line command.

```
EDIT ---- TSO1234.EXAMPLE.DATA(BLKSIZE) - 01.03 ------------- COLUMNS 001 072
COMMAND ===>                                                   SCROLL ===> CSR
****** ************************** TOP OF DATA ******************************
000001                        Block Size Chart
000002
000003  ----------------------  ------------------------------------
000004        3380            Device            3390
000005                        Blocks Per
000006      Min.      Max.      Track        Min.      Max.
000007
0U0008    23477     47476         1          27999     56664
000009        a
000010      single
000011          character
000012              is enough
d4_                 to
000014                  retain
000015                        a
000016                        line
000017    15477     23476         2          18453     27998
000018    11477     15476         3          13683     18452
000019     9077     11476         4          10797     13682
000020     7477      9076         5           8907     10796
000021     6357      7476         6           7549      8906
```

Figure 11.11 Command to delete four lines.

```
EDIT ---- TSO1234.EXAMPLE.DATA(BLKSIZE) - 01.03 ------------- COLUMNS 001 072
COMMAND ===>                                                   SCROLL ===> CSR
****** ************************** TOP OF DATA ******************************
000001                     Block Size Chart
000002
000003  ------------------------------------------------------------------
000004          3380                Device              3390
000005                            Blocks Per
000006      Min.      Max.          Track          Min.      Max.
000007
000008     23477     47476            1            27999     56664
dd           a
000010        single
000011           character
dd_                             is enough
000013     15477     23476            2            18453     27998
000014     11477     15476            3            13683     18452
000015      9077     11476            4            10797     13682
000016      7477      9076            5             8907     10796
000017      6357      7476            6             7549      8906
000018      5493      6356            7             6519      7548
000019      4821      5492            8             5727      6518
000020      4277      4820            9             5065      5726
000021      3861      4276           10
```

Figure 11.12   Block delete line command.

```
EDIT ---- TSO1234.EXAMPLE.DATA(BLKSIZE) - 01.03 ------------- COLUMNS 001 072
COMMAND ===>                                                   SCROLL ===> CSR
****** ************************** TOP OF DATA ******************************
000001                     Block Size Chart
000002
000003  ------------------------------------------------------------------
000004          3380                Device              3390
000005                            Blocks Per
000006      Min.      Max.          Track          Min.      Max.
000007
000008     23477     47476            1            27999     56664
000009     15477     23476            2            18453     27998
000010     11477     15476            3            13683     18452
000011      9077     11476            4            10797     13682
000012      7477      9076            5             8907     10796
000013      6357      7476            6             7549      8906
000014      5493      6356            7             6519      7548
000015      4821      5492            8             5727      6518
000016      4277      4820            9             5065      5726
000017      3861      4276           10
000018      3477
000019
000020
****** ************************** BOTTOM OF DATA ***************************
```

Figure 11.13   Result of block delete line command.

Figure 11.13 shows the result of the block delete command. Again, the line command area is automatically renumbered after the lines are removed. It's also possible to start the block form of the delete command on one screen and finish it on another. Normal scrolling methods can be used to find the other end of the block of lines to be deleted. The ISPF editor will issue a warning that a command has been started and is still pending. No lines will be deleted as a result of the block delete command until the second DD pair has been specified and the ENTER (or PF key) has been pressed.

When deleting all subsequent lines past a certain point in a data set, it's not necessary to use the block format of the command. The numeric form can be used with a value equal to or greater than the number of remaining lines. Because there's no adverse consequence to specifying more than the number of remaining lines, it's typical to type D99999 on the first of the lines to be deleted. That way, it's not necessary to know how many more lines exist or to scroll all the way to the bottom of the data set.

12

Basic Edit Line Commands
Section 2

Repeat Line Command

The repeat line command is used to replicate data lines. Repeated lines are placed immediately after the line or lines they're created from. All three forms of the repeat line command are available, but with a significant difference. When the numeric form of the command is used, it describes the number of times a line is replicated rather than the number of lines to replicate. This is true with the singular form of the command and with the block form of the command.

In Figure 12.1, the repeat line command is used to repeat line 12. Using the single form of the command will produce an identical line right below the one repeated. Figure 12.2 shows the result of repeating a single line and seeks to repeat the newly created line seven more times using the single form of the line command followed by the numeric value 7.

The block format of the repeat line command tags both the start and end lines of the block to be repeated (Figure 12.3). The start and end lines need not be on the same screen. Once the start or end line has been tagged, it's possible to scroll up or down to locate the other end of the block.

The entire block of lines is repeated as an entity rather than just defining a range of single lines to repeat. This causes the sequence of repeated lines to be retained, as seen in Figure 12.4. The same figure contains another block repeat command. That block command has the numeric value 4 to cause the block of lines to be repeated 4 times. The numeric value can be specified on either of the RR pairs or both. If specified on both, the numeric values, must, of course, agree with each other.

Figure 12.5 shows the result of repeating a block of lines four times. Another line command, copy, acts like repeat, except that the repeated result must be specifically

```
EDIT ---- TSO1234.EXAMPLE.DATA(BLKSIZE) - 01.05 ------------- COLUMNS 001 072
COMMAND ===>                                              SCROLL ===> CSR
****** *************************** TOP OF DATA ***************************
000001  -------------------------------------------------------------------
000002  |                      Block Size Chart                            |
000003  |                                                                  |
000004  |-----------------------------------------------------------------|
000005  |       3380           |     Device     |       3390              |
000006  |                      |   Blocks Per   |                         |
000007  |   Min.   |   Max.    |     Track      |   Min.   |   Max.       |
000008  |----------------------|----------------|-------------------------|
000009 | 23477    | 47476      |       1        | 27999    | 56664       |
000010 | 15477    | 23476      |       2        | 18453    | 27998       |
000011 | 11477    | 15476      |       3        | 13683    | 18452       |
r_     |  9077    | 11476      |       4        | 10797    | 13682       |
000013 |  7477    |  9076      |       5        |  8907    | 10796       |
000014 |  6357    |  7476      |       6        |  7549    |  8906       |
000015 |  5493    |  6356      |       7        |  6519    |  7548       |
000016 |  4821    |  5492      |       8        |  5727    |  6518       |
000017 |  4277    |  4820      |       9        |  5065    |  5726       |
000018 |  3861    |  4276      |      10        |  4567    |  5064       |
000019 |  3477    |  3860      |      11        |  4137    |  4566       |
000020 |  3189    |  3476      |      12        |  3769    |  4136       |
000021 |  2933    |  3188      |      13        |  3441    |  3768       |
```

Figure 12.1 Repeat line command.

```
EDIT ---- TSO1234.EXAMPLE.DATA(BLKSIZE) - 01.06 ------------- COLUMNS 001 072
COMMAND ===>                                              SCROLL ===> CSR
****** *************************** TOP OF DATA ***************************
000001  -------------------------------------------------------------------
000002  |                      Block Size Chart                            |
000003  |                                                                  |
000004  |-----------------------------------------------------------------|
000005  |       3380           |     Device     |       3390              |
000006  |                      |   Blocks Per   |                         |
000007  |   Min.   |   Max.    |     Track      |   Min.   |   Max.       |
000008  |----------------------|----------------|-------------------------|
000009 | 23477    | 47476      |       1        | 27999    | 56664       |
000010 | 15477    | 23476      |       2        | 18453    | 27998       |
000011 | 11477    | 15476      |       3        | 13683    | 18452       |
000012 |  9077    | 11476      |       4        | 10797    | 13682       |
r7_    |  9077    | 11476      |       4        | 10797    | 13682       |
000014 |  7477    |  9076      |       5        |  8907    | 10796       |
000015 |  6357    |  7476      |       6        |  7549    |  8906       |
000016 |  5493    |  6356      |       7        |  6519    |  7548       |
000017 |  4821    |  5492      |       8        |  5727    |  6518       |
000018 |  4277    |  4820      |       9        |  5065    |  5726       |
000019 |  3861    |  4276      |      10        |  4567    |  5064       |
000020 |  3477    |  3860      |      11        |  4137    |  4566       |
000021 |  3189    |  3476      |      12        |  3769    |  4136       |
```

Figure 12.2 Command to repeat one line seven times.

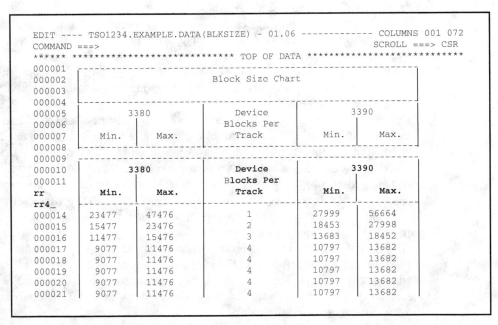

```
EDIT ---- TSO1234.EXAMPLE.DATA(BLKSIZE) - 01.06 ------------- COLUMNS 001 072
COMMAND ===>                                                  SCROLL ===> CSR
****** *************************** TOP OF DATA ***************************
000001 ,---------------------------------------------------------------------.
000002 |                         Block Size Chart                             |
000003 |                                                                     |
rr     |-----------------------+-----------------------+---------------------|
000005 |         3380          |        Device         |         3390        |
000006 |                       |      Blocks Per       |                     |
000007 |   Min.    |   Max.    |       Track           |   Min.    |   Max.  |
rr_    |-----------+-----------+-----------------------+-----------+---------|
000009 | 23477     | 47476     |         1             | 27999     | 56664   |
000010 | 15477     | 23476     |         2             | 18453     | 27998   |
000011 | 11477     | 15476     |         3             | 13683     | 18452   |
000012 |  9077     | 11476     |         4             | 10797     | 13682   |
000013 |  9077     | 11476     |         4             | 10797     | 13682   |
000014 |  9077     | 11476     |         4             | 10797     | 13682   |
000015 |  9077     | 11476     |         4             | 10797     | 13682   |
000016 |  9077     | 11476     |         4             | 10797     | 13682   |
000017 |  9077     | 11476     |         4             | 10797     | 13682   |
000018 |  9077     | 11476     |         4             | 10797     | 13682   |
000019 |  9077     | 11476     |         4             | 10797     | 13682   |
000020 |  9077     | 11476     |         4             | 10797     | 13682   |
000021 |  7477     |  9076     |         5             |  8907     | 10796   |
```

Figure 12.3 Block repeat line command.

```
EDIT ---- TSO1234.EXAMPLE.DATA(BLKSIZE) - 01.06 ------------- COLUMNS 001 072
COMMAND ===>                                                  SCROLL ===> CSR
****** *************************** TOP OF DATA ***************************
000001 ,---------------------------------------------------------------------.
000002 |                         Block Size Chart                             |
000003 |                                                                     |
000004 |-----------------------+-----------------------+---------------------|
000005 |         3380          |        Device         |         3390        |
000006 |                       |      Blocks Per       |                     |
000007 |   Min.    |   Max.    |       Track           |   Min.    |   Max.  |
000008 |-----------+-----------+-----------------------+-----------+---------|
000009 |-----------------------+-----------------------+---------------------|
000010 |         3380          |        Device         |         3390        |
000011 |                       |      Blocks Per       |                     |
rr     |   Min.    |   Max.    |       Track           |   Min.    |   Max.  |
rr4_   |-----------+-----------+-----------------------+-----------+---------|
000014 | 23477     | 47476     |         1             | 27999     | 56664   |
000015 | 15477     | 23476     |         2             | 18453     | 27998   |
000016 | 11477     | 15476     |         3             | 13683     | 18452   |
000017 |  9077     | 11476     |         4             | 10797     | 13682   |
000018 |  9077     | 11476     |         4             | 10797     | 13682   |
000019 |  9077     | 11476     |         4             | 10797     | 13682   |
000020 |  9077     | 11476     |         4             | 10797     | 13682   |
000021 |  9077     | 11476     |         4             | 10797     | 13682   |
```

Figure 12.4 Block repeat command repeated four times.

placed. A similar line command, move, as well as the before and after line commands will be discussed next.

Before and After Line Commands

The line commands that have been discussed so far have all been autonomous. They do not require the execution of any other line command. The rest of the basic line commands, however, only function with another command. The before and after line commands, for example, do nothing themselves. They merely point to where something else will take place. Both line commands are used with the data movement commands move and copy. That's true with the MOVE and COPY primary commands as well as the move and copy line commands.

Before and after are designated using the letters B and A respectively. As line commands, they point to where data will be moved or copied. Both commands can also be used with a numeric value. When used, the numeric value indicates how many times the moved or copied data should be repeated.

Copy Line Command

The copy line command is used to copy lines of data. It's like the repeat command, except that the copied lines must be placed somewhere using either before or after. All three line command modes are supported, and so it's possible to copy a single line, a specified number of lines, or a block of lines. In Figure 12.6, a single line of data is copied after the fifth line of data.

The same result could have been obtained by using the before line command on line six (rather than after on line five). The copy line command, like repeat, doesn't affect the source data lines, and so the copied line is now in two places (Figure 12.7). On the same screen is a set of line commands to copy two lines using the numeric form of the command. The two lines starting at line five will be placed after line 17 using the after line command.

Figure 12.8 shows the result of having copied two lines after the currently visible data. On that screen, the third form of the copy line command is also used. The first four lines of the data set are tagged as a block using CC pairs on the first and last lines of the block. Just as with the repeat line command, the order in which the line commands are typed is not important. The after line command has been used on line 17 to designate where the copied lines are to be placed. Figure 12.9 shows the result of the block copy command. The four lines at the top of the data set have been copied to the bottom of the currently visible screen.

All of the data copied to this point has been on a single screen. It's also possible to copy data that's not currently on the screen when it's within the numeric range specified with the numeric form of the copy command, or the data can be accessed by scrolling to other screens after the initial block copy designation has been made in the third form of the command.

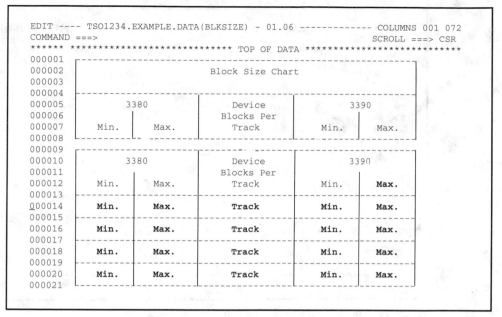

Figure 12.5 Result of repeating a block four times.

```
EDIT ---- TSO1234.EXAMPLE.DATA(BLKSTZE) - 01.04 ------------- COLUMNS 001 072
COMMAND ===>                                                SCROLL ===> CSR
****** *************************** TOP OF DATA ***************************
000001                        Block Size Chart
c          ----------------------------------------------------------------
000003          3380                Device                3390
000004                            Blocks Per
a_          Min.     Max.          Track        Min.     Max.
000006     23477    47476            1          27999    56664
000007     15477    23476            2          18453    27998
000008     11477    15476            3          13683    18452
000009      9077    11476            4          10797    13682
000010      7477     9076            5           8907    10796
000011      6357     7476            6           7549     8906
000012      5493     6356            7           6519     7548
000013      4821     5492            8           5727     6518
000014      4277     4820            9           5065     5726
000015      3861     4276           10
000016      3477
000017
000018
****** *************************** BOTTOM OF DATA ***************************
```

Figure 12.6 Copy line command.

```
EDIT ---- TSO1234.EXAMPLE.DATA(BLKSIZE) - 01.04 ------------- COLUMNS 001 072
COMMAND ===>                                                  SCROLL ===> CSR
****** ************************** TOP OF DATA ***************************
000001                       Block Size Chart
000002 ----------------------------------------------------------------
000003        3380             Device              3390
000004                        Blocks Per
c2       Min.     Max.         Track          Min.     Max.
000006 ----------------------------------------------------------------
000007  23477    47476           1            27999    56664
000008  15477    23476           2            18453    27998
000009  11477    15476           3            13683    18452
000010   9077    11476           4            10797    13682
000011   7477     9076           5             8907    10796
000012   6357     7476           6             7549     8906
000013   5493     6356           7             6519     7548
000014   4821     5492           8             5727     6518
000015   4277     4820           9             5065     5726
000016   3861     4276          10
a_       3477
000018
000019
****** ************************** BOTTOM OF DATA ***************************
```

Figure 12.7 Numeric form of copy command.

```
EDIT ---- TSO1234.EXAMPLE.DATA(BLKSIZE) - 01.04 ------------- COLUMNS 001 072
COMMAND ===>                                                  SCROLL ===> CSR
****** ************************** TOP OF DATA ***************************
cc                           Block Size Chart
000002 ----------------------------------------------------------------
000003        3380             Device              3390
cc                            Blocks Per
000005   Min.     Max.         Track          Min.     Max.
000006 ----------------------------------------------------------------
000007  23477    47476           1            27999    56664
000008  15477    23476           2            18453    27998
000009  11477    15476           3            13683    18452
000010   9077    11476           4            10797    13682
U00011   7477     9076           5             8907    10796
000012   6357     7476           6             7549     8906
000013   5493     6356           7             6519     7548
000014   4821     5492           8             5727     6518
000015   4277     4820           9             5065     5726
000016   3861     4276          10
a_       3477
000018   Min.     Max.         Track          Min.     Max.
000019 ----------------------------------------------------------------
000020
000021
```

Figure 12.8 Block copy line command.

```
EDIT ---- TSO1234.EXAMPLE.DATA(BLKSIZE) - 01.04 ------------- COLUMNS 001 072
COMMAND ===>                                                  SCROLL ===> CSR
****** ************************** TOP OF DATA ******************************
000001                         Block Size Chart
000002 ------------------------------------------------------------------
000003        3380                 Device                 3390
000004                           Blocks Per
000005     Min.      Max.          Track         Min.      Max.
000006 ------------------------------------------------------------------
000007    23477     47476            1           27999     56664
000008    15477     23476            2           18453     27998
000009    11477     15476            3           13683     18452
000010     9077     11476            4           10797     13682
000011     7477      9076            5            8907     10796
000012     6357      7476            6            7549      8906
000013     5493      6356            7            6519      7548
000014     4821      5492            8            5727      6518
000015     4277      4820            9            5065      5726
000016     3861      4276           10
000017     3477
000018                         Block Size Chart
000019 ------------------------------------------------------------------
000020        3380                 Device                 3390
000021                           Blocks Per
```

Figure 12.9 Result of block copy line command.

Move Command

The move line command is used to move lines of data. It's just like the copy line command except that the data lines will be taken from their original position in the data set. Like the copy command, all three line command modes are supported, and so it's possible to move a single line, a specified number of lines, or a block of lines.

In the first example of the move line command (Figure 12.10), line 16 is designated as the source line. The before line command is used on line 24 to show where the moved line should be placed. Figure 12.11 shows the result of moving the single line and also shows the numeric form of the command. A different feature is used in this particular example. It's the numeric form of the after line command. The effect will be to move two lines (lines 16 and 17) but to repeat the pair of lines four times as they're placed after line 23.

The result of the move line command is shown in Figure 12.12. The two lines have been taken from their initial place in the data set and placed four times at the bottom of the screen. The numeric repeat value can, of course, also be used on the before line command.

The block form of the move line command is available, just as it is with the repeat and copy commands. Just like those other line commands, it's also possible to scroll up or down to find the other end of the data to be moved before finishing the command.

```
EDIT ---- TSO1234.EXAMPLE.DATA(BLKSIZE) - 01.04 ------------- COLUMNS 001 072
COMMAND ===>                                                SCROLL ===> CSR
000012     6357      7476           6           7549      8906
000013     5493      6356           7           6519      7548
000014     4821      5492           8           5727      6518
000015     4277      4820           9           5065      5726
m          3861      4276          10
000017     3477
000018                    Block Size Chart
000019     ----------------------------------------------------------
000020         3380           Device              3390
000021                        Blocks Per
000022     Min.     Max.       Track          Min.      Max.
000023     ----------------------------------------------------------
b_
000025
****** ************************* BOTTOM OF DATA ***************************
```

Figure 12.10 Move line command.

```
EDIT ---- TSO1234.EXAMPLE.DATA(BLKSIZE) - 01.04 ------------- COLUMNS 001 072
COMMAND ===>                                                SCROLL ===> CSR
000012     6357      7476           6           7549      8906
000013     5493      6356           7           6519      7548
000014     4821      5492           8           5727      6518
000015     4277      4820           9           5065      5726
m2         3477
000017                    Block Size Chart
000018     ----------------------------------------------------------
000019         3380           Device              3390
000020                        Blocks Per
000021     Min.     Max.       Track          Min.      Max.
000022     ----------------------------------------------------------
a4_        3861      4276          10
000024
000025
****** ************************* BOTTOM OF DATA ***************************
```

Figure 12.11 Numeric form of move line command.

Multiple Line Commands

Multiple line commands can be executed at one time. This is an efficient way to conduct an edit session, but make sure that commands don't conflict. This usually entails one command overlapping the scope of another. It would not be possible, for example, to repeat lines within a block being deleted. It also would not be possible to have more than one block of a given command since the ISPF editor would not know which of the pair designators to match up. Several line commands have been entered in Figure 12.13. The editor will execute the commands from top to bottom. The result of those line commands is displayed in Figure 12.14.

```
EDIT ---- TSO1234.EXAMPLE.DATA(BLKSIZE) - 01.04 ------------- COLUMNS 001 072
COMMAND ===>                                                  SCROLL ===> CSR
000012     6357      7476              6          7549     8906
000013     5493      6356              7          6519     7548
000014     4821      5492              8          5727     6518
000015     4277      4820              9          5065     5726
000016  ------------------------------------------------------------
000017         3380                Device              3390
000018                           Blocks Per
000019     Min.      Max.          Track        Min.      Max.
000020  ------------------------------------- -------------------------
000021     3861      4276             10
000022     3477
000023                          Block Size Chart
000024     3477
000025                          Block Size Chart
000026     3477
000027                          Block Size Chart
000028     3477
000029                          Block Size Chart
000030
000031
****** *********************** BOTTOM OF DATA ***************************
```

Figure 12.12   Result of numeric form of move line command.

```
EDIT ---- TSO1234.EXAMPLE.DATA(BLKSIZE) - 01.04 ------------- COLUMNS 001 072
COMMAND ===>                                                  SCROLL ===> CSR
000012     6357      7476              6          7549     8906
000013     5493      6356 .            7          6519     7548
000014     4821      5492              8          5727     6518
a          4277      4820              9          5065     5726
000016  ------------------------------------------------------------
000017         3380                Device              3390
000018                           Blocks Per
000019     Min.      Max.          Track        Min.      Max.
000020  ------------------------------------------------------------
000021     3861      4276             10
000022     3477
m                               Block Size Chart
000024     3477
d                               Block Size Chart
r3_        3477
d                               Block Size Chart
000028     3477
dd                              Block Size Chart
000030
dd
****** *********************** BOTTOM OF DATA ***************************
```

Figure 12.13   Entering multiple different line commands.

```
EDIT ---- TSO1234.EXAMPLE.DATA(BLKSIZE) - 01.04 ------------- COLUMNS 001 072
COMMAND ===>                                              SCROLL ===> CSR
000012   6357      7476              6           7549     8906
000013   5493      6356              7           6519     7548
000014   4821      5492              8           5727     6518
000015   4277      4820              9           5065     5726
000016                        Block Size Chart
000017 -----------------------------------------------------------------
000018        3380               Device                 3390
000019                         Blocks Per
000020   Min.      Max.           Track        Min.      Max.
000021 -----------------------------------------------------------------
000022   3861      4276             10
000023   3477
000024   3477
000025   3477
000026   3477
000027   3477
000028   3477
000029   3477
****** ************************* BOTTOM OF DATA ****************************
```

Figure 12.14 Result of entering multiple line commands.

13

Advanced Edit Line Commands
Section 1

MASK Line Command

The MASK line command is used to display the mask line. The mask line itself is used with the insert line command. Each inserted line resembles the mask, which, as a default, is blank. Figure 13.1 shows the MASK line command being invoked. Display of the mask line is noted in the line command area in Figure 13.2. The line is currently blank, and so any inserted lines would also be blank.

Anything entered on the mask line will remain there until the line is again altered. Figure 13.3 shows vertical bars typed on the mask line. Any lines inserted at this point should contain the new mask. The altered mask line need not be displayed for this to be true. The line command to insert three lines is entered in Figure 13.4.

The result of the insert line command shows three insert type lines (Figure 13.5). Each line contains the vertical bars added earlier to the mask line. Notice that, as a result of the insert command, the cursor has automatically been placed in alignment with other first-column data.

In Figure 13.6, data has been added to two of the three insert lines. Like any type of insert line, the lines not used will be removed from the display when the ENTER key is pressed. Information placed on the line by the mask does not, by itself, constitute use of the line.

In Figure 13.7, the extra insert line has been removed (since no data was entered on the line). The same screen also shows the delete line command used to remove the mask line from the display. There is no harm in leaving the mask line as part of the data display. The mask line will not be saved with the data.

In Figure 13.8, the mask line has been removed. Other lines can still be inserted with the last mask setting since the mask line need not be displayed to be effective. The

```
EDIT ---- TSO1234.EXAMPLE.DATA(BLKSIZE) - 01.03 ------------- COLUMNS 001 072
COMMAND ===>                                                   SCROLL ===> CSR
000005                              Blocks Per
000006      Min.       Max.          Track          Min.       Max.
000007
000008    23477      47476             1            27999      56664
000009    15477      23476             2            18453      27998
000010    11477      15476             3            13683      18452
000011     9077      11476             4            10797      13682
000012     7477       9076             5             8907      10796
000013     6357       7476             6             7549       8906
mask_      5493       6356             7             6519       7548
000015     4821       5492             8             5727       6518
000016     4277       4820             9             5065       5726
000017     3861       4276            10
000018     3477
000019
000020
****** ************************** BOTTOM OF DATA ***************************
```

Figure 13.1 The MASK line command.

```
EDIT ---- TSO1234.EXAMPLE.DATA(BLKSIZE) - 01.03 ------------- COLUMNS 001 072
COMMAND ===>                                                   SCROLL ===> CSR
000005                              Blocks Per
000006      Min.       Max.          Track          Min.       Max.
000007
000008    23477      47476             1            27999      56664
000009    15477      23476             2            18453      27998
000010    11477      15476             3            13683      18452
000011     9077      11476             4            10797      13682
000012     7477       9076             5             8907      10796
000013     6357       7476             6             7549       8906
=MASK>
000014     5493       6356             7             6519       7548
000015     4821       5492             8             5727       6518
000016     4277       4820             9             5065       5726
000017     3861       4276            10
000018     3477
000019
000020
****** ************************** BOTTOM OF DATA ***************************
```

Figure 13.2 Display of initial mask line.

MASK line command is issued on this screen to bring the mask line back to the display.

Re-display of the mask (Figure 13.9) shows that it has retained its value. The mask line is in fact stored with the edit profile and therefore retained between ISPF sessions. With the mask line displayed, its value can again be changed. In Figure 13.10, the cursor has been brought into the data area, and the ERASE EOF key used to blank out the mask line. That will reset the mask to its blank, default value. If multiple mask lines are displayed, they are all changed to reflect the last change to any mask line.

When there is more than one mask line displayed (there is no limit for how often the command can be invoked), ISPF will keep all mask lines current with the last changed mask line. This includes the mask line that is optionally displayed with the edit profile.

```
EDIT ---- TSO1234.EXAMPLE.DATA(BLKSIZE) - 01.03 ------------- COLUMNS 001 072
COMMAND ===>                                                  SCROLL ===> CSR
000005                              Blocks Per
000006      Min.      Max.           Track        Min.      Max.
000007
000008    23477     47476              1         27999     56664
000009    15477     23476              2         18453     27998
000010    11477     15476              3         13683     18452
000011     9077     11476              4         10797     13682
000012     7477      9076              5          8907     10796
000013     6357      7476              6          7549      8906
=MASK>   I         I           I               I         I         I_
000014     5493      6356              7          6519      7548
000015     4821      5492              8          5727      6518
000016     4277      4820              9          5065      5726
000017     3861      4276             10
000018     3477
000019
000020
****** ************************** BOTTOM OF DATA ***************************
```

Figure 13.3 Update of the mask line.

```
EDIT ---- TSO1234.EXAMPLE.DATA(BLKSIZE) - 01.03 ------------- COLUMNS 001 072
COMMAND ===>                                                  SCROLL ===> CSR
000005                              Blocks Per
000006      Min.      Max.           Track        Min.      Max.
000007
000008    23477     47476              1         27999     56664
000009    15477     23476              2         18453     27998
000010    11477     15476              3         13683     18452
000011     9077     11476              4         10797     13682
000012     7477      9076              5          8907     10796
000013     6357      7476              6          7549      8906
=MASK>   I         I           I               I         I         I
000014     5493      6356              7          6519      7548
000015     4821      5492              8          5727      6518
000016     4277      4820              9          5065      5726
000017     3861      4276             10
i3_        3477
000019
000020
****** ************************** BOTTOM OF DATA ***************************
```

Figure 13.4 The command to insert three lines.

```
EDIT ---- TSO1234.EXAMPLE.DATA(BLKSIZE) - 01.03 ------------- COLUMNS 001 072
COMMAND ===>                                            SCROLL ===> CSR
000005                                Blocks Per
000006     Min.       Max.             Track           Min.        Max.
000007
000008    23477      47476                1             27999      56664
000009    15477      23476                2             18453      27998
000010    11477      15476                3             13683      18452
000011     9077      11476                4             10797      13682
000012     7477       9076                5              8907      10796
000013     6357       7476                6              7549       8906
=MASK>  |          |            |                    |          |            |
000014     5493       6356                7              6519       7548
000015     4821       5492                8              5727       6518
000016     4277       4820                9              5065       5726
000017     3861       4276               10
000018     3477
''''''  |     —    |            |                    |          |            |
''''''  |          |            |                    |          |            |
''''''  |          |            |                    |          |            |
000019
000020
****** ************************** BOTTOM OF DATA ****************************
```

Figure 13.5 Lines inserted with new mask value.

```
EDIT ---- TSO1234.EXAMPLE.DATA(BLKSIZE) - 01.03 ------------- COLUMNS 001 072
COMMAND ===>                                            SCROLL ===> CSR
000005                                Blocks Per
000006     Min.       Max.             Track           Min.        Max.
000007
000008    23477      47476                1             27999      56664
000009    15477      23476                2             18453      27998
000010    11477      15476                3             13683      18452
000011     9077      11476                4             10797      13682
000012     7477       9076                5              8907      10796
000013     6357       7476                6              7549       8906
=MASK>  |          |            |                    |          |            |
000014     5493       6356                7              6519       7548
000015     4821       5492                8              5727       6518
000016     4277       4820                9              5065       5726
000017     3861       4276               10
000018     3477
''''''  |   3189   |    3476    |        12          |   3769   |    4136    |
''''''  |   2933   |    3188    |        13          |   3441   |    3768_   |
''''''
000019
000020
****** ************************** BOTTOM OF DATA ****************************
```

Figure 13.6 Data entered on insert lines.

```
EDIT ---- TSO1234.EXAMPLE.DATA(BLKSIZE) - 01.04 ------------- COLUMNS 001 072
COMMAND ===>                                                 SCROLL ===> CSR
000005                                  Blocks Per
000006      Min.        Max.            Track           Min.        Max.
000007
000008     23477       47476              1             27999       56664
000009     15477       23476              2             18453       27998
000010     11477       15476              3             13683       18452
000011      9077       11476              4             10797       13682
000012      7477        9076              5              8907       10796
000013      6357        7476              6              7549        8906
dMASK>  |          |           |              |             |           |
000014      5493        6356              7              6519        7548
000015      4821        5492              8              5727        6518
000016      4277        4820              9              5065        5726
000017      3861        4276             10
000018      3477
000019  |   3189    |   3476    |         12    |         3769    |   4136    |
000020  |   2933    |   3188    |         13    |         3441    |   3768    |
000021
000022
****** ************************** BOTTOM OF DATA ****************************
```

Figure 13.7   Deleting the mask line.

```
EDIT ---- TSO1234.EXAMPLE.DATA(BLKSIZE) - 01.04 ------------- COLUMNS 001 072
COMMAND ===>                                                 SCROLL ===> CSR
000005                                  Blocks Per
000006      Min.        Max.            Track           Min.        Max.
000007
000008     23477       47476              1             27999       56664
000009     15477       23476              2             18453       27998
000010     11477       15476              3             13683       18452
000011      9077       11476              4             10797       13682
000012      7477        9076              5              8907       10796
000013      6357        7476              6              7549        8906
mask_       5493        6356              7              6519        7548
000015      4821        5492              8              5727        6518
000016      4277        4820              9              5065        5726
000017      3861        4276             10
000018      3477
000019  |   3189    |   3476    |         12    |         3769    |   4136    |
000020  |   2933    |   3188    |         13    |         3441    |   3768    |
000021
000022
****** ************************** BOTTOM OF DATA ****************************
```

Figure 13.8   Recalling the mask line.

```
EDIT ---- TSO1234.EXAMPLE.DATA(BLKSIZE) - 01.04 ------------- COLUMNS 001 072
COMMAND ===>                                             SCROLL ===> CSR
000005                               Blocks Per
000006       Min.      Max.            Track           Min.      Max.
000007
000008      23477     47476              1             27999     56664
000009      15477     23476              2             18453     27998
000010      11477     15476              3             13683     18452
000011       9077     11476              4             10797     13682
000012       7477      9076              5              8907     10796
000013       6357      7476              6              7549      8906
=MASK>   |           |              |              |           |           |
000014       5493      6356              7              6519      7548
000015       4821      5492              8              5727      6518
000016       4277      4820              9              5065      5726
000017       3861      4276             10
000018       3477
000019   |   3189   |   3476      |   12      |   3769   |   4136   |
000020   |   2933   |   3188      |   13      |   3441   |   3768   |
000021
000022
****** ************************* BOTTOM OF DATA ***************************
```

Figure 13.9 Redisplay of the mask line.

```
EDIT ---- TSO1234.EXAMPLE.DATA(BLKSIZE) - 01.04 ------------- COLUMNS 001 072
COMMAND ===>                                             SCROLL ===> CSR
000005                               Blocks Per
000006       Min.      Max.            Track           Min.      Max.
000007
000008      23477     47476              1             27999     56664
000009      15477     23476              2             18453     27998
000010      11477     15476              3             13683     18452
000011       9077     11476              4             10797     13682
000012       7477      9076              5              8907     10796
000013       6357      7476              6              7549      8906
=MASK>   _
000014       5493      6356              7              6519      7548
000015       4821      5492              8              5727      6518
000016       4277      4820              9              5065      5726
000017       3861      4276             10
000018       3477
000019   |   3189   |   3476      |   12      |   3769   |   4136   |
000020   |   2933   |   3188      |   13      |   3441   |   3768   |
000021
000022
****** ************************* BOTTOM OF DATA ***************************
```

Figure 13.10 Returning to a default mask.

The Overlay Command

The overlay line command is much like the before and after line commands. It works with the line commands move and copy to show where data is to be placed. In this case, however, data is moved or copied over existing data lines. This could be considered a line merge function to combine the contents of the line that's moved or copied with the line that it's placed on. In Figure 13.11, the line commands are issued to copy a single line over the line that precedes it.

The line commands can be entered in any order, with the effect shown in Figure 13.12, where the changed portion of line 18 is highlighted. Notice that the four-digit number that was on the original line remained unchanged. Information is only overlaid onto a line where significant data doesn't already exist. In that way, existing data will not be lost.

Any of the commands used in the overlay process can be used in the numeric mode (the line command followed by a numeric value) or in the block mode (the line command specified in double letter pairs). The block form of overlay is shown in Figure 13.13, where a single line is moved over a block of lines.

The source line value is repeated enough to cover the block specified, as shown in Figure 13.14. This is also true when there's more than a single source line. When there are more source lines than there are target lines, the extra source lines simply are not used. Notice too that the source line was deleted because the move line command was used rather than copy.

```
EDIT ---- TSO1234.EXAMPLE.DATA(BLKSIZE) - 01.04 ------------- COLUMNS 001 072
COMMAND ===>                                               SCROLL ===> CSR
000005                                Blocks Per
000006      Min.        Max.            Track            Min.        Max.
000007
000008     23477       47476              1              27999       56664
000009     15477       23476              2              18453       27998
000010     11477       15476              3              13683       18452
000011      9077       11476              4              10797       13682
000012      7477        9076              5               8907       10796
000013      6357        7476              6               7549        8906
000014      5493        6356              7               6519        7548
000015      4821        5492              8               5727        6518
000016      4277        4820              9               5065        5726
000017      3861        4276             10
o_          3477
c        |  3189   |   3476     |        12      |        3769   |    4136   |
000020   |  2933   |   3188     |        13      |        3441   |    3768   |
000021
000022
****** ************************** BOTTOM OF DATA ****************************
```

Figure 13.11 Copying one line over another.

```
EDIT ---- TSO1234.EXAMPLE.DATA(BLKSIZE) - 01.04 ------------- COLUMNS 001 072
COMMAND ===>                                              SCROLL ===> CSR
000005                                Blocks Per
000006     Min.      Max.             Track          Min.      Max.
000007
000008    23477     47476               1            27999     56664
000009    15477     23476               2            18453     27998
000010    11477     15476               3            13683     18452
000011     9077     11476               4            10797     13682
000012     7477      9076               5             8907     10796
000013     6357      7476               6             7549      8906
000014     5493      6356               7             6519      7548
000015     4821      5492               8             5727      6518
000016     4277      4820               9             5065      5726
000017     3861      4276              10
000018 |   3477 |    3476 |            12 |           3769 |    4136 |
000019 |   3189 |    3476 |            12 |           3769 |    4136 |
000020 |   2933 |    3188 |            13 |           3441 |    3768 |
000021
000022
****** ************************* BOTTOM OF DATA ***************************
```

Figure 13.12   Copy/overlay result.

```
EDIT ---- TSO1234.EXAMPLE.DATA(BLKSIZE) - 01.04 ------------- COLUMNS 001 072
COMMAND ===>                                              SCROLL ===> CSR
oo                                    Blocks Per
000006     Min.      Max.             Track          Min.      Max.
000007
000008    23477     47476               1            27999     56664
000009    15477     23476               2            18453     27998
000010    11477     15476               3            13683     18452
000011     9077     11476               4            10797     13682
000012     7477      9076               5             8907     10796
000013     6357      7476               6             7549      8906
000014     5493      6356               7             6519      7548
000015     4821      5492               8             5727      6518
000016     4277      4820               9             5065      5726
oo         3861      4276              10
m_
000019 |   3477 |    3476 |            12 |           3769 |    4136 |
000020 |   3189 |    3476 |            12 |           3769 |    4136 |
000021 |   2933 |    3188 |            13 |           3441 |    3768 |
000022
000023
****** ********************^************ BOTTOM OF DATA ***************************
```

Figure 13.13   Block overlay command.

```
EDIT ---- TSO1234.EXAMPLE.DATA(BLKSIZE) - 01.04 ------------- COLUMNS 001 072
  COMMAND ===>                                                SCROLL ===> CSR
  m
  o_       Min.      Max.            Blocks Per       Min.       Max.
                                      Track
000007
000008    23477     47476              1           27999       56664
000009    15477     23476              2           18453       27998
000010    11477     15476              3           13683       18452
000011     9077     11476              4           10797       13682
000012     7477      9076              5            8907       10796
000013     6357      7476              6            7549        8906
000014     5493      6356              7            6519        7548
000015     4821      5492              8            5727        6518
000016     4277      4820              9            5065        5726
000017     3861      4276             10
000018     3477      3476             12            3769        4136
000019     3189      3476             12            3769        4136
000020     2933      3188             13            3441        3768
000021
000022
****** ************************** BOTTOM OF DATA ****************************
```

Figure 13.14 Result of block overlay.

On the same screen another command sequence is started. In this case, an attempt is made to move the contents of one line over another, which could not accept all of the data.

As in a prior example, existing data is not overlaid (Figure 13.15), but neither is the source line deleted. The editor has sensed that some of the data from the source line has not been placed on the target line. Because of that, it didn't delete the source line as it typically would in a move/overlay sequence. The short message area indicates that the source line was not deleted.

Column Indicators

Just as in the browse function, it's possible to display column indicators to help determine the proper placement of data. Unlike the browse function, however, COLS (which can be abbreviated COL) is used as a line command in edit. Another difference is that the column indicators remain in a fixed position relative to the data and scroll right along with the data. Figure 13.16 shows the COLS line command issued near the top of the data set.

The columns indicators are displayed before the line that the command was typed on (Figure 13.17). The column values displayed adjust to left and right scrolling to indicate the current columns displayed. They should be used with the column values displayed in the short message area to determine the range of columns shown. Notice that no data is disrupted by using the command, and that even the number sequence in the line command area is maintained. The column indicators are specially

```
EDIT ---- TSO1234.EXAMPLE.DATA(BLKSIZE) - 01.04 ------------ LINE NOT DELETED
COMMAND ===>                                             SCROLL ===> CSR
000005                               Blocks Per
000006  |  Min.   |   Max.   |      BlTrackPer  |    Min.   |   Max.
000007
000008 |  23477  |  47476   |         1        |   27999   |  56664
000009 |  15477  |  23476   |         2        |   18453   |  27998
000010 |  11477  |  15476   |         3        |   13683   |  18452
000011 |   9077  |  11476   |         4        |   10797   |  13682
000012 |   7477  |   9076   |         5        |    8907   |  10796
000013 |   6357  |   7476   |         6        |    7549   |   8906
000014 |   5493  |   6356   |         7        |    6519   |   7548
000015 |   4821  |   5492   |         8        |    5727   |   6518
000016 |   4277  |   4820   |         9        |    5065   |   5726
000017 |   3861  |   4276   |        10        |
000018 |   3477  |   3476   |        12        |    3769   |   4136
000019 |   3189  |   3476   |        12        |    3769   |   4136
000020 |   2933  |   3188   |        13        |    3441   |   3768
000021
000022
****** ************************* BOTTOM OF DATA *****************************
```

Figure 13.15 Line not deleted warning.

```
EDIT ---- TSO1234.EXAMPLE.DATA(BLKSIZE) - 01.04 ------------- COLUMNS 001 072
COMMAND ===>                                             SCROLL ===> CSR
****** ************************* TOP OF DATA ********************************
000001 -------------------------------------------------------------------
000002 |                       Block Size Chart                           |
cols_  |                                                                  |
000004 |------------------------------------------------------------------|
000005 |       3380         |    Device     |       3390                  |
000006 |                    |  Blocks Per   |                             |
000007 |  Min.   |   Max.   |    Track      |    Min.   |   Max.          |
000008 |------------------------------------------------------------------|
000009 | 23477  |  47476   |      1        |   27999   |  56664
000010 | 15477  |  23476   |      2        |   18453   |  27998
000011 | 11477  |  15476   |      3        |   13683   |  18452
000012 |  9077  |  11476   |      4        |   10797   |  13682
000013 |  7477  |   9076   |      5        |    8907   |  10796
000014 |  6357  |   7476   |      6        |    7549   |   8906
000015 |  5493  |   6356   |      7        |    6519   |   7548
000016 |  4821  |   5492   |      8        |    5727   |   6518
000017 |  4277  |   4820   |      9        |    5065   |   5726
000018 |  3861  |   4276   |     10        |    4567   |   5064
000019 |  3477  |   3860   |     11        |    4137   |   4566
000020 |  3189  |   3476   |     12        |    3769   |   4136
000021 |  2933  |   3188   |     13        |    3441   |   3768
```

Figure 13.16 COLS line command.

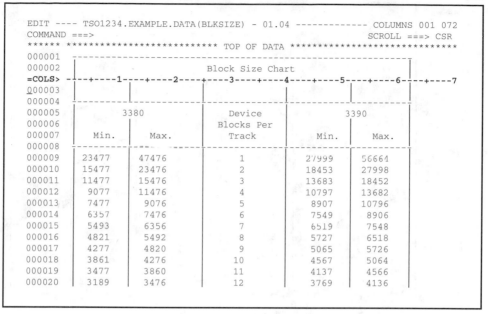

```
EDIT ---- TSO1234.EXAMPLE.DATA(BLKSIZE) - 01.04 ------------- COLUMNS 001 072
COMMAND ===>                                                  SCROLL ===> CSR
****** ************************** TOP OF DATA ******************************
000001   -------------------------------------------------------------------
000002   |                          Block Size Chart                        |
=COLS> --|--+----1----+----2----+----3----+----4----+----5----+----6--|--+----7
000003   |           |           |           |           |           |
000004   --------------------------------------------------------------------
000005   |      3380           |      Device       |      3390           |
000006   |                     |    Blocks Per     |                     |
000007   |   Min.  |   Max.    |     Track         |   Min.  |   Max.    |
000008   --------------------------- ------------------------------------
000009   | 23477   | 47476     |       1           | 27999   | 56664     |
000010   | 15477   | 23476     |       2           | 18453   | 27998     |
000011   | 11477   | 15476     |       3           | 13683   | 18452     |
000012   |  9077   | 11476     |       4           | 10797   | 13682     |
000013   |  7477   |  9076     |       5           |  8907   | 10796     |
000014   |  6357   |  7476     |       6           |  7549   |  8906     |
000015   |  5493   |  6356     |       7           |  6519   |  7548     |
000016   |  4821   |  5492     |       8           |  5727   |  6518     |
000017   |  4277   |  4820     |       9           |  5065   |  5726     |
000018   |  3861   |  4276     |      10           |  4567   |  5064     |
000019   |  3477   |  3860     |      11           |  4137   |  4566     |
000020   |  3189   |  3476     |      12           |  3769   |  4136     |
```

Figure 13.17 Column indicator display.

designated by =COLS> in the line command area, much like the designation for the special mask line discussed earlier. Neither display line is retained with the data when it's saved, however, either could be turned into a permanent data line using the MD (make data) line command.

Even though it's not a permanent data line, the column indicator can be treated as if it were. In Figure 13.18, the move line command is used on the special line containing the column indicators to move it after the ninth line of data.

Figure 13.19 shows the new placement of the column indicator line. The COLS line command can also be used any number of times, whether on the same screen or on different screens after scrolling. In Figure 13.19, the COLS line command is invoked a second time.

Rather than move or copy the column indicator line, additional column lines can easily be created at any point in the data set (Figure 13.20). In the same figure, the delete line command is used to show one way of removing a column indicator line.

Figure 13.21 shows that one of the two column indicator lines has been deleted. All column indicator lines can be deleted at one time using the RESET primary command. This, however, would affect all other special line displays, including excluded lines. Because they're not saved with the data, deleting column indicator lines is not necessary. Deleting the extra lines will, however, allow more data lines to be displayed on a given screen.

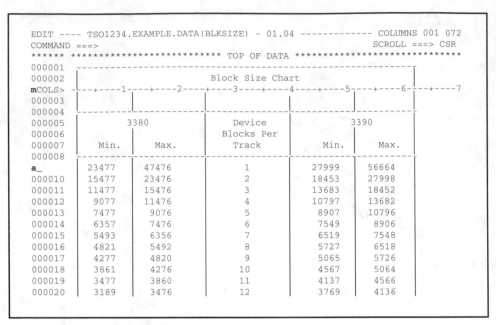

```
EDIT ---- TSO1234.EXAMPLE.DATA(BLKSIZE) - 01.04 ------------- COLUMNS 001 072
COMMAND ===>                                                   SCROLL ===> CSR
****** ************************** TOP OF DATA ***************************
000001 -----------------------------------------------------------------|
000002 |                      Block Size Chart                          |
mCOLS> ----+----1----+----2----+----3----+----4----+----5----+----6----+----7
000003 |            |            |            |            |            |
000004 ----------------------------------------------------------------|
000005 |         3380          |   Device   |         3390             |
000006 |                       | Blocks Per |                          |
000007 |   Min.  |    Max.     |   Track    |   Min.   |    Max.       |
000008 --------------------------------------------------------------|
a_     |   23477 |   47476     |     1      |  27999   |   56664       |
000010 |   15477 |   23476     |     2      |  18453   |   27998       |
000011 |   11477 |   15476     |     3      |  13683   |   18452       |
000012 |    9077 |   11476     |     4      |  10797   |   13682       |
000013 |    7477 |    9076     |     5      |   8907   |   10796       |
000014 |    6357 |    7476     |     6      |   7549   |    8906       |
000015 |    5493 |    6356     |     7      |   6519   |    7548       |
000016 |    4821 |    5492     |     8      |   5727   |    6518       |
000017 |    4277 |    4820     |     9      |   5065   |    5726       |
000018 |    3861 |    4276     |    10      |   4567   |    5064       |
000019 |    3477 |    3860     |    11      |   4137   |    4566       |
000020 |    3189 |    3476     |    12      |   3769   |    4136       |
```

Figure 13.18 Moving the column indicator line.

```
EDIT ---- TSO1234.EXAMPLE.DATA(BLKSIZE) - 01.04 ------------- COLUMNS 001 072
COMMAND ===>                                                   SCROLL ===> CSR
****** ************************** TOP OF DATA ***************************
000001 -----------------------------------------------------------------|
000002 |                      Block Size Chart                          |
000003 |                                                                |
000004 ----------------------------------------------------------------|
000005 |         3380          |   Device   |         3390             |
000006 |                       | Blocks Per |                          |
000007 |   Min.  |    Max.     |   Track    |   Min.   |    Max.       |
000008 --------------------------------------------------------------|
000009 |   23477 |   47476     |     1      |  27999   |   56664       |
=COLS> ----+----1----+----2----+----3----+----4----+----5----+----6----+----7
000010 |   15477 |   23476     |     2      |  18453   |   27998       |
000011 |   11477 |   15476     |     3      |  13683   |   18452       |
000012 |    9077 |   11476     |     4      |  10797   |   13682       |
000013 |    7477 |    9076     |     5      |   8907   |   10796       |
000014 |    6357 |    7476     |     6      |   7549   |    8906       |
cols_  |    5493 |    6356     |     7      |   6519   |    7548       |
000016 |    4821 |    5492     |     8      |   5727   |    6518       |
000017 |    4277 |    4820     |     9      |   5065   |    5726       |
000018 |    3861 |    4276     |    10      |   4567   |    5064       |
000019 |    3477 |    3860     |    11      |   4137   |    4566       |
000020 |    3189 |    3476     |    12      |   3769   |    4136       |
```

Figure 13.19 Second COLS line command.

```
EDIT ---- TSO1234.EXAMPLE.DATA(BLKSIZE) - 01.04 ------------ COLUMNS 001 072
COMMAND ===>                                               SCROLL ===> CSR
****** ************************** TOP OF DATA ******************************
000001 ------------------------------------------------------------------
000002 |                        Block Size Chart                         |
000003 |                                                                 |
000004 |-----------------------------------------------------------------|
000005 |       3380        |      Device       |       3390              |
000006 |                   |    Blocks Per      |                         |
000007 |  Min.  |   Max.   |     Track         |   Min.  |   Max.        |
000008 |--------|----------|-------------------|---------|---------------|
000009 | 23477  |  47476   |        1          |  27999  |  56664        |
dCOLS> -+--+----1-+---+----2-+----3----+----4--+--+----5-+---+----6-+--+----7
000010 | 15477  |  23476   |        2          |  18453  |  27998        |
000011 | 11477  |  15476   |        3          |  13683  |  18452        |
000012 |  9077  |  11476   |        4          |  10797  |  13682        |
000013 |  7477  |   9076   |        5          |   8907  |  10796        |
000014 |  6357  |   7476   |        6          |   7549  |   8906        |
=COLS> -+--+----1-+---+----2----+----3----+----4--+--+----5-+---+----6-+--+----7
000015 |  5493  |   6356   |        7          |   6519  |   7548        |
000016 |  4821  |   5492   |        8          |   5727  |   6518        |
000017 |  4277  |   4820   |        9          |   5065  |   5726        |
000018 |  3861  |   4276   |       10          |   4567  |   5064        |
000019 |  3477  |   3860   |       11          |   4137  |   4566        |
```

Figure 13.20 Deleting a column indicator line.

```
EDIT ---- TSO1234.EXAMPLE.DATA(BLKSIZE) - 01.04 ------------ COLUMNS 001 072
COMMAND ===>                                               SCROLL ===> CSR
****** ************************** TOP OF DATA ******************************
000001 ------------------------------------------------------------------
000002 |                        Block Size Chart                         |
000003 |                                                                 |
000004 |-----------------------------------------------------------------|
000005 |       3380        |      Device       |       3390              |
000006 |                   |    Blocks Per      |                         |
000007 |  Min.  |   Max.   |     Track         |   Min.  |   Max.        |
000008 |--------|----------|-------------------|---------|---------------|
000009 | 23477  |  47476   |        1          |  27999  |  56664        |
000010 | 15477  |  23476   |        2          |  18453  |  27998        |
000011 | 11477  |  15476   |        3          |  13683  |  18452        |
000012 |  9077  |  11476   |        4          |  10797  |  13682        |
000013 |  7477  |   9076   |        5          |   8907  |  10796        |
000014 |  6357  |   7476   |        6          |   7549  |   8906        |
=COLS> -+--+----1-+---+----2----+----3----+----4--+--+----5-+---+----6-+--+----7
000015 |  5493  |   6356   |        7          |   6519  |   7548        |
000016 |  4821  |   5492   |        8          |   5727  |   6518        |
000017 |  4277  |   4820   |        9          |   5065  |   5726        |
000018 |  3861  |   4276   |       10          |   4567  |   5064        |
000019 |  3477  |   3860   |       11          |   4137  |   4566        |
000020 |  3189  |   3476   |       12          |   3769  |   4136        |
```

Figure 13.21 Result of deleting a column indicator line.

Advanced Edit Line Commands
Section 2

The BNDS Line Command

The bounds line command is used to set boundaries that are used to limit several other edit commands. These commands include line commands for data and column shifting as well as line overlay. Affected primary commands include FIND and CHANGE as well as SORT and EXCLUDE. The BNDS command can be issued anywhere in the line command area (as in Figure 14.1) and can be abbreviated BND.

The bounds display line shows the current boundary settings (Figure 14.2). The bounds line is also displayed when the edit profile is displayed, but the bounds line is only displayed when the boundaries are not at the default settings or when the PROFILE primary command is used to force the display of special lines. Initially, the bounds are set at default values, which depend on the profile type and the record length of the data. The left boundary is visible in column 1 of Figure 14.2, while the right boundary is at column 80 and could be viewed after scrolling to the right.

New boundaries are set by placing the symbols < for the left boundary and > for the right boundary in the desired column of the bounds line. The old boundary indicators can be erased before setting the new ones, or they'll automatically be removed after the new bounds are entered. A new right boundary is set at column 33 in Figure 14.3, showing that it's not necessary to see the current boundary when setting it.

To demonstrate the effect of the new (now restricted) bounds, a block copy line command is used in Figure 14.4 to overlay three blank lines. Only data within the new bounds settings was overlaid onto the blank lines, as seen in Figure 14.5. The boundary settings also affect the scope of the edit primary commands FIND, CHANGE,

```
EDIT ---- TSO1234.EXAMPLE.DATA(BLKSIZE) - 01.05 ------------- COLUMNS 001 072
   COMMAND ===>                                                 SCROLL ===> CSR
   000012  |  9077  |  11476  |          4        |  10797  |  13682  |
   000013  |  7477  |  9076   |          5        |  8907   |  10796  |
   000014  |  6357  |  7476   |          6        |  7549   |  8906   |
   =COLS> ----+----1----+----2---+----3----+----4---+----5---+----6---+----7
   000015  |  5493  |  6356   |          7        |  6519   |  7548   |
   000016  |  4821  |  5492   |          8        |  5727   |  6518   |
   000017  |  4277  |  4820   |          9        |  5065   |  5726   |
   bnds_   |  3861  |  4276   |         10        |  4567   |  5064   |
   000019  |  3477  |  3860   |         11        |  4137   |  4566   |
   000020  |  3189  |  3476   |         12        |  3769   |  4136   |
   000021  |  2933  |  3188   |         13        |  3441   |  3768   |
   000022
   000023
   000024
   000025
   000026
   000027
   ****** *************************** BOTTOM OF DATA ***************************
```

Figure 14.1 BNDS line command.

```
EDIT ---- TSO1234.EXAMPLE.DATA(BLKSIZE) - 01.05 ------------- COLUMNS 001 072
   COMMAND ===>                                                 SCROLL ===> CSR
   000012  |  9077  |  11476  |          4        |  10797  |  13682  |
   000013  |  7477  |  9076   |          5        |  8907   |  10796  |
   000014  |  6357  |  7476   |          6        |  7549   |  8906   |
   =COLS> ----+----1----+----2---+----3----+----4---+----5---+----6---+----7
   000015  |  5493  |  6356   |          7        |  6519   |  7548   |
   000016  |  4821  |  5492   |          8        |  5727   |  6518   |
   000017  |  4277  |  4820   |          9        |  5065   |  5726   |
   =BNDS>  <
   000018  |  3861  |  4276   |         10        |  4567   |  5064   |
   000019  |  3477  |  3860   |         11        |  4137   |  4566   |
   000020  |  3189  |  3476   |         12        |  3769   |  4136   |
   000021  |  2933  |  3188   |         13        |  3441   |  3768   |
   000022
   000023
   000024
   000025
   000026
   000027
   ****** *************************** BOTTOM OF DATA ***************************
```

Figure 14.2 Display of default boundaries.

```
EDIT ---- TSO1234.EXAMPLE.DATA(BLKSIZE) - 01.05 ------------- COLUMNS 001 072
COMMAND ===>                                              SCROLL ===> CSR
000012 │ 9077  │ 11476 │         4         │ 10797 │ 13682 │
000013 │ 7477  │ 9076  │         5         │ 8907  │ 10796 │
000014 │ 6357  │ 7476  │         6         │ 7549  │ 8906  │
=COLS> ---+----1---+----2---+----3----+----4---+----5---+----6---+----7
000015 │ 5493  │ 6356  │         7         │ 6519  │ 7548  │
000016 │ 4821  │ 5492  │         8         │ 5727  │ 6518  │
000017 │ 4277  │ 4820  │         9         │ 5065  │ 5726  │
=BNDS> <                       >_
000018 │ 3861  │ 4276  │        10         │ 4567  │ 5064  │
000019 │ 3477  │ 3860  │        11         │ 4137  │ 4566  │
000020 │ 3189  │ 3476  │        12         │ 3769  │ 4136  │
000021 │ 2933  │ 3188  │        13         │ 3441  │ 3768  │
000022
000023
000024
000025
000026
000027
****** ************************** BOTTOM OF DATA ***************************
```

Figure 14.3 Setting new boundaries.

```
EDIT ---- TSO1234.EXAMPLE.DATA(BLKSIZE) - 01.05 ------------- COLUMNS 001 072
COMMAND ===>                                              SCROLL ===> CSR
000012 │ 9077  │ 11476 │         4         │ 10797 │ 13682 │
000013 │ 7477  │ 9076  │         5         │ 8907  │ 10796 │
000014 │ 6357  │ 7476  │         6         │ 7549  │ 8906  │
=COLS> ---+----1---+----2---+----3----+----4---+----5---+----6---+----7
000015 │ 5493  │ 6356  │         7         │ 6519  │ 7548  │
000016 │ 4821  │ 5492  │         8         │ 5727  │ 6518  │
000017 │ 4277  │ 4820  │         9         │ 5065  │ 5726  │
=BNDS> <                       >
cc     │ 3861  │ 4276  │        10         │ 4567  │ 5064  │
000019 │ 3477  │ 3860  │        11         │ 4137  │ 4566  │
000020 │ 3189  │ 3476  │        12         │ 3769  │ 4136  │
cc     │ 2933  │ 3188  │        13         │ 3441  │ 3768  │
000022
o3_
000024
000025
000026
000027
****** ************************** BOTTOM OF DATA ***************************
```

Figure 14.4 Data overlay within restricted bounds.

```
EDIT ---- TSO1234.EXAMPLE.DATA(BLKSIZE)  - 01.05 ---------- NOT ALL DATA COPIED
COMMAND ===>                                               SCROLL ===> CSR
000012 |   9077  |  11476  |        4        |  10797  |  13682  |
000013 |   7477  |   9076  |        5        |   8907  |  10796  |
000014 |   6357  |   7476  |        6        |   7549  |   8906  |
=COLS> ----+----1----+----2----+----3----+----4----+----5----+----6----+----7
000015 |   5493  |   6356  |        7        |   6519  |   7548  |
000016 |   4821  |   5492  |        8        |   5727  |   6518  |
000017 |   4277  |   4820  |        9        |   5065  |   5726  |
=BNDS> <                            >
000018 |   3861  |   4276  |       10        |   4567  |   5064  |
000019 |   3477  |   3860  |       11        |   4137  |   4566  |
000020 |   3189  |   3476  |       12        |   3769  |   4136  |
000021 |   2933  |   3188  |       13        |   3441  |   3768  |
000022
000023 |   3861  |   4276  |       10
000024 |   3477  |   3860  |       11
000025 |   3189  |   3476  |       12
000026
000027
****** ************************** BOTTOM OF DATA ******************************
```

Figure 14.5 Result of data overlay within restricted bounds.

SORT, and EXCLUDE when those commands are issued without parameters that indicate column numbers. Boundary settings affect text editing commands, and their effect on commands that shift data will be demonstrated later in this chapter.

In Figure 14.6, the cursor has been moved past the left boundary, and the ERASE EOF key has been used to erase the > symbol marking the right boundary. When the Enter key is pressed, any missing boundaries (here the right boundary) will be reset to the default for the profile type and record length.

Column Shifting

Column shifting refers to the processing of shifting data to the left or right and maintaining the internal spacing of the data within the shifted lines. When the column shift line commands are used, the information on the line is moved one way or the other without data compression, whether it's in column format or not. A column shift is specified using the special characters "(" and ")."

The characters are used to indicate the direction of the shift, much as if the characters were arrows (like those used in data shifting commands). The "(" character therefore indicates that data is to be shifted to the left, while ")" indicates that data is to be shifted to the right. Figure 14.7 shows the line command to shift a single line eight columns to the right.

Figure 14.8 shows the result of having shifted a line eight columns to the right. When no numeric value is used on the line command, the default value of two is used. Data can also be shifted in blocks of lines using pairs of the double shift character. Figure 14.8 also shows the block form of the command as it's used to shift six more lines, eight columns to the right.

```
EDIT ---- TSO1234.EXAMPLE.DATA(BLKSIZE) - 01.05 ------------- COLUMNS 001 072
COMMAND ===>                                              SCROLL ===> CSR
000012   | 9077  | 11476  |         4       |10797  |13682  |
000013   | 7477  | 9076   |         5       | 8907  |10796  |
000014   | 6357  | 7476   |         6       | 7549  | 8906  |
=COLS> --+----1--+----2--+----3----+----4--+----5--+----6--+----7
000015   | 5493  | 6356   |         7       | 6519  | 7548  |
000016   | 4821  | 5492   |         8       | 5727  | 6518  |
000017   | 4277  | 4820   |         9       | 5065  | 5726  |
=BNDS> <_
000018   | 3861  | 4276   |        10       | 4567  | 5064  |
000019   | 3477  | 3860   |        11       | 4137  | 4566  |
000020   | 3189  | 3476   |        12       | 3769  | 4136  |
000021   | 2933  | 3188   |        13       | 3441  | 3768  |
000022
000023   | 3861  | 4276   |        10
000024   | 3477  | 3860   |        11
000025   | 3189  | 3476   |        12
000026
000027
****** ************************* BOTTOM OF DATA *****************************
```

Figure 14.6 Obtaining default bound settings.

```
EDIT ---- TSO1234.EXAMPLE.DATA(BLKSIZE) - 01.05 ------------- COLUMNS 001 072
COMMAND ===>                                              SCROLL ===> CSR
000012   | 9077  | 11476  |         4       |10797  |13682  |
000013   | 7477  | 9076   |         5       | 8907  |10796  |
000014   | 6357  | 7476   |         6       | 7549  | 8906  |
=COLS> -+----1--+----2--+----3----+----4--+----5--+----6--+----7
000015   | 5493  | 6356   |         7       | 6519  | 7548  |
000016   | 4821  | 5492   |         8       | 5727  | 6518  |
000017   | 4277  | 4820   |         9       | 5065  | 5726  |
=BNDS> <
000018   | 3861  | 4276   |        10       | 4567  | 5064  |
)8_      | 3477  | 3860   |        11       | 4137  | 4566  |
000020   | 3189  | 3476   |        12       | 3769  | 4136  |
000021   | 2933  | 3188   |        13       | 3441  | 3768  |
000022
000023   | 3861  | 4276   |        10
000024   | 3477  | 3860   |        11
000025   | 3189  | 3476   |        12
000026
000027
****** ************************* BOTTOM OF DATA *****************************
```

Figure 14.7 Single line column shift.

```
EDIT ---- TSO1234.EXAMPLE.DATA(BLKSIZE)  - 01.05 ------------- COLUMNS 001 072
COMMAND ===>                                                  SCROLL ===> CSR
000012  |  9077  | 11476  |           4          | 10797  | 13682  |
000013  |  7477  |  9076  |           5          |  8907  | 10796  |
000014  |  6357  |  7476  |           6          |  7549  |  8906  |
=COLS> -|--+----1-|--+----2-|--+----3----+----4-|--+----5-|--+----6-|--+----7
000015  |  5493  |  6356  |           7          |  6519  |  7548  |
000016  |  4821  |  5492  |           8          |  5727  |  6518  |
000017  |  4277  |  4820  |           9          |  5065  |  5726  |
=BNDS> <
000018  |  3861  |  4276  |          10          |  4567  |  5064  |
000019            |  3477 |  3860  |          11          |  4137 |  4566   |
))        |  3189  |  3476  |          12          |  3769  |  4136  |
000021  |  2933  |  3188  |          13          |  3441  |  3768  |
000022
000023  |  3861  |  4276  |          10
000024  |  3477  |  3860  |          11
))8_     |  3189  |  3476  |          12
000026
000027
****** ************************** BOTTOM OF DATA ****************************
```

Figure 14.8 Result of a single line column shift.

The numeric value indicating how many columns are to be shifted can be specified on either of the tagged lines or on both of them, as in Figure 14.9. When the value is specified on both ends of the block, the value must, of course, be the same on both lines. In Figure 14.9, the data will be shifted 40 columns to the left.

Figure 14.10 shows the result of shifting the last block of data. What might not be immediately obvious, though, is that data has been lost as a result of the last command. Data has been shifted under the left boundary and is no longer part of the edit session. In Figure 14.11, the command is issued to shift the same block of data back 40 columns to the right.

In Figure 14.12, it's rather apparent, now, that data has been lost. There are certain instances when it's desirable to use such a shifting technique (known as a destructive column shift) to get rid of unwanted data. If, however, the data was inadvertently lost, it would be time to use the UNDO primary command to back out the last change to the data. If the UNDO command can't be used (because edit recovery is turned off) the CANCEL primary command can be used (if necessary) to terminate the edit session and return to the last saved version of the data.

Adjusting the edit bounds can make a destructive column shift even more practical to use. In Figure 14.13, the bounds have been reset to columns 21 and 29 respectively. In that way, column shifting will only affect data that lies between the bounds. In the same figure, the command is issued to shift a block of seven lines nine bytes to the left.

The result of a destructive column shift with restricted bounds was to destroy only the column of data that fell within the bounds (Figure 14.14). Data outside of the new bounds on the shifted lines remains unaffected.

```
EDIT ---- TSO1234.EXAMPLE.DATA(BLKSIZE) - 01.05 ------------- COLUMNS 001 072
COMMAND ===>                                                  SCROLL ===> CSR
000012 | 9077  | 11476 |            4 | 10797 | 13682 |
000013 | 7477  | 9076  |            5 | 8907  | 10796 |
((40   | 6357  | 7476  |            6 | 7549  | 8906  |
=COLS> -|---+----1-|---+----2-|---+----3----+----4-|---+----5-|---+----6-|---+----7
000015 | 5493  | 6356  |            7 | 6519  | 7548  |
000016 | 4821  | 5492  |            8 | 5727  | 6518  |
000017 | 4277  | 4820  |            9 | 5065  | 5726  |
=BNDS> <
((40_  | 3861  | 4276  |           10 | 4567  | 5064  |
000019 |       | 3477  | 3860 |     11 | 4137  | 4566  |
000020 |       | 3189  | 3476 |     12 | 3769  | 4136  |
000021 |       | 2933  | 3188 |     13 | 3441  | 3768  |
000022 |
000023 |       | 3861  | 4276 |     10 |       |       |
000024 |       | 3477  | 3860 |     11 |       |       |
000025 |       | 3189  | 3476 |     12 |       |       |
000026 |
000027 |
****** ************************** BOTTOM OF DATA ***************************
```

Figure 14.9 Block column shift.

```
EDIT ---- TSO1234.EXAMPLE.DATA(BLKSIZE) - 01.05 ------------- COLUMNS 001 072
COMMAND --->                                                  SCROLL ===> CSR
000012 | 9077  | 11476 |            4 | 10797 | 13682 |
000013 | 7477  | 9076  |            5 | 8907  | 10796 |
000014 | 7549  | 8906  |
=COLS> -|---+----1-|---+----2-|---+----3----+----4----+----5----+----6----+----7
000015 | 6519  | 7548  |
000016 | 5727  | 6518  |
000017 | 5065  | 5726  |
=BNDS> <
000018 | 4567  | 5064  |
000019 |       | 3477  | 3860 |     11 | 4137  | 4566  |
000020 |       | 3189  | 3476 |     12 | 3769  | 4136  |
000021 |       | 2933  | 3188 |     13 | 3441  | 3768  |
000022 |
000023 |       | 3861  | 4276 |     10 |
000024 |       | 3477  | 3860 |     11 |
000025 |       | 3189  | 3476 |     12 |
000026 |
000027 |
****** ************************** BOTTOM OF DATA ***************************
```

Figure 14.10 Result of block column shift.

```
EDIT ---- TSO1234.EXAMPLE.DATA(BLKSIZE) - 01.05 ------------- COLUMNS 001 072
COMMAND ===>                                                  SCROLL ===> CSR
000012   | 9077   | 11476   |        4        | 10797   | 13682   |
000013   | 7477   | 9076    |        5        | 8907    | 10796   |
))       | 7549   | 8906
=COLS> -|---+----1---+----2-|--+----3----+----4----+----5----+----6---+----7
000015   | 6519   | 7548    |
000016   | 5727   | 6518    |
000017   | 5065   | 5726    |
=BNDS> <
))40_    | 4567   | 5064    |
000019   |        | 3477    | 3860   |    11   | 4137   | 4566   |
000020   |        | 3189    | 3476   |    12   | 3769   | 4136   |
000021   |        | 2933    | 3188   |    13   | 3441   | 3768   |
000022
000023   |        | 3861    | 4276   |    10
000024   |        | 3477    | 3860   |    11
000025   |        | 3189    | 3476   |    12
000026
000027
****** ************************** BOTTOM OF DATA ***************************
```

Figure 14.11 Return column shift.

```
EDIT ---- TSO1234.EXAMPLE.DATA(BLKSIZE) - 01.05 ------------- COLUMNS 001 072
COMMAND ===>                                                  SCROLL ===> CSR
000012   | 9077   | 11476   |        4        | 10797   | 13682   |
000013   | 7477   | 9076    |        5        | 8907    | 10796   |
000014                                        | 7549    | 8906    |
=COLS> ----+----1----+----2----+----3----+----4---+----5---+----6---+----7
000015                                        | 6519    | 7548    |
000016                                        | 5727    | 6518    |
000017                                        | 5065    | 5726    |
=BNDS> <
000018                                        | 4567    | 5064    |
000019   |        | 3477    | 3860   |    11   | 4137   | 4566   |
000020   |        | 3189    | 3476   |    12   | 3769   | 4136   |
000021   |        | 2933    | 3188   |    13   | 3441   | 3768   |
000022
000023   |        | 3861    | 4276   |    10
000024   |        | 3477    | 3860   |    11
000025   |        | 3189    | 3476   |    12
000026
000027
****** ************************** BOTTOM OF DATA ***************************
```

Figure 14.12 Result of return column shift.

```
EDIT ---- TSO1234.EXAMPLE.DATA(BLKSIZE) - 01.05 ------------- COLUMNS 001 072
COMMAND ===>                                                  SCROLL ===> CSR
000012  |  9077   |  11476  |            4      |  10797  |  13682  |
000013  |  7477   |  9076   |            5      |   8907  |  10796  |
000014                                             7549      8906
=COLS> ----+----1----+----2----+----3----+----4--|--+----5--|--+----6--|--+----7
000015                                             6519      7548
000016                                             5727      6518
000017                                             5065      5726
=BNDS>                      <         >
000018                                          |  4567   |  5064   |
( (            |  3477   |  3860   |           11      |  4137   |  4566   |
000020         |  3189   |  3476   |           12      |  3769   |  4136   |
000021         |  2933   |  3188   |           13      |  3441   |  3768   |
000022
000023         |  3861   |  4276   |           10
000024         |  3477   |  3860   |           11
( (9_          |  3189   |  3476   |           12
000026
000027
****** ************************** BOTTOM OF DATA ***************************
```

Figure 14.13 Column shift within restrictive bounds.

```
EDIT ---- TSO1234.EXAMPLE.DATA(BLKSIZE) - 01.05 ------------- COLUMNS 001 072
COMMAND ===>                                                  SCROLL ===> CSR
000012  |  9077   |  11476  |            4      |  10797  |  13682  |
000013  |  7477   |  9076   |            5      |   8907  |  10796  |
000014                                             7549      8906
=COLS> ----+----1----+----2----+----3----+----4--|--+----5--|--+----6--|--+----7
000015                                             6519      7548
000016                                             5727      6518
000017                                             5065      5726
=BNDS>                      <         >
000018                                          |  4567   |  5064   |
000019         |  3477   |         |           11      |  4137   |  4566   |
000020         |  3189   |         |           12      |  3769   |  4136   |
000021         |  2933   |         |           13      |  3441   |  3768   |
000022
000023         |  3861   |         |           10
000024         |  3477   |         |           11
000025         |  3189   |         |           12
000026
000027
****** ************************** BOTTOM OF DATA ***************************
```

Figure 14.14 Result of column shift within restrictive bounds.

Data Shifting

Data shifting is implemented in the same way as column shifting, except that it uses the symbols < and >. Data shifting is different from column shifting in that it will never destroy the significant (non-blank) information on the data line. Normal text data might, however, have spaces compressed out during data shifting. In Figure 14.15, part of a paragraph is shifted six positions to the left. The result of the data shift is shown in Figure 14.16. In this particular instance, there would be no difference in the result if the column shift technique had been used.

In Figure 14.17, another block of data is shifted to the left. In this case, however, the request is to shift the data 99 positions to the left. If this were a column shift, all the data on those lines would be lost since the data being edited is only 80 bytes wide.

The effect of the data shift is to move the data as much as possible without destroying it. In Figure 14.18, the block of data has been moved to the left boundary of the edit session and a warning message has been issued to indicate that it could not shift the data as much as had been specified. Each line that could not be fully shifted (in this case all of them) also contains the characters ==ERR> in the line command area. This points out which lines in the designated block ran into the left boundary before they could be fully shifted.

```
EDIT ---- TSO1234.EXAMPLE.DATA(CLIST) - 01.02 --------------- COLUMNS 001 072
COMMAND ===>                                                  SCROLL ===> CSR
****** ************************** TOP OF DATA ******************************
000001
000002                           CLIST Execution
000003
000004
000006            Modes Of CLIST Execution
<<[Shift 1->] There are four modes of CLIST execution, explicit, modified ex
000008            implicit, and modified implicit. CLIST execution is made possi
000009            the TSO command, EXEC. That command can also be abbreviated as
000010            Because the command is explicitly stated in the first two mode
000011            are known as explicit modes. The implicit modes do not contain
000012            EXEC as part of the command syntax. They also differ in their
000013            upon a special file to identify which CLIST code to execute.
000014
000015            CLISTS are invoked at the TSO prompter or an interface to it.
<<6[Shift 1->]  those who have ISPF installed, this could also be OPTION 6 as
000017            most Productivity Development Facility (PDF) panels that have
000018            command line. When a CLIST (or TSO command for that matter) is
000019            from a PDF panel it should be preceded by the word TSO. This i
000020            required from PDF Option 6 because it was designed to accept T
000021            commands and CLISTS.
```

Figure 14.15 Data shift command.

```
EDIT ---- TSO1234.EXAMPLE.DATA(CLIST) - 01.02 -------------- COLUMNS 001 072
COMMAND ===>                                               SCROLL ===> CSR
****** ************************* TOP OF DATA *****************************
000001
000002                         CLIST Execution
000003
000004
000005                     Modes Of CLIST Execution
000006
000007   There are four modes of CLIST execution, explicit, modified explicit
000008   implicit, and modified implicit. CLIST execution is made possible by
000009   the TSO command, EXEC. That command can also be abbreviated as EX.
000010   Because the command is explicitly stated in the first two modes, the
000011   are known as explicit modes. The implicit modes do not contain EX or
000012   EXEC as part of the command syntax. They also differ in their relian
000013   upon a special file to identify which CLIST code to execute.
000014
000015   CLISTS are invoked at the TSO prompter or an interface to it. For
000016   those who have ISPF installed, this could also be OPTION 6 as well a
000017       most Productivity Development Facility (PDF) panels that have
000018       command line. When a CLIST (or TSO command for that matter) is
000019       from a PDF panel it should be preceded by the word TSO. This i
000020       required from PDF Option 6 because it was designed to accept T
000021       commands and CLISTS.
```

Figure 14.16 Result of data shift command.

```
EDIT ---- TSO1234.EXAMPLE.DATA(CLIST) - 01.02 -------------- COLUMNS 001 072
COMMAND ===>                                               SCROLL ===> CSR
****** ************************* TOP OF DATA *****************************
000001
000002                         CLIST Execution
000003
000004
000005                     Modes Of CLIST Execution
000006
000007   There are four modes of CLIST execution, explicit, modified explicit
000008   implicit, and modified implicit. CLIST execution is made possible by
000009   the TSO command, EXEC. That command can also be abbreviated as EX.
000010   Because the command is explicitly stated in the first two modes, the
000011   are known as explicit modes. The implicit modes do not contain EX or
000012   EXEC as part of the command syntax. They also differ in their relian
000013   upon a special file to identify which CLIST code to execute.
000014
000015   CLISTS are invoked at the TSO prompter or an interface to it. For
000016   those who have ISPF installed, this could also be OPTION 6 as well a
<<       most Productivity Development Facility (PDF) panels that have
000018       command line. When a CLIST (or TSO command for that matter) is
000019       from a PDF panel it should be preceded by the word TSO. This i
000020       required from PDF Option 6 because it was designed to accept T
<<99_        commands and CLISTS.
```

Figure 14.17 Shifting into a bound.

```
EDIT ---- TSO1234.EXAMPLE.DATA(CLIST) - 01.02 ------ DATA SHIFTING INCOMPLETE
COMMAND ===>                                              SCROLL ===> CSR
000001
000002                        CLIST Execution
000003
000004
000005                      Modes Of CLIST Execution
000006
000007   There are four modes of CLIST execution, explicit, modified explicit
000008   implicit, and modified implicit. CLIST execution is made possible by
000009   the TSO command, EXEC. That command can also be abbreviated as EX.
000010   Because the command is explicitly stated in the first two modes, the
000011   are known as explicit modes. The implicit modes do not contain EX or
000012   EXEC as part of the command syntax. They also differ in their relian
000013   upon a special file to identify which CLIST code to execute.
000014
000015   CLISTS are invoked at the TSO prompter or an interface to it. For
000016    those who have ISPF installed, this could also be OPTION 6 as well a
==ERR>   most Productivity Development Facility (PDF) panels that have a
==ERR>   command line. When a CLIST (or TSO command for that matter) is entere
==ERR>   from a PDF panel it should be preceded by the word TSO. This is not
==ERR>   required from PDF Option 6 because it was designed to accept TSO
==ERR>   commands and CLISTS.
000022
```

Figure 14.18 Result of shifting into a bound.

Despite the error messages, this is a valid shifting technique. The error messages can be removed using the RESET primary command. Because the last block command included the last visible line, the screen was automatically scrolled down one line to show the full effect of the command.

The bounds setting also affects data shifting away from the bound. Just like column shifting, only data within the bounds will be shifted. Figure 14.19 shows a block data shift of seven lines of data starting in column 1.

The unexpected result of shifting the data (Figure 14.20) was caused because the first word of each line is "stuck" on the left boundary. Since the first word on each line started in the same column as the left boundary, anything after the first space on the line could be shifted and indeed was. Since data is never destroyed in a data shift, the data can easily be restored by shifting the data back (also shown in Figure 14.20).

With the data in its original format (Figure 14.21), it would be advisable to first use the column shift to move the data off the current bound. Shifting the data even a single byte to the right using the column shift function would be enough to move the data off the bound. It would then be possible to return to the safer technique of column shifting.

```
EDIT ---- TSO1234.EXAMPLE.DATA(CLIST) - 01.01 -------------- COLUMNS 001 072
COMMAND ===>                                              SCROLL ===> CSR
****** ************************** TOP OF DATA ****************************
000001
000002                        CLIST Execution
000003
000004
000005                     Modes Of CLIST Execution
000006
>>      There are four modes of CLIST execution, explicit, modified explicit,
000008 implicit, and modified implicit. CLIST execution is made possible by
000009 the TSO command, EXEC. That command can also be abbreviated as EX.
000010 Because the command is explicitly stated in the first two modes, they
000011 are known as explicit modes. The implicit modes do not contain EX or
000012 EXEC as part of the command syntax. They also differ in their reliance
>>4_    upon a special file to identify which CLIST code to execute.
000014
000015 CLISTS are invoked at the TSO prompter or an interface to it. For
000016 those who have ISPF installed, this could also be OPTION 6 as well as
000017 most Productivity Development Facility (PDF) panels that have a
000018 command line. When a CLIST (or TSO command for that matter) is entered
000019 from a PDF panel it should be preceded by the word TSO. This is not
000020 required from PDF Option 6 because it was designed to accept TSO
000021 commands and CLISTS.
```

Figure 14.19 Shifting away from a bound.

```
EDIT ---- TSO1234.EXAMPLE.DATA(CLIST) - 01.02 -------------- COLUMNS 001 072
COMMAND ===>                                              SCROLL ===> CSR
****** ************************** TOP OF DATA ***************************
000001
000002                        CLIST Execution
000003
000004
000005                     Modes Of CLIST Execution
000006
<<      There       are four modes of CLIST execution, explicit, modified explic
000008 implicit,       and modified implicit. CLIST execution is made possible
000009 the        TSO command, EXEC. That command can also be abbreviated as EX.
000010 Because       the command is explicitly stated in the first two modes, t
000011 are        known as explicit modes. The implicit modes do not contain EX
000012 EXEC       as part of the command syntax. They also differ in their reli
<<4_    upon       a special file to identify which CLIST code to execute.
000014
000015 CLISTS are invoked at the TSO prompter or an interface to it. For
000016 those who have ISPF installed, this could also be OPTION 6 as well as
000017 most Productivity Development Facility (PDF) panels that have a
000018 command line. When a CLIST (or TSO command for that matter) is entered
000019 from a PDF panel it should be preceded by the word TSO. This is not
000020 required from PDF Option 6 because it was designed to accept TSO
000021 commands and CLISTS.
```

Figure 14.20 Result of shifting away from a bound.

```
EDIT ---- TSO1234.EXAMPLE.DATA(CLIST) - 01.02 -------------- COLUMNS 001 072
COMMAND ===>                                               SCROLL ===> CSR
****** ************************** TOP OF DATA ****************************
000001
000002                      CLIST Execution
000003
000004
000005                   Modes Of CLIST Execution
000006
000007 There are four modes of CLIST execution, explicit, modified explicit,
000008 implicit, and modified implicit. CLIST execution is made possible by
000009 the TSO command, EXEC. That command can also be abbreviated as EX.
000010 Because the command is explicitly stated in the first two modes, they
000011 are known as explicit modes. The implicit modes do not contain EX or
000012 EXEC as part of the command syntax. They also differ in their reliance
000013 upon a special file to identify which CLIST code to execute.
000014
000015 CLISTS are invoked at the TSO prompter or an interface to it. For
000016 those who have ISPF installed, this could also be OPTION 6 as well as
000017 most Productivity Development Facility (PDF) panels that have a
000018 command line. When a CLIST (or TSO command for that matter) is entered
000019 from a PDF panel it should be preceded by the word TSO. This is not
000020 required from PDF Option 6 because it was designed to accept TSO
000021 commands and CLISTS.
```

Figure 14.21 Data shifted into previous position.

15

Advanced Edit Line Commands
Section 3

The Exclude Command

The exclude line command (X, XX, Xn) is used to temporarily remove lines from the edit display. Excluded lines are still part of the data set being edited, but they're represented on the screen as a line of dashes with a number indicating how many consecutive excluded lines are "hidden" from the display. There are several reasons for excluding lines. The first is to bring separate sections of edit data closer together. That allows sections of noncontiguous data (data not excluded) to be displayed on a single screen. This in turn facilitates visual comparisons as well as movement of data and other changes to the visible data. Figure 15.1 shows the numeric form of the command to exclude 506 lines. It would, of course, also be possible to use the block form of the command and scroll to the end of the block to be excluded.

Figure 15.2 shows the result of having excluded the lines from the display, which now shows data from two disparate areas of the data set. Not only would this facilitate a visual comparison of the two pieces of data on either side of the excluded block, but scrolling would also be minimized if data were to be moved or copied from one portion of the visible data to the other.

The lines that have been removed from the display are now represented by a single line entry that says 506 LINE(S) NOT DISPLAYED. If the edit session were ended at this point or the data were saved, those 506 lines would be written back to disk just as if they were not excluded. The lines can also be redisplayed so that they can be modified with normal edit functions. There are three different line commands that can be used to redisplay excluded lines. Each of the three has a different effect. The Last (L, Ln) line command is used to display the last line or last n lines of an excluded block. This is shown in Figure 15.2 where L5 has been typed in the line com-

```
EDIT ---- TSO1234.EXAMPLE.DATA(CLIST) - 01.01 -------------- COLUMNS 001 072
COMMAND ===>                                          SCROLL ===> CSR
000004
000005                        Modes Of CLIST Execution
000006
000007 There are four modes of CLIST execution, explicit, modified explicit,
000008 implicit, and modified implicit. CLIST execution is made possible by
000009 the TSO command, EXEC. That command can also be abbreviated as EX.
000010 Because the command is explicitly stated in the first two modes, they
000011 are known as explicit modes. The implicit modes do not contain EX or
000012 EXEC as part of the command syntax. They also differ in their reliance
000013 upon a special file to identify which CLIST code to execute.
000014
x506_  CLISTS are invoked at the TSO prompter or an interface to it. For
000016 those who have ISPF installed, this could also be OPTION 6 as well as
000017 most Productivity Development Facility (PDF) panels that have a
000018 command line. When a CLIST (or TSO command for that matter) is entered
000019 from a PDF panel it should be preceded by the word TSO. This is not
000020 required from PDF Option 6 because it was designed to accept TSO
000021 commands and CLISTS.
000022
000023 The modes of CLIST execution will now be covered in more detail. The
000024 next few examples, used to demonstrate that execution, will assume
000025 that there is a partitioned data set, TSO1234.SAMPLE.CLIST, that
```

Figure 15.1 Exclude line command.

mand area corresponding to the excluded block of lines.

Figure 15.3 shows the result of displaying the last five excluded lines (two of them are blank lines) as well as the line command First. The First (F, Fn) line command is used to display the first line or first n lines of an excluded block.

Figure 15.4 shows the result of showing the first four excluded lines. The numeric value on the excluded block line is automatically adjusted to reflect the number of lines still in the excluded block. The third line command to display excluded lines is Show (S Sn). The Show line command displays lines based upon indentation, giving priority to data that's further to the left. Priority is from top to bottom for lines with the same indentation.

Excluding lines can also make it easier to perform other changes to a group of data lines. Many edit line commands can be executed against an excluded block to affect each line of the block. This again reduces the amount of scrolling required to make changes. This is demonstrated in Figure 15.4 where a block data shift includes both excluded and nonexcluded lines. The same command used against only the block of excluded lines would have been coded)8 in the line command area corresponding to the block of excluded lines.

The result of the block column shift is shown in Figure 15.5. Seven displayed lines and 497 excluded lines have been shifted, but the change will not be fully apparent until the lines are redisplayed. The RESET primary command will redisplay all excluded groups of lines. At the same time, however, it might remove special display lines (such as column indicators) and negate commands already started.

After the lines are redisplayed, it's apparent that lines in the excluded block (highlighted in Figure 15.6) were also shifted. Excluded lines throughout the data set

```
EDIT ---- TSO1234.EXAMPLE.DATA(CLIST) - 01.01 --------------- COLUMNS 001 072
COMMAND ===>                                              SCROLL ===> CSR
000004
000005                     Modes Of CLIST Execution
000006
000007 There are four modes of CLIST execution, explicit, modified explicit,
000008 implicit, and modified implicit. CLIST execution is made possible by
000009 the TSO command, EXEC. That command can also be abbreviated as EX.
000010 Because the command is explicitly stated in the first two modes, they
000011 are known as explicit modes. The implicit modes do not contain EX or
000012 EXEC as part of the command syntax. They also differ in their reliance
000013 upon a special file to identify which CLIST code to execute.
000014
15_ - - - - - - - - - - - - - - - - - 506 LINE(S) NOT DISPLAYED
000521                     Data Driven Parameters
000522
000523 As a final consideration for which type of parameter to use, we will
000524 look at the kind of data each will accept. Positional parameters will
000525 accept all data, including quotes. The quotes are treated as part of
000526 the data as it is conveyed to the variable. The ability to tolerate
000527 parentheses and retain quotes makes positional parameters ideally
000528 suited to convey data set names. Positional parameters have problems,
000529 however, accepting data that contains embedded spaces or commas since
000530 they both serve as delimiters to separate parameters.
```

Figure 15.2 Result of excluding lines.

```
EDIT ---- TSO1234.EXAMPLE.DATA(CLIST) - 01.01 --------------- COLUMNS 001 072
COMMAND ===>                                              SCROLL ===> CSR
000004
000005                     Modes Of CLIST Execution
000006
000007 There are four modes of CLIST execution, explicit, modified explicit,
000008 implicit, and modified implicit. CLIST execution is made possible by
000009 the TSO command, EXEC. That command can also be abbreviated as EX.
000010 Because the command is explicitly stated in the first two modes, they
000011 are known as explicit modes. The implicit modes do not contain EX or
000012 EXEC as part of the command syntax. They also differ in their reliance
000013 upon a special file to identify which CLIST code to execute.
000014
f4_ - - - - - - - - - - - - - - - - - 501 LINE(S) NOT DISPLAYED
000516 turning the list function on if its value was "TRACE". If the word
000517 TRACE had not been typed on the statement that invokes the HARDCOPY
000518 CLIST, the variable &TRACE would have contained spaces.
000519
000520
000521                     Data Driven Parameters
000522
000523 As a final consideration for which type of parameter to use, we will
000524 look at the kind of data each will accept. Positional parameters will
000525 accept all data, including quotes. The quotes are treated as part of
```

Figure 15.3 Result of showing last five lines.

```
EDIT ---- TSO1234.EXAMPLE.DATA(CLIST) - 01.01 -------------- COLUMNS 001 072
COMMAND ===>                                                SCROLL ===> CSR
000004
000005                         Modes Of CLIST Execution
000006
000007 There are four modes of CLIST execution, explicit, modified explicit,
000008 implicit, and modified implicit. CLIST execution is made possible by
000009 the TSO command, EXEC. That command can also be abbreviated as EX.
000010 Because the command is explicitly stated in the first two modes, they
000011 are known as explicit modes. The implicit modes do not contain EX or
000012 EXEC as part of the command syntax. They also differ in their reliance
000013 upon a special file to identify which CLIST code to execute.
000014
))        CLISTS are invoked at the TSO prompter or an interface to it. For
000016 those who have ISPF installed, this could also be OPTION 6 as well as
000017 most Productivity Development Facility (PDF) panels that have a
000018 command line. When a CLIST (or TSO command for that matter) is entered
- - - - - - - - - - - - - - - - - - - - - 497 LINE(S) NOT DISPLAYED
000516 turning the list function on if its value was "TRACE". If the word
000517 TRACE had not been typed on the statement that invokes the HARDCOPY
))8_   CLIST, the variable &TRACE would have contained spaces.
000519
000520
000521                         Data Driven Parameters
```

Figure 15.4 Result of showing first four lines.

```
EDIT ---- TSO1234.EXAMPLE.DATA(CLIST) - 01.02 -------------- COLUMNS 001 072
COMMAND ===> reset_                                         SCROLL ===> CSR
000004
000005                         Modes Of CLIST Execution
000006
000007 There are four modes of CLIST execution, explicit, modified explicit,
000008 implicit, and modified implicit. CLIST execution is made possible by
000009 the TSO command, EXEC. That command can also be abbreviated as EX.
000010 Because the command is explicitly stated in the first two modes, they
000011 are known as explicit modes. The implicit modes do not contain EX or
000012 EXEC as part of the command syntax. They also differ in their reliance
000013 upon a special file to identify which CLIST code to execute.
000014
000015           CLISTS are invoked at the TSO prompter or an interface to it.
000016           those who have ISPF installed, this could also be OPTION 6 as
000017           most Productivity Development Facility (PDF) panels that have
000018           command line. When a CLIST (or TSO command for that matter) is
- - - - - - - - - - - - - - - - - - - - - 497 LINE(S) NOT DISPLAYED
000516           turning the list function on if its value was "TRACE". If the
000517           TRACE had not been typed on the statement that invokes the HAR
000518           CLIST, the variable &TRACE would have contained spaces.
000519
000520
000521                         Data Driven Parameters
```

Figure 15.5 Resetting excluded lines.

would also be redisplayed, whether visible on the current screen or not.

Lines can also be excluded to highlight data. Take, for example, a situation where all edit lines are excluded, as in Figure 15.7. A FIND ALL command can be used to redisplay all lines with a certain characteristic (in this case all lines containing the character string PROC).

Lines that contain the text string (from the FIND command) would essentially be highlighted (Figure 15.8), since only those lines would be redisplayed. That makes it much easier to scan or change the data. In this situation it would be much easier to use the RESET primary command to redisplay the data, since the alternative would be several dozen line commands (S, F, or L) and considerable scrolling.

Lines can also be excluded to create a dichotomy. Excluded lines can then be treated differently from nonexcluded lines, and vice versa. The difference created by excluded lines can be used by several edit primary commands, including CHANGE, DELETE, FIND, and SORT. These commands use parameters X and NX to reference excluded and nonexcluded lines respectively.

Edit Labels

Labels assigned in an edit session work much like they do in a browse session, and so only the differences will be discussed here. The first significant difference is in how the labels are assigned. In edit, the label is merely typed into the line command area for the line that it's to be assigned to. In Figure 15.9, the label .MODE is assigned to line number five.

The LOCATE command is used as a primary command in the same way it's used in the browse function (Figure 15.10). Figure 15.11 shows that the located label has

```
EDIT ---- TSO1234.EXAMPLE.DATA(CLIST) - 01.02 --------------- COLUMNS 001 072
COMMAND ===> _                                           SCROLL ===> CSR
000004
000005                      Modes Of CLIST Execution
000006
000007 There are four modes of CLIST execution, explicit, modified explicit,
000008 implicit, and modified implicit. CLIST execution is made possible by
000009 the TSO command, EXEC. That command can also be abbreviated as EX.
000010 Because the command is explicitly stated in the first two modes, they
000011 are known as explicit modes. The implicit modes do not contain EX or
000012 EXEC as part of the command syntax. They also differ in their reliance
000013 upon a special file to identify which CLIST code to execute.
000014
000015        CLISTS are invoked at the TSO prompter or an interface to it.
000016        those who have ISPF installed, this could also be OPTION 6 as
000017        most Productivity Development Facility (PDF) panels that have
000018        command line. When a CLIST (or TSO command for that matter) is
000019        from a PDF panel it should be preceded by the word TSO. This i
000020        required from PDF Option 6 because it was designed to accept T
000021        commands and CLISTS.
000022
000023        The modes of CLIST execution will now be covered in more detai
000024        next few examples, used to demonstrate that execution, will as
000025        that there is a partitioned data set, TSO1234.SAMPLE.CLIST, th
```

Figure 15.6 Result of resetting excluded lines.

```
EDIT ---- TSO1234.EXAMPLE.DATA(CLIST) - 01.02 --------------- COLUMNS 001 072
COMMAND ===> f proc all_                                      SCROLL ===> CSR
****** ************************** TOP OF DATA **************************
- - - - - - - - - - - - - - - - - - - 639 LINE(S) NOT DISPLAYED
****** ************************** BOTTOM OF DATA **************************
```

Figure 15.7 FIND ALL with all lines excluded.

```
EDIT ---- TSO1234.EXAMPLE.DATA(CLIST) - 01.02 --------------- 53 CHARS 'PROC'
COMMAND ===>                                                   SCROLL ===> CSR
****** ************************** TOP OF DATA **************************
- - - - - - - - - - - - - - - - - - -     52 LINE(S) NOT DISPLAYED
000053      Before proceeding to the second execution mode, it is necessar
- - - - - - - - - - - - - - - - - - -     98 LINE(S) NOT DISPLAYED
000152      library or libraries to the SYSPROC file. The process of alloc
- - - - - - - - - - - - - - - - - - -      3 LINE(S) NOT DISPLAYED
000156      allocated to the SYSPROC file are searched in the order they w
- - - - - - - - - - - - - - - - - - -      5 LINE(S) NOT DISPLAYED
000162      library in the SYSPROC file. The contents of the like named me
- - - - - - - - - - - - - - - - - - -      2 LINE(S) NOT DISPLAYED
000165      this fashion, only to find yourself in a totally different pro
- - - - - - - - - - - - - - - - - - -     13 LINE(S) NOT DISPLAYED
000179      CLIST can now be found by searching the SYSPROC file, all we w
- - - - - - - - - - - - - - - - - - -      9 LINE(S) NOT DISPLAYED
000189      the member will come only from a search of the SYSPROC file. T
- - - - - - - - - - - - - - - - - - -      1 LINE(S) NOT DISPLAYED
000191      TSO command by mistake, because only the libraries in the SYSP
- - - - - - - - - - - - - - - - - - -      4 LINE(S) NOT DISPLAYED
000196      libraries are not searched before those defined to the SYSPROC
- - - - - - - - - - - - - - - - - - -     11 LINE(S) NOT DISPLAYED
000208      they set up JCL cataloged procedure libraries. These are very
- - - - - - - - - - - - - - - - - - -      6 LINE(S) NOT DISPLAYED
```

Figure 15.8 Result of the FIND ALL command.

```
EDIT ---- TSO1234.EXAMPLE.DATA(CLIST) - 01.01 -------------- COLUMNS 001 072
COMMAND ===>                                               SCROLL ===> CSR
****** *************************** TOP OF DATA ****************************
000001
000002                       CLIST Execution
000003
000004
.mode_                     Modes Of CLIST Execution
000006
000007 There are four modes of CLIST execution, explicit, modified explicit,
000008 implicit, and modified implicit. CLIST execution is made possible by
000009 the TSO command, EXEC. That command can also be abbreviated as EX.
000010 Because the command is explicitly stated in the first two modes, they
000011 are known as explicit modes. The implicit modes do not contain EX or
000012 EXEC as part of the command syntax. They also differ in their reliance
000013 upon a special file to identify which CLIST code to execute.
000014
000015 CLISTS are invoked at the TSO prompter or an interface to it. For
000016 those who have ISPF installed, this could also be OPTION 6 as well as
000017 most Productivity Development Facility (PDF) panels that have a
000018 command line. When a CLIST (or TSO command for that matter) is entered
000019 from a PDF panel it should be preceded by the word TSO. This is not
000020 required from PDF Option 6 because it was designed to accept TSO
000021 commands and CLISTS.
```

Figure 15.9 Setting an edit session label.

been brought to the top of the data set, where another difference has become apparent. In edit, the label is retained in the line command area rather than being noted in the short message area (as in the browse function).

Other built-in labels already exist and can be referenced as in Figure 15.12. There, the command is issued to locate the label .ZLAST, which corresponds to the last line of the data set.

When the locate command is entered, the data set is automatically scrolled to place the last line at the top of the display (Figure 15.13). On the same screen, the locate command is issued with the label abbreviation for the first line of the data set.

Figure 15.14 shows the edit session positioned at the first line of the data set. This is the result of having located the label .ZF, which is an abbreviated version of the label .ZFIRST. Labels can also be used to create ranges that work with edit primary commands. The commands FIND, CHANGE, EXCLUDE, SORT, SUBMIT, DELETE, REPLACE, and RESET can use label ranges. The label ranges define the scope of the command and thereby limit the lines affected by the command much the same way that columns or bounds might be specified to limit their effect within a line.

Labels can be changed by typing the new label name over the old one. They can be erased by spacing over the label or using the ERASE EOF key in the line command area. The RESET primary command can also be used to erase labels.

The TABS Line Command

The TABS line command is used to display the current tab setting. The command is

```
EDIT — TSO1234.EXAMPLE.DATA(CLIST) - 01.01 --------------- COLUMNS 001 072
COMMAND ===> l .mode_                                       SCROLL ===> CSR
000027
000028
000029                          Explicit Mode
000030
000031 The first execution mode uses the TSO command EXEC followed by the
000032 complete name of the data set that contains the CLIST. That can
000033 optionally be followed by two types of parameter information that will
000034 be discussed later. The TSO EXEC command can also be abbreviated EX, a
000035 has the following syntax:
000036
000037    EXEC clist-name 'positional-parameters(s) keyword-parameter(s)'
000038
000039 Using our sample CLIST library, the explicit mode of the EXEC command
000040 followed by the CLIST name might look like the following:
000041
000042    EX 'TSO1234.SAMPLE.CLIST(HARDCOPY)'
000043
000044 This mode of execution might also be considered explicit because it
000045 pinpoints the name of the CLIST being executed. The same syntax will
000046 work for a CLIST contained in a sequential data set except, of course,
000047 that no member name is specified. You may be pleased to know that, as
000048 we progress, the syntax for CLIST execution becomes shorter.
```

Figure 15.10 Locating an edit session label.

```
EDIT ---- TSO1234.EXAMPLE.DATA(CLIST) - 01.01 --------------- COLUMNS 001 072
COMMAND ===> _                                             SCROLL ===> CSR
.MODE                         Modes Of CLIST Execution
000006
000007 There are four modes of CLIST execution, explicit, modified explicit,
000008 implicit, and modified implicit. CLIST execution is made possible by
000009 the TSO command, EXEC. That command can also be abbreviated as EX.
000010 Because the command is explicitly stated in the first two modes, they
000011 are known as explicit modes. The implicit modes do not contain EX or
000012 EXEC as part of the command syntax. They also differ in their reliance
000013 upon a special file to identify which CLIST code to execute.
000014
000015 CLISTS are invoked at the TSO prompter or an interface to it. For
000016 those who have ISPF installed, this could also be OPTION 6 as well as
000017 most Productivity Development Facility (PDF) panels that have a
000018 command line. When a CLIST (or TSO command for that matter) is entered
000019 from a PDF panel it should be preceded by the word TSO. This is not
000020 required from PDF Option 6 because it was designed to accept TSO
000021 commands and CLISTS.
000022
000023 The modes of CLIST execution will now be covered in more detail. The
000024 next few examples, used to demonstrate that execution, will assume
000025 that there is a partitioned data set, TSO1234.SAMPLE.CLIST, that
000026 contains several executable CLISTS.
```

Figure 15.11 Result of locating an edit session label.

```
EDIT ---- TSO1234.EXAMPLE.DATA(CLIST) - 01.01 -------------- COLUMNS 001 072
COMMAND ===> l .zlast_                                SCROLL ===> CSR
.MODE                      Modes Of CLIST Execution
000006
000007 There are four modes of CLIST execution, explicit, modified explicit,
000008 implicit, and modified implicit. CLIST execution is made possible by
000009 the TSO command, EXEC. That command can also be abbreviated as EX.
000010 Because the command is explicitly stated in the first two modes, they
000011 are known as explicit modes. The implicit modes do not contain EX or
000012 EXEC as part of the command syntax. They also differ in their reliance
000013 upon a special file to identify which CLIST code to execute.
000014
000015 CLISTS are invoked at the TSO prompter or an interface to it. For
000016 those who have ISPF installed, this could also be OPTION 6 as well as
000017 most Productivity Development Facility (PDF) panels that have a
000018 command line. When a CLIST (or TSO command for that matter) is entered
000019 from a PDF panel it should be preceded by the word TSO. This is not
000020 required from PDF Option 6 because it was designed to accept TSO
000021 commands and CLISTS.
000022
000023 The modes of CLIST execution will now be covered in more detail. The
000024 next few examples, used to demonstrate that execution, will assume
000025 that there is a partitioned data set, TSO1234.SAMPLE.CLIST, that
000026 contains several executable CLISTS.
```

Figure 15.12 Locating a built-in label.

```
EDIT ---- TSO1234.EXAMPLE.DATA(CLIST) - 01.01 -------------- COLUMNS 001 072
 COMMAND ===> l .zf_                                  SCROLL ===> CSR
 000639
 ****** *************************** BOTTOM OF DATA ***************************
```

Figure 15.13 Using the abbreviated label form.

```
EDIT ---- TSO1234.EXAMPLE.DATA(CLIST) - 01.01 -------------- COLUMNS 001 072
COMMAND ===> _                                          SCROLL ===> CSR
000001
000002                       CLIST Execution
000003
000004
.MODE                    Modes Of CLIST Execution
000006
000007 There are four modes of CLIST execution, explicit, modified explicit,
000008 implicit, and modified implicit. CLIST execution is made possible by
000009 the TSO command, EXEC. That command can also be abbreviated as EX.
000010 Because the command is explicitly stated in the first two modes, they
000011 are known as explicit modes. The implicit modes do not contain EX or
000012 EXEC as part of the command syntax. They also differ in their reliance
000013 upon a special file to identify which CLIST code to execute.
000014
000015 CLISTS are invoked at the TSO prompter or an interface to it. For
000016 those who have ISPF installed, this could also be OPTION 6 as well as
000017 most Productivity Development Facility (PDF) panels that have a
000018 command line. When a CLIST (or TSO command for that matter) is entered
000019 from a PDF panel it should be preceded by the word TSO. This is not
000020 required from PDF Option 6 because it was designed to accept TSO
000021 commands and CLISTS.
```

Figure 15.14 Result of locating the .ZF label.

```
EDIT ---- TSO1234.EXAMPLE.DATA(BLKSIZE) - 01.04 ------------- COLUMNS 001 072
COMMAND ===>                                            SCROLL ===> CSR
000010 | 15477 | 23476 |        2        | 18453 | 27998 |
000011 | 11477 | 15476 |        3        | 13683 | 18452 |
000012 | 9077  | 11476 |        4        | 10797 | 13682 |
tabs_  | 7477  | 9076  |        5        | 8907  | 10796 |
000014 | 6357  | 7476  |        6        | 7549  | 8906  |
000015 | 5493  | 6356  |        7        | 6519  | 7548  |
000016 | 4821  | 5492  |        8        | 5727  | 6518  |
000017 | 4277  | 4820  |        9        | 5065  | 5726  |
000018 | 3861  | 4276  |       10        | 4567  | 5064  |
000019 | 3477  | 3860  |       11        | 4137  | 4566  |
000020 | 3189  | 3476  |       12        | 3769  | 4136  |
000021 | 2933  | 3188  |       13        | 3441  | 3768  |
000022
000023
****** ************************** BOTTOM OF DATA *************************
```

Figure 15.15 TABS line command.

issued in the line command area (see Figure 15.15) and can be abbreviated TAB. The special line that's displayed (Figure 15.16) is like that displayed for the mask. Like the mask line, the tabs display line allows the settings to be altered. Unlike the mask, however, the tabs displayed are not automatically active. Hardware tabs are activated, and changes to the tab line become effective after the TABS primary command is issued. The complete process of tabbing is discussed in Chapter 23. What can be determined from the tab line display at this point is that if tabs were turned on, there would be 5 tab stops (designated by the asterisks) in addition to the automatic tab stop established in column 1.

```
EDIT ---- TSO1234.EXAMPLE.DATA(BLKSIZE) - 01.04 ------------- COLUMNS 001 072
COMMAND ===>                                                  SCROLL ===> CSR
000010 | 15477 | 23476 |          2 |          | 18453 | 27998 |
000011 | 11477 | 15476 |          3 |          | 13683 | 18452 |
000012 |  9077 | 11476 |          4 |          | 10797 | 13682 |
=TABS>      *       *              *              *       *
000013 |  7477 |  9076 |          5 |          |  8907 | 10796 |
000014 |  6357 |  7476 |          6 |          |  7549 |  8906 |
000015 |  5493 |  6356 |          7 |          |  6519 |  7548 |
000016 |  4821 |  5492 |          8 |          |  5727 |  6518 |
000017 |  4277 |  4820 |          9 |          |  5065 |  5726 |
000018 |  3861 |  4276 |         10 |          |  4567 |  5064 |
000019 |  3477 |  3860 |         11 |          |  4137 |  4566 |
000020 |  3189 |  3476 |         12 |          |  3769 |  4136 |
000021 |  2933 |  3188 |         13 |          |  3441 |  3768 |
000022
000023
****** *************************** BOTTOM OF DATA ***************************
```

Figure 15.16 TABS display line.

Edit Primary Commands

The HEX Command

The HEX command is used to turn the hexadecimal display on and off. Without any parameters, the HEX command turns the hexadecimal display on. The hexadecimal display will remain on for a given period until turned off by specifying HEX OFF. Figure 16.1 shows the command used to turn the hexadecimal display on.

In Figure 16.2, the edit session data is now displayed in both character and hexadecimal formats. Because each line of data is now represented by three lines on the display, much less data is actually displayed on a given screen. The first of the three lines is the same as before the hex mode was turned on. The next two lines show the hexadecimal equivalent of the first line. The hexadecimal representation is given in a vertical display, which is the default. The display can also be explicitly stated or changed to display vertically with the command HEX ON VERT. Using the command HEX ON DATA, the hexadecimal portion of the display can be changed to display horizontally. Again, when the hexadecimal display is turned on, it remains on for a given period until turned off. The command HEX OFF can be used to return to a normal character display.

The data displayed in Figure 16.2 was grouped to make it obvious how letters and numbers were drawn from ranges of hexadecimal codes known as the *extended binary code for decimal interchange*. This is also known as the *EBCIDIC code*. The data displayed would not need to be displayed in hexadecimal format because it can easily be changed in normal display format. Often the hexadecimal display mode is used when a data set contains data that can't readily be displayed. In many such instances, the information is stored in binary or packed format.

With the hexadecimal format turned on, each byte of data can be updated by changing the normal display portion of the line (lined up with the line command area) or the hexadecimal portion. Each portion of the display is updated to reflect changes in the other portion after the ENTER key is pressed.

```
EDIT ---- TSO1234.HEX.DATA - 01.01 ------------------------ COLUMNS 001 072
COMMAND ===> hex on_                                        SCROLL ===> CSR
****** *************************** TOP OF DATA ****************************
000001
000002     ABCDEFGHI   JKLMNOPQR   STUVWXYZ   0123456789
000003
000004     abcdefghi   jklmnopqr   stuvwxyz   {}\
000005
000006     ¢.<(+|&      !$*);¬-/    |,%_>?      :#@'="
000007
****** *************************** BOTTOM OF DATA *************************
```

Figure 16.1 Edit HEX command.

```
EDIT ---- TSO1234.HEX.DATA - 01.01 ------------------------ COLUMNS 001 072
COMMAND ===>  _                                             SCROLL ===> CSR
****** *************************** TOP OF DATA ****************************
000001
       4444444444444444444444444444444444444444444444444444444444444444444444
       0000000000000000000000000000000000000000000000000000000000000000000000
000002     ABCDEFGHI   JKLMNOPQR   STUVWXYZ   0123456789
       4444CCCCCCCCC444DDDDDDDDD444EEEEEEEE444FFFFFFFFFF44444444444444444444444
       0000123456789000123456789000234567890000123456789000000000000000000000
000003
       4444444444444444444444444444444444444444444444444444444444444444444444
       0000000000000000000000000000000000000UUU000000000000000000000000000000
000004     abcdefghi   jklmnopqr   stuvwxyz   {}\
       4444888888888444999999999444AAAAAAAA444CDE444444444444444444444444444444
       0000123456789000123456789000234567890000000000000000000000000000000000
000005
       4444444444444444444444444444444444444444444444444444444444444444444444
       0000000000000000000000000000000000000000000000000000000000000000000000
000006     ¢.<(+|&      !$*);¬-/    |,%_>?      :#@'="
       44444444445444455555556644446666644444777777444444444444444444444444444
       0000ABCDEF000000ABCDEF010000ABCDEF00000ABCDEF000000000000000000000000000
000007
       4444444444444444444444444444444444444444444444444444444444444444444444
       0000000000000000000000000000000000000000000000000000000000000000000000
```

Figure 16.2 Hexadecimal display of edit data.

The FIND Command

The FIND command works the same in edit as it does in browse. In the edit context, two additional features can be added to facilitate use of the FIND command. In edit, the FIND command can be used with excluded lines and bounds, both of which serve to limit the scope of the command.

The previous chapter showed how the FIND command could be used with excluded lines. In the example, FIND was used to highlight all of the lines containing a particular character string. Another FIND command operating on only the non-excluded lines would essentially represent a multiple condition within a given line (that which caused the line to be redisplayed and the subject of the second FIND command). The parameter X designates an excluded line, while NX designates a non-excluded line. Like all other FIND command parameters, these can be specified in any order (with regard to other parameters). When the parameter X is specified, only the non-displayed lines are searched. When the parameter NX is specified, only the displayed lines are searched, but each line containing found text is redisplayed as the text is found.

In Figure 16.3 all data lines have been excluded. The FIND command has the ALL parameter included to find every instance of the character string COUNT.

As a result of executing the FIND command, all lines that contain the character string are redisplayed. This can then become the basis for treating excluded lines in a different manner than non-excluded lines. It can also be a way to further isolate the context of data, as in Figure 16.4, where a second FIND command is issued to operate only within non-excluded lines. The result of this second FIND command (Figure 16.5) essentially shows an instance where both the string COUNT (from the first FIND command) and the string DO (from the second FIND command) occur on the same line (line 57).

Edit FIND commands also work within the current bounds. This has the same effect as specifying start and end columns, but is not as obvious because the BNDS line usually is not displayed. In Figure 16.6, a FIND command is issued with restrictive bounds (which are displayed at the top of the data area).

The result of the FIND command (Figure 16.7) was to find the string on line 12. Five other instances of the string were bypassed because they fell outside of the bounds. (See Table 16.1).

TABLE 16.1 FIND Command Syntax Summary

| FIND
F | string
* | **NEXT**
PREV
FIRST
LAST
ALL | **CHARS**
PREFIX
SUFFIX
WORD | [start-col] | [end-col] | X
NX | label-
range |

```
EDIT ---- TSO1234.CLIST(REFORMAT) - 01.00 ------------------- COLUMNS 001 072
COMMAND ===> f all count_                                    SCROLL ===> CSR
****** ************************** TOP OF DATA ******************************
- - - - - - - - - - - - - - - - - - - -  79 LINE(S) NOT DISPLAYED
****** ************************** BOTTOM OF DATA ******************************
```

Figure 16.3 FIND command with all lines excluded.

```
EDIT ---- TSO1234.CLIST(REFORMAT) - 01.00 ------------------ 10 CHARS 'COUNT'
COMMAND ===> f do nx_                                        SCROLL ===> CSR
****** ************************** TOP OF DATA ******************************
- - - - - - - - - - - - - - - - - - - -  33 LINE(S) NOT DISPLAYED
000034 /***  SET THE LOOP_COUNT VARIABLE TO DETERMINE HOW MANY RECORDS
- - - - - - - - - - - - - - - - - - - -   2 LINE(S) NOT DISPLAYED
000037 SET &LOOP_COUNT = &LEN /  &LRECL
- - - - - - - - - - - - - - - - - - - -  12 LINE(S) NOT DISPLAYED
000050   SET &COUNT  = 0
- - - - - - - - - - - - - - - - - - - -   3 LINE(S) NOT DISPLAYED
000054 /***  WHILE LOOP_COUNT IS LESS THAN COUNT THERE ARE MORE
- - - - - - - - - - - - - - - - - - - -   2 LINE(S) NOT DISPLAYED
000057   DO WHILE &COUNT < &LOOP_COUNT
- - - - - - - - - - - - - - - - - - - -   3 LINE(S) NOT DISPLAYED
000061 /*** OF THE NEXT RECORD. INCREMENT THE VARIABLE &COUNT FOR
- - - - - - - - - - - - - - - - - - - -   2 LINE(S) NOT DISPLAYED
000064     SET &COUNT = &COUNT + 1
- - - - - - - - - - - - - - - - - - - -  15 LINE(S) NOT DISPLAYED
****** ************************** BOTTOM OF DATA ******************************
```

Figure 16.4 FIND command limited to non-excluded lines.

```
EDIT ---- TSO1234.CLIST(REFORMAT) - 01.00 ----------------- CHARS 'DO' FOUND
COMMAND ===>                                           SCROLL ===> CSR
****** ************************** TOP OF DATA *****************************
_ _ _ _ _ _ _ _ _ _ _ _ _ _ _ _ _ _ _ _   33 LINE(S) NOT DISPLAYED
000034 /***  SET THE LOOP_COUNT VARIABLE TO DETERMINE HOW MANY RECORDS
_ _ _ _ _ _ _ _ _ _ _ _ _ _ _ _ _ _ _ _   2 LINE(S) NOT DISPLAYED
000037 SET &LOOP_COUNT = &LEN /  &LRECL
_ _ _ _ _ _ _ _ _ _ _ _ _ _ _ _ _ _ _ _   12 LINE(S) NOT DISPLAYED
000050   SET &COUNT  = 0
_ _ _ _ _ _ _ _ _ _ _ _ _ _ _ _ _ _ _ _   3 LINE(S) NOT DISPLAYED
000054 /***  WHILE LOOP_COUNT IS LESS THAN COUNT THERE ARE MORE
_ _ _ _ _ _ _ _ _ _ _ _ _ _ _ _ _ _ _ _   2 LINE(S) NOT DISPLAYED
000057   DO WHILE &COUNT < &LOOP_COUNT
_ _ _ _ _ _ _ _ _ _ _ _ _ _ _ _ _ _ _ _   3 LINE(S) NOT DISPLAYED
000061 /*** OF THE NEXT RECORD. INCREMENT THE VARIABLE &COUNT FOR
_ _ _ _ _ _ _ _ _ _ _ _ _ _ _ _ _ _ _ _   2 LINE(S) NOT DISPLAYED
000064   SET &COUNT = &COUNT + 1
_ _ _ _ _ _ _ _ _ _ _ _ _ _ _ _ _ _ _ _   15 LINE(S) NOT DISPLAYED
****** ************************** BOTTOM OF DATA **************************
```

Figure 16.5 Result of FIND NX.

```
EDIT ---- TSO1234.EXAMPLE.DATA(PDF) - 01.00 ----------------- COLUMNS 001 072
COMMAND ===> f pdf_                                        SCROLL ===> CSR
****** ************************** TOP OF DATA *****************************
=BNDS>                      <                 >
000001
000002    PDF 1
000003
000004      PDF 2
000005
000006        PDF 3
000007
000008          PDF 4
000009
000010         PDF 5
000011
000012          PDF 6
000013
000014           PDF 7
000015
000016          PDF 8
000017
000018
****** ************************** BOTTOM OF DATA **************************
```

Figure 16.6 FIND command within restrictive bounds.

```
EDIT ---- TSO1234.EXAMPLE.DATA(PDF) - 01.00 --------------- CHARS 'PDF' FOUND
COMMAND ===>                                                SCROLL ===> CSR
****** ************************** TOP OF DATA ********************************
=BNDS>                         <                   >
000001
000002    PDF  1
000003
000004       PDF  2
000005
000006          PDF  3
000007
000008             PDF  4
000009
000010                PDF  5
000011
000012                   PDF  6
000013
000014                      PDF  7
000015
000016                         PDF  8
000017
000018
****** ************************** BOTTOM OF DATA ****************************
```

Figure 16.7 Result of FIND command within restrictive bounds.

The LOCATE Command

Just as in the browse function, the LOCATE command (abbreviated LOC or simply L) can be used to locate line numbers as well as any labels that have been set. When line numbers are used, leading zeros need not be specified. When the line number is specified as six digits or less, the line command area is searched for the line number. When the line number is specified as seven or eight digits, the data area is searched for the line number and is dependent on the current profile number mode.

When the LOCATE command is used to search for a label, it uses the user-defined labels typed into the line command area. LOCATE can also use the built-in labels .ZFIRST, .ZLAST, and .ZCUR. The LOCATE command can also be used to search for a particular class of line. The following parameters can be used with the LOCATE command to specify which generic class of line to search for.

CHANGE (CHG)   To locate change flagged lines.

COMMAND (CMD)   To locate pending line commands.

ERROR (ERR)   To locate error flagged lines.

EXCLUDED (X)   To locate excluded lines.

LABEL (LAB)   To locate labels (any rather than a specific label).

SPECIAL (SPE)   To locate special lines (like NOTE PROF COLS or TABS).

Like the FIND command, LOCATE has NEXT and PREV parameters that can be used to provide the direction the command will operate in when searching for a class of line. When not used, the default is to search for the next instance. Parameters FIRST and LAST can also be used to set the direction with the advantage that the search will stop at the top or bottom of the data set respectively. In this mode, it's also possible to specify a label range to be searched.

For example, the following LOCATE command will search for the previous label that's already in the range defined by user labels .F and .L:

```
LOC PREV LABEL .F .L
```

With the search direction specified first, it also shows that the parameters can be specified in any order. (See Table 16.2.)

TABLE 16.2 LOCATE Command Syntax Summary

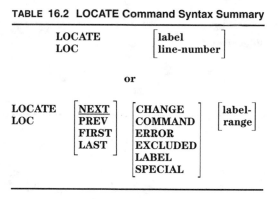

The RESET Command

The RESET command is used to remove special lines from the edit display. In Figure 16.8, the RESET command is used in an effort to remove the four message lines at the top of the display as well as the column and bounds display lines.

Figure 16.9 shows the edit session after the RESET command has been executed. All six special display lines have been removed. The RESET command can also be abbreviated RES. In Figure 16.10, the RESET command is used to remove pending line commands (commands that have been typed but not entered).

Figure 16.11 shows that the line commands have been reset. This is much more convenient than erasing the values in the line command area, and this will affect pending line commands throughout the data set whether they're currently visible or not.

As mentioned previously, the RESET command also affects excluded lines. In Figure 16.12, the RESET command is used with a label range to reshow all but the first three excluded blocks of lines. The user-defined label .MID is specified as the starting point for the command. The built-in label .ZL (for .ZLAST) is used to reference the last line of the data set.

The result of the RESET command (Figure 16.13) is that all excluded blocks from the label .MID to the end of the data set are redisplayed. Notice that excluded blocks before the specified range remain unchanged. The RESET command also has op-

```
EDIT ---- TSO1234.CNTL(COMPRESS) -------------------------- COLUMNS 001 072
COMMAND ===> reset_                                         SCROLL ===> CSR
****** **************************** TOP OF DATA ****************************
==MSG> -CAUTION- PROFILE CHANGED TO "CAPS ON"  (FROM "CAPS OFF") BECAUSE THE
==MSG>          DATA DOES NOT CONTAIN ANY LOWER CASE CHARACTERS.
==MSG> -WARNING- THE UNDO COMMAND IS NOT AVAILABLE UNTIL YOU CHANGE
==MSG>          YOUR EDIT PROFILE USING THE COMMAND "RECOVERY ON".
010000 //TSO1234A JOB 'SAMPLE JOB',
012000 //   CLASS=A,MSGCLASS=T,NOTIFY=TSO1234
013000 //COMPRESS   EXEC PGM=IEBCOPY
=COLS> ----+----1----+----2----+----3----+----4----+----5----+----6----+----7
014000 //SYSPRINT DD SYSOUT=*
015000 //SYSUT1    DD UNIT=3380,SPACE=(TRK,(5,5))
=BNDS> <
016000 //PDS       DD DSN=TSO1234.CLIST,DISP=OLD
016100 //SYSIN     DD *
016200   COPY INDD=PDS,OUTDD=PDS
****** **************************** BOTTOM OF DATA ****************************
```

Figure 16.8 Edit RESET command.

```
EDIT --- TSO1234.CNTL(COMPRESS) - 01.00 ---------------------- COLUMNS 001 072
COMMAND ===> _                                               SCROLL ===> CSR
****** **************************** TOP OF DATA ****************************
000100 //TSO1234A JOB 'SAMPLE JOB',
000120 //   CLASS=A,MSGCLASS=T,NOTIFY=TSO1234
000130 //COMPRESS   EXEC PGM=IEBCOPY
000140 //SYSPRINT DD SYSOUT=*
000150 //SYSUT1    DD UNIT=3380,SPACE=(TRK,(5,5))
000160 //PDS       DD DSN=TSO1234.CLIST,DISP=OLD
000161 //SYSIN     DD *
000162   COPY INDD=PDS,OUTDD=PDS
****** **************************** BOTTOM OF DATA ****************************
```

Figure 16.9 Reset edit session.

```
EDIT ---- TSO1234.CNTL(COMPRESS) - 01.00 -------------------- COLUMNS 001 072
COMMAND ===> res_                                         SCROLL ===> CSR
****** *************************** TOP OF DATA ****************************
rr       //TSO1234A JOB 'SAMPLE JOB',
rr5      //  CLASS=A,MSGCLASS=T,NOTIFY=TSO1234
000130 //COMPRESS   EXEC PGM=IEBCOPY
000140 //SYSPRINT DD SYSOUT=*
d9       //SYSUT1    DD UNIT=3380,SPACE=(TRK,(5,5))
000160 //PDS        DD DSN=TSO1234.CLIST,DISP=OLD
000161 //SYSIN      DD *
000162    COPY INDD=PDS,OUTDD=PDS
****** ************************** BOTTOM OF DATA **************************
```

Figure 16.10 Abbreviated form of RESET command.

```
EDIT ---- TSO1234.CNTL(COMPRESS) - 01.00 -------------------- COLUMNS 001 072
COMMAND ===> _                                           SCROLL ===> CSR
****** *************************** TOP OF DATA ****************************
000100 //TSO1234A JOB 'SAMPLE JOB',
000120 //  CLASS=A,MSGCLASS=T,NOTIFY=TSO1234
000130 //COMPRESS   EXEC PGM=IEBCOPY
000140 //SYSPRINT DD SYSOUT=*
000150 //SYSUT1    DD UNIT=3380,SPACE=(TRK,(5,5))
000160 //PDS        DD DSN=TSO1234.CLIST,DISP=OLD
000161 //SYSIN      DD *
000162    COPY INDD=PDS,OUTDD=PDS
****** ************************** BOTTOM OF DATA **************************
```

Figure 16.11 Edit session with line commands Reset.

```
EDIT ---- TSO1234.CLIST(REFORMAT) - 01.00 ------------------- COLUMNS 001 072
COMMAND ===> res .mid .zl                                    SCROLL ===> CSR
****** ************************** TOP OF DATA ******************************
- - - - - - - - - - - - - - - - - - - - - - - -  33 LINE(S) NOT DISPLAYED
000034 /***   SET THE LOOP_COUNT VARIABLE TO DETERMINE HOW MANY RECORDS
- - - - - - - - - - - - - - - - - - - - - - - -   2 LINE(S) NOT DISPLAYED
000037 SET &LOOP_COUNT = &LEN /  &LRECL
- - - - - - - - - - - - - - - - - - - - - - - -  12 LINE(S) NOT DISPLAYED
.MID     SET &COUNT  = 0
- - - - - - - - - - - - - - - - - - - - - - - -   3 LINE(S) NOT DISPLAYED
000054 /***  WHILE LOOP_COUNT IS LESS THAN COUNT THERE ARE MORE
- - - - - - - - - - - - - - - - - - - - - - - -   2 LINE(S) NOT DISPLAYED
000057   DO WHILE &COUNT < &LOOP_COUNT
- - - - - - - - - - - - - - - - - - - - - - - -   3 LINE(S) NOT DISPLAYED
000061 /*** OF THE NEXT RECORD. INCREMENT THE VARIABLE &COUNT FOR
- - - - - - - - - - - - - - - - - - - - - - - -   2 LINE(S) NOT DISPLAYED
000064     SET &COUNT = &COUNT + 1
- - - - - - - - - - - - - - - - - - - - - - - -  15 LINE(S) NOT DISPLAYED
****** ************************** BOTTOM OF DATA ***************************
```

Figure 16.12 RESET through a label range.

```
EDIT ---- TSO1234.CLIST(REFORMAT) - 01.00 ------------------- COLUMNS 001 072
COMMAND ===>                                                 SCROLL ===> CSR
****** ************************** TOP OF DATA ******************************
- - - - - - - - - - - - - - - - - - - - - - - -  33 LINE(S) NOT DISPLAYED
000034 /***   SET THE LOOP_COUNT VARIABLE TO DETERMINE HOW MANY RECORDS
- - - - - - - - - - - - - - - - - - - - - - - -   2 LINE(S) NOT DISPLAYED
000037 SET &LOOP_COUNT = &LEN /   &LRECL
- - - - - - - - - - - - - - - - - - - - - - - -  12 LINE(S) NOT DISPLAYED
.MID     SET &COUNT  = 0
000051   SET &START  = 1
000052   SET &END    = &LRECL
000053 /***
000054 /***  WHILE LOOP_COUNT IS LESS THAN COUNT THERE ARE MORE
000055 /***  OUTPUT RECORDS TO GENERATE.
000056 /***
000057   DO WHILE &COUNT < &LOOP_COUNT
000058     SET &NEWDATA = &SUBSTR(&START:&END,&CUT)
000059 /***
000060 /*** ADVANCE POSITION IN THE INPUT RECORD TO GET THE CONTENTS
000061 /*** OF THE NEXT RECORD. INCREMENT THE VARIABLE &COUNT FOR
000062 /*** EACH OUTPUT RECORD GENERATED.
000063 /***
000064     SET &COUNT = &COUNT + 1
000065     SET &START = &START + &LRECL
```

Figure 16.13 Effect of resetting all lines in a label range.

tional parameters to identify a particular type of line to reset. These parameters are the same as with the LOCATE command and are:

CHANGE (CHG)   To reset change flags.

COMMAND (CMD)   To reset pending line commands.

ERROR (ERR)   To reset error flags.

EXCLUDED (X)   To reset excluded lines.

LABEL (LAB)   To reset labels.

SPECIAL (SPE)   To reset special lines (like NOTE PROF COLS or TABS).

When one of the parameters is used, only that type of line is reset, leaving the other line types unchanged. The parameters can also be used when a label range is specified.

The SUBMIT Command

The SUBMIT command is used to read JCL jobstreams into the computer for background execution. The jobstream is read from the current edit session and therefore need not first be saved to disk as would be necessary with the TSO SUBMIT command. Since the data need not be saved to submit it, it's possible and often desirable to make edit changes to a jobstream, submit it, and cancel the edit session. In that way, the background job can be tailored to the particular needs of that execution and the original job contents retained as well. Figure 16.14 shows the SUBMIT command used to read a compress job into the operating system.

```
EDIT ---- TSO1234.CNTL(COMPRESS) - 01.01 -------------------- COLUMNS 001 072
 COMMAND ===> sub_                                       SCROLL ===> CSR
****** ************************** TOP OF DATA **************************
000100 //TSO1234A JOB 'SAMPLE JOB',
000120 //   CLASS=A,MSGCLASS=T,NOTIFY=TSO1234
000130 //COMPRESS   EXEC PGM=IEBCOPY
000140 //SYSPRINT DD SYSOUT=*
000150 //SYSUT1    DD UNIT=3380,SPACE=(TRK,(5,5))
000160 //PDS       DD DSN=TSO1234.CLIST,DISP=OLD
000161 //SYSIN     DD *
000162    COPY INDD=PDS,OUTDD=PDS
****** ************************** BOTTOM OF DATA **************************
```

Figure 16.14 Edit SUBMIT command.

The message at the bottom of the screen (Figure 16.15) indicates that the jobstream has been read into the operating system. The message includes the jobname and JES (Job Entry Subsystem) number, which can be used to track the job throughout the system. An edit member could contain multiple jobstreams. Each would have its own jobcard and merely follow the statements for the previous job. When the SUBMIT command is issued, all jobstreams in the current edit session would be read into the system at once. Conversely, established edit labels can be specified with the SUBMIT command to limit which lines of the edit session are actually read into the system.

```
EDIT ---- TSO1234.CNTL(COMPRESS) - 01.01 -------------------- COLUMNS 001 072
COMMAND ===> sub                                          SCROLL ===> CSR
****** **************************** TOP OF DATA ****************************
000100 //TSO1234A JOB 'SAMPLE JOB',
000120 //   CLASS=A,MSGCLASS=T,NOTIFY=TSO1234
000130 //COMPRESS  EXEC PGM=IEBCOPY
000140 //SYSPRINT DD SYSOUT=*
000150 //SYSUT1    DD UNIT=3380,SPACE=(TRK,(5,5))
000160 //PDS       DD DSN=TSO1234.CLIST,DISP=OLD
000161 //SYSIN     DD *
000162   COPY INDD=PDS,OUTDD=PDS
****** **************************** BOTTOM OF DATA ****************************




JOB TSO1234(JOB09370) SUBMITTED
***_
```

Figure 16.15 SUBMIT command message.

17

Advanced
Edit Primary Commands

The EXCLUDE Command

Like the exclude line command, the EXCLUDE command (abbreviated X) is used to exclude lines. The syntax for the EXCLUDE command, however, is virtually identical to the FIND command. This allows the EXCLUDE command to exclude lines of data based on the data content. When used in this fashion, a character string would be specified, and any line containing the string (within any optional specified parameters) would be excluded from the display. All FIND command parameters except X and NX are available with the EXCLUDE command.

In Figure 17.1, the EXCLUDE command is used to exclude all lines that have /* (the standard for designating a comment in CLIST code) in columns one through eight. The type of line that's being targeted by this command is also highlighted.

Figure 17.2 shows the result of the EXCLUDE command. The command caused 29 lines to be excluded, as evidenced by the short message. Twenty of those excluded lines are contained in three blocks on the current screen. With the comment lines excluded, it's easier to see the executable CLIST code. It will also be possible to treat excluded and non-excluded lines differently in other edit primary commands.

The EXCLUDE command can also be used to exclude lines by label range rather than a character string, as in the following example:

```
EXCLUDE .HERE .THERE
```

where .HERE and .THERE are edit labels that have been previously defined. It's also possible to execute the command as X ALL without any other parameters to exclude all lines in the data set. (See Table 17.1.)

```
EDIT ---- TSO1234.CLIST(REFORMAT) - 01.00 ------------------- COLUMNS 001 072
COMMAND ===> x all /* 1 8_                                   SCROLL ===> CSR
****** ************************** TOP OF DATA ****************************
000001 PROC 1 DSN LRECL(80)
000002 /***********************************************************
000003 /***                                                      *
000004 /***   FUNCTION: THIS CLIST WILL REFORMAT THE RECORD       *
000005 /***   LENGTH OF RECORDS IT READS. THE NEW RECORDS ARE     *
000006 /***   PLACED IN A NEW DATA SET CONTAINING A DATE AND      *
000007 /***   TIME STAMP. THE NEW RECORD LENGTH CAN BE MADE       *
000008 /***   LARGER OR SMALLER THAN THE ORIGINAL RECORD          *
000009 /***   LENGTH.                                             *
000010 /***                                                      *
000011 /***********************************************************
000012 CONTROL NOFLUSH
000013 SET &RC = 0
000014 ALLOC F(CUT) DA(&DSN) SHR REUSE
000015 /***
000016 /***   USE DATA AND TIME INFORMATION TO CREATE QUALIFIERS
000017 /***   FOR THE OUTPUT DATA SET. THE DATE AND TIME THAT THE
000018 /***   CLIST IS EXECUTED WILL CAUSE EACH NEW DSNAME TO BE
000019 /***   UNIQUE.
000020 /***
000021 SET &DATE = D&SUBSTR(1:2,&SYSDATE)+
```

Figure 17.1 EXCLUDE primary command.

```
EDIT ---- TSO1234.CLIST(REFORMAT) - 01.00 -------------------- 29 CHARS '/*'
COMMAND ===> _                                              SCROLL ===> CSR
****** ************************** TOP OF DATA ****************************
000001 PROC 1 DSN LRECL(80)
- - - - - - - - - - - - - - - - - - -  10 LINE(S) NOT DISPLAYED
000012 CONTROL NOFLUSH
000013 SET &RC = 0
000014 ALLOC F(CUT) DA(&DSN) SHR REUSE
- - - - - - - - - - - - - - - - - - -  6 LINE(S) NOT DISPLAYED
000021 SET &DATE = D&SUBSTR(1:2,&SYSDATE)+
000022    &SUBSTR(4:5,&SYSDATE)&SUBSTR(7:8,&SYSDATE)
000023 SET &TIME = T&SUBSTR(1:2,&SYSTIME)+
000024    &SUBSTR(4:5,&SYSTIME)&SUBSTR(7:8,&SYSTIME)
000025 SET &DSN2 = &SYSUID..&DATE..&TIME
000026 SET &BLKSIZE = 23476 / &LRECL * &LRECL
000027 ALLOC F(NEWDATA) DA('&DSN2') SPACE(5 5) TRACK RELEASE CATALOG +
000028    RECFM(F B) LRECL(&LRECL) BLKSIZE(&BLKSIZE) REUSE
000029 OPENFILE CUT
000030 OPENFILE NEWDATA OUTPUT
000031 GETFILE CUT
000032 SET &LEN = &LENGTH(&STR(&CUT))
- - - - - - - - - - - - - - - - - - -  4 LINE(S) NOT DISPLAYED
000037 SET &LOOP_COUNT = &LEN /  &LRECL
000038 SET &REMAIN     = &LEN // &LRECL
```

Figure 17.2 Result of EXCLUDE command execution.

TABLE 17.1 EXCLUDE Command Syntax Summary

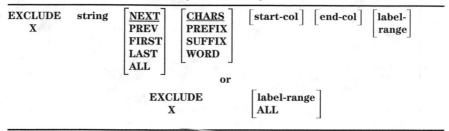

The DELETE Command

The DELETE primary command is a convenient way to delete all lines in a specified label range. The command can be abbreviated DEL, and so the command DEL ALL .HERE .THERE would delete all lines in that label range (including the labels themselves). Using the ALL parameter and the parameters X or NX, the DELETE command can also be used to delete all excluded lines or all non-excluded lines. When the label range is again added, the DELETE command could be used to delete all excluded lines or all non-excluded lines within the label range.

In Figure 17.3, the DELETE command is used to delete all of the excluded lines in the data set (the lines excluded earlier with the EXCLUDE primary command). Figure 17.4 shows the edit session after excluded lines are deleted. The excluded blocks no longer display, and the short message indicates that a total of 29 lines were deleted throughout the data set.

```
EDIT ---- TSO1234.CLIST(REFORMAT) - 01.00 ------------------- COLUMNS 001 072
COMMAND ===> del all x_                                    SCROLL ===> CSR
****** ************************** TOP OF DATA ******************************
000001 PROC 1 DSN LRECL(80)
- - - - - - - - - - - - - - - - - - -  10 LINE(S) NOT DISPLAYED
000012 CONTROL NOFLUSH
000013 SET &RC = 0
000014 ALLOC F(CUT) DA(&DSN) SHR REUSE
- - - - - - - - - - - - - - - - - - -  6 LINE(S) NOT DISPLAYED
000021 SET &DATE = D&SUBSTR(1:2,&SYSDATE)+
000022    &SUBSTR(4:5,&SYSDATE)&SUBSTR(7:8,&SYSDATE)
000023 SET &TIME = T&SUBSTR(1:2,&SYSTIME)+
000024    &SUBSTR(4:5,&SYSTIME)&SUBSTR(7:8,&SYSTIME)
000025 SET &DSN2 = &SYSUID..&DATE..&TIME
000026 SET &BLKSIZE = 23476 / &LRECL * &LRECL
000027 ALLOC F(NEWDATA) DA('&DSN2') SPACE(5 5) TRACK RELEASE CATALOG +
000028    RECFM(F B) LRECL(&LRECL) BLKSIZE(&BLKSIZE) REUSE
000029 OPENFILE CUT
000030 OPENFILE NEWDATA OUTPUT
000031 GETFILE CUT
000032 SET &LEN = &LENGTH(&STR(&CUT))
- - - - - - - - - - - - - - - - - - -  4 LINE(S) NOT DISPLAYED
000037 SET &LOOP_COUNT = &LEN /  &LRECL
000038 SET &REMAIN    = &LEN // &LRECL
```

Figure 17.3 DELETE primary command.

```
EDIT ---- TSO1234.CLIST(REFORMAT) - 01.01 ------------------ 29 LINES DELETED
COMMAND ===> _                                             SCROLL ===> CSR
****** ************************* TOP OF DATA *****************************
000001 PROC 1 DSN LRECL(80)
000002 CONTROL NOFLUSH
000003 SET &RC = 0
000004 ALLOC F(CUT) DA(&DSN) SHR REUSE
000005 SET &DATE = D&SUBSTR(1:2,&SYSDATE)+
000006    &SUBSTR(4:5,&SYSDATE)&SUBSTR(7:8,&SYSDATE)
000007 SET &TIME = T&SUBSTR(1:2,&SYSTIME)+
000008    &SUBSTR(4:5,&SYSTIME)&SUBSTR(7:8,&SYSTIME)
000009 SET &DSN2 = &SYSUID..&DATE..&TIME
000010 SET &BLKSIZE = 23476 / &LRECL * &LRECL
000011 ALLOC F(NEWDATA) DA('&DSN2') SPACE(5 5) TRACK RELEASE CATALOG +
000012    RECFM(F B) LRECL(&LRECL) BLKSIZE(&BLKSIZE) REUSE
000013 OPENFILE CUT
000014 OPENFILE NEWDATA OUTPUT
000015 GETFILE CUT
000016 SET &LEN = &LENGTH(&STR(&CUT))
000017 SET &LOOP_COUNT = &LEN /  &LRECL
000018 SET &REMAIN     = &LEN // &LRECL
000019 ERROR +
000020    DO
000021      SET &RC = &LASTCC
```

Figure 17.4 Result of DELETE command execution.

The SORT Command

The SORT command is used to resequence data. Data is placed in collating sequence in either ascending or descending order. The order or collating sequence is determined by the hexadecimal value of a particular character. The lower the hexadecimal value, the lower the character appears in the sort order. A look back at Figure 16.2 (in the previous chapter) and the hexadecimal values it contains will help to visualize the sort sequence. The order is special characters, lowercase letters, uppercase letters, and finally numbers.

The SORT command has no required parameters. In practice, however, it's common to specify at least one range of columns to serve as the sort field. Data within that range of columns would then be used to resequence the edit data. In Figure 17.5, the SORT command is used to sort data in columns four through eight.

When the sort order is not specified (A for ascending and D for descending), the default of ascending is used. Figure 17.6 shows the same data after sorting columns four through eight in ascending sequence. A comparison of lines six and seven gives some idea where spaces fit in the collating sequence. Obviously, spaces sort lower than numbers, but with a hexadecimal value of 40 they also sort lower than the special characters.

The SORT command can make use of a label range or the difference between excluded and non-excluded lines to sort some data lines while not sorting others. Figure 17.7 shows the exclude line command used on data that's apparently in report format.

As seen in Figure 17.8, excluding heading and blank lines leaves only lines with raw data still visible (non-excluded). The command to sort columns four through

```
EDIT ---- TSO1234.EXAMPLE.DATA(BLKSIZE4) - 01.01 ------------ COLUMNS 001 072
COMMAND ===> sort 4 8_                                    SCROLL ===> CSR
****** *************************** TOP OF DATA ***************************
=COLS> ----+----1----+----2----+----3----+----4----+----5----+----6----+----7
000001    23477      47476            1          27999     56664
000002    15477      23476            2          18453     27998
000003    11477      15476            3          13683     18452
000004     9077      11476            4          10797     13682
000005     7477       9076            5           8907     10796
000006     6357       7476            6           7549      8906
000007     5493       6356            7           6519      7548
000008     4821       5492            8           5727      6518
000009     4277       4820            9           5065      5726
****** *************************** BOTTOM OF DATA ***************************
```

Figure 17.5 Edit SORT command.

```
EDIT ---- TSO1234.EXAMPLE.DATA(BLKSIZE4) - 01.02 ------------ COLUMNS 001 072
COMMAND ===> _                                            SCROLL ===> CSR
****** *************************** TOP OF DATA ***************************
=COLS> ----+----1----+----2----+----3----+----4----+----5----+----6----+----7
000001     4277       4820            9           5065      5726
000002     4821       5492            8           5727      6518
000003     5493       6356            7           6519      7548
000004     6357       7476            6           7549      8906
000005     7477       9076            5           8907     10796
000006     9077      11476            4          10797     13682
000007    11477      15476            3          13683     18452
000008    15477      23476            2          18453     27998
000009    23477      47476            1          27999     56664
****** *************************** BOTTOM OF DATA ***************************
```

Figure 17.6 Result of edit SORT command.

```
EDIT ---- TSO1234.EXAMPLE.DATA(BLKSIZE4) - 01.02 ------------ COLUMNS 001 072
COMMAND ===>                                            SCROLL ===> CSR
****** ***************************** TOP OF DATA *****************************
XX                             Block Size Chart
000002
000003          3380                  Device               3390
000004                                Blocks Per
000005      Min.        Max.          Track         Min.        Max.
XX
=COLS> ----+----1----+----2----+----3----+----4----+----5----+----6----+----7
000007    4277        4820            9            5065        5726
000008    4821        5492            8            5727        6518
000009    5493        6356            7            6519        7548
000010    6357        7476            6            7549        8906
000011    7477        9076            5            8907        10796
000012    9077        11476           4            10797       13682
000013    11477       15476           3            13683       18452
000014    15477       23476           2            18453       27998
000015    23477       47476           1            27999       56664
X2_
000017
****** *************************** BOTTOM OF DATA ***************************
```

Figure 17.7 Excluding non-data lines.

```
EDIT ---- TSO1234.EXAMPLE.DATA(BLKSIZE4) - 01.02 ------------ COLUMNS 001 072
COMMAND ===> sort nx 4 8 d_                             SCROLL ===> CSR
****** ***************************** TOP OF DATA *****************************
- - - - - - - - - - - - - - - - - - - - - - - - 6 LINE(S) NOT DISPLAYED
=COLS> ----+----1----+----2----+----3----+----4----+----5----+----6----+----7
000007    4277        4820            9            5065        5726
000008    4821        5492            8            5727        6518
000009    5493        6356            7            6519        7548
000010    6357        7476            6            7549        8906
000011    7477        9076            5            8907        10796
000012    9077        11476           4            10797       13682
000013    11477       15476           3            13683       18452
000014    15477       23476           2            18453       27998
000015    23477       47476           1            27999       56664
- - - - - - - - - - - - - - - - - - - - - - - - 2 LINE(S) NOT DISPLAYED
****** *************************** BOTTOM OF DATA ***************************
```

Figure 17.8 Sorting non-excluded lines.

eight is issued again. This time, however, two parameters have been added. The first parameter, NX, specifies that only non-excluded lines should be affected. Excluded lines would be specified using the letter X. The second added parameter D signifies that the sorted data should be placed in descending order (high to low values).

Figure 17.9 shows how the visible data has been resequenced. On the same screen, the RESET command is issued to redisplay all excluded blocks of lines. The redisplayed lines (Figure 17.10) show that they were not intermixed with the sorted lines and are still in their original order.

Up to five sort fields can be specified. The first column range specified is considered the primary sort field. Other column ranges help to determine the sort order within the primary sort field. The sort direction, ascending or descending, is independent for each field.

If only a single column is specified, it's interpreted as the start column. The right bound would then mark the end of the sort field. If no columns are specified, the sort will operate within the current bounds. The effect will be to treat all data within the current bounds as one contiguous sort field.

Recursive Edit

Like the browse function, edit can be invoked recursively. While in edit, as in Figure 17.11, the EDIT command can be used to start another edit session. In this instance, a member name is specified to indicate the desire to edit an existing member in the same PDS or to create that member if it doesn't already exist.

```
EDIT ---   TSO1234.EXAMPLE.DATA(BLKSIZE4) - 01.02 ------------ COLUMNS 001 072
COMMAND ===> reset_                                      SCROLL ===> CSR
****** ************************** TOP OF DATA ***************************
- - - - - - - - - - - - - - - - - - - 6 LINE(S) NOT DISPLAYED
=COLS> ----+----1----+----2----+----3----+----4----+----5----+----6----+----7
000007    23477      47476            1           27999      56664
000008    15477      23476            2           18453      27998
000009    11477      15476            3           13683      18452
000010     9077      11476            4           10797      13682
000011     7477       9076            5            8907      10796
000012     6357       7476            6            7549       8906
000013     5493       6356            7            6519       7548
000014     4821       5492            8            5727       6518
000015     4277       4820            9            5065       5726
- - - - - - - - - - - - - - - - - - - 2 LINE(S) NOT DISPLAYED
****** ************************** BOTTOM OF DATA ***************************
```

Figure 17.9 Result of sorting non-excluded lines.

```
EDIT ---- TSO1234.EXAMPLE.DATA(BLKSIZE4) - 01.02 ------------ COLUMNS 001 072
COMMAND ===> _                                            SCROLL ===> CSR
****** **************************** TOP OF DATA ****************************
000001                        Block Size Chart
000002
000003           3380              Device               3390
000004                           Blocks Per
000005       Min.      Max.         Track         Min.      Max.
000006
000007      23477     47476           1           27999     56664
000008      15477     23476           2           18453     27998
000009      11477     15476           3           13683     18452
000010       9077     11476           4           10797     13682
000011       7477      9076           5            8907     10796
000012       6357      7476           6            7549      8906
000013       5493      6356           7            6519      7548
000014       4821      5492           8            5727      6518
000015       4277      4820           9            5065      5726
000016
000017
****** ************************* BOTTOM OF DATA **************************
```

Figure 17.10 Redisplayed lines following SORT.

```
EDIT ---- TSO1234.EXAMPLE.DATA(EDITING) - 01.00 ------------- COLUMNS 001 072
COMMAND ===> edit blksize_                                 SCROLL ===> CSR
****** **************************** TOP OF DATA ****************************
000001
000002     Recursive edit can be used with other members of the same PDS
000003
000004     or it can be used with different libraries and sequential data sets
000005
000006
000007
****** ************************* BOTTOM OF DATA **************************
```

Figure 17.11 Editing another member of the same PDS.

In Figure 17.12, editing of the member EDITING has been suspended and the member BLKSIZE placed in the active edit session. Recursive edit can be invoked as many times as allocated computer memory (also known as region) will support. In Figure 17.12, it's invoked a second time without specifying a member name.

When recursive edit's invoked without a member name, the edit menu is displayed, as in Figure 17.13. All of the options available from the edit menu can be used, providing great latitude about which data is selected. The menu could be used to specify a member or display a member list. The list could be from the last library accessed or it could be from a different library. Of course, it's also possible to specify a sequential data set at this point. In Figure 17.13 a different library and member combination is specified. Figure 17.14 shows the third edit session.

The return path is identical to that used to get here. When the last edit session is terminated, the edit menu is again displayed (Figure 17.15). Another data set can be specified here, or the END command can be invoked to return to the second edit session.

Using the END command again returns to the second edit session (Figure 17.16). After the necessary changes were made, the END command or the CANCEL command could be used to terminate the session. In this case, the END PF key is pressed to end the session.

After pressing the END PF key, the second session is terminated, revealing the initial edit session (Figure 17.17). The jump function can also be used to exit out of multiple edit sessions. If the jump function is used, the current edit session will be saved if changes have been made. Other edit sessions are only redisplayed if they too have changes that could be saved.

```
EDIT ---- TSO1234.EXAMPLE.DATA(BLKSIZE) - 01.05 ------------- COLUMNS 001 072
COMMAND ===> edit_                                         SCROLL ===> CSR
****** *************************** TOP OF DATA ****************************
000001  ----------------------------------------------------------------
000002  |                         Block Size Chart                      |
000003  |                                                               |
000004  ----------------------------------------------------------------
000005  |          3380        |    Device    |          3390          |
000006  |                      |  Blocks Per  |                        |
000007  |  Min.    |   Max.    |  Disk Track  |  Min.     |   Max.     |
000008  ----------------------------------------------------------------
000009  | 23477    |  47476    |      1       |  27999    |   56664    |
000010  | 15477    |  23476    |      2       |  18453    |   27998    |
000011  | 11477    |  15476    |      3       |  13683    |   18452    |
000012  |  9077    |  11476    |      4       |  10797    |   13682    |
000013  |  7477    |   9076    |      5       |   8907    |   10796    |
000014  |  6357    |   7476    |      6       |   7549    |    8906    |
000015  |  5493    |   6356    |      7       |   6519    |    7548    |
000016  |  4821    |   5492    |      8       |   5727    |    6518    |
000017  |  4277    |   4820    |      9       |   5065    |    5726    |
000018  |  3861    |   4276    |     10       |   4567    |    5064    |
000019  |  3477    |   3860    |     11       |   4137    |    4566    |
000020  |  3189    |   3476    |     12       |   3769    |    4136    |
000021  |  2933    |   3188    |     13       |   3441    |    3768    |
```

Figure 17.12 EDIT command without a member name.

```
----------------------- EDIT COMMAND - ENTRY PANEL -----------------------
COMMAND ===>

ISPF LIBRARY:
   PROJECT ===> TSO1234
   GROUP   ===> EXAMPLE  ===>           ===>           ===>
   TYPE    ===> DATA
   MEMBER  ===>              (Blank or pattern for member selection list)

OTHER PARTITIONED OR SEQUENTIAL DATA SET:
   DATA SET NAME ===> CNTL(COMPRESS)_
   VOLUME SERIAL ===>           (If not cataloged)

DATA SET PASSWORD ===>          (If password protected)

PROFILE NAME      ===>          (Blank defaults to data set type)

INITIAL MACRO     ===>      LOCK       ===> YES    (YES, NO or NEVER)

FORMAT LINE       ===>      MIXED MODE ===> NO     (YES or NO)
```

Figure 17.13 The edit menu following recursive edit.

```
EDIT ---- TSO1234.CNTL(COMPRESS) - 01.01 -------------------- COLUMNS 001 072
COMMAND ===> _                                              SCROLL ===> CSR
****** **************************** TOP OF DATA ****************************
000100 //TSO1234A JOB 'SAMPLE JOB',
000120 //   CLASS=A,MSGCLASS=T,NOTIFY=TSO1234
000130 //COMPRESS   EXEC PGM=IEBCOPY
000140 //SYSPRINT DD SYSOUT=*
000150 //SYSUT1    DD UNIT=3380,SPACE=(TRK,(5,5))
000160 //PDS       DD DSN=TSO1234.CLIST,DISP=OLD
000161 //SYSIN     DD *
000162    COPY INDD=PDS,OUTDD=PDS
****** *************************** BOTTOM OF DATA **************************
```

Figure 17.14 Third edit session.

```
------------------------- EDIT COMMAND - ENTRY PANEL  -----------------------
COMMAND ===>

ISPF LIBRARY:
   PROJECT ===> TSO1234
   GROUP   ===> EXAMPLE   ===>              ===>              ===>
   TYPE    ===> DATA
   MEMBER  ===>                    (Blank or pattern for member selection list)

OTHER PARTITIONED OR SEQUENTIAL DATA SET:
   DATA SET NAME   ===> CNTL(COMPRESS)
   VOLUME SERIAL   ===>              (If not cataloged)

DATA SET PASSWORD ===>              (If password protected)

PROFILE NAME      ===>              (Blank defaults to data set type)

INITIAL MACRO     ===>         LOCK     ===> YES    (YES, NO or NEVER)

FORMAT NAME       ===>         MIXED MODE ===> NO   (YES or NO)
```

Figure 17.15 Return to edit menu.

```
EDIT ---- TSO1234.EXAMPLE.DATA(BLKSIZE) - 01.05 ------------- COLUMNS 001 072
COMMAND ===> _                                              SCROLL ===> CSR
****** **************************** TOP OF DATA ****************************
000001  ----------------------------------------------------------------
000002  |                       Block Size Chart                        |
000003  |                                                               |
000004  ----------------------------------------------------------------
000005  |           3380         |  Device   |         3390            |
000006  |                        | Blocks Per |                        |
000007  |    Min.   |   Max.     | Disk Track |   Min.   |   Max.      |
000008  ----------------------------------------------------------------
000009  |   23477   |  47476     |     1      |  27999   |  56664      |
000010  |   15477   |  23476     |     2      |  18453   |  27998      |
000011  |   11477   |  15476     |     3      |  13683   |  18452      |
000012  |    9077   |  11476     |     4      |  10797   |  13682      |
000013  |    7477   |   9076     |     5      |   8907   |  10796      |
000014  |    6357   |   7476     |     6      |   7549   |   8906      |
000015  |    5493   |   6356     |     7      |   6519   |   7548      |
000016  |    4821   |   5492     |     8      |   5727   |   6518      |
000017  |    4277   |   4820     |     9      |   5065   |   5726      |
000018  |    3861   |   4276     |    10      |   4567   |   5064      |
000019  |    3477   |   3860     |    11      |   4137   |   4566      |
000020  |    3189   |   3476     |    12      |   3769   |   4136      |
000021  |    2933   |   3188     |    13      |   3441   |   3768      |
```

Figure 17.16 Return to the second edit session.

```
EDIT ---- TSO1234.EXAMPLE.DATA(EDITING) - 01.00 ------------- COLUMNS 001 072
 COMMAND ===> _                                              SCROLL ===> CSR
****** **************************** TOP OF DATA ****************************
000001
000002     Recursive edit can be used with other members of the same PDS
000003
000004     or it can be used with different libraries and sequential data sets
000005
000006
000007
****** **************************** BOTTOM OF DATA *************************
```

Figure 17.17 Return to original edit session.

18

The CHANGE Command

The CHANGE command is used to change one character string value to another. This command is closely tied to the FIND command in function and syntax. The CHANGE command can be spelled out, abbreviated as CHG, or, more commonly, abbreviated with the letter C. Command execution must also specify the string that's to be changed and what it will be changed to. Either of the strings should be enclosed in single or double quotes when they might otherwise be confused with one of the optional parameters. That's because parameters are reserved words rather than being position specific. Pure numeric values should also be enclosed in quotes because they could be confused with start and end column specifications. CHANGE command strings should also be enclosed in quotes when they contain embedded spaces.

The search for the string to be changed will start at the current cursor position on the current screen (not at the top of the data) and work toward the bottom of the data. Figure 18.1 shows a CHANGE command that will change the string PDF into the three words PROGRAM DEVELOPMENT FACILITY. In this instance, the old string can be either uppercase or lowercase characters. The new string will only be uppercase characters. Notice that the new string must be enclosed in quotes because it contains spaces that would otherwise serve to delimit CHANGE command parameters.

If the string is not found, a message will be issued to indicate that. Once a string has been found and changed, however, the cursor is positioned at the end of the character string. The screen contents will be scrolled when necessary to show the context of the string within the data set. Figure 18.2 shows the result of the CHANGE command. The short message indicates that the string has been changed and even represents the string exactly as it was (all capital letters). The numeral following the string has been pushed to the right to make room for the new, larger string.

```
EDIT ---- TSO1234.EXAMPLE.DATA(PDF) - 01.00 ----------------- COLUMNS 001 072
COMMAND ===> c pdf 'PROGRAM DEVELOPMENT FACILITY'            SCROLL ===> CSR
****** ************************* TOP OF DATA ******************************
000001
000002              PDF 1
000003
000004              PDF 2
000005
000006              PDF 3
000007
000008              PDF 4
000009
000010              PDF 5
000011
000012              PDF 6
000013
000014              PDF 7
000015
000016              PDF 8
000017
000018
****** ************************* BOTTOM OF DATA ***************************
```

Figure 18.1 Edit CHANGE command.

```
EDIT ---- TSO1234.EXAMPLE.DATA(PDF) - 01.00 ------------- CHARS 'PDF' CHANGED
COMMAND ===>                                             SCROLL ===> CSR
****** ************************* TOP OF DATA ******************************
000001
000002              PROGRAM DEVELOPMENT FACILITY 1
000003
000004              PDF 2
000005
000006              PDF 3
000007
000008              PDF 4
000009
000010              PDF 5
000011
000012              PDF 6
000013
000014              PDF 7
000015
000016              PDF 8
000017
000018
****** ************************* BOTTOM OF DATA ***************************
```

Figure 18.2 Result of the edit CHANGE command.

The Repeat Change Function

After a change has been made, the same change can be applied to other strings using the RCHANGE command, which will "remember" the old and new strings until they're changed in subsequent command executions. The process can be repeated until the search for the old string reaches the bottom of the data set. When this happens, a message will be issued indicating that the bottom of the data has been reached. If the repeat change function is used after reaching the bottom of the data, the search for the old string will continue from the top of the data.

Implementing the repeat change function is made easier when RCHANGE is assigned to a PF key. That allows the current cursor position to be retained and each subsequent search to be started with a single keystroke. RCHANGE is the default function assigned to PF keys 6 and 18. The search direction and any other parameters specified with the initial change command are retained with the repeat change function, which has been invoked from the screen shown in Figure 18.2. The result of the RCHANGE command is shown in Figure 18.3.

Applying Selective Changes

Changing a string actually involves two functions: finding the string and then making the modification. This allows the terminal operator the opportunity to apply the functions separately. This in turn allows changes to be applied selectively, meaning that the string can be located before deciding whether or not to change it. Selective

```
EDIT ---- TSO1234.EXAMPLE.DATA(PDF) - 01.00 ------------- CHARS 'PDF' CHANGED
COMMAND ===>                                              SCROLL ===> CSR
****** ********************** TOP OF DATA ***************************
000001
000002              PROGRAM DEVELOPMENT FACILITY 1
000003
000004              PROGRAM DEVELOPMENT FACILITY_2
000005
000006              PDF 3
000007
000008              PDF 4
000009
000010              PDF 5
000011
000012              PDF 6
000013
000014              PDF 7
000015
000016              PDF 8
000017
000018
****** ************************ BOTTOM OF DATA ***************************
```

Figure 18.3 Result of the RCHANGE command.

changes are applied by first using the RFIND command (usually by way of a PF key like PF key 5 or 17) to find the string. Once the string has been located, the RCHANGE command can be applied (usually by way of a PF key like PF key 6 or 18) to change the string. Or, the RFIND command could instead be used again to find the next occurrence of the string, leaving the present string unchanged. In Figure 18.3, the RFIND command is invoked using PF5 to start the selective change process.

Figure 18.4 shows that the next occurrence of the old string has been located with the cursor positioned at the first character of the string. Pressing PF6 at this point would cause the string to change as it had with previous strings. In this case, however, PF5 is used again to find the next string occurrence.

Having passed one of the old strings means that it will not be changed in this sequence of commands entered using PF5 (to find) and PF6 (to change). The cursor is now positioned on the fourth instance of the string in Figure 18.5. PF6 is pressed, and, because the command direction is still next, the string at the current cursor position will be changed.

Figure 18.6 shows the changed string as well as the changed message in the short message area. With the two PF keys, each subsequent string can be examined before it's changed. The command combination just demonstrated is much more important when the string to be changed is hard to see or is completely off the page.

CHANGE ALL

All of the occurrences of a string can be changed at once by including the ALL parameter. The ALL parameter (as well as the entire primary command area) is used

```
EDIT ---- TSO1234.EXAMPLE.DATA(PDF) - 01.00 --------------- CHARS 'PDF' FOUND
COMMAND ===>                                            SCROLL ===> CSR
****** *************************** TOP OF DATA ***************************
000001
000002              PROGRAM DEVELOPMENT FACILITY 1
000003
000004              PROGRAM DEVELOPMENT FACILITY 2
000005
000006              PDF 3
000007
000008              PDF 4
000009
000010              PDF 5
000011
000012              PDF 6
000013
000014              PDF 7
000015
000016              PDF 8
000017
000018
****** *************************** BOTTOM OF DATA ***************************
```

Figure 18.4 Result of the RFIND command.

```
EDIT ---- TSO1234.EXAMPLE.DATA(PDF) - 01.00 --------------- CHARS 'PDF' FOUND
COMMAND ===>                                             SCROLL ===> CSR
****** ************************** TOP OF DATA ******************************
000001
000002                 PROGRAM DEVELOPMENT FACILITY 1
000003
000004                 PROGRAM DEVELOPMENT FACILITY 2
000005
000006                 PDF 3
000007
000008                 PDF 4
000009
000010                 PDF 5
000011
000012                 PDF 6
000013
000014                 PDF 7
000015
000016                 PDF 8
000017
000018
****** ************************** BOTTOM OF DATA ****************************
```

Figure 18.5 Using RFIND again to skip a change.

```
EDIT ---- TSO1234.EXAMPLE.DATA(PDF) - 01.00 ------------- CHARS 'PDF' CHANGED
COMMAND ===>                                             SCROLL ===> CSR
****** ************************** TOP OF DATA ******************************
000001
000002                 PROGRAM DEVELOPMENT FACILITY 1
000003
000004                 PROGRAM DEVELOPMENT FACILITY 2
000005
000006                 PDF 3
000007
000008                 PROGRAM DEVELOPMENT FACILITY_4
000009
000010                 PDF 5
000011
000012                 PDF 6
000013
000014                 PDF 7
000015
000016                 PDF 8
000017
000018
****** ************************** BOTTOM OF DATA ****************************
```

Figure 18.6 Second repeat change.

for the CHANGE command in Figure 18.7. In this case, the command line doesn't provide sufficient space to enter the complete new string. This problem will be addressed shortly.

Change flags have been written in the line command area for every line where a change was made (Figure 18.8). This is a unique feature when the ALL parameter is used. The change flags are used because the cursor can only be used to identify changes made one at a time. The change flags are particularly important because many of the changes might take place off the visible screen.

Because the new string in the last CHANGE command is longer than the old string, it was necessary to push existing text on line six farther to the right. This was not necessary on line nine, where there was ample space before the next significant text. Notice too that there was not enough space on line four to make the change at all. That line was left in its original state, and an error flag was placed in the line command area. In addition, the short message area contains text regarding the error.

When the new string is shorter than the old string, making a change might cause the subsequent portion of the line to shift to the left. Whether or not the remainder of the line is shifted to the left (when the new string is shorter) is determined by the number of spaces following the old string. A single space following the string represents a normal text situation. Under that circumstance, the remainder of the line will be shifted, if necessary, to preserve the text characteristic. When more than a single space follows the string, it takes on the characteristic of column data, which the editor will try to preserve.

The CHANGE command also tries to maintain the spacing of column data when the new string is longer than the old string. The command will, however, displace

```
EDIT ---- TSO1234.EXAMPLE.DATA(CHANGE) - 01.01 -------------- COLUMNS 001 072
COMMAND ===> c all ispf 'Interactive System Productivity Fac'_SCROLL ===> CSR
****** ************************** TOP OF DATA **************************
000001
000002                 ISPF
000003
000004                                                         ISPF
000005
000006 The product is called ISPF and it runs under TSO
000007
000008
000009  ISPF                                       TSO
000010
000011
****** ************************** BOTTOM OF DATA **************************
```

Figure 18.7 CHANGE ALL command.

```
EDIT ---- TSO1234.EXAMPLE.DATA(CHANGE) - 01.01 --------- ERROR - CHARS 'ISPF'
COMMAND ===>                                              SCROLL ===> CSR
****** *************************** TOP OF DATA ****************************
000001
==CHG>                    Interactive System Productivity Fac_
000003
==ERR>                                                   ISPF
000005
==CHG> The product is called Interactive System Productivity Fac and it runs
000007
000008
==CHG>    Interactive System Productivity Fac          TSO
000010
000011
****** *************************** BOTTOM OF DATA ************************
```

Figure 18.8 Result of CHANGE ALL command.

column data ahead of the string if that's absolutely necessary to make the change. The only reason for not making a particular change is when there's insufficient room on the subsequent portion of the line for the added characters. The room available to add characters is affected by the bounds settings, since the change must be made within the bounds.

When there's insufficient room to make a change within text data, it's advisable to use the TF (text flow) line command to increase the size of the right margin. The TF line command can make more space available at the end of each line. After CHANGE command modifications are made, the TF command can be used to re-establish appropriate margins.

Representing a Previous String Value

An asterisk can be used to represent the previous string value for the old and/or new string. This fact can save typing string values in subsequent CHANGE commands, or it can be used to save space in the command area, as in the next example. In Figure 18.9, the special character % is used as the old string value. That character was chosen because it's not already in the data set and it leaves the maximum amount of space for the new string to be entered. The command was entered in this way to establish the proper string for the new string value without making an actual change. This is one of several techniques that can be used when the command area is not large enough to accept all of the necessary command parameters.

```
EDIT ---- TSO1234.EXAMPLE.DATA(CHANGE) - 01.01 -------------- COLUMNS 001 072
COMMAND ===> c % 'Interactive System Productivity Facility'_ SCROLL ===> CSR
****** *************************** TOP OF DATA ***************************
000001
000002                ISPF
000003
000004                                                        ISPF
000005
000006 The product is called ISPF and it runs under TSO
000007
000008
000009  ISPF                                     TSO
000010
000011
****** *************************** BOTTOM OF DATA ***************************
```

Figure 18.9 Change technique to accommodate large values.

Pressing the ENTER key fails to make any changes because the special character % could not be found in the data set (Figure 18.10). Using the PF5 key would also be ideal here since it would only attempt to find a string and not change it. Since the new string has just been used in a CHANGE command, it can be represented in the next one using an asterisk. The string ISPF is specified before the asterisk to represent the old string. At the same time, the ALL parameter has been added to change all string occurrences in the data set.

The result of the change command is shown in Figure 18.11. Two lines (line four and line six) contain strings that could not be changed because there was not enough room left on the line. Both lines are marked with error flags.

When it's necessary to include an asterisk as one of the strings rather than use it to designate the previous string, the asterisk should be enclosed in single or double quotes. This is not necessary when the asterisk is enclosed in or otherwise part of a larger string.

Case Sensitive Search

Searching for the existing string is done in text mode, which is not case sensitive. Text mode can only be used with the old string. It's specified by enclosing the old string in quotes and preceding it with the letter T. The text string is seldom specified, however, since it's the default. The command will find a string in uppercase or lowercase, as demonstrated in Figure 18.12, where the existing string is entered in lowercase letters.

```
EDIT ---- TSO1234.EXAMPLE.DATA(CHANGE) - 01.01 ----------- NO CHARS '%' FOUND
COMMAND ===> c ISPF * all_                                  SCROLL ===> CSR
****** *************************** TOP OF DATA ****************************
000001
000002                    ISPF
000003
000004                                                       ISPF
000005
000006 The product is called ISPF and it runs under TSO
000007
000008
000009  ISPF                                       TSO
000010
000011
****** *************************** BOTTOM OF DATA ****************************
```

Figure 18.10 Change using previous value.

```
EDIT ---- TSO1234.EXAMPLE.DATA(CHANGE) - 01.01 --------- ERROR - CHARS 'ISPF'
COMMAND ===>                                                SCROLL ===> CSR
****** *************************** TOP OF DATA ****************************
000001
==CHG>                    Interactive System Productivity Facility_
000003
==ERR>                                                      ISPF
000005
==ERR> The product is called ISPF and it runs under TSO
000007
000008
==CHG>   Interactive System Productivity Facility           TSO
000010
000011
****** *************************** BOTTOM OF DATA ****************************
```

Figure 18.11 Result of change using previous values.

```
EDIT ---- TSO1234.EXAMPLE.DATA(CHANGE) - 01.00 -------------- COLUMNS 001 072
COMMAND ===> c lowercase UPPERCASE all_                    SCROLL ===> CSR
****** *************************** TOP OF DATA ****************************
000001
000002  lowercase
000003  LOWERCASE
000004  lowercase
000005  LOWERCASE
000006  lowercase
000007  LOWERCASE
000008
000009
000010
****** *************************** BOTTOM OF DATA **************************
```

Figure 18.12   CHANGE ALL for uppercase and lowercase strings.

The result of the CHANGE command is shown in Figure 18.13. It shows that all instances of the old string were changed, even though every other instance was initially in uppercase letters. Notice that the result of the change in each case is uppercase letters. The new string doesn't have the same latitude that the old string does and is literally taken from the new string parameter.

When it's necessary to obtain an exact match on uppercase and lowercase characters for a particular string, the character string feature can be specified. This merely requires the letter C in front of the string itself. The string is enclosed in quotes to separate it from the parameter, as shown in Figure 18.14.

In this case, only the three strings that contained lowercase letters were actually matched and therefore changed to the new string (Figure 18.15). Character string mode can be specified for the new string but is not required since the case of the new string is taken literally.

Changing Hexadecimal Strings

The CHANGE command supports changing data by its hexadecimal representation. The data can still be referenced in a CHANGE command using its hexadecimal representation. The letter X immediately preceding or following the character string identifies it as a hexadecimal value. The string value must be specified with quotes to separate it from the hex parameter. Hex string values must also be specified in pairs since two base 16 values represent one byte of data. To specify an odd number

```
EDIT ---- TSO1234.EXAMPLE.DATA(CHANGE) - 01.01 ----- CHARS 'LOWERCASE' CHANGE
COMMAND ===>                                           SCROLL ===> CSR
****** ************************** TOP OF DATA **************************
000001
==CHG>    UPPERCASE_
==CHG>    UPPERCASE
==CHG>    UPPERCASE
==CHG>    UPPERCASE
==CHG>    UPPERCASE
==CHG>    UPPERCASE
000008
000009
000010
****** ************************** BOTTOM OF DATA ************************^**
```

Figure 18.13 Result of CHANGE ALL for uppercase and lowercase strings.

```
EDIT ---- TSO1234.EXAMPLE.DATA(CHANGE) - 01.00 -------------- COLUMNS 001 072
COMMAND ===> c c'lowercase' UPPERCASE all_              SCROLL ===> CSR
****** ***********^***************** TOP OF DATA **************************
000001
000002    lowercase
000003    LOWERCASE
000004    lowercase
000005    LOWERCASE
000006    lowercase
000007    LOWERCASE
000008
000009
000010
****** ************************** BOTTOM OF DATA ************************
```

Figure 18.14 CHANGE ALL for only lowercase strings.

```
EDIT ---- TSO1234.EXAMPLE.DATA(CHANGE) - 01.01 ----- CHARS 'lowercase' CHANGE
COMMAND ===>                                          SCROLL ===> CSR
****** ************************** TOP OF DATA ***************************
000001
==CHG>    UPPERCASE_
000003    LOWERCASE
==CHG>    UPPERCASE
000005    LOWERCASE
==CHG>    UPPERCASE
000007    LOWERCASE
000008
000009
000010
****** ************************** BOTTOM OF DATA ************************
```

Figure 18.15   Result of CHANGE ALL for only lowercase strings.

of values or values other than 0 through 9 and A through F would constitute an error. The following CHANGE command is used to change hex zeros (known as low values) into spaces:

```
CHANGE ALL X'00' X'40'
```

While low values would have to be specified this way, the new string would not since it could easily be represented as ' ' or " ".

CHANGE Using Picture Strings

A picture string is a special designation just like a hex or character string. The picture string supports a number of special characters that are used to represent a class of characters rather than a specific character itself. This allows a search to be conducted for that particular class. For example, a period is used in a picture string (Figure 18.16) to represent any non-display character (those mentioned in the message at the top of the data set).

The CHANGE command would change all non-display characters to spaces. In Figure 18.17, the effect of the command is not apparent since the non-display characters were never visible. The only indications that a change has been made are the change flags and the short message. The message at the top of the data portion will not appear the next time edit is invoked for this data set.

```
EDIT ---- TSO1234.EXAMPLE.DATA(COLUMNS) - 01.01 ------------- COLUMNS 001 072
COMMAND ===> c   p'.'   ' '   all_                           SCROLL ===> CSR
****** ************************** TOP OF DATA *******************************
==MSG> -CAUTION- DATA CONTAINS INVALID (NON-DISPLAY) CHARACTERS.  USE COMMAND
==MSG>        ===> FIND P'.'       TO POSITION CURSOR TO THESE CHARACTERS.
000001
000002
000003            000123.57
000004            000435.98
000005            000555.12
000006            000473.53
000007            000258.09
000008            000407.50
000009            000617.00
000010            000238.40
000011            000527.27
000012            000357.22
000013            000117.67
000014            000310.33
000015            000272.00
000016
000017
****** ************************** BOTTOM OF DATA ****************************
```

Figure 18.16 Command to change non-display characters to blanks.

```
EDIT ---- TSO1234.EXAMPLE.DATA(COLUMNS) - 01.01 ----------- CHARS '.' CHANGED
COMMAND ===> _                                              SCROLL ===> CSR
****** ************************** TOP OF DATA *******************************
==MSG> -CAUTION- DATA CONTAINS INVALID (NON-DISPLAY) CHARACTERS.  USE COMMAND
==MSG>        ===> FIND P'.'       TO POSITION CURSOR TO THESE CHARACTERS.
==CHG>
==CHG>
000003            000123.57
000004            000435.98
000005            000555.12
000006            000473.53
000007            000258.09
000008            000407.50
000009            000617.00
000010            000238.40
000011            000527.27
000012            000357.22
000013            000117.67
000014            000310.33
000015            000272.00
==CHG>
==CHG>
****** ************************** BOTTOM OF DATA ****************************
```

Figure 18.17 Result of changing non-display characters to blanks.

The special characters =, <, > can be used in the new string as well as the old. This allows the CHANGE command in Figure 18.18 to be used to change lowercase characters (designated P'<') into uppercase characters (designated P'>'). Figure 18.19 shows the result of the command to change all lowercase letters to uppercase. In the figure, only the changed characters are highlighted.

The special characters that are used in a picture string to represent a type of character can also be used with literal data. The length of the new string should be the same as the old string. Table 18.1 shows the use of special characters within the picture string context.

TABLE 18.1 Picture String Symbols

String symbol	Use within a picture string
=	Any character
T	Any non-blank character
#	Any numeric character
-	Any non-numeric character
@	Any alphabetic character
$	Any special character
>	Any uppercase alphabetic character
<	Any lowercase alphabetic character
•	Any non-display character

```
EDIT ---- TSO1234.EXAMPLE.DATA(CLIST) - 01.01 --------------- COLUMNS 001 072
COMMAND ===> c   p'<'   p'>'   all_                           SCROLL ===> CSR
****** *************************** TOP OF DATA ***************************
000001
000002                        CLIST Execution
000003
000004
000005                    Modes Of CLIST Execution
000006
000007 There are four modes of CLIST execution, explicit, modified explicit,
000008 implicit, and modified implicit. CLIST execution is made possible by
000009 the TSO command, EXEC. That command can also be abbreviated as EX.
000010 Because the command is explicitly stated in the first two modes, they
000011 are known as explicit modes. The implicit modes do not contain EX or
000012 EXEC as part of the command syntax. They also differ in their reliance
000013 upon a special file to identify which CLIST code to execute.
000014
000015 CLISTS are invoked at the TSO prompter or an interface to it. For
000016 those who have ISPF installed, this could also be OPTION 6 as well as
000017 most Productivity Development Facility (PDF) panels that have a
000018 command line. When a CLIST (or TSO command for that matter) is entered
000019 from a PDF panel it should be preceded by the word TSO. This is not
000020 required from PDF Option 6 because it was designed to accept TSO
000021 commands and CLISTS.
```

Figure 18.18 Command to change lowercase to uppercase.

```
EDIT ---- TSO1234.EXAMPLE.DATA(CLIST) - 01.02 ------------ CHARS '<' CHANGED
COMMAND ===>                                              SCROLL ===> CSR
****** *************************** TOP OF DATA ***************************
000001
==CHG>                          CLIST EXECUTION
000003
000004
==CHG>                       MODES OF CLIST EXECUTION
000006
==CHG> THERE ARE FOUR MODES OF CLIST EXECUTION, EXPLICIT, MODIFIED EXPLICIT,
==CHG> IMPLICIT, AND MODIFIED IMPLICIT. CLIST EXECUTION IS MADE POSSIBLE BY
==CHG> THE TSO COMMAND, EXEC. THAT COMMAND CAN ALSO BE ABBREVIATED AS EX.
==CHG> BECAUSE THE COMMAND IS EXPLICITLY STATED IN THE FIRST TWO MODES, THEY
==CHG> ARE KNOWN AS EXPLICIT MODES. THE IMPLICIT MODES DO NOT CONTAIN EX OR
==CHG> EXEC AS PART OF THE COMMAND SYNTAX. THEY ALSO DIFFER IN THEIR RELIANCE
==CHG> UPON A SPECIAL FILE TO IDENTIFY WHICH CLIST CODE TO EXECUTE.
000014
==CHG> CLISTS ARE INVOKED AT THE TSO PROMPTER OR AN INTERFACE TO IT. FOR
==CHG> THOSE WHO HAVE ISPF INSTALLED, THIS COULD ALSO BE OPTION 6 AS WELL AS
==CHG> MOST PRODUCTIVITY DEVELOPMENT FACILITY (PDF) PANELS THAT HAVE A
==CHG> COMMAND LINE. WHEN A CLIST (OR TSO COMMAND FOR THAT MATTER) IS ENTERED
==CHG> FROM A PDF PANEL IT SHOULD BE PRECEDED BY THE WORD TSO. THIS IS NOT
==CHG> REQUIRED FROM PDF OPTION 6 BECAUSE IT WAS DESIGNED TO ACCEPT TSO
==CHG> COMMANDS AND CLISTS.
```

Figure 18.19 Result of command to change lowercase to uppercase.

19

CHANGE Command Parameters

CHANGE command parameters are generally used to limit the scope of the command. Parameters are used to define the context and direction of the string search and limit the lines and columns that the command operates within. When they're specified, optional parameters can be listed in any order and are separated by blanks or commas.

Specifying the Change Direction

The default is to change the next occurrence of a string. Since NEXT is the default direction for the CHANGE command, NEXT is never required as a parameter. To reverse the normal command direction, PREV can be specified. The current cursor position on the current screen is still used as the starting position, but the search for the old string is conducted up toward the top of the data. If the top of the data set is reached before a string (to be changed) is found, the editor will issue a message stating so. If the repeat change function is used after reaching the top of the data, the search will restart at the bottom of the data.

Two parameters, FIRST and LAST, can be used instead of NEXT and PREV to determine the direction in which the command will operate. FIRST, for example, will start at the top of the data and search down into the data set for a string to change. This is true no matter what the current position is in the data. Using the parameter FIRST, it's not necessary to first scroll to the top of the data. The implied direction for the repeat find function is NEXT or down. Conversely, LAST will start at the bottom of the data to search up into the data set for a string to change. The first string it changes is then the last such string in the data set. With LAST, the implied direction for the repeat change function is PREV or up.

Specifying the Change Context

Additional CHANGE command parameters can be used to specify the string context. They help to limit changes to strings used as a word prefix (PREFIX or PRE), a word suffix (SUFFIX or SUF), or the entire word (WORD). The default CHARS will find the string no matter what the context is. CHARS includes all three parameters, as well as strings that are embedded within a word. Word in this context merely means characters grouped together with spaces on both sides. Most special characters (except @, #, and $) have the same effect as spaces in this context. No check is made to ensure that a particular group of characters is part of the English language. The group could in fact contain numbers or special characters and still qualify as a word. Table 19.1 illustrates the effect of the context parameters.

TABLE 19.1 Effect of Context Parameters on CHANGE Command

C ant ANT PRE (PREFIX)	C ant ANT SUF (SUFFIX)	C ant ANT WORD (WORD)	C ant ANT (CHARS)
ANTerior	anterior	anterior	**ANT**erior
significant	signific**ANT**	significant	signific**ANT**
ant	ant	**ANT**	**ANT**
planted	planted	planted	pl**ANT**ed

Limiting Columns Searched

Limiting the columns searched for a particular string can make processing more efficient. It can also help to differentiate or isolate one use of a particular string from another when their use differs by column position (as in some programming languages). Both a starting column number and an ending column number can be specified. When only one column value is specified, it's interpreted as the start column. In this case, the string will only be changed if it starts in that particular column. When two columns are specified, the second column number represents the end column. The entire string must then fall within the column range created by the two values before it will be changed.

In Figure 19.1, a CHANGE command is issued to change all zeros to spaces. The command includes a single column number that will limit the scope of the command. Since only one column number was entered, it serves as the starting column number. The effect will be to limit changes to zeros in column 11.

Figure 19.2 shows the result of the CHANGE command. Only the zeros in column 11 were changed. Also in Figure 19.2, the command is entered again with two column values that form a range (albeit a short one).

When the CHANGE command is executed, zeros from both columns in the range are changed to spaces. The short message, as usual, indicates that changes have been made. The HELP command is issued in Figure 19.3 to cause the corresponding long message to display.

```
EDIT ---- TSO1234.EXAMPLE.DATA(COLUMNS) - 01.01 ------------- COLUMNS 001 072
COMMAND ===> c  '0'  ' '  11  all_                           SCROLL ===> CSR
****** ************************** TOP OF DATA ****************************
000001
=COLS> ----+----1----+----2----+----3----+----4----+----5----+----6----+----7
000002
000003            000123.57
000004            000435.98
000005            000555.12
000006            000473.53
000007            000258.09
000008            000407.50
000009            000617.00
000010            000238.40
000011            000527.27
000012            000357.22
000013            000117.67
000014            000310.33
000015            000272.00
000016
000017
****** ************************** BOTTOM OF DATA ****************************
```

Figure 19.1 CHANGE command with start column specified.

```
EDIT ---- TSO1234.EXAMPLE.DATA(COLUMNS) - 01.02 ----------- CHARS '0' CHANGED
COMMAND ===> c  '0'  ' '  12  13  all_                      SCROLL ===> CSR
****** ************************** TOP OF DATA ****************************
000001
=COLS> ----+----1----+----2-- -+----3----+----4----+----5----+----6----+----7
000002
==CHG>            00123.57
==CHG>            00435.98
==CHG>            00555.12
==CHG>            00473.53
==CHG>            00258.09
==CHG>            00407.50
==CHG>            00617.00
==CHG>            00238.40
==CHG>            00527.27
==CHG>            00357.22
==CHG>            00117.67
==CHG>            00310.33
==CHG>            00272.00
000016
000017
****** ************************** BOTTOM OF DATA ****************************
```

Figure 19.2 CHANGE command with column range specified.

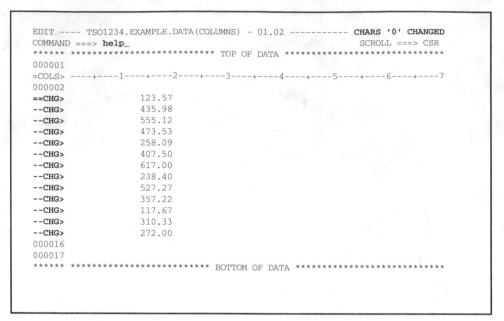

```
EDIT ---- TSO1234.EXAMPLE.DATA(COLUMNS) - 01.02 ----------- CHARS '0' CHANGED
COMMAND ===> help_                                          SCROLL ===> CSR
****** ************************** TOP OF DATA ******************************
000001
=COLS> ----+----1----+----2----+----3----+----4----+----5----+----6----+----7
000002
==CHG>             123.57
--CHG>             435.98
--CHG>             555.12
--CHG>             473.53
--CHG>             258.09
--CHG>             407.50
--CHG>             617.00
--CHG>             238.40
--CHG>             527.27
--CHG>             357.22
--CHG>             117.67
--CHG>             310.33
--CHG>             272.00
000016
000017
****** ************************** BOTTOM OF DATA ***************************
```

Figure 19.3 Result of CHANGE command with column range specified.

The long message display (Figure 19.4) indicates that 26 zeros were changed on 13 data lines. This information can be useful after a CHANGE ALL command is issued because many times changes are made off the visible screen and the magnitude of a change might not be readily apparent.

CHANGE within Bounds

The current bounds act to restrict the scope of a CHANGE command in the same fashion as if a column range had been specified. To see the effect that bounds have on the command, restrictive bounds have been set in Figure 19.5. A CHANGE command is then issued to change each blank to a dollar sign. Figure 19.6 shows the result of the CHANGE command. Only the blanks within the bounds have been changed.

CHANGE X/NX

As previously demonstrated, the CHANGE command can be limited to particular columns by specifying those columns or by operating within the current bounds. The scope of the CHANGE command can also be limited to particular lines. This is done in two ways. The first method is to exclude lines within the data set and change only the excluded (or only the non-excluded) lines. The lines can be excluded either because they represent a range of lines that the CHANGE command should operate within or because they have some characteristic that makes them unique.

```
EDIT ---- TSO1234.EXAMPLE.DATA(COLUMNS) - 01.02 ----------- CHARS '0' CHANGED
COMMAND ===> _                                             SCROLL ===> CSR
CHARS '0' - CHANGED TO ' ' 26 TIMES ON 13 LINE(S).
000001
=COLS> ----+----1----+----2----+----3----+----4----+----5----+----6----+----7
000002
--CHG>          123.57
==CHG>          435.98
==CHG>          555.12
==CHG>          473.53
==CHG>          258.09
==CHG>          407.50
==CHG>          617.00
==CHG>          238.40
==CHG>          527.27
==CHG>          357.22
==CHG>          117.67
==CHG>          310.33
==CHG>          272.00
000016
000017
****** ************************* BOTTOM OF DATA ***************************
```

Figure 19.4 Long message regarding CHANGE command.

```
EDIT ---- TSO1234.EXAMPLE.DATA(BLANK) - 01.00 -------------- COLUMNS 001 072
COMMAND ===> c ' ' $ all                                    SCROLL ===> CSR
****** ************************* TOP OF DATA ***************************
=BNDS>               <                             >
000001
000002
000003
000004
000005
000006
000007
000008
000009
000010
000011
000012
000013
000014
000015
000016
000017
000018
****** ************************* BOTTOM OF DATA ***************************
```

Figure 19.5 CHANGE ALL command within restrictive bounds.

```
EDIT ---- TSO1234.EXAMPLE.DATA(BLANK) - 01.00 ------------- CHARS ' ' CHANGED
COMMAND ===>                                                SCROLL ===> CSR
****** ************************** TOP OF DATA **************************
=BNDS>               <                                      >
==CHG>               $$$$$$$$$$$$$$$$$$$$$$$$$$$$$$$$$$$$$$$
==CHG>               $$$$$$$$$$$$$$$$$$$$$$$$$$$$$$$$$$$$$$$
==CHG>               $$$$$$$$$$$$$$$$$$$$$$$$$$$$$$$$$$$$$$$
==CHG>               $$$$$$$$$$$$$$$$$$$$$$$$$$$$$$$$$$$$$$$
==CHG>               $$$$$$$$$$$$$$$$$$$$$$$$$$$$$$$$$$$$$$$
==CHG>               $$$$$$$$$$$$$$$$$$$$$$$$$$$$$$$$$$$$$$$
==CHG>               $$$$$$$$$$$$$$$$$$$$$$$$$$$$$$$$$$$$$$$
==CHG>               $$$$$$$$$$$$$$$$$$$$$$$$$$$$$$$$$$$$$$$
==CHG>               $$$$$$$$$$$$$$$$$$$$$$$$$$$$$$$$$$$$$$$
==CHG>               $$$$$$$$$$$$$$$$$$$$$$$$$$$$$$$$$$$$$$$
==CHG>               $$$$$$$$$$$$$$$$$$$$$$$$$$$$$$$$$$$$$$$
==CHG>               $$$$$$$$$$$$$$$$$$$$$$$$$$$$$$$$$$$$$$$
==CHG>               $$$$$$$$$$$$$$$$$$$$$$$$$$$$$$$$$$$$$$$
==CHG>               $$$$$$$$$$$$$$$$$$$$$$$$$$$$$$$$$$$$$$$
==CHG>               $$$$$$$$$$$$$$$$$$$$$$$$$$$$$$$$$$$$$$$
==CHG>               $$$$$$$$$$$$$$$$$$$$$$$$$$$$$$$$$$$$$$$
****** ************************** BOTTOM OF DATA **************************
```

Figure 19.6 Result of CHANGE ALL command within restrictive bounds.

In Figure 19.7, the exclude line command is used to exclude all of the lines from line eight to the end of the data set. A CHANGE command can now operate on these excluded lines using the parameter X. Conversely, the non-excluded lines can be affected using the parameter NX.

Figure 19.8 shows a CHANGE command with the parameter X. With this parameter included, the command can only affect the 11 lines in the excluded block. Notice too that the optional parameters ALL and X have been placed on both sides of the change strings and will still be properly interpreted. After the change is made (Figure 19.9), the changed lines are redisplayed. Only the strings in the excluded group were affected.

CHANGE within Label Limits

The second way to limit the lines that are affected by the CHANGE command is to use labels. The labels must be specified in pairs. In Figure 19.10, the command is issued again to change each space to a dollar sign. This time, however, a label range has been specified using the labels .FIRST and .LAST.

Figure 19.11 shows that the CHANGE command has only been applied to the nine lines that fall within the label range. Figure 19.11 also shows the RESET command used to reset only the change flags. With the change flags reset (Figure 19.12), the labels .FIRST and .LAST are again visible. Table 19.2 shows the CHANGE command syntax for edit. Brackets indicate optional parameters. Underscored parameters are defaults and need not be specified.

```
EDIT ---- TSO1234.EXAMPLE.DATA(PDF) - 01.01 ---------------- COLUMNS 001 072
COMMAND ===>                                          SCROLL ===> CSR
****** ************************** TOP OF DATA ******************************
000001
000002              PDF 1
000003
000004              PDF 2
000005
000006              PDF 3
000007
x99_                PDF 4
000009
000010              PDF 5
000011
000012              PDF 6
000013
000014              PDF 7
000015
000016              PDF 8
000017
000018
****** ************************* BOTTOM OF DATA ****************************
```

Figure 19.7 Line command to exclude a group of lines.

```
EDIT ---- TSO1234.EXAMPLE.DATA(PDF) - 01.01 ---------------- COLUMNS 001 072
COMMAND ===> c all pdf 'PROGRAM DEVELOPMENT FACILITY' x  _   SCROLL ===> CSR
****** ************************** TOP OF DATA ******************************
000001
000002              PDF 1
000003
000004              PDF 2
000005
000006              PDF 3
000007
- - - - - - - - - - - - - - - - - - - - - 11 LINE(S) NOT DISPLAYED
****** ************************* BOTTOM OF DATA ****************************
```

Figure 19.8 Command to change excluded lines.

```
EDIT ---- TSO1234.EXAMPLE.DATA(PDF) - 01.01 ------------- CHARS 'PDF' CHANGED
COMMAND ===> _                                        SCROLL ===> CSR
****** ************************** TOP OF DATA ******************************
000001
000002              PDF 1
000003
000004              PDF 2
000005
000006              PDF 3
000007
==CHG>              PROGRAM DEVELOPMENT FACILITY 4
- - - - - - - - - - - - - - - - - - - - - - 1 LINE(S) NOT DISPLAYED
==CHG>              PROGRAM DEVELOPMENT FACILITY 5
- - - - - - - - - - - - - - - - - - - - - - 1 LINE(S) NOT DISPLAYED
==CHG>              PROGRAM DEVELOPMENT FACILITY 6
- - - - - - - - - - - - - - - - - - - - - - 1 LINE(S) NOT DISPLAYED
==CHG>              PROGRAM DEVELOPMENT FACILITY 7
- - - - - - - - - - - - - - - - - - - - - - 1 LINE(S) NOT DISPLAYED
==CHG>              PROGRAM DEVELOPMENT FACILITY 8
- - - - - - - - - - - - - - - - - - - - - - 2 LINE(S) NOT DISPLAYED
****** ************************** BOTTOM OF DATA ***************************
```

Figure 19.9 Result of command to change excluded lines.

```
EDIT ---- TSO1234.EXAMPLE.DATA(BLANK) - 01.00 --------------- COLUMNS 001 072
COMMAND ===> c ' ' $ all .first .last  _             SCROLL ===> CSR
****** ************************** TOP OF DATA ******************************
000001
000002
000003
.FIRST
000005
000006
000007
U00008
000009
000010
000011
.LAST
000013
000014
000015
000016
000017
000018
****** ************************** BOTTOM OF DATA ***************************
```

Figure 19.10 CHANGE ALL within label range.

```
EDIT ---- TSO1234.EXAMPLE.DATA(BLANK) - 01.00 ------------ CHARS ' ' CHANGED
COMMAND ===> res chg __                                    SCROLL ===> CSR
****** ************************* TOP OF DATA ****************************
000001
000002
000003
==CHG> $$$$$$$$$$$$$$$$$$$$$$$$$$$$$$$$$$$$$$$$$$$$$$$$$$$$$$$$$$$$$$$$$$$$
==CHG> $$$$$$$$$$$$$$$$$$$$$$$$$$$$$$$$$$$$$$$$$$$$$$$$$$$$$$$$$$$$$$$$$$$$
==CHG> $$$$$$$$$$$$$$$$$$$$$$$$$$$$$$$$$$$$$$$$$$$$$$$$$$$$$$$$$$$$$$$$$$$$
==CHG> $$$$$$$$$$$$$$$$$$$$$$$$$$$$$$$$$$$$$$$$$$$$$$$$$$$$$$$$$$$$$$$$$$$$
==CHG> $$$$$$$$$$$$$$$$$$$$$$$$$$$$$$$$$$$$$$$$$$$$$$$$$$$$$$$$$$$$$$$$$$$$
==CHG> $$$$$$$$$$$$$$$$$$$$$$$$$$$$$$$$$$$$$$$$$$$$$$$$$$$$$$$$$$$$$$$$$$$$
==CHG> $$$$$$$$$$$$$$$$$$$$$$$$$$$$$$$$$$$$$$$$$$$$$$$$$$$$$$$$$$$$$$$$$$$$
==CHG> $$$$$$$$$$$$$$$$$$$$$$$$$$$$$$$$$$$$$$$$$$$$$$$$$$$$$$$$$$$$$$$$$$$$
==CHG> $$$$$$$$$$$$$$$$$$$$$$$$$$$$$$$$$$$$$$$$$$$$$$$$$$$$$$$$$$$$$$$$$$$$
000013
000014
000015
000016
000017
000018
****** ************************* BOTTOM OF DATA *************************
```

Figure 19.11 Result of CHANGE ALL within label range.

```
EDIT ---- TSO1234.EXAMPLE.DATA(BLANK) - 01.00 --------------- COLUMNS 001 072
COMMAND ===> __                                            SCROLL ===> CSR
****** ************************* TOP OF DATA ****************************
000001
000002
000003
.FIRST $$$$$$$$$$$$$$$$$$$$$$$$$$$$$$$$$$$$$$$$$$$$$$$$$$$$$$$$$$$$$$$$$$$$
000005 $$$$$$$$$$$$$$$$$$$$$$$$$$$$$$$$$$$$$$$$$$$$$$$$$$$$$$$$$$$$$$$$$$$$
000006 $$$$$$$$$$$$$$$$$$$$$$$$$$$$$$$$$$$$$$$$$$$$$$$$$$$$$$$$$$$$$$$$$$$$
000007 $$$$$$$$$$$$$$$$$$$$$$$$$$$$$$$$$$$$$$$$$$$$$$$$$$$$$$$$$$$$$$$$$$$$
000008 $$$$$$$$$$$$$$$$$$$$$$$$$$$$$$$$$$$$$$$$$$$$$$$$$$$$$$$$$$$$$$$$$$$$
000009 $$$$$$$$$$$$$$$$$$$$$$$$$$$$$$$$$$$$$$$$$$$$$$$$$$$$$$$$$$$$$$$$$$$$
000010 $$$$$$$$$$$$$$$$$$$$$$$$$$$$$$$$$$$$$$$$$$$$$$$$$$$$$$$$$$$$$$$$$$$$
000011 $$$$$$$$$$$$$$$$$$$$$$$$$$$$$$$$$$$$$$$$$$$$$$$$$$$$$$$$$$$$$$$$$$$$
.LAST  $$$$$$$$$$$$$$$$$$$$$$$$$$$$$$$$$$$$$$$$$$$$$$$$$$$$$$$$$$$$$$$$$$$$
000013
000014
000015
000016
000017
000018
****** ************************* BOTTOM OF DATA *************************
```

Figure 19.12 Edit session with RESET change flags.

TABLE 19.2 CHANGE Command Syntax Summary

CHANGE	old	new	NEXT	CHARS	[start-col]	[end-col]	X
CHG	string	string	PREV	PREFIX			NX
C			FIRST	SUFFIX			
	*	*	LAST	WORD			
			ALL		[label1 label2]		

Changes Involving Quotes

There are times when it's necessary to change from one type of quotation mark to the other in the edit data. Figure 19.13 shows what might logically be done to change a single quote to a double quote. The command as entered could not be executed (Figure 19.14). The short message indicates that the string is incomplete, and so information must be added that will assist in the interpretation of the command.

The command has been amended in Figure 19.15 to include quotes around the quotes that form the old and new strings. The opposite type of quote has been used to avoid confusion and to make the command easier to read. Each outer quote pair uses the same type of quote. The ALL parameter has also been added to allow the command to affect all three single quotes in the data. Figure 19.16 shows the result of the CHANGE ALL command. The single quote has been changed three times on two lines of data.

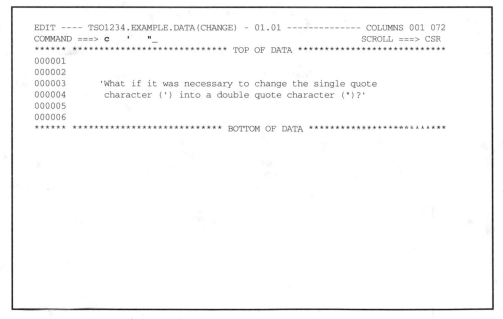

Figure 19.13 Attempt to change single quotes.

```
EDIT ---- TSO1234.EXAMPLE.DATA(CHANGE) - 01.01 ------------ INCOMPLETE STRING
COMMAND ===> c    '_    "                                    SCROLL ===> CSR
****** **************************** TOP OF DATA ****************************
000001
000002
000003      'What if it was necessary to change the single quote
000004       character (') into a double quote character (")?'
000005
000006
****** **************************** BOTTOM OF DATA ************************
```

Figure 19.14 Result of attempt to change single quotes.

```
EDIT ---- TSO1234.EXAMPLE.DATA(CHANGE) - 01.01 ------------ INCOMPLETE STRING
COMMAND ===> c      "'"    '"' all_                          SCROLL ===> CSR
****** **************************** TOP OF DATA ****************************
000001
000002
000003      'What if it was necessary to change the single quote
000004       character (') into a double quote character (")?'
000005
000006
****** **************************** BOTTOM OF DATA ************************
```

Figure 19.15 Revised command to change single quotes.

```
EDIT ---- TSO1234.EXAMPLE.DATA(CHANGE) - 01.01 -------------- CHARS ' CHANGED
COMMAND ===>                                              SCROLL ===> CSR
****** *************************** TOP OF DATA ***************************
000001
000002
==CHG>      "What if it was necessary to change the single quote
==CHG>      character (") into a double quote character (")?"
000005
000006
****** *************************** BOTTOM OF DATA ***************************
```

Figure 19.16 Result of revised command to change single quotes.

```
EDIT ---- TSO1234.EXAMPLE.DATA(BLKSIZE) - 01.04 ------------- COLUMNS 001 072
COMMAND ===> c   p'=' ' ' ' '   13   18   all   nx_        SCROLL ===> CSR
****** *************************** TOP OF DATA ***************************
- - - - - - - - - - - - - - - - - - - - 7 LINE(S) NOT DISPLAYED
=COLS> ----+----1----+----2----+----3----+----4----+----5----+----6----+----7
- - - - - - - - - - - - - - - - - - - - 1 LINE(S) NOT DISPLAYED
000009 | 23477 | 47476 |            1 |       | 27999 | 56664 |
000010 | 15477 | 23476 |            2 |       | 18453 | 27998 |
000011 | 11477 | 15476 |            3 |       | 13683 | 18452 |
000012 | 9077  | 11476 |            4 |       | 10797 | 13682 |
000013 | 7477  | 9076  |            5 |       | 8907  | 10796 |
000014 | 6357  | 7476  |            6 |       | 7549  | 8906  |
000015 | 5493  | 6356  |            7 |       | 6519  | 7548  |
000016 | 4821  | 5492  |            8 |       | 5727  | 6518  |
000017 | 4277  | 4820  |            9 |       | 5065  | 5726  |
000018 | 3861  | 4276  |           10 |       | 4567  | 5064  |
000019 | 3477  | 3860  |           11 |       | 4137  | 4566  |
000020 | 3189  | 3476  |           12 |       | 3769  | 4136  |
000021 | 2933  | 3188  |           13 |       | 3441  | 3768  |
000022
000023
****** *************************** BOTTOM OF DATA **********************
```

Figure 19.17 CHANGE command to remove column data.

```
EDIT ---- TSO1234.EXAMPLE.DATA(BLKSIZE) - 01.04 ----------- CHARS '=' CHANGED
COMMAND ===>                                                 SCROLL ===> CSR
****** **************************** TOP OF DATA ****************************
- - - - - - - - - - - - - - - - - - - 7 LINE(S) NOT DISPLAYED
=COLS> ----+----1----+----2----+----3----+----4----+----5----+----6----+----7
- - - - - - - - - - - - - - - - - - - 1 LINE(S) NOT DISPLAYED
==CHG>  | 23477   |  _      |         1 |   27999 |   56664 |
==CHG>  | 15477   |         |         2 |   18453 |   27998 |
==CHG>  | 11477   |         |         3 |   13683 |   18452 |
==CHG>  |  9077   |         |         4 |   10797 |   13682 |
==CHG>  |  7477   |         |         5 |    8907 |   10796 |
==CHG>  |  6357   |         |         6 |    7549 |    8906 |
==CHG>  |  5493   |         |         7 |    6519 |    7548 |
==CHG>  |  4821   |         |         8 |    5727 |    6518 |
==CHG>  |  4277   |         |         9 |    5065 |    5726 |
==CHG>  |  3861   |         |        10 |    4567 |    5064 |
==CHG>  |  3477   |         |        11 |    4137 |    4566 |
==CHG>  |  3189   |         |        12 |    3769 |    4136 |
==CHG>  |  2933   |         |        13 |    3441 |    3768 |
==CHG>
==CHG>
****** **************************** BOTTOM OF DATA ****************************
```

Figure 19.18 Result of CHANGE command to remove column data.

Removing Column Data

A combination of CHANGE command parameters can be used together to remove column data. Figure 19.17 shows a CHANGE command that uses a picture string as well as start and end columns. The command also includes parameters that specify all occurrences while limiting the command to non-excluded data. The data targeted by the command is highlighted in the example.

Figure 19.18 shows the result of the CHANGE command. All of the data in columns 13 through 18 has been removed, but only in the non-excluded lines. In this instance, the picture string could also have specified non-blank or numeric characters, and the same result would have been obtained.

20

Data Storage Commands

The SAVE Command

When an edit session is started, the computer reads data from disk into memory. The edit session is conducted in memory, and the data is only written back to disk when the SAVE primary command is issued or when AUTOSAVE (a default edit profile characteristic) causes the data to be written while terminating an edit session. In either case, the old data is overlaid. If the edit session involves a new member, it's added to the PDS being edited. When terminating a session where no changes were made, the memory used to conduct the edit session is released without rewriting the data to disk. When it's desirable to explicitly write changes to disk, the SAVE command can be used, as in Figure 20.1.

The only indication that the data has been saved is the message in the short message area (Figure 20.2). The complete edit session is written to disk and is independent of the current position in the data set. Editing can be resumed with the advantage that data recovery might be made easier (especially when edit recovery is turned off) if the edit session is interrupted.

The CANCEL Command

When AUTOSAVE is left to default, edit changes are always saved. If an error is made during an edit session or for some other reason, the changes should not be saved; the CANCEL primary command can be used to terminate the edit session without saving the changes. That command can also be abbreviated CAN and will ensure that the data is not written over the existing data set. The data set will then look like it did after the last normally ended edit session or the last save. When CANCEL is used to terminate an edit session involving a new PDS member, that member is not created.

```
EDIT ---- TSO1234.EXAMPLE.DATA(BLKSIZE) - 01.04 ------------- COLUMNS 001 072
COMMAND ===> save_                                           SCROLL ===> CSR
****** *************************** TOP OF DATA ***************************
000001 ------------------------------------------------------------------
000002 |                        Block Size Chart                         |
000003 |                                                                 |
000004 |----------------------------------------------------------------|
000005 |        3380         |       Device        |        3390         |
000006 |                     |     Blocks Per      |                     |
000007 |   Min.  |   Max.    |       Track         |   Min.  |   Max.    |
000008 |---------------------|---------------------|---------------------|
000009 | 23477   | 47476     |         1           | 27999   | 56664     |
000010 | 15477   | 23476     |         2           | 18453   | 27998     |
000011 | 11477   | 15476     |         3           | 13683   | 18452     |
000012 | 9077    | 11476     |         4           | 10797   | 13682     |
000013 | 7477    | 9076      |         5           | 8907    | 10796     |
000014 | 6357    | 7476      |         6           | 7549    | 8906      |
000015 | 5493    | 6356      |         7           | 6519    | 7548      |
000016 | 4821    | 5492      |         8           | 5727    | 6518      |
000017 | 4277    | 4820      |         9           | 5065    | 5726      |
000018 | 3861    | 4276      |        10           | 4567    | 5064      |
000019 | 3477    | 3860      |        11           | 4137    | 4566      |
000020 | 3189    | 3476      |        12           | 3769    | 4136      |
000021 | 2933    | 3188      |        13           | 3441    | 3768      |
```

Figure 20.1 SAVE primary command.

```
EDIT ---- TSO1234.EXAMPLE.DATA(BLKSIZE) - 01.04 -------- MEMBER BLKSIZE SAVED
COMMAND ===> _                                               SCROLL ===> CSR
****** *************************** TOP OF DATA ***************************
000001 ------------------------------------------------------------------
000002 |                        Block Size Chart                         |
000003 |                                                                 |
000004 |----------------------------------------------------------------|
000005 |        3380         |       Device        |        3390         |
000006 |                     |     Blocks Per      |                     |
000007 |   Min.  |   Max.    |       Track         |   Min.  |   Max.    |
000008 |---------------------|---------------------|---------------------|
000009 | 23477   | 47476     |         1           | 27999   | 56664     |
000010 | 15477   | 23476     |         2           | 18453   | 27998     |
000011 | 11477   | 15476     |         3           | 13683   | 18452     |
000012 | 9077    | 11476     |         4           | 10797   | 13682     |
000013 | 7477    | 9076      |         5           | 8907    | 10796     |
000014 | 6357    | 7476      |         6           | 7549    | 8906      |
000015 | 5493    | 6356      |         7           | 6519    | 7548      |
000016 | 4821    | 5492      |         8           | 5727    | 6518      |
000017 | 4277    | 4820      |         9           | 5065    | 5726      |
000018 | 3861    | 4276      |        10           | 4567    | 5064      |
000019 | 3477    | 3860      |        11           | 4137    | 4566      |
000020 | 3189    | 3476      |        12           | 3769    | 4136      |
000021 | 2933    | 3188      |        13           | 3441    | 3768      |
```

Figure 20.2 Result of the SAVE command.

In Figure 20.3, line commands are issued that will radically change the edit data. These commands are issued right after having just saved the data. Figure 20.4 shows what the data set looks like after the line commands are executed. It also contains the CANCEL primary command to terminate the edit session without saving the changes to disk. Under normal circumstances, this is the only way to ensure that the changes don't become permanent.

In terminating the edit session, the CANCEL command causes a return to the previous screen. This is typically a member list or the edit menu. When the data is again placed in an edit session (Figure 20.5), it's obvious that the data is the previously saved version.

EDIT Recovery

Another edit profile characteristic is RECOVERY. When it's turned on, edit transactions during the session are saved. These transactions can be automatically reapplied to the last saved version of the data to reconstruct the edit session up to the point where it was disrupted. Usually, that disruption is some sort of system or terminal problem, but pressing the SYS REQ key would also do nicely. The edit session can be reconstructed up to the last time the ENTER or any PF key was used. That presents a problem for installations that cancel TSO sessions that appear to be inactive because it's those very keys that make a session appear active. The result is data that's lost and can only be recreated by manually re-entering the data or changes.

```
EDIT ---- TSO1234.EXAMPLE.DATA(BLKSIZE) - 01.04 -------- MEMBER BLKSIZE SAVED
COMMAND ===>                                              SCROLL ===> CSR
****** *************************** TOP OF DATA ***********************
000001  ----------------------------------------------------------------
r9                               Block Size Chart
000003  |
000004  ----------------------------------------------------------------
000005  |       3380        |    Device     |       3390        |
000006  |                   |  Blocks Per   |                   |
000007  |  Min.  |   Max.   |    Track      |   Min.  |   Max.  |
000008  -------------------------------------------------------
d99999 _  23477     47476         1           27999     56664
000010    15477     23476         2           18453     27998
000011    11477     15476         3           13683     18452
000012     9077     11476         4           10797     13682
000013     7477      9076         5            8907     10796
000014     6357      7476         6            7549      8906
000015     5493      6356         7            6519      7548
000016     4821      5492         8            5727      6518
000017     4277      4820         9            5065      5726
000018     3861      4276        10            4567      5064
000019     3477      3860        11            4137      4566
000020     3189      3476        12            3769      4136
000021     2933      3188        13            3441      3768
```

Figure 20.3 Line commands to change the data set.

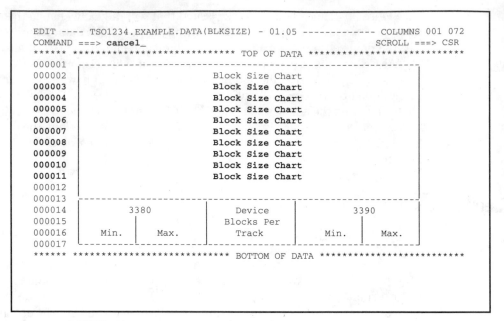

```
EDIT ---- TSO1234.EXAMPLE.DATA(BLKSIZE) - 01.05 ------------- COLUMNS 001 072
COMMAND ===> cancel_                                 SCROLL ===> CSR
****** ************************** TOP OF DATA *************************
000001 ---------------------------------------------------------------
000002                      Block Size Chart
000003                      Block Size Chart
000004                      Block Size Chart
000005                      Block Size Chart
000006                      Block Size Chart
000007                      Block Size Chart
000008                      Block Size Chart
000009                      Block Size Chart
000010                      Block Size Chart
000011                      Block Size Chart
000012
000013 ---------------------------------------------------------------
000014       3380              Device              3390
000015                       Blocks Per
000016   Min.    Max.          Track         Min.     Max.
000017 ---------------------------------------------------------------
****** ************************** BOTTOM OF DATA **************************
```

Figure 20.4 CANCEL primary command.

```
EDIT ---- TSO1234.EXAMPLE.DATA(BLKSIZE) - 01.04 ------------- COLUMNS 001 072
COMMAND ===> _                                       SCROLL ===> CSR
****** ************************** TOP OF DATA *************************
000001 ---------------------------------------------------------------
000002                      Block Size Chart
000003
000004 ---------------------------------------------------------------
000005       3380              Device              3390
000006                       Blocks Per
000007   Min.    Max.          Track         Min.     Max.
000008 ---------------------------------------------------------------
000009  23477   47476           1            27999    56664
000010  15477   23476           2            18453    27998
000011  11477   15476           3            13683    18452
000012   9077   11476           4            10797    13682
000013   7477    9076           5             8907    10796
000014   6357    7476           6             7549     8906
000015   5493    6356           7             6519     7548
000016   4821    5492           8             5727     6518
000017   4277    4820           9             5065     5726
000018   3861    4276          10             4567     5064
000019   3477    3860          11             4137     4566
000020   3189    3476          12             3769     4136
000021   2933    3188          13             3441     3768
```

Figure 20.5 Result of the CANCEL command.

When returning from a disrupted edit session, the terminal user should go straight to Option 2, since edit recovery is not supported from the Option 3.4 (the DSLIST Utility) edit line command, nor from most custom edit interfaces. If recovery was active at the time of the disruption, recovery options will be presented on the edit recovery screen shown in Figure 20.6. The name of the data set being modified at the time the edit session was disrupted is displayed so a decision can be made as to whether or not the session should be recovered. Since multiple edit sessions can be conducted (by splitting the screen and by using recursive edit), there might be more than one recovery pending. Each will display the unique name of the data set affected.

One of available options is to resume the edit session from where it was disrupted. This option is selected by merely pressing the ENTER key when presented with the recovery options. A second recovery option allows the decision about edit recovery to be deferred until later. If the data is important, however, it would be prudent to secure it using the edit recovery process before starting another edit session. This would bar the possibility of any problems arising in the recovery table or recovery data sets that make up the recovery mechanism. A third recovery option is to cancel that particular edit recovery. This option would only be chosen if the edit changes were no longer needed. It would cause the edit recovery data set to be deleted and the corresponding entry to be removed from the edit recovery table.

Recovery Suspended

Recovery mode can be suspended when there's not enough disk space to support the recovery data sets. The potential for this problem is much greater when editing large data sets. At that point, a message is issued and backup edit transactions are no

```
----------------------------- EDIT - RECOVERY -----------------------------
COMMAND ===>

                    *******************************************
                    *          EDIT AUTOMATIC RECOVERY        *
                    *******************************************


The following data set was being edited when a system failure or
task abend occurred:

Data set: TSO1234.EXAMPLE.DATA(BLKSIZE)


Instructions:
     Press ENTER key to continue editing the data set, or
     Enter END command to return to the primary option menu, or
     Enter DEFER command to defer recovery of the specified data set, or
     Enter CANCEL command to cancel recovery of the data set.

To continue editing a password protected data set, specify:

     DATA SET PASSWORD ===>
```

Figure 20.6 Edit recovery screen.

longer stored. It's possible to turn recovery off for the active profile type using the edit primary command RECOVERY OFF (abbreviated REC OFF). This will avoid the repeated display of error messages. The terminal user should then explicitly save the data at regular intervals using the SAVE command. The amount of time given to each interval would determine the maximum time that would be required to reconstruct the data should a system disruption occur. Edit recovery could later be turned on (REC ON) when disk space is available or other conditions warrant. Note that some installations set default profiles to RECOVERY OFF to avoid the extra overhead that it consumes.

Another solution would be to try to allocate larger recovery data sets or place them where sufficient disk space can be found. The characteristics of such a recovery data set should be modeled from those that ISPF creates automatically. If they're not needed to recover an edit session, the recovery data sets are automatically deleted when exiting ISPF. It will be necessary to allocate new recovery data sets before each ISPF session if this is the method used to circumvent recovery errors.

The UNDO Command

The UNDO command allows edit transactions to be backed out. The same recovery data set is used, and so recovery must be set on to make use of the UNDO command. When an edit session is started without recovery, messages are written to the top of the edit session to warn that the UNDO function is not available. The command REC OFF NOWARN can be used to leave recovery off and suppress the UNDO warning message. The UNDO command works backward from the most recent edit transaction to pull changes out one at a time.

Transactions can be removed up to the point that the data was last saved. This is the version of the data that's written to disk and might represent the way the data looked at the start of the edit session. It could also represent an intermediate form of the data that was placed on disk during the edit session using the SAVE command.

To demonstrate how the UNDO command works, two changes will first be made to the data set. The first change is shown in Figure 20.7 where the bulk of the data set is deleted. The next change (Figure 20.8) involves repeating one of the lines nine times. The changes were applied one at a time so they could be backed out that way too. Figure 20.9 shows a radically different data set where the repeated lines are highlighted. The figure also shows the UNDO command to back out the most recent change.

Figure 20.10 shows the result of the UNDO command. The last change has been backed out, removing the nine repeated lines. A second UNDO command is issued to back out the previous change. After UNDO is executed a second time, the first of the two changes is also backed out. Figure 20.11 shows the edit session with the deleted lines replaced. If the UNDO command were issued again, the message NO MORE TO UNDO would be displayed because only two changes were made since the data was last saved.

The message UNDO NOT AVAILABLE is an indication that the UNDO command can't be used because edit recovery is turned off. It will not be possible to "undo" any past changes. At that point, recovery can be turned on to allow subsequent changes to be backed out, but that leaves only the CANCEL command to deal with unwanted changes already made to the data.

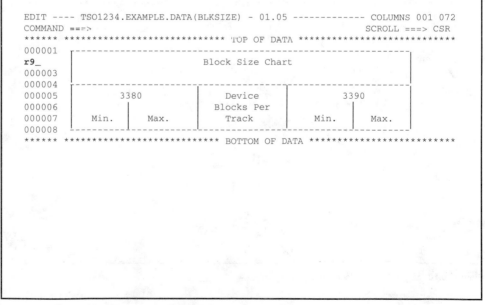

```
EDIT ---- TSO1234.EXAMPLE.DATA(BLKSIZE) - 01.04 ------------- COLUMNS 001 072
COMMAND ===>                                                 SCROLL ===> CSR
****** ************************** TOP OF DATA **************************
000001  ----------------------------------------------------------------
000002  |                         Block Size Chart                      |
000003  |                                                               |
000004  ----------------------------------------------------------------
000005  |        3380         |     Device      |        3390           |
000006  |                     |   Blocks Per    |                       |
000007  |    Min.  |   Max.   |     Track       |    Min.   |   Max.    |
000008  ----------------------------------------------------------------
d99999 _|   23477  |  47476   |       1         |   27999   |  56664    |
000010  |   15477  |  23476   |       2         |   18453   |  27998    |
000011  |   11477  |  15476   |       3         |   13683   |  18452    |
000012  |    9077  |  11476   |       4         |   10797   |  13682    |
000013  |    7477  |   9076   |       5         |    8907   |  10796    |
000014  |    6357  |   7476   |       6         |    7549   |   8906    |
000015  |    5493  |   6356   |       7         |    6519   |   7548    |
000016  |    4821  |   5492   |       8         |    5727   |   6518    |
000017  |    4277  |   4820   |       9         |    5065   |   5726    |
000018  |    3861  |   4276   |      10         |    4567   |   5064    |
000019  |    3477  |   3860   |      11         |    4137   |   4566    |
000020  |    3189  |   3476   |      12         |    3769   |   4136    |
000021  |    2933  |   3188   |      13         |    3441   |   3768    |
```

Figure 20.7 First line command to alter data.

```
EDIT ---- TSO1234.EXAMPLE.DATA(BLKSIZE) - 01.05 ------------- COLUMNS 001 072
COMMAND ===>                                                 SCROLL ===> CSR
****** ************************** TOP OF DATA **************************
000001  ----------------------------------------------------------------
r9 _    |                         Block Size Chart                      |
000003  |                                                               |
000004  ----------------------------------------------------------------
000005  |        3380         |     Device      |        3390           |
000006  |                     |   Blocks Per    |                       |
000007  |    Min.  |   Max.   |     Track       |    Min.   |   Max.    |
000008  ----------------------------------------------------------------
****** ************************** BOTTOM OF DATA **************************
```

Figure 20.8 Second line command to alter data.

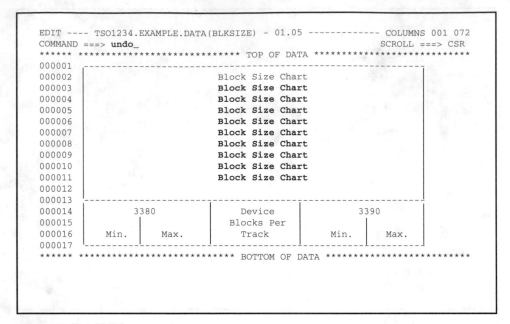

Figure 20.9 First UNDO command.

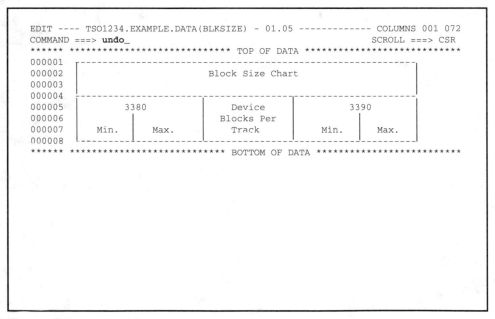

Figure 20.10 Second UNDO command.

```
EDIT ---- TSO1234.EXAMPLE.DATA(BLKSIZE) - 01.04 ------------- COLUMNS 001 072
COMMAND ===> _                                                SCROLL ===> CSR
****** ***************************** TOP OF DATA *****************************
000001  .----------------------------------------------------------------.
000002  |                          Block Size Chart                       |
000003  |                                                                 |
000004  .----------------------------------------------------------------.
000005  |       3380        |      Device      |        3390             |
000006  |                   |   Blocks Per     |                         |
000007  |  Min.  |   Max.   |     Track        |   Min.    |   Max.      |
000008  .--------.----------.------------------.-----------.-------------.
000009  | 23477  |  47476   |       1          |   27999   |   56664     |
000010  | 15477  |  23476   |       2          |   18453   |   27998     |
000011  | 11477  |  15476   |       3          |   13683   |   18452     |
000012  |  9077  |  11476   |       4          |   10797   |   13682     |
000013  |  7477  |   9076   |       5          |    8907   |   10796     |
000014  |  6357  |   7476   |       6          |    7549   |    8906     |
000015  |  5493  |   6356   |       7          |    6519   |    7548     |
000016  |  4821  |   5492   |       8          |    5727   |    6518     |
000017  |  4277  |   4820   |       9          |    5065   |    5726     |
000018  |  3861  |   4276   |      10          |    4567   |    5064     |
000019  |  3477  |   3860   |      11          |    4137   |    4566     |
000020  |  3189  |   3476   |      12          |    3769   |    4136     |
000021  |  2933  |   3188   |      13          |    3441   |    3768     |
```

Figure 20.11 Edit data after changes have been backed out.

21

Data Movement Commands

The ISPF editor has four commands that support the movement of data between data sets. The commands MOVE and COPY are used to bring data into an edit session, while the commands CREATE and REPLACE are used to write data out from the current edit session. Any of the four commands can access data from the same PDS (the same PDS as the data being edited) or from other partitioned and sequential data sets.

The COPY Command

Data from the same PDS can be referenced entirely from the command line. As shown in Figure 21.1, the COPY command is issued to bring data to the current edit session from the member COMPRESS. COMPRESS must be in the same PDS for the command to work in this format.

Figure 21.2 shows the result of the COPY command. The entire contents of the member COMPRESS has been copied into the empty edit session. Because the edit session initially contained the insert lines of a new member, it was not necessary to place the copied data. When the current edit session already contains data, however, it will be necessary to use the before (B) or after (A) lines commands to designate where the data is to be copied to.

In some cases it's even possible to copy a member (or sequential data set) onto itself. This is only possible with an edit session using existing data and is made possible because the data is not changed on disk until it's saved. This fact can be important for accessing deleted data where the UNDO command is not available or its use would destroy other valuable changes.

```
EDIT ---- TSO1234.CNTL(COPYTEST) - 01.00 -------------------- COLUMNS 001 072
COMMAND ===> copy compress_                                   SCROLL ===> CSR
****** *************************** TOP OF DATA ****************************
''''''
''''''
''''''
''''''
''''''
''''''
''''''
''''''
''''''
''''''
''''''
''''''
''''''
''''''
''''''
''''''
''''''
''''''
****** *************************** BOTTOM OF DATA *************************
```

Figure 21.1 COPY primary command.

```
EDIT ---- TSO1234.CNTL(COPYTEST) - 01.00 ------------- MEMBER COMPRESS COPIED
COMMAND ===> _                                               SCROLL ===> CSR
****** *************************** TOP OF DATA ****************************
000100 //TSO1234A JOB 'SAMPLE JOB',
000110 //   CLASS=A,MSGCLASS=T,NOTIFY=TSO1234
000120 //COMPRESS  EXEC PGM=IEBCOPY
000130 //SYSPRINT DD SYSOUT-*
000140 //SYSUT1    DD UNIT=3380,SPACE=(TRK,(5,5))
000150 //PDS       DD DSN=TSO1234.CLIST,DISP=OLD
000160 //SYSIN     DD *
000170   COPY INDD=PDS,OUTDD=PDS
****** *************************** BOTTOM OF DATA *************************
```

Figure 21.2 Result of COPY primary command.

The MOVE Command

The MOVE command is just like the COPY command, except that the source data set is removed. If the source data set is a member of a PDS, that member is deleted after the data is successfully transferred into the current edit session. If the source data set is sequential, the entire sequential data set is deleted after the data is successfully transferred. Deletion of the source data set is independent of whether or not the current edit data (including the data that has been moved in) is ever saved. Canceling the edit session will, therefore, not restore the moved data source.

The latter fact allows the MOVE command to be used to delete unwanted members while in edit mode (since deleting all of the members' lines would still leave an empty member). Even though members are best deleted using the library utility (Option 3.1), it's sometimes convenient to create a new member and move unwanted members into it. The edit session containing the new member can then be canceled with the result that neither the new member nor those moved into it will exist when the process is finished.

The CREATE Command

The CREATE command is used to transfer data in the opposite direction. Figure 21.3 shows the command used to create a new member called JOB. The CREATE command (which can be abbreviated CRE) uses the MOVE (M) or COPY (C) line commands to identify the data lines to be transferred. If MOVE is specified, the lines are removed from the current edit session and placed in the other data set. If COPY is specified, as in this case, the lines are retained in the current edit session and they're also placed in the other data set. The line command in the example requests that nine lines be copied, starting with the third line of the data set. Since there are only six lines from that point to the end of the data set, they will all be copied.

Figure 21.4 shows the result of the CREATE command. The only indication that the command has worked is the message in the short message area. Again, if MOVE instead of COPY had been used as the line command, the affected lines would also have been removed from the data set.

The CREATE command can only be used to create new members and therefore will never overlay existing data. If the specified member already exists, the command will fail. A message will be issued indicating that the member already exists. If the member contents must truly be overlaid, the REPLACE command should be used in place of CREATE.

The CREATE command cannot be used to transfer data to a sequential data set. A sequential data set must already exist if it's to be the target of a data movement command. The fact that the data set already exists and is a single entity means that it could already contain data that should not be overlaid. This instance too would indicate use of the REPLACE command instead of CREATE.

The REPLACE Command

The counterpart to the CREATE command is REPLACE. It's used when the target data set (either sequential or specific member of a PDS) already exists. The RE-

```
EDIT ---- TSO1234.CNTL(COPYTEST) - 01.00 -------------------- COLUMNS 001 072
COMMAND ===> create job                                       SCROLL ===> CSR
****** *************************** TOP OF DATA ***************************
000100 //TSO1234A JOB 'SAMPLE JOB',
000110 //   CLASS=A,MSGCLASS=T,NOTIFY=TSO1234
c9_    //COMPRESS  EXEC PGM=IEBCOPY
000130 //SYSPRINT DD SYSOUT=*
000140 //SYSUT1   DD UNIT=3380,SPACE=(TRK,(5,5))
000150 //PDS      DD DSN=TSO1234.CLIST,DISP=OLD
000160 //SYSIN    DD *
000170    COPY INDD=PDS,OUTDD=PDS
****** *************************** BOTTOM OF DATA ***************************
```

Figure 21.3 CREATE primary command.

```
EDIT ---- TSO1234.CNTL(COPYTEST) - 01.00 ----------------- MEMBER JOB CREATED
COMMAND ===> _                                                SCROLL ===> CSR
****** *************************** TOP OF DATA ***************************
000100 //TSO1234A JOB 'SAMPLE JOB',
000110 //   CLASS=A,MSGCLASS=T,NOTIFY=TSO1234
000120 //COMPRESS  EXEC PGM=IEBCOPY
000130 //SYSPRINT DD SYSOUT=*
000140 //SYSUT1   DD UNIT=3380,SPACE=(TRK,(5,5))
000150 //PDS      DD DSN=TSO1234.CLIST,DISP=OLD
000160 //SYSIN    DD *
000170    COPY INDD=PDS,OUTDD=PDS
****** *************************** BOTTOM OF DATA ***************************
```

Figure 21.4 Result of CREATE primary command.

PLACE command (which can be abbreviated REP) causes the current content of the target data set to be replaced with the lines being moved or copied. Figure 21.5 shows the REPLACE command used to replace the member JOB in the same PDS (that member was just created in the previous example using the CREATE command). The block move command is used to identify two lines to move over the current contents of the member JOB.

As a result of the REPLACE command, the first two lines of the current edit session have been deleted (Figure 21.6). The short message area indicates that the member has been replaced. If the member didn't exist prior to the execution of the command, the message wording would have been changed to "MEMBER JOB CREATED" to reflect that fact.

Specifying Other Data Sources

Data from another source can be accessed by COPY or MOVE by omitting the member name. This is also true for the object of CREATE and REPLACE commands. When the member name is omitted, a second screen is presented that allows the same or another data set to be specified. In Figure 21.7, the COPY command is used without a member name. Because the current edit session already contains data, it's also necessary to specify where the copied data will be placed. The after line command (A) is used to specify that the copied data be placed after the top-of-data marker.

When the COPY command is executed, the absence of a member name causes the edit copy screen to be displayed (Figure 21.8). With this screen, the COPY command is no longer limited to accessing data from the same PDS. The same is true of the

```
EDIT ---- TSO1234.CNTL(COPYTEST) - 01.00 -------------------- COLUMNS 001 072
COMMAND ===> replace job                                    SCROLL ===> CSR
****** **************************** TOP OF DATA *****************************
mm        //TSO1234A JOB 'SAMPLE JOB',
mm_       //   CLASS=A,MSGCLASS=T,NOTIFY=TSO1234
000120 //COMPRESS  EXEC PGM=IEBCOPY
000130 //SYSPRINT DD SYSOUT=*
000140 //SYSUT1    DD UNIT=3380,SPACE=(TRK,(5,5))
000150 //PDS       DD DSN=TSO1234.CLIST,DISP=OLD
000160 //SYSIN     DD *
000170    COPY INDD=PDS,OUTDD=PDS
****** **************************** BOTTOM OF DATA *************************
```

Figure 21.5 REPLACE primary command.

```
EDIT ---- TSO1234.CNTL(COPYTEST) - 01.00 --------------- MEMBER JOB REPLACED
COMMAND ===> _                                        SCROLL ===> CSR
****** *************************** TOP OF DATA ***************************
000120 //COMPRESS  EXEC PGM=IEBCOPY
000130 //SYSPRINT DD SYSOUT=*
000140 //SYSUT1    DD UNIT=3380,SPACE=(TRK,(5,5))
000150 //PDS       DD DSN=TSO1234.CLIST,DISP=OLD
000160 //SYSIN     DD *
000170    COPY INDD=PDS,OUTDD=PDS
****** *************************** BOTTOM OF DATA ***************************
```

Figure 21.6 Result of REPLACE primary command.

```
EDIT ---- TSO1234.CNTL(COPYTEST) - 01.00 ------------------- COLUMNS 001 072
COMMAND ===> copy                                     SCROLL ===> CSR
a****** *************************** TOP OF DATA ***************************
000120 //COMPRESS  EXEC PGM=IEBCOPY
000130 //SYSPRINT DD SYSOUT=*
000140 //SYSUT1    DD UNIT=3380,SPACE=(TRK,(5,5))
000150 //PDS       DD DSN=TSO1234.CLIST,DISP=OLD
000160 //SYSIN     DD *
000170    COPY INDD-PDS,OUTDD=PDS
****** *************************** BOTTOM OF DATA ***************************
```

Figure 21.7 COPY command without member name.

```
------------------------------- EDIT - COPY --------------------------------
COMMAND ===>
"CURRENT" DATA SET: TSO1234.CNTL(COPYTEST)

FROM ISPF LIBRARY:
    PROJECT ===> TSO1234
    GROUP   ===> EXAMPLE  ===>           ===>          ===>
    TYPE    ===> DATA
    MEMBER  ===>                    (Blank or pattern for member selection list)

FROM OTHER PARTITIONED OR SEQUENTIAL DATA SET:
    DATA SET NAME  ===> jcl.cntl(sort)
    VOLUME SERIAL  ===>             (If not cataloged)

DATA SET PASSWORD ===>             (If password protected)

LINE NUMBERS                       (Blank for entire member or seq. data set)
    FIRST LINE   ===> 1
    LAST LINE    ===> 3
    NUMBER TYPE  ===> r_           (STANDARD, ISPFSTD, COBOL, or RELATIVE)

Press ENTER key to copy.
Enter END command to cancel copy.
```

Figure 21.8 Edit copy screen.

MOVE, CREATE, and REPLACE commands. The equivalent screens will allow data to be pulled from or written to any PDS or sequential data set.

Another advantage to this mode of processing is that a PDS can be specified without a member name forcing the member list to display. A member can then be selected from the list. This is a distinct advantage since it's usually easier to recognize a particular member than it is to remember its name.

Yet another advantage inherent in the edit copy screen in particular is that the screen allows particular lines to be copied. This feature is not available with the corresponding MOVE primary command. In Figure 21.8, a particular PDS and member combination is specified in the DATA SET NAME field. As in all screens that contain this alternate data set name field, its value is used over that contained in the PROJECT, GROUP, and TYPE fields.

Fields at the bottom of the screen are used to specify which lines will be copied. If these fields are not used, the entire data set is copied. In this instance, however, only the first three lines are needed. That's indicated by specifying the start and end line numbers as 1 and 3 respectively. The line type used here is relative (R) meaning relative to the start of the data set. Other line types can be used depending on the data type and the numbering options that its data was saved with.

Figure 21.9 shows the result of the copy operation. Only the first three lines of the specified data set were copied into the current edit session. The short message is also adjusted to reflect that a line copy operation was completed.

```
EDIT ---- TSO1234.CNTL(COPYTEST) - 01.00 ---------- REQUESTED LINE(S) COPIED
COMMAND ===> _                                        SCROLL ===> CSR
****** ************************** TOP OF DATA *****************************
000100 //TSO1234S JOB 'SAMPLE JOB',
000110 //   MSGLEVEL=(1,1),
000111 //   CLASS=A,MSGCLASS=T,NOTIFY=TSO1234
000120 //COMPRESS  EXEC PGM=IEBCOPY
000130 //SYSPRINT DD SYSOUT=*
000140 //SYSUT1    DD UNIT=3380,SPACE=(TRK,(5,5))
000150 //PDS       DD DSN=TSO1234.CLIST,DISP=OLD
000160 //SYSIN     DD *
000170    COPY INDD=PDS,OUTDD=PDS
****** ************************** BOTTOM OF DATA *************************
```

Figure 21.9 Result of copying selected lines.

Truncation and Padding

When data is transferred between data sets with different record lengths, the data will be padded or truncated as necessary. Figure 21.10 shows the start of a process to replace the contents of a sequential data set with a shorter record length.

Since the REPLACE command was issued without a member name, the edit replace menu is displayed as in Figure 21.11. On this screen, the name of a sequential data set SHORT.DATA is specified.

ISPF will issue a full screen warning when data must be padded or truncated to accommodate the record length of the receiving data set. In Figure 21.12, the target data set is shorter (72 bytes) than the current data set (80 bytes). The data must then be truncated as it's copied to the target data set. The replace process can be terminated at this point by using the END command. Pressing ENTER from this screen confirms the user's intent to truncate data.

After pressing the ENTER key, the short message in Figure 21.13 indicates that the process to replace the sequential data set is complete. The last eight bytes of each record was truncated as the record was written to the data set.

The MODEL Command

The MODEL command is very different from the others mentioned in this chapter and also supports the movement of data. The difference is the source of that data and what it's typically used for. The MODEL command is generally used to copy into

```
EDIT ---- TSO1234.CNTL(COPYTEST) - 01.00 -------------------- COLUMNS 001 072
COMMAND ===> rep                                            SCROLL ===> CSR
****** ************************* TOP OF DATA *****************************
c99_    //TSO1234S JOB 'SAMPLE JOB',
000110 //  MSGLEVEL=(1,1),
000111 //   CLASS=A,MSGCLASS=T,NOTIFY=TSO1234
000120 //COMPRESS  EXEC PGM=IEBCOPY
000130 //SYSPRINT DD SYSOUT=*
000140 //SYSUT1   DD UNIT=3380,SPACE=(TRK,(5,5))
000150 //PDS      DD DSN=TSO1234.CLIST,DISP=OLD
000160 //SYSIN    DD *
000170   COPY INDD=PDS,OUTDD=PDS
****** ************************* BOTTOM OF DATA ***************************
```

Figure 21.10 Start of replace sequence.

```
------------------------- -- EDIT - REPLACE ---------------------------
COMMAND ===>
"CURRENT" DATA SET: TSO1234.CNTL(COPYTEST)

TO ISPF LIBRARY:
   PROJECT ===> TSO1234
   GROUP   ===> EXAMPLE
   TYPE    ===> DATA
   MEMBER  ===>

TO OTHER SEQUENTIAL DATA SET OR PARTITIONED DATA SET MEMBER:
   DATA SET NAME  ===> short.data_
   VOLUME SERIAL  ===>          (If not cataloged)

DATA SET PASSWORD ===>          (If password protected)

SPECIFY PACK OPTION FOR "REPLACE" DATA SET ===> NO    (YES or NO)

Press ENTER key to replace.
Enter END command to cancel replace.
```

Figure 21.11 Specifying the target data set.

```
----------------------- EDIT - CONFIRM REPLACE  --------------------------
COMMAND ===> _

Data set attributes are inconsistent.  Truncation may result in
the right-most portions of some records if replace is performed.

   "Target" data set attributes:
       Data set name: TSO1234.SHORT.DATA
       Record format: FIXED
       Record length: 72

   "Current" data set attributes:
       Data set name: TSO1234.CNTL(COPYTEST)
       Record format: FIXED
       Record length: 80

Press ENTER key to allow replace with truncation.
Enter END command to cancel replace.
```

Figure 21.12 Confirm truncation screen.

```
EDIT ---- TSO1234.CNTL(COPYTEST) - 01.00 ------------------ DATA SET REPLACED
COMMAND ===>                                               SCROLL ===> CSR
****** ************************** TOP OF DATA *****************************
000100 _/TSO1234S JOB 'SAMPLE JOB',
000110 //   MSGLEVEL=(1,1),
000111 //   CLASS=A,MSGCLASS-T,NOTIFY=TSO1234
000120 //COMPRESS   EXEC PGM=IEBCOPY
000130 //SYSPRINT DD SYSOUT=*
000140 //SYSUT1     DD UNIT=3380,SPACE=(TRK,(5,5))
000150 //PDS        DD DSN=TSO1234.CLIST,DISP=OLD
000160 //SYSIN      DD *
000170   COPY INDD=PDS,OUTDD=PDS
****** ************************** BOTTOM OF DATA *************************
```

Figure 21.13 End of replace sequence.

an edit session programming statements that are unique to the ISPF dialog management product. These statements then serve as the basis for invoking dialog management services. Some installations have added other types of data to this command, which is sensitive to the type of data being edited. If the MODEL command can't match the current data type with models that it supports, the command will display the menu shown in Figure 21.14. This is the standard menu supplied with ISPF. The descriptive qualifier (in this case NOSUCH) from the data set being edited is automatically displayed in the option field, and a warning message is issued. The appropriate language type can be selected by name or by its corresponding number. Selecting a particular type provides access to other menus with more detailed topic areas.

Shown in context, the MODEL command is used in the new CLIST member EDITMOD in Figure 21.15. If the letter and number combination for a specific example is known, it can be specified following the MODEL command. Like the MOVE and COPY primary commands, it would be necessary to place the command output if the current edit session already contains data. This is done with before (B) and after (A) line commands.

The data set low-level or descriptive qualifier indicates the data type. The descriptive qualifier of the data set being edited is CLIST. Since the CLIST data type is a standard for the MODEL command, the menu for the CLIST language is displayed (Figure 21.16). The various models are grouped under letter codes. It's also possible for a particular code (in this case T1 representing table processing functions) to represent a whole different menu system with other detail choices. In the example, M4 is selected to copy the edit function model into the current edit session.

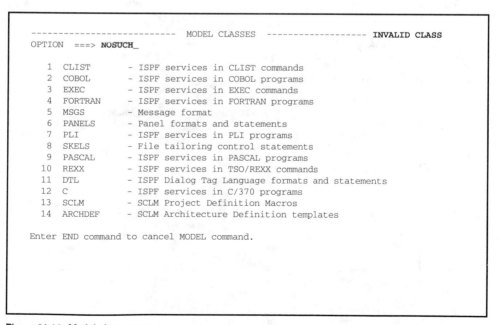

```
------------------------------  MODEL CLASSES  ------------------  INVALID CLASS
    OPTION  ===> NOSUCH_

        1   CLIST      - ISPF services in CLIST commands
        2   COBOL      - ISPF services in COBOL programs
        3   EXEC       - ISPF services in EXEC commands
        4   FORTRAN    - ISPF services in FORTRAN programs
        5   MSGS       - Message format
        6   PANELS     - Panel formats and statements
        7   PLI        - ISPF services in PLI programs
        8   SKELS      - File tailoring control statements
        9   PASCAL     - ISPF services in PASCAL programs
       10   REXX       - ISPF services in TSO/REXX commands
       11   DTL        - ISPF Dialog Tag Language formats and statements
       12   C          - ISPF services in C/370 programs
       13   SCLM       - SCLM Project Definition Macros
       14   ARCHDEF    - SCLM Architecture Definition templates

    Enter END command to cancel MODEL command.
```

Figure 21.14 Model class menu.

```
EDIT ---- TSO1234.CLIST(EDITMOD) - 01.00 ------------------ COLUMNS 001 072
COMMAND ===> model_                                    SCROLL ===> CSR
****** ************************** TOP OF DATA ******************************
'''''''
'''''''
'''''''
'''''''
'''''''
'''''''
'''''''
'''''''
'''''''
'''''''
'''''''
'''''''
'''''''
'''''''
'''''''
'''''''
'''''''
'''''''
****** ************************** BOTTOM OF DATA ****************************
```

Figure 21.15 MODEL primary command.

```
---------------------------- CLIST MODELS ----------------------------
OPTION  ===> m4_

  VARIABLES            MISCELLANEOUS        LIBRARY ACCESS
  V1    VGET           M1    SELECT         L1    LMCLOSE      L16   LMRENAME
  V2    VPUT           M2    CONTROL        L2    LMERASE      L17   LMHIER
  V3    VERASE         M3    BROWSE         L3    LMFREE       L18   LMACT
                       M4    EDIT           L4    LMGET        L19   LMDEACT
  DISPLAY              M5    LOG            L5    LMINIT       L20   LMREVIEW
  D1    DISPLAY        M6    GETMSG         L6    LMMADD       L21   LMMDISP
  D2    TBDISPL        M7    EDREC          L7    LMMDEL       L22   LMMOVE
  D3    SETMSG         M8    LIBDEF         L8    LMMFIND      L23   LMCOPY
  D4    PQUERY         M9    LIST           L9    LMMLIST      L24   LMCOMP
  D5    ADDPOP                              L10   LMMREN       L25   LMMSTATS
  D6    REMPOP         FILE TAILORING       L11   LMMREP       L26   LMPRINT
                       F1    FTOPEN         L12   LMOPEN       L27   LMDINIT
  TABLES               F2    FTINCL         L13   LMPROM       L28   LMDLIST
  T1    TABLES         F3    FTCLOSE        L14   LMPUT        L29   LMDFREE
                       F4    FTERASE        L15   LMQUERY


  Enter END command to cancel MODEL command.
```

Figure 21.16 CLIST model menu.

Figure 21.17 shows the result of the MODEL command. The edit session now contains an example of the command that would be used to invoke a standard edit session from a CLIST. A new type of line, the note line, is shown in the example. The note lines are part of the edit function model for CLIST code. They're temporary lines used to describe the other model statements and will not be saved with the data.

Scrolling down into the data set reveals additional note lines (Figure 21.18). The make data line command (MD) can be used to turn the temporary note lines (as well as other temporary display lines) into permanent data lines. The MD line command is used here to turn the last several note lines into permanent data lines that can be retained (saved) in the data set. In addition to the numeric format used here, the make data line command can also be used in the single line format (MD) or in the block line command format (MD pairs).

Figure 21.19 shows the result of the make data line command. The converted lines now show normal sequence numbers in the line command area and will be retained in the data set if it's saved. All note lines will be deleted when the edit session is terminated or when the RESET primary command is used.

```
EDIT ---- TSO1234.CLIST(EDITMOD) - 01.00 ------------------ COLUMNS 001 072
COMMAND ===> _                                          SCROLL ===> CSR
****** ************************* TOP OF DATA *****************************
000001    ISPEXEC   EDIT DATASET(DSNAME)   VOLUME(SERIAL) PASSWORD(PSWD)    +
000002                        PANEL(PANELID)    MACRO(MACNAME) PROFILE(PROFNAME) +
000003                        FORMAT(FORM-NAM) MIXED(NO)      LOCK(YES)
=NOTE=                   OR
000004    ISPEXEC   EDIT DATAID(DATA-ID)   MEMBER(MBRNAME)    PANEL(PANELID) +
000005                        MACRO(MACNAME)    PROFILE(PROFNAME)            +
000006                        FORMAT(FORM-NAM) MIXED(NO)          LOCK(YES)
=NOTE=
=NOTE=        DSNAME    - NAME, IN TSO SYNTAX, OF DATA SET TO BE EDITED.
=NOTE=        SERIAL    - OPTIONAL, VOLUME SERIAL ON WHICH THE DATA SET RESIDES.
=NOTE=        PSWD      - OPTIONAL, IF DATA SET HAS OS PASSWORD PROTECTION.
=NOTE=        DATA-ID   - REQUIRED IF DSNAME NOT SPECIFIED. NAME RETURNED FROM
=NOTE=                    LMINIT.
=NOTE=        MBRNAME   - OPTIONAL, MEMBER NAME TO BE USED WITH DATA-ID.
=NOTE=        PANELID   - OPTIONAL, NAME OF THE PANEL TO BE USED FOR DISPLAYING
=NOTE=                    THE DATA.
=NOTE=        MACNAME   - OPTIONAL, NAME OF THE INITIAL MACRO TO BE EXECUTED
=NOTE=                    AFTER THE DATA IS READ.
=NOTE=        PROFNAME  - OPTIONAL, NAME OF THE EDIT PROFILE TO BE USED. DEFAULT
=NOTE=                    IS ISPF LIBRARY "TYPE" OR LAST QUALIFIER OF "OTHER"
=NOTE=
```

Figure 21.17 Result of MODEL command.

```
EDIT ---- TSO1234.CLIST(EDITMOD) - 01.00 ------------------- COLUMNS 001 072
COMMAND ===>                                                SCROLL ===> CSR
=NOTE=                   DATA SET NAME.
=NOTE=       FORM-NAM - OPTIONAL, NAME OF THE FORMATTED DATA.
=NOTE=       MIXED    - OPTIONAL, CHOOSE ONE
=NOTE=         YES    - TREAT AS DBCS DATA.
=NOTE=         NO     - DEFAULT, TREAT AS SBCS DATA.
=NOTE=       LOCK     - OPTIONAL, CHOOSE ONE
=NOTE=         YES    - DEFAULT, EDIT LOCK THE MEMBER.
=NOTE=         NO     - DO NOT EDIT LOCK THE MEMBER.
md9_
=NOTE=       EXAMPLES:
=NOTE=         ISPEXEC  EDIT DATASET('PAYROLL.INP.PLI(PAY303)') +
=NOTE=                       VOLUME(SCRTH1) PASSWORD(SECRET)
=NOTE=                              OR
=NOTE=         ISPEXEC  EDIT DATAID(&MYID ) MBRNAME(PAY303)
=NOTE=
000007    IF &LASTCC ¬= 0 THEN   /* RETURN CODES                       */ +
000008      DO                   /*  4 - DATA NOT SAVED                */
000009      END                  /* 14 - MEMBER IN USE OR DATA SET IN USE */
000010    ELSE                   /* 16 - NO MEMBERS IN LIBRARY         */ +
000011                           /* 20 - SEVER ERROR                   */
****** ************************** BOTTOM OF DATA ****************************
```

Figure 21.18 Make data line command.

```
EDIT ---- TSO1234.CLIST(EDITMOD) - 01.00 ------------------- COLUMNS 001 072
COMMAND ===> _                                              SCROLL ===> CSR
=NOTE=                   DATA SET NAME.
=NOTE=       FORM-NAM - OPTIONAL, NAME OF THE FORMATTED DATA.
=NOTE=       MIXED    - OPTIONAL, CHOOSE ONE
=NOTE=         YES    - TREAT AS DBCS DATA.
=NOTE=         NO     - DEFAULT, TREAT AS SBCS DATA.
=NOTE=       LOCK     - OPTIONAL, CHOOSE ONE
=NOTE=         YES    - DEFAULT, EDIT LOCK THE MEMBER.
=NOTE=         NO     - DO NOT EDIT LOCK THE MEMBER.
000007
000008      EXAMPLES:
000009        ISPEXEC  EDIT DATASET('PAYROLL.INP.PLI(PAY303)') +
000010                      VOLUME(SCRTH1) PASSWORD(SECRET)
000011                             OR
000012        ISPEXEC  EDIT DATAID(&MYID ) MBRNAME(PAY303)
000013
000014    IF &LASTCC ¬= 0 THEN   /* RETURN CODES                       */ +
000015      DO                   /*  4 - DATA NOT SAVED                */
000016      END                  /* 14 - MEMBER IN USE OR DATA SET IN USE */
000017    ELSE                   /* 16 - NO MEMBERS IN LIBRARY         */ +
000018                           /* 20 - SEVER ERROR                   */
****** ************************** BOTTOM OF DATA ****************************
```

Figure 21.19 Result of make data command.

22

Text Editing Commands

The Text Edit Line Command

The text entry line command (TE) can be used to start a special text entry mode. The entry mode allows text to be entered without regard for the end of the line. Text that's entered will automatically wrap around to the next line. When the text entry process is finished, letters that were separated during the wrap process are rejoined into words. At the end of the text entry process, paragraphs are also reformatted to make spacing uniform. The TE command is used in Figure 22.1 in a virtually empty member.

From Figure 22.2 it's obvious that the special text entry mode is made possible by the removal of the line command area. This is done automatically as a result of executing the text entry command. Without any parameters, the command creates a text entry area to the bottom of the screen. A vertical bar (located in the lower right corner) signifies the end of the text entry area.

As text is entered, the cursor automatically jumps from the end of one line to the beginning of the next (Figure 22.3). No provision is yet made for word boundaries; characters are literally placed in the next available position.

When the ENTER key is pressed, words are reconnected and paragraphs are reformatted to correct spacing (Figure 22.4). Two spaces are used to separate sentences when they're moved to a new line (as on line 7) but not when they're not moved during the reformatting process (as on line 5, which had only one space to begin with).

Blank lines with text are retained. Blank lines at the end of the text area, however, are like insert lines and are not retained if they're not used. At least a space would have to be typed on such a line to cause it to be retained. The line command area has been reinstated now that the edit session is no longer in a special text entry mode.

```
EDIT ---- TSO1234.EXAMPLE.DATA(TEXTEDIT) - 01.01 ------------ COLUMNS 001 072
COMMAND ===>                                                  SCROLL ===> CSR
**** **************************** TOP OF DATA ****************************
0001
0002                         TEXT ENTRY
te_
**** **************************** BOTTOM OF DATA ****************************
```

Figure 22.1 Text entry line command.

```
EDIT ---- TSO1234.EXAMPLE.DATA(TEXTEDIT) - 01.01 ----------------- ENTER TEXT
COMMAND ===>                                                  SCROLL ===> CSR
**** **************************** TOP OF DATA ****************************
0001
0002                           TEXT ENTRY
0003_
```

Figure 22.2 Result of text entry line command.

```
EDIT ---- TSO1234.EXAMPLE.DATA(TEXTEDIT) - 01.01 ---------------- ENTER TEXT
COMMAND ===>                                          SCROLL ===> CSR
**** ************************** TOP OF DATA ****************************
0001
0002                              TEXT ENTRY
0003
     WITH THE REMAINDER OF THE SCREEN BLANKED OUT, TEXT CAN BE ENTERED WITHOU
     T REGARD FOR THE END OF THE LINE. THE CURSOR, AND THEREFORE THE SUBSEQUE
     NT TEXT WILL AUTOMATICALLY BE PLACED AT THE BEGINNING OF THE NEXT LINE.
     WHEN THE ENTER KEY (OR ANY PF KEY) IS PRESSED, THE TEXT WILL BE REFORMAT
     TED INTO PARAGRAPHS WITHIN THE CURRENT BOUNDARY SETTINGS.

     LEAVING A BLANK LINE IN THE TEXT THAT IS ENTERED, WILL ALSO LEAVE A BLAN
     K LINE IN THE RESULTANT TEXT._
```

Figure 22.3 Data entered in text entry area.

```
EDIT ---- TSO1234.EXAMPLE.DATA(TEXTEDIT) - 01.01 ------------ COLUMNS 001 072
COMMAND ===> _                                        SCROLL ===> CSR
**** ************************** TOP OF DATA ****************************
0001
0002                              TEXT ENTRY
0003
0004 WITH THE REMAINDER OF THE SCREEN BLANKED OUT, TEXT CAN BE ENTERED
0005 WITHOUT REGARD FOR THE END OF THE LINE. THE CURSOR, AND THEREFORE THE
0006 SUBSEQUENT TEXT WILL AUTOMATICALLY BE PLACED AT THE BEGINNING OF THE
0007 NEXT LINE.  WHEN THE ENTER KEY (OR ANY PF KEY) IS PRESSED, THE TEXT WILL
0008 BE REFORMATTED INTO PARAGRAPHS WITHIN THE CURRENT BOUNDARY SETTINGS.
0009
0010 LEAVING A BLANK LINE IN THE TEXT THAT IS ENTERED, WILL ALSO LEAVE A
0011 BLANK LINE IN THE RESULTANT TEXT.
**** ************************** BOTTOM OF DATA ****************************
```

Figure 22.4 Reflowed text entry data.

The Text Split Line Command

Other text editing commands are useful in processing existing data. One such command, the text split line command (TS) is used to split an existing line and allow room for additional text entry. Figure 22.5 shows the text split command. Notice that after the command is typed, the cursor is moved into the data line before pressing the ENTER key. It's the cursor position that determines where the line will be split. In this case, the cursor has been placed under the first letter of the start of a sentence on line 14.

Figure 22.6 shows the result of the command execution. The portion of the line starting at the cursor position has been left justified and placed on a separate line. The cursor remains positioned for additional text to be entered, and an insert line is placed just below to accommodate additional text.

If the cursor is left on the insert line when the ENTER key is pressed, an additional insert line will be generated. The insert process can be repeated as often as necessary. As long as the cursor is still on the last insert line, pressing the ENTER key will generate another insert line. The process is terminated by moving the cursor off the last insert line, as in Figure 22.7.

When the ENTER key is pressed again, the insert cycle is stopped (Figure 22.8). All lines are now permanent edit lines, but the text is no longer in neat paragraph alignment.

The text split line command can also be issued with a numeric value. The numeric value indicates how many insert lines should follow the split line. This would be a more efficient way to add multiple lines than pressing ENTER for each insert line.

The Text Flow Line Command

Yet another text editing command can be used to restore the alignment of the paragraph being worked on. That command is the text flow line command (TF). That command is specified in Figure 22.9 followed by the number 65. The 65 indicates that text is to be reflowed through (but not past) column 65.

The text flow command will reformat text up to the first blank line. The scope of the command can also be limited by line indentation. Reformatting will stop before a line that doesn't share the same starting position (starts further left or right than the line before it).

Figure 22.10 shows the effect of the text flow command. Notice that none of the text extends beyond the column specified (column 65). Even though the command was issued at the start of the paragraph, not all of the text needed to be reformatted. The portion of the text that was changed is highlighted in Figure 22.10.

The text flow command is also closely tied to the bounds settings. The bounds have been displayed in Figure 22.11, and the data has been shifted to coincide with the left bound. The right bound has been set to column 71, and the text flow command has been entered without a column value. Under these circumstances, the right boundary will set the right-hand margin when the text is reformatted.

With the new, wider limits, the entire paragraph is reformatted (Figure 22.12). The editor will ensure that two spaces separate each sentence on any line that it moves in the process of reformatting. The spacing is not changed between sentences that are not moved to a new line.

```
EDIT ---- TSO1234.EXAMPLE.DATA(TEXTEDIT) - 01.02 ------------ COLUMNS 001 072
COMMAND ===>                                              SCROLL ===> CSR
****** ************************** TOP OF DATA ****************************
000001
000002
000003                    TSO Naming Conventions
000004
000005
000006      When data set names are not literally specified (enclosed
000007      in single quotes), TSO will append a prefix in front of
000008      the data set name.  This prefix is usually the
000009      individual's user-id, but can be changed by any TSO user,
000010      by using the TSO PROFILE command.  Based upon the context
000011      in which it is used, TSO can also detect special data set
000012      types and attach an appropriate suffix.  This too will
000013      only occur when the data set name is not literally
ts          specified.  This last qualifier (which precedes the
000015      member name, if any) is also known as the descriptive
000016      qualifier.  Two such descriptive qualifiers that pertain
000017      especially to CLIST execution are .CLIST for CLIST data
000018      sets and .LOAD for load module libraries.  The former is
000019      the basis for the modified explicit execution mode, while
000020      the latter will be discussed  later with the resource
000021      controlling aspects of CLISTS.  Finally, if a CLIST
```

Figure 22.5 Text split line command.

```
EDIT -- - TSO1234.EXAMPLE.DATA(TEXTEDIT) - 01.02 ------------ COLUMNS 001 072
COMMAND ===>                                              SCROLL ===> CSR
****** ************************** TOP OF DATA ****************************
000001
000002
000003                    TSO Naming Conventions
000004
000005
000006      When data set names are not literally specified (enclosed
000007      in single quotes), TSO will append a prefix in front of
000008      the data set name.  This prefix is usually the
000009      individual's user-id, but can be changed by any TSO user,
000010      by using the TSO PROFILE command.  Based upon the context
000011      in which it is used, TSO can also detect special data set
000012      types and attach an appropriate suffix.  This too will
000013      only occur when the data set name is not literally
000014      specified.  _
''''''
000015      This last qualifier (which precedes the
000016      member name, if any) is also known as the descriptive
000017      qualifier.  Two such descriptive qualifiers that pertain
000018      especially to CLIST execution are .CLIST for CLIST data
000019      sets and .LOAD for load module libraries.  The former is
000020      the basis for the modified explicit execution mode, while
```

Figure 22.6 Result of text split line command.

```
EDIT ---- TSO1234.EXAMPLE.DATA(TEXTEDIT) - 01.03 ------------ COLUMNS 001 072
COMMAND ===>                                             SCROLL ===> CSR
****** ************************* TOP OF DATA ******************************
000001
000002
000003                     TSO Naming Conventions
000004
000005
000006        When data set names are not literally specified (enclosed
000007        in single quotes), TSO will append a prefix in front of
000008        the data set name.  This prefix is usually the
000009        individual's user-id, but can be changed by any TSO user,
000010        by using the TSO PROFILE command.  Based upon the context
000011        in which it is used, TSO can also detect special data set
000012        types and attach an appropriate suffix.  This too will
000013        only occur when the data set name is not literally
000014        specified.  This suffix would become the last data set
''''''        qualifier.
000015        This last qualifier (which precedes the
000016        member name, if any) is also known as the descriptive
000017        qualifier.  Two such descriptive qualifiers that pertain
000018        especially to CLIST execution are .CLIST for CLIST data
000019        sets and .LOAD for load module libraries.  The former is
000020        the basis for the modified explicit execution mode, while
```

Figure 22.7 Data entered in space provided by text split command.

```
EDIT ---- TSO1234.EXAMPLE.DATA(TEXTEDIT) - 01.03 ------------ COLUMNS 001 072
COMMAND ===>                                             SCROLL ===> CSR
****** ************************* TOP OF DATA ******************************
000001
000002
000003                     TSO Naming Conventions
000004
000005
000006        When data set names are not literally specified (enclosed
000007        in single quotes), TSO will append a prefix in front of
000008        the data set name.  This prefix is usually the
000009        individual's user-id, but can be changed by any TSO user,
000010        by using the TSO PROFILE command.  Based upon the context
000011        in which it is used, TSO can also detect special data set
000012        types and attach an appropriate suffix.  This too will
000013        only occur when the data set name is not literally
000014        specified.  This suffix would become the last data set
000015        qualifier.
000016        This last qualifier (which precedes the
000017        member name, if any) is also known as the descriptive
000018        qualifier.  Two such descriptive qualifiers that pertain
000019        especially to CLIST execution are .CLIST for CLIST data
000020        sets and .LOAD for load module libraries.  The former is
000021        the basis for the modified explicit execution mode, while
```

Figure 22.8 End of text split sequence.

```
EDIT ---- TSO1234.EXAMPLE.DATA(TEXTEDIT) - 01.03 ------------ COLUMNS 001 072
COMMAND ===>                                              SCROLL ===> CSR
000003                      TSO Naming Conventions
000004
=COLS> ----+----1----+----2----+----3----+----4----+----5----+----6----+----7
000005
tf65_           When data set names are not literally specified (enclosed
000007          in single quotes), TSO will append a prefix in front of
000008          the data set name.  This prefix is usually the
000009          individual's user-id, but can be changed by any TSO user,
000010          by using the TSO PROFILE command.  Based upon the context
000011          in which it is used, TSO can also detect special data set
000012          types and attach an appropriate suffix.  This too will
000013          only occur when the data set name is not literally
000014          specified.  This suffix would become the last data set
000015          qualifier.
000016          This last qualifier (which precedes the
000017          member name, if any) is also known as the descriptive
000018          qualifier.  Two such descriptive qualifiers that pertain
000019          especially to CLIST execution are .CLIST for CLIST data
000020          sets and .LOAD for load module libraries.  The former is
000021          the basis for the modified explicit execution mode, while
000022          the latter will be discussed later with the resource
000023          controlling aspects of CLISTS.  Finally, if a CLIST
```

Figure 22.9 The text flow line command.

```
EDIT ---- TSO1234.EXAMPLE.DATA(TEXTEDIT) - 01.03 ------------ COLUMNS 001 072
 COMMAND ===>                                             SCROLL ===> CSR
 000003                      TSO Naming Conventions
 000004
=COLS> ----+----1----+----2----+----3----+----4----+----5----+----6----+----7
 000005
 000006          When data set names are not literally specified (enclosed
 000007          in single quotes), TSO will append a prefix in front of
 000008          the data set name.  This prefix is usually the
 000009          individual's user-id, but can be changed by any TSO user,
 000010          by using the TSO PROFILE command.  Based upon the context
 000011          in which it is used, TSO can also detect special data set
 000012          types and attach an appropriate suffix.  This too will
 000013          only occur when the data set name is not literally
 000014          specified.  This suffix would become the last data set
 000015          **qualifier.  This last qualifier (which precedes the member**
 000016          **name, if any) is also known as the descriptive qualifier.**
 000017          **Two such descriptive qualifiers that pertain especially to**
 000018          **CLIST execution are .CLIST for CLIST data sets and .LOAD**
 000019          **for load module libraries.  The former is the basis for**
 000020          **the modified explicit execution mode, while the latter**
 000021          **will be discussed later with the resource controlling**
 000022          **aspects of CLISTS.  Finally, if a CLIST library is**
 000023          **specified but the member name is omitted, TSO will assume**
```

Figure 22.10 Result of the text flow line command.

```
EDIT ---- TSO1234.EXAMPLE.DATA(TEXTEDIT) - 01.03 ------------ COLUMNS 001 072
 COMMAND ===>                                                SCROLL ===> CSR
 00003                        TSO Naming Conventions
 00004
 COLS> ----+----1----+----2----+----3----+----4----+----5----+----6----+----7-
 BNDS> <                                                                      >
 00005
 tf_    When data set names are not literally specified (enclosed
 00007 in single quotes), TSO will append a prefix in front of
 00008 the data set name.  This prefix is usually the
 00009 individual's user-id, but can be changed by any TSO user,
 00010 by using the TSO PROFILE command.  Based upon the context
 00011 in which it is used, TSO can also detect special data set
 00012 types and attach an appropriate suffix.  This too will
 00013 only occur when the data set name is not literally
 00014 specified.  This suffix would become the last data set
 00015 qualifier.  This last qualifier (which precedes the member
 00016 name, if any) is also known as the descriptive qualifier.
 00017 Two such descriptive qualifiers that pertain especially to
 00018 CLIST execution are .CLIST for CLIST data sets and .LOAD
 00019 for load module libraries.  The former is the basis for
 00020 the modified explicit execution mode, while the latter
 00021 will be discussed later with the resource controlling
 00022 aspects of CLISTS.  Finally, if a CLIST library is
```

Figure 22.11 Text flow within bounds.

```
EDIT ---- TSO1234.EXAMPLE.DATA(TEXTEDIT) - 01.03 ------------ COLUMNS 001 072
 COMMAND ===>                                                SCROLL ===> CSR
 00003                        TSO Naming Conventions
 00004
 COLS> ----+----1----+----2----+----3----+----4----+----5----+----6----+----7-
 BNDS> <                                                                      >
 00005
 00006 When data set names are not literally specified (enclosed in single
 00007 quotes), TSO will append a prefix in front of the data set name.  This
 00008 prefix is usually the individual's user-id, but can be changed by any
 00009 TSO user, by using the TSO PROFILE command.  Based upon the context in
 00010 which it is used, TSO can also detect special data set types and attach
 00011 an appropriate suffix.  This too will only occur when the data set name
 00012 is not literally specified.  This suffix would become the last data set
 00013 qualifier.  This last qualifier (which precedes the member name, if
 00014 any) is also known as the descriptive qualifier.  Two such descriptive
 00015 qualifiers that pertain especially to CLIST execution are .CLIST for
 00016 CLIST data sets and .LOAD for load module libraries.  The former is the
 00017 basis for the modified explicit execution mode, while the latter will
 00018 be discussed later with the resource controlling aspects of CLISTS.
 00019 Finally, if a CLIST library is specified but the member name is
 00020 omitted, TSO will assume that a member name of TEMPNAME is to be
 00021 applied.
 00022
```

Figure 22.12 Result of text flow within bounds.

Limited Text Entry

The text entry command was used previously to create a large area for automatic wrap typing. The command made use of the entire subsequent portion of the screen. It can also be used to provide a finite number of lines for text entry. This is accomplished by adding a numeric value to the command. The value represents the number of lines to be formatted for text entry. Figure 22.13 shows the command used to create three text entry lines.

Figure 22.14 shows the result of the text entry line command. Three blank lines have been made available for text entry. As before, the cursor has been placed in the data portion aligned with the start column of the line before it. The vertical bar at the end of the third line marks the end of the text entry area.

In Figure 22.15, data has been entered on all three lines without regard for the end of the line. The cursor has automatically repositioned at the start of the next line, so typing is uninterrupted. When the ENTER key is pressed, the data on the text entry lines is reformatted so that words are no longer split across different lines (Figure 22.16). The text flow command can again be used to reset the paragraph margins.

Uppercase Command

The uppercase line command is used to convert lowercase characters into uppercase characters. The command is designated UC and can be used in the single format, the numeric format, or the block format. When used in the block format, the line command is specified in UCUC pairs and can be completed after scrolling.

```
EDIT ---  TSO1234.EXAMPLE.DATA(TEXTEDIT) - 01.03 ------------ COLUMNS 001 072
COMMAND ===>                                          SCROLL ===> CSR
00003                          TSO Naming Conventions
00004
COLS> ----+----1----+----2----+----3----+----4----+----5----+----6----+----7-
BNDS> <                                                                      >
00005
00006 When data set names are not literally specified (enclosed in single
00007 quotes), TSO will append a prefix in front of the data set name.  This
00008 prefix is usually the individual's user-id, but can be changed by any
00009 TSO user, by using the TSO PROFILE command.  Based upon the context in
00010 which it is used, TSO can also detect special data set types and attach
00011 an appropriate suffix.  This too will only occur when the data set name
00012 is not literally specified.  This suffix would become the last data set
00013 qualifier.  This last qualifier (which precedes the member name, if
00014 any) is also known as the descriptive qualifier.  Two such descriptive
00015 qualifiers that pertain especially to CLIST execution are .CLIST for
00016 CLIST data sets and .LOAD for load module libraries.  The former is the
00017 basis for the modified explicit execution mode, while the latter will
te3_  be discussed later with the resource controlling aspects of CLISTS.
00019 Finally, if a CLIST library is specified but the member name is
00020 omitted, TSO will assume that a member name of TEMPNAME is to be
00021 applied.
00022
```

Figure 22.13 Text entry for three lines.

```
EDIT ---- TSO1234.EXAMPLE.DATA(TEXTEDIT) - 01.03 ---------------- ENTER TEXT
COMMAND ===>                                          SCROLL ===> CSR
00003                        TSO Naming Conventions
00004
COLS> ----+----1----+----2----+----3----+----4----+----5----+----6----+----7-
BNDS> <                                                                      >
00005
00006 When data set names are not literally specified (enclosed in single
00007 quotes), TSO will append a prefix in front of the data set name.  This
00008 prefix is usually the individual's user-id, but can be changed by any
00009 TSO user, by using the TSO PROFILE command.  Based upon the context in
00010 which it is used, TSO can also detect special data set types and attach
00011 an appropriate suffix.  This too will only occur when the data set name
00012 is not literally specified.  This suffix would become the last data set
00013 qualifier.  This last qualifier (which precedes the member name, if
00014 any) is also known as the descriptive qualifier.  Two such descriptive
00015 qualifiers that pertain especially to CLIST execution are .CLIST for
00016 CLIST data sets and .LOAD for load module libraries.  The former is the
00017 basis for the modified explicit execution mode, while the latter will
00018 be discussed later with the resource controlling aspects of CLISTS.
          _

                                                                           |
00019 Finally, if a CLIST library is specified but the member name is
```

Figure 22.14   Three-line text entry area.

```
EDIT ---- TSO1234.EXAMPLE.DATA(TEXTEDIT) - 01.03 ---------------- ENTER TEXT
COMMAND ===>                                          SCROLL ===> CSR
00003                        TSO Naming Conventions
00004
COLS> ----+----1----+----2----+----3----+----4----+----5----+----6----+----7-
BNDS> <                                                                      >
00005
00006 When data set names are not literally specified (enclosed in single
00007 quotes), TSO will append a prefix in front of the data set name.  This
00008 prefix is usually the individual's user-id, but can be changed by any
00009 TSO user, by using the TSO PROFILE command.  Based upon the context in
00010 which it is used, TSO can also detect special data set types and attach
00011 an appropriate suffix.  This too will only occur when the data set name
00012 is not literally specified.  This suffix would become the last data set
00013 qualifier.  This last qualifier (which precedes the member name, if
00014 any) is also known as the descriptive qualifier.  Two such descriptive
00015 qualifiers that pertain especially to CLIST execution are .CLIST for
00016 CLIST data sets and .LOAD for load module libraries.  The former is the
00017 basis for the modified explicit execution mode, while the latter will
00018 be discussed later with the resource controlling aspects of CLISTS.
         Where it is necessary to enter greater amounts of data and especially w
         here it is not necessary to break an existing line, the text entry line
            command should be used._
                                                                           |
00019 Finally, if a CLIST library is specified but the member name is
```

Figure 22.15   Data entered into limited text entry area.

```
EDIT ---- TSO1234.EXAMPLE.DATA(TEXTEDIT) - 01.03 ------------ COLUMNS 001 072
COMMAND ===>                                              SCROLL ===> CSR
00003                         TSO Naming Conventions
00004
COLS> ----+----1----+----2----+----3----+----4----+----5----+----6----+----7-
BNDS> <                                                                      >
00005
00006 When data set names are not literally specified (enclosed in single
00007 quotes), TSO will append a prefix in front of the data set name.  This
00008 prefix is usually the individual's user-id, but can be changed by any
00009 TSO user, by using the TSO PROFILE command.  Based upon the context in
00010 which it is used, TSO can also detect special data set types and attach
00011 an appropriate suffix.  This too will only occur when the data set name
00012 is not literally specified.  This suffix would become the last data set
00013 qualifier.  This last qualifier (which precedes the member name, if
00014 any) is also known as the descriptive qualifier.  Two such descriptive
00015 qualifiers that pertain especially to CLIST execution are .CLIST for
00016 CLIST data sets and .LOAD for load module libraries.  The former is the
00017 basis for the modified explicit execution mode, while the latter will
00018 be discussed later with the resource controlling aspects of CLISTS.
00019 Where it is necessary to enter greater amounts of data and especially
00020 where it is not necessary to break an existing line, the text entry
00021 line command should be used.
00022 Finally, if a CLIST library is specified but the member name is
```

Figure 22.16 Reflow of text entry data.

```
EDIT ---- TSO1234.EXAMPLE.DATA(CLIST) - 01.01 -------------- COLUMNS 001 072
COMMAND ===>                                              SCROLL ===> CSR
****** ************************** TOP OF DATA ****************************
==MSG> -CAUTION- PROFILE CHANGED TO "CAPS OFF" (FROM "CAPS ON") BECAUSE DATA
==MSG>         CONTAINS LOWER CASE CHARACTERS.
000001
000002                         CLIST Execution
000003
000004
000005                       Modes Of CLIST Execution
000006
uc7_   There are four modes of CLIST execution, explicit, modified explicit,
000008 implicit, and modified implicit. CLIST execution is made possible by
000009 the TSO command, EXEC. That command can also be abbreviated as EX.
000010 Because the command is explicitly stated in the first two modes, they
000011 are known as explicit modes. The implicit modes do not contain EX or
000012 EXEC as part of the command syntax. They also differ in their reliance
000013 upon a special file to identify which CLIST code to execute.
000014
000015 CLISTS are invoked at the TSO prompter or an interface to it. For
000016 those who have ISPF installed, this could also be OPTION 6 as well as
000017 most Productivity Development Facility (PDF) panels that have a
000018 command line. When a CLIST (or TSO command for that matter) is entered
000019 from a PDF panel it should be preceded by the word TSO. This is not
```

Figure 22.17 Uppercase line command.

```
EDIT ---- TSO1234.EXAMPLE.DATA(CLIST) - 01.02 -------------- COLUMNS 001 072
COMMAND ===>                                            SCROLL ===> CSR
****** *************************** TOP OF DATA ***************************
==MSG> -CAUTION- PROFILE CHANGED TO "CAPS OFF" (FROM "CAPS ON") BECAUSE DATA
==MSG>          CONTAINS LOWER CASE CHARACTERS.
000001
000002                         CLIST Execution
000003
000004
000005                     Modes Of CLIST Execution
000006
1c7_    THERE ARE FOUR MODES OF CLIST EXECUTION, EXPLICIT, MODIFIED EXPLICIT,
000008  IMPLICIT, AND MODIFIED IMPLICIT. CLIST EXECUTION IS MADE POSSIBLE BY
000009  THE TSO COMMAND, EXEC. THAT COMMAND CAN ALSO BE ABBREVIATED AS EX.
000010  BECAUSE THE COMMAND IS EXPLICITLY STATED IN THE FIRST TWO MODES, THEY
000011  ARE KNOWN AS EXPLICIT MODES. THE IMPLICIT MODES DO NOT CONTAIN EX OR
000012  EXEC AS PART OF THE COMMAND SYNTAX. THEY ALSO DIFFER IN THEIR RELIANCE
000013  UPON A SPECIAL FILE TO IDENTIFY WHICH CLIST CODE TO EXECUTE.
000014
000015  CLISTS are invoked at the TSO prompter or an interface to it. For
000016  those who have ISPF installed, this could also be OPTION 6 as well as
000017  most Productivity Development Facility (PDF) panels that have a
000018  command line. When a CLIST (or TSO command for that matter) is entered
000019  from a PDF panel it should be preceded by the word TSO. This is not
```

Figure 22.18 Result of uppercase command.

```
EDIT ---- TSO1234.EXAMPLE.DATA(CLIST) - 01.02 -------------- COLUMNS 001 072
COMMAND ===>                                            SCROLL ===> CSR
****** *************************** TOP OF DATA ***************************
==MSG> -CAUTION- PROFILE CHANGED TO "CAPS OFF" (FROM "CAPS ON") BECAUSE DATA
==MSG>          CONTAINS LOWER CASE CHARACTERS.
000001
000002                         CLIST Execution
000003
000004
000005                     Modes Of CLIST Execution
000006
000007  there are four modes of clist execution, explicit, modified explicit,
000008  implicit, and modified implicit. clist execution is made possible by
000009  the tso command, exec. that command can also be abbreviated as ex.
000010  because the command is explicitly stated in the first two modes, they
000011  are known as explicit modes. the implicit modes do not contain ex or
000012  exec as part of the command syntax. they also differ in their reliance
000013  upon a special file to identify which clist code to execute.
000014
000015  CLISTS are invoked at the TSO prompter or an interface to it. For
000016  those who have ISPF installed, this could also be OPTION 6 as well as
000017  most Productivity Development Facility (PDF) panels that have a
000018  command line. When a CLIST (or TSO command for that matter) is entered
000019  from a PDF panel it should be preceded by the word TSO. This is not
```

Figure 22.19 Result of lowercase command.

Figure 22.17 shows the numeric form of the uppercase command. It's used to convert seven lines of data (the first paragraph) to uppercase characters. Figure 22.18 shows the result of the uppercase line command. Characters in the paragraph that were a mixture of uppercase and lowercase are now all uppercase. In the same figure, the equivalent lowercase command is used.

Lowercase Command

The LC (lowercase) command uses the same three formats that the UC command does. The result of its use is shown in Figure 22.19. Obviously, the normal capitalization of the original data has been lost by the conversions. The CAPS mode of the edit session should be turned off (CAPS OFF) to retain converted lowercase characters. Neither command (uppercase or lowercase) would, by itself, affect the CAPS setting maintained in the profile.

23

Text Editing Examples

With the ISPF editor, commands are always available to support what must be done. Occasionally, however, commands must be used with other editor commands, a little planning, and a lot of imagination to achieve the desired result. This chapter contains two examples of how text editing commands can be combined into a practical application.

Creating Column Data

In the first example, a string of words is reformatted into three columns across the page. This several-step process is started in Figure 23.1 by issuing the line command TF9 on the fourth line. That command specifies that text is to be flowed through column nine. This is not really enough positions to account for the maximum-size word in the current data, but the intent is merely to create a single column with each line containing a single word.

In Figure 23.2, the text has been reformatted into a single column of data and now extends past the current screen display. By excluding groups of lines, it will be possible to work with all of the data on a single screen and not have to scroll.

The data now includes three blocks of excluded lines (Figure 23.3). Lines were left displayed between excluded blocks to create distinct groups that will ultimately be made into columns. These excluded blocks can be treated as if they were single lines, and this condenses the data into a small area that will be easy to work with. Line commands to shift the data (including two excluded blocks) are issued to start creating additional columns.

In Figure 23.4, the data has been shifted, and the last group of lines is tagged in the same fashion to shift them 20 positions further to the right. All shifting has been completed to create three distinct columns of data (Figure 23.5). One excluded block is then merged with another using the move and overlay line commands.

```
EDIT ---- TSO1234.SAMPLE.DATA - 01.01 ---------------------- COLUMNS 001 072
COMMAND ===>                                                 SCROLL ===> CSR
****** *************************** TOP OF DATA ***************************
000001
000002    The following is a list of foreground linkage editor parameters:
=COLS> ----+----1----+----2----+----3----+----4----+----5----+----6----+----7
000003
tf9_      AC AMODE COBLIB DC DCBS FORTLIB LET LIB LIST LOAD MAP NCAL NE
000005    NONE OL OVLY PLIBASE PLICMIX PLILIB PRINT REFR RENT REUS RMODE
000006    SCTR SIZE TERM TEST XCAL XREF
000007
****** *************************** BOTTOM OF DATA ***************************
```

Figure 23.1 Text flow line command.

```
EDIT ---- TSO1234.SAMPLE.DATA - 01.01 ---------------------- COLUMNS 001 072
COMMAND ===>                                                 SCROLL ===> CSR
****** *************************** TOP OF DATA ***************************
000001
000002    The following is a list of foreground linkage editor parameters:
=COLS> ----+----1----+----2----+----3----+----4----+----5----+----6----+----7
000003
000004        AC
x9            AMODE
000006        COBLIB
000007        DC
000008        DCBS
000009        FORTLIB
000010        LET
000011        LIB
000012        LIST
000013        LOAD
000014        MAP
x9_           NCAL
000016        NE
000017        NONE
000018        OL
000019        OVLY
000020        PLIBASE
```

Figure 23.2 Exclude line commands.

```
EDIT ---- TSO1234.SAMPLE.DATA - 01.01 ---------------------- COLUMNS 001 072
COMMAND ===>                                                 SCROLL ===> CSR
****** ************************** TOP OF DATA ***************************
000001
000002     The following is a list of foreground linkage editor parameters:
=COLS> ----+----1----+----2----+----3----+----4----+----5----+----6----+----7
000003
000004     AC
- - - - - - - - - - - - - - - - - - - - -   9 LINE(S) NOT DISPLAYED
))         MAP
- - - - - - - - - - - - - - - - - - - - -   9 LINE(S) NOT DISPLAYED
000024     REFR
))20_ - - - - - - - - - - - - - - -   9 LINE(S) NOT DISPLAYED
000034
****** ************************** BOTTOM OF DATA **************************
```

Figure 23.3 Column shift line command.

```
EDIT ---- TSO1234.SAMPLE.DATA - 01.01 ---------------------- COLUMNS 001 072
COMMAND ===>                                                 SCROLL ===> CSR
****** ************************** TOP OF DATA ***************************
000001
000002     The following is a list of foreground linkage editor parameters:
=COLS> ----+----1----+----2----+----3----+----4----+----5----+----6----+----7
000003
000004     AC
- - - - - - - - - - - - - - - - - - - - -   9 LINE(S) NOT DISPLAYED
000014                         MAP
- - - - - - - - - - - - - - - - - - - - -   9 LINE(S) NOT DISPLAYED
))                            REFR
))20_ - - - - - - - - - - - - - - -   9 LINE(S) NOT DISPLAYED
000034
****** ************************** BOTTOM OF DATA **************************
```

Figure 23.4 Shifting the last group of lines.

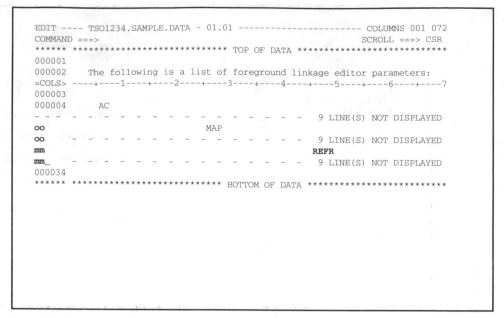

Figure 23.5 Move/overlay line commands.

Figure 23.6 shows two excluded blocks of data merged together. In the same figure, blocks will be combined with the first excluded block using the same line commands. Figure 23.7 shows the result of merging the last two excluded blocks together. In the same figure, the RESET primary command is issued to display all excluded lines. The RESET session shows the result of having shifted and merged the data lines together (Figure 23.8). The primary command RESET has also removed the special column indicator line.

Column Relocation

The next example is also centered around column data. This example attempts to relocate a column of data. Since there's no single command to do this, several editor commands are used in combination with each other. The specific objective of this example is to move the last column of data so that it becomes the second column. There's no one correct way to do this, but the approach taken here will use the following steps:

1. Reduce the data to an easily managed size.

2. Repeat the data.

3. Isolate the data to be relocated in one copy of the data.

4. Make room for the data to be relocated in the other.

5. Overlay the separate pieces of data.

6. Reset the special edit characteristics.

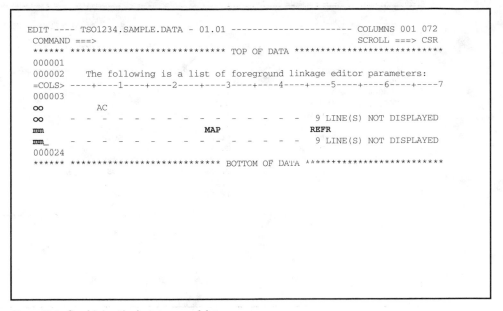

```
EDIT ---- TSO1234.SAMPLE.DATA - 01.01 ---------------------- COLUMNS 001 072
 COMMAND ===>                                            SCROLL ===> CSR
 ****** *************************** TOP OF DATA ***************************
 000001
 000002    The following is a list of foreground linkage editor parameters:
 =COLS> ----+----1----+----2----+----3----+----4----+----5----+----6----+----7
 000003
 oo          AC
 oo     - - - - -  - - - - -  - - - -  9 LINE(S) NOT DISPLAYED
 mm                            MAP              REFR
 mm_    - - - - -  - - - - -  - - - -  9 LINE(S) NOT DISPLAYED
 000024
 ****** *************************** BOTTOM OF DATA ***************************
```

Figure 23.6 Combining the last groups of data.

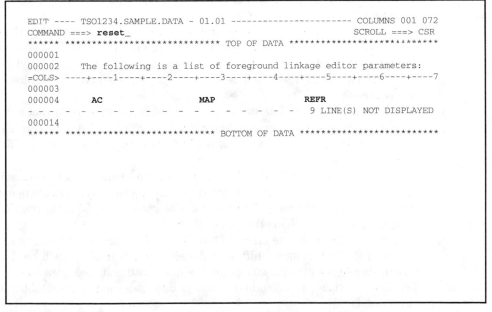

```
 EDIT ---- TSO1234.SAMPLE.DATA - 01.01 ---------------------- COLUMNS 001 072
 COMMAND ===> reset_                                     SCROLL ===> CSR
 ****** *************************** TOP OF DATA ***************************
 000001
 000002    The following is a list of foreground linkage editor parameters:
 =COLS> ----+----1----+----2----+----3----+----4----+----5----+----6----+----7
 000003
 000004    AC                   MAP              REFR
 - - - - -  - - - - -  - - - - -  9 LINE(S) NOT DISPLAYED
 000014
 ****** *************************** BOTTOM OF DATA ***************************
```

Figure 23.7 RESET primary command.

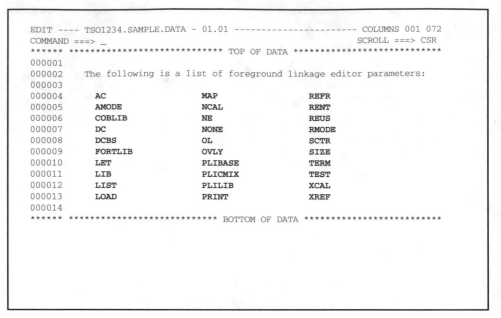

```
EDIT ---- TSO1234.SAMPLE.DATA - 01.01 ---------------------- COLUMNS 001 072
COMMAND ===> _                                            SCROLL ===> CSR
****** *************************** TOP OF DATA ***************************
000001
000002    The following is a list of foreground linkage editor parameters:
000003
000004    AC                  MAP                 REFR
000005    AMODE               NCAL                RENT
000006    COBLIB              NE                  REUS
000007    DC                  NONE                RMODE
000008    DCBS                OL                  SCTR
000009    FORTLIB             OVLY                SIZE
000010    LET                 PLIBASE             TERM
000011    LIB                 PLICMIX             TEST
000012    LIST                PLILIB              XCAL
000013    LOAD                PRINT               XREF
000014
****** *************************** BOTTOM OF DATA ***************************
```

Figure 23.8 Result of formatting COLUMNS.

In Figure 23.9, the exclude line command is used on the fifth line of data. This will reduce the data to fit on a single screen and make it easier to work with. At the same time, the COLS line command is issued to display column indicators.

Figure 23.10 shows the result of the exclude line command. Lines of data have been excluded and can now be treated as a single entity. While only 41 lines are excluded, the concept of treating them as a single entity can work as well for hundreds or thousands of lines. Some data lines were not excluded so they could give visibility to the changes being made and delimit one copy of the data from another as the data is repeated.

In Figure 23.11, the data has been replicated. Even the lines that were excluded are maintained in the repeated block. Labels are placed before and after the first copy of the data to allow commands to be issued against one group of lines without affecting the other.

In Figure 23.12, the CHANGE command is used to blank out the last column in the first group of data lines. The command uses the picture string to change any character in columns 63 through 69 to a blank. The command is further restricted to lines 1 through 46 by specifying the labels .F and .L.

Figure 23.13 shows the effect of the CHANGE command. The same effect can be achieved through column shifting with restricted bounds, as will be demonstrated shortly. While the change was made, the lines with changed data were redisplayed. The line command to exclude 41 lines of data is issued to re-establish two similar blocks of data.

```
EDIT ---- TSO1234.EXAMPLE.MEMBERS -------------------------- COLUMNS 001 072
COMMAND ===>                                                  SCROLL ===> CSR
****** ************************** TOP OF DATA ******************************
cols
000002 ALLOC         01.01 91/12/04 91/12/11 17:04   270   270   0 TSO1906
000003 ALTLIB        01.01 91/12/04 91/12/11 17:10   329   327   0 TSO1234
000004 ATTRIB        01.00 91/12/04 91/12/04 17:48   102   102   0 TSO1234
x99_   BLKSIZE       01.05 91/12/11 91/12/21 23:15    23    18   0 TSO1906
000006 CALL          01.01 91/12/04 91/12/11 17:05    31    31   0 TSO7854
000007 CANCEL        01.00 91/12/04 91/12/04 17:49    20    20   0 TSO1234
000008 CLIST         01.01 91/12/11 91/12/11 17:16   639   655   0 TSO1906
000009 COPY          01.00 91/12/04 91/12/04 17:50    68    68   0 TSO1234
000010 DEFINE        01.00 91/12/04 91/12/04 17:51   545   545   0 TSO1234
000011 DELETE        01.03 91/12/04 91/12/11 17:06   123   123   0 TSO7854
000012 EDIT          01.00 91/12/04 91/12/04 17:52   106   106   0 TSO1234
000013 EXEC          01.00 91/12/04 91/12/04 17:53    48    48   0 TSO1234
000014 FORMAT        01.00 91/12/04 91/12/04 17:54    60    60   0 TSO1234
000015 FREE          01.00 91/12/04 91/12/04 17:44    55    55   0 TSO1234
000016 LINK          01.00 91/12/04 91/12/04 17:55   116   116   0 TSO1234
000017 LIST          01.00 91/12/04 91/12/04 17:56    38    38   0 TSO1234
000018 LISTALC       01.00 91/12/04 91/12/04 17:56    22    22   0 TSO1234
000019 LISTBC        01.00 91/12/04 91/12/04 17:57    27    27   0 TSO1234
000020 LISTCAT       01.00 91/12/04 91/12/04 17:57   104   104   0 TSO1234
000021 LISTDS        01.00 91/12/04 91/12/04 17:58    29    29   0 TSO1234
```

Figure 23.9 Excluding lines of data.

```
EDIT ---- TSO1234.EXAMPLE.MEMBERS -------------------------- COLUMNS 001 072
COMMAND ===>                                                  SCROLL ===> CSR
****** ************************** TOP OF DATA ******************************
bnds   ----+----1----+----2----+----3----+----4----+----5----+----6----+--- 7
rr
000002 ALLOC         01.01 91/12/04 91/12/11 17:04   270   270   0 TSO1906
000003 ALTLIB        01.01 91/12/04 91/12/11 17:10   329   327   0 TSO1234
000004 ATTRIB        01.00 91/12/04 91/12/04 17:48   102   102   0 TSO1234
rr_ -  -  -  -  -  -  -  -  -  -  -  -  -  -  -  -  41 LINE(S) NOT DISPLAYED
****** ************************** BOTTOM OF DATA ***************************
```

Figure 23.10 Replicating the data.

```
EDIT ---- TSO1234.EXAMPLE.MEMBERS ------------------------ COLUMNS 001 072
COMMAND ===>                                             SCROLL ===> CSR
****** ************************** TOP OF DATA ****************************
=BNDS> <
=COLS> ----+----1----+----2----+----3----+----4----+----5----+----6----+----7
.f
000002 ALLOC        01.01 91/12/04 91/12/11 17:04   270   270    0 TSO1906
000003 ALTLIB       01.01 91/12/04 91/12/11 17:10   329   327    0 TSO1234
000004 ATTRIB       01.00 91/12/04 91/12/04 17:48   102   102    0 TSO1234
- - - - - - - - - - - - - - - - - - - 41 LINE(S) NOT DISPLAYED
.1_
000047 ALLOC        01.01 91/12/04 91/12/11 17:04   270   270    0 TSO1906
000048 ALTLIB       01.01 91/12/04 91/12/11 17:10   329   327    0 TSO1234
000049 ATTRIB       01.00 91/12/04 91/12/04 17:48   102   102    0 TSO1234
- - - - - - - - - - - - - - - - - - - 41 LINE(S) NOT DISPLAYED
****** ************************** BOTTOM OF DATA ************************
```

Figure 23.11 Placing labels around the first block of data.

```
EDIT ---- TSO1234.EXAMPLE.MEMBERS ------------------------ COLUMNS 001 072
COMMAND ===> c all p'=' ' ' .f .1 63 69_                   SCROLL ===> CSR
****** ************************** TOP OF DATA ****************************
=BNDS> <
=COLS> ----+----1----+----2----+----3----+----4----+----5----+----6----+----7
.F
000002 ALLOC        01.01 91/12/04 91/12/11 17:04   270   270    0 TSO1906
000003 ALTLIB       01.01 91/12/04 91/12/11 17:10   329   327    0 TSO1234
000004 ATTRIB       01.00 91/12/04 91/12/04 17:48   102   102    0 TSO1234
- - - - - - - - - - - - - - - - - - - 41 LINE(S) NOT DISPLAYED
.L
000047 ALLOC        01.01 91/12/04 91/12/11 17:04   270   270    0 TSO1906
000048 ALTLIB       01.01 91/12/04 91/12/11 17:10   329   327    0 TSO1234
000049 ATTRIB       01.00 91/12/04 91/12/04 17:48   102   102    0 TSO1234
- - - - - - - - - - - - - - - - - - - 41 LINE(S) NOT DISPLAYED
****** ************************** BOTTOM OF DATA ************************
```

Figure 23.12 Removing a column of data.

```
EDIT ---- TSO1234.EXAMPLE.MEMBERS ----------------------- CHARS '=' CHANGED
COMMAND ===>                                              SCROLL ===> CSR
****** ************************** TOP OF DATA ******************************
=BNDS> <
=COLS> ----+----1----+----2----+----3----+----4----+----5----+----6----+----7
==CHG>
==CHG>   ALLOC        01.01 91/12/04 91/12/11 17:04    270    270    0
==CHG>   ALTLIB       01.01 91/12/04 91/12/11 17:10    329    327    0
==CHG>   ATTRIB       01.00 91/12/04 91/12/04 17:48    102    102    0
x41_     BLKSIZE      01.05 91/12/11 91/12/21 23:15     23     18    0
==CHG>   CALL         01.01 91/12/04 91/12/11 17:05     31     31    0
==CHG>   CANCEL       01.00 91/12/04 91/12/04 17:49     20     20    0
==CHG>   CLIST        01.01 91/12/11 91/12/11 17:16    639    655    0
==CHG>   COPY         01.00 91/12/04 91/12/04 17:50     68     68    0
==CHG>   DEFINE       01.00 91/12/04 91/12/04 17:51    545    545    0
==CHG>   DELETE       01.03 91/12/04 91/12/11 17:06    123    123    0
==CHG>   EDIT         01.00 91/12/04 91/12/04 17:52    106    106    0
==CHG>   EXEC         01.00 91/12/04 91/12/04 17:53     48     48    0
==CHG>   FORMAT       01.00 91/12/04 91/12/04 17:54     60     60    0
==CHG>   FREE         01.00 91/12/04 91/12/04 17:44     55     55    0
==CHG>   LINK         01.00 91/12/04 91/12/04 17:55    116    116    0
==CHG>   LIST         01.00 91/12/04 91/12/04 17:56     38     38    0
==CHG>   LISTALC      01.00 91/12/04 91/12/04 17:56     22     22    0
==CHG>   LISTBC       01.00 91/12/04 91/12/04 17:57     27     27    0
```

Figure 23.13 Result of picture string change.

In Figure 23.14, the column shift is used to shift the second block of data 61 columns to the left. This will be used to isolate the last column of data, since all of the data before it will be shifted under the left bound and thereby destroyed.

Now that the column to be moved has been isolated, it can be shifted into the position that it will ultimately occupy. This is done in Figure 23.15 again using the block column shift. It's used to shift the data 13 columns back to the right.

In Figure 23.16, the column shift is used to make room for the isolated column of data. The block of data is shifted 10 columns to the right within newly set bounds. The left bound was set at column 14 so that the first column of data would not be shifted with the rest of the data.

Now that the columns are properly positioned, the two blocks of data can be brought back together. This is done using block move and overlay line commands in Figure 23.17. Maintaining the two blocks of data at a consistent size and appearance helps to ensure that the lines from one block are applied in the proper place in the other block. Also in Figure 23.17, the left bound setting has been erased so that it will return to its default value when the ENTER key is pressed.

The last step is not really required. In Figure 23.18, the RESET command is used to redisplay the data and to remove special lines from the display. This will help show the effect of the changes but is not part of making them permanent. Figure 23.19 shows the final result of the series of commands.

```
EDIT ---- TSO1234.EXAMPLE.MEMBERS -------------------------- COLUMNS 001 072
COMMAND ===>                                              SCROLL ===> CSR
****** ************************** TOP OF DATA ***************************
=BNDS> <
=COLS> ----+----1----+----2----+----3----+----4----+----5----+----6----+----7
==CHG>
==CHG>  ALLOC      01.01 91/12/04 91/12/11 17:04    270    270      0
==CHG>  ALTLIB     01.01 91/12/04 91/12/11 17:10    329    327      0
==CHG>  ATTRIB     01.00 91/12/04 91/12/04 17:48    102    102      0
- - - - - - - - - - - - - - - - - - -  41 LINE(S) NOT DISPLAYED
==CHG>
((      ALLOC      01.01 91/12/04 91/12/11 17:04    270    270      0 TSO1906
000048  ALTLIB     01.01 91/12/04 91/12/11 17:10    329    327      0 TSO1234
000049  ATTRIB     01.00 91/12/04 91/12/04 17:48    102    102      0 TSO1234
((61_ - - - - - - - - - - - - - - -  41 LINE(S) NOT DISPLAYED
****** ************************** BOTTOM OF DATA ************************
```

Figure 23.14 Destructive data shift.

```
EDIT ---- TSO1234.EXAMPLE.MEMBERS -------------------------- COLUMNS 001 072
COMMAND ===>                                              SCROLL ===> CSR
****** ************************** TOP OF DATA ***************************
=BNDS> <
=COLS> ----+----1----+----2----+----3----+----4----+----5 ---+----6----+----7
==CHG>
==CHG>  ALLOC      01.01 91/12/04 91/12/11 17:04    270    270      0
==CHG>  ALTLIB     01.01 91/12/04 91/12/11 17:10    329    327      0
==CHG>  ATTRIB     01.00 91/12/04 91/12/04 17:48    102    102      0
- - - - - - - - - - - - - - - - - - -  41 LINE(S) NOT DISPLAYED
==CHG>
))      TSO1906
000048  TSO1234
000049  TSO1234
))13_ - - - - - - - - - - - - - - -  41 LINE(S) NOT DISPLAYED
****** ************************** BOTTOM OF DATA ************************
```

Figure 23.15 Positioning column data.

```
EDIT ---- TSO1234.EXAMPLE.MEMBERS -------------------------- COLUMNS 001 072
COMMAND ===>                                                SCROLL ===> CSR
****** ************************* TOP OF DATA ****************************
=BNDS>                    <
=COLS> ----+----1----+----2----+----3----+----4----+----5----+----6----+----7
==CHG>
))     ALLOC       01.01 91/12/04 91/12/11 17:04    270    270     0
==CHG> ALTLIB      01.01 91/12/04 91/12/11 17:10    329    327     0
==CHG> ATTRIB      01.00 91/12/04 91/12/04 17:48    102    102     0
))10_  - - - - - - - - - - - - - - - - - - 41 LINE(S) NOT DISPLAYED
=-CHG>
000047             TSO1234
000048             TSO1234
000049             TSO1234
- - - - - - - - - - - - - - - - - - - - 41 LINE(S) NOT DISPLAYED
****** ************************* BOTTOM OF DATA *************************
```

Figure 23.16 Shifting column data.

```
EDIT ---- TSO1234.EXAMPLE.MEMBERS -------------------------- COLUMNS 001 072
COMMAND ===>                                                SCROLL ===> CSR
****** ************************* TOP OF DATA ****************************
=BNDS>
=COLS> ----+----1----+----2----+----3----+----4----+----5----+----6----+----7
oo_
000002 ALLOC                01.01 91/12/04 91/12/11 17:04    270    270     0
==CHG> ALTLIB               01.01 91/12/04 91/12/11 17:10    329    327     0
==CHG> ATTRIB               01.00 91/12/04 91/12/04 17:48    102    102     0
oo     - - - - - - - - - - - - - - - - - - 41 LINE(S) NOT DISPLAYED
mm
000047             TSO1906
000048             TSO1234
000049             TSO1234
mm     - - - - - - - - - - - - - - - - - - 41 LINE(S) NOT DISPLAYED
****** ************************* BOTTOM OF DATA *************************
```

Figure 23.17 Merging blocks of data.

```
EDIT ---- TSO1234.EXAMPLE.MEMBERS ------------------------- COLUMNS 001 072
COMMAND ===> res_                                    SCROLL ===> CSR
****** ************************** TOP OF DATA ****************************
=BNDS> <
=COLS> ----+----1----+----2----+----3----+----4----+----5----+----6----+----7
.F
000002  ALLOC      TSO1906   01.01 91/12/04 91/12/11 17:04    270    270     0
==CHG>  ALTLIB     TSO1234   01.01 91/12/04 91/12/11 17:10    329    327     0
==CHG>  ATTRIB     TSO1234   01.00 91/12/04 91/12/04 17:48    102    102     0
- -- - -  -  -  -   -  -  -  -  -  -  -  -  - - 41 LINE(S) NOT DISPLAYED
****** ************************** BOTTOM OF DATA ***************************
```

Figure 23.18 Resetting the edit session.

```
EDIT ---- TSO1234.EXAMPLE.MEMBERS ------------------------- COLUMNS 001 072
COMMAND ===> _                                       SCROLL ===> CSR
****** ************************** TOP OF DATA ****************************
.F
000002  ALLOC      TSO1906   01.01 91/12/04 91/12/11 17:04    270    270     0
000003  ALTLIB     TSO1234   01.01 91/12/04 91/12/11 17:10    329    327     0
000004  ATTRIB     TSO1234   01.00 91/12/04 91/12/04 17:48    102    102     0
000005  BLKSIZE    TSO1906   01.05 91/12/11 91/12/21 23:15     23     18     0
000006  CALL       TSO7854   01.01 91/12/04 91/12/11 17:05     31     31     0
000007  CANCEL     TSO1234   01.00 91/12/04 91/12/04 17:49     20     20     0
000008  CLIST      TSO1906   01.01 91/12/11 91/12/11 17:16    639    655     0
000009  COPY       TSO1234   01.00 91/12/04 91/12/04 17:50     68     68     0
000010  DEFINE     TSO1234   01.00 91/12/04 91/12/04 17:51    545    545     0
000011  DELETE     TSO7854   01.03 91/12/04 91/12/11 17:06    123    123     0
000012  EDIT       TSO1234   01.00 91/12/04 91/12/04 17:52    106    106     0
000013  EXEC       TSO1234   01.00 91/12/04 91/12/04 17:53     48     48     0
000014  FORMAT     TSO1234   01.00 91/12/04 91/12/04 17:54     60     60     0
000015  FREE       TSO1234   01.00 91/12/04 91/12/04 17:44     55     55     0
000016  LINK       TSO1234   01.00 91/12/04 91/12/04 17:55    116    116     0
000017  LIST       TSO1234   01.00 91/12/04 91/12/04 17:56     38     38     0
000018  LISTALC    TSO1234   01.00 91/12/04 91/12/04 17:56     22     22     0
000019  LISTBC     TSO1234   01.00 91/12/04 91/12/04 17:57     27     27     0
000020  LISTCAT    TSO1234   01.00 91/12/04 91/12/04 17:57    104    104     0
000021  LISTDS     TSO1234   01.00 91/12/04 91/12/04 17:58     29     29     0
```

Figure 23.19 Result of column relocation.

24

Tabbing Techniques

Default Tabs

The editor tab functions are designed to facilitate cursor placement for data entry. Two tabbing features that are inherent in the edit function are always available. The first tabbing feature places an attribute byte between the line command area and the data portion of the edit session. That attribute byte serves as a permanent tab stop and is the reason data can't be entered in that position. (Trying to enter data in that position will lock the terminal.) This feature facilitates movement of the cursor from the line command area into the data area. Forward and backward tab keys will alternately position the cursor at the first data column and the first column of the line command area. When necessary, movement to the next line or previous line will occur automatically to locate the next tab.

Another form of tabbing is automatically performed every time the ENTER key is pressed. When the cursor is in the data area, it's moved to the next line and positioned under the first character of the preceding line. If the preceding line is blank, the first character of the following line is instead used to determine where the cursor should be placed.

Explicitly Defined Tabs

There are three distinctly different types of user-defined tabs in an edit session. The tabbing methods are known as *hardware tabs*, *software tabs,* and *logical tabs*. Hardware and logical tabs have both a line command component and a primary command component. The TABS line command is used to establish the tab type and position, while the TABS primary command is used to turn those tab positions on and off. Both the primary command and the line command can be specified as TAB as well as TABS. The TABS primary command must also be used to incorporate changed hardware and logical tab settings (even when tabs are already turned on).

The tab display line (created by the TABS line command) can be deleted using the delete line command. Or, the tab display line can be removed from the display using the RESET primary command. Tabs might very well be active, however, even when the special line is not displayed, since the line need not be displayed when tabs are used.

Hardware Tabs

Hardware tabs are implemented by placing an attribute byte in front of where the cursor is to stop. Each attribute byte is defined on the tab display line using an asterisk. In Figure 24.1, the TABS line command is executed to cause the tabs line to be displayed.

After the tabs line is displayed (Figure 24.2) it's possible to define where the hardware tabs will be placed. Previous tabs, if any, can be retained or erased. Tabs should be placed just before the first data position. For example, if data is to be typed in column four, the tab should be placed in column three. Tabs can be defined beyond the currently visible screen after scrolling to the right. Those tabs, however, will only be accessible while scrolled to the right. There's no automatic scrolling function to access tabs that are not within the current logical screen.

The primary command TABS ON STD is used to turn the tabs on. The parameters ON and STD are optional, since they're defaults. TABS as a primary command must be used to incorporate any changes to the tab display line even when tabs are already turned on. It's possible to have more than one tab display line (including that

```
EDIT ---- TSO1234.EXAMPLE.DATA(BLKSIZE) - 01.00 ------------- COLUMNS 001 072
COMMAND ===>                                                  SCROLL ===> CSR
****** ************************** TOP OF DATA ****************************
000001
000002                       Block Size Chart
000003
000004         3380              Device              3390
000005                         Blocks Per
000006   Min.      Max.          Track        Min.      Max.
000007
tabs_
000009
000010
000011
000012
000013
000014
****** ************************ BOTTOM OF DATA **************************
```

Figure 24.1 TABS line command.

```
EDIT ---- TSO1234.EXAMPLE.DATA(BLKSIZE) - 01.00 ------------- COLUMNS 001 072
COMMAND ===> tabs on_                                       SCROLL ===> CSR
****** ************************* TOP OF DATA *****************************
000001
000002                      Block Size Chart
000003
000004          3380                Device              3390
000005                           Blocks Per
000006    Min.      Max.           Track        Min.      Max.
000007
=TABS>    *         *                *          *         *
000008
000009
000010
000011
000012
000013
000014
****** ************************* BOTTOM OF DATA ***************************
```

Figure 24.2 TABS primary command.

contained in a profile display). When any one tab display line is updated, all others are also automatically updated.

Hardware tabs are efficient to use. They are, as their name implies, implemented as a hardware function through the terminal control unit. Because it's not necessary to interact with the computer itself, hardware tabs are not prone to most response-time problems. Figure 24.3 shows the sequence of cursor positions each time the forward tab key is pressed from the current cursor position on line eight. Using the backward tab key, the cursor still positions to the right of the attribute byte, but the direction of cursor movement is exactly opposite.

Figure 24.4 shows how a value can be entered and the cursor positioned at the next data entry point by pressing the forward tab key once. After entering the next value, the cursor can again be advanced using the forward tab key (Figure 24.5). The process can be repeated before entering new data or to get to existing data.

The effect of using standard hardware tabs is different when tabbing through lines that already contain data. This is because attribute bytes are not placed in a given line at positions that contain data. Since existing data might keep many attribute bytes from being placed, tabbing through that data might appear to have erratic results.

The ALL Parameter

The ALL parameter can be used in place of STD to create uniform tabs on all data lines (Figure 24.6). This forces all tabs to be available. When tabs are turned on with the ALL parameter, it will make data in the same column disappear from the display

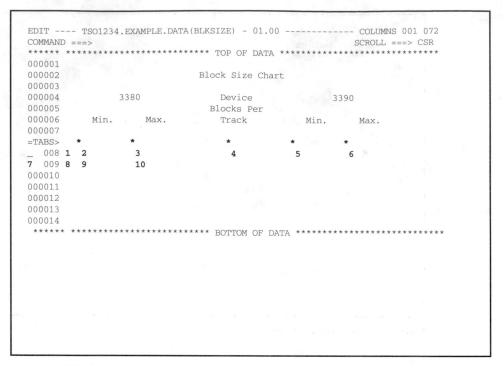

```
EDIT ---- TSO1234.EXAMPLE.DATA(BLKSIZE) - 01.00 ------------- COLUMNS 001 072
COMMAND ===>                                              SCROLL ===> CSR
***** ************************** TOP OF DATA *****************************
000001
000002                        Block Size Chart
000003
000004        3380                 Device                 3390
000005                         Blocks Per
000006     Min.      Max.          Track         Min.      Max.
000007
=TABS>      *         *             *            *         *
_   008 1  2        3              4            5         6
7   009 8  9       10
000010
000011
000012
000013
000014
****** ************************** BOTTOM OF DATA ***************************
```

Figure 24.3 Tab stop sequence.

```
EDIT ---- TSO1234.EXAMPLE.DATA(BLKSIZE) - 01.00 ------------- COLUMNS 001 072
COMMAND ===>                                              SCROLL ===> CSR
***** ************************** TOP OF DATA *****************************
000001
000002                        Block Size Chart
000003
000004        3380                 Device                 3390
000005                         Blocks Per
000006     Min.      Max.          Track         Min.      Max.
000007
=TABS>      *         *             *            *         *
000008    23477      _
000009
000010
000011
000012
000013
000014
****** ************************** BOTTOM OF DATA ***************************
```

Figure 24.4 Result of forward tab.

```
EDIT ---- TSO1234.EXAMPLE.DATA(BLKSIZE) - 01.00 ------------- COLUMNS 001 072
COMMAND ===>                                                 SCROLL ===> CSR
****** ************************** TOP OF DATA ****************************
000001
000002                         Block Size Chart
000003
000004        3380              Device          . 3390
000005                        Blocks Per
000006    Min.       Max.        Track          Min.       Max.
000007
=TABS>    *          *                *          *          *
000008   23477      47476            _
000009
000010
000011
000012
000013
000014
****** ************************** BOTTOM OF DATA ****************************
```

Figure 24.5 Result of a second forward tab.

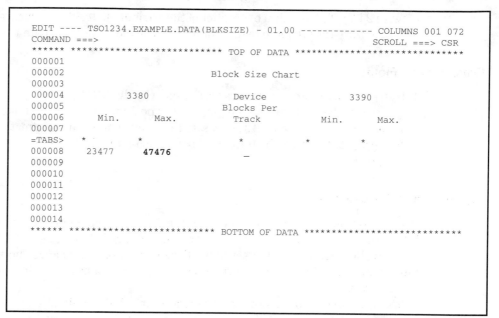

```
EDIT ---- TSO1234.CLIST(MODEL) ----------------------------- COLUMNS 001 072
COMMAND ===> tabs on all_                                    SCROLL ===> CSR
****** ************************** TOP OF DATA ****************************
000001   ISPEXEC LIBDEF LIB-TYPE DATASET |LIBRARY |EXCLDATA |EXCLLIBR      +
000002                           TD(DATASET-LIST) |ID(LIBNAME)             +
000003                           COND |UNCOND                              +
=TABS>        *          * *      *    *      *       *      *       *
000004
000005      LIB-TYPE     - TYPE OF ISPF DDNAME APPLICATION-LEVEL LIBRARY
000006                     DEFINITION, ISPPLIB, ISPMLIB, ETC.
000007      CHOOSE ONE:
000008       DATASET     - INDICATES THAT THE ID SPECIFIES A LIST OF CATALOGE
000009                     DATA SET NAMES
000010       LIBRARY     - INDICATES THAT THE ID SPECIFIES A LIBRARY NAME
000011                     (DDNAME)
000012       EXCLDATA    - INDICATES THAT THE ID SPECIFIES A LIST OF CATALOGE
000013                     DATA SET NAMES, CAN ONLY BE USED WITH ISPLLIB
000014       EXCLLIBR    - INDICATES THAT THE ID SPECIFIES A LIBRARY NAME
000015                     (DDNAME)
000016      DATASET-LIST - INDICATES A LIST OF DATASETS TO BE SEARCHED FOR TH
000017                     APPLICATION. USED WITH DATASET OR EXCLDATA. IF NOT
000018                     SPECIFIED, THEN THE EXISTING LIBDEF IS REMOVED.
000019      LIBNAME      - SPECIFIES THE NAME OF A DD STATEMENT THAT DEFINE
000020                     THE APPLICATION LIBRARY(S). USED WITH LIBRARY OR
```

Figure 24.6 TABS command with ALL parameter.

(Figure 24.7). This is only a byproduct of the attribute bytes themselves, and no data is lost, nor are the attribute bytes stored with the data when the data is saved.

Erasing Data Fields

Tab attribute bytes create barriers with respect to the ERASE EOF key. The effect is to erase only the data from the current cursor position up to the next attribute byte. This can be beneficial when it's necessary to remove part of the information on a line. If necessary, the tabs can be turned off before using the ERASE EOF key to broaden its scope.

Typing over Tab Positions

It's not normally possible to enter data in a column occupied by an attribute byte. When that's necessary, the primary command TABS OFF can be used. That command will deactivate the tab settings. It's not necessary to change the tabs on the tabs display line. Tabs can be turned back on after data has been entered over the tab positions.

It's also possible to temporarily deactivate tabs. This would also allow data to be entered in a tab column. This can be accomplished, as in Figure 24.8, by erasing the line command area of a particular line and pressing the ENTER key.

Turning tabs off on a line will redisplay data on that line, as on line eight of Figure 24.9. Data can then be typed over any tab position on that line. When the ENTER key is pressed again, the attribute bytes will return and mask any data in the same column.

```
 EDIT ---- TSO1234.CLIST(MODEL) ----------------------------- COLUMNS 001 072
 COMMAND ===> _                                               SCROLL ===> CSR
 ****** ************************** TOP OF DATA ****************************
 000001    IS EXEC LIBDEF  I -TYP  D TASE | LIBRA Y|EXC DATA|E CLLIBR      +
 000002                            I (DAT SET-LI T)|ID LIBNAM )            +
 000003                            C ND| U COND                           +
 =TABS>       *              * *    * *     *       *       *        *
 000004
 000005    LIB-TYPE      - TYPE OF ISPF DDNAME APPLI ATION- EVEL LIBRARY
 000006                    DEFI IT ON,  SPPLIB  ISPM IB, ET .
 000007    CHOOSE ONE:
 000008      DATASET     - INDI AT S TH T THE  D SPE IFIES   LIST OF CATALOGE
 000009                    DATA SE  NAM S
 000010      LIBRARY     - INDI AT S TH T THE  D SPE IFIES    LIBRARY NAME
 000011                    (DDN ME
 000012      EXCLDATA    - INDI AT S TH T THE  D SPE IFIES   LIST OF CATALOGE
 000013                    DATA SE  NAM S, CAN ONLY  E USED WITH ISPLLIB
 000014      EXCLLIBR    - INDI AT S TH T THE  D SPE IFIES    LIBRARY NAME
 000015                    (DDN ME
 000016    DATASET-LIST - INDI AT S A  IST OF DATAS TS TO  E SEARCHED FOR TH
 000017                    APPL CA ION. USED W TH DA ASET O  EXCLDATA. IF NOT
 000018                    SPEC FI D, T EN THE EXIST NG LIB EF IS REMOVED.
 000019    LIBNAME      - SPEC FI S TH  NAME  F A D  STATE ENT THAT DEFINE
 000020                    THE  PP ICAT ON LIB ARY(S . USED WITH LIBRARY OR
```

Figure 24.7 Data masked by tabs.

```
EDIT ---- TSO1234.CLIST(MODEL) ---------------------------- COLUMNS 001 072
COMMAND ===>                                                SCROLL ===> CSR
****** *************************** TOP OF DATA ***************************
000001     IS EXEC LIBDEF  I -TYP  D TASE| LIBRA Y| EXC DATA| E CLLIBR      +
000002                     I (DAT SET-LI T)|ID LIBNAM )                     +
000003                     C ND|U COND                                      +
=TABS>         *               * *    * *    *       *       *       *
000004
000005     LIB-TYPE      - TYPE OF ISPF DDNAME APPLI ATION- EVEL LIBRARY
000006                    DEFI IT ON,  SPPLIB  ISPM IB, ET .
000007     CHOOSE ONE:
_            DATASET    - INDI AT S TH T THE  D SPE IFIES   LIST OF CATALOGE
000009                    DATA SE  NAM S
000010       LIBRARY    - INDI AT S TH T THE  D SPE IFIES   LIBRARY NAME
000011                    (DDN ME
000012       EXCLDATA   - INDI AT S TH T THE  D SPE IFIES   LIST OF CATALOGE
000013                    DATA SE  NAM S, CAN ONLY  E USED WITH ISPLLIB
000014       EXCLLIBR   - INDI AT S TH T THE  D SPE IFIES   LIBRARY NAME
000015                    (DDN ME
000016     DATASET-LIST - INDI AT S A  IST OF DATAS TS TO  E SEARCHED FOR TH
000017                    APPL CA ION. USED W TH DA ASET O  EXCLDATA. IF NOT
000018                    SPEC FI D, T EN THE EXIST NG LIB EF IS REMOVED.
000019     LIBNAME      - SPEC FI S TH  NAME  F A D  STATE ENT THAT DEFINE
000020                    THE  PP ICAT ON LIB ARY(S . USED WITH LIBRARY OR
```

Figure 24.8 Deactivating tabs, method one.

```
EDIT ---- TSO1234.CLIST(MODEL) ---------------------------- COLUMNS 001 072
COMMAND ===>                                                SCROLL ===> CSR
****** *************************** TOP OF DATA ***************************
000001     IS EXEC LIBDEF  I -TYP  D TASE | LIBRA Y| EXC DATA| E CLLIBR     +
000002                     I (DAT SET-LI T)|ID LIBNAM )                     +
000003                     C ND|U COND                                      +
=TABS>         *               * *    * *    *       *       *       *
000004
000005     LIB-TYPE      - TYPE OF ISPF DDNAME APPLI ATION- EVEL LIBRARY
000006                    DEFI IT ON,  SPPLIB  ISPM IB, ET .
000007     CHOOSE ONE:
000008       DATASET    - INDI**CATE**S TH**AT** THE **ID** SPE**C**IFIES **A** LIST OF CATALOGE
000009                    DATA SE  NAM S
000010       LIBRARY    - INDI AT S TH T THE  D SPE IFIES   LIBRARY NAME
000011                    (DDN ME
000012       EXCLDATA   - INDI AT S TH T THE  D SPE IFIES   LIST OF CATALOGE
000013                    DATA SE  NAM S, CAN ONLY  E USED WITH ISPLLIB
000014       EXCLLIBR   - INDI AT S TH T THE  D SPE IFIES   LIBRARY NAME
000015                    (DDN ME
000016     DATASET-LIST - INDI AT S A  IST OF DATAS TS TO  E SEARCHED FOR TH
000017                    APPL CA ION. USED W TH DA ASET O  EXCLDATA. IF NOT
000018                    SPEC FI D, T EN THE EXIST NG LIB EF IS REMOVED.
000019     LIBNAME      - SPEC FI S TH  NAME  F A D  STATE ENT THAT DEFINE
000020                    THE  PP ICAT ON LIB ARY(S . USED WITH LIBRARY OR
```

Figure 24.9 Tabs deactivated on line eight.

The tabs on any line can also be deactivated by placing the cursor in a tab column and pressing the ENTER key (Figure 24.10). The tabs on that line will then be deactivated until the ENTER key is again pressed. Figure 24.11 shows tabs temporarily deactivated on line 12. Data in tab columns is revealed while the tabs are turned off.

Turning tabs off need not involve the tab line display. The tab indicators can be left there for future use. The TABS primary command can be used as in Figure 24.12 to turn the tabs off. When the tabs are turned off, data is redisplayed in the tab columns (Figure 24.13). The data in these columns will be saved whether the tabs are turned on or off.

Creating Entry Fields

The fact that data can't normally be typed in the same column as an attribute byte can be used to good advantage. In Figure 24.14, tab characters are added to include positions between the data columns.

When the last digit's entered in the first column of data, the cursor automatically jumps to the start of the next column of data (Figure 24.15). It does this because of the continuous string of attribute bytes between the two data columns.

After the second column of data is entered, the cursor jumps to the third data column (Figure 24.16). This method of defining tabs provides an automatic tabbing effect, and it prohibits the entry of data outside of the intended columns.

```
EDIT ---- TSO1234.CLIST(MODEL) ----------------------------- COLUMNS 001 072
COMMAND ===>                                                 SCROLL ===> CSR
****** ************************** TOP OF DATA ******************************
000001    IS EXEC LIBDEF  I -TYP  D TASE LIBRA|Y|EXC DATA|E CLLIBR      +
000002                            I (DAT SET-LI T)|ID LIBNAM )          +
000003                            C ND|U COND                           +
=TABS>     *              * *    *  *     *        *       *       *
000004
000005    LIB-TYPE       - TYPE OF ISPF DDNAME APPLI ATION- EVEL LIBRARY
000006                     DEFI IT ON,  SPPLIB  ISPM IB, ET .
000007    CHOOSE ONE:
000008     DATASET       - INDI AT S TH T THE  D SPE IFIES   LIST OF CATALOGE
000009                     DATA SE  NAM S
000010     LIBRARY       - INDI AT S TH T THE  D SPE IFIES   LIBRARY NAME
000011                     (DDN ME
000012    _ EXCLDATA     - INDI AT S TH T THE  D SPE IFIES   LIST OF CATALOGE
000013                     DATA SE  NAM S, CAN ONLY  E USED WITH ISPLLIB
000014     EXCLLIBR      - INDI AT S TH T THE  D SPE IFIES   LIBRARY NAME
000015                     (DDN ME
000016    DATASET-LIST - INDI AT S A  IST OF DATAS TS TO  E SEARCHED FOR TH
000017                     APPL CA ION. USED W TH DA ASET O  EXCLDATA. IF NOT
000018                     SPEC F  D, T EN THE EXIST NG LIB EF IS REMOVED.
000019    LIBNAME       - SPEC FI S TH  NAME  F A D  STATE ENT THAT DEFINE
000020                     THE  PP ICAT ON LIB ARY(S . USED WITH LIBRARY OR
```

Figure 24.10 Deactivating tabs, method two.

```
EDIT ---- TSO1234.CLIST(MODEL) ----------------------------- COLUMNS 001 072
COMMAND ===>                                            SCROLL ===> CSR
****** ************************* TOP OF DATA ***************************
000001    IS EXEC LIBDEF  I -TYP  D TASE  LIBRA|Y|EXC DATA|E CLLIBR    +
000002                        I (DAT SET-LI T)|ID LIBNAM )           +
000003                        C ND|U COND                           +
=TABS>       *            * *    *   *    *       *       *       *
000004
000005       LIB-TYPE      - TYPE OF ISPF DDNAME APPLI ATION- EVEL LIBRARY
000006                       DEFI IT ON,  SPPLIB  ISPM IB, ET .
000007       CHOOSE ONE:
000008         DATASET     - INDI AT S TH T THE  D SPE IFIES   LIST OF CATALOG
000009                       DATA SE  NAM S
000010         LIBRARY     - INDI AT S TH T THE  D SPE IFIES   LIBRARY NAME
000011                       (DDN ME
000012    _    EXCLDATA    - INDICATES THAT THE ID SPECIFIES A LIST OF CATALOG
000013                       DATA SE  NAM S, CAN ONLY  E USED WITH ISPLLIB
000014         EXCLLIBR    - INDI AT S TH T THE  D SPE IFIES   LIBRARY NAME
000015                       (DDN ME
000016       DATASET-LIST - INDI AT S A  IST OF DATAS TS TO  E SEARCHED FOR TH
000017                       APPL CA ION. USED W TH DA ASET O  EXCLDATA. IF NOT
000018                       SPEC FI D, T EN THE EXIST NG LIB EF IS REMOVED.
000019       LIBNAME       - SPEC FI S TH  NAME  F A D  STATE ENT THAT DEFINE
000020                       THE  PP ICAT ON LIB ARY(S . USED WITH LIBRARY OR
```

Figure 24.11 Tabs deactivated on line 12.

```
EDIT ---- TSO1234.CLIST(MODEL) ----------------------------- COLUMNS 001 072
COMMAND ===> tabs off_                                  SCROLL ===> CSR
****** ************************* TOP OF DATA ***************************
000001    IS EXEC LIBDEF  I -TYP  D TASE | LIBRA Y|EXC DATA|E CLLIBR    +
000002                        I (DAT SET-LI T)|ID LIBNAM )           +
000003                        C ND|U COND                           +
=TABS>       *            * *    *   *    *       *       *       *
000004
000005       LIB-TYPE      - TYPE OF ISPF DDNAME APPLI ATION- EVEL LIBRARY
000006                       DEFI IT ON,  SPPLIB  ISPM IB, ET .
000007       CHOOSE ONE:
000008         DATASET     - INDI AT S TH T THE  D SPE IFIES   LIST OF CATALOG
000009                       DATA SE  NAM S
000010         LIBRARY     - INDI AT S TH T THE  D SPE IFIES   LIBRARY NAME
000011                       (DDN ME
000012         EXCLDATA    - INDICATES THAT THE ID SPECIFIES A LIST OF CATALOG
000013                       DATA SE  NAM S, CAN ONLY  E USED WITH ISPLLIB
000014         EXCLLIBR    - INDI AT S TH T THE  D SPE IFIES   LIBRARY NAME
000015                       (DDN ME
000016       DATASET-LIST - INDI AT S A  IST OF DATAS TS TO  E SEARCHED FOR TH
000017                       APPL CA ION. USED W TH DA ASET O  EXCLDATA. IF NOT
000018                       SPEC FI D, T EN THE EXIST NG LIB EF IS REMOVED.
000019       LIBNAME       - SPEC FI S TH  NAME  F A D  STATE ENT THAT DEFINE
000020                       THE  PP ICAT ON LIB ARY(S . USED WITH LIBRARY OR
```

Figure 24.12 TABS OFF command.

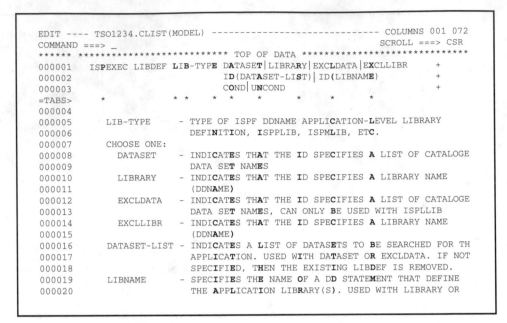

```
EDIT ---- TSO1234.CLIST(MODEL) ------------------------------- COLUMNS 001 072
COMMAND ===> _                                            SCROLL ===> CSR
****** ************************** TOP OF DATA ******************************
000001    ISPEXEC LIBDEF LIB-TYPE DATASET|LIBRARY|EXCLDATA|EXCLLIBR      +
000002                            ID(DATASET-LIST)| ID(LIBNAME)          +
000003                            COND| UNCOND                           +
=TABS>         *           * *    *    *    *       *       *       *
000004
000005         LIB-TYPE     - TYPE OF ISPF DDNAME APPLICATION-LEVEL LIBRARY
000006                        DEFINITION, ISPPLIB, ISPMLIB, ETC.
000007         CHOOSE ONE:
000008          DATASET     - INDICATES THAT THE ID SPECIFIES A LIST OF CATALOGE
000009                        DATA SET NAMES
000010          LIBRARY     - INDICATES THAT THE ID SPECIFIES A LIBRARY NAME
000011                        (DDNAME)
000012          EXCLDATA    - INDICATES THAT THE ID SPECIFIES A LIST OF CATALOGE
000013                        DATA SET NAMES, CAN ONLY BE USED WITH ISPLLIB
000014          EXCLLIBR    - INDICATES THAT THE ID SPECIFIES A LIBRARY NAME
000015                        (DDNAME)
000016         DATASET-LIST - INDICATES A LIST OF DATASETS TO BE SEARCHED FOR TH
000017                        APPLICATION. USED WITH DATASET OR EXCLDATA. IF NOT
000018                        SPECIFIED, THEN THE EXISTING LIBDEF IS REMOVED.
000019          LIBNAME     - SPECIFIES THE NAME OF A DD STATEMENT THAT DEFINE
000020                        THE APPLICATION LIBRARY(S). USED WITH LIBRARY OR
```

Figure 24.13 Result of TABS OFF command.

```
EDIT ---- TSO1234.EXAMPLE.DATA(BLKSIZE) - 01.00 ------------- COLUMNS 001 072
COMMAND ===> tabs on_                                     SCROLL ===> CSR
****** ************************** TOP OF DATA ******************************
000001
000002                        Block Size Chart
000003
000004          3380              Device              3390
000005                        Blocks Per
000006      Min.      Max.         Track         Min.      Max.
000007
=TABS> ***       *****    ************* ***********    *****     ***********
000008 23477    47476              1         27999    56664
000009
000010
000011
000012
000013
000014
****** ************************** BOTTOM OF DATA ***************************
```

Figure 24.14 Creating limited entry fields.

```
EDIT ---- TSO1234.EXAMPLE.DATA(BLKSIZE) - 01.00 ------------- COLUMNS 001 072
COMMAND ===>                                           SCROLL ===> CSR
****** ************************** TOP OF DATA ****************************
000001
000002                      Block Size Chart
000003
000004           3380              Device              3390
000005                           Blocks Per
000006      Min.      Max.         Track        Min.      Max.
000007
=TABS> ***      *****     ************* *******^^***     *****    ***********
000008   23477    47476             1          27999    56664
000009   15477       _
000010
000011
000012
000013
000014
****** ************************** BOTTOM OF DATA *************************
```

Figure 24.15 Automatic skip to next field.

```
EDIT ---- TSO1234.EXAMPLE.DATA(BLKSIZE) - 01.00 ------------- COLUMNS 001 072
COMMAND ===>                                           SCROLL ===> CSR
****** ************************** TOP OF DATA ****************************
000001
000002                      Block Size Chart
000003
000004           3380              Device              3390
000005                           Blocks Per
000006      Min.      Max.         Track        Min.      Max.
000007
=TABS> ***      *****     ************* ***********     *****    ***********
000008   23477    47476             1          27999    56664
000009   15477    23476             _
000010
000011
000012
000013
000014
****** ************************** BOTTOM OF DATA *************************
```

Figure 24.16 Skip to next field.

Logical Tabs

Logical tabs are a variation of hardware tabs. Tab positions are still defined using asterisks on the tabs display line, and the tabs are still turned on with the TABS primary command. One difference, however, is that the TABS primary command includes a tab character. The tab character should be a special character that will not be used as part of the data being entered. In Figure 24.17, the TABS command is issued with a dollar sign as the tab character.

The major difference between logical tabs and hardware tabs is the way in which data is entered. Rather than tab to each column position, data is entered in a continuous format. The tab character is placed before any piece of data that's to be positioned after a tab. In Figure 24.18, three lines of data have been entered. Each column of data has been preceded by the established tab character $.

When the ENTER key is pressed, each tab character locates and aligns with the next attribute byte. The data after the tab character, therefore, aligns behind the attribute byte (Figure 24.19). When any given line includes more tab characters than are defined, the extra tabs characters will be applied to the attribute bytes on subsequent lines. The data in Figure 24.20 includes two tab characters together to account for the permanent tab stop positioned before data column number one and the first user-defined tab. After the ENTER key is pressed, the data aligns behind the tabs. The extra tab characters caused data to go to a second line in Figure 24.21.

```
EDIT ---- TSO1234.EXAMPLE.DATA(BLKSIZE) - 01.00 ------------- COLUMNS 001 072
COMMAND ===> tabs on $_                                      SCROLL ===> CSR
****** ************************** TOP OF DATA ******************************
000001
000002                       Block Size Chart
000003
000004           3380              Device              3390
000005                          Blocks Per
000006      Min.      Max.         Track        Min.      Max.
000007
000008     23477     47476          1          27999     56664
000009     15477     23476          2          18453     27998
000010     11477     15476          3          13683     18452
000011      9077     11476          4          10797     13682
000012      7477      9076          5           8907     10796
=TABS>     *         *             *           *         *
000013
000014
000015
000016
000017
000018
****** ************************** BOTTOM OF DATA ***************************
```

Figure 24.17 Setting logical tabs.

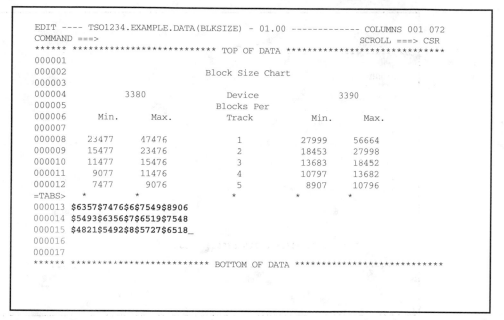

```
EDIT ---- TSO1234.EXAMPLE.DATA(BLKSIZE) - 01.00 ------------- COLUMNS 001 072
COMMAND ===>                                              SCROLL ===> CSR
****** ************************** TOP OF DATA ****************************
000001
000002                      Block Size Chart
000003
000004          3380              Device              3390
000005                           Blocks Per
000006      Min.      Max.        Track          Min.      Max.
000007
000008    23477     47476           1           27999     56664
000009    15477     23476           2           18453     27998
000010    11477     15476           3           13683     18452
000011     9077     11476           4           10797     13682
000012     7477      9076           5            8907     10796
=TABS>        *         *            *              *         *
000013 $6357$7476$6$7549$8906
000014 $5493$6356$7$6519$7548
000015 $4821$5492$8$5727$6518_
000016
000017
****** ************************** BOTTOM OF DATA ****************************
```

Figure 24.18 Data entered in logical tab format.

```
EDIT ---- TSO1234.EXAMPLE.DATA(BLKSIZE) - 01.00 ------------- COLUMNS 001 072
COMMAND ===>                                              SCROLL ===> CSR
****** ************************** TOP OF DATA ****************************
000001
000002                      Block Size Chart
000003
000004          3380              Device              3390
000005                           Blocks Per
000006      Min.      Max.        Track          Min.      Max.
000007
000008    23477     47476           1           27999     56664
000009    15477     23476           2           18453     27998
000010    11477     15476           3           13683     18452
000011     9077     11476           4           10797     13682
000012     7477      9076           5            8907     10796
=TABS>        *         *            *              *         *
000013     6357      7476           6            7549      8906
000014     5493      6356           7            6519      7548
000015     4821      5492           8            5727      6518
000016        _
000017
****** ************************** BOTTOM OF DATA ****************************
```

Figure 24.19 Result of logical tabbing.

```
EDIT ---- TSO1234.EXAMPLE.DATA(BLKSIZE) - 01.00 ------------- COLUMNS 001 072
COMMAND ===>                                            SCROLL ===> CSR
****** ************************** TOP OF DATA *****************************
000001
000002                      Block Size Chart
000003
000004          3380              Device              3390
000005                          Blocks Per
000006    Min.       Max.         Track       Min.       Max.
000007
000008   23477      47476            1         27999      56664
000009   15477      23476            2         18453      27998
000010   11477      15476            3         13683      18452
000011    9077      11476            4         10797      13682
000012    7477       9076            5          8907      10796
=TABS>    *          *              *          *          *
000013    6357       7476            6          7549       8906
000014    5493       6356            7          6519       7548
000015    4821       5492            8          5727       6518
000016 $4277$4820$9$5065$5726$$3861$4276$10_
000017
****** ************************** BOTTOM OF DATA **************************
```

Figure 24.20 Excess data entered in logical tab format.

```
EDIT ---- TSO1234.EXAMPLE.DATA(BLKSIZE) - 01.00 ------------- COLUMNS 001 072
COMMAND ===>                                            SCROLL ===> CSR
****** ************************** TOP OF DATA *****************************
000001
000002                      Block Size Chart
000003
000004          3380              Device              3390
000005                          Blocks Per
000006    Min.       Max.         Track       Min.       Max.
000007
000008   23477      47476            1         27999      56664
000009   15477      23476            2         18453      27998
000010   11477      15476            3         13683      18452
000011    9077      11476            4         10797      13682
000012    7477       9076            5          8907      10796
=TABS>    *          *              *          *          *
000013    6357       7476            6          7549       8906
000014    5493       6356            7          6519       7548
000015    4821       5492            8          5727       6518
000016    4277       4820            9          5065       5726
000017    3861       4276           10
000018    _
****** ************************** BOTTOM OF DATA **************************
```

Figure 24.21 Logical tabs over multiple lines.

Software Tabs

Software tabs are not as efficient to use as hardware tabs. Their use consumes CPU time and is only as fast as that interaction will allow (meaning that it might be dramatically slower during peak periods of computer usage). Software tabs are defined on the same tabs display line that hardware tabs are defined on. In fact, hardware and software tabs can be defined together. Software tabs are designated with a hyphen, as in Figure 24.22. The TABS primary command is not required to activate software tabs because they don't rely on the use of attribute bytes.

Software tabs are defined with a single hyphen or underscore character where the cursor is to be positioned (rather than on the space before it). When the ENTER key is pressed, the cursor positions itself in the next tab-defined column. The cursor will stay in the data area and will move to the next line when necessary to get to the next tab.

When multiple hyphens are placed together (as in Figure 24.23), they define a tab group. When the ENTER key is pressed, the cursor will position at the first non-blank position within the tab group. If there are no characters in the next tab group, the cursor will be positioned in the first byte of the tab group.

Software tabs don't inhibit the entry of data in any way and certainly would not be useful if data could not be entered in the same column as the tab character. In Figure 24.23, a group of numbers is typed, and the ENTER key is pressed. As a result of software tabbing, the cursor is placed in the first column of the second tab group (Figure 24.24). The process can be repeated to move the cursor across the line as well as from the last tab group on one line to the first tab group on the next line.

```
EDIT ---- TSO1234.EXAMPLE.DATA(BLKSIZE) - 01.01 ------------- COLUMNS 001 072
COMMAND ===> _                                              SCROLL ===> CSR
****** ************************** TOP OF DATA ***************************
000001                          Block Size Chart
000002
000003          3380                Device              3390
000004                           Blocks Per
000005     Min.      Max.          Track        Min.      Max.
000006
000007   23477     47476            1          27999     56664
000008   15477     23476            2          18453     27998
000009   11477     15476            3          13683     18452
000010    9077     11476            4          10797     13682
000011    7477      9076            5           8907     10796
000012    6357      7476            6           7549      8906
000013    5493      6356            7           6519      7548
000014    4821      5492            8           5727      6518
000015    4277      4820            9           5065      5726
000016    3861      4276           10
=TABS>    -         -               -           -         -
000017
000018
000019
****** ************************** BOTTOM OF DATA ***************************
```

Figure 24.22 Defining software tabs.

```
EDIT ---- TSO1234.EXAMPLE.DATA(BLKSIZE) - 01.01 ------------- COLUMNS 001 072
COMMAND ===>                                               SCROLL ===> CSR
****** ************************** TOP OF DATA ******************************
000001                      Block Size Chart
000002
000003          3380            Device              3390
000004                         Blocks Per
000005     Min.      Max.        Track       Min.        Max.
000006
000007   23477     47476          1         27999       56664
000008   15477     23476          2         18453       27998
000009   11477     15476          3         13683       18452
000010    9077     11476          4         10797       13682
000011    7477      9076          5          8907       10796
000012    6357      7476          6          7549        8906
000013    5493      6356          7          6519        7548
000014    4821      5492          8          5727        6518
000015    4277      4820          9          5065        5726
000016    3861      4276         10
=TABS>   ----      ----          --         ----        ----
000017   3477_
000018
000019
****** ************************** BOTTOM OF DATA ***************************
```

Figure 24.23 Start of software tab sequence.

```
EDIT ---- TSO1234.EXAMPLE.DATA(BLKSIZE) - 01.01 ------------- COLUMNS 001 072
COMMAND ===>                                               SCROLL ===> CSR
****** ************************** TOP OF DATA ******************************
000001                      Block Size Chart
000002
000003          3380            Device              3390
000004                         Blocks Per
000005     Min.      Max.        Track       Min.        Max.
000006
000007   23477     47476          1         27999       56664
000008   15477     23476          2         18453       27998
000009   11477     15476          3         13683       18452
000010    9077     11476          4         10797       13682
000011    7477      9076          5          8907       10796
000012    6357      7476          6          7549        8906
000013    5493      6356          7          6519        7548
000014    4821      5492          8          5727        6518
000015    4277      4820          9          5065        5726
000016    3861      4276         10
=TABS>   ----      ----          --         ----        ----
000017   3477      _
000018
000019
****** ************************** BOTTOM OF DATA ***************************
```

Figure 24.24 Position after using software tabs.

25

The Edit Profile

The edit profile is used to save the characteristics of an edit session. Profile characteristics are set by various edit primary and line commands. The editor itself can even change some of the profile characteristics. The characteristics are available between ISPF sessions because they're saved in a member of the ISPF profile data set (which contains more than just edit information). Edit profiles are made unique by a data-set low-level qualifier. Every data set ending in the qualifier DATA would share one edit profile, while all of the data sets with a last qualifier of TEXT would share another profile.

By default, up to 25 different edit profiles can be maintained. The number of profiles maintained can be changed by any installation. When necessary, profiles will be reused. The least-used profiles will be reused first, and unlocked profiles will be used before locked profiles.

Displaying the Edit Profile

The current profile is displayed using the PROFILE primary command, as in Figure 25.1. The command can also be abbreviated PROF or PRO. The profile displays at the top of the edit session, as shown in Figure 25.2. It shows the settings created by several already-discussed primary commands like HEX, NULLS, RECOVERY, and TABS. The profile is affected by many other primary commands that will be covered shortly.

When special lines have values that are not default settings, they're automatically displayed with the profile. These special lines include the tabs, bounds, and mask settings and are all affected by edit line commands. In Figure 25.2, the tabs line is displayed with the profile since it contains user-defined hardware tabs. When any special line is displayed, the column indicators are also automatically displayed so it will be easier to determine the position of the special line settings. In the same figure, the TABS line command is issued.

```
EDIT ---- TSO1234.EXAMPLE.DATA(BLKSIZE) - 01.04 ------------ COLUMNS 001 072
COMMAND ===> profile_                                   SCROLL ===> CSR
***** ***************************** TOP OF DATA *****************************
000001  ------------------------------------------------------------------
000002  |                       Block Size Chart                          |
000003  |                                                                 |
000004  ------------------------------------------------------------------
000005  |       3380       |      Device      |        3390       |
000006  |                  |   Blocks Per     |                   |
000007  |   Min.  |  Max.  |     Track        |   Min.  |  Max.   |
000008  ------------------------------------------------------------------
000009   23477    47476           1            27999    56664
000010   15477    23476           2            18453    27998
000011   11477    15476           3            13683    18452
000012    9077    11476           4            10797    13682
000013    7477     9076           5             8907    10796
000014    6357     7476           6             7549     8906
000015    5493     6356           7             6519     7548
000016    4821     5492           8             5727     6518
000017    4277     4820           9             5065     5726
000018    3861     4276          10             4567     5064
000019    3477     3860          11             4137     4566
000020    3189     3476          12             3769     4136
000021    2933     3188          13             3441     3768
```

Figure 25.1 PROFILE primary command.

```
EDIT ---- TSO1234.EXAMPLE.DATA(BLKSIZE) - 01.04 ------------ COLUMNS 001 072
COMMAND ===>                                            SCROLL ===> CSR
***** ***************************** TOP OF DATA *****************************
=PROF> ....DATA (FIXED - 80)....RECOVERY ON....NUMBER OFF...................
=PROF> ....CAPS OFF....HEX OFF....NULLS OFF....TABS OFF.....................
=PROF> ....AUTOSAVE ON....AUTONUM OFF....AUTOLIST OFF....STATS ON...........
=PROF> ....PROFILE UNLOCK....IMACRO NONE....PACK OFF....NOTE ON.............
=TABS>       *          *            *           *          *
=COLS> ----+----1----+----2----+----3----+----4----+----5----+----6----+----7
000001  ------------------------------------------------------------------
000002  |                       Block Size Chart                          |
000003  |                                                                 |
000004  ------------------------------------------------------------------
000005  |       3380       |      Device      |        3390       |
000006  |                  |   Blocks Per     |                   |
000007  |   Min.  |  Max.  |     Track        |   Min.  |  Max.   |
000008  ------------------------------------------------------------------
000009   23477    47476           1            27999    56664
000010   15477    23476           2            18453    27998
000011   11477    15476           3            13683    18452
tabs_     9077    11476           4            10797    13682
000013    7477     9076           5             8907    10796
000014    6357     7476           6             7549     8906
000015    5493     6356           7             6519     7548
```

Figure 25.2 Edit profile display.

The display created by the TABS line command (Figure 25.3) shows the same tab settings. Changes to one tab line will automatically be made to the other. This is also true of the other special lines (BNDS and MASK) and is independent of how many times or where that line type is displayed. It's also possible to specify how many lines of the profile are to be displayed. This is done by specifying the number of lines (a value from 0 to 8) with the PROFILE command. This can be used to force the display of special lines that contain default values, as in the example where all eight lines are requested.

After specifying the PROFILE command with the number eight, all special lines are displayed (Figure 25.4). The mask and bounds lines have been added to the display, even though they have default values. Specifying a lower value can be used to suppress the display of special lines that would otherwise display. The value 0 is available to allow the profile to be changed without causing the new profile to be displayed.

Many commands affect the profile. This becomes more apparent when the profile is displayed. In Figure 25.5, the TABS primary command is used to turn tabs on. The current profile display shows that they're turned off. After the TABS primary command is issued, the profile display is changed to show the new status (Figure 25.6). The profile display can also be used in this way to view what the tabbing character is when logical tabs are used.

The CAPS command also affects the profile. It's used to control whether or not information typed into the data area is converted to capital letters. The current setting CAPS OFF has allowed data in the active edit session to remain in lowercase. When capital letters are required, they're created using the shift key as the letter is typed.

```
EDIT ---- TSO1234.EXAMPLE.DATA(BLKSIZE) - 01.04 ------------- COLUMNS 001 072
COMMAND ===> pro 8_                                           SCROLL ===> CSR
****** *************************** TOP OF DATA ***************************
=PROF> ....DATA (FIXED - 80)....RECOVERY ON....NUMBER OFF..................
=PROF> ....CAPS OFF....HEX OFF....NULLS OFF....TABS OFF.....................
=PROF> ....AUTOSAVE ON....AUTONUM OFF....AUTOLIST OFF....STATS ON...........
=PROF> ....PROFILE UNLOCK....IMACRO NONE....PACK OFF....NOTE ON.............
=TABS>      *           *              *              *           *
=COLS> ----+----1----+----2----+----3----+----4----+----5----+----6----+----7
000001  -------------------------------------------------------------------
000002  |                        Block Size Chart                         |
000003  |                                                                 |
000004  -------------------------------------------------------------------
000005  |        3380        |     Device      |        3390        |
000006  |                    |   Blocks Per    |                    |
000007  |  Min.  |   Max.    |     Track       |   Min.   |   Max.  |
000008  -------------------------------------------------------------------
000009  | 23477  |  47476    |       1         |  27999   |  56664  |
000010  | 15477  |  23476    |       2         |  18453   |  27998  |
000011  | 11477  |  15476    |       3         |  13683   |  18452  |
=TABS>     *        *                *              *         *
000012  |  9077  |  11476    |       4         |  10797   |  13682  |
000013  |  7477  |   9076    |       5         |   8907   |  10796  |
000014  |  6357  |   7476    |       6         |   7549   |   8906  |
```

Figure 25.3 Specifying all profile lines.

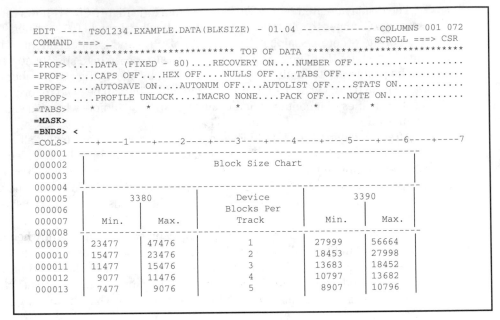

```
EDIT ---- TSO1234.EXAMPLE.DATA(BLKSIZE) - 01.04 ------------- COLUMNS 001 072
COMMAND ===> _                                            SCROLL ===> CSR
****** **************************** TOP OF DATA ***************************
=PROF> ....DATA (FIXED - 80)....RECOVERY ON....NUMBER OFF....................
=PROF> ....CAPS OFF....HEX OFF....NULLS OFF....TABS OFF......................
=PROF> ....AUTOSAVE ON....AUTONUM OFF....AUTOLIST OFF....STATS ON............
=PROF> ....PROFILE UNLOCK....IMACRO NONE....PACK OFF....NOTE ON..............
=TABS>    *         *              *              *         *
=MASK>
=BNDS> <
=COLS> ----+----1----+----2----+----3----+----4----+----5----+----6----+---7
000001 ------------------------------------------------------------------
000002 |                         Block Size Chart                        |
000003 |                                                                 |
000004 ------------------------------------------------------------------
000005 |       3380        |      Device       |       3390        |
000006 |                   |    Blocks Per     |                   |
000007 |   Min.  |  Max.   |     Track         |   Min.  |   Max.  |
000008 ------------------------------------------------------------------
000009 | 23477   | 47476   |        1          | 27999   | 56664   |
000010 | 15477   | 23476   |        2          | 18453   | 27998   |
000011 | 11477   | 15476   |        3          | 13683   | 18452   |
000012 |  9077   | 11476   |        4          | 10797   | 13682   |
000013 |  7477   |  9076   |        5          |  8907   | 10796   |
```

Figure 25.4 Display of extra profile lines.

```
EDIT ---- TSO1234.EXAMPLE.DATA(BLKSIZE) - 01.04 ------------- COLUMNS 001 072
COMMAND ===> tabs on_                                     SCROLL ===> CSR
****** **************************** TOP OF DATA ***************************
=PROF> ....DATA (FIXED - 80)....RECOVERY ON....NUMBER OFF....................
=PROF> ....CAPS OFF....HEX OFF....NULLS OFF....TABS OFF......................
=PROF> ....AUTOSAVE ON....AUTONUM OFF....AUTOLIST OFF....STATS ON............
=PROF> ....PROFILE UNLOCK....IMACRO NONE....PACK OFF....NOTE ON..............
=TABS>    *         *              *              *         *
=COLS> ----+----1----+----2----+----3----+----4----+----5----+----6----+---7
000001 ------------------------------------------------------------------
000002 |                         Block Size Chart                        |
000003 |                                                                 |
000004 ------------------------------------------------------------------
000005 |       3380        |      Device       |       3390        |
000006 |                   |    Blocks Per     |                   |
000007 |   Min.  |  Max.   |     Track         |   Min.  |   Max.  |
000008 ------------------------------------------------------------------
000009 | 23477   | 47476   |        1          | 27999   | 56664   |
000010 | 15477   | 23476   |        2          | 18453   | 27998   |
000011 | 11477   | 15476   |        3          | 13683   | 18452   |
000012 |  9077   | 11476   |        4          | 10797   | 13682   |
000013 |  7477   |  9076   |        5          |  8907   | 10796   |
000014 |  6357   |  7476   |        6          |  7549   |  8906   |
000015 |  5493   |  6356   |        7          |  6519   |  7548   |
```

Figure 25.5 TABS ON primary command.

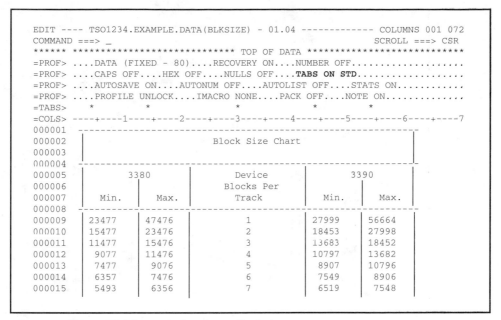

```
EDIT ---- TSO1234.EXAMPLE.DATA(BLKSIZE) - 01.04 ------------- COLUMNS 001 072
COMMAND ===> _                                                 SCROLL ===> CSR
****** **************************** TOP OF DATA ****************************
=PROF> ....DATA (FIXED - 80)....RECOVERY ON....NUMBER OFF....................
=PROF> ....CAPS OFF....HEX OFF....NULLS OFF....TABS ON STD...................
=PROF> ....AUTOSAVE ON....AUTONUM OFF....AUTOLIST OFF....STATS ON............
=PROF> ....PROFILE UNLOCK....IMACRO NONE....PACK OFF....NOTE ON..............
=TABS>    *         *              *              *          *
=COLS> ----+----1----+----2----+----3----+----4----+----5----+----6----+----7
000001 ------------------------------------------------------------------
000002 |                        Block Size Chart                         |
000003 |                                                                 |
000004 ------------------------------------------------------------------
000005 |       3380       |      Device      |        3390       |
000006 |                  |   Blocks Per     |                   |
000007 |  Min.  |  Max.   |     Track        |  Min.  |  Max.    |
000008 ------------------------------------------------------------------
000009 | 23477  | 47476   |       1          | 27999  | 56664    |
000010 | 15477  | 23476   |       2          | 18453  | 27998    |
000011 | 11477  | 15476   |       3          | 13683  | 18452    |
000012 |  9077  | 11476   |       4          | 10797  | 13682    |
000013 |  7477  |  9076   |       5          |  8907  | 10796    |
000014 |  6357  |  7476   |       6          |  7549  |  8906    |
000015 |  5493  |  6356   |       7          |  6519  |  7548    |
```

Figure 25.6 Effect of TABS command on the profile display.

In Figure 25.7, the CAPS primary command is used to turn caps mode on. ON is the default when the CAPS command is issued and therefore need not be specified.

Figure 25.8 shows the resultant change to the edit profile. The effect of the command is also demonstrated, as lowercase information is added to the third data line. When the ENTER key is pressed, the lowercase information just entered is converted to capital letters (Figure 25.9). Notice that data entered before the CAPS command was issued is still a mixture of uppercase and lowercase characters. Only data entered after caps are turned on will be converted. The LC and UC line commands can be used to convert existing data to lowercase and uppercase respectively. Conversion to uppercase characters can be turned off using the primary command CAPS OFF.

An edit session is not restricted to the profile it's given. Any other existing profile can be used, or new profiles can be created. The PROFILE command is used to switch to a different profile. Figure 25.10 shows the PROFILE command to switch to a profile named CNTL from the existing profile, which is called DATA (based on the last qualifier of the data set name).

When a new profile name (one that doesn't already exist) is used, a new profile is created. A new profile starts with the installation default values that can be tailored. Those values are saved with the profile and can be used in subsequent edit sessions. The value 0 can be used with the PROFILE command to switch to a different profile but not have the profile display.

Figure 25.11 shows the new profile. The name of the profile (CNTL) is the first entry on the first line. The characteristics of this second profile will now control the

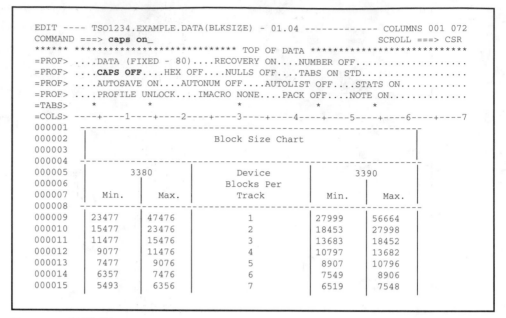

```
EDIT ---- TSO1234.EXAMPLE.DATA(BLKSIZE) - 01.04 ------------- COLUMNS 001 072
COMMAND ===> caps on_                                          SCROLL ===> CSR
****** ************************** TOP OF DATA ***************************
=PROF> ....DATA (FIXED - 80)....RECOVERY ON....NUMBER OFF...................
=PROF> ....CAPS OFF....HEX OFF....NULLS OFF....TABS ON STD..................
=PROF> ....AUTOSAVE ON....AUTONUM OFF....AUTOLIST OFF....STATS ON...........
=PROF> ....PROFILE UNLOCK....IMACRO NONE....PACK OFF....NOTE ON.............
=TABS>      *           *              *            *           *
=COLS> ----+----1----+----2----+----3----+----4----+----5----+----6----+----7
000001 -----------------------------------------------------------------
000002 |                        Block Size Chart                        |
000003 |                                                                |
000004 -----------------------------------------------------------------
000005 |       3380       |         Device         |       3390        |
000006 |                  |       Blocks Per       |                   |
000007 |  Min.  |  Max.   |         Track          |  Min.   |  Max.   |
000008 -----------------------------------------------------------------
000009 | 23477  | 47476   |           1            | 27999   | 56664   |
000010 | 15477  | 23476   |           2            | 18453   | 27998   |
000011 | 11477  | 15476   |           3            | 13683   | 18452   |
000012 |  9077  | 11476   |           4            | 10797   | 13682   |
000013 |  7477  |  9076   |           5            |  8907   | 10796   |
000014 |  6357  |  7476   |           6            |  7549   |  8906   |
000015 |  5493  |  6356   |           7            |  6519   |  7548   |
```

Figure 25.7 CAPS ON primary command.

```
EDIT ---- TSO1234.EXAMPLE.DATA(BLKSIZE) - 01.05 ------------- COLUMNS 001 072
COMMAND ===>                                                  SCROLL ===> CSR
****** ************************** TOP OF DATA ***************************
=PROF> ....DATA (FIXED - 80)....RECOVERY ON....NUMBER OFF...................
=PROF> ....CAPS ON....HEX OFF....NULLS OFF....TABS ON STD...................
=PROF> ....AUTOSAVE ON....AUTONUM OFF....AUTOLIST OFF....STATS ON...........
=PROF> ....PROFILE UNLOCK....IMACRO NONE....PACK OFF....NOTE ON.............
=TABS>      *           *              ^            *           *
=COLS> ----+----1----+----2----+----3----+----4----+----5----+----6----+----7
000001 -----------------------------------------------------------------
000002 |                        Block Size Chart                        |
000003 |  new data will convert to caps_                                |
000004 -----------------------------------------------------------------
000005 |       3380       |         Device         |       3390        |
000006 |                  |       Blocks Per       |                   |
000007 |  Min.  |  Max.   |         Track          |  Min.   |  Max.   |
000008 -----------------------------------------------------------------
000009 | 23477  | 47476   |           1            | 27999   | 56664   |
000010 | 15477  | 23476   |           2            | 18453   | 27998   |
000011 | 11477  | 15476   |           3            | 13683   | 18452   |
000012 |  9077  | 11476   |           4            | 10797   | 13682   |
000013 |  7477  |  9076   |           5            |  8907   | 10796   |
000014 |  6357  |  7476   |           6            |  7549   |  8906   |
000015 |  5493  |  6356   |           7            |  6519   |  7548   |
```

Figure 25.8 Data entered in lowercase letters.

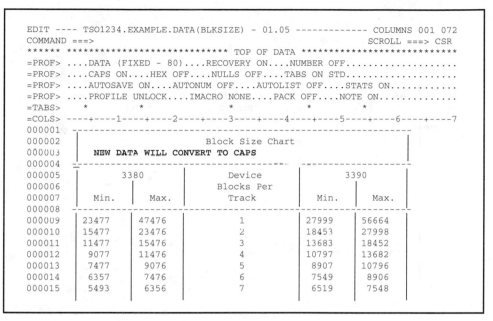

```
EDIT ---- TSO1234.EXAMPLE.DATA(BLKSIZE) - 01.05 ------------- COLUMNS 001 072
COMMAND ===>                                               SCROLL ===> CSR
****** ************************** TOP OF DATA ****************************
=PROF> ....DATA (FIXED - 80)....RECOVERY ON....NUMBER OFF...................
=PROF> ....CAPS ON....HEX OFF....NULLS OFF....TABS ON STD..................
=PROF> ....AUTOSAVE ON....AUTONUM OFF....AUTOLIST OFF....STATS ON...........
=PROF> ....PROFILE UNLOCK....IMACRO NONE....PACK OFF....NOTE ON.............
=TABS>     *         *              *              *         *
=COLS> ----+----1----+----2----+----3----+----4----+----5----+----6----+----7
000001 ---------------------------------------------------------------------
000002                          Block Size Chart
000003       NEW DATA WILL CONVERT TO CAPS
000004 =-------------------------------------------==-  -------------------=
000005 |        3380        |       Device        |        3390        |
000006 |                    |     Blocks Per      |                    |
000007 |  Min.   |  Max.    |       Track         |  Min.   |  Max.    |
000008 --------------------------------------------------------------------
000009 | 23477   | 47476    |         1           | 27999   | 56664    |
000010 | 15477   | 23476    |         2           | 18453   | 27998    |
000011 | 11477   | 15476    |         3           | 13683   | 18452    |
000012 |  9077   | 11476    |         4           | 10797   | 13682    |
000013 |  7477   |  9076    |         5           |  8907   | 10796    |
000014 |  6357   |  7476    |         6           |  7549   |  8906    |
000015 |  5493   |  6356    |         7           |  6519   |  7548    |
```

Figure 25.9 Data converted to uppercase characters.

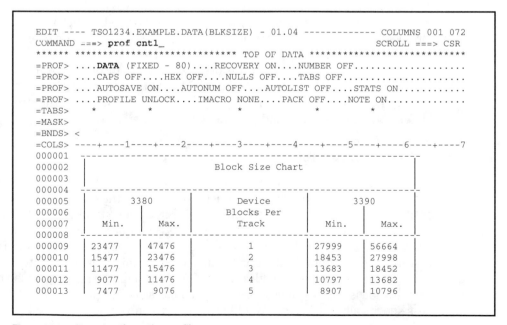

```
EDIT ---- TSO1234.EXAMPLE.DATA(BLKSIZE) - 01.04 ------------- COLUMNS 001 072
COMMAND ===> prof cntl_                                    SCROLL ===> CSR
****** ************************** TOP OF DATA ****************************
=PROF> ....DATA (FIXED - 80)....RECOVERY ON....NUMBER OFF...................
=PROF> ....CAPS OFF....HEX OFF....NULLS OFF....TABS OFF.....................
=PROF> ....AUTOSAVE ON....AUTONUM OFF....AUTOLIST OFF....STATS ON...........
=PROF> ....PROFILE UNLOCK....IMACRO NONE....PACK OFF....NOTE ON.............
=TABS>     *         *              *              *         *
=MASK>
=BNDS> <
=COLS> ----+----1----+----2----+----3----+----4----+----5----+----6----+----7
000001 ---------------------------------------------------------------------
000002                          Block Size Chart
000003
000004 --------------------------------------------------------------------
000005 |        3380        |       Device        |        3390        |
000006 |                    |     Blocks Per      |                    |
000007 |  Min.   |  Max.    |       Track         |  Min.   |  Max.    |
000008 --------------------------------------------------------------------
000009 | 23477   | 47476    |         1           | 27999   | 56664    |
000010 | 15477   | 23476    |         2           | 18453   | 27998    |
000011 | 11477   | 15476    |         3           | 13683   | 18452    |
000012 |  9077   | 11476    |         4           | 10797   | 13682    |
000013 |  7477   |  9076    |         5           |  8907   | 10796    |
```

Figure 25.10 Changing the active profile.

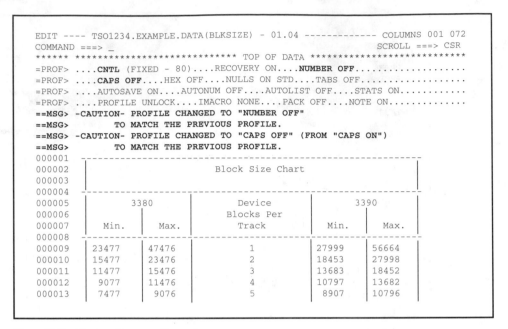

```
EDIT ---- TSO1234.EXAMPLE.DATA(BLKSIZE) - 01.04 ------------- COLUMNS 001 072
COMMAND ===> _                                               SCROLL ===> CSR
****** **************************** TOP OF DATA ****************************
=PROF> ....CNTL (FIXED - 80)....RECOVERY ON....NUMBER OFF...................
=PROF> ....CAPS OFF....HEX OFF....NULLS ON STD....TABS OFF...................
=PROF> ....AUTOSAVE ON....AUTONUM OFF....AUTOLIST OFF....STATS ON............
=PROF> ....PROFILE UNLOCK....IMACRO NONE....PACK OFF....NOTE ON..............
==MSG> -CAUTION- PROFILE CHANGED TO "NUMBER OFF"
==MSG>          TO MATCH THE PREVIOUS PROFILE.
==MSG> -CAUTION- PROFILE CHANGED TO "CAPS OFF" (FROM "CAPS ON")
==MSG>          TO MATCH THE PREVIOUS PROFILE.
000001 ------------------------------------------------------------
000002 |                        Block Size Chart                   |
000003 |                                                           |
000004 ------------------------------------------------------------
000005 |      3380        |      Device       |       3390         |
000006 |                  |    Blocks Per     |                    |
000007 |  Min.  |  Max.   |      Track        |  Min.   |  Max.    |
000008 ------------------------------------------------------------
000009 | 23477  | 47476   |        1          | 27999   | 56664    |
000010 | 15477  | 23476   |        2          | 18453   | 27998    |
000011 | 11477  | 15476   |        3          | 13683   | 18452    |
000012 |  9077  | 11476   |        4          | 10797   | 13682    |
000013 |  7477  |  9076   |        5          |  8907   | 10796    |
```

Figure 25.11 Display of new profile.

edit session. Two of the characteristics were automatically changed in the CNTL profile to be congruent with those in the previous profile, DATA. A message just below the profile describes which characteristics were changed. Notice too that the actual profile display is only four lines, indicating that all special lines have default settings.

It's also possible to specify an alternate profile name on the edit menu. Figure 25.12 shows the edit menu that was originally used to invoke the edit session. Specifying the value CNTL in the PROFILE NAME field would make use of the CNTL profile as the edit session is started. When this field is left blank, the profile used is determined by the last qualifier of the data set name.

Automatic Changes to the Profile

There are times when changes are automatically made to the edit profile. These changes are made apparent by messages at the top of the edit session as it's started. The changes are made by the editor when certain incongruities exist between the profile and the data in the current edit session. For example, the editor would change the profile to CAPS OFF if an edit session were started that didn't contain lowercase characters. In addition to caps, changes might be made automatically for number mode, member statistics, and the pack option. The message at the top of the edit session is the only indication of this change, since the profile is not displayed unless specifically invoked by the PROFILE command.

Locking the Profile

A profile can be locked to prohibit permanent changes from being made to it. This is done with the primary command PROFILE LOCK. After a profile is locked, changes can still be made to the profile, but the changes are not permanently stored. The change can be explicit changes caused by edit primary and line commands or the type of changes that occur automatically when new or copied edit data disagrees with the profile settings. The primary command PROFILE UNLOCK can be used to unlock the profile and allow the current profile setting to be permanently stored. The lock status of a profile is displayed on the fourth line of the profile display.

```
--------  ------------------  EDIT - ENTRY PANEL  ---------------------------
COMMAND ===>

ISPF LIBRARY:
    PROJECT ===> TSO1234
    GROUP   ===> EXAMPLE   ===>            ===>            ===>
    TYPE    ===> DATA
    MEMBER  ===> BLKSIZE            (Blank or pattern for member selection list)

OTHER PARTITIONED OR SEQUENTIAL DATA SET:
    DATA SET NAME   ===>
    VOLUME SERIAL   ===>            (If not cataloged)

DATA SET PASSWORD ===>             (If password protected)

PROFILE NAME        ===> cnt1_     (Blank defaults to data set type)

INITIAL MACRO       ===>           LMF LOCK   ===> YES    (YES, NO or NEVER)

FORMAT NAME         ===>           MIXED MODE ===> NO     (YES or NO)
```

Figure 25.12 Profile change from edit menu.

26

Changing
Edit Characteristics

I've already discussed several line commands that affect the edit session and that store information in the edit profile. These commands include TABS, BNDS, and MASK. I've also mentioned several primary commands, including: CAPS, HEX, NULLS, PROFILE, RECOVERY, and TABS. Beyond this, many other primary commands also affect the edit session and the profile. I detail those commands in the following.

AUTOLIST

The autolist function determines whether or not edit data is printed. When autolist is turned on, the saved result of an edit session is automatically printed when the edit session is terminated. The print data is sent to the list data set, which must be processed further before it's actually printed. The AUTOLIST command can be used with values ON and OFF to turn the autolist function on or off. ON is the default when the command is issued and therefore need not be specified. The current autolist setting can be determined by displaying the edit profile. The autolist setting is listed on the third line of the profile display.

AUTONUM

The autonum function determines whether or not sequence numbers within edit data are automatically renumbered. This is also dependent on the number mode used. The AUTONUM command can be used with values ON and OFF to turn the autonum function on or off. ON is the default when the command is issued and therefore need not be specified. When autonum is turned on, sequence numbers within the data portion (generally used with various source languages) are automatically renumbered when the data is saved. The current autonum setting can be determined by displaying the edit profile. The autonum setting is listed on the third line of the profile display.

AUTOSAVE

The autosave function determines whether or not edit data is automatically saved when an edit session is terminated. This is only a consideration when changes have been made to the data. The AUTOSAVE command can be used with values ON and OFF to turn the autosave function on or off. ON is the default when the command is issued and therefore need not be specified. ON is also the recommended setting to avoid inadvertent loss of data.

When OFF is specified, the additional parameters PROMPT and NOPROMPT can be specified. PROMPT is the default when OFF is specified, and PROMPT therefore need not be specified. It would warn when changes have been made and force either SAVE (followed by END) or CANCEL to be used to end the edit session. NO-PROMPT would allow the edit session to be terminated using END without saving the data. The current autosave setting can be determined by displaying the edit profile. The autosave setting is listed on the third line of the profile display.

LEVEL

The LEVEL primary command is used to set the modification level of the member currently being edited. The LEVEL command is specified with a numeric value from 0 to 99. The number specified with the LEVEL command becomes the new modification level that's displayed in the member statistics. The modification level is also displayed on the title line of the edit session.

NONUMBER

The primary command NONUMBER turns number mode off. The command can be abbreviated NONUM and is one of the few commands that have no parameters at all. NONUMBER is actually provided as a convenient alternative to the NUMBER primary command used with the OFF parameter. With number mode turned off, new sequence numbers are not generated, and existing line numbers are not renumbered.

NOTES

The NOTES primary command controls whether or not notes are included in MODEL command output. The MODEL command is used to copy dialog management examples into an edit session. Notes are included with most model information to explain how the dialog management statements are used and what the parameters represent. The NOTES command can be used with the values ON and OFF to include or omit model notes. ON is the default when the command is issued and therefore need not be specified. The current notes setting can be determined by displaying the edit profile. The notes setting is listed on the fourth line of the profile display.

Figure 26.1 shows the MODEL command used with notes turned off. The specific code (M8) is included to elicit model information for the LIBDEF function. Figure 26.2 shows the result of the model command. The edit session contains no notes because notes have been turned off. The same figure shows the NOTES command used to turn notes on. At the same time, the delete line command is used to delete the current MODEL command output. The same MODEL command is issued in Figure 26.3. The after line command is used in this case to place the command result.

With notes turned on, the permanent lines supplied by the MODEL command are supplemented by note lines that further describe the subject (Figure 26.4). When necessary, note lines can be made into permanent data lines using the make data (MD) line command.

NUMBER

The number function determines whether or not sequence numbers are maintained in the edit data. When number mode is turned on, sequence numbers are created or maintained in the data portion of the edit session. The number function is controlled with the NUMBER primary command. The NUMBER command can be abbreviated NUM and can be used with the values ON and OFF to turn the number mode on or off. ON is the default when the command is issued and therefore need not be specified.

When number mode is turned on, three different numbering modes can be used.

STD Indicates that numbers will be maintained in the right sequence number area. In an 80-byte data set, this would be columns 73 through 80. STD is the default when numbers are turned on and therefore need not be specified.

```
EDIT ---- TSO1234.CLIST(MODEL) ---------------------------- COLUMNS 001 072
COMMAND ===> model m8_                                      SCROLL ===> CSR
******* ************************* TOP OF DATA *****************************
''''''
''''''
''''''
''''''
''''''
''''''
''''''
''''''
''''''
''''''
''''''
''''''
''''''
''''''
''''''
''''''
''''''
''''''
''''''
****** ************************* BOTTOM OF DATA **************************
```

Figure 26.1 MODEL command with notes turned off.

```
EDIT ---- TSO1234.CLIST(MODEL) ----------------------------- COLUMNS 001 072
COMMAND ===> note on_                                        SCROLL ===> CSR
****** ************************** TOP OF DATA ******************************
d99       ISPEXEC LIBDEF LIB-TYPE DATASET |LIBRARY|EXCLDATA|EXCLLIBR      +
000002                             ID(DATASET-LIST)|ID(LIBNAME)           +
000003                             COND|UNCOND                            +
000004 /* SPECIFY THE APPLICATION PANEL LIBRARY NEEDED */
000005
000006    ISPEXEC LIBDEF ISPPLIB DATASET ID('PROJECT.ABC.PANELS')
000007
000008    IF &LASTCC = 0 THEN                                             +
000009      ISPEXEC DISPLAY PANEL(PNAME )
000010    ELSE                        /* RETURN CODES              */+
000011                                /*  4 - APPLICATION LIBRARY DOES NOT  */
000012                                /*      EXIST FOR THIS TYPE IF A       */
000013                                /*  8 - APPLICATION ALREADY EXIST FOR  */
000014                                /*      THIS TYPE ID, COND SPECIFIED   */
000015                                /* 12 - ISPPROF WAS SPECIFIED AS THE   */
000016                                /*      LIB-TYPE OR EXCLDATA OR         */
000017                                /*      EXCLLIBR WAS SPECIFIED WITH     */
000018                                /*      LIB-TYPE OTHER THAN ISPXLIB OR */
000019                                /*      ISPLLIB                         */
000020                                /* 16 - A LIBNAME WAS NOT ALLOCATED OR */
000021                                /*      THE DATASET-LIST IS INCOMPLETE */
```

Figure 26.2 Result of MODEL command with notes turned off.

```
EDIT ---- TSO1234.CLIST(MODEL) ----------------------------- COLUMNS 001 072
COMMAND ===> model m8_                                       SCROLL ===> CSR
a***** ************************** TOP OF DATA ******************************
****** ************************** BOTTOM OF DATA ***************************
```

Figure 26.3 MODEL command with notes turned on.

```
EDIT ---- TSO1234.CLIST(MODEL) ---------------------------- COLUMNS 001 072
COMMAND ===> _                                              SCROLL ===> CSR
****** *********************** TOP OF DATA ***********************
000001   ISPEXEC LIBDEF LIB-TYPE DATASET|LIBRARY| EXCLDATA| EXCLLIBR      +
000002                           ID(DATASET-LIST)| ID(LIBNAME)            +
000003                           COND|UNCOND                              +
=NOTE=
=NOTE=     LIB-TYPE     - TYPE OF ISPF DDNAME APPLICATION-LEVEL LIBRARY
=NOTE=                    DEFINITION, ISPPLIB, ISPMLIB, ETC.
=NOTE=     CHOOSE ONE:
=NOTE=       DATASET    - INDICATES THAT THE ID SPECIFIES A LIST OF CATALOGE
=NOTE=                    DATA SET NAMES
=NOTE=       LIBRARY    - INDICATES THAT THE ID SPECIFIES A LIBRARY NAME
=NOTE=                    (DDNAME)
=NOTE=       EXCLDATA   - INDICATES THAT THE ID SPECIFIES A LIST OF CATALOGE
=NOTE=                    DATA SET NAMES, CAN ONLY BE USED WITH ISPLLIB
=NOTE=       EXCLLIBR   - INDICATES THAT THE ID SPECIFIES A LIBRARY NAME
=NOTE=                    (DDNAME)
=NOTE=     DATASET-LIST - INDICATES A LIST OF DATASETS TO BE SEARCHED FOR TH
=NOTE=                    APPLICATION. USED WITH DATASET OR EXCLDATA. IF NOT
=NOTE=                    SPECIFIED, THEN THE EXISTING LIBDEF IS REMOVED.
=NOTE=     LIBNAME      - SPECIFIES THE NAME OF A DD STATEMENT THAT DEFINE
=NOTE=                    THE APPLICATION LIBRARY(S). USED WITH LIBRARY OR
=NOTE=                    EXCLLIBR. IF NOT SPECIFIED, THEN THE EXISTING
```

Figure 26.4 Result of MODEL command with notes turned on.

COBOL   Indicates that numbers will be maintained in the left sequence number area. This would be columns one through six. This is the default in a COBOL data set (a data set with a descriptive qualifier of COBOL) and might also be specified as COB.

STD COBOL   Indicates that numbers will be maintained in both the standard and the COBOL sequence areas. This would maintain numbers in both the left and right sequence number areas.

Another NUMBER command parameter, DISPLAY, can be used when the number mode is turned on to increase the width of the edit window. This will include the line sequence area on terminals that are capable of displaying more than 80 columns. Take care to ensure that turning the number mode on will not destroy data that might already exist in the line sequence area that will be affected. The current number mode setting can be determined by displaying the edit profile. The number mode setting is listed on the first line of the profile display.

In Figure 26.5, the data display is scrolled to the extreme right of the data set to show that line sequence numbers don't currently exist. The NUMBER command is issued to set the number mode on with standard line numbers. STD and ON are both defaults, and so neither need be specified.

Following the command, the data is automatically scrolled left to display column one of the data. Scrolling back to the right reveals the line numbers added to the data in columns 73 through 80 (Figure 26.6).

COBOL numbers are maintained in columns one through six. No matter which number type is used, care should be used to avoid placing line numbers over useful

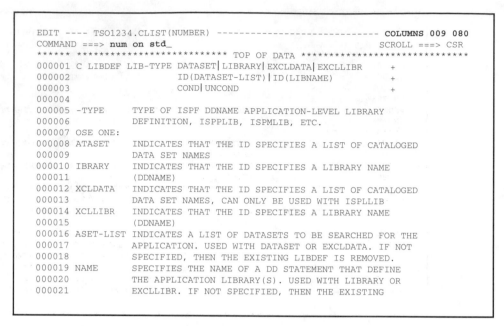

```
EDIT ---- TSO1234.CLIST(NUMBER) --------------------------- COLUMNS 009 080
COMMAND ===> num on std_                                    SCROLL ===> CSR
****** ************************* TOP OF DATA ******************************
000001 C LIBDEF LIB-TYPE DATASET|LIBRARY|EXCLDATA|EXCLLIBR      +
000002                    ID(DATASET-LIST)|ID(LIBNAME)          +
000003                    COND|UNCOND                           +
000004
000005 -TYPE     TYPE OF ISPF DDNAME APPLICATION-LEVEL LIBRARY
000006           DEFINITION, ISPPLIB, ISPMLIB, ETC.
000007 OSE ONE:
000008 ATASET    INDICATES THAT THE ID SPECIFIES A LIST OF CATALOGED
000009           DATA SET NAMES
000010 IBRARY    INDICATES THAT THE ID SPECIFIES A LIBRARY NAME
000011           (DDNAME)
000012 XCLDATA   INDICATES THAT THE ID SPECIFIES A LIST OF CATALOGED
000013           DATA SET NAMES, CAN ONLY BE USED WITH ISPLLIB
000014 XCLLIBR   INDICATES THAT THE ID SPECIFIES A LIBRARY NAME
000015           (DDNAME)
000016 ASET-LIST INDICATES A LIST OF DATASETS TO BE SEARCHED FOR THE
000017           APPLICATION. USED WITH DATASET OR EXCLDATA. IF NOT
000018           SPECIFIED, THEN THE EXISTING LIBDEF IS REMOVED.
000019 NAME      SPECIFIES THE NAME OF A DD STATEMENT THAT DEFINE
000020           THE APPLICATION LIBRARY(S). USED WITH LIBRARY OR
000021           EXCLLIBR. IF NOT SPECIFIED, THEN THE EXISTING
```

Figure 26.5 NUMBER command to create standard line numbers.

```
EDIT ---- TSO1234.CLIST(NUMBER) --------------------------- COLUMNS 009 080
COMMAND ===> _                                              SCROLL ===> CSR
****** ************************* TOP OF DATA ******************************
000100 C LIBDEF LIB-TYPE DATASET |LIBRARY |EXCLDATA |EXCLLIBR   +   00000100
000200                    ID(DATASET-LIST)|ID(LIBNAME)          +   00000200
000300                    COND|UNCOND                           +   00000300
000400                                                              00000400
000500 -TYPE     TYPE OF ISPF DDNAME APPLICATION-LEVEL LIBRARY       00000500
000600           DEFINITION, ISPPLIB, ISPMLIB, ETC.                  00000600
000700 OSE ONE:                                                      00000700
000800 ATASET    INDICATES THAT THE ID SPECIFIES A LIST OF CATALOGED 00000800
000900           DATA SET NAMES                                      00000900
001000 IBRARY    INDICATES THAT THE ID SPECIFIES A LIBRARY NAME      00001000
001100           (DDNAME)                                            00001100
001200 XCLDATA   INDICATES THAT THE ID SPECIFIES A LIST OF CATALOGED 00001200
001300           DATA SET NAMES, CAN ONLY BE USED WITH ISPLLIB       00001300
001400 XCLLIBR   INDICATES THAT THE ID SPECIFIES A LIBRARY NAME      00001400
001500           (DDNAME)                                            00001500
001600 ASET-LIST INDICATES A LIST OF DATASETS TO BE SEARCHED FOR THE 00001600
001700           APPLICATION. USED WITH DATASET OR EXCLDATA. IF NOT  00001700
001800           SPECIFIED, THEN THE EXISTING LIBDEF IS REMOVED.     00001800
001900 NAME      SPECIFIES THE NAME OF A DD STATEMENT THAT DEFINE    00001900
002000           THE APPLICATION LIBRARY(S). USED WITH LIBRARY OR    00002000
002100           EXCLLIBR. IF NOT SPECIFIED, THEN THE EXISTING       00002100
```

Figure 26.6 Result of NUM ON STD command.

data. Figure 26.7 shows the NUMBER command used to create COBOL numbers. Notice that columns one through six currently contain data.

Figure 26.8 shows the data after line numbers have been added. Some of the data has been overlaid by the line numbers. On the same screen, the UNNUMBER command is issued to remove the numbers just added and to turn number mode off.

The UNNUMBER command has removed the COBOL line numbers (Figure 26.9) that were just created. With the numbers removed, it's obvious that the data from those positions is missing. This is a permanent change to the data that can only be rectified by canceling the edit session or by using the UNDO command to back out the changes.

A third choice for number type is to include both standard and COBOL numbers. This is accomplished by including both the STD and COBOL parameters on the NUMBER command.

Figure 26.10 shows the standard line numbers created from the command NUM ON STD COB. Notice that less of the data is displayed here. The display would normally start in column nine.

Scrolling to the left reveals the COBOL type numbers added by the command NUM ON STD COB (Figure 26.11). Again, fewer columns are actually displayed here (the normal display would include columns one through 72).

In many cases, line numbers are not required. This is usually determined by how the data is used. Some language compilers, for example, disregard the existing line numbers and create their own. As demonstrated, the line numbers can always be added later after ensuring that they will not destroy any of the existing data.

```
EDIT ---- TSO1234.CLIST(NUMBER) ---------------------------- COLUMNS 001 072
COMMAND ===> num on cob_                                      SCROLL ===> CSR
****** **********************▲▲▲▲▲********** TOP OF DATA ****************************
000001    ISPEXEC LIBDEF LIB-TYPE DATASET |LIBRARY|EXCLDATA|EXCLLIBR      +
000002                            ID(DATASET-LIST)|ID(LIBNAME)            +
000003                            COND|UNCOND                             +
000004
000005    LIB-TYPE       TYPE OF ISPF DDNAME APPLICATION-LEVEL LIBRARY
000006                   DEFINITION, ISPPLIB, ISPMLIB, ETC.
000007    CHOOSE ONE:
000008     DATASET       INDICATES THAT THE ID SPECIFIES A LIST OF CATALOGED
000009                   DATA SET NAMES
000010     LIBRARY       INDICATES THAT THE ID SPECIFIES A LIBRARY NAME
000011                   (DDNAME)
000012     EXCLDATA      INDICATES THAT THE ID SPECIFIES A LIST OF CATALOGED
000013                   DATA SET NAMES, CAN ONLY BE USED WITH ISPLLIB
000014     EXCLLIBR      INDICATES THAT THE ID SPECIFIES A LIBRARY NAME
000015                   (DDNAME)
000016    DATASET-LIST INDICATES A LIST OF DATASETS TO BE SEARCHED FOR THE
000017                   APPLICATION. USED WITH DATASET OR EXCLDATA. IF NOT
000018                   SPECIFIED, THEN THE EXISTING LIBDEF IS REMOVED.
000019     LIBNAME       SPECIFIES THE NAME OF A DD STATEMENT THAT DEFINE
000020                   THE APPLICATION LIBRARY(S). USED WITH LIBRARY OR
000021                   EXCLLIBR. IF NOT SPECIFIED, THEN THE EXISTING
```

Figure 26.7 NUM ON COB command.

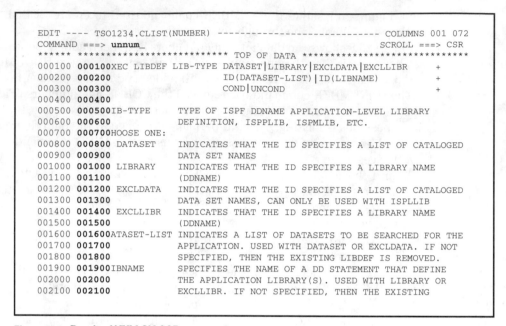

```
EDIT ---- TSO1234.CLIST(NUMBER) ----------------------------- COLUMNS 001 072
COMMAND ===> unnum_                                          SCROLL ===> CSR
****** ************************** TOP OF DATA ******************************
000100 000100XEC LIBDEF LIB-TYPE DATASET|LIBRARY|EXCLDATA|EXCLLIBR      +
000200 000200             ID(DATASET-LIST)|ID(LIBNAME)                  +
000300 000300             COND|UNCOND                                   +
000400 000400
000500 000500IB-TYPE      TYPE OF ISPF DDNAME APPLICATION-LEVEL LIBRARY
000600 000600             DEFINITION, ISPPLIB, ISPMLIB, ETC.
000700 000700HOOSE ONE:
000800 000800 DATASET     INDICATES THAT THE ID SPECIFIES A LIST OF CATALOGED
000900 000900             DATA SET NAMES
001000 001000 LIBRARY     INDICATES THAT THE ID SPECIFIES A LIBRARY NAME
001100 001100             (DDNAME)
001200 001200 EXCLDATA    INDICATES THAT THE ID SPECIFIES A LIST OF CATALOGED
001300 001300             DATA SET NAMES, CAN ONLY BE USED WITH ISPLLIB
001400 001400 EXCLLIBR    INDICATES THAT THE ID SPECIFIES A LIBRARY NAME
001500 001500             (DDNAME)
001600 001600ATASET-LIST INDICATES A LIST OF DATASETS TO BE SEARCHED FOR THE
001700 001700             APPLICATION. USED WITH DATASET OR EXCLDATA. IF NOT
001800 001800             SPECIFIED, THEN THE EXISTING LIBDEF IS REMOVED.
001900 001900IBNAME       SPECIFIES THE NAME OF A DD STATEMENT THAT DEFINE
002000 002000             THE APPLICATION LIBRARY(S). USED WITH LIBRARY OR
002100 002100             EXCLLIBR. IF NOT SPECIFIED, THEN THE EXISTING
```

Figure 26.8 Result of NUM ON COB command.

```
EDIT ---- TSO1234.CLIST(NUMBER) ----------------------------- COLUMNS 001 072
COMMAND ===> num on std cob_                                 SCROLL ===> CSR
****** ************************** TOP OF DATA ******************************
000001        XEC LIBDEF LIB-TYPE DATASET|LIBRARY|EXCLDATA|EXCLLIBR     +
000002                     ID(DATASET-LIST)|ID(LIBNAME)                 +
000003                     COND|UNCOND                                  +
000004
000005        IB-TYPE      TYPE OF ISPF DDNAME APPLICATION-LEVEL LIBRARY
000006                     DEFINITION, ISPPLIB, ISPMLIB, ETC.
000007        HOOSE ONE:
000008         DATASET     INDICATES THAT THE ID SPECIFIES A LIST OF CATALOGED
000009                     DATA SET NAMES
000010         LIBRARY     INDICATES THAT THE ID SPECIFIES A LIBRARY NAME
000011                     (DDNAME)
000012         EXCLDATA    INDICATES THAT THE ID SPECIFIES A LIST OF CATALOGED
000013                     DATA SET NAMES, CAN ONLY BE USED WITH ISPLLIB
000014         EXCLLIBR    INDICATES THAT THE ID SPECIFIES A LIBRARY NAME
000015                     (DDNAME)
000016        ATASET-LIST INDICATES A LIST OF DATASETS TO BE SEARCHED FOR THE
000017                     APPLICATION. USED WITH DATASET OR EXCLDATA. IF NOT
000018                     SPECIFIED, THEN THE EXISTING LIBDEF IS REMOVED.
000019         TBNAME      SPECIFIES THE NAME OF A DD STATEMENT THAT DEFINE
000020                     THE APPLICATION LIBRARY(S). USED WITH LIBRARY OR
000021                     EXCLLIBR. IF NOT SPECIFIED, THEN THE EXISTING
```

Figure 26.9 Result of UNNUMBER command.

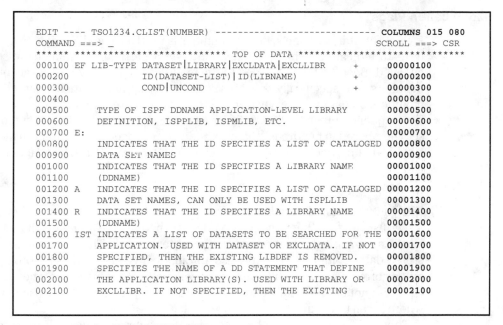

```
EDIT ---- TSO1234.CLIST(NUMBER) --------------------------- COLUMNS 015 080
COMMAND ===> _                                            SCROLL ===> CSR
****** ************************* TOP OF DATA ****************************
000100 EF LIB-TYPE DATASET|LIBRARY|EXCLDATA|EXCLLIBR       +    00000100
000200           ID(DATASET-LIST)|ID(LIBNAME)             +    00000200
000300           COND|UNCOND                              +    00000300
000400                                                          00000400
000500     TYPE OF ISPF DDNAME APPLICATION-LEVEL LIBRARY       00000500
000600     DEFINITION, ISPPLIB, ISPMLIB, ETC.                 00000600
000700 E:                                                      00000700
000800     INDICATES THAT THE ID SPECIFIES A LIST OF CATALOGED 00000800
000900     DATA SET NAMES                                     00000900
001000     INDICATES THAT THE ID SPECIFIES A LIBRARY NAME     00001000
001100     (DDNAME)                                           00001100
001200 A   INDICATES THAT THE ID SPECIFIES A LIST OF CATALOGED 00001200
001300     DATA SET NAMES, CAN ONLY BE USED WITH ISPLLIB      00001300
001400 R   INDICATES THAT THE ID SPECIFIES A LIBRARY NAME     00001400
001500     (DDNAME)                                           00001500
001600 IST INDICATES A LIST OF DATASETS TO BE SEARCHED FOR THE 00001600
001700     APPLICATION. USED WITH DATASET OR EXCLDATA. IF NOT 00001700
001800     SPECIFIED, THEN THE EXISTING LIBDEF IS REMOVED.    00001800
001900     SPECIFIES THE NAME OF A DD STATEMENT THAT DEFINE   00001900
002000     THE APPLICATION LIBRARY(S). USED WITH LIBRARY OR   00002000
002100     EXCLLIBR. IF NOT SPECIFIED, THEN THE EXISTING      00002100
```

Figure 26.10 Result of NUM ON STD COB command.

```
EDIT ---- TSO1234.CLIST(NUMBER) --------------------------- COLUMNS 001 066
COMMAND ===> _                                            SCROLL ===> CSR
****** ************************* TOP OF DATA ****************************
000100 000100XEC LIBDEF LIB-TYPE DATASET|LIBRARY|EXCLDATA|EXCLLIBR    +
000200 000200                     ID(DATASET-LIST)|ID(LIBNAME)       +
000300 000300                     COND|UNCOND                        +
000400 000400
000500 000500IB-TYPE     TYPE OF ISPF DDNAME APPLICATION-LEVEL LIBRARY
000600 000600            DEFINITION, ISPPLIB, ISPMLIB, ETC.
000700 000700HOOSE ONE:
000800 000800 DATASET    INDICATES THAT THE ID SPECIFIES A LIST OF CATA
000900 000900            DATA SET NAMES
001000 001000 LIBRARY    INDICATES THAT THE ID SPECIFIES A LIBRARY NAME
001100 001100            (DDNAME)
001200 001200 EXCLDATA   INDICATES THAT THE ID SPECIFIES A LIST OF CATA
001300 001300            DATA SET NAMES, CAN ONLY BE USED WITH ISPLLIB
001400 001400 EXCLLIBR   INDICATES THAT THE ID SPECIFIES A LIBRARY NAME
001500 001500            (DDNAME)
001600 001600ATASET-LIST INDICATES A LIST OF DATASETS TO BE SEARCHED FO
001700 001700            APPLICATION. USED WITH DATASET OR EXCLDATA. IF
001800 001800            SPECIFIED, THEN THE EXISTING LIBDEF IS REMOVED
001900 001900IBNAME      SPECIFIES THE NAME OF A DD STATEMENT THAT DEFI
002000 002000            THE APPLICATION LIBRARY(S). USED WITH LIBRARY
002100 002100            EXCLLIBR. IF NOT SPECIFIED, THEN THE EXISTING
```

Figure 26.11 Further result of NUM ON STD COB command.

Modification Flags

Part of the standard line sequence number is used as a modification flag. This flag is used to indicate at which modification level a particular statement was added or changed. Because the flag is tied to the modification level, it's only available for PDS members, and specifically only those members that have statistics turned on. When modification flags are present, they're the last two bytes of the standard line number. The sequence number 00040015, for example, indicates the fourth line of the data set (numbered in hundreds) that was added or changed at the fifteenth modification level of that particular member. That can be quite useful to track changes to the data.

PACK

The pack function determines whether or not edit data is compressed or packed as it's written to disk. When the pack mode is turned on, the saved result of an edit session is automatically compressed as it's written to disk. This will save disk space for stored data. Compressed data is also automatically expanded as it's brought into an edit or browse session. There are, however, many other instances where edit data is used and not automatically expanded. Do not compress data that's used in a context where it can't be expanded.

The PACK command can be used with the values ON and OFF to turn the compression feature on or off. ON is the default when the command is issued and therefore need not be specified. When necessary, compressed data can be stored in standard format by issuing the command PACK OFF before saving the data. The current setting for the pack feature can be determined by displaying the edit profile. The setting is listed on the fourth line of the profile display.

RENUM

The RENUM command renumbers the line sequence numbers in the data area. It has the same parameters that the NUMBER command has to designate standard numbers (STD), COBOL numbers (COBOL or COB), or both number types (STD COBOL). Figure 26.12 shows an edit session where the numbers in the line command area are no longer incremented by 100.

Scrolling to the right shows the same numbers in the standard line number area of the data (Figure 26.13). Here, the RENUM command is used to resequence both areas. The parameters ON and STD are defaults and will apply even though not specified.

Use of the RENUM command will automatically turn the number mode on. Figure 26.14 shows the data display adjusted to start in column one. The line command area is now uniformly numbered.

Scrolling right again shows that the line numbers in the data have also been renumbered (Figure 26.15). The same caution should be exercised in using the RENUM command as is used with the NUMBER command. If the line sequence area contains data, that data will be destroyed when numbers are added.

RENUM OFF merely turns the number mode off, just as the command NUM OFF would. The RENUM command parameter, DISPLAY, can be used to increase the width of the edit window to include the line sequence area on terminals that are capable of displaying more than 80 columns.

```
EDIT ---- TSO1234.CLIST(CUT) - 01.01 ----------------------- COLUMNS 001 072
COMMAND ===> _                                        SCROLL ===> CSR
****** ************************** TOP OF DATA *****************************
000100 PROC 1 DSN LRECL(80)
000200 CONTROL NOFLUSH
000300 SET &RC = 0
000400 ALLOC F(CUT) DA(&DSN) SHR REUSE
000500 SET &DATE = D&SUBSTR(1:2,&SYSDATE)+
000501    &SUBSTR(4:5,&SYSDATE)&SUBSTR(7:8,&SYSDATE)
000502 SET &TIME = T&SUBSTR(1:2,&SYSTIME)+
000503    &SUBSTR(4.5,&SYSTIME)&SUBSTR(7:8,&SYSTIME)
000504 SET &DSN2 = &SYSUID..&DATE..&TIME
000505 SET &BLKSIZE = 23476 / &LRECL * &LRECL
000506 ALLOC F(NEWDATA) DA('&DSN2') SPACE(5 5) TRACK RELEASE CATALOG +
000507    RECFM(F B) LRECL(&LRECL) BLKSIZE(&BLKSIZE) REUSE
000508 OPENFILE CUT
000509 OPENFILE NEWDATA OUTPUT
000530 GETFILE CUT
000600 SET &LEN = &LENGTH(&STR(&CUT))
000700 SET &LOOP_COUNT = &LEN / &LRECL
000800 SET &REMAIN    = &LEN // &LRECL
000900 ERROR +
001000    DO
001100       SET &RC = &LASTCC
```

Figure 26.12 Non-uniform numbers.

```
EDIT ---- TSO1234.CLIST(CUT) - 01.01 ---------- ------------- COLUMNS 009 080
COMMAND ===> renum_                                   SCROLL ==-> CSR
****** ************************** TOP OF DATA *****************************
000100 SN LRECL(80)                                              00010001
000200 NOFLUSH                                                   00020001
000300 = 0                                                       00030001
000400 CUT) DA(&DSN) SHR REUSE                                   00040001
000500 E = D&SUBSTR(1:2,&SYSDATE)+                               00050001
000501 R(4:5,&SYSDATE)&SUBSTR(7:8,&SYSDATE)                      00050101
000502 E = T&SUBSTR(1:2,&SYSTIME)+                               00050201
000503 R(4:5,&SYSTIME)&SUBSTR(7:8,&SYSTIME)                      00050301
000504 2 = &SYSUID..&DATE..&TIME                                 00050401
000505 SIZE = 23476 / &LRECL * &LRECL                            00050501
000506 NEWDATA) DA('&DSN2') SPACE(5 5) TRACK RELEASE CATALOG +   00050601
000507 F B) LRECL(&LRECL) BLKSIZE(&BLKSIZE) REUSE                00050701
000508    CUT                                                    00050801
000509    NEWDATA OUTPUT                                         00050901
000530 CUT                                                       00053001
000600    = &LENGTH(&STR(&CUT))                                  00060001
000700 P_COUNT = &LEN / &LRECL                                   00070001
000800 AIN    = &LEN // &LRECL                                   00080001
000900                                                           00090001
001000                                                           00100001
001100 &RC = &LASTCC                                             00110001
```

Figure 26.13 RENUM primary command.

```
EDIT ---- TSO1234.CLIST(CUT) - 01.01 ----------------------- COLUMNS 001 072
COMMAND ===> _                                              SCROLL ===> CSR
****** ************************* TOP OF DATA ****************************
000100 PROC 1 DSN LRECL(80)
000200 CONTROL NOFLUSH
000300 SET &RC = 0
000400 ALLOC F(CUT) DA(&DSN) SHR REUSE
000500 SET &DATE = D&SUBSTR(1:2,&SYSDATE)+
000600    &SUBSTR(4:5,&SYSDATE)&SUBSTR(7:8,&SYSDATE)
000700 SET &TIME = T&SUBSTR(1:2,&SYSTIME)+
000800    &SUBSTR(4:5,&SYSTIME)&SUBSTR(7:8,&SYSTIME)
000900 SET &DSN2 = &SYSUID..&DATE..&TIME
001000 SET &BLKSIZE = 23476 / &LRECL * &LRECL
001100 ALLOC F(NEWDATA) DA('&DSN2') SPACE(5 5) TRACK RELEASE CATALOG +
001200    RECFM(F B) LRECL(&LRECL) BLKSIZE(&BLKSIZE) REUSE
001300 OPENFILE CUT
001400 OPENFILE NEWDATA OUTPUT
001500 GETFILE CUT
001600 SET &LEN = &LENGTH(&STR(&CUT))
001700 SET &LOOP_COUNT = &LEN /  &LRECL
001800 SET &REMAIN     = &LEN // &LRECL
001900 ERROR +
002000    DO
002100      SET &RC = &LASTCC
```

Figure 26.14 Result of RENUM command.

```
EDIT ---- TSO1234.CLIST(CUT) - 01.01 ----------------------- COLUMNS 009 080
COMMAND ===> _                                              SCROLL ===> CSR
****** ************************* TOP OF DATA ****************************
000100 SN LRECL(80)                                              00010001
000200 NOFLUSH                                                   00020001
000300 = 0                                                       00030001
000400 CUT) DA(&DSN) SHR REUSE                                   00040001
000500 E = D&SUBSTR(1:2,&SYSDATE)+                               00050001
000600 R(4:5,&SYSDATE)&SUBSTR(7:8,&SYSDATE)                      00060001
000700 E = T&SUBSTR(1:2,&SYSTIME)+                               00070001
000800 R(4:5,&SYSTIME)&SUBSTR(7:8,&SYSTIME)                      00080001
000900 2 = &SYSUID..&DATE..&TIME                                 00090001
001000 SIZE = 23476 / &LRECL * &LRECL                            00100001
001100 NEWDATA) DA('&DSN2') SPACE(5 5) TRACK RELEASE CATALOG +   00110001
001200 F B) LRECL(&LRECL) BLKSIZE(&BLKSIZE) REUSE                00120001
001300   CUT                                                     00130001
001400   NEWDATA OUTPUT                                          00140001
001500 CUT                                                       00150001
001600 = &LENGTH(&STR(&CUT))                                     00160001
001700 P_COUNT = &LEN /  &LRECL                                  00170001
001800 AIN     = &LEN // &LRECL                                  00180001
001900                                                           00190001
002000                                                           00200001
002100 &RC = &LASTCC                                             00210001
```

Figure 26.15 Resequenced line number area.

STATS

The STATS primary command is used to turn member statistics on and off. Statistics are stored in the PDS directory, and so they're only maintained for partitioned data sets. The statistics are very useful, especially for determining when a member was last updated. Member list displays can also be sorted by the statistics that are generated when statistics are turned on.

The STATS command can be used with values ON and OFF to turn the statistics on or off. ON is the default when the command is issued and therefore need not be specified. STATS can be turned off as a temporary measure when the current edit data can't be saved because the PDS directory is full. The partitioned data set should later be reallocated with more directory blocks. When statistics are turned on, a minimum of five members can be stored in each directory block. When statistics are turned off, a maximum of 22 members can be stored in each directory block.

The statistics mode is subject to automatic change by the editor. This will occur when the statistics mode is off and the member already has statistics. Under this circumstance, the profile will be changed to STATS ON. The current setting for this feature is displayed on the third line of the profile.

UNNUMBER

The UNNUMBER primary command is used to remove all line sequence numbers from the data and turn the number mode off. The command has no parameters. It can also be specified as UNNUM. The type of line numbers that are removed depends on the currently established number mode. To use the UNNUMBER command, the profile must already be in number mode. If the number mode is turned off but the edit session still has sequence numbers, turn the number mode on before using the UNNUMBER command. Use of the UNNUMBER command will automatically turn the number mode off. Following the command, the data display will automatically be repositioned to display column one of the data.

VERSION

The VERSION primary command is used to set the version number of the member currently being edited. The VERSION command is specified with a numeric value from 1 to 99. The number specified with the VERSION command becomes the new version number that's displayed in the member statistics. The version number is also displayed on the title line of the edit session. (See Table 26.1.)

TABLE 26.1 Summary of Commands in This Chapter

AUTOLIST	ON OFF	AUTONUM	ON OFF
AUTOSAVE	ON OFF	LEVEL	number

TABLE 26.1 Summary of Commands in This Chapter (continued).

NONUMBER				NOTES	<u>ON</u>	
NONUM					OFF	
NUMBER	OFF			PACK	<u>ON</u>	
NUM	<u>ON</u>	<u>STD</u>	DISPLAY		OFF	
		COBOL				
		STD COBOL				
RENUM	OFF			STATS	ON	
	ON	<u>STD</u>	DISPLAY		OFF	
		COBOL				
		STD COBOL				
UNNUMBER				VERSION	number	
UNNUM						

ISPF Utilities

27

Data Management Concepts

The basis for storing information is the *data set*. A data set is loosely defined as a collection of related data records. *Data management* is the term used to describe the process of creating, maintaining, and deleting data sets. The data set is created with a name that's also used to reference the data when it's needed.

Data Set Characteristics

Each data set is created with certain characteristics that are determined by what information it will contain and how that information will be used. One of the characteristics used in defining a data set is the device type. There are many devices that can be used to store the records that make up a data set. The type used depends largely on how accessible the data set must be. Further discussions will concentrate on the most accessible and commonly used form of storage—disk devices. Data sets are stored on disk when they must be readily available for use. The disk device is meant to be constantly connected to the system and therefore requires no manual intervention to make the device ready for use.

One of the data set characteristics that's peculiar to disk data sets is space. Some portion of the disk device must be reserved for the data set as it's created. It's also a good idea to request additional space that will allow the data set to expand during later use.

Other aspects are common to all data sets. These include the data set organization (an indication of how the data will be processed), its physical attributes (what it looks like), and volume residence (where it will be placed). All aspects of data set creation and use will be covered individually in more detail before describing how they're specified on ISPF screens.

Data Set Organization

The data set organization determines the access method that will be used to read from and write to the data set. The data set organization also determines how the data set can be accessed. The two organizations supported by ISPF are sequential, which is also known as QSAM (Queued Sequential Access Method), and partitioned, which is also known as BPAM (Basic Partitioned Access Method). A *sequential data set* is a single collection of records that are accessed in order (sequentially). A sequential data set can be specified with a DSORG value of PS. A partitioned data set is a collection of sequential data sets organized under a single directory. Each sequential data set in a partitioned data set or PDS is given a unique name known as a member name. A partitioned data set can be specified with a DSORG value of PO. Other data set organizations are supported in a limited sense by ISPF; these include BDAM (Basic Direct Access Method), ISAM (Indexed Sequential Access Method), and VSAM (Virtual Storage Access Method).

Record Format

The record format describes the basic nature of the data set. Codes represent the data as fixed (F) or variable (V) in length. Fixed-length records are all the same length. Variable records are allowed to vary in length and contain a special four-byte field at the beginning of each record describing how long it is. Either record format can also be blocked (B) or spanned (S). Blocking seeks to place multiple logical records together in larger physical records. Spanned records are allowed to span from one such physical record to another.

Record formats are also able to designate the presence of carriage control characters in the data records. The carriage control could be either ANSI (A) or machine code (M). Either would be a character in column one of the data set that would direct printer line spacing. Another fairly common designation (U) represents an undefined record format. This format is used, for example, for executable load code.

Record Length

The *record length* is merely how long the logical record is. For fixed-length records, this is simply the length of each record. For variable-length records, the record length describes the maximum record length. This includes the RDW (Record Descriptor Word), which is the first four bytes of a variable-length record. The RDW contains the length of the record as a binary value.

Blocksize

Records are considered to be *blocked* when two or more logical records are stored together in a physical record or block. The *blocksize* is then the size of the physical record or block. For fixed-length records, the blocksize is a multiple of the record length. For variable-length records, the blocksize need not be a multiple of the blocksize, but it should be at least four bytes larger than the maximum record length to allow for a BDW. A BDW (Block Descriptor Word) is like an RDW, except that it describes the length of a block of data.

Blocking records makes I/O processing more efficient since an entire block of data is transferred at one time. Effective blocksizes also reduce the amount of space required to store data. Effective blocksizes for sequential data sets approach the number 27,998 for 3390 disk devices and 23,476 for 3380 disk devices. The recommendation for partitioned data sets is to approach the number 6144. For variable-length records, those values can be used. For fixed-length records, the number is first divided by the record length. The integer result is then multiplied by the record length.

```
device-dependent-number / record-length = integer-result
integer-result * record-length = blocksize
```

An example for 80-byte records for a sequential data set on a 3380 disk device would be calculated in the following manner, arriving at a blocksize of 23440.

```
23476 / 80 = 293.45
293 * 80 = 23440
```

Unit Type

The unit type is used to determine what type of device the data is written to. Most ISPF functions will be limited to the use of disk devices (as opposed to tape devices). There might, however, be more than one kind of disk device available. An installation might, for example, use both 3380 and 3390 disk devices. Then too, many installations group similar devices together under generic or esoteric device names. Groupings might imply other characteristics like permanent versus temporary storage, or large versus small data sets. Either esoteric or device specifications will help to determine where data is stored.

Volume Residence

When data must be placed on a specific device, a volume serial number can be specified. These volume designations are peculiar to a given installation. In most cases, the volume serial number will be omitted and a generic unit specified. Unit and volume residence information is typically stored in the system catalog so the individual doesn't have to remember where data sets were placed.

Space

Space for a data set must be reserved on a disk volume before data can be written to it. Specifications for how space is allocated and how much space is reserved is actually specified through several parameters. The basic parameters include space units, primary space quantity, secondary space quantity, and sometimes directory blocks. I will cover each of these subjects in turn.

Space Units

The space units parameter indicates the size of a space unit to be allocated. The three choices in increasing size are blocks, tracks, and cylinders. Assuming that a 3380 device will be used and that the blocksize is 23440, a track is twice as big as a block. The relationship to other blocksizes would have to be determined from a device-dependent chart like that shown in many of the edit examples. A cylinder is always 15 times larger than a track on a 3380 device, and so is 30 times larger than the blocksize used here.

When discussed in terms of record capacity, a block of 23440 bytes would hold 293 records (calculated previously in the section on blocksizes). A track would hold 586 records, and a cylinder would hold 8790. When space is requested in blocks, it's rounded up to complete tracks. If a single 23440-byte block were requested, two would be allocated because a track is the minimum allocation unit. When space is requested in cylinders, it can be more efficient to read from and write to, but that might make it more difficult to release unused space.

Primary Space Quantity

The primary space quantity requests a certain number of space units at the time that the data set is created. If available, the primary space is obtained from a single area on the disk. If space is constrained or fragmented, the primary space allocation might be spread to as many as five places or extents on the disk volume. If the primary space allocation can't be satisfied in five extents, the request for space will be denied.

Secondary Space Quantity

The secondary space quantity requests a certain number of space units each time that the data set runs out of space while being extended. Whatever secondary space quantity is requested can be applied up to 15 times. The data set as a whole is allowed up to 16 extents. Since the primary allocation might be from one to five extents, the secondary allocation might be from 11 to 15 extents. The secondary space quantity is optional, but should routinely be used to help keep the data set from running out of space.

Directory Blocks

Directory blocks are also an optional part of space allocation. When directory blocks are included, they define a partitioned data set. A numeric value is used to indicate how many directory blocks will be formatted at the beginning of the primary space allocation. Each block is 256 bytes and can accommodate from 5 to 22 members, depending on whether or not member statistics are kept.

Partitioned Data Set Organization

Multiple sequential data sets can be grouped together within a single data set known as a PDS. This type of data set organization, also referred to as a library, has advantages and disadvantages over regular sequential data sets. The main advantage comes from being able to group logically related data under a single data set name. For example, an individual could store all of their text in one PDS, JCL in another, and COBOL source code in yet another. These libraries could, in turn, each contain many members. ISPF provides ways to scan and select from lists of members, making any piece of data easy to find. ISPF also stores statistics about much of the member data, making it easy to determine, from the member list, things like who last updated a particular member, when it was last updated, and how many lines it contains.

Partitioned data sets also store small amounts of data more efficiently since it allows different pieces of data to share the same track. It does this using the directory in the front of the data set to keep track of the members. The directory is what differentiates a PDS from a regular sequential data set. The directory retains the member statistics mentioned above and the addresses of all current members. While partitioned data sets are preferable for storing many types of data, they're actually required for storing executable load code.

One drawback encountered in using a PDS is that it must periodically be compressed. This stems from the fact that data is always written to the next available data space. This is true even when updating an existing member (which also prohibits a PDS member from being written to in an extend mode). Over time, portions of the data space will be consumed by deleted members as well as older copies of existing members. The only way to make this space available again is to compress the data set. This rewrites the existing members to the beginning of the data space, leaving room for them to be written as they're updated or new members are added.

The System Catalog

The system catalog is a special data set that keeps track of data set placement. Roughly analogous to a phone book, the operating system can use the system catalog to find what volume a data set has been placed on. This is a significant convenience because it would be very difficult to remember where each data set has been placed. Most TSO and ISPF functions work on the assumption that data sets are cataloged, although some provide a way to specify a volume serial number. The LIST-CAT (also abbreviated LISTC) TSO command can be used to list catalog information. Many rely on it to display what data sets they have as well as where they're located.

Storage Management Subsystem

Storage Management Subsystem (SMS) software can be installed with other operating system software (Data Facility Product or DFP) to influence the placement of data. Perhaps it would be better understood if it were called system managed storage, since each installation can use SMS to control things like data set placement, migration, and backup patterns. All data on SMS-managed volumes must be cataloged. For the average user, this is not a problem, since different forms of the same data can easily be stored using different data set names.

With SMS comes a new form of partitioned data set known as *PDS/E*. This type of data set can only be maintained on an SMS-managed volume. One advantage it has is that it doesn't need to be compressed. When writing back onto one of its existing members, it actually replaces the member rather than writing a new version. The PDSE format will also not run out of directory space since directory information is stored with the data itself rather than in a separate directory area.

Specifying Data Set Information

Figure 27.1 shows a screen that's part of the data set utility (Option 3.2). The screen has fields for entering data set information that will be used to create the data set. The data set will have a maximum size of 33 tracks (3 primary tracks + (2 secondary tracks * 15 extents)). The data set will be partitioned because 20 directory blocks are requested.

Use of ISPF Utilities

The ISPF utilities are available under option 3. The first of the listed utilities is the library utility (option 3.1). It's used mainly to maintain the members of an existing PDS. It also has functions that can affect the entire PDS like the print and compress functions.

The data set utility (option 3.2) is so named because it deals exclusively with the entire data set, whether it's partitioned or sequential. The data set utility has options to create, delete, rename, catalog, uncatalog, or list the attributes of a data set.

```
----------------------- ALLOCATE NEW DATA SET -----------------------------
COMMAND ===>

DATA SET NAME: TSO1234.SAMPLE.PDS

     VOLUME SERIAL       ===> DISK1A    (Blank for authorized default volume) *
     GENERIC UNIT        ===> _         (Generic group name or unit address) *
     SPACE UNITS         ===> TRACK     (BLKS, TRKS, or CYLS)
     PRIMARY QUANTITY    ===> 3         (In above units)
     SECONDARY QUANTITY  ===> 2         (In above units)
     DIRECTORY BLOCKS    ===> 20        (Zero for sequential data set)
     RECORD FORMAT       ===> FB
     RECORD LENGTH       ===> 80
     BLOCK SIZE          ===> 6160
     EXPIRATION DATE     ===>           (YY/MM/DD, YYYY/MM/DD
                                         YY.DDD, YYYY.DDD in Julian form
                                         DDDD for retention period in days
                                         or blank)

     ( * Only one of these fields may be specified)
```

Figure 27.1 Specifying data-set characteristics.

The move/copy utility (option 3.3) is used to move or copy sequential data sets or members of a PDS. Again, this option only works with existing data sets. A browse function is also included so members can be examined before they're moved or copied.

The data set list utility (option 3.4) is used to generate a list of data sets, and allows basic utility functions to be applied to those data sets. A particular option is applied using its letter code in front of the data set to be affected. These utilities will be discussed in the next four chapters.

28

The Data Set Utility

The data set utility is not the first of the listed ISPF utilities, but logically it comes first because it's used to create the data sets that are used in many of the other options. The data set utility is option 3.2, and so it can be accessed by entering 3.2 on the primary option menu or by entering 3 to invoke the utility menu before entering suboption 2.

The data set utility has several functions. As just mentioned, it's used to create data sets. These data sets can be either partitioned or sequential. The data set utility is also used to delete, rename, catalog, uncatalog, and list the characteristics of data sets. These functions apply to all non-VSAM data sets.

Listing Data Set Information

To list the characteristics of an existing data set, the processing option is left blank. The data set name is specified in either ISPF or TSO format, and the volume serial number is specified when the data set is not cataloged. The data set must be on a mounted device so the data set label can be read. In Figure 28.1, the name of data set to be displayed is specified in ISPF format.

Information for a disk data set is pulled from the disk VTOC (Volume Table Of Contents). The *VTOC* is a collection of data set labels for all of the data sets on a particular disk volume. For a partitioned data set, information is also pulled from the PDS directory.

Figure 28.2 shows the data set information display. The display includes unit and volume residence information as well as the characteristics of the data set. The right side of the display details the space usage for the data set. Because the data set listed is partitioned, the space usage also includes information on the PDS directory. For a discussion of data set characteristics and space use, see Chapter 27.

```
-------------------------- DATA SET UTILITY ----------------------------
OPTION ===>

   A - Allocate new data set          C - Catalog data set
   R - Rename entire data set         U - Uncatalog data set
   D - Delete entire data set         S - Data set information (short)
   blank - Data set information

ISPF LIBRARY:
   PROJECT ===> tso1234
   GROUP   ===> test
   TYPE    ===> cntl_

OTHER PARTITIONED OR SEQUENTIAL DATA SET:
   DATA SET NAME  ===>
   VOLUME SERIAL  ===>         (If not cataloged, required for option "C")

DATA SET PASSWORD ===>         (If password protected)
```

Figure 28.1 Listing data set information.

```
-------------------------- DATA SET INFORMATION ------------------------
COMMAND ===> _

DATA SET NAME:  TS01234.TEST.CNTL

GENERAL DATA:                          CURRENT ALLOCATION:
   Volume serial:      DISK11             Allocated blocks:        21
   Device type:        3380               Allocated extents:        1
   Organization:       PO                 Maximum dir. blocks:     20
   Record format:      FB
   Record length:      80
   Block size:         6160            CURRENT UTILIZATION:
   1st extent blocks:  21                 Used blocks:              6
   Secondary blocks:   11                 Used extents:             1
                                          Used dir. blocks:         2
   Creation date:      1992/12/11         Number of members:        7
   Expiration date:    ***NONE***
```

Figure 28.2 List of data set information.

Processing option S from the data set utility menu will also list data set information. When option S is used, the PDS directory is not accessed, and directory information is, therefore, omitted from the display. Since the data set is not opened (to get directory information), there should not be an access problem in listing data set information.

Deleting a Data Set

An existing data set can be deleted using processing option D. This removes the data set label (or VTOC entry) and usually the catalog entry as well. When a volume serial number is specified, the catalog entry, if any, is not deleted. In Figure 28.3, the data set utility is used to delete the data set just listed. The only difference here is that the processing option is now the letter D.

Pressing the ENTER key causes a second screen to appear (Figure 28.4). This screen is used to confirm the delete process because, once deleted, the data set can no longer be accessed. The END command can be issued to cancel the delete request, and the data set will be retained. Pressing the ENTER key from this screen will serve as confirmation that the data set is to be deleted.

Yet another screen might be involved. This screen (shown in Figure 28.5) is only displayed if the data set has an expiration date, and that date (displayed on the screen) has not yet arrived. This screen is just like the Confirm Delete screen. Using the END command here or entering NO in the PURGE DATA SET field will cause the data set to be retained. Entering a value of YES will override the data set expiration date and cause the data set to be deleted.

```
--------------------------- DATA SET UTILITY ----------------------------
OPTION  ===> d_

   A - Allocate new data set          C - Catalog data set
   R - Rename entire data set         U - Uncatalog data set
   D - Delete entire data set         S - Data set information (short)
   blank - Data set information

ISPF LIBRARY:
   PROJECT ===> TSO1234
   GROUP   ===> TEST
   TYPE    ===> CNTL


OTHER PARTITIONED OR SEQUENTIAL DATA SET:
   DATA SET NAME  ===>
   VOLUME SERIAL  ===>        (If not cataloged, required for option "C")

DATA SET PASSWORD ===>        (If password protected)
```

Figure 28.3 Deleting a data set.

```
--------------------------- CONFIRM DELETE ---------------------------------
COMMAND ===> _

DATA SET NAME: TSO1234.TEST.CNTL
VOLUME:        DISK11
CREATION DATE: 1992/12/11


INSTRUCTIONS:

    Press ENTER key to confirm delete request.
        (The data set will be deleted and uncataloged.)

    Enter END command to cancel delete request.
```

Figure 28.4 Confirm delete screen.

```
--------------------------- CONFIRM PURGE  ---------------------------------
COMMAND ===>

 The data set being deleted has an expiration date which has not expired.

DATA SET NAME:    TSO1234.TEST.CNTL
VOLUME:           DISK11
CREATION DATE:    1992/02/11
EXPIRATION DATE:  1999/01/17

PURGE DATA SET ===> yes_   (YES or NO)

INSTRUCTIONS:

    Enter YES to confirm the purge request.
        (A request will be issued for the data set
          to be deleted and uncataloged)

    Enter NO or END command to cancel the purge request.
```

Figure 28.5 Screen to purge unexpired data sets.

Once the data set is deleted, the data set utility menu is again displayed (Figure 28.6). The short message area indicates that the data set has been deleted. The data set utility is used to delete an entire data set. The library utility (option 3.1) can be used to delete members from a given data set.

Modeling a Data Set

The process of creating a new data set is often made easier if there's a model to follow. The data set utility presents just such a feature. The key to its use is that the characteristics of the last viewed data set are retained. To take advantage of that fact, the name of an existing data set (CNTL) is specified in the DATA SET NAME field in Figure 28.7.

Once the data set characteristics are displayed (Figure 28.8), they're retained until another data set is listed. The characteristics of the model data set need not exactly match the one being created. The closer its characteristics are, however, the easier the task of creating the new data set. Modeling data set characteristics can also help to create compatibility between data sets in future use.

Creating a Data Set

Whether or not the characteristics of an existing data set have been displayed, the rest of the process is the same. A processing option of A is used to create or allocate a data set. The name of the new data set is specified, just as with the listing option (Figure 28.9).

```
-------------------------- DATA SET UTILITY ------------ DATA SET DELETED
OPTION  ==->  _

    A - Allocate new data set          C - Catalog data set
    R - Rename entire data set         U - Uncatalog data set
    D - Delete entire data set         S - Data set information (short)
    blank - Data set information

ISPF LIBRARY:
    PROJECT ===> TSO1234
    GROUP   ===> TEST
    TYPE    ===> CNTL

OTHER PARTITIONED OR SEQUENTIAL DATA SET:
    DATA SET NAME  ===>
    VOLUME SERIAL  ===>          (If not cataloged, required for option "C")

DATA SET PASSWORD ===>          (If password protected)
```

Figure 28.6 End of data set delete process.

```
-------------------------- DATA SET UTILITY  --------------------------
OPTION  ===>

   A - Allocate new data set          C - Catalog data set
   R - Rename entire data set         U - Uncatalog data set
   D - Delete entire data set         S - Data set information (short)
   blank - Data set information

ISPF LIBRARY:
   PROJECT ===> TSO1234
   GROUP   ===> JCL
   TYPE    ===> CNTL

OTHER PARTITIONED OR SEQUENTIAL DATA SET:
   DATA SET NAME  ===> cntl_
   VOLUME SERIAL  ===>            (If not cataloged, required for option "C")

DATA SET PASSWORD ===>           (If password protected)
```

Figure 28.7 Listing the characteristics of a model data set.

```
-------------------------- DATA SET INFORMATION  --------------------------
COMMAND ===> _

DATA SET NAME: TSO1234.CNTL

GENERAL DATA:                          CURRENT ALLOCATION:
   Volume serial:      DISK1A             Allocated tracks:        3
   Device type:        3380               Allocated extents:       1
   Organization:       PO                 Maximum dir. blocks:    20
   Record format:      FB
   Record length:      80
   Block size:         6160            CURRENT UTILIZATION:
   1st extent tracks:  3                  Used tracks:             1
   Secondary tracks:   2                  Used extents:            1
                                          Used dir. blocks:        2
   Creation date:      1992/10/09         Number of members:       6
   Expiration date:    ***NONE***
```

Figure 28.8 Display of model data set characteristics.

Figure 28.10 shows the name of the data set being created, with the characteristics of the old (last viewed) data set. If it was not necessary to change any of the characteristics, the ENTER key could be pressed to create the data set.

Allowing the new data set to be allocated on the same volume as the model data set is not necessarily a good idea. Ideally data sets should be spread across different volumes to minimize disk head movement of data sets used at the same time. Allowing data sets to be placed on different volumes will also minimize the effect of a volume outage (where the loss of a single volume would otherwise cause all of an individual's data sets to be inaccessible). For those reasons (and because space might not be available on that volume) the volume serial number has been erased (Figure 28.11).

When both volume serial number and generic unit (the next field down) are omitted, the operating system will determine the appropriate volume for the data set. This is done according to defaults defined at each installation and generally has advantages in being able to find enough disk space for the data set.

The one field that should almost always be left blank is the expiration date. Most think that the expiration date keeps a data set from being deleted. It actually only makes it slightly more difficult to delete the data set. In practice, however, it's very difficult to update an unexpired data set. For that reason, it's not recommended that expiration dates be applied to disk data sets.

After changes are made to any of the fields, the ENTER key is pressed to continue the allocation process. The END command could instead be issued to end the sequence without creating the data set. The short message in Figure 28.12 shows that the data set has been allocated.

```
----------------------------- DATA SET UTILITY  ----------------------------
OPTION  ===> a_

   A - Allocate new data set           C - Catalog data set
   R - Rename entire data set          U - Uncatalog data set
   D - Delete entire data set          S - Data set information (short)
   blank - Data set information

ISPF LIBRARY:
   PROJECT ===> tso1234
   GROUP   ===> jcl
   TYPE    ===> cntl

OTHER PARTITIONED OR SEQUENTIAL DATA SET:
   DATA SET NAME  ===>
   VOLUME SERIAL  ===>            (If not cataloged, required for option "C")

DATA SET PASSWORD ===>           (If password protected)
```

Figure 28.9 Creating a new data set.

```
------------------------  ALLOCATE NEW DATA SET  ----------------------------
COMMAND ===>

DATA SET NAME: TSO1234.JCL.CNTL

      VOLUME SERIAL      ===> DISK1A    (Blank for authorized default volume) *
      GENERIC UNIT       ===> _         (Generic group name or unit address) *
      SPACE UNITS        ===> TRACK     (BLKS, TRKS, or CYLS)
      PRIMARY QUANTITY   ===> 3         (In above units)
      SECONDARY QUANTITY ===> 2         (In above units)
      DIRECTORY BLOCKS   ===> 20        (Zero for sequential data set)
      RECORD FORMAT      ===> FB
      RECORD LENGTH      ===> 80
      BLOCK SIZE         ===> 6160
      EXPIRATION DATE    ===>           (YY/MM/DD, YYYY/MM/DD
                                        YY.DDD, YYYY.DDD in Julian form
                                        DDDD for retention period in days
                                        or blank)

      ( * Only one of these fields may be specified)
```

Figure 28.10 Modeled data set characteristics.

```
------------------------  ALLOCATE NEW DATA SET  ----------------------------
COMMAND ===>

DATA SET NAME: TSO1234.JCL.CNTL

      VOLUME SERIAL      ===> _         (Blank for authorized default volume) *
      GENERIC UNIT       ===>           (Generic group name or unit address) *
      SPACE UNITS        ===> TRACK     (BLKS, TRKS, or CYLS)
      PRIMARY QUANTITY   ===> 3         (In above units)
      SECONDARY QUANTITY ===> 2         (In above units)
      DIRECTORY BLOCKS   ===> 20        (Zero for sequential data set)
      RECORD FORMAT      ===> FB
      RECORD LENGTH      ===> 80
      BLOCK SIZE         ===> 6160
      EXPIRATION DATE    ===>           (YY/MM/DD, YYYY/MM/DD
                                        YY.DDD, YYYY.DDD in Julian form
                                        DDDD for retention period in days
                                        or blank)

      ( * Only one of these fields may be specified)
```

Figure 28.11 Removing the volume serial number.

```
-------------------------------- DATA SET UTILITY  --------- DATA SET ALLOCATED
OPTION  ===> _

    A - Allocate new data set              C - Catalog data set
    R - Rename entire data set             U - Uncatalog data set
    D - Delete entire data set             S - Data set information (short)
    blank - Data set information

ISPF LIBRARY:
    PROJECT ===> TSO1234
    GROUP   ===> JCL
    TYPE    ===> CNTL

OTHER PARTITIONED OR SEQUENTIAL DATA SET:
    DATA SET NAME  ===>
    VOLUME SERIAL  ===>            (If not cataloged, required for option "C")

DATA SET PASSWORD ===>            (If password protected)
```

Figure 28.12 End of allocation sequence.

The allocate option only supports cataloged data sets. (This is also the industry trend.) If an uncataloged data set must be maintained, the data set can be uncataloged using option U right after it's created.

Renaming a Data Set

A data set can be renamed using processing option R, as in Figure 28.13. The only other required information is the current name of the data set to be renamed. That information has been supplied in the PROJECT, GROUP, and TYPE fields. When the ENTER key is pressed, a second screen is displayed where the new data set name is specified.

The second screen used in the rename process is shown in Figure 28.14. The name of the data set being renamed is displayed at the top of the screen. The data set name was also carried forward, from the previous screen, to the PROJECT, GROUP, and TYPE fields. In this instance, the second data set qualifier is changed from OLD to NEW, and the ENTER key is again pressed. The END command can be used instead to return to the previous screen without renaming the data set.

After pressing the ENTER key, the data set utility menu is redisplayed (Figure 28.15). The message in the short message area indicates that the data set has been renamed. The name returned in the PROJECT, GROUP, and TYPE fields is the new name of the data set.

The data set utility is used to rename at the data set level. This would typically be a sequential data set or an entire PDS. Members of a PDS are renamed using the library utility, which is discussed in the next chapter.

```
--------------------------- DATA SET UTILITY -----------------------------
OPTION  ===> r

   A - Allocate new data set          C - Catalog data set
   R - Rename entire data set         U - Uncatalog data set
   D - Delete entire data set         S - Data set information (short)
   blank - Data set information

ISPF LIBRARY:
   PROJECT ===> tso1234
   GROUP   ===> old
   TYPE    ===> pds_

OTHER PARTITIONED OR SEQUENTIAL DATA SET:
   DATA SET NAME  ===>
   VOLUME SERIAL  ===>          (If not cataloged, required for option "C")

DATA SET PASSWORD ===>          (If password protected)
```

Figure 28.13 Renaming a data set.

```
--------------------------- RENAME DATA SET ------------------------------
COMMAND ===>

DATA SET NAME: TSO1234.OLD.PDS
VOLUME:        DISK13

ENTER NEW NAME BELOW:    (The data set will be recataloged.)

ISPF LIBRARY:
   PROJECT ===> TSO1234
   GROUP   ===> new_
   TYPE    ===> PDS

OTHER PARTITIONED OR SEQUENTIAL DATA SET:
   DATA SET NAME  ===>
```

Figure 28.14 Specifying the new data set name.

```
--------------------------- DATA SET UTILITY ------------ DATA SET RENAMED
OPTION  ===> _

    A - Allocate new data set           C - Catalog data set
    R - Rename entire data set          U - Uncatalog data set
    D - Delete entire data set          S - Data set information (short)
    blank - Data set information

ISPF LIBRARY:
    PROJECT ===> TSO1234
    GROUP   ===> NEW
    TYPE    ===> PDS

OTHER PARTITIONED OR SEQUENTIAL DATA SET:
    DATA SET NAME  ===>
    VOLUME SERIAL  ===>           (If not cataloged, required for option "C")

DATA SET PASSWORD ===>           (If password protected)
```

Figure 28.15   End of the rename process.

Catalog Maintenance

The data set utility can also be used to perform catalog maintenance. The utility has options to catalog or uncatalog a data set. Uncataloging a data set is as easy as specifying the processing option U with the data set to be uncataloged. The data set itself is not changed; only its catalog entry is removed. It will still be possible to access the data set by specifying its volume serial number.

Cataloging a data set is only slightly more difficult. The volume serial number must be known before a data set can be cataloged, since it must be specified with processing option C. The data set utility will use the data set name and volume serial number supplied to create a catalog entry. The volume that the data set is being cataloged to must be mounted so that information about the device type can be obtained and placed in the catalog entry as well.

29

Library Utilities

The library utility is used to maintain an existing partitioned data set or library. Most functions operate at the member level, allowing members to be browsed, printed, deleted, and renamed. Functions that affect the entire PDS include the printing of all members, the printing of all member names, and library compression. The function to print an entire data set also works for sequential data sets. The library utility includes options that allow data set information to be displayed much like the data set utility. The library utility is option 3.1, and so it can be accessed by entering 3.1 on the primary option menu or by entering 3 to invoke the utility menu before entering suboption 1.

Member Rename

The initial screen of the library utility can be used to rename a member. In Figure 29.1, the name of a partitioned data set is specified in ISPF format along with a member name. The field just below the MEMBER field is used to specify the new member name.

When the ENTER key is pressed, the member is renamed, as reflected in the short message area in Figure 29.2. The data set need not have three qualifiers to be used in the library utility. Figure 29.2 shows a two-qualifier data set referenced in the DATA SET NAME field. Remember that when quotes are omitted in this field, the TSO prefix is automatically appended to form the data set name. The data set name in this field takes precedence over that specified in the PROJECT, GROUP, and TYPE FIELDS. The new member name is still specified in the NEWNAME field.

The short message area in Figure 29.3 shows that this member has also been renamed. Both the PDS name and the member name specified in the DATA SET NAME field have been retained. This would aid activities performed against other like-named members.

```
--------------------------- LIBRARY UTILITY ----------------------------
OPTION  ===>  r

   blank - Display member list        B - Browse member
   C - Compress data set              P - Print member
   X - Print index listing            R - Rename member
   L - Print entire data set          D - Delete member
   I - Data set information           S - Data set information (short)

ISPF LIBRARY:
   PROJECT ===> tso1234
   GROUP   ===> example   ===>          ===>          ===>
   TYPE    ===> data
   MEMBER  ===> alloc          (If "P", "R", "D", "B", or blank selected)
   NEWNAME ===> allocate _     (If "R" selected)

OTHER PARTITIONED OR SEQUENTIAL DATA SET:
   DATA SET NAME  ===>
   VOLUME SERIAL  ===>         (If not cataloged)

DATA SET PASSWORD ===>         (If password protected)
```

Figure 29.1   Renaming a PDS member.

```
--------------------------- LIBRARY UTILITY  --------- MEMBER ALLOC RENAMED
OPTION  ===>  r_

   blank - Display member list        B - Browse member
   C - Compress data set              P - Print member
   X - Print index listing            R - Rename member
   L - Print entire data set          D - Delete member
   I - Data set information           S - Data set information (short)

ISPF LIBRARY:
   PROJECT ===> TSO1234
   GROUP   ===> EXAMPLE   ===>          ===>          ===>
   TYPE    ===> DATA
   MEMBER  ===>                (If "P", "R", "D", "B", or blank selected)
   NEWNAME ===> job2           (If "R" selected)

OTHER PARTITIONED OR SEQUENTIAL DATA SET:
   DATA SET NAME  ===> cntl(job)
   VOLUME SERIAL  ===>         (If not cataloged)

DATA SET PASSWORD ===>         (If password protected)
```

Figure 29.2   Alternate data set specified for rename.

```
------------------- LIBRARY UTILITY ------------------- MEMBER JOB RENAMED
  OPTION  ===>

      blank - Display member list       B - Browse member
      C - Compress data set             P - Print member
      X - Print index listing           R - Rename member
      L - Print entire data set         D - Delete member
      I - Data set information          S - Data set information (short)

  ISPF LIBRARY:
      PROJECT ===> TSO1234
      GROUP   ===> EXAMPLE   ===>            ===>            ===>
      TYPE    ===> DATA
      MEMBER  ===>                  (If "P", "R", "D", "D", or blank selected)
      NEWNAME ===>                  (If "R" selected)

  OTHER PARTITIONED OR SEQUENTIAL DATA SET:
      DATA SET NAME   ===> CNTL(JOB)_
      VOLUME SERIAL   ===>          (If not cataloged)

  DATA SET PASSWORD ===>            (If password protected)
```

Figure 29.3 Result of renaming a PDS member.

Member Deletion

A processing option of D is used to delete a member. The library and member name can be specified in either format, just as with the rename function. In Figure 29.4, the delete function is used to delete a member within the first referenced PDS.

The short message in Figure 29.5 indicates that the member has been deleted. The other member-oriented options, B for browse and P for print, can be used against individual members in the same way. Any of the member-oriented options can also be applied from the member list, which is generated when the member name and processing option are both omitted.

Member List Processing

The member-oriented options of browse, print, delete, and rename can also be used from the member list. The member list supports multiple commands and executes them from the top of the list to the bottom. With the browse function, members can be examined before other options are applied against them. Figure 29.6 shows three different commands applied to eight members. Notice that when the rename function is used from the member list, a field called RENAME is used to specify the new member name.

After the ENTER key is pressed, all of the commands entered on the member list are executed (Figure 29.7). The status of those commands is listed in the RENAME field next to the affected member. Upon leaving the member list, the library utility screen is again displayed (Figure 29.8). The short message indicates the number of members processed while in the member list.

```
------------------------------  LIBRARY UTILITY  ------------------------------
OPTION  ===> d

    blank - Display member list        B - Browse member
    C - Compress data set              P - Print member
    X - Print index listing            R - Rename member
    L - Print entire data set          D - Delete member
    I - Data set information           S - Data set information (short)

ISPF LIBRARY:
    PROJECT ===> TSO1234
    GROUP   ===> EXAMPLE    ===>              ===>              ===>
    TYPE    ===> DATA
    MEMBER  ===> c5_            (If "P", "R", "D", "B", or blank selected)
    NEWNAME ===>                (If "R" selected)

OTHER PARTITIONED OR SEQUENTIAL DATA SET:
    DATA SET NAME  ===>
    VOLUME SERIAL  ===>         (If not cataloged)

DATA SET PASSWORD ===>          (If password protected)
```

Figure 29.4   Deleting a PDS member.

```
------------------------------  LIBRARY UTILITY  ------------  MEMBER C5 DELETED
OPTION  ===> _

    blank - Display member list        B - Browse member
    C - Compress data set              P - Print member
    X - Print index listing            R - Rename member
    L - Print entire data set          D - Delete member
    I - Data set information           S - Data set information (short)

ISPF LIBRARY:
    PROJECT ===> TSO1234
    GROUP   ===> EXAMPLE    ===>              ===>              ===>
    TYPE    ===> DATA
    MEMBER  ===>                (If "P", "R", "D", "B", or blank selected)
    NEWNAME ===>                (If "R" selected)

OTHER PARTITIONED OR SEQUENTIAL DATA SET:
    DATA SET NAME  ===>
    VOLUME SERIAL  ===>         (If not cataloged)

DATA SET PASSWORD ===>          (If password protected)
```

Figure 29.5   Result of deleting a PDS member.

```
LIBRARY - TSO1234.EXAMPLE.DATA ------------------------- ROW 00001 OF 00062
COMMAND ===>                                              SCROLL ===> CSR
  NAME      RENAME    VV.MM  CREATED     CHANGED      SIZE  INIT  MOD   ID
  ALLOCATE            01.01  91/12/04  91/12/11 17:04  270   270    0  TSO1234
  ALTLIB             01.01  91/12/04  91/12/11 17:10  329   327    0  TSO1234
  ATTRIB             01.00  91/12/04  91/12/04 17:48  102   102    0  TSO1234
  BLKSIZE            01.05  91/12/11  91/12/21 23:15   23    18    0  TSO1234
  BLKSIZE2           01.00  91/12/14  91/12/14 14:22   19    19    0  TSO1234
  BLKSIZE3           01.00  91/12/14  91/12/14 15:32   22    22    0  TSO1234
d BLKSIZE4           01.02  91/12/19  91/12/19 17:53   17    19    0  TSO1234
  CALL               01.01  91/12/04  91/12/11 17:05   31    31    0  TSO1234
p CANCEL             01.00  91/12/04  91/12/04 17:49   20    20    0  TSO1234
p CLIST              01.01  91/12/11  91/12/11 17:16  639   655    0  TSO1234
d COLUMNS            01.01  92/02/01  92/02/01 23:24   17    17    0  TSO1234
  COPY               01.00  91/12/04  91/12/04 17:50   68    68    0  TSO1234
r C1        copy1    01.00  91/12/21  91/12/21 23:08   11    11    0  TSO1234
r C2        copy2    01.00  91/12/21  91/12/21 23:17   10    10    0  TSO1234
d C3                 01.01  91/12/21  91/12/21 23:32   11    11    0  TSO1234
d C4                 01.00  91/12/21  91/12/21 23:31   11    11    0  TSO1234
  DATASETS           01.00  92/02/01  92/02/01 23:40   15    15    0  TSO1234
  DEFINE             01.00  91/12/04  91/12/04 17:51  545   545    0  TSO1234
  DELETE             01.03  91/12/04  91/12/11 17:06  123   123    0  TSO1234
  EDIT               01.00  91/12/04  91/12/04 17:52  106   106    0  TSO1234
  EXEC               01.00  91/12/04  91/12/04 17:53   48    48    0  TSO1234
```

Figure 29.6 Commands applied to the member list.

```
LIBRARY - TSO1234.EXAMPLE.DATA ------------------------- ROW 00001 OF 00062
COMMAND ===> _                                           SCROLL ===> CSR
  NAME      RENAME    VV.MM  CREATED     CHANGED      SIZE  INIT  MOD   ID
  ALLOCATE            01.01  91/12/04  91/12/11 17:04  270   270    0  TSO1234
  ALTLIB             01.01  91/12/04  91/12/11 17:10  329   327    0  TSO1234
  ATTRIB             01.00  91/12/04  91/12/04 17:48  102   102    0  TSO1234
  BLKSIZE            01.05  91/12/11  91/12/21 23:15   23    18    0  TSO1234
  BLKSIZE2           01.00  91/12/14  91/12/14 14:22   19    19    0  TSO1234
  BLKSIZE3           01.00  91/12/14  91/12/14 15:32   22    22    0  TSO1234
  BLKSIZE4 *DELETED
  CALL               01.01  91/12/04  91/12/11 17:05   31    31    0  TSO1234
  CANCEL   *PRINTED  01.00  91/12/04  91/12/04 17:49   20    20    0  TSO1234
  CLIST    *PRINTED  01.01  91/12/11  91/12/11 17:16  639   655    0  TSO1234
  COLUMNS  *DELETED
  COPY               01.00  91/12/04  91/12/04 17:50   68    68    0  TSO1234
  C1       *RENAMED
  C2       *RENAMED
  C3       *DELETED
  C4       *DELETED
  DATASETS           01.00  92/02/01  92/02/01 23:40   15    15    0  TSO1234
  DEFINE             01.00  91/12/04  91/12/04 17:51  545   545    0  TSO1234
  DELETE             01.03  91/12/04  91/12/11 17:06  123   123    0  TSO1234
  EDIT               01.00  91/12/04  91/12/04 17:52  106   106    0  TSO1234
  EXEC               01.00  91/12/04  91/12/04 17:53   48    48    0  TSO1234
```

Figure 29.7 Result of executing multiple commands.

```
-------------------------------- LIBRARY UTILITY  ----------  8 MEMBERS PROCESSED
OPTION  ===> x_

   blank - Display member list        B - Browse member
   C - Compress data set              P - Print member
   X - Print index listing            R - Rename member
   L - Print entire data set          D - Delete member
   I - Data set information           S - Data set information (short)

ISPF LIBRARY:
   PROJECT ===> TSO1234
   GROUP   ===> EXAMPLE    ===>           ===>           ===>
   TYPE    ===> DATA
   MEMBER  ===>                    (If "P", "R", "D", "B", or blank selected)
   NEWNAME ===>                    (If "R" selected)

OTHER PARTITIONED OR SEQUENTIAL DATA SET:
   DATA SET NAME  ===>
   VOLUME SERIAL  ===>             (If not cataloged)

DATA SET PASSWORD ===>             (If password protected)
```

Figure 29.8 Printing the PDS index.

Commands that affect the entire PDS must be executed from the utility menu. One example is the function that prints the index. This prints information about the PDS and its members to the list data set.

Figure 29.9 shows the message issued after the index has been printed to the list data set. The list data set must be processed further to obtain actual hard-copy output. Also in Figure 29.9, the command is issued to compress the PDS.

Figure 29.10 shows that the PDS has been successfully compressed. This is a process of rewriting the member data to make more room available in the PDS. It's the first course of action to be taken following a space abend involving the PDS.

Using Member Patterns

In Chapter 6, I mentioned that the characters % and * could be used in member names to represent any single character or series of characters, respectively. This sort of member pattern can be used from the initial menu of many options to generate a filtered list of members. Member patterns can also be used in the library utility from within the member list, as in Figure 29.11. There it's used with the SELECT primary command to delete all members starting with the letters LIST. The letter D represents the library utility line command that's to be applied to all of the selected members.

Figure 29.12 shows the result of the SELECT primary command. Four members on the current screen show a status of DELETED in the rename column. Other members not on the current screen could have also been affected by the command.

```
------------------------------- LIBRARY UTILITY ---------------- INDEX PRINTED
OPTION  ===> C_

      blank - Display member list          B - Browse member
      C - Compress data set                P - Print member
      X - Print index listing              R - Rename member
      L - Print entire data set            D - Delete member
      I - Data set information             S - Data set information (short)

   ISPF LIBRARY:
      PROJECT ===> TSO1234
      GROUP   ===> EXAMPLE  ===>            ===>            ===>
      TYPE    ---> DATA
      MEMBER  ===>               (If "P", "R", "D", "B", or blank selected)
      NEWNAME ===>               (If "R" selected)

   OTHER PARTITIONED OR SEQUENTIAL DATA SET:
      DATA SET NAME   ===>
      VOLUME SERIAL   ===>       (If not cataloged)

   DATA SET PASSWORD ===>        (If password protected)
```

Figure 29.9 Compressing a PDS.

```
------------------------------- LIBRARY UTILITY ---------- COMPRESS SUCCESSFUL
OPTION  ===> _

      blank - Display member list          B - Browse member
      C - Compress data set                P - Print member
      X - Print index listing              R - Rename member
      L - Print entire data set            D - Delete member
      I - Data set information             S - Data set information (short)

   ISPF LIBRARY:
      PROJECT ===> TSO1234
      GROUP   ===> EXAMPLE  ===>            ===>            ===>
      TYPE    ===> DATA
      MEMBER  ===>               (If "P", "R", "D", "B", or blank selected)
      NEWNAME ===>               (If "R" selected)

   OTHER PARTITIONED OR SEQUENTIAL DATA SET:
      DATA SET NAME   ===>
      VOLUME SERIAL   ===>       (If not cataloged)

   DATA SET PASSWORD ===>        .   (If password protected)
```

Figure 29.10 Result of PDS compression.

```
LIBRARY - TSO1234.TEST.DATA ----------------------------- ROW 00001 OF 00048
COMMAND ===> s list* d_                              SCROLL ===> CSR
   NAME     RENAME    VV.MM  CREATED    CHANGED       SIZE  INIT   MOD   ID
   ALLOC              01.01  92/12/04 92/12/11 17:04   270   270    0 TSO1234
   ALTLIB             01.01  92/12/04 92/12/11 17:10   329   327    0 TSO1234
   ATTRIB             01.00  92/12/04 92/12/04 17:48   102   102    0 TSO1234
   BLKSIZE            01.04  92/12/11 92/12/14 18:19    23    18    0 TSO1234
   BLKSIZE2           01.00  92/12/14 92/12/14 14:22    19    19    0 TSO1234
   BLKSIZE3           01.00  92/12/14 92/12/14 15:32    22    22    0 TSO1234
   CALL               01.01  92/12/04 92/12/11 17:05    31    31    0 TSO1234
   CANCEL             01.00  92/12/04 92/12/04 17:49    20    20    0 TSO1234
   CLIST              01.01  92/12/11 92/12/11 17:16   639   655    0 TSO1234
   COPY               01.00  92/12/04 92/12/04 17:50    68    68    0 TSO1234
   DEFINE             01.00  92/12/04 92/12/04 17:51   545   545    0 TSO1234
   DELETE             01.03  92/12/04 92/12/11 17:06   123   123    0 TSO1234
   EDIT               01.00  92/12/04 92/12/04 17:52   106   106    0 TSO1234
   EXEC               01.00  92/12/04 92/12/04 17:53    48    48    0 TSO1234
   FORMAT             01.00  92/12/04 92/12/04 17:54    60    60    0 TSO1234
   FREE               01.00  92/12/04 92/12/04 17:44    55    55    0 TSO1234
   LINK               01.00  92/12/04 92/12/04 17:55   116   116    0 TSO1234
   LIST               01.00  92/12/04 92/12/04 17:56    38    38    0 TSO1234
   LISTALC            01.00  92/12/04 92/12/04 17:56    22    22    0 TSO1234
   LISTBC             01.00  92/12/04 92/12/04 17:57    27    27    0 TSO1234
   LISTCAT            01.00  92/12/04 92/12/04 17:57   104   104    0 TSO1234
```

Figure 29.11 Specifying a member pattern.

```
LIBRARY - TSO1234.TEST.DATA ----------------------------- ROW 00001 OF 00048
COMMAND ===> _                                       SCROLL ===> CSR
   NAME     RENAME    VV.MM  CREATED    CHANGED       SIZE  INIT   MOD   ID
   ALLOC              01.01  92/12/04 92/12/11 17:04   270   270    0 TSO1234
   ALTLIB             01.01  92/12/04 92/12/11 17:10   329   327    0 TSO1234
   ATTRIB             01.00  92/12/04 92/12/04 17:48   102   102    0 TSO1234
   BLKSIZE            01.04  92/12/11 92/12/14 18:19    23    18    0 TSO1234
   BLKSIZE2           01.00  92/12/14 92/12/14 14:22    19    19    0 TSO1234
   BLKSIZE3           01.00  92/12/14 92/12/14 15:32    22    22    0 TSO1234
   CALL               01.01  92/12/04 92/12/11 17:05    31    31    0 TSO1234
   CANCEL             01.00  92/12/04 92/12/04 17:49    20    20    0 TSO1234
   CLIST              01.01  92/12/11 92/12/11 17:16   639   655    0 TSO1234
   COPY               01.00  92/12/04 92/12/04 17:50    68    68    0 TSO1234
   DEFINE             01.00  92/12/04 92/12/04 17:51   545   545    0 TSO1234
   DELETE             01.03  92/12/04 92/12/11 17:06   123   123    0 TSO1234
   EDIT               01.00  92/12/04 92/12/04 17:52   106   106    0 TSO1234
   EXEC               01.00  92/12/04 92/12/04 17:53    48    48    0 TSO1234
   FORMAT             01.00  92/12/04 92/12/04 17:54    60    60    0 TSO1234
   FREE               01.00  92/12/04 92/12/04 17:44    55    55    0 TSO1234
   LINK               01.00  92/12/04 92/12/04 17:55   116   116    0 TSO1234
   LIST     *DELETED
   LISTALC  *DELETED
   LISTBC   *DELETED
   LISTCAT  *DELETED
```

Figure 29.12 Result of the SELECT primary command.

Indeed, upon leaving the member list, a message is issued that five members were processed. This is displayed in the short message area in Figure 29.13. Pressing the ENTER key generates a new member list, which is displayed in Figure 29.14. The members previously deleted (those starting with LIST) no longer appear on the list. The same figure shows that the SELECT command can be used with an asterisk to represent all members. The result of the SELECT command was to delete all of the members of the PDS as shown in Figure 29.15.

Using the END command to return to the library utility menu shows that 43 members were affected. This again is displayed in the short message area (Figure 29.16). The PDS now contains no active members.

The Member Statistics Utility

The member statistics utility is option 3.5. It's used to create and maintain member statistics. The utility can be accessed by entering 3.5 on the primary option menu or by entering 3 to invoke the utility menu before entering suboption 5.

Resetting Member Statistics

Member statistics can be created or reset in this option. This is useful where members don't already have statistics or where statistics should be reset to start a new change history. Either process will incorporate the current date and time into the fields CREATED and CHANGED (fields that display on the member list). Member

```
--------------------------- LIBRARY UTILITY  ---------- 5 MEMBERS PROCESSED
OPTION ===> _

    blank - Display member list        B - Browse member
    C - Compress data set              P - Print member
    X - Print index listing            R - Rename member
    L - Print entire data set          D - Delete member
    I - Data set information           S - Data set information (short)

ISPF LIBRARY:
    PROJECT ===> TSO1234
    GROUP   ===> TEST      ===>          ===>          ===>
    TYPE    ===> DATA
    MEMBER  ===>                 (If "P", "R", "D", "B", or blank selected)
    NEWNAME ===>                 (If "R" selected)

OTHER PARTITIONED OR SEQUENTIAL DATA SET:
    DATA SET NAME   ===>
    VOLUME SERIAL   ===>         (If not cataloged)

DATA SET PASSWORD ===>           (If password protected)
```

Figure 29.13 Message indicating the number of members processed.

```
LIBRARY - TSO1234.TEST.DATA ------------------------------ ROW 00001 OF 00043
COMMAND ===> s * d_                                       SCROLL ===> CSR
   NAME      RENAME    VV.MM  CREATED      CHANGED       SIZE  INIT  MOD   ID
   ALLOC               01.01 92/12/04 92/12/11 17:04     270   270    0 TSO1234
   ALTLIB              01.01 92/12/04 92/12/11 17:10     329   327    0 TSO1234
   ATTRIB              01.00 92/12/04 92/12/04 17:48     102   102    0 TSO1234
   BLKSIZE             01.04 92/12/11 92/12/14 18:19      23    18    0 TSO1234
   BLKSIZE2            01.00 92/12/14 92/12/14 14:22      19    19    0 TSO1234
   BLKSIZE3            01.00 92/12/14 92/12/14 15:32      22    22    0 TSO1234
   CALL                01.01 92/12/04 92/12/11 17:05      31    31    0 TSO1234
   CANCEL              01.00 92/12/04 92/12/04 17:49      20    20    0 TSO1234
   CLIST               01.01 92/12/11 92/12/11 17:16     639   655    0 TSO1234
   COPY                01.00 92/12/04 92/12/04 17:50      68    68    0 TSO1234
   DEFINE              01.00 92/12/04 92/12/04 17:51     545   545    0 TSO1234
   DELETE              01.03 92/12/04 92/12/11 17:06     123   123    0 TSO1234
   EDIT                01.00 92/12/04 92/12/04 17:52     106   106    0 TSO1234
   EXEC                01.00 92/12/04 92/12/04 17:53      48    48    0 TSO1234
   FORMAT              01.00 92/12/04 92/12/04 17:54      60    60    0 TSO1234
   FREE                01.00 92/12/04 92/12/04 17:44      55    55    0 TSO1234
   LINK                01.00 92/12/04 92/12/04 17:55     116   116    0 TSO1234
   LOADGO              01.00 92/12/04 92/12/04 17:59      68    68    0 TSO1234
   LOGOFF              01.00 92/12/04 92/12/04 17:59      16    16    0 TSO1234
   MERGE               01.00 92/12/04 92/12/04 18:00      68    68    0 TSO1234
   NAME                01.00 92/12/10 92/12/10 19:13      31    31    0 TSO1234
```

Figure 29.14 SELECT command to delete all members.

```
LIBRARY - TSO1234.TEST.DATA ------------------------------ ROW 00001 OF 00043
COMMAND ===> _                                            SCROLL ===> CSR
   NAME      RENAME    VV.MM  CREATED      CHANGED       SIZE  INIT  MOD   ID
   ALLOC     *DELETED
   ALTLIB    *DELETED
   ATTRIB    *DELETED
   BLKSIZE   *DELETED
   BLKSIZE2  *DELETED
   BLKSIZE3  *DELETED
   CALL      *DELETED
   CANCEL    *DELETED
   CLIST     *DELETED
   COPY      *DELETED
   DEFINE    *DELETED
   DELETE    *DELETED
   EDIT      *DELETED
   EXEC      *DELETED
   FORMAT    *DELETED
   FREE      *DELETED
   LINK      *DELETED
   LOADGO    *DELETED
   LOGOFF    *DELETED
   MERGE     *DELETED
   NAME      *DELETED
```

Figure 29.15 Result of the SELECT * command.

```
--------------------------- LIBRARY UTILITY --------- 43 MEMBERS PROCESSED
OPTION ===> _

   blank - Display member list        B - Browse member
   C - Compress data set              P - Print member
   X - Print index listing            R - Rename member
   L - Print entire data set          D - Delete member
   I - Data set information            S - Data set information (short)

ISPF LIBRARY:
   PROJECT -==> TSO1234
   GROUP   ===> TEST        ===>          =-->           ===>
   TYPE    ===> DATA
   MEMBER  ===>                    (If "P", "R", "D", "B", or blank selected)
   NEWNAME ===>                    (If "R" selected)

OTHER PARTITIONED OR SEQUENTIAL DATA SET:
   DATA SET NAME  ===>
   VOLUME SERIAL  ===>             (If not cataloged)

DATA SET PASSWORD ===>             (If password protected)
```

Figure 29.16 Message for number of members processed.

statistics are reset using option R (Figure 29.17). Information about the statistics is specified at the top of the screen, while data set information is specified in normal format further down.

Statistics can be reset for a single member by specifying the member name in the MEMBER field. An asterisk in the same field would cause all member statistics to be reset. In this case, however, the field is left blank to force the member list to be displayed.

Figure 29.18 shows a part of the member list after scrolling down. It's quite apparent which members don't already have statistics. Each of the members on the current screen that doesn't have statistics has been selected using the letter S.

Figure 29.19 shows the result of having reset statistics. The current date and time has been applied to the columns labeled CREATED and CHANGED. Upon returning to the initial screen, a message is displayed in the short message area (Figure 29.20). It indicates that statistics for 15 members were reset.

Deleting Member Statistics

Member statistics can be helpful in determining who last made a change to a member or when it was last changed. When a member list is sorted by the CHANGED column, statistics can also be used to show what members have last been changed in the PDS. When the directory is full, however, it might be convenient to delete some of the member statistics until the directory can be enlarged. Member statistics can be deleted using a processing option of D rather than R. The rest of the process is the same as resetting member statistics, whether a single member is specified on the initial screen or all members are affected. The member list can also be used as in the previous example. The letter S would be used to select each member to be affected.

```
-------------------------- RESET ISPF STATISTICS --------------------------
OPTION  ===> r

   R - Reset (create/update) ISPF statistics
   D - Delete ISPF statistics

NEW USERID              ===> tso1234 (If userid is to be changed)
NEW VERSION NUMBER      ===>         (If version number is to be changed)
   RESET MOD LEVEL      ===> YES     (YES or NO)
   RESET SEQ NUMBERS    ===> YES     (YES or NO)

ISPF LIBRARY:
   PROJECT ===> tso1234
   GROUP   ===> example
   TYPE    ===> data  _
   MEMBER  ===>                  (Blank or pattern for member selection
                                  list, '*' for all members)

OTHER PARTITIONED DATA SET:
   DATA SET NAME   ===>
   VOLUME SERIAL   ===>          (If not cataloged)

DATA SET PASSWORD ===>           (If password protected)
```

Figure 29.17 Resetting member statistics.

```
RESET - TSO1234.EXAMPLE.DATA --------------------------- ROW 00023 OF 00043
COMMAND ===>                                       SCROLL ===> CSR
   NAME           VV.MM  CREATED      CHANGED      SIZE  INIT  MOD   ID
 s NAME
   OUTDES         01.00 92/12/04 92/12/04 18:00    329   329    0 TSO1234
   OUTPUT         01.00 92/12/04 92/12/04 18:01     99    99    0 TSO1234
   PRINT          01.00 92/12/04 92/12/04 18:01    113   113    0 TSO1234
   PRINTDS        01.00 92/12/04 92/12/04 17:42    434   434    0 TSO1234
   PROTECT        01.00 92/12/04 92/12/04 18:02     56    56    0 TSO1234
 s RECEIVE
   RENAME         01.00 92/12/04 92/12/04 18:03     15    15    0 TSO1234
 s REPRO
 s RUN
 s SEND
 s STATUS
 s SUBMIT
 s TERMINAL
 s TEST
 s TIME
 s TRANSMIT
 s TSOEXEC
 s UNALLOC
 s VERIFY
 s WHEN
   _
```

Figure 29.18 Selective resetting of member statistics.

```
RESET -  TSO1234.EXAMPLE.DATA -------------------------- ROW 00023 OF 00043
COMMAND ===> _                                         SCROLL ===> CSR
   NAME              VV.MM  CREATED      CHANGED      SIZE  INIT  MOD  ID
   NAME      *RESET  01.00  92/12/10  92/12/10 19:13   31    31   0  TSO1234
   OUTDES            01.00  92/12/04  92/12/04 18:00  329   329   0  TSO1234
   OUTPUT            01.00  92/12/04  92/12/04 18:01   99    99   0  TSO1234
   PRINT             01.00  92/12/04  92/12/04 18:01  113   113   0  TSO1234
   PRINTDS           01.00  92/12/04  92/12/04 17:42  434   434   0  TSO1234
   PROTECT           01.00  92/12/04  92/12/04 18:02   56    56   0  TSO1234
   RECEIVE   *RESET  01.00  92/12/10  92/12/10 19:13  371   371   0  TSO1234
   RENAME            01.00  92/12/04  92/12/04 18:03   15    15   0  TSO1234
   REPRO     *RESET  01.00  92/12/10  92/12/10 19:13  294   294   0  TSO1234
   RUN       *RESET  01.00  92/12/10  92/12/10 19:13    7     7   0  TSO1234
   SEND      *RESET  01.00  92/12/10  92/12/10 19:13   49    49   0  TSO1234
   STATUS    *RESET  01.00  92/12/10  92/12/10 19:13   20    20   0  TSO1234
   SUBMIT    *RESET  01.00  92/12/10  92/12/10 19:13  105   105   0  TSO1234
   TERMINAL  *RESET  01.00  92/12/10  92/12/10 19:13   94    94   0  TSO1234
   TEST      *RESET  01.00  92/12/10  92/12/10 19:13   99    99   0  TSO1234
   TIME      *RESET  01.00  92/12/10  92/12/10 19:13   13    13   0  TSO1234
   TRANSMIT  *RESET  01.00  92/12/10  92/12/10 19:13  557   557   0  TSO1234
   TSOEXEC   *RESET  01.00  92/12/10  92/12/10 19:13   16    16   0  TSO1234
   UNALLOC   *RESET  01.00  92/12/10  92/12/10 19:13   55    55   0  TSO1234
   VERIFY    *RESET  01.00  92/12/10  92/12/10 19:13   31    31   0  TSO1234
   WHEN      *RESET  01.00  92/12/10  92/12/10 19:13   25    25   0  TSO1234
```

Figure 29.19 Result of resetting selected member statistics.

```
------------------------- RESET ISPF STATISTICS ------- 15 MEMBERS RESET
OPTION  ===> r_


   R - Reset (create/update) ISPF statistics
   D - Delete ISPF statistics

NEW USERID            ===> TSO1234 (If userid is to be changed)
NEW VERSION NUMBER    ===>         (If version number is to be changed)
   RESET MOD LEVEL    ===> YES     (YES or NO)
   RESET SEQ NUMBERS  ===> YES     (YES or NO)

ISPF LIBRARY:
   PROJECT ===> TSO1234
   GROUP   ===> EXAMPLE
   TYPE    ===> DATA
   MEMBER  ===>                    (Blank or pattern for member selection
                                   list, '*' for all members)


OTHER PARTITIONED DATA SET:
   DATA SET NAME  ===>
   VOLUME SERIAL  ===>             (If not cataloged)

DATA SET PASSWORD ===>             (If password protected)
```

Figure 29.20 Reset message.

30

The Move/Copy Utility

The move/copy utility is option 3.3, and it can be accessed by entering 3.3 on the primary option menu or by entering 3 to invoke the utility menu before entering suboption 3. The move/copy utility is used to move or copy data from one disk data set to another. The data sets involved can be either partitioned or sequential. When copy is specified, the data is left in the "FROM" data set as it's copied to the "TO" data set. When move is specified, the data is removed from the "FROM" data set as it's placed in the "TO" data set.

Individual members of a PDS can be copied by specifying the member name in the field provided below the data set name. While this is certainly acceptable for copying one or even a few members, it's not practical for many copy instances. All members of a PDS can be copied by using an asterisk in place of the member name, as in Figure 30.1.

After pressing the ENTER key, a second screen is displayed (Figure 30.2). This screen is used to specify the target or "TO" data set. The source or "FROM" data set name is displayed on the screen title line. Notice that there's no special field here for the member name. In this form of move or copy, the member name is supplied by the source library.

A field near the bottom of the screen specifies what's to happen when a particular member name already exists in the target library. This field must be specified when copying to a PDS. YES indicates that target members with the same name will be replaced. This will write over the contents of all such duplicate named members. NO indicates that like-named members will not be replaced, while all other members can still be written to the target library. Either value can be abbreviated and will be automatically translated by ISPF.

After pressing ENTER again, the first screen is redisplayed (Figure 30.3). The short message indicates that 44 members were copied. Representing those 44 mem-

```
--------------------------- MOVE/COPY UTILITY ---------------------------
OPTION  ===> c

   C - Copy data set or member(s)        CP - Copy and print
   M - Move data set or member(s)        MP - Move and print
   L - Copy and LMF lock member(s)       LP - Copy, LMF lock, and print
   P - LMF Promote data set or member(s) PP - LMF Promote and print

SPECIFY "FROM" DATA SET BELOW, THEN PRESS ENTER KEY

FROM ISPF LIBRARY:          —— Options C, CP, L, and LP only ——-
   PROJECT ===> tso1234    |                                    |
   GROUP   ===> example  ===> TEST      ===>           ===>
   TYPE    ===> data
   MEMBER  ===> *_              (Blank or pattern for member selection list,
                                 '*' for all members)


FROM OTHER PARTITIONED OR SEQUENTIAL DATA SET:
   DATA SET NAME  ===>
   VOLUME SERIAL  ===>          (If not cataloged)

DATA SET PASSWORD ===>         (If password protected)
```

Figure 30.1 Copy from screen.

```
COPY --- FROM TSO1234.EXAMPLE.DATA(*) -----------------------------------------
COMMAND ===>

SPECIFY "TO" DATA SET BELOW.

TO ISPF LIBRARY:
   PROJECT ===> tso1234
   GROUP   ===> script
   TYPE    ===> text_

TO OTHER PARTITIONED OR SEQUENTIAL DATA SET:
   DATA SET NAME  ===>
   VOLUME SERIAL  ===>          (If not cataloged)

DATA SET PASSWORD ===>         (If password protected)

"TO" DATA SET OPTIONS:
   IF PARTITIONED, REPLACE LIKE-NAMED MEMBERS ===> YES    (YES or NO)
   IF SEQUENTIAL, "TO" DATA SET DISPOSITION   ===>        (OLD or MOD)
   SPECIFY PACK OPTION FOR "TO" DATA SET      ===>        (YES, NO or blank)
```

Figure 30.2 Copy to screen.

```
------------------------- MOVE/COPY UTILITY ------------ 44 MEMBERS COPIED
OPTION  ===> c

   C - Copy data set or member(s)        CP - Copy and print
   M - Move data set or member(s)        MP - Move and print
   L - Copy and LMF lock member(s)       LP - Copy, LMF lock, and print
   P - LMF Promote data set or member(s) PP - LMF Promote and print

SPECIFY "FROM" DATA SET BELOW, THEN PRESS ENTER KEY

FROM ISPF LIBRARY:          ------ Options C, CP, L, and LP only -------
   PROJECT ===> TSO1234    |                                          |
   GROUP   ===> EXAMPLE    ===>            ===>            ===>
   TYPE    ===> DATA
   MEMBER  ===> _             (Blank or pattern for member selection list,
                               '*' for all members)

FROM OTHER PARTITIONED OR SEQUENTIAL DATA SET:
   DATA SET NAME   ===>
   VOLUME SERIAL   ===>          (If not cataloged)

DATA SET PASSWORD ===>          (If password protected)
```

Figure 30.3 Result of member copy.

bers with the single character * is the easiest way to copy them. The data set values are retained on the screen to make it easier to start subsequent copy operations.

When nothing is specified in the member field, as in Figure 30.4, ISPF will eventually display the member list. Members can then be selectively copied from the member list. Pressing the ENTER key again causes the "COPY TO" screen to display (Figure 30.5). Here too, the same target data set is specified, and the REPLACE LIKE-NAMED MEMBERS field value of YES is retained.

Because the member name was omitted, the member list is displayed (Figure 30.6). One of the advantages to using the member list is that members can be browsed before they're copied. This might help to determine which members to copy. A member is browsed by placing a B in front of the member name and pressing the ENTER key. The END command is then used to return from browse mode to the member list.

Perhaps the biggest advantages of working from the member list is that it's not necessary to remember the member names, and members can be selectively copied. This is shown in Figure 30.6, where an S is used to select each member to be copied.

Yet another advantage is demonstrated with the first selected member. That member (ALLOC) will be copied to a different member name (ALLOCATE). A new name is supplied to a moved or copied member by specifying the new name in the RE-NAME field adjacent to any particular member name. The forward tab key can be used to expedite movement to the RENAME field.

```
--------------------------- MOVE/COPY UTILITY -----------------------------
OPTION  ===> C_

   C - Copy data set or member(s)            CP - Copy and print
   M - Move data set or member(s)            MP - Move and print
   L - Copy and LMF lock member(s)           LP - Copy, LMF lock, and print
   P - LMF Promote data set or member(s)     PP - LMF Promote and print

SPECIFY "FROM" DATA SET BELOW, THEN PRESS ENTER KEY

FROM ISPF LIBRARY:          ------ Options C, CP, L, and LP only -------
   PROJECT ===> TSO1234    |                                           |
   GROUP   ===> EXAMPLE   ===>           ===>            ===>
   TYPE    ===> DATA
   MEMBER  ===>                 (Blank or pattern for member selection list,
                                '*' for all members)


FROM OTHER PARTITIONED OR SEQUENTIAL DATA SET:
   DATA SET NAME   ===>
   VOLUME SERIAL   ===>         (If not cataloged)

DATA SET PASSWORD ===>         (If password protected)
```

Figure 30.4 Selective member copy from screen.

```
COPY --- FROM TSO1234.EXAMPLE.DATA ---------------------------------------
COMMAND ===>

SPECIFY "TO" DATA SET BELOW.

TO ISPF LIBRARY:
   PROJECT ===> TSO1234
   GROUP   ===> SCRIPT
   TYPE    ===> TEXT_

TO OTHER PARTITIONED OR SEQUENTIAL DATA SET:
   DATA SET NAME   ===>
   VOLUME SERIAL   ===>         (If not cataloged)

DATA SET PASSWORD ===>         (If password protected)

"TO" DATA SET OPTIONS:
   IF PARTITIONED, REPLACE LIKE-NAMED MEMBERS ===> YES    (YES or NO)
   IF SEQUENTIAL, "TO" DATA SET DISPOSITION   ===>        (OLD or MOD)
   SPECIFY PACK OPTION FOR "TO" DATA SET      ===>        (YES, NO or blank)
```

Figure 30.5 Selective member copy to screen.

```
COPY --- TSO1234.EXAMPLE.DATA TO TSO1234.SCRIPT.TEXT ----- ROW 00001 OF 00044
COMMAND ===>                                                 SCROLL ===> CSR
    NAME      RENAME     VV.MM  CREATED    CHANGED     SIZE  INIT  MOD   ID
  s ALLOC     allocate   01.01  92/12/04 92/12/11 17:04  270   270    0 TSO1234
  s ALTLIB               01.01  92/12/04 92/12/11 17:10  329   327    0 TSO1234
    ATTRIB               01.00  92/12/04 92/12/04 17:48  102   102    0 TSO1234
  s CALL                 01.01  92/12/04 92/12/11 17:05   31    31    0 TSO1234
    CANCEL               01.00  92/12/04 92/12/04 17:49   20    20    0 TSO1234
    CLIST                01.01  92/12/11 92/12/11 17:16  639   655    0 TSO1234
    COPY                 01.00  92/12/04 92/12/04 17:50   68    68    0 TSO1234
    DEFINE               01.00  92/12/04 92/12/04 17:51  545   545    0 TSO1234
  s DELETE               01.03  92/12/04 92/12/11 17:06  123   123    0 TSO1234
    EDIT                 01.00  92/12/04 92/12/04 17:52  106   106    0 TSO1234
    EXEC                 01.00  92/12/04 92/12/04 17:53   48    48    0 TSO1234
    FORMAT               01.00  92/12/04 92/12/04 17:54   60    60    0 TSO1234
    FREE                 01.00  92/12/04 92/12/04 17:44   55    55    0 TSO1234
    LINK                 01.00  92/12/04 92/12/04 17:55  116   116    0 TSO1234
    LIST                 01.00  92/12/04 92/12/04 17:56   38    38    0 TSO1234
    LISTALC              01.00  92/12/04 92/12/04 17:56   22    22    0 TSO1234
    LISTBC               01.00  92/12/04 92/12/04 17:57   27    27    0 TSO1234
    LISTCAT              01.00  92/12/04 92/12/04 17:57  104   104    0 TSO1234
    LISTDS               01.00  92/12/04 92/12/04 17:58   29    29    0 TSO1234
    LOADGO               01.00  92/12/04 92/12/04 17:59   68    68    0 TSO1234
    LOGOFF               01.00  92/12/04 92/12/04 17:59   16    16    0 TSO1234
```

Figure 30.6 Member list for selective copy.

The result of the selective copy is shown in Figure 30.7. It points out yet another advantage. From the member list, it's possible to see which members are replaced rather than copied (remember that all of the members had previously been copied to the target library). It's also possible to see which members are not moved or copied (like when the target data set runs out of space or when NO is specified in the RE-PLACE field).

It's also possible to use the primary command version of SELECT. Any single member can be copied by specifying the member name after the SELECT primary command. It's also possible to specify a member pattern, as in Figure 30.8. There, the command is used to select every member that starts with the letters LIST.

Figure 30.9 shows the result of the SELECT primary command. It caused five members to be copied, replacing like-named members in the target library. Member patterns can also be specified from the initial MOVE/COPY screen. Either form of data set name (ISPF or TSO) can be used to specify such a pattern.

Truncation and Padding

When the record lengths of the source and target data sets differ, the move/copy utility will compensate by truncating or padding the source data. Figure 30.10 shows the screen that would appear when trying to copy into a data set another data set that's smaller. This is, of course, the worse situation since it presents the possibility of losing valid data. The screen shows the names of the data sets involved as well as their characteristics. The copy process can be continued by pressing the ENTER key. Use of the END command will terminate the copy process without copying any data.

```
COPY --- TSO1234.EXAMPLE.DATA TO TSO1234.SCRIPT.TEXT ----- ROW 00001 OF 00044
COMMAND ===> _                                          SCROLL ===> CSR
   NAME     RENAME     VV.MM  CREATED    CHANGED       SIZE INIT  MOD   ID
   ALLOC    *COPIED    01.01 92/12/04 92/12/11 17:04    270  270    0 TSO1234
   ALTLIB   *REPL      01.01 92/12/04 92/12/11 17:10    329  327    0 TSO1234
   ATTRIB              01.01 92/12/04 92/12/11 17:48    102  102    0 TSO1234
   CALL     *REPL      01.01 92/12/04 92/12/11 17:05     31   31    0 TSO1234
   CANCEL             01.00 92/12/04 92/12/04 17:49     20   20    0 TSO1234
   CLIST              01.01 92/12/11 92/12/11 17:16    639  655    0 TSO1234
   COPY               01.00 92/12/04 92/12/04 17:50     68   68    0 TSO1234
   DEFINE             01.00 92/12/04 92/12/04 17:51    545  545    0 TSO1234
   DELETE   *REPL     01.03 92/12/04 92/12/11 17:06    123  123    0 TSO1234
   EDIT               01.00 92/12/04 92/12/04 17:52    106  106    0 TSO1234
   EXEC               01.00 92/12/04 92/12/04 17:53     48   48    0 TSO1234
   FORMAT             01.00 92/12/04 92/12/04 17:54     60   60    0 TSO1234
   FREE               01.00 92/12/04 92/12/04 17:44     55   55    0 TSO1234
   LINK               01.00 92/12/04 92/12/04 17:55    116  116    0 TSO1234
   LIST               01.00 92/12/04 92/12/04 17:56     38   38    0 TSO1234
   LISTALC            01.00 92/12/04 92/12/04 17:56     22   22    0 TSO1234
   LISTBC             01.00 92/12/04 92/12/04 17:57     27   27    0 TSO1234
   LISTCAT            01.00 92/12/04 92/12/04 17:57    104  104    0 TSO1234
   LISTDS             01.00 92/12/04 92/12/04 17:58     29   29    0 TSO1234
   LOADGO             01.00 92/12/04 92/12/04 17:59     68   68    0 TSO1234
   LOGOFF             01.00 92/12/04 92/12/04 17:59     16   16    0 TSO1234
```

Figure 30.7 Result of selective member copy.

```
COPY --- TSO1234.EXAMPLE.DATA TO TSO1234.SCRIPT.TEXT ----- ROW 00001 OF 00044
COMMAND ===> s list*_                                   SCROLL ===> CSR
   NAME     RENAME     VV.MM  CREATED    CHANGED       SIZE INIT  MOD   ID
   ALLOC              01.01 92/12/04 92/12/11 17:04    270  270    0 TSO1234
   ALTLIB             01.01 92/12/04 92/12/11 17:10    329  327    0 TSO1234
   ATTRIB             01.00 92/12/04 92/12/04 17:48    102  102    0 TSO1234
   CALL               01.01 92/12/04 92/12/11 17:05     31   31    0 TSO1234
   CANCEL             01.00 92/12/04 92/12/04 17:49     20   20    0 TSO1234
   CLIST              01.01 92/12/11 92/12/11 17:16    639  655    0 TSO1234
   COPY               01.00 92/12/04 92/12/04 17:50     68   68    0 TSO1234
   DEFINE             01.00 92/12/04 92/12/04 17:51    545  545    0 TSO1234
   DELETE             01.03 92/12/04 92/12/11 17:06    123  123    0 TSO1234
   EDIT               01.00 92/12/04 92/12/04 17:52    106  106    0 TSO1234
   EXEC               01.00 92/12/04 92/12/04 17:53     48   48    0 TSO1234
   FORMAT             01.00 92/12/04 92/12/04 17:54     60   60    0 TSO1234
   FREE               01.00 92/12/04 92/12/04 17:44     55   55    0 TSO1234
   LINK               01.00 92/12/04 92/12/04 17:55    116  116    0 TSO1234
   LIST               01.00 92/12/04 92/12/04 17:56     38   38    0 TSO1234
   LISTALC            01.00 92/12/04 92/12/04 17:56     22   22    0 TSO1234
   LISTBC             01.00 92/12/04 92/12/04 17:57     27   27    0 TSO1234
   LISTCAT            01.00 92/12/04 92/12/04 17:57    104  104    0 TSO1234
   LISTDS             01.00 92/12/04 92/12/04 17:58     29   29    0 TSO1234
   LOADGO             01.00 92/12/04 92/12/04 17:59     68   68    0 TSO1234
   LOGOFF             01.00 92/12/04 92/12/04 17:59     16   16    0 TSO1234
```

Figure 30.8 Selecting by member pattern.

```
COPY --- TSO1234.EXAMPLE.DATA TO TSO1234.SCRIPT.TEXT ----- ROW 00001 OF 00044
COMMAND ===> _                                             SCROLL ===> CSR
   NAME     RENAME     VV.MM  CREATED     CHANGED     SIZE  INIT  MOD   ID
   ALLOC               01.01  92/12/04  92/12/11 17:04  270   270   0  TSO1234
   ALTLIB              01.01  92/12/04  92/12/11 17:10  329   327   0  TSO1234
   ATTRIB              01.00  92/12/04  92/12/04 17:48  102   102   0  TSO1234
   CALL                01.01  92/12/04  92/12/11 17:05   31    31   0  TSO1234
   CANCEL              01.00  92/12/04  92/12/04 17:49   20    20   0  TSO1234
   CLIST               01.01  92/12/11  92/12/11 17:16  639   655   0  TSO1234
   COPY                01.00  92/12/04  92/12/04 17:50   68    68   0  TSO1234
   DEFINE              01.00  92/12/04  92/12/04 17:51  545   545   0  TSO1234
   DELETE              01.03  92/12/04  92/12/11 17:06  123   123   0  TSO1234
   EDIT                01.00  92/12/04  92/12/04 17:52  106   106   0  TSO1234
   EXEC                01.00  92/12/04  92/12/04 17:53   48    48   0  TSO1234
   FORMAT              01.00  92/12/04  92/12/04 17:54   60    60   0  TSO1234
   FREE                01.00  92/12/04  92/12/04 17:44   55    55   0  TSO1234
   LINK                01.00  92/12/04  92/12/04 17:55  116   116   0  TSO1234
   LIST     *REPL      01.00  92/12/04  92/12/04 17:56   38    38   0  TSO1234
   LISTALC  *REPL      01.00  92/12/04  92/12/04 17:56   22    22   0  TSO1234
   LISTBC   *REPL      01.00  92/12/04  92/12/04 17:57   27    27   0  TSO1234
   LISTCAT  *REPL      01.00  92/12/04  92/12/04 17:57  104   104   0  TSO1234
   LISTDS   *REPL      01.00  92/12/04  92/12/04 17:58   29    29   0  TSO1234
   LOADGO              01.00  92/12/04  92/12/04 17:59   68    68   0  TSO1234
   LOGOFF              01.00  92/12/04  92/12/04 17:59   16    16   0  TSO1234
```

Figure 30.9 Result of selecting by member pattern.

```
------------------------- MOVE/COPY - CONFIRM ----------------------------
COMMAND ===> _

Data set attributes are inconsistent.  Truncation may result in the
right-most portions of some "from" records if COPY is performed.

    "From" data set attributes:
        Data set name:   TSO1234.LONG.TEXT
        Record format:   FBA
        Data length:     133

    "To" data set attributes:
        Data set name:   TSO1234.SHORT.TEXT
        Record format:   FB
        Data length:     80

Press ENTER key to allow COPY with truncation.
Press END key to cancel COPY
```

Figure 30.10 Confirm truncation screen.

Copying Sequential Data

Copying sequential data is just like copying partitioned data except that no member names are specified. When a move operation is performed from a sequential data set, the source data set is deleted. A sequential target data set has other options besides replace/noreplace. A sequential data set can be completely replaced, or the data placed there can be appended to any data already in the data set. These latter options are specified in a field labeled SEQUENTIAL "TO" DATA SET DISPOSITION. If a disposition of OLD is specified, the target sequential data set is completely overlaid. If a disposition of MOD is specified, moved or copied data is added to the existing end of the target sequential data set.

Copying Partitioned to Sequential

Obviously, a single PDS member can be copied to a sequential data set. It's not obvious, however, that multiple members of a partitioned data set can be moved or copied to a sequential data set. When this is done, all members selected are written to the data set, one after the other. This might be desirable when portions of the data have been assembled in different members and need to be consolidated. It can also be helpful when preparing to transfer data to computers (including PCs) that don't support partitioned data sets. The drawback is that the individual members will lose their identity when placed in a single sequential data set. There's no difference in how the members are copied. It's not even necessary to switch to a sequential disposition of MOD, which is the normal way to append data to the end of a sequential data set.

Printing Transferred Data

Both the move and copy options have companion options that print the data as it's moved or copied. These are designated with the same letters: M and C, with the letter P for print. When transferred data is printed, the print form of the data is first placed in the list data set. The list data set must then be printed to obtain the actual printout.

While it might seem very convenient to copy and print data at the same time, it can also be the cause of some frustration. List data sets are often allocated to accommodate minimal printing. When a large data set is copied, the list data set could easily run out of space and cause the copy process to be interrupted. Under most circumstances, it would be better to use a separate function like the PRINTDS command (which can go straight to a printer), or option 3.1 to print the data.

Enlarging a PDS

Occasionally, data sets must be enlarged. This applies to the directory of a PDS as well as its data space. It's a good idea to keep track of the space that's available to the data set before processing is disrupted by a system B37, D37, or E37 abend. An attempt should first be made to compress a PDS (using option 3.1) before deciding that it's too small. The number of available extents or space just after the library has been compressed is most indicative of whether or not the data set should be enlarged.

When a data set must be enlarged, the features of the data set utility (option 3.2) are combined with the move or copy functions to replicate the data. Specifically, a new, larger data set will be created so the current contents can be copied to it. When successfully replicated, the old data set is then deleted so the new data set can be renamed (to use the old name). A sequential data set is enlarged in the same way. The only difference is that the copy process involves the single content of the sequential data set rather than discrete members of a PDS. The rest of this chapter demonstrates the steps that can be used to enlarge a PDS.

The sequence to enlarge a PDS can be started by displaying the current data set contents. That will allow the current data set characteristics to serve as a model in creating the new PDS. Figure 30.11 shows option 3.2 with the processing option left blank. The name of the current PDS is specified, and the ENTER key is pressed.

Figure 30.12 shows a display of the current data set characteristics. The data set is currently consuming 14 of the 16 extents available to it. While it's not yet completely out of space, this data set should probably be enlarged. Enlarging the data set will also tend to bring the data set together in fewer, larger pieces. That will, in turn, increase the efficiency of input and output processing.

Pressing the ENTER key causes a return to the data set utility menu (Figure 30.13). The new data set can be created by selecting a processing option of A and specifying the new data set name. Pressing ENTER causes the old data set characteristics to display in the input fields (Figure 30.14). These modeled characteristics can then serve as a starting point to make new specifications.

```
-------------------- ------ DATA SET UTILITY  ----------------------------
OPTION  ===> _

   A - Allocate new data set          C - Catalog data set
   R - Rename entire data set         U - Uncatalog data set
   D - Delete entire data set         S - Data set information (short)
   blank - Data set information

ISPF LIBRARY:
   PROJECT ===> tso1234
   GROUP   ===> current
   TYPE    ===> pds

OTHER PARTITIONED OR SEQUENTIAL DATA SET:
   DATA SET NAME   ===>
   VOLUME SERIAL   ===>          (If not cataloged, required for option "C")

DATA SET PASSWORD ===>          (If password protected)
```

Figure 30.11 Displaying the current data set characteristics.

```
-------------------------- DATA SET INFORMATION --------------------------
COMMAND ===> _

DATA SET NAME: TSO1234.CURRENT.PDS

GENERAL DATA:                              CURRENT ALLOCATION:
   Volume serial:        DISK1C               Allocated tracks:        14
   Device type:          3380                 Allocated extents:       14
   Organization:         PO                   Maximum dir. blocks:     15
   Record format:        FB
   Record length:        80
   Block size:           6160              CURRENT UTILIZATION:
   1st extent tracks:    1                    Used tracks:             14
   Secondary tracks:     1                    Used extents:            14
                                              Used dir. blocks:        11
   Creation date:        1992/03/16           Number of members:       63
   Expiration date:      ***NONE***
```

Figure 30.12 Characteristics of the current data set.

```
-------------------------- DATA SET UTILITY --------------------------
OPTION  ===> a

   A - Allocate new data set          C - Catalog data set
   R - Rename entire data set         U - Uncatalog data set
   D - Delete entire data set         S - Data set information (short)
   blank - Data set information

ISPF LIBRARY:
   PROJECT ===> TSO1234
   GROUP   ===> larger_
   TYPE    ===> PDS2

OTHER PARTITIONED OR SEQUENTIAL DATA SET:
   DATA SET NAME  ===>
   VOLUME SERIAL  ===>            (If not cataloged, required for option "C")

DATA SET PASSWORD ===>            (If password protected)
```

Figure 30.13 Creating the new PDS.

```
----------------------- ALLOCATE NEW DATA SET  ----------------------------
COMMAND ===> _

DATA SET NAME: TSO1234.LARGER.PDS

   VOLUME SERIAL       ===> DISK1C   (Blank for authorized default volume) *
   GENERIC UNIT        ===>          (Generic group name or unit address) *
   SPACE UNITS         ===> TRACK    (BLKS, TRKS, or CYLS)
   PRIMARY QUANTITY    ===> 1        (In above units)
   SECONDARY QUANTITY  ===> 1        (In above units)
   DIRECTORY BLOCKS    ===> 15       (Zero for sequential data set)
   RECORD FORMAT       ===> FB
   RECORD LENGTH       ===> 80
   BLOCK SIZE          ===> 6160
   EXPIRATION DATE     ===>          (YY/MM/DD, YYYY/MM/DD
                                      YY.DDD, YYYY.DDD in Julian form
                                      DDDD for retention period in days
                                      or blank)

   ( * Only one of these fields may be specified)
```

Figure 30.14 Characteristics modeled from the existing PDS.

In Figure 30.15, the values from the old data set are changed to make the new data set larger. The primary space has been changed from one to 15 tracks to account for all of the data currently in the data set. Secondary space will still be maintained, but has been changed from one track to two. The maximum size of the new data set will be 30 tracks, which is almost twice the size of the old PDS. Because much of the space will be obtained from secondary extents, it will not be allocated to the data set until it's actually needed. The directory space for the PDS has also been expanded (from 15 to 20 blocks) to account for future growth.

Pressing the ENTER key again, causes the data set to be created as indicated in the short message area of Figure 30.16. The PDS, TSO1234.LARGER.PDS, is now an expanded (although empty) copy of the data set to be enlarged. The jump function is used in the OPTION field to invoke the move/copy utility. The existing members must now be moved or copied to the new PDS. This is shown in Figure 30.17 where all of the members are specified in a copy operation.

Pressing ENTER reveals the next copy screen, where the target data set is specified (Figure 30.18). The target data set is the new PDS that was just created. Pressing ENTER again starts the copy operation.

When all members have been copied, the first screen is redisplayed. The short message indicates that 63 members have been copied. This coincides with the statistic displayed in Figure 30.19 for the number of members in the old data set. On the same screen, the jump function is used to return to the data set utility.

```
------------------------ ALLOCATE NEW DATA SET ---------------------------
COMMAND ===>

DATA SET NAME: TSO1234.LARGER.PDS

    VOLUME SERIAL        ===>              (Blank for authorized default volume) *
    GENERIC UNIT         ===>              (Generic group name or unit address) *
    SPACE UNITS          ===> TRACK        (BLKS, TRKS, or CYLS)
    PRIMARY QUANTITY     ===> 15           (In above units)
    SECONDARY QUANTITY   ===> 2            (In above units)
    DIRECTORY BLOCKS     ===> 20_          (Zero for sequential data set)
    RECORD FORMAT        ===> FB
    RECORD LENGTH        ===> 80
    BLOCK SIZE           ===> 6160
    EXPIRATION DATE      ===>              (YY/MM/DD, YYYY/MM/DD
                                            YY.DDD, YYYY.DDD in Julian form
                                            DDDD for retention period in days
                                            or blank)


    ( * Only one of these fields may be specified)
```

Figure 30.15 Changing the data set characteristics.

```
-------------------------- DATA SET UTILITY ---------- **DATA SET ALLOCATED**
OPTION  ===> =3.3_

   A - Allocate new data set              C - Catalog data set
   R - Rename entire data set             U - Uncatalog data set
   D - Delete entire data set             S - Data set information (short)
   blank - Data set information

ISPF LIBRARY:
   PROJECT ===> TSO1234
   GROUP   ===> LARGER
   TYPE    ===> PDS

OTHER PARTITIONED OR SEQUENTIAL DATA SET:
   DATA SET NAME  ===>
   VOLUME SERIAL  ===>              (If not cataloged, required for option "C")

DATA SET PASSWORD ===>          (If password protected)
```

Figure 30.16 Result of creating the new PDS.

```
------------------------------ MOVE/COPY UTILITY ----------------------------
OPTION  ===> c

   C - Copy data set or member(s)        CP - Copy and print
   M - Move data set or member(s)        MP - Move and print
   L - Copy and LMF lock member(s)       LP - Copy, LMF lock, and print
   P - LMF Promote data set or member(s) PP - LMF Promote and print

SPECIFY "FROM" DATA SET BELOW, THEN PRESS ENTER KEY

FROM ISPF LIBRARY:         ------ Options C, CP, L, and LP only -------
   PROJECT ===> tso1234    |                                    |
   GROUP   ===> current    ===>          ===>          ===>
   TYPE    ===> pds
   MEMBER  ===> *_             (Blank or pattern for member selection list,
                               '*' for all members)

FROM OTHER PARTITIONED OR SEQUENTIAL DATA SET:
   DATA SET NAME  ===>
   VOLUME SERIAL  ===>            (If not cataloged)

DATA SET PASSWORD ===>           (If password protected)
```

Figure 30.17 Requesting that all members be copied.

```
COPY --- FROM TSO1234.CURRENT.PDS(*) ----------------------------------------
COMMAND ===>

SPECIFY "TO" DATA SET BELOW.

TO ISPF LIBRARY:
   PROJECT ===> TSO1234
   GROUP   ===> larger_
   TYPE    ===> PDS

TO OTHER PARTITIONED OR SEQUENTIAL DATA SET:
   DATA SET NAME  ===>
   VOLUME SERIAL  ===>            (If not cataloged)

DATA SET PASSWORD ===>           (If password protected)

"TO" DATA SET OPTIONS:
   IF PARTITIONED, REPLACE LIKE-NAMED MEMBERS ===> YES    (YES or NO)
   IF SEQUENTIAL, "TO" DATA SET DISPOSITION   ===> OLD    (OLD or MOD)
   SPECIFY PACK OPTION FOR "TO" DATA SET      ===>        (YES, NO or blank)
```

Figure 30.18 Specifying the target data set.

```
--------------------------- MOVE/COPY UTILITY  ----------- 63 MEMBERS COPIED
OPTION  ===> C

   C - Copy data set or member(s)          CP - Copy and print
   M - Move data set or member(s)          MP - Move and print
   L - Copy and LMF lock member(s)         LP - Copy, LMF lock, and print
   P - LMF Promote data set or member(s)   PP - LMF Promote and print

SPECIFY "FROM" DATA SET BELOW, THEN PRESS ENTER KEY

FROM ISPF LIBRARY:          ------ Options C, CP, L, and LP only -------
   PROJECT ===> TSO1234    |                                          |
   GROUP   ===> CURRENT ===>            ===>            ===>
   TYPE    ===> PDS
   MEMBER  ===> =3.2_           (Blank or pattern for member selection list,
                                '*' for all members)

FROM OTHER PARTITIONED OR SEQUENTIAL DATA SET:
   DATA SET NAME  ===>
   VOLUME SERIAL  ===>          (If not cataloged)

DATA SET PASSWORD ===>          (If password protected)
```

Figure 30.19 Result of member copy.

```
--------------------------- DATA SET UTILITY  ----------------------------
OPTION  ===> d

   A - Allocate new data set        C   Catalog data set
   R - Rename entire data set       U - Uncatalog data set
   D - Delete entire data set       S - Data set information (short)
   blank - Data set information

ISPF LIBRARY:
   PROJECT ===> TSO1234
   GROUP   ===> current_
   TYPE    ===> PDS

OTHER PARTITIONED OR SEQUENTIAL DATA SET:
   DATA SET NAME  ===>
   VOLUME SERIAL  ===>          (If not cataloged, required for option "C")

DATA SET PASSWORD ===>          (If password protected)
```

Figure 30.20 Deleting the old PDS.

```
----------------------------- CONFIRM DELETE  -------------------------------
COMMAND ===> _

DATA SET NAME: TSO1234.CURRENT.PDS
VOLUME:        DISK1C
CREATION DATE: 1992/03/16


INSTRUCTIONS:

   Press ENTER key to confirm delete request.
      (The data set will be deleted and uncataloged.)

   Enter END command to cancel delete request.
```

Figure 30.21 Delete confirmation screen.

```
------------ --------------- DATA SET UTILITY ------------ DATA SET DELETED
OPTION  ===> r

   A - Allocate new data set         C - Catalog data set
   R - Rename entire data set        U - Uncatalog data set
   D - Delete entire data set        S - Data set information (short)
   blank - Data set information

ISPF LIBRARY:
   PROJECT ===> TSO1234
   GROUP   ===> larger_
   TYPE    ===> PDS

OTHER PARTITIONED OR SEQUENTIAL DATA SET:
   DATA SET NAME  ===>
   VOLUME SERIAL  ===>            (If not cataloged, required for option "C")

DATA SET PASSWORD ===>           (If password protected)
```

Figure 30.22 Renaming the new PDS.

```
------------------------------ RENAME DATA SET ------------------------------
COMMAND ===>

DATA SET NAME: TSO1234.LARGER.PDS
VOLUME:        DISK13

ENTER NEW NAME BELOW:     (The data set will be recataloged.)

ISPF LIBRARY:
    PROJECT ===> TSO1234
    GROUP   ===> current_
    TYPE    ===> PDS

OTHER PARTITIONED OR SEQUENTIAL DATA SET:
    DATA SET NAME  ===>
```

Figure 30.23 Supplying the old PDS name.

```
------------------------- DATA SET UTILITY ------------ DATA SET RENAMED
OPTION  ===> _

    A - Allocate new data set          C - Catalog data set
    R - Rename entire data set         U - Uncatalog data set
    D - Delete entire data set         S - Data set information (short)
    blank - Data set information

ISPF LIBRARY:
    PROJECT ===> TSO1234
    GROUP   =-=> CURRENT
    TYPE    ===> PDS

OTHER PARTITIONED OR SEQUENTIAL DATA SET:
    DATA SET NAME  ===>
    VOLUME SERIAL  ===>          (If not cataloged, required for option "C")

DATA SET PASSWORD ===>          (If password protected)
```

Figure 30.24 Data set renamed to old PDS name.

Now that the old library has been replicated, it can be deleted. This is indicated in Figure 30.20 by a processing option of D, specified with the old data set name. Pressing the ENTER key causes the delete confirmation screen to display (Figure 30.21). Pressing ENTER from this screen confirms the desire to delete the data set.

Figure 30.22 shows that the old PDS has been deleted (indicated in the short message area). The new PDS can now be renamed to use the old PDS name. That's done using processing option R with the new PDS name. The second screen of the rename process is used in Figure 30.23 to specify the old PDS name. Pressing the ENTER key will complete the rename process.

Figure 30.24 marks the end of the process. It took several steps, but the result is as if the old PDS were merely enlarged.

31

The Data Set
List Utility

The data set list utility is option 3.4, and it can be accessed by entering 3.4 on the primary option menu or by entering 3 to invoke the utility menu before entering suboption 4. The data set list utility is not like the other utility functions or any other ISPF function. The typical ISPF function relies on finding the necessary option and supplying the information that it needs. Often, the information is the name of a data set that the function will operate on. The data set list utility is just the opposite. It provides a means of generating data set names and then specifying which option will be used against a particular data set.

The data set list utility can make it easier to affect multiple data sets or apply several functions to a single data set. The utility makes many of the fundamental data management functions and the two most widely used functions, browse and edit, available from a single screen. The available functions and their letter codes are listed on the initial screen in Figure 31.1. The object of the initial screen is to accept a data set name pattern that can be applied to the system catalog. Data set names that fit the pattern will become part of a list that options can be applied against.

The data set list utility is also different from other options in not using quotes around the data set name. That's because the data set name serves as a search specification rather than as an actual data set name. The data set level specified in Figure 31.1 is the same as the current user-id. It will cause all cataloged data sets that start with that high-level qualifier to be listed. More levels of qualification can be used to limit the number of data sets listed. It's also possible to use an asterisk to represent one or more characters within a qualifier.

```
------------------------- DATA SET LIST UTILITY -------------------------
OPTION  ===>

   blank - Display data set list *        P  - Print data set list
   V     - Display VTOC information only   PV - Print VTOC information only

Enter one or both of the parameters below:
   DSNAME LEVEL  ===> tso1234_
   VOLUME       ===>


   INITIAL DISPLAY VIEW     ===> VOLUME    (VOLUME,SPACE,ATTRIB,TOTAL)
   CONFIRM DELETE REQUEST   ===> YES       (YES or NO)

 * The following line commands will be available when the list is displayed:

 B - Browse data set       C - Catalog data set     F - Free unused space
 E - Edit data set         U - Uncatalog data set   = - Repeat last command
 D - Delete data set       P - Print data set
 R - Rename data set       X - Print index listing
 I - Data set information M - Display member list
 S - Information (short)   Z - Compress data set     TSO cmd, CLIST or REXX exec
```

Figure 31.1 Generating a data set list.

After a data set pattern is entered, matching entries are pulled from the catalog and listed in data set name order (Figure 31.2). The short message indicates the starting data set number as well as the total number of data sets in the list. Across from each data set name is the volume serial number of the device it's on (these all happen to be disk data sets). If the data set is a multivolume data set (spread across multiple disks or tapes), only the first volume is listed. Multiple options can be specified (at the same time), as in Figure 31.2, where a different option has been specified for all but the last data set.

When the data set list option was invoked, the initial display view was set to VOLUME. That meant that the volume serial number would be the only other information that displayed with the data set names. This is the most efficient way to bring up a data set list since only the catalog is searched. Other display options SPACE, ATTRIB, and TOTAL require that each disk VTOC be searched (in addition to the catalog) to obtain the additional information from the data set labels.

Each option specified behaves in a different fashion. Virtually all of them leave the data set list to allow the selected option to operate. Each option specified is executed in turn from top to bottom without returning to the list until after the last option is executed. Figure 31.3 shows the data set list after all of the options have been executed. The last of those functions was to rename the data set TSO1234.SCREENS.DATA. The new data set name is now part of the list (with middle qualifier SCREEN rather than SCREENS), and the short message makes mention of the rename. The message field of the data set list indicates the last activity for each of the data sets in the list.

```
DSLIST - DATA SETS BEGINNING WITH TSO1234 --------------------- ROW 1 OF 8
COMMAND ===>                                        SCROLL ===> CSR

COMMAND    NAME                                  MESSAGE        VOLUME
--------------------------------------------------------------------------
e          TSO1234.CLIST                                        DISK1C
z          TSO1234.CNTL                                         DISK1A
m          TSO1234.FORT.LOAD                                    DISK1A
d          TSO1234.ISPF.PROFILE                                 DISK16
i          TSO1234.PROFILE                                      DISK19
b          TSO1234.JCL.SYSOUT                                   DISK18
r_         TSO1234.SCREENS.DATA                                 DISK12
           TSO1234.SPF3.LIST                                    DISK13
**************************** END OF DATA SET LIST **************************
```

Figure 31.2 Specifying multiple options.

```
DSLIST - DATA SETS BEGINNING WITH TSO1234 ----------------- DATA SET RENAMED
COMMAND ===>                                        SCROLL ===> CSR

COMMAND    NAME                                  MESSAGE        VOLUME
--------------------------------------------------------------------------
           TSO1234.CLIST                         EDITED         DISK1C
           TSO1234.CNTL                          COMPRESSED     DISK1A
           TSO1234.FORT.LOAD                     MEMBER LIST    DISK1A
           TSO1234.ISPF.PROFILE                  DELETED        ??????
           TSO1234.PROFILE                       INFO - I       DISK19
           TSO1234.JCL.SYSOUT                    BROWSED        DISK18
   _       TSO1234.SCREEN.DATA                   RENAMED        DISK12
           TSO1234.SPF3.LIST                                    DISK13
**************************** END OF DATA SET LIST **************************
```

Figure 31.3 Data set list showing command messages.

The one command available in option 3.4 that has not been discussed elsewhere is the command to free unused space. That command is executed using the letter F. It frees the space that's not used by a data set. If a data set had seven tracks allocated to it but was only using four, three would be released. The data set would then have only four tracks allocated to it. It could still obtain secondary extents, however, when they were required.

The member list option is like option 3.1, except that it also supports the editing of members. In addition to the listed options, the data set list allows TSO commands, CLISTs, and REXX EXECs to be applied against a particular data set. The general requirement is that it be a function that accepts a data set name as its first parameter. Additional flexibility is gained by another feature that allows the data set name to be represented by a slash. Sometimes the start of the initial line has a data set name like:

```
TSO1234.CLIST
```

Then the command can be typed over the data set name, using a slash to represent the data set name:

```
listc ent(/) all_LIST
```

It's not necessary to erase the old line contents (the string LIST remains from the displayed data set name) to execute the command, which, as it's executed, would essentially appear as:

```
LISTC ENT('TSO1234.CLIST') ALL
```

Another helpful feature is the ability to represent the last executed command with an equal sign in the line command area. An equal sign used with the last data set in the list would cause the same command to execute with the new data set name:

```
LISTC ENT('TSO1234.SPF3.LIST'„) ALL
```

Showing Commands before Execution

Yet another feature of the data set list utility allows commands to be expanded before they're executed. This feature is activated by using the primary command SHOWCMD ON or simply SHOWCMD, as in Figure 31.4.

After the SHOWCMD command is executed, line commands will not be executed directly. This is indicated in the short message area in Figure 31.5. On that screen, a TSO command is placed in front of the first data set name.

Pressing the ENTER key doesn't execute the command. Instead, a second screen is displayed that contains the command and the data set name (Figure 31.6). The command syntax can then be modified, if necessary, as in Figure 31.7. The way the command is entered in this example is exactly the same as the previous command example that used the forward slash.

```
DSLIST - DATA SETS BEGINNING WITH TSO1234 ---------------- DATA SET RENAMED
COMMAND ===> showcmd_                                  SCROLL ===> CSR

COMMAND     NAME                              MESSAGE        VOLUME
-----------------------------------------------------------------------------
            TSO1234.CLIST                     EDITED         DISK1C
            TSO1234.CNTL                      COMPRESSED     DISK1A
            TSO1234.FORT.LOAD                 MEMBER LIST    DISK1A
            TSO1234.ISPF.PROFILE              DELETED        ??????
            TSO1234.PROFILE                   INFO - I       DISK19
            TSO1234.JCL.SYSOUT                BROWSED        DISK18
            TSO1234.SCREEN.DATA               RENAMED        DISK12
            TSO1234.SPF3.LIST                                DISK13
            **************************** END OF DATA SET LIST ***************************
```

Figure 31.4 SHOWCMD primary command.

```
DSLIST - DATA SETS BEGINNING WITH TSO1234 ----------- COMMANDS WILL BE SHOWN
COMMAND ===>                                           SCROLL ===> CSR

COMMAND     NAME                              MESSAGE        VOLUME
-----------------------------------------------------------------------------
listc_      TSO1234.CLIST                     EDITED         DISK1C
            TSO1234.CNTL                      COMPRESSED     DISK1A
            TSO1234.FORT.LOAD                 MEMBER LIST    DISK1A
            TSO1234.ISPF.PROFILE              DELETED        ??????
            TSO1234.PROFILE                   INFO - I       DISK19
            TSO1234.JCL.SYSOUT                BROWSED        DISK18
            TSO1234.SCREEN.DATA               RENAMED        DISK12
            TSO1234.SPF3.LIST                                DISK13
            **************************** END OF DATA SET LIST ***************************
```

Figure 31.5 Activating the SHOW command feature.

```
-------------------------- DATA SET LIST UTILITY --------------------------
COMMAND ===> _

Data Set Name: TSO1234.CLIST

Command before expansion:
     LISTC

Command after expansion:
===> LISTC 'TSO1234.CLIST'



The expanded command field shown above can be modified.


Press ENTER key to process the command.
Enter END command to return without processing the command.
```

Figure 31.6 Screen to expand command execution.

```
-------------------------- DATA SET LIST UTILITY --------------------------
COMMAND ===>

Data Set Name: TSO1234.CLIST

Command before expansion:
     LISTC

Command after expansion:
===> LISTC ent('TSO1234.CLIST') all_



The expanded command field shown above can be modified.


Press ENTER key to process the command.
Enter END command to return without processing the command.
```

Figure 31.7 Command after expansion.

Following execution of the command and its display output, the data set list is again displayed (Figure 31.8). The message field on that line indicates the new last status for that line (execution of the LISTC command with a return code of zero). The option to show a command before its execution can be turned off using the primary command SHOWCMD OFF.

Restricting the Data Set List

The list of data sets displayed by option 3.4 can be limited by specifying additional levels of qualification. Only data sets with those additional qualifiers are placed in the list that's displayed. This filtering technique is augmented by the use of the character * to represent any series of characters. An asterisk can be used at the beginning or end of a data set qualifier. In fact, an asterisk can even be used at both the beginning and end of the same data set qualifier.

The data set list can also be limited to list only the data sets that reside on a particular volume. This is shown on Figure 31.9, where a disk volume serial number has been added. The resultant list shows only the data sets that start with the specified high-level qualifier and reside on disk volume DISK1A (Figure 31.10). Since a volume serial number has been specified, the disk VTOC is searched rather than the catalog. This would allow uncataloged and cataloged data sets on a volume to be displayed.

```
DSLIST - DATA SETS BEGINNING WITH TSO1234 --------------------- ROW 1 OF 8
COMMAND ===>                                            SCROLL ===> CSR

COMMAND     NAME                                 MESSAGE          VOLUME
-----------------------------------------------------------------------
  _         TSO1234.CLIST                        LISTC     RC=0   DISK1C
            TSO1234.CNTL                         COMPRESSED       DISK1A
            TSO1234.FORT.LOAD                    MEMBER LIST      DISK1A
            TSO1234.ISPF.PROFILE                 DELETED          ??????
            TSO1234.PROFILE                      INFO - I         DISK19
            TSO1234.JCL.SYSOUT                   BROWSED          DISK18
            TSO1234.SCREEN.DATA                  RENAMED          DISK12
            TSO1234.SPF3.LIST                                     DISK13
**************************** END OF DATA SET LIST **************************
```

Figure 31.8 Return after LISTC command.

```
------------------------ DATA SET LIST UTILITY ---------------------------
OPTION  ===>

  blank - Display data set list *        P  - Print data set list
  V     - Display VTOC information only   PV - Print VTOC information only

Enter one or both of the parameters below:
  DSNAME LEVEL  ===> TSO1234
  VOLUME        ===> disk1a_


  INITIAL DISPLAY VIEW   ===> VOLUME   (VOLUME,SPACE,ATTRIB,TOTAL)
  CONFIRM DELETE REQUEST  ===> YES      (YES or NO)

* The following line commands will be available when the list is displayed:

B - Browse data set     C - Catalog data set    F - Free unused space
E - Edit data set       U - Uncatalog data set  = - Repeat last command
D - Delete data set     P - Print data set
R - Rename data set     X - Print index listing
I - Data set information M - Display member list
S - Information (short)  Z - Compress data set   TSO cmd, CLIST or REXX exec
```

Figure 31.9 Listing data sets from a single volume.

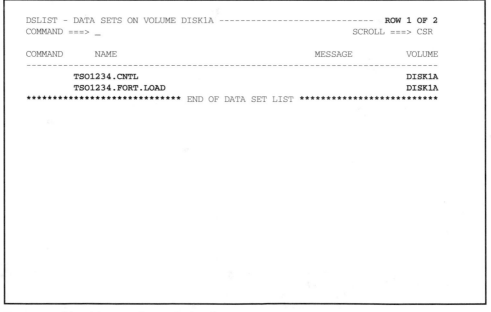

```
DSLIST - DATA SETS ON VOLUME DISK1A ----------------------------- ROW 1 OF 2
COMMAND ===> _                                         SCROLL ===> CSR

COMMAND     NAME                                 MESSAGE        VOLUME
-----------------------------------------------------------------------------
        TSO1234.CNTL                                            DISK1A
        TSO1234.FORT.LOAD                                       DISK1A
**************************** END OF DATA SET LIST ***************************
```

Figure 31.10 List of data sets from a single volume source.

Displaying Additional Data Set Characteristics

Whether limited to a particular volume or not, additional data set information can be displayed by pressing the scroll right key. Figure 31.11 shows the result of pressing the scroll right key. Additional information about the space consumed, the data set attributes, and create and last reference dates are now displayed. This is equivalent to having specified TOTAL in the INITIAL DISPLAY VIEW field of the initial option 3.4 screen.

When the volume serial number is specified but the data set level field is left blank, all of the data sets on the volume will be listed. This is shown in Figure 31.12. The field labeled INITIAL DISPLAY VIEW has been given a value of space to list out the space use of each data set. Again, the catalog will not be used because a volume serial number has been specified.

Figure 31.13 shows the list of all data sets on the volume specified. The initial screen shows the first 19 of 6,042 data sets on the volume. The number of data sets is indicated by the row counter in the short message area. The data set list can be scrolled just like a member list.

Sorting the Data Set List

The data sets in Figure 31.13 are in order by data set name and also contain information about space use. The SORT command is used here to resequence the list by the number of tracks that the data set has allocated to it. The SORT command can be used on any of the labeled column headings to sort the list by the information in that particular field.

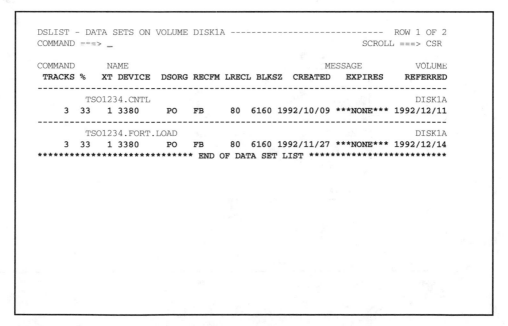

```
DSLIST - DATA SETS ON VOLUME DISK1A ---------------------------- ROW 1 OF 2
COMMAND ===> _                                           SCROLL ===> CSR

COMMAND     NAME                                    MESSAGE          VOLUME
 TRACKS %   XT DEVICE  DSORG RECFM LRECL BLKSZ  CREATED   EXPIRES   REFERRED
-------------------------------------------------------------------------
           TSO1234.CNTL                                             DISK1A
    3  33   1 3380      PO   FB     80   6160 1992/10/09 ***NONE*** 1992/12/11
-------------------------------------------------------------------------
           TSO1234.FORT.LOAD                                        DISK1A
    3  33   1 3380      PO   FB     80   6160 1992/11/27 ***NONE*** 1992/12/14
**************************** END OF DATA SET LIST **************************
```

Figure 31.11 Expanded data set list information.

```
------------------------- DATA SET LIST UTILITY -------------------------
OPTION  ===>

  blank - Display data set list *      P  - Print data set list
  V     - Display VTOC information only  PV - Print VTOC information only

Enter one or both of the parameters below:
  DSNAME LEVEL  ===>
  VOLUME        ===> disk1a


  INITIAL DISPLAY VIEW   ===> space_   (VOLUME,SPACE,ATTRIB,TOTAL)
  CONFIRM DELETE REQUEST ===> YES      (YES or NO)

* The following line commands will be available when the list is displayed:

B - Browse data set      C - Catalog data set     F - Free unused space
E - Edit data set        U - Uncatalog data set   = - Repeat last command
D - Delete data set      P - Print data set
R - Rename data set      X - Print index listing
I - Data set information M - Display member list
S - Information (short)   Z - Compress data set    TSO cmd, CLIST or REXX exec
```

Figure 31.12 Listing all data sets from a volume.

```
DSLIST - DATA SETS ON VOLUME DISK1A ------------------------- ROW 1 OF 6042
COMMAND ===> sort tracks_                             SCROLL ===> CSR

COMMAND     NAME                              TRACKS %USED XT  DEVICE
--------------------------------------------------------------------------
            ACCT053.FTP.APRDATA               1443   100   5  3380
            ACCT053.FTP.MARDATA                  2     ?   1  3380
            ACCT072.BATCH01                      1   100   1  3380
            ACCT252.FORT492.QCKRUN               1   100   1  3380
            DEVL015.BMP2.DP1.TEST2.DATA          5   100   1  3380
            DEVL015.BMP2.DP2.TEST3A.DATA         3   100   1  3380
            DEVL015.TEST3A.TEMP                  3   100   1  3380
            FINANCE.APR                          2   100   1  3380
            FINANCE.APROLD                      20    45   1  3380
            FINANCE.APRRUN                       1   100   1  3380
            FINANCE.LEDNOV                       1   100   1  3380
            FINANCE.NOV3.DATA                    1   100   1  3380
            FINANCE.OUT.APR                      5    20   1  3380
            FINANCE.OUT.APRRUN                   2   100   2  3380
            ENGR256.C370                         1   100   1  3380
            ENGR327.CLIST                        1   100   1  3380
            ENGR327.DATA                         1   100   1  3380
            ENGR327.MAIL                         1   100   1  3380
            ENGR327.PROFILE                      1   100   1  3380
```

Figure 31.13 Data set list SORT command.

In Figure 31.14, the data set list has been resequenced to show the largest data sets first. The command SORT NAME or SORT (since NAME is the default) can be used, if necessary, to again display the list in data set name order.

The LOCATE Command

The LOCATE command helps to locate a data set by the data set name or one of the other displayed characteristics. The command works in the data set list just as it does within a member list. The string to be located is applied to the sorted column. By default, this is the data set name column, and the string specified would be a data set name prefix. When sorted by a different column, a value that's appropriate to that column should be specified. That's also true for the alternate columns that can be listed in the data set list utility. For any column, the leading characters of the column value are specified.

The FIND Command

The FIND command can be used to find a character string within the list of data sets. Unlike the LOCATE command, the object of the FIND command can occur anywhere within the data set name. In Figure 31.15, the FIND command (abbreviated with the letter F) is used to find the string CNTL.

```
DSLIST - DATA SETS ON VOLUME DISK1A ------------------------- ROW 1 OF 6042
COMMAND ===> _                                         SCROLL ===> CSR

COMMAND     NAME                               TRACKS  %USED  XT  DEVICE
------------------------------------------------------------------------
            TSO2345.TEST                         1876    63    2  3380
            ACCT053.FTP.APRDATA                  1443   100    5  3380
            TSO3307.CPSTEST.SYSTEM                794   100    2  3380
            TSO3307.WORKFILE                      477   100    2  3380
            TSO3307.SASA.DATA                     405    99    1  3380
            TSO4123.NLS.DATA                      353   100    1  3380
            TSO5431.MAURA.DATA                    323   100    1  3380
            TSO2151.CHECK                         300    73   16  3380
            TSO2345.KATHY.DATA                    300     1    1  3380
            TSO4001.PSB.TEMP                      290   100   16  3380
            TSO2151.FORT                          272   100   16  3380
            TSO2100.RESLIB                        264    30    1  3380
            TSO2345.OUTDATA                       250     0    1  3380
            TSO2100.VSAM01.UNLOAD                 226   100    1  3380
            TSO2775.PROD.EXTRACT                  200   100    4  3380
            TSO2151.OUTLIST                       200     0    1  3380
            TSO2151.LOAD                          195    96    4  3380
            TSO3307.SAS.VERSION6.TESTDATA         156   100    4  3380
            TSO4001.DASD.REPORT                   151     7   16  3380
```

Figure 31.14 Data set list in track order.

```
DSLIST - DATA SETS ON VOLUME DISK1A --------------------------  ROW 1 OF 6042
COMMAND ===> f cnt1_                                  SCROLL ===> CSR

COMMAND     NAME                                 MESSAGE       VOLUME
-----------------------------------------------------------------------------
            ACCT053.FTP.APRDATA                                DISK1A
            ACCT053.FTP.MARDATA                                DISK1A
            ACCT072.BATCH01                                    DISK1A
            ACCT252.FORT492.QCKRUN                             DISK1A
            DEVL015.BMP2.DP1.TEST2.DATA                        DISK1A
            DEVL015.BMP2.DP2.TEST3A.DATA                       DISK1A
            DEVL015.TEST3A.TEMP                                DISK1A
            FINANCE.APR                                        DISK1A
            FINANCE.APROLD                                     DISK1A
            FINANCE.APRRUN                                     DISK1A
            FINANCE.LEDNOV                                      DISK1A
            FINANCE.NOV3.DATA                                  DISK1A
            FINANCE.OUT.APR                                    DISK1A
            FINANCE.OUT.APRRUN                                 DISK1A
            ENGR256.C370                                       DISK1A
            ENGR327.CLIST                                      DISK1A
            ENGR327.DATA                                       DISK1A
            ENGR327.MAIL                                       DISK1A
            ENGR327.PROFILE                                    DISK1A
```

Figure 31.15 Data set list FIND command.

Figure 31.16 shows the result of the FIND command just executed. The next occurrence of the string (in this case also the first occurrence) was found, and the short message was changed to reflect that. At the same time, the data set list was scrolled to show the data set name containing the string.

FIND command parameters can be used to specify the search direction and context. The parameters NEXT, ALL, FIRST, LAST, and PREV are used to indicate the search direction. NEXT is the default and so would only be required to change the current direction. The parameters CHARS, PREFIX, SUFFIX, and WORD can be used to specify the string context. CHARS is the default for the string context. The RFIND command can be executed to find the next occurrence of the string (in whatever direction is established).

Start and end columns can also be used with the FIND command. When only a single column number is specified, it's interpreted as the start column. The string would have to start in the column specified (within the data set name) before it will be found. When two column numbers are specified, the string must fall within the range of columns to be found.

Additional Primary Commands

The SAVE command can be used to write out the data set list. This is like the same function used from a member list. Data set information is retrieved so that information about space and attributes can be included. When specified by itself, the SAVE command writes the data set information to the list data set, where it can later be printed. This would be like specifying processing option P from the initial screen of the data set list utility. When SAVE is specified with a one-character to eight-character name, data set information is written to a data set. The one-character to eight-character name specified becomes the middle qualifier of the data set that the information is written to. Because it becomes a data set name qualifier, the name must conform to the rules for forming a simple name. The first qualifier of the data set is the current profile prefix, and the last qualifier is the word DATASETS.

The CONFIRM primary command is used to control whether or not the delete confirmation screen is displayed each time the data set list utility is used to delete a data set. By default, the delete confirmation screen is displayed. The field CONFIRM DELETE REQUEST can be used from the initial 3.4 screen to indicate whether or not the confirmation screen should be displayed. The command CONFIRM OFF can be issued from the data set list to suppress the display of the confirmation screen and thereby expedite the process of deleting data sets. CONFIRM ON or CONFIRM (since ON is the default) can be used to indicate that the confirmation screen should be displayed.

Displaying VTOC Information

At times it might be necessary to display VTOC information. This used to be handled in option 3.7 but was subsequently incorporated in the data set list utility (which is why there currently is no option 3.7). Processing option V is used to request the VTOC information rather than list all of the data sets on a volume. Processing option V is specified in Figure 31.17, along with the volume serial number of the disk to be listed.

```
DSLIST - DATA SETS ON VOLUME DISK1A --------------------- CHARS 'CNTL' FOUND
COMMAND ===>                                              SCROLL ===> CSR

COMMAND      NAME                                 MESSAGE          VOLUME
--------------------------------------------------------------------------------
  _          TSO1234.CNTL                                          DISK1A
             TSO1234.FORT.LOAD                                     DISK1A
             TSO1235.JCL.CNTL                                      DISK1A
             TSO1237.PROFILE                                       DISK1A
             TSO1240.FINAL.TEXT                                    DISK1A
             TSO1245.HWRK3.TXT                                     DISK1A
             TSO1258.PROJECT1                                      DISK1A
             TSO1301.PROFILE                                       DISK1A
             TSO1314.PROFILE                                       DISK1A
             TSO1317.PROGRAM2.CLIST                                DISK1A
             TSO1317.PROGRAM2.MSGS                                 DISK1A
             TSO1317.PROGRAM2.PANELS                               DISK1A
             TSO1317.PROGRAM2.SKELS                                DISK1A
             TSO1317.PROGRAM2.TABLES                               DISK1A
             TSO1317.RUN.PROGRAM2.RESULT1                          DISK1A
             TSO1317.RUN.PROGRAM2.RESULT2                          DISK1A
             TSO1317.RUN.PROGRAM2.RESULT3                          DISK1A
             TSO1317.RUN.PROGRAM2.RESULT4                          DISK1A
             TSO1317.RUN.PROGRAM2.RESULT5                          DISK1A
```

Figure 31.16 Result of the FIND command.

```
------------------------- DATA SET LIST UTILITY -------------------------
OPTION  ===>  v_

  blank - Display data set list *        P  - Print data set list
  V    - Display VTOC information only   PV - Print VTOC information only

Enter one or both of the parameters below:
  DSNAME LEVEL  ===>
  VOLUME        ===>  DISK1A


  INITIAL DISPLAY VIEW   ===> VOLUME   (VOLUME,SPACE,ATTRIB,TOTAL)
  CONFIRM DELETE REQUEST ===> YES      (YES or NO)

* The following line commands will be available when the list is displayed:

B - Browse data set       C - Catalog data set     F - Free unused space
E - Edit data set         U - Uncatalog data set   = - Repeat last command
D - Delete data set       P - Print data set
R - Rename data set       X - Print index listing
I - Data set information  M - Display member list
S - Information (short)    Z - Compress data set    TSO cmd, CLIST or REXX exec
```

Figure 31.17 Requesting VTOC information.

```
VTOC SUMMARY INFORMATION FOR VOLUME DISK1A ----------------------------------
COMMAND ===> _

UNIT:  3380

VOLUME DATA:            VTOC DATA          FREE SPACE:    TRACKS    CYLS
  TRACKS:    39,825       TRACKS:    210     SIZE:        7,371     322
  %USED:         81       %USED:      56     LARGEST:       226      14
  TRKS/CYLS:     15       FREE DSCBS: 4,946

                                            FREE EXTENTS:   417
```

Figure 31.18 VTOC information display.

The VTOC information is displayed in Figure 31.18. It shows the device type and capacity information. The volume listed is a 3380 device with a total capacity of 39,825 tracks. The volume is currently 81 percent full. The second column of data is directed to the VTOC itself. It shows that the VTOC is 210 tracks and is just over half full. The last two columns show the amount of free space in both tracks and cylinders. Included is the largest single extent in terms of contiguous tracks or cylinders.

Displaying the VTOC for a volume will show whether or not the volume can support the space required for a particular data set. DASD administrators will be interested in the volume's free space as well as volume fragmentation. The latter situation is indicated by sufficient free space that's spread in so many small pieces (extents) that data set allocation becomes difficult.

32

Printing

I've made numerous references to printing with ISPF. These references, however, typically refer to ISPF creating the print image and storing it in the list data set. Actual printing (including printing the list data set) involves copying information from storage media (like a disk) to a print device. In this chapter, I'll discuss several methods of printing, but first I'll discuss concepts that are common to printing in general.

Print Classes

A *print class* is a single letter or number designation. It might carry with it special features that determine when, where, or how material will print. An installation can design print classes around things like the sensitivity of printed material. This could allow different output classes to be labeled differently or printed only in secure surroundings. Classes could also be based on the source of input, whether that's different companies, different departments, company production, or individual production. An installation could even set print classes to determine distribution points.

Print classes can also be designed around physical characteristics like the location of the printer to be used, the type of printer to be used, the use of special forms, or distribution and post-processing requirements. An installation can, for example, reset their printers at a particular time of day to print only production-designated output to ensure that it can be printed and delivered on time. Special forms classes can be held until the forms can be loaded into the printer. Output for one class could print on a laser printer while a different class output is directed to an impact printer.

Print Destination

The *print destination* is an indication of where information is to print. It's often mistaken for where the printed material finally ends up. This is more often a distribution issue and might only be indirectly related to where the information was printed. The print destination could be one of a group of eligible printers or one printer in particular. The print destination can cause printing to occur at physically remote sites, or it can be used to direct information to a printer with distinct print characteristics. Again, this could mean the difference between printing on an impact printer or a laser printer. The print destination could also be used to differentiate between similar printers with some slight difference like the type of form it typically prints.

Printer Carriage Control

Printer carriage control can be used to determine the spacing on an output document. The characters –, 0, and + can be used to triple space, double space, and print without advancing when used in the first byte of a data set defined to contain ANSI carriage control characters (defined by the letter A in the data set record format RECFM). A blank or invalid character will cause single spacing before printing. Number designations 1 through 9 and A through C can be used in the same first byte of data to represent channel skips. The first channel skip is defined to the first line that will be printed on a page (known as head of form). The other 11 channel skips might be defined to different places on a form or page to facilitate print positioning. Their placement must be coordinated with the carriage control information loaded in the printer to achieve proper print positioning.

Changing Print Characteristics

The ability to change print characteristics varies by printer type. With impact printers, for example, it might only be practical to change the number of lines per inch (and therefore the number of lines per page) without physically changing the print chain (or similar printer part). Laser printers, on the other hand, can easily accommodate other characteristic changes like the size and style of print character. These characteristics, as well as channel skips, can be incorporated in a forms control buffer or FCB. Reference to a particular FCB while printing is then an easy way to determine the print characteristic.

ISPF Hardcopy Utility

The hardcopy utility can be used to print sequential data sets as well as individual members of a PDS. This utility allows the print class to be specified, but no other parameters for changing print characteristics or number of copies. Because the jobcard is available, however, JES statements can be used to determine where the print is routed as well as the number of copies. It's also essential that the jobcard syntax is correct to avoid a JCL error. To discern proper jobcard syntax, look to other options that might have been used previously like the background options (primary option 5) or the log/list default screen (option 0.2). Most jobcards can also be viewed by displaying the ISPF variables (option 7.3) that store them. See Appendix A for a discussion of jobcard parameters.

The name of the data set to be printed is specified in normal TSO format. In this option, a PDS can't be specified without also specifying a member name. Two print options are included so the data set can either be retained after printing (option PK) or printed and deleted (option PD). The one character print class is specified to determine which output class will be used. No check is made against this field since valid print classes are installation specific. It's important to adhere to installation standards to ensure that the data set is printed at all, let alone with the proper characteristics.

Figure 32.1 shows the hardcopy utility. When executed in a batch or background mode, JCL is generated using the specified data set name as input and the print class as output. That JCL is combined with the jobcard information at the bottom of the screen and is then ready to be submitted.

Figure 32.2 shows the next screen with the jobcard filled in. The short message indicates that the JCL has been created from the information on the previous screen. The data set name field can be used to print additional data sets. Each time a new data set name is entered, additional JCL is created and added to that already generated. Each data set or member will be processed in a separate step but will appear to print together.

Although not intended for that purpose, the CLASS field can be used to specify additional print information. Using a substitution concept that's common to JCL procedures, additional parameters can be added in such a way that the end result is still syntactically correct. The following shows the FCB keyword added to the print class:

```
SYSOUT CLASS ===> A),FCB=(STD3
```

```
    -------------------------- HARDCOPY UTILITY ----------------------------
  OPTION ===> PK

    PK - Print and keep data set
    PD - Print and delete data set



  DATA SET NAME ===> EXAMPLE.TEXT(MEMO1)   _
    VOLUME SERIAL      ===>                (If not cataloged)
    DATA SET PASSWORD ===>                 (If password protected PDS)


  PRINT MODE         ===> BATCH           (BATCH or LOCAL)

  SYSOUT CLASS       ===> A
  LOCAL PRINTER ID   ===>

  JOB STATEMENT INFORMATION: (If not to local printer verify before proceeding)
    ===> //useridA  JOB (ACCOUNT),'NAME'
    ===> //*
    ===> //*
    ===> //*
```

Figure 32.1 The hardcopy utility.

```
--------------------------  HARDCOPY UTILITY  ---------------- JCL GENERATED
OPTION ===> PK

  PK - Print and keep data set
  PD - Print and delete data set
  CANCEL - Exit without submitting job


DATA SET NAME ===> EXAMPLE.TEXT(MEMO1)
  VOLUME SERIAL     ===>                    (If not cataloged)
  DATA SET PASSWORD ===>                    (If password protected PDS)

PRINT MODE           ===> BATCH           (BATCH or LOCAL)

SYSOUT CLASS         ===> A
LOCAL PRINTER ID     ===>

JOB STATEMENT INFORMATION: (If not to local printer verify before proceeding)
  ===> //TSO1234A JOB (TSO12349999),'PRINT JOB',
  ===> //   CLASS=A,MSGCLASS=H,NOTIFY=TSO1234   _
  ===> //*
  ===> //*
```

Figure 32.2 The hardcopy utility (screen two).

Multiple parameters can be added as in the following example:

```
SYSOUT CLASS ===> A),FCB=STD3,COPIES=2,DEST=(R17
```

Parentheses are a normal part of the JCL that's constructed. With multiple parameters, it's necessary to move the left parenthesis to the last keyword value. The JCL statement might look like the following after substitution:

```
//SYSUT1 DD SYSOUT=(A),FCB=STD3,COPIES=2,DEST=(R17)
```

This type of extended substitution can also be used in other print instances such as printing the log and list data sets.

Option PK will direct the JCL to print and keep the data set. Option PD will direct the JCL to delete the data set after printing it. The END function will cause the JCL to be submitted, or CANCEL can be specified to terminate the print process without printing.

PRINTDS Command

The PRINTDS command can be used to print regular sequential or partitioned data sets, or the PRINTDS command can reference a file name and print the data set or data sets that are allocated to that particular file. As a TSO command, PRINTDS shares certain keyword parameters that have the same use in other commands.

When a PDS is printed, the member contents, the member name list, or both can be printed. The mutually exclusive parameters for those options are MEMBERS, DI-RECTORY, and ALL, respectively. Selected members can be printed, or, by default, all members of the PDS will be printed. The ability to automatically print all of the members of a PDS makes this a very useful command.

Titles are added, by default, to the data that's printed. An exception to this is when a data set is printed that's defined to contain carriage control characters. In this latter case, an assumption is made that the data is already formatted into an acceptable print format. Titles are also omitted when the parameter NOTITLES is included when the command is invoked. Conversely, titles can be forced to print by including the TITLES parameter. The title created by PRINTDS contains the data set name, member name (if any), date, time, and page number.

The following example shows the PRINTDS command used to print an entire PDS:

```
PRINTDS DATASET(REPORT.PDS) CLASS(A) DEST(R17) FCB(STD4)
```

The data set name is specified in TSO format and so, in this instance, would have the current prefix added as a high-level qualifier. Keyword parameters are used to specify the print class (CLASS), the print characteristics (FCB), and the location of the printer (DEST). Some of the other print option parameters are specified in Table 32.1.

TABLE 32.1 Print Option Parameters

TODATASET	- This keyword allows the data set contents to be written to another data set. This is particularly useful to unload a partitioned data set into a sequential data set. If the data set referenced in the TODATASET keyword does not already exist, the PRINTDS command will create it. Below is an example of how an entire PDS can be unloaded into a sequential data set. **PRINTDS DATASET(REPORT.PDS) TODATASET(NEW.REPORT)** The member contents of the PDS, REPORT.PDS, will be unloaded into the sequential data set, NEW.REPORT. If the data set, NEW.REPORT, does not already exist, the PRINTDS command will create it based upon the characteristics of REPORT.PDS. The keyword, TODSNAME, can also be used in place of the keyword, TODATASET.
FILE	- This keyword allows data to be printed by file name. When the FILE keyword is used in place of the DATASET keyword, the data set currently allocated to the file specified will be printed. If more than one data set is concatenated to the file, all of those data sets will be printed. The keyword, DDNAME, can be used in place of the keyword, FILE.
COLUMNS	- This keyword allows particular columns of the data to be printed. The columns are specified by start and end columns separated by a colon. Multiple column specifications are separated by blanks or commas. This keyword can, therefore, be used to print only selected parts of a line of data, or it can be used to change the order of the data within the line as it is written out. The example below does both, using the abbreviation for the command, PR, and an abbreviation for the DATASET keyword, DA. **PR DA(SEQUENTL.DATA) CLASS(A) COLUMNS(1:10 37:43 60:80 15:20)**
LINES	- The LINES keyword allows specific lines of the data set to be printed. Both starting line

TABLE 32.1 Print Option Parameters (Continued)

	number, and optionally, ending line number can be specified. If both line numbers are specified, they are separated by a colon.
TRUNCATE	- This keyword will cause the print output to be truncated at the column value specified with this parameter. When used, no data beyond the column value specified will be printed.
FOLD	- This keyword is used to cause the data to wrap at the column specified. Subsequent data is written on successive lines. This can be used when the data is longer than the print characteristic can print on a single line of output.
PAGELEN	- This keyword specifies the number of lines to be printed on each page. This would be used to change the default value from 60 lines per page where a data set was not already using carriage control characters.
LMARGIN	- This keyword specifies the left margin to be maintained when printing the data set. The value is specified in column positions.
TMARGIN	- This keyword specifies the top margin to be maintained when printing the data set. The value is specified in number of lines.
BMARGIN	- This keyword specifies the bottom margin to be maintained when printing the data set. The value is also specified in number of lines.

Printing Using JCL

A standard piece of JCL can easily be maintained to print most sequential data sets. The advantage is that more control can be exercised in this environment than with the ISPF print utility. The JCL could also allow tape data to be printed. Changing the data set reference in the JCL would allow different data sets to be printed. The JCL below uses a standard utility, IEBGENER. It reads from file SYSUT1 and writes to file SYSUT2:

```
//TSO1234A JOB TSO9999,'SEQ DSN PRINT',
// CLASS=A,MSGCLASS=A,NOTIFY=TSO1234
//PRINT    EXEC PGM=IEBGENER
//SYSPRINT DD SYSOUT=A
//SYSUT1   DD DSN=TSO1234.FINANCE.REPORT,DISP=SHR
//SYSUT2   DD SYSOUT=A,FCB=STD2,DEST=PRT3,COPIES=2
//SYSIN    DD DUMMY
```

This JCL is, in fact, very similar to that generated by the ISPF hardcopy utility. The data set to be printed in the JCL example is TSO1234.FINANCE.REPORT. The data set name on the SYSUT1 statement can be changed to print other sequential data sets. It can also be changed to print a member of a PDS:

```
//SYSUT1 DD DSN=TSO1234.TEXT(CHAPTER1),DISP=SHR
```

It can also be concatenated to print multiple data sets or members.

```
//SYSUT1 DD DSN=TSO1234.TEXT(CHAPTER1),DISP=SHR
//       DD DSN=TSO1234.TEXT(CHAPTER2),DISP=SHR
//       DD DSN=TSO1234.TEXT(CHAPTER3),DISP=SHR
//       DD DSN=TSO1234.TEXT(CHAPTER4),DISP=SHR
```

No titles or reference to the data set name will be added to the data printed. It's therefore advisable to retain the JCL output with the data printed to identify what data was printed and when it was printed. The SYSUT2 parameter, SYSOUT, is similar to the CLASS parameter of the PRINTDS command. It identifies the print class to be used. The other parameters used on the SYSUT2 statement are the same as they were with the PRINTDS command. The format is different since JCL keywords are noted with an equal sign rather than being enclosed in parentheses.

If the data set being printed was not defined as containing carriage control, this can be specified in the JCL. For example, if a data set uses the first data position for carriage control but was created with a record format of FB rather than FBA, the data set can be printed with the following slight modification:

```
//SYSUT2 DD SYSOUT=A,FCB=STD2,DEST=PRT3,COPIES=2,
//           DCB=RECFM=FBA
```

The added RECFM parameter indicates that the data records are fixed-length records that are blocked and contain ANSI carriage control characters.

Other utilities can be used that would allow an entire PDS to be printed. None would be any easier to use nor provide as many features as the PRINTDS command discussed earlier. JCL can be used to invoke the TSO program in a background mode and execute TSO commands like PRINTDS:

```
//TSO1234B JOB TSO9999,'PDS PRINT',
//    CLASS=A,MSGCLASS=A,NOTIFY=TSO1234
//PDSPRINT EXEC PGM=IKJEFT01
//SYSTSPRT DD SYSOUT=A
//SYSTSIN  DD *
PRINTDS DA('TSO1234.TEXT') CLASS(A) FCB(STD2) DEST(PRT3)
/*
```

TSO commands are input to the SYSTSIN file. In the previous example, the DSPRINT command will print the entire PDS, TSO1234.TEXT, to output class A using the forms control buffer STD2. The output will be routed to printer PRT3 to print. Other message output from the DSPRINT command and TSO will be directed to the SYSTSPRT file.

Either JCL jobstream can be submitted for execution using the editor SUBMIT command or the TSO SUBMIT command. The advantage to background printing is that it leaves the terminal free for other work. This is especially important when printing large data sets. Background printing can also be used to schedule printing tasks around data availability by deferring or delaying execution of the background job.

Advanced
ISPF Utilities

33

Compare and Search Utilities

Comparing Data Sets

The compare utilities are options 3.12 and 3.13. In option 3.12, the new data set is specified on the first screen, and the data set it's being compared with is specified on a second screen. Either partitioned or sequential data sets can be compared. Comparisons can be made to display only the changed lines (DELTA), the entire data set (LONG), a general summary (OVSUM), or no list at all (NOLIST). Also, the option CHNG can be used to display the changed lines within the context of the previous and following 10 lines. The type of compare can range from file level at the high end down to a byte-level compare.

The compare utility available with option 3.13 has the same compare features as 3.12, but option 3.13 provides many additional options. The compare examples in this chapter will be taken exclusively from option 3.13. In option 3.13, both data sets to be compared are specified on a single screen. Figure 33.1 shows two partitioned data sets being compared. An asterisk is used in the Member List field to indicate that all members will be included.

The browse option causes the compare output data set to be displayed (Figure 33.2). The result of the compare shows three members to be common to both data sets. These three members also have the same content in both libraries, as shown first by the DIFF and SAME columns, and then shown by the number of bytes and lines in each member and their generated hash totals. Statistics for both libraries are shown with N to designate the "new" library and O to designate the "old." The lower part of the screen also shows that there are seven uniquely named members (four members in one library and three in the other).

```
---------------------------- SUPERCE UTILITY ----------------------------
OPTION  ===>

blank - Compare Data Sets                    P - Select Process Options
  B   - Submit Batch Data Set Compare        E - Edit Statements Data Set
  S   - Extended Search-For Compare Utility  A - Activate/Create Profiles

New DS Name    ===> cntl
Old DS Name    ===> jcl.cntl
PDS Member List ===> *_        (blank/pattern - member list, * - compare all)
   (Leave New/Old Dsn "blank" for concatenated-uncataloged-password panel)
                       Optional Section
Compare Type   ===> FILE              (FILE/ LINE /WORD/BYTE)
Listing Type   ===> DELTA             (OVSUM/ DELTA /CHNG/LONG/NOLIST)
Listing Dsn    ===> SUPERC.LIST
Process Options ===>
               ===>
Statements Dsn ===>
Update  Dsn    ===>
BROWSE  Output ===> YES               ( YES /NO/COND/UPD)
```

Figure 33.1 Comparing partitioned data sets.

```
BROWSE -- TSO1234.SUPERC.LIST --------------------- LINE 00000000 COL 001 080
COMMAND ===> _                                         SCROLL ===> CSR
****************************** TOP OF DATA ********************************
      SUPERC - FILE/LINE/WORD/BYTE COMPARE PGM - V2.7(87/03/27)  92/12/10
NEW: TSO1234.CNTL                                      OLD:  TSO1234.JCL.

                  MEMBER SUMMARY LISTING (FILE COMPARE)

DIFF SAME    MEMBER-NAME    N-BYTES  O-BYTES N-LINES O-LINES N-HASH-SUM O-HAS

       **    COMPILE           1360     1360      17      17 734DCAEB   734D
       **    COMPRESS           640      640       8       8 18C00747   18C0
       **    SORT              1120     1120      14      14 6B7BA620   6B7B
             --------------  ------- ------- ------- -------
             MEMBER TOTALS     3120     3120      39      39


   3   TOTAL MEMBER(S) PROCESSED AS A PDS
   0   TOTAL MEMBER(S) PROCESSED HAD CHANGES
   3   TOTAL MEMBER(S) PROCESSED HAD NO CHANGES
   4   TOTAL NEW FILE MEMBER(S) NOT PAIRED
   3   TOTAL OLD FILE MEMBER(S) NOT PAIRED

    SUPERC - FILE/LINE/WORD/BYTE COMPARE PGM - V2.7(87/03/27)   92/12/10
```

Figure 33.2 Compare output.

The second page of the output (shown in Figure 33.3) shows the members from each PDS that had no counterpart in the other library. The four members listed on the left side of the screen appear in the "new" library, but not in the "old" one. The three members listed on the right side of the screen appear in the "old" library but not in the "new" one.

Detail Comparisons

In Figure 33.4, another comparison is made. Here, two members of the same PDS are compared at the line level. The long format is requested to display any differences within the context of the entire data set.

The LONG option shows the data set differences in normal sequence with the lines that surround them (Figure 33.5). The lines with differences are marked by a code at the left margin. The letter R represents REFORMATTED, while letters N and O represent NEW and OLD, respectively. The letter I represents an inserted line, while D represents a deleted line.

Page two of the compare output (Figure 33.6) shows summary information. That information indicates that of the 11 lines compared, 8 of the lines matched exactly. Two of the lines where essentially the same except for the spacing on the line. Only one line was significantly different. This is noted as both a one-line insertion and one-line deletion. This should be interpreted as one line would have to be deleted from the old version to get to the new version. At the same time, one line would have to be inserted into the old version to get to the new version.

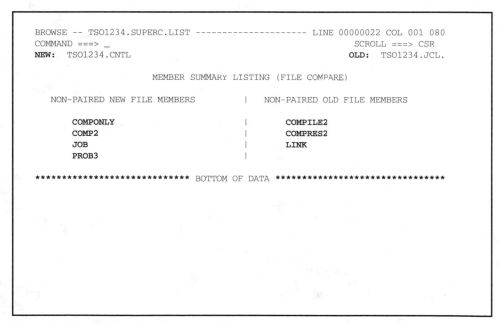

```
BROWSE -- TSO1234.SUPERC.LIST -------------------- LINE 00000022 COL 001 080
COMMAND ===> _                                          SCROLL ===> CSR
NEW:   TSO1234.CNTL                           OLD:   TSO1234.JCL.

                    MEMBER SUMMARY LISTING (FILE COMPARE)

   NON-PAIRED NEW FILE MEMBERS        |    NON-PAIRED OLD FILE MEMBERS

       COMPONLY                       |        COMPILE2
       COMP2                          |        COMPRES2
       JOB                            |        LINK
       PROB3                          |

****************************** BOTTOM OF DATA ********************************
```

Figure 33.3 Second page of compare output.

```
----------------------------- SUPERCE UTILITY -----------------------------
OPTION  ===>

blank - Compare Data Sets                    P - Select Process Options
  B   - Submit Batch Data Set Compare        E - Edit Statements Data Set
  S   - Extended Search-For Compare Utility  A - Activate/Create Profiles

New DS Name    ===> fort(newrate2)
Old DS Name    ===> fort(newrate)
PDS Member List ===>          (blank/pattern - member list, * - compare all)
    (Leave New/Old Dsn "blank" for concatenated-uncataloged-password panel)
                        Optional Section
Compare Type   ===> line                  (FILE/ LINE /WORD/BYTE)
Listing Type   ===> long _                (OVSUM/ DELTA /CHNG/LONG/NOLIST)
Listing Dsn    ===> SUPERC.LIST
Process Options ===>
               ===>
Statements Dsn ===>
Update  Dsn    ===>
BROWSE  Output ===> YES                    ( YES /NO/COND/UPD)
```

Figure 33.4 Line-level comparison.

```
BROWSE -- TSO1234.SUPERC.LIST -------------------- LINE 00000000 COL 001 080
COMMAND ===> _                                            SCROLL ===> CSR
****************************** TOP OF DATA **********************************
      SUPERC - FILE/LINE/WORD/BYTE COMPARE PGM - V2.7(87/03/27)   92/12/10
NEW:  TSO1234.FORT(NEWRATE2)                        OLD:  TSO1234.FORT

                    LISTING OUTPUT SECTION (LINE COMPARE)

ID      SOURCE LINES
    ----+----1----+----2----+----3----+----4----+----5----+----6----+----7---
      100 FORMAT(F5.2)                                                      0
          OPEN (1,FILE='BASERATE')                                         0
          OPEN (3,FILE='NEWRATES')                                         0
RN-       READ (1,100) RATE                                               0
RO-       READ(1,100)RATE                                                 0
RN-       WRITE (3,100) RATE                                              0
RO-       WRITE(3,100)RATE                                                0
          DO 10 I=1,9                                                      0
I -       RATE = RATE * 1.3                                               0
D -       RATE = RATE * 1.1                                               0
          WRITE(3,100)RATE                                                 0
       10 CONTINUE                                                         0
          STOP                                                             0
          END                                                              0
```

Figure 33.5 Line-level comparison output.

Compare Processing Options

Using processing options, the way a compare is conducted can be altered. The options themselves are accessed by specifying option P in the primary command area, as in Figure 33.7. The processing options are presented over three different screens. Options can be selected by placing an S in front of the option. Removing the S from in front of an option will cause it to be deactivated. The short message in Figure 33.8 shows that this is the first of the three screens. The ENTER key can be used to page forward to the other option screens.

In Figure 33.9, the NOPRTCC option is selected. This option will cause headings and carriage control to be omitted from subsequent pages of the output. Pressing ENTER from the third and final options screen (Figure 33.10) will cause all selected options to be captured.

Additional Processing Instructions

In Figure 33.11, the selected processing option has been carried forward to the initial screen and placed in the field labeled Process Options. Valid processing options can be specified in this field without using menu selection P and the previous three screens. Additional processing instructions can be specified in the statements data set. The data set can be accessed by selecting option E for edit.

Option E causes the statements data set to be displayed in standard edit mode (Figure 33.12). Because a data set was not specified (in the previous screen field labeled Statements Dsn), the extended compare utility will create one under a default data set name.

```
BROWSE -- TSO1234.SUPERC.LIST -------------------- LINE 00000022 COL 001 080
COMMAND ===> _                                        SCROLL ===> CSR
        SUPERC - FILE/LINE/WORD/BYTE COMPARE PGM - V2.7(87/03/27)   92/12/10
NEW:  TSO1234.FORT(NEWRATE2)                          OLD:  TSO1234.FORT

                    LINE COMPARE SUMMARY AND STATISTICS

        8 NUMBER OF LINE MATCHES       3  TOTAL CHANGES (PAIRED+NONPAIRED
        2 REFORMATTED LINES            3  PAIRED CHANGES (REFM+PAIRED INS
        1 NEW FILE LINE INSERTIONS     0  NON-PAIRED INSERTS
        1 OLD FILE LINE DELETIONS      0  NON-PAIRED DELETES
       11 NEW FILE LINES PROCESSED
       11 OLD FILE LINES PROCESSED

LISTING-TYPE = LONG      COMPARE-COLUMNS =   1:72       LONGEST-LINE = 80
PROCESS OPTIONS USED: SEQ(DEFAULT)

***************************** BOTTOM OF DATA ********************************
```

Figure 33.6 Second page of line-level comparison output.

```
------------------------------ SUPERCE UTILITY -----------------------------
OPTION  ===> p_

blank - Compare Data Sets                    P - Select Process Options
  B   - Submit Batch Data Set Compare        E - Edit Statements Data Set
  S   - Extended Search-For Compare Utility  A - Activate/Create Profiles

New DS Name      ===> FORT(NEWRATE2)
Old DS Name      ===> FORT(NEWRATE)
PDS Member List ===>           (blank/pattern - member list, * - compare all)
   (Leave New/Old Dsn "blank" for concatenated-uncataloged-password panel)
                          Optional Section
Compare Type     ===> LINE               (FILE/ LINE /WORD/BYTE)
Listing Type     ===> LONG               (OVSUM/ DELTA /CHNG/LONG/NOLIST)
Listing Dsn      ===> SUPERC.LIST
Process Options ===>
                 ===>
Statements Dsn   ===>
Update  Dsn      ===>
BROWSE  Output   ===> YES                 ( YES /NO/COND/UPD)
```

Figure 33.7 Access to processing options.

```
------------------ SUPERCE - LINE COMPARE PROCESS OPTIONS --------- (1 of 3)
COMMAND ===> _

Select Process Option(s) or "blank" to remove.  Press  ENTER to continue.

                    Input Process Control Options
   SEQ      - Ignore FB 80/VB 255 standard sequence number columns, or
   NOSEQ    - Process FB 80/VB 255 standard sequence number columns as data
   COBOL    - Ignore sequence number columns 1-6 in FB 80 records.
   ANYC     - Process Lower case as Upper case input characters.

                    Don't Process Control Options
   DPPLCMT  - Don't process /* ... */ comments and blank compare lines.
   DPPSCMT  - Don't process (* ... *) comments and blank compare lines.
   DPADCMT  - Don't process "--" comments and blank compare lines.
   DPACMT   - Don't process "assembler" lines with "*" in column 1.
   DPFTCMT  - Don't process lines with "C" in column 1.
   DPCBCMT  - Don't process lines with "*" in column 7.
   DPBLKCL  - Don't process blank compare lines.
                     (continued on next page)
```

Figure 33.8 First screen of processing options.

```
------------------- SUPERCE - LINE COMPARE PROCESS OPTIONS --------- (2 of 3)
COMMAND ===>

Select Process Option(s) or "blank" to remove.  Press  ENTER to continue.

                       Output Process Control Options
     REFMOVR  - Reformat override.  Don't flag reformatted lines in listing.
     DLREFM   - Don't list reformatted old DS lines. Only new DS reformats.
     DLMDUP   - Don't list matched old DS lines in side-by-side listing.
     FMVLNS   - Flag Insert/Delete moved lines.
     LOCS     - List only changed and non-paired members in PDS summary list.
     CNPML      Count all lines including non-paired members in PDS summary.

                       Listing Control Options
     WIDE     - Up to 80 columns side-by-side. Line length = 202/203, or
     NARROW   - Up to 55 columns side-by-side. Line length = 132/133, or
     LONGLN   - Lists up to 176 columns. Line length = 202/203.
  s _NOPRTCC  - No print control column and page separators.
     APNDLST  - Append listing report to listing data set.
                       (continued on next page)
```

Figure 33.9 Selecting a processing option.

```
------------------- SUPERCE - LINE COMPARE PROCESS OPTIONS --------- (3 of 3)
COMMAND ===> _

Select Process Option(s) or "blank" to remove.  Press  ENTER to continue.

                       Update Data Set Options
     APNDUPD  - Append update report to update data set.

     UPDSUMO  - Overall summary statistics listed in a single line format, or
     UPDCMS8  - Cntl and new DS source using cols 73-80 (for CMS UPDATE), or
     UPDMVS8  - Cntl and new DS source using cols 73-80 (for MVS IEBUPDTE), or
     UPDSEQ0  - Cntl and new DS source using relative line numbers, or
     UPDCNTL  - Ins, del and mat control records using relative line numbers or
     UPDPDEL  - Prefixed delta lines (maximum 32K columns in output line).
```

Figure 33.10 Third screen of processing options.

```
------------------------------ SUPERCE UTILITY ------------------------------
OPTION ===> e_

blank - Compare Data Sets                    P - Select Process Options
  B   - Submit Batch Data Set Compare        E - Edit Statements Data Set
  S   - Extended Search-For Compare Utility  A - Activate/Create Profiles

New DS Name     ===> FORT(NEWRATE2)
Old DS Name     ===> FORT(NEWRATE)
PDS Member List ===>            (blank/pattern - member list, * - compare all)
   (Leave New/Old Dsn "blank" for concatenated-uncataloged-password panel)
                          Optional Section
Compare Type    ===> LINE                 (FILE/ LINE /WORD/BYTE)
Listing Type    ===> LONG                 (OVSUM/ DELTA /CHNG/LONG/NOLIST)
Listing Dsn     ===> SUPERC.LIST
Process Options ===> NOPRTCC
                ===>
Statements Dsn  ===>
Update  Dsn     ===>
BROWSE  Output  ===> YES                   ( YES /NO/COND/UPD)
```

Figure 33.11 Accessing the statements data set.

```
 EDIT ----- TSO1234.SUPERC.STMTS ---------------------------- COLUMNS 001 072
 COMMAND ===>                                                 SCROLL ===> CSR

     Enter or change Process Statements in the EDIT window below:
****** ************************** TOP OF DATA ******************************
==MSG> -WARNING- THE UNDO COMMAND IS NOT AVAILABLE UNTIL YOU CHANGE
==MSG>          YOUR EDIT PROFILE USING THE COMMAND "RECOVERY ON".
'''''' cmpcolm 1:30_
''''''
''''''
****** ************************** BOTTOM OF DATA ***************************
    Examples                        Explanation
 CMPCOLM 5:60  75:90         Compare using two column compare ranges
 LSTCOLM 25:90               List columns 25:90 from input
 DPLINE  'PAGE '             Exclude line if "PAGE " found anywhere on line
 DPLINE  'PAGE ',87:95       Exclude if "PAGE " found within columns 87:99
 SELECT  MEM1,NMEM2:OMEM2    Compare MEM1 with MEM1 and NMEM2 with OMEM2
 CMPLINE NTOP 'MACRO'        Start comparing after string found in new DSN
 LNCT    66                  Set lines per page to 66
 Others: DPLINEC  CMPBOFS  CMPCOLMN  CMPCOLMO  NTITLE  OTITLE  SLIST
         NCHGT    OCHGT    comment-lines ("*" and ".*")
```

Figure 33.12 Specifying compare instructions.

On the same screen, the instruction to restrict comparisons to column 1 through 30 is entered on the first insert line. The instructions can be modeled from those displayed below the edit area. The HELP command can also be executed to reveal more detail about the instructions.

Using the END command saves the instructions typed into the data set (indicated in the short message area) and returns to the screen shown in Figure 33.13. The name of the statements data set now appears in the field labeled Statements Dsn. The compare can now be started in the foreground by leaving the OPTION field blank and pressing the ENTER key, as in the first compare example. In this instance, however, the letter B is used to specify batch (or background) execution.

Since only foreground output can be directed to the terminal, a screen is then presented for specifying the form that the output should take (Figure 33.14). The output can be directed to a print class or to a data set. When the processing option is left blank, the output is directed to the SYSOUT class that's specified. This can also be a held print queue so the output can ultimately be viewed from the terminal.

In this instance, option 1 is selected to place the result in a data set. The data set name is specified in the field labeled DATA SET NAME. ISPF will automatically create the data set if it doesn't already exist. A third option allows the output to be directed to a JCL DD statement. The JCL parameters would have to be supplied in the two lines specified. This would allow the output to be directed to SYSOUT or a data set. When SYSOUT parameters are specified, this option would allow additional print parameters to be specified.

```
--------------------------------- SUPERCE UTILITY ----------- STATEMENTS DS SAVED
OPTION  ===> b_

blank - Compare Data Sets                   P - Select Process Options
   B   - Submit Batch Data Set Compare      E - Edit Statements Data Set
   S   - Extended Search-For Compare Utility  A - Activate/Create Profiles

New DS Name    ===> FORT(NEWRATE2)
Old DS Name    ===> FORT(NEWRATE)
PDS Member List ===>           (blank/pattern - member list, * - compare all)
    (Leave New/Old Dsn "blank" for concatenated-uncataloged-password panel)
                      Optional Section
Compare Type   ===> LINE               (FILE/ LINE /WORD/BYTE)
Listing Type   ===> LONG               (OVSUM/ DELTA /CHNG/LONG/NOLIST)
Listing Dsn    ===> SUPERC.LIST
Process Options ===> NOPRTCC
               ===>
Statements Dsn ===> SUPERC.STMTS
Update  Dsn    ===>
BROWSE  Output ===> YES                ( YES /NO/COND/UPD)
```

Figure 33.13 Specifying background execution.

```
-------------------- SUPERC UTILITY - SUBMIT BATCH JOBS --------------------
OPTION  ===> 1

blank  - Generate output listing to SYSOUT CLASS below.
  1    - Generate output listing to DATA SET NAME below.
  2    - Generate output listing using completed  //OUTDD DD  below.

SYSOUT CLASS  ===> A

DATA SET NAME ===> compare.data_

//OUTDD  DD   ===>
//            ===>
                            LRECL for the Listing Output will be 132

JOB STATEMENT INFORMATION: (Required - Enter/Verify JOB control statements)
 ===> //TSO1234D JOB ,'COMPARE EXAMPLE',
 ===> //    CLASS=A,MSGCLASS=A,NOTIFY=TSO1234
 ===> //*
 ===>
```

Figure 33.14 Specifying the output format.

Having pressed the ENTER key, the JCL to execute the background compare is constructed and added to the jobcard at the bottom of Figure 33.14. This includes parameters passed to the program and the statements data set that further refine the compare. The job is submitted for execution and the initial screen is redisplayed (Figure 33.15). The short message area indicates that the job has been submitted. When the background job has finished executing, the compare results can be viewed in the data set specified in Figure 33.14.

The Search Utility

The search utility is option 3.14. It can be accessed by entering 3.14 on the primary option menu or by entering 3 to invoke the utility menu before entering suboption 14. Both browse and edit have facilities for finding or isolating character strings in a sequential data set or a member of a PDS. What makes the search utility so useful is its ability to search through all or multiple members of a PDS. This can help to identify which members will need to be changed. It can also be used to find a particular member based on a unique string that it's known to contain.

A string to be searched for (EXEC) is specified in the first of the utility fields in Figure 33.16. No other strings will be used in the search, as indicated by the next field. The alternate form for data set is used here to specify all of the members of a PDS. The last two fields indicate: the name of the data set that the results will be written to, and that the search will be conducted in the foreground. If this were a large PDS, it would be prudent to instead submit the search as a background job.

```
---------------------------- SUPERCE UTILITY ---------------- JOB SUBMITTED
OPTION  ===> B

blank - Compare Data Sets                 P - Select Process Options
  B   - Submit Batch Data Set Compare     E - Edit Statements Data Set
  S   - Extended Search-For Compare Utility  A - Activate/Create Profiles

New DS Name    ===> FORT(NEWRATE2)
Old DS Name    ===> FORT(NEWRATE)
PDS Member List ===>            (blank/pattern - member list, * - compare all)
   (Leave New/Old Dsn "blank" for concatenated-uncataloged-password panel)
                        Optional Section
Compare Type   ===> LINE             (FILE/ LINE /WORD/BYTE)
Listing Type   ===> LONG             (OVSUM/ DELTA /CHNG/LONG/NOLIST)
Listing Dsn    ===> SUPERC.LIST
Process Options ===> NOPRTCC
               ===>
Statements Dsn ===> SUPERC.STMTS
Update  Dsn    ===>
BROWSE  Output ===> YES              ( YES /NO/COND/UPD)
```

Figure 33.15 Submitting a batch compare job.

```
----------- ----------------- SEARCH-FOR UTILITY ---------------------------
COMMAND ===>

SEARCH STRING    ===> exec

MULTIPLE STRINGS ===> NO   (Yes to specify additional search strings)

ISPF LIBRARY:
   PROJECT ===>
   GROUP   ===>        ===>          ===>          ===>
   TYPE    ===>
   MEMBER  ===>                  (Blank or pattern for member selection list,
                                  '*' for all members)

OTHER PARTITIONED OR SEQUENTIAL DATA SET:
   DATA SET NAME  ===> cntl(*)_
   VOLUME SERIAL  ===>          (If not cataloged)

DATA SET PASSWORD ===>          (If password protected)

LISTING DSNAME    ===> SRCHFOR.LIST

MODE             ===> F        (F - foreground, B - batch)
```

Figure 33.16 Searching all members.

At the end of the search, the data set containing the result is automatically displayed (Figure 33.17). The column at the left lists the name of the member containing the string. Just below that is the number of the line within the member that contains the string. The actual line that contains the string is also displayed.

Additional lines containing the string are revealed after scrolling down (Figure 33.18). Summary information is displayed at the bottom of the screen. It shows that 8 lines containing the string EXEC were found in 96 lines of the 7 members searched.

The extended compare utility can be used when it's necessary to specify additional processing options (as in the extended compare example). Processing option S would be used to access that function from the utility located in option 3.13.

Entering Multiple Search Strings

If additional search strings are specified, they can be considered in AND or OR fashion. Multiple strings can be specified by entering YES in the field labeled MULTIPLE STRINGS. This is shown in Figure 33.19, where all other parameters are the same as the previous execution.

Pressing the ENTER key causes a second screen to display. The string specified on the previous screen (EXEC) is carried forward where other strings and parameters can be added. Figure 33.20 shows a parameter added to the original string that will require the string to be in a word context. The parameters PREFIX, WORD, and SUFFIX can be used to qualify a search string just as they would be with the FIND and CHANGE commands discussed in browse and edit.

```
BROWSE -- TSO1234.SRCHFOR.LIST -------------------- LINE 00000000 COL 001 080
COMMAND ===> _                                          SCROLL ===> CSR
**************************** TOP OF DATA *********************************
     SUPERC - FILE/LINE/WORD/BYTE COMPARE PGM - V2.7(87/03/27)   92/12/10
   LINE-#  SOURCE SECTION                     SRCH DSN: TSO1234.CNTL


   COMPILE                 ---------- STRING(S) FOUND -------------------

        4  //    EXEC FORTVCL,RC=2000K,PARM.LKED='LIST,NOMAP',FVPOPT=0

   COMPONLY                ---------- STRING(S) FOUND -------------------

        4  //    EXEC FORTVCL,RC=2000K,COND.LKED=(0,LE),FVPOPT=0

   COMPRESS                ---------- STRING(S) FOUND -------------------

        3  //COMPRESS  EXEC PGM=IEBCOPY

   COMP2                   ---------- STRING(S) FOUND -------------------

        4  //    EXEC FORTVCL

   JOB                     ---------- STRING(S) FOUND -------------------
```

Figure 33.17 Result of searching all members.

```
BROWSE -- TSO1234.SRCHFOR.LIST ------------------ LINE 00000022 COL 001 080
COMMAND ===> _                                          SCROLL ===> CSR

      4  //   EXEC PGM=IEFBR14
             *

 PROB3                    ---------- STRING(S) FOUND ------------------

      5  //STEP1    EXEC PGM=VALIDATE,REGION=1088K
     17  //STEP2    EXEC PGM=BILLING,PARM='REGION 4 BILLS',REGION=2048K

 SORT                     ---------- STRING(S) FOUND ------------------

      5  //STEP1    EXEC PGM=SYNCSORT

       SUPERC - FILE/LINE/WORD/BYTE COMPARE PGM - V2.7(87/03/27)   92/12/10
          SUMMARY SECTION                SRCH DSN: TSO1234.CNTL

 LINES-FOUND  MEMBERS-W/LNS  MEMBERS-PROC  LINES-PROC COMPARE-COLS LONGEST-LIN
      8             7             7            96        1: 80           80

 PROCESS OPTIONS USED: ANYC

 THE FOLLOWING PROCESS STATEMENT(S) WERE PROCESSED:
```

Figure 33.18 Second page of search results.

```
-------------------- ----- SEARCH-FOR UTILITY ----------------------------
COMMAND ===>

SEARCH STRING    ===> EXEC

MULTIPLE STRINGS ===> y_   (Yes to specify additional search strings)

ISPF LIBRARY:
   PROJECT ===>
   GROUP   ===>        ===>        ===>          ===>
   TYPE    ===>
   MEMBER  ===>              (Blank or pattern for member selection list,
                             '*' for all members)

OTHER PARTITIONED OR SEQUENTIAL DATA SET:
   DATA SET NAME   ===> CNTL(*)
```

Figure 33.19 Requesting a multiple string search.

Figure 33.19 Requesting a multiple string search.

```
SEARCH --- CNTL(*) -------------------------------------------------------
COMMAND ===>


Specify 1 or more SEARCH STRINGS below:

  ===> EXEC word
  ===> sort c_
  ===>
  ===>
  ===>
  ===>
  ===>
  ===>
  ===>

Press ENTER to start search or END command to exit.
```

Figure 33.20 Specifying additional search strings.

```
BROWSE -- TSO1234.SRCHFOR.LIST -------------------- LINE 00000000 COL 001 080
COMMAND ===> _                                        SCROLL ===> CSR
***************************** TOP OF DATA ********************************
      SUPERC - FILE/LINE/WORD/BYTE COMPARE PGM - V2.7(87/03/27)   92/03/31
  LINE-#  SOURCE SECTION                  SRCH DSN: TSO1234.CNTL


  SORT                 ---------- STRING(S) FOUND -------------------

      5  //STEP1    EXEC PGM=SYNCSORT

      SUPERC - FILE/LINE/WORD/BYTE COMPARE PGM - V2.7(87/03/27)   92/03/31
        SUMMARY SECTION                    SRCH DSN: TSO1234.CNTL

LINES-FOUND  MEMBERS-W/LNS  MEMBERS-PROC  LINES-PROC COMPARE-COLS LONGEST-LIN
     1            1             9           107       1: 80          80

PROCESS OPTIONS USED: ANYC

THE FOLLOWING PROCESS STATEMENT(S) WERE PROCESSED:
   SRCHFOR  'EXEC',W
   SRCHFORC 'SORT'

***************************** BOTTOM OF DATA ****************************
```

Figure 33.21 Result of multiple string search.

The second line contains a second string to search for. The default is to search for all strings specified, and display a line if it contains any of them. The C at the end of the second line in Figure 33.20 signifies a continuation. As a continuation, the string on that line must appear on the same data line as the first string to be found.

Figure 33.21 shows that one line of one member meets the string qualifications set. The line contains both strings (EXEC and SORT), with the first string used in a word context. Strings can also be enclosed in single quotes when the string contains embedded spaces or apostrophes. In the latter situation, two single quotes or apostrophes are used to represent a single quote or apostrophe within the string.

34

Job Processing Systems

The Outlist Utility

The outlist utility is used to view held job output. Such held output is the result of background job execution where job output is sent to a special SYSOUT class. That SYSOUT class designator is different at each installation, but it automatically places output in a held queue. The advantage to using such a special SYSOUT class is that the job output can be viewed online before it's printed. In many cases, job output is viewed merely to ensure that it ran correctly. Once verified, the output can often be deleted, and this saves the various costs associated with printing, handling, and storing hardcopy output.

The initial screen of the outlist utility (shown in Figure 34.1) shows the options available. From this screen, job output can be displayed (by leaving the processing option blank), deleted (D), printed (P), or requeued (R) to a different print class. The job name (and sometimes the JES number as well) must be known before a job can be processed. Processing option L can be used to list the status of background jobs as well as what jobs are available to be processed.

Displaying a list of held jobs

The L processing option can be used to help determine what jobs have run. It produces the same information as the TSO STATUS command. The L option works with whatever job name and JES number are specified in the screen fields. These values should be modified to produce the information required at the time. By omitting the JES number (as in Figure 34.1), the L option would list the status of all jobs with the job name TSO1234A. Status information includes jobs that are in the input queue or executing, as well as those that are on the output queue.

```
-------------------------- OUTLIST UTILITY ----------------------------
OPTION ===>

    L - List job names/id's via the TSO STATUS command
    D - Delete job output from SYSOUT hold queue
    P - Print job output and delete from SYSOUT hold queue
    R - Requeue job output to a new output class
    blank - Display job output

FOR JOB TO BE SELECTED:
    JOBNAME ===> tso1234a_
    CLASS   ===>
    JOBID   ===>

FOR JOB TO BE REQUEUED:
    NEW OUTPUT CLASS ===>

FOR JOB TO BE PRINTED:                    (A for ANSI    )
    PRINTER CARRIAGE CONTROL ===>         (M for machine )
                                          (Blank for none)
```

Figure 34.1   Request for job display.

When duplicate job names exist, they must be processed using the JES number as well. The JES number is a unique number that the job entry subsystem assigns to a particular job. The JES number can be used to uniquely identify job TSO1234A, for example, when more than one job is in the system at the same time. The JES number is specified in the field labeled JOBID. When used, it must be preceded with the word JOB or the letter J. Because the JES number will be much harder to remember than the job name, it's advisable and expedient to use a different job name with each job submitted. Usually this is a simple matter of changing the last letter in the job name since most installations use a seven-character user-id as the base for creating a job name. An alternative that might be useful when the same job must be repeated is to delete the last job output before submitting the next. Where available, a product like SDSF (System Display and Search Facility) can be used to facilitate locating and selecting jobs. This optional product is discussed later in this chapter.

Viewing held job output

The held output of a batch job is displayed by leaving the processing option blank. The only information that's generally required is the job name. It's not generally necessary to place a value in the CLASS field. If one is used, it should correspond to the installation's held output class. Again, the JOBID field is only required to select from jobs that have the same job name. In Figure 34.1, the complete job name TSO1234A has been specified without a JES number because it's unique in the system.

The outlist utility turns information on the output spool file into a data set just like the TSO OUTPUT command does. Each time the utility is used, it uses a new data set and increments the numeric portion of the data set by one. Once the job output has been written to the data set, the data set is displayed in a normal browse mode. Figure 34.2 shows the browse session, including the name of the data set on the first line of the display. The job display starts with the JES log. That's immediately followed by the JCL image (the Job Control Language statements) and the termination/allocation messages.

The job output data set can be scrolled up and down as well as left and right. Scrolling down reveals more of the message output (Figure 34.3) as well as the start of the program message output. The short message indicates that the current screen display starts with line 22 of the data set. Notice that column one of the data set contains carriage control characters that will be used as line feed information if the data set is subsequently printed.

Scrolling again reveals the end of job output (Figure 34.4). The end of the data set is marked by the line containing "BOTTOM OF DATA." While the job output is in data set form, it can be copied to other data sets using a number of ISPF and TSO functions. Splitting the screen will allow the data set to be retained while information is copied from it. Generally though, it's not necessary to save job output in this way, and the data set will be deleted when the browse session is terminated.

Printing held job contents

Even though the temporary display data set has been deleted, the original job is still on the output queue. It can be printed using option P from the 3.8 screen (Figure 34.5). This will cause the job output to be placed in a data set, just as with the display function.

```
BROWSE -- TSO1234.SPF117.OUTLIST ----------------- LINE 00000000 COL 001 080
COMMAND ===> _                                              SCROLL ===> CSR
****************************** TOP OF DATA ********************************
1                  J E S 2   J O B   L O G  --  S Y S T E M   C P U 1  --  N O D
0
 17.40.54 JOB07950  $HASP373 TSO1234A STARTED - INIT 18 - CLASS A - SYS CPU1
 17.42.12 JOB07950  $HASP395 TSO1234A ENDED
0------ JES2 JOB STATISTICS ------
-     13 NOV 92 JOB EXECUTION DATE
-            9 CARDS READ
-           82 SYSOUT PRINT RECORDS
-            0 SYSOUT PUNCH RECORDS
-            6 SYSOUT SPOOL KBYTES
-         1.30 MINUTES EXECUTION TIME
        1 //TSO1234A JOB 'SAMPLE JOB',
         //   CLASS=A,MSGCLASS=T,NOTIFY=TSO1234
         //* $ACFJ219 ACF2 ACTIVE
        2 //COMPRESS  EXEC PGM=IEBCOPY
        3 //SYSPRINT DD SYSOUT=*
        4 //SYSUT1    DD UNIT=3380,SPACE=(TRK,(5,5))
        5 //PDS       DD DSN=TSO1234.CLIST,DISP=OLD
        6 //SYSIN     DD *
IEF236I ALLOC. FOR TSO1234A COMPRESS
IEF237I JES2 ALLOCATED TO SYSPRINT
```

Figure 34.2 Display of held job output.

```
BROWSE -- TSO1234.SPF117.OUTLIST ---------------- LINE 00000022 COL 001 080
COMMAND ===> _                                            SCROLL ===> CSR
 IEF237I VIO  ALLOCATED TO SYSUT1
 IEF237I 2C0  ALLOCATED TO PDS
 IEF237I JES2 ALLOCATED TO SYSIN
 IEF142I TSO1234A COMPRESS - STEP WAS EXECUTED - COND CODE 0000
 IEF285I   JES2.JOB07950.O0000102               SYSOUT
 IEF285I   SYS92317.T174054.RA000.TSO1234A.R0083816     DELETED
 IEF285I   TSO1234.CLIST                        KEPT
 IEF285I   VOL SER NOS= DISK1C.
 IEF285I   JES2.JOB07950.I0000101               SYSIN
 IEF373I STEP /COMPRESS/ START 92317.1740
 IEF374I STEP /COMPRESS/ STOP  92317.1742 CPU  0MIN 00.07SEC SRB    0MIN 00.0
 IEF375I  JOB /TSO1234A/ START 92317.1740
 IEF376I  JOB /TSO1234A/ STOP  92317.1742 CPU  0MIN 00.07SEC SRB    0MIN 00.0
1                                      IEBCOPY MESSAGES AND CONTROL STATEMEN
-IEB1035I TSO1234A  COMPRESS 17:42:12 WED 13 NOV 1992 PARM='' 05/16/92HDP3320
 IEB1057I VL GETMAIN REQUESTED 17920 TO 1024K BYTES. OBTAINED 916K. WILL RELE
- COPY INDD=PDS,OUTDD=PDS                                       000162
 IEB161I COMPRESS TO BE DONE USING INDD NAMED PDS
0IEB1018I COMPRESSING PDS  OUTDD=PDS      VOL=DISK1C DSN=TSO1234.CLIST
 IEB152I ON        COMPRESSED - WAS ALREADY IN PLACE AND NOT MOVED
 IEB167I FOLLOWING MEMBER(S) COPIED FROM INPUT DATASET REFERENCED BY PDS
 IEB154I DELACC   HAS BEEN SUCCESSFULLY COPIED
```

Figure 34.3 Page two of held job output.

```
BROWSE -- TSO1234.SPF117.OUTLIST ---------------- LINE 00000044 COL 001 080
COMMAND ===> _                                            SCROLL ===> CSR
 IEB154I LISTACC  HAS BEEN SUCCESSFULLY COPIED
 IEB154I ON       HAS BEEN SUCCESSFULLY COPIED
 IEB154I PERMIT   HAS BEEN SUCCESSFULLY COPIED
 IEB144I THERE ARE 2 UNUSED TRACKS IN OUTPUT DATASET REFERENCED BY PDS
 IEB149I THERE ARE 19 UNUSED DIRECTORY BLOCKS IN OUTPUT DIRECTORY
 IEB1056I RELEASED 908K ADDITIONAL BYTES.
 IEB147I END OF JOB - 0 WAS HIGHEST SEVERITY CODE
************************************* BOTTOM OF DATA *****************************
```

Figure 34.4 End of held job output.

```
------------------------------ OUTLIST UTILITY ------------------------------
OPTION  ===> P_

     L - List job names/id's via the TSO STATUS command
     D - Delete job output from SYSOUT hold queue
     P - Print job output and delete from SYSOUT hold queue
     R - Requeue job output to a new output class
     blank - Display job output

  FOR JOB TO BE SELECTED:
     JOBNAME ===> TSO1234A
     CLASS   ===>
     JOBID   ===>

  FOR JOB TO BE REQUEUED:
     NEW OUTPUT CLASS ===>

  FOR JOB TO BE PRINTED:                     (A for ANSI    )
     PRINTER CARRIAGE CONTROL ===>           (M for machine )
                                             (Blank for none)
```

Figure 34.5 Requesting print of held output.

Once the data set has been created, a second screen is displayed (Figure 34.6). This screen has processing options that will submit a background job to print the data set just created. For either of the batch print options, valid jobcard information must be specified at the bottom of the screen. A mistake in the jobcard would likely cause the print job to be flushed from the system. If that happens, the data set will be retained but not printed. A valid print class must also be specified. This is the output class that will be used to print the job output. It would therefore be useless to again specify the held SYSOUT class because that output would also be held for viewing. It would be equally futile to specify a SYSOUT class that's not assigned to print. It's therefore important to know an installation's standards for print classes and adhere to them.

Notice in Figure 34.6 that the data set name has changed. The data set used to display the job in the first place was deleted when the browse function was terminated. Each activity is treated separately because it's not possible to determine that the same job will be processed again, nor would it be desirable to leave job output data sets to consume valuable disk space.

At this point, the original job output has been deleted. The data set represents the only form of job output. The print options allow the data set to be retained or deleted after it's printed. Most often, the option PD will be used to print and delete the data set. Other options allow the data set to be retained (K for keep) or deleted (D) without printing it.

```
------------------------ FOREGROUND PRINT OPTIONS ------------------------
OPTION  ===> PD_

  PK - Print data set and keep        K - Keep data set (without printing)
  PD - Print data set and delete      D - Delete data set (without printing)

  If END command is entered, data set is kept without printing.

DATA SET NAME: TSO1234.SPF118.OUTLIST

PRINT MODE   ===> BATCH            (BATCH or LOCAL)

SYSOUT CLASS ===> A
PRINTER ID   ===>                  (For 328x printer)

JOB STATEMENT INFORMATION:        (Required for system printer)
  ===> //TSO1234  JOB  ,'SAMPLE JOB',
  ===> //    CLASS=A,MSGCLASS=A,NOTIFY=TSO1234
  ===> /*ROUTE  PRINT  R27
  ===>
```

Figure 34.6 Completing print request.

Requeuing held job contents

Job output can also be requeued. This causes the original output to be assigned to a different output class. By choosing an output class that's assigned to print, it's not necessary to convert the output to a data set nor run another background job. When a new output class is assigned, the original job output is immediately available to print. Again, it's important to specify the letter or number that will actually print at a particular installation.

Deleting held jobs

The outlist utility can also be used to delete held job output. Installations often do this automatically by clearing the held output queue entirely or by the age of output it contains. It's prudent, however, for each individual to clean up their own held output. In that way, they will not have to search through old jobs to find the one they want. They would also be less likely to have to specify a JES number to distinguish which job they wanted to process. Held output can be deleted by using the D processing option from the original 3.8 screen.

System Display and Search Facility

The System Display and Search Facility (more commonly known as SDSF) is an optional product that serves the same function as the outlist utility (option 3.8). SDSF has additional functions that go beyond the capabilities of option 3.8 in dealing with different Job Entry Subsystem (JES) components. Depending on the installation, the SDSF function might be available as a menu selection or by executing the command SDSF, or both. The SDSF primary menu is displayed in Figure 34.7.

An option can be invoked from the primary menu or the primary command area of an SDSF option by specifying the new option letter. The display of options that deal with input and output classes can be restricted by following the option letter with the classes that are to be displayed. When input or output classes are specified, only jobs assigned to those classes will be shown when the new option is displayed. The jobs displayed can also be filtered using the PREFIX command. That command is used to specify the jobnames that are to be displayed. The specification can include the symbols * and % to represent any series or any single character, respectively. The PREFIX command issued by itself will open the display to all jobs in the system.

SDSF job display

The advantage that SDSF has over option 3.8 is that it gives much greater visibility to jobs. Jobs are displayed in one of three different suboptions, depending on whether they're in an input queue, an output queue, or the held output queue. Jobs in any of the three queues are displayed in a scrollable list. Jobs that are active (currently being executed or printed) are highlighted. Certain fields can be modified right from the list of jobs, making it easy to change print information or the job class. Processing any of the jobs is made simple by placing letter codes in front of the desired job.

Figure 34.8 shows a list of selected jobs in the hold queue. Additional job information can be displayed using a question mark in the primary command area. This

```
-------------- --------- SDSF PRIMARY OPTION MENU  -------------------------
COMMAND INPUT ===> _                                      SCROLL ===> CSR

Type an option or command and press Enter.

    LOG        - Display the system log
    DA         - Display active users of the system
    I          - Display jobs in the JES2 input queue
    O          - Display jobs in the JES2 output queue
    H          - Display jobs in the JES2 held output queue
    ST         - Display status of jobs in the JES2 queues
    PR         - Display JES2 printers on this system
    INIT       - Display JES2 initiators on this system

    TUTOR      - Short course on SDSF (ISPF only)
    END        - Exit SDSF

Use Help Key for more information.

5665-488 (C) COPYRIGHT IBM CORP. 1981, 1990. ALL RIGHTS RESERVED
```

Figure 34.7 SDSF primary menu.

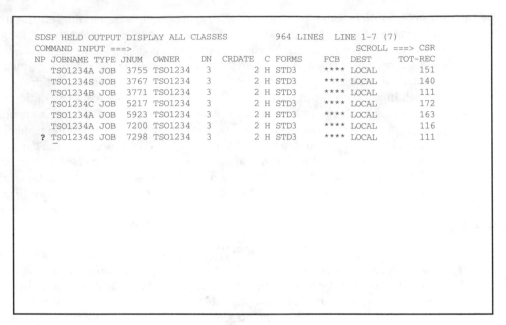

```
  SDSF HELD OUTPUT DISPLAY ALL CLASSES              964 LINES   LINE 1-7 (7)
  COMMAND INPUT ===>                                           SCROLL ===> CSR
  NP JOBNAME TYPE JNUM  OWNER    DN  CRDATE  C FORMS    FCB  DEST     TOT-REC
     TSO1234A JOB  3755 TSO1234  3        2 H STD3      **** LOCAL        151
     TSO1234S JOB  3767 TSO1234  3        2 H STD3      **** LOCAL        140
     TSO1234B JOB  3771 TSO1234  3        2 H STD3      **** LOCAL        111
     TSO1234C JOB  5217 TSO1234  3        2 H STD3      **** LOCAL        172
     TSO1234A JOB  5923 TSO1234  3        2 H STD3      **** LOCAL        163
     TSO1234A JOB  7200 TSO1234  3        2 H STD3      **** LOCAL        116
   ? TSO1234S JOB  7298 TSO1234  3        2 H STD3      **** LOCAL        111
     ‾
```

Figure 34.8 Job list display.

activates an alternate field display. Additional job information (like start and end times) can be viewed by scrolling the job list to the right. In addition, a question mark can be used as a line command to display the individual JES data sets that make up a particular jobstream.

Display of individual JES data sets

Figure 34.9 shows the display of JES data sets belonging to a single job. Using a question mark instead of a letter code caused a separate display to be created that lists all of the JES data sets that make up the job. This particular display includes separate entries for the JES log, the JCL image, the termination/allocation messages, and a single SYSOUT DD statement. An individual JES data set can then be selected to be viewed. This can be used to isolate the salient information from the rest of the job output.

Common line commands

The common letter codes used for background jobs and the queues that they're used in are listed in the following. Each line command would be specified in the NP column before the job that the command is to affect.

S—Select a job to be viewed (Input Output and Hold).
C—Cancel a job (Input).
P—Purge a job (Input Output and Hold).
O—Output a held job (Hold).
H—Place a job in hold (Input) or no select (Output) status.
A—Release a job in hold (Input) or from no select status (Output).

Additional job processing options

The ST (STatus) option allows jobs in any of the three previously mentioned queues to be displayed. The obvious advantage of the option is that the one screen shows both input and output processing. The option display is formatted differently and includes a field that shows the status of the job.

The DA (Display Active) option displays what's active on the system. This includes background jobs and foreground sessions. The display shows the step that each is in as well as the EXCP (input and output) count and CPU time for the step. The option will not display jobs that are active on other connected systems.

SDSF primary commands

The FIND command can be used in SDSF as it would be in browse mode. Parameters can be used to limit the columns searched as well as the search direction (NEXT, PREV, FIRST, LAST, and ALL). The parameters CHARS, PREFIX, WORD, and SUFFIX can be used to define the search context. The defaults are CHARS and NEXT. Just as in browse mode, scrolling can occur to reveal the strings that are found.

The FINDLIM command can be used to limit the number of lines searched by the FIND command. The FINDLIM command is followed by the number of lines (from 1000 to 9999999) that will serve as the search limit. Once the search limit is reached, the repeat find function can be used to resume the search from that point.

Instream data is spooled into separate JES data sets and is not normally displayed with the jobstream it was submitted with. The INPUT command can be used to cause that data to also be displayed. The parameters ON and OFF are used to control whether or not instream data is displayed.

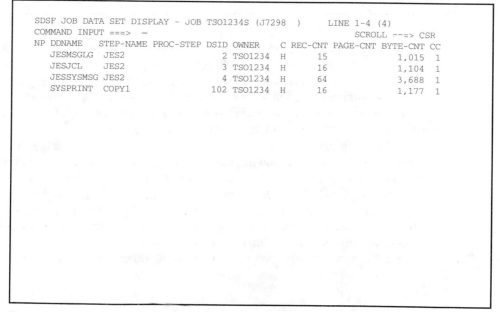

```
SDSF JOB DATA SET DISPLAY - JOB TSO1234S (J7298  )     LINE 1-4 (4)
COMMAND INPUT ===>  -                                  SCROLL ---=> CSR
NP DDNAME   STEP-NAME PROC-STEP DSID OWNER   C REC-CNT PAGE-CNT BYTE-CNT CC
   JESMSGLG  JES2                  2 TSO1234 H    15              1,015  1
   JESJCL    JES2                  3 TSO1234 H    16              1,104  1
   JESSYSMSG JES2                  4 TSO1234 H    64              3,688  1
   SYSPRINT  COPY1               102 TSO1234 H    16              1,177  1
```

Figure 34.9 Display of individual JES data sets.

LOCATE can be used to locate a particular line number. This can be especially useful in functions like LOG, where it's necessary to return to a particular line number.

The commands NEXT and PREV can be used to expedite movement to the next or previous JES data set within a job display. Either command can be abbreviated using the first letter, and either command can be followed by at least one space and a numeric value to indicate how many data sets will be involved in repositioning the display.

The PRINT command allows SDSF displayed data to be printed. Before printing, the print output is assigned to an output class or a data set using either the OPEN or ODSN parameters. Printing can include the entire log or job display or only certain specified lines. The CLOSE parameter is used with the PRINT command to make the printed material available to an output device. When the print material is written to an existing data set, the data set would be available following close processing. Where a list is displayed, the PRINT command will serve to print the current screen just as the standard ISPF PRINT command would. PRINT SCREEN will also cause the current screen image to be printed. The print parameters are listed in Table 34.1.

TABLE 34.1 Print Parameters

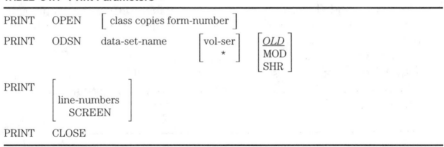

The PREFIX, DEST, and OWNER commands are used to filter the list of jobs that are displayed in the SDSF options. Only the jobs matching the specified criteria (established using these commands) will be displayed when a new list of jobs is generated. The commands can make use of the characters * and % to represent any series of characters and any single character respectively. Each command can also be used without a value to effectively turn that particular filter off.

The SET command can be used to affect the display characteristics. SET HEX ON would, for example, cause job information to display in both character and hexadecimal. The hexadecimal display could be turned off by specifying SET HEX OFF. The command SET SCREEN allows the screen display attributes to be changed. The command provides access to a screen where the color, intensity, and highlight characteristics of certain lines can be changed. The highlight characteristics include normal display, reverse video, blinking, and underscored.

The SET command also has a parameter that will cause the current prefix, DEST, and owner settings to be displayed. SET DISPLAY ON will cause those settings to be displayed at the top of the job list. The line used to display the settings will remain displayed until the command SET DISPLAY OFF is used.

The commands DEST, FINDLIM, OWNER, PREFIX, and SYSID can all be used with a question mark to query the current value established by those commands. For example, the command PREFIX ? would display the current prefix used to filter the job display. The WHO command can be issued to display the current TSO user-id, their logon procedure name, and their terminal name or address.

System support options

SDSF provides other JES-related functions that are directed more toward system support than to specific job processing. Three such options are briefly discussed in the following. An installation can tailor an individual's view of SDSF to make certain commands or options unavailable.

The INIT option is used to display JES initiators. The scrollable display shows what classes are assigned to each initiator as well as the initiator status and active job, if any. Those who are authorized can issue commands to affect the initiators.

The PR option is used to display JES printers. The scrollable display shows what classes are assigned to each printer as well as the printer status and the job it's currently printing, if any. Those who are authorized can issue commands to affect the printers.

The LOG option is used to display the system log. It typically contains a log of the messages that are written to the system console as well as the information that's written to individual JES job logs. The SYSID primary command can be used to switch to a different system log in a multisystem environment.

35

The ISPF Tutorial

ISPF is equipped with an extensive network of help screens. Collectively, these are known as the tutorial. Context-sensitive help is available using the help function. The active screen or last message displayed will cause ISPF to display the relevant portion of the tutorial when the HELP command is issued (or when a PF key assigned to HELP is pressed). Figure 35.1 shows the HELP command issued from an edit session.

The edit context (that the HELP command was entered from) helps to restrict which part of the tutorial text ISPF will display. Figure 35.2 shows the initial tutorial screen displayed as a result of invoking the help function. The screen gives a choice of high-level edit topics, or the topics will be presented in order as the ENTER key is used to page through them.

A more specific topic can be accessed following an error. In Figure 35.3, the END function has been invoked to return to the edit session, where a deliberate error (a CHANGE command with no "to" and "from" strings) has been made. The short message gives the first indication of the error.

By invoking the help function (default PF keys 1 and 13), the long message is also displayed, as in Figure 35.4. By invoking the help function a second time following the error, the tutorial network is entered. Entry into the tutorial is at a point more specific than the previous instance because the CHANGE command error created a more specific context. The section of the tutorial that addresses the CHANGE command is displayed as in Figure 35.5. It provides basic information and provides access to additional topics. By way of example, option 1 has been selected, since it pertains most directly to the error encountered (specifying/omitting the character string).

The subject chosen is complex enough that it too contains suboptions. In Figure 35.6, suboption 3 is selected to view information on picture strings. Figure 35.7

```
EDIT ---- TSO1234.EXAMPLE.DATA(CLIST) - 01.01 -------------- COLUMNS 001 072
COMMAND ===> help_                                    SCROLL ===> CSR
****** ************************** TOP OF DATA ******************************
000001
000002                         CLIST Execution
000003
000004
000005                     Modes Of CLIST Execution
000006
000007 There are four modes of CLIST execution, explicit, modified explicit,
000008 implicit, and modified implicit. CLIST execution is made possible by
000009 the TSO command, EXEC. That command can also be abbreviated as EX.
000010 Because the command is explicitly stated in the first two modes, they
000011 are known as explicit modes. The implicit modes do not contain EX or
000012 EXEC as part of the command syntax. They also differ in their reliance
000013 upon a special file to identify which CLIST code to execute.
000014
000015 CLISTS are invoked at the TSO prompter or an interface to it. For
000016 those who have ISPF installed, this could also be OPTION 6 as well as
000017 most Productivity Development Facility (PDF) panels that have a
000018 command line. When a CLIST (or TSO command for that matter) is entered
000019 from a PDF panel it should be preceded by the word TSO. This is not
000020 required from PDF Option 6 because it was designed to accept TSO
000021 commands and CLISTS.
```

Figure 35.1 The HELP command.

```
TUTORIAL ------------------------- EDIT -------------------------- TUTORIAL
OPTION  ===> _


               ------------------------------------
               |                 EDIT              |
               ------------------------------------

   Edit allows you to create or change source data.

The following topics are presented in sequence, or may be selected by number:
    0 - General introduction      8 - Display modes (CAPS/HEX/NULLS)
    1 - Types of data sets        9 - Tabbing (hardware/software/logical)
    2 - Edit entry panel         10 - Automatic recovery
    3 - SCLM edit entry panel    11 - Edit profiles
    4 - Member selection list    12 - Edit line commands
    5 - Display screen format    13 - Edit primary commands
    6 - Scrolling data           14 - Labels and line ranges
    7 - Sequence numbering       15 - Ending an edit session

The following topics will be presented only if selected by number:
   16 - Interaction between LMF and SCLM
   17 - Edit models
   18 - Miscellaneous notes about edit
```

Figure 35.2 High-level edit topics.

```
EDIT ---- TSO1234.EXAMPLE.DATA(CLIST) - 01.01 ------- REQUIRED STRING MISSING
COMMAND ===> C_                                      SCROLL ===> CSR
****** ************************** TOP OF DATA ******************************
000001
000002                          CLIST Execution
000003
000004
000005                     Modes Of CLIST Execution
000006
000007 There are four modes of CLIST execution, explicit, modified explicit,
000008 implicit, and modified implicit. CLIST execution is made possible by
000009 the TSO command, EXEC. That command can also be abbreviated as EX.
000010 Because the command is explicitly stated in the first two modes, they
000011 are known as explicit modes. The implicit modes do not contain EX or
000012 EXEC as part of the command syntax. They also differ in their reliance
000013 upon a special file to identify which CLIST code to execute.
000014
000015 CLISTS are invoked at the TSO prompter or an interface to it. For
000016 those who have ISPF installed, this could also be OPTION 6 as well as
000017 most Productivity Development Facility (PDF) panels that have a
000018 command line. When a CLIST (or TSO command for that matter) is entered
000019 from a PDF panel it should be preceded by the word TSO. This is not
000020 required from PDF Option 6 because it was designed to accept TSO
000021 commands and CLISTS.
```

Figure 35.3 Invoking help after an error.

```
EDIT ---- TSO1234.EXAMPLE.DATA(CLIST) - 01.01 ------- REQUIRED STRING MISSING
COMMAND ===> C_                                      SCROLL ===> CSR
THE CHANGE COMMAND REQUIRES THE SPECIFICATION OF A TARGET STRING.
000001
000002                          CLIST Execution
000003
000004
000005                     Modes Of CLIST Execution
000006
000007 There are four modes of CLIST execution, explicit, modified explicit,
000008 implicit, and modified implicit. CLIST execution is made possible by
000009 the TSO command, EXEC. That command can also be abbreviated as EX.
000010 Because the command is explicitly stated in the first two modes, they
000011 are known as explicit modes. The implicit modes do not contain EX or
000012 EXEC as part of the command syntax. They also differ in their reliance
000013 upon a special file to identify which CLIST code to execute.
000014
000015 CLISTS are invoked at the TSO prompter or an interface to it. For
000016 those who have ISPF installed, this could also be OPTION 6 as well as
000017 most Productivity Development Facility (PDF) panels that have a
000018 command line. When a CLIST (or TSO command for that matter) is entered
000019 from a PDF panel it should be preceded by the word TSO. This is not
000020 required from PDF Option 6 because it was designed to accept TSO
000021 commands and CLISTS.
```

Figure 35.4 Long message display.

```
TUTORIAL ----------------- EDIT - 'CHANGE' COMMAND ---------------- TUTORIAL
OPTION  ===> 1_

    The CHANGE command is used to find and change the next occurrence of a
    character string in the data being edited.
        COMMAND ===> change xxx yyy          changes the next "xxx" to "yyy"

    The cursor is placed at the end of the changed string.  Automatic
    scrolling will be performed, if necessary, to bring the string into view.

Topics are presented in the following sequence, or may be selected by number:
    1 - Specifying the character string
    2 - Limiting the search to a specified range of lines
    3 - Limiting the search to specified columns
    4 - Optional parameters that can be used to indicate the direction and
          starting point of the search ( next, prev, first, last, all )
    5 - Optional parameters that can be used to limit the strings to be
          found ( chars, prefix, suffix, word )
    6 - Optional parameters that can be used to limit the lines to be
          searched ( x, nx )
    7 - Using the RFIND (repeat find) and the RCHANGE (repeat change) commands
    8 - Error and information messages
    9 - Syntax rules when using optional parameters
```

Figure 35.5 Context-specific help text.

```
TUTORIAL -------------------- 'CHANGE' STRINGS --------------------- TUTORIAL
OPTION  ===> 3_

    On every CHANGE command, you must specify a "from" string and a "to"
    string.  In most cases you simply enter CHANGE or its abbreviations
    CHG or C, followed by the two character strings.
        Example - ===> change demo test

    If you want to use the same string that was used in the previous CHANGE
    command, use an * (asterisk).
        Example - ===> chg * * 40 60     (change demo to test in cols 40 to 60)

    In some cases, you want to change a string of characters that cannot be
    entered in the simple format shown above.  For these cases, special
    strings can be entered.  For example, to change the expression "a = b" to
    "c = d" you must use delimited strings as the expressions contain blanks.
        Example - ===> c 'a = b' 'c = d'

The following topics are presented in sequence, or may be selected by number:
    1 - Delimited strings           4 - Text strings
    2 - Hex strings                 5 - Character strings
    3 - Picture strings
```

Figure 35.6 Selecting a subtopic.

```
TUTORIAL --------------------- 'CHANGE' STRINGS -------------------- TUTORIAL
COMMAND ===> _

   A picture string is used to describe the type of string to be changed
   instead of the exact characters to be changed.

      Example -  ===> chg all p'^' 'x' 72     change all non-blanks in column
                                              72 to the character "x"

   A picture string is a quoted string that is preceded or followed by the
   letter "P".  It can contain blanks, alphabetic and numeric characters
   which represent themselves, or any of the special characters listed
   below, each of which represents a class of characters.
   The special characters that can be used in a "from" picture string are:
      =  - any character                  .  - invalid characters
      @  - alphabetic characters          -  - non-numeric characters
      #  - numeric characters             <  - lower case alphabetics
      $  - special characters             >  - upper case alphabetics
      ^  - non-blank characters
   The special characters that can be used in a "to" picture string are:
      =  - any character                  <  - lower case alphabetics
      >  - upper case alphabetics
                          (continued on next page)
```

Figure 35.7 Lowest-level help text.

represents the final or lowest level in this particular path through the tutorial. It describes the picture strings that can be used with the CHANGE command to represent a class of character rather than a specific character. Using the END function returns in one step to the screen that was active before the tutorial function was entered (Figure 35.8). The process of obtaining help, therefore, doesn't disrupt the processing already started.

Using the help function is a convenient way to isolate the help text for the current function. It's also possible to enter the tutorial network as a separate option. The tutorial is option T from the primary option menu. Figure 35.9 shows the first screen of the tutorial system.

Initial tutorial screens explain how to use the tutorial. They explain the two major ways to find subject areas: the table of contents and the index. These are just like the corresponding parts of a book. The table of contents would be used to get to general topic areas, while the index provides access to more specific topics. Pressing the ENTER key from the first screen displays information on the commands that are available to navigate the tutorial (Figure 35.10).

Pressing the ENTER key again displays additional tutorial commands (Figure 35.11) and shows the default PF key assignments for tutorial mode processing. LEFT and RIGHT functions are used to display previous and next pages, respectively. BACK is also used to display the previous page, and ENTER is also used to move forward into the tutorial. UP and DOWN apply to levels within the tutorial, and END exits the tutorial completely. This is a departure from the normal way of navi-

```
EDIT ---- TSO1234.EXAMPLE.DATA(CLIST) - 01.01 ------- REQUIRED STRING MISSING
COMMAND ===> c_                                        SCROLL ===> CSR
THE CHANGE COMMAND REQUIRES THE SPECIFICATION OF A TARGET STRING.
000001
000002                           CLIST Execution
000003
000004
000005                       Modes Of CLIST Execution
000006
000007 There are four modes of CLIST execution, explicit, modified explicit,
000008 implicit, and modified implicit. CLIST execution is made possible by
000009 the TSO command, EXEC. That command can also be abbreviated as EX.
000010 Because the command is explicitly stated in the first two modes, they
000011 are known as explicit modes. The implicit modes do not contain EX or
000012 EXEC as part of the command syntax. They also differ in their reliance
000013 upon a special file to identify which CLIST code to execute.
000014
000015 CLISTS are invoked at the TSO prompter or an interface to it. For
000016 those who have ISPF installed, this could also be OPTION 6 as well as
000017 most Productivity Development Facility (PDF) panels that have a
000018 command line. When a CLIST (or TSO command for that matter) is entered
000019 from a PDF panel it should be preceded by the word TSO. This is not
000020 required from PDF Option 6 because it was designed to accept TSO
000021 commands and CLISTS.
```

Figure 35.8 Return to the active function.

```
------------------------------ ISPF TUTORIAL --------------------------------
COMMAND ===> _

                     ISPF PROGRAM DEVELOPMENT FACILITY

                                 TUTORIAL

     This tutorial provides on-line information about the features and
     operation of the ISPF program development facility (ISPF/PDF).  You can
     view the tutorial sequentially, or you can choose selected topics from
     lists that are displayed on many of the tutorial pages.

     The table of contents contains a list of major topics. Subsequent pages
     contain additional lists that lead you through more specific levels of
     detail.  You can also select topics from the tutorial index.

     The next two pages contain a description of how to use this tutorial.

         Press ENTER key to proceed to the next page, or
         Enter UP command to go directly to the table of contents, or
         Enter END command to return to the primary option menu.
```

Figure 35.9 The initial tutorial screen.

```
---------------------------- INTRODUCTION ----------------------------
COMMAND ===> _

   You may view the tutorial sequentially by leaving the command/option
   field blank and repeatedly pressing the ENTER key.  Alternatively, you
   may select topics from lists that are displayed on many of the tutorial
   pages. For example enter:

       OPTION  ===> 3    to select topic 3.

   You may also enter one of the following commands on any tutorial page:

       BACK  or B - to back up to the previously viewed page.
       SKIP  or S - to skip the current topic and go on to the next topic.
       UP    or U - to display a higher level list of topics.
       TOC   or T - to display the table of contents.
       INDEX or I - to display the tutorial index.

                        (continued on next page)
```

Figure 35.10 Tutorial commands.

```
TUTORIAL ----------------- INTRODUCTION (CONTINUED) -----------------TUTORIAL
COMMAND ===> _
```

	DEFAULT ARRANGEMENT FOR PF KEY PAD		
You may use the following program function (PF)	--------	--------	--------
	HELP PF1 or Pf13		END PF3 or PF15
HELP - to get help on how to use the tutorial.	--------	--------	--------
END - to end the tutorial.			
UP - to display a higher level list of topics			
DOWN - to go on to the next topic (skip).			
LEFT - to display the previous page (back).	--------	--------	--------
RIGHT - to display the next page, which is the same as pressing ENTER.	UP PF7 or PF19	DOWN PF8 or PF20	
	--------	--------	--------
	LEFT PF10 or PF22	RIGHT PF11 or PF23	
	--------	--------	--------

Figure 35.11 Additional tutorial commands.

gating an ISPF hierarchy. The commands TOC and INDEX are also available to expedite moving to those functions.

Pressing the ENTER key again displays the table of contents (Figure 35.12). Notice that it's structured like the ISPF options themselves and therefore looks much like the primary option menu. Any of the listed options can be selected (just as if it were the primary option menu). In this case, the index function is selected using the letter I.

The first page of the tutorial index (Figure 35.13) describes its use. Essentially, access to any topic is gained by first displaying the screen that lists that topic, and then entering the two- or three-character code that corresponds to that topic. The ENTER key can be used to page through the index topics, or a letter can be specified in the primary command area to go to the portion of the index that starts with that letter.

Use of the ENTER key reveals the first of the index topics. In Figure 35.14, the topic of ABEND codes is selected by entering its code: A1. Figure 35.15 shows the content of the help text covering ABEND codes. This is a subject area that's not unique to ISPF. Other more involved ISPF topics might involve a sequence or hierarchy of screens like that shown earlier for the CHANGE command. Such topics are often divided into subtopics that can be accessed in the sequence listed, or individual subtopics can be randomly selected using a number or letter code.

The UP command (or corresponding PF key) can be used to return to the index. In Figure 35.16, the letter D is specified to go to that portion of the index without having to page through intervening screens. From this portion of the index, a code

```
 TUTORIAL -------------------- TABLE OF CONTENTS --------------------TUTORIAL
 OPTION  ===> i_
                 ---------------------------------------------------
                | ISPF PROGRAM DEVELOPMENT FACILITY TUTORIAL |
                 ---------------------------------------------------
    The following topics are presented in sequence, or may be selected by
    entering a selection code in the option field:
       G  GENERAL      - General information about ISPF
       0  ISPF PARMS   - Specify terminal and user parameters
       1  BROWSE       - Display source data or output listings
       2  EDIT         - Create or change source data
       3  UTILITIES    - Perform utility functions
       4  FOREGROUND   - Invoke language processors in foreground
       5  BATCH        - Submit job for language processing
       6  COMMAND      - Enter TSO command, CLIST, or REXX exec
       7  DIALOG TEST  - Perform dialog testing
       8  LM UTILITY   - Perform library administrator utility functions
       9  IBM PRODUCTS- Use additional IBM program development products
      10  SCLM         - Software Configuration and Library Manager
       X  EXIT         - Terminate ISPF using log and list defaults
    The following topics will be presented only if selected by number:
       A  APPENDICES   - Dynamic allocation errors and ISPF listing formats
       I  INDEX        - Alphabetic index of tutorial topics
```

Figure 35.12 Tutorial table of contents.

```
TUTORIAL ---------------------  INDEX  ----------------------------TUTORIAL
COMMAND ===>  _

                    ----------------------------------
                   |              INDEX               |
                    ----------------------------------

     Selected topics discussed in the tutorial can be found in this index.

     To use the index, enter the first letter of the topic of interest.  The
     index page containing subjects starting with that letter is displayed.
     On an index page, any subject can be selected by entering the two
     character option preceding that selection.

     When you are on one index page, you can access any other index page by
     entering its letter identification.  If you are in the tutorial but not
     on an index page, you can get to the index by entering INDEX or I in
     the command field.

     The index pages are presented in sequence if you press the ENTER key.
```

Figure 35.13 Introduction to the tutorial index.

```
TUTORIAL ------------- -------- INDEX - 'A' -----------------------TUTORIAL
OPTION  ===> a1_

     To select a topic, enter code (letter and number) in the option field:

      A1 - ABEND codes
      A2 - Access control (LMF)
      A3 - ACTIONS command
      A4 - Activate controls (LMF)
      A5 - Activity log, delete type from member log (LMF)
      A6 - Activity log, empty administrator log (LMF)
      A7 - Activity log function (LMF)
      A8 - Activity log - Member log information (LMF)
      A9 - Activity log - Administrator log information (LMF)
     A10 - Activity log type list (LMF)
     A11 - Activity log, logging (LMF)
     A12 - Add after table row
     A13 - Administrator activity log (LMF)
     A14 - After A line command (edit)
     A15 - Allocate new data set
     A16 - Alternate projects (SCLM)

                          (continued on next page)
```

Figure 35.14 Alphabetic tutorial index.

```
TUTORIAL -------------------- COMMON ABEND CODES --------------------TUTORIAL
COMMAND ===> _

                  ----------------------------
                 |     COMMON ABEND CODES      |
                  ----------------------------
    The following list contains some common ABEND codes.  For more information
    about these codes and for information about other abend codes, see "MVS/370
    Message Library: System Completion Codes" (#GC38-1008) or "MVS/XA Message
    Library: System Completion Codes" (#GC28-1157).  For abends resulting from
    other products, refer to the appropriate product's message library.

    001 - I/O ERROR                    706 - NON-EXECUTABLE PROGRAM
    002 - I/O INVALID RECORD           804 - INSUFFICIENT VIRTUAL STORAGE
    004 - OPEN ERROR                   806 - UNABLE TO LOAD (LINK ETC) PROGRAM
    008 - I/O SYNAD ERROR              80A - INSUFFICIENT VIRTUAL STORAGE
    013 - OPEN ERROR                   878 - INSUFFICIENT VIRTUAL STORAGE
    028 - PAGING I/O ERROR             737 - I/O ERROR
    0CX - PROGRAM CHECK EXCEPTIONS:    A14 - I/O ERROR
      0C1 - OPERATION,                 B37 - INSUFFICIENT DASD SPACE
      0C4 - PROTECTION / ADDRESSING,   D37 - INSUFFICIENT DASD SPACE
      0C5 - ADDRESSING,                E37 - INSUFFICIENT DASD SPACE
      0C6 - SPECIFICATION,
      0C7 - DATA
```

Figure 35.15 Tutorial abend code list.

```
TUTORIAL --------------------- INDEX - 'A' ----------------------TUTORIAL
OPTION  ===> d_

To select a topic, enter code (letter and number) in the option field:

 A1 - ABEND codes
 A2  Access control (LMF)
 A3 - ACTIONS command
 A4 - Activate controls (LMF)
 A5 - Activity log, delete type from member log (LMF)
 A6 - Activity log, empty administrator log (LMF)
 A7 - Activity log function (LMF)
 A8 - Activity log - Member log information (LMF)
 A9 - Activity log - Administrator log information (LMF)
A10 - Activity log type list (LMF)
A11 - Activity log, logging (LMF)
A12 - Add after table row
A13 - Administrator activity log (LMF)
A14 - After A line command (edit)
A15 - Allocate new data set
A16 - Alternate projects (SCLM)

                    (continued on next page)
```

Figure 35.16 Alphabetic tutorial index.

```
TUTORIAL --------------------- INDEX - 'D' ---------------------- TUTORIAL
OPTION ===> d1_

To select a topic, enter code (letter and number) in the option field:

 D1 - DAIR return codes
 D2 - Data base contents utility (SCLM)
 D3 - Data entry panels
 D4 - Data set compare - Standard compare dialog
 D5 - Data set compare - Extended function dialog
 D6 - Data set compare - Profiles, creating
 D7 - Data set compare - Profiles, using
 D8 - Data set compare - Report format
 D9 - Data set full action (LMF)
D10 - Data set List Utility
D11 - Data set List Utility - line commands
D12 - Data set List Utility - primary commands
D13 - Data set passwords
D14 - Data set search for a string utility - Search-For
D15 - Data set specification
D16 - Data set utility

                    (continued on next page)
```

Figure 35.17 Alphabetic tutorial index.

```
TUTORIAL -- ----------------------------------------------------------TUTORIAL
COMMAND ===> _




  CODE MEANING
  ---- -------
    0  DAIR COMPLETED SUCCESSFULLY.  SECONDARY ERROR CODE IN DARC FIELD.
    4  INVALID PARAMETER LIST PASSED TO DAIR.
    8  CATALOG MANAGEMENT ERROR.  ERROR CODE IN CTRC FIELD.
   12  DYNAMIC ALLOCATION ERROR.  ERROR CODE IN CTRC FIELD.
   16  NO TIOT ENTRIES WERE AVAILABLE FOR USE.
   20  THE DDNAME REQUESTED IS UNAVAILABLE
   24  THE DDNAME REQUESTED IS A MEMBER OF A CONCATENATED GROUP.
   28  SPECIFIED DDNAME OR DSNAME NOT ALLOCATED, OR ATTR LIST NAME NOT FOUND.
   32  DISP=NEW SPECIFIED FOR PREVIOUSLY PERMANENTLY ALLOCATED DATA SET.
   36  CATALOG INFORMATION ROUTINE ERROR.
   40  MORE INDEX BLOCKS EXIST THAN PROGRAM PROVIDED ROOM FOR.
   44  DISP=OLD, MOD, OR SHR FOR DATA SET PREVIOUSLY ALLOCATED FOR DELETE.
   48  RESERVED.
   52  REQUEST DENIED BY INSTALLATION EXIT.

  (error codes in DARC (dynamic allocation return codes) on next page)
```

Figure 35.18 Dynamic allocation (DAIR) return codes.

can be specified to display the help text for that topic. It's also possible to start paging through subsequent index pages. In Figure 35.17, the code D1 is used to display information on DAIR return codes.

The first of several pages of dynamic allocation (DAIR) return codes is displayed in Figure 35.18. Additional codes can be displayed by paging forward with the ENTER key or the RIGHT command. The END command can be issued at any time to terminate the tutorial.

What makes the index function so easy to use is that it has discrete functions that are listed separately. This is particularly helpful in gaining access to information on a particular topic. For example, to look for information on the bounds command, first locate the "B" section of the index. For information on tabs, list the "T" section of the index. The individual topics can then be selected from those listed.

Access to tutorial information was designed solely for online use. There's no print function that can be used to organize and print the tutorial information. Individual screen prints can be made using the PRINT command and processing the list data set that those screen images are placed in.

Customizing
the ISPF Environment

36

Setting ISPF Program Function Keys

The program function (PF) keys have special significance in ISPF applications. The commands assigned to the PF keys can be invoked with a single keystroke. On some keyboard models, use of the ALT key might also be required to uniquely identify the use of a particular PF key. PF key default values are set by an installation, but any individual can change their own key assignments. Also, different sets of key values can be maintained for each different environment (known as an *application-id*) established within ISPF. That allows ISPF users to customize their keys in certain specialized functions without affecting the key settings that exist for most of the ISPF functions.

Displaying Key Settings

Program function key settings can be displayed in several different ways. The basic key settings (those that are active in most ISPF functions) can be displayed and changed in option 0.3. That's the sole function of that particular option, which will be discussed briefly in the next chapter. The key values can also be accessed from option 7.3, which is the dialog test option that displays profile variables. PF key assignments are stored as variable values in the ISPF profile. The variables that represent the PF keys are ZPF01 through ZPF24. The main focus of this chapter, however, will be on commands that can be entered from any ISPF option to access PF key settings. In that way, both the standard PF keys (those available with most ISPF options) and the keys that are unique to particular options can be accessed.

The KEYS Command

The KEYS command can be used from the primary command area of any ISPF screen. That allows the command to display the keys that are currently active rather than the basic keys that apply to most ISPF options. In Figure 36.1, the KEYS command is entered from the primary command area of an edit session.

The command causes the current PF key settings to display as in Figure 36.2. This is the same type of display that's generated from option 0.3. The keys listed here, however, are specific to the option that the command was invoked from. The initial display shows PF keys 13 through 24 and the labels assigned to those keys.

Pressing the ENTER key causes the other 12 PF keys to display with their label values (Figure 36.3). The initial display of alternate keys (PF keys 1 through 12) was identical to that for PF keys 13 through 24. Because the key values are duplicated across the two displays, key values on one of the screens can be changed while retaining the default values on the other. It would not be prudent to remove certain crucial key settings. At least one of the PF keys should remain set to the END command, for example, because of how often it's used.

Three of the key values in Figure 36.3 have been changed to show how they might be used in the edit session that the KEYS command was invoked from. Of particular note is the use of special characters within the three values assigned. A semicolon is used to chain multiple commands together in the value for PF1. The value for PF4 starts with the character ">" to help identify it as an edit primary command. The value for PF12 starts with the character ":" to help identify it as an edit line command. The label values for the changed keys have also been changed. This is not required when changing PF key values, but its value will become apparent when the PFSHOW command is discussed.

Pressing PF15 causes the KEYS command to terminate and return to the edit session that it was invoked from. From that screen the PF1 key was pressed to invoke the two commands that were just assigned to that key (X ALL and F ALL C'EXEC'). The result in Figure 36.4 shows what the edit session looks like after excluding all of the lines (X ALL) and finding all occurrences of the character string EXEC (F ALL C'EXEC'). The short message area reflects the result of the latter of the two commands.

Pressing the PF4 key causes the command placed there (RESET) to be executed to redisplay all excluded line groups in the edit session (Figure 36.5). On the same screen, the cursor has been moved down to line eight before using the last altered key, PF12.

Figure 36.6 shows the result of executing the line command I5 to insert five lines. The effect of such a line command will start from the current cursor position. PF keys can also be set to execute TSO commands. In setting the key value, the word TSO should precede the command to be executed.

The PFSHOW Command

The PFSHOW command can be used to display the PF key values. The command is executed in Figure 36.7 to cause the key values to display on the screen. ON is the default value when the command is issued and therefore need not be specified.

```
EDIT ---- TSO1234.EXAMPLE.DATA(CLIST) - 01.01 -------------- COLUMNS 001 072
COMMAND ===> keys_                                        SCROLL ===> CSR
****** *************************** TOP OF DATA ***************************
000001
000002                          CLIST Execution
000003
000004
000005                      Modes Of CLIST Execution
000006
000007 There are four modes of CLIST execution, explicit, modified explicit,
000008 implicit, and modified implicit. CLIST execution is made possible by
000009 the TSO command, EXEC. That command can also be abbreviated as EX.
000010 Because the command is explicitly stated in the first two modes, they
000011 are known as explicit modes. The implicit modes do not contain EX or
000012 EXEC as part of the command syntax. They also differ in their reliance
000013 upon a special file to identify which CLIST code to execute.
000014
000015 CLISTS are invoked at the TSO prompter or an interface to it. For
000016 those who have ISPF installed, this could also be OPTION 6 as well as
000017 most Productivity Development Facility (PDF) panels that have a
000018 command line. When a CLIST (or TSO command for that matter) is entered
000019 from a PDF panel it should be preceded by the word TSO. This is not
000020 required from PDF Option 6 because it was designed to accept TSO
000021 commands and CLISTS.
```

Figure 36.1 The KEYS command.

```
---------------- PF KEY DEFINITIONS AND LABELS - PRIMARY KEYS ---------------
COMMAND ===> _

NUMBER OF PF KEYS ===> 24                       TERMINAL TYPE ===> 3278

PF13 ===> HELP
PF14 ===> SPLIT
PF15 ===> END
PF16 ===> RETURN
PF17 ===> RFIND
PF18 ===> RCHANGE
PF19 ===> UP
PF20 ===> DOWN
PF21 ===> SWAP
PF22 ===> LEFT
PF23 ===> RIGHT
PF24 ===> RETRIEVE

PF13 LABEL ===>          PF14 LABEL ===>          PF15 LABEL ===>
PF16 LABEL ===>          PF17 LABEL ===>          PF18 LABEL ===>
PF19 LABEL ===>          PF20 LABEL ===>          PF21 LABEL ===>
PF22 LABEL ===>          PF23 LABEL ===>          PF24 LABEL ===>

Press ENTER key to display alternate keys.  Enter END command to exit.
```

Figure 36.2 Initial PF key display.

```
--------------- PF KEY DEFINITIONS AND LABELS - ALTERNATE KEYS -------------
COMMAND ===>

NOTE The definitions and labels below apply only to terminals with 24 PF keys

PF1  ===> x all;f all c'EXEC'
PF2  ===> SPLIT
PF3  ===> END
PF4  ===> >reset
PF5  ===> RFIND
PF6  ===> RCHANGE
PF7  ===> UP
PF8  ===> DOWN
PF9  ===> SWAP
PF10 ===> LEFT
PF11 ===> RIGHT
PF12 ===> :i5_

PF1  LABEL ===> Highlite   PF2  LABEL ===>        PF3  LABEL ===>
PF4  LABEL ===> Redispla   PF5  LABEL ===>        PF6  LABEL ===>
PF7  LABEL ===>            PF8  LABEL ===>        PF9  LABEL ===>
PF10 LABEL ===>            PF11 LABEL ===>        PF12 LABEL ===> Insert

Press ENTER key to display primary keys.  Enter END command to exit.
```

Figure 36.3 Alternate key display.

```
EDIT ---- TSO1234.EXAMPLE.DATA(CLIST) - 01.01 --------------- 13 CHARS 'EXEC'
COMMAND ===>                                               SCROLL ===> CSR
****** ***************************** TOP OF DATA *****************************
- - - -  -   -   -  -   -   -  -   -   -  -   -   -  - 8 LINE(S) NOT DISPLAYED
000009 the TSO command, EXEC. That command can also be abbreviated as EX.
- - - -  -   -   -  -   -   -  -   -   -  -   -   -  - 2 LINE(S) NOT DISPLAYED
000012 EXEC as part of the command syntax. They also differ in their reliance
- - - -  -   -   -  -   -   -  -   -   -  -   -   -  -18 LINE(S) NOT DISPLAYED
000031 The first execution mode uses the TSO command EXEC followed by the
- - - -  -   -   -  -   -   -  -   -   -  -   -   -  - 2 LINE(S) NOT DISPLAYED
000034 be discussed later. The TSO EXEC command can also be abbreviated EX an
- - - -  -   -   -  -   -   -  -   -   -  -   -   -  - 2 LINE(S) NOT DISPLAYED
000037    EXEC clist-name 'positional-parameters(s) keyword-parameter(s)'
- - - -  -   -   -  -   -   -  -   -   -  -   -   -  - 1 LINE(S) NOT DISPLAYED
000039 Using our sample CLIST library, the explicit mode of the EXEC command
- - - -  -   -   -  -   -   -  -   -   -  -   -   -  -38 LINE(S) NOT DISPLAYED
000078 data set name. Inclusion of the data set name in an EXEC command
- - - -  -   -   -  -   -   -  -   -   -  -   -   -  -38 LINE(S) NOT DISPLAYED
000117 EXEC statement
- - - -  -   -   -  -   -   -  -   -   -  -   -   -  - 2 LINE(S) NOT DISPLAYED
000120    Name Specified In EXEC         Resultant Name
- - - -  -   -   -  -   -   -  -   -   -  -   -   -  -13 LINE(S) NOT DISPLAYED
000134    Name Specified In EXEC         Resultant Name
- - - -  -   -   -  -   -   -  -   -   -  -   -   -  - 457 LINE(S) NOT DISPLAYED
```

Figure 36.4 Invoking commands set to PF1.

```
EDIT ---- TSO1234.EXAMPLE.DATA(CLIST) - 01.01 --------------- COLUMNS 001 072
COMMAND ===>                                                 SCROLL ===> CSR
****** *************************** TOP OF DATA ***************************
000001
000002                              CLIST Execution
000003
000004
000005                           Modes Of CLIST Execution
000006
000007 There are four modes of CLIST execution, explicit, modified explicit,
000008 implicit, and modified implicit. CLIST execution is made possible by
000009 the TSO command, EXEC. That command can also be abbreviated as EX.
000010 Because the command is explicitly stated in the first two modes, they
000011 are known as explicit modes. The implicit modes do not contain EX or
000012 EXEC as part of the command syntax. They also differ in their reliance
000013 upon a special file to identify which CLIST code to execute.
000014
000015 CLISTS are invoked at the TSO prompter or an interface to it. For
000016 those who have ISPF installed, this could also be OPTION 6 as well as
000017 most Productivity Development Facility (PDF) panels that have a
000018 command line. When a CLIST (or TSO command for that matter) is entered
000019 from a PDF panel it should be preceded by the word TSO. This is not
000020 required from PDF Option 6 because it was designed to accept TSO
000021 commands and CLISTS.
```

Figure 36.5 Using the PF key set to insert five lines.

```
EDIT ---- TSO1234.EXAMPLE.DATA(CLIST) - 01.01 --------------- COLUMNS 001 072
COMMAND ===>                                                 SCROLL ===> CSR
****** *************************** TOP OF DATA ***************************
000001
000002                              CLIST Execution
000003
000004
000005                           Modes Of CLIST Execution
000006
000007 There are four modes of CLIST execution, explicit, modified explicit,
000008 implicit, and modified implicit. CLIST execution is made possible by
'''''' _
''''''
''''''
''''''
''''''
000009 the TSO command, EXEC. That command can also be abbreviated as EX.
000010 Because the command is explicitly stated in the first two modes, they
000011 are known as explicit modes. The implicit modes do not contain EX or
000012 EXEC as part of the command syntax. They also differ in their reliance
000013 upon a special file to identify which CLIST code to execute.
000014
000015 CLISTS are invoked at the TSO prompter or an interface to it. For
000016 those who have ISPF installed, this could also be OPTION 6 as well as
```

Figure 36.6 Result of using the PF key to insert five lines.

```
EDIT ---- TSO1234.EXAMPLE.DATA(CLIST) - 01.01 --------------- COLUMNS 001 072
COMMAND ===> pfshow on_                                          SCROLL ===> CSR
****** **************************** TOP OF DATA ****************************
000001
000002                            CLIST Execution
000003
000004
000005                        Modes Of CLIST Execution
000006
000007 There are four modes of CLIST execution, explicit, modified explicit,
000008 implicit, and modified implicit. CLIST execution is made possible by
''''''
''''''
''''''
''''''
''''''
000009 the TSO command, EXEC. That command can also be abbreviated as EX.
000010 Because the command is explicitly stated in the first two modes, they
000011 are known as explicit modes. The implicit modes do not contain EX or
000012 EXEC as part of the command syntax. They also differ in their reliance
000013 upon a special file to identify which CLIST code to execute.
000014
000015 CLISTS are invoked at the TSO prompter or an interface to it. For
000016 those who have ISPF installed, this could also be OPTION 6 as well as
```

Figure 36.7 PFSHOW command.

As a result of the command, the settings for PF keys 13 through 24 are displayed at the bottom of the screen (Figure 36.8). The key values will remain displayed on this and other screens until turned off.

In Figure 36.9, the PFSHOW command is entered again. Here, the optional parameter TAILOR has been added to allow modification of the PF key display. The screen displayed by using the TAILOR option is shown in Figure 36.10. That screen allows the display characteristics to be modified, including the number of keys displayed on a line and which of the keys are displayed. The latter charactcristic is changed here by changing the DISPLAY SET value from PRI to ALT. That will cause the alternate keys (PF keys 1 through 12) to be displayed instead of the primary keys (PF keys 13 through 24).

When the END command is used, the tailored characteristics are saved and the previous screen is redisplayed. Figure 36.11 shows the display of the alternate keys. These show the altered labels for the changed key values.

In Figure 36.12, the KEYS command is issued to again gain access to the PF key settings. When the PF keys are again displayed, the changed keys can be reset or any key value altered.

Default PF Key Settings

The default value can, of course, be typed back into the PF key field. It would be much easier, however, to erase the value of a given key. After its value is erased, any PF key will return to its installation default value. When a label value is erased, the

```
EDIT ---- TSO1234.EXAMPLE.DATA(CLIST) - 01.01 -------------- COLUMNS 001 072
COMMAND ===> _                                          SCROLL ===> CSR
****** *************************** TOP OF DATA ***************************
000001
000002                          CLIST Execution
000003
000004
000005                     Modes Of CLIST Execution
000006
000007 There are four modes of CLIST execution, explicit, modified explicit,
000008 implicit, and modified implicit. CLIST execution is made possible by
''''''
''''''
''''''
''''''
''''''
000009 the TSO command, EXEC. That command can also be abbreviated as EX.
000010 Because the command is explicitly stated in the first two modes, they
000011 are known as explicit modes. The implicit modes do not contain EX or
000012 EXEC as part of the command syntax. They also differ in their reliance
000013 upon a special file to identify which CLIST code to execute.
000014
F13=HELP      F14=SPLIT     F15=END       F16=RETURN    F17=RFIND     F18=RCHANGE
F19=UP        F20=DOWN      F21=SWAP      F22=LEFT      F23=RIGHT     F24=RETRIEVE
```

Figure 36.8 Display of PF key settings.

```
EDIT ---- TSO1234.EXAMPLE.DATA(CLIST) - 01.01 -------------- COLUMNS 001 072
COMMAND ===> pfshow tailor_                             SCROLL ===> CSR
****** *************************** TOP OF DATA ***************************
000001
000002                          CLIST Execution
000003
000004
000005                     Modes Of CLIST Execution
000006
000007 There are four modes of CLIST execution, explicit, modified explicit,
000008 implicit, and modified implicit. CLIST execution is made possible by
000009 the TSO command, EXEC. That command can also be abbreviated as EX.
000010 Because the command is explicitly stated in the first two modes, they
000011 are known as explicit modes. The implicit modes do not contain EX or
000012 EXEC as part of the command syntax. They also differ in their reliance
000013 upon a special file to identify which CLIST code to execute.
000014
000015 CLISTS are invoked at the TSO prompter or an interface to it. For
000016 those who have ISPF installed, this could also be OPTION 6 as well as
000017 most Productivity Development Facility (PDF) panels that have a
000018 command line. When a CLIST (or TSO command for that matter) is entered
000019 from a PDF panel it should be preceded by the word TSO. This is not
F13=HELP      F14=SPLIT     F15=END       F16=RETURN    F17=RFIND     F18=RCHANGE
F19=UP        F20=DOWN      F21=SWAP      F22=LEFT      F23=RIGHT     F24=RETRIEVE
```

Figure 36.9 TAILOR option of PFSHOW.

```
------------------- TAILOR PF KEY DEFINITION DISPLAY ----------------------
COMMAND ===>

For all terminals:
   KEYS PER LINE ===> SIX         (SIX - six keys per line)
                                  (MAX - maximum possible keys per line)
                                  (MAX forced when CUA MODE ===> YES specified)

   PRIMARY RANGE ===> UPP         (LOW - keys 1 to 12 are primary keys)
                                  (UPP - keys 13 to 24 are primary keys)

For terminals with 24 PF keys:
   DISPLAY SET    ===> alt_        (PRI - display primary keys 13 to 24)
                                  (ALT - display alternate keys 1 to 12)
                                  (ALL - display all keys 1 to 24)
                                  (ignored for terminals with 12 PF keys)

Press ENTER key to save changes.  Enter END command to save changes and exit.




   F13=HELP     F14=SPLIT    F15=END      F16=RETURN   F17=RFIND    F18=RCHANGE
   F19=UP       F20=DOWN     F21=SWAP     F22=LEFT     F23=RIGHT    F24=RETRIEVE
```

Figure 36.10 Tailoring the PFSHOW display.

```
EDIT ---- TSO1234.EXAMPLE.DATA(CLIST) - 01.01 --------------- COLUMNS 001 072
COMMAND ===> _                                              SCROLL ===> CSR
****** **************************** TOP OF DATA ****************************
000001
000002                          CLIST Execution
000003
000004
000005                      Modes Of CLIST Execution
000006
000007 There are four modes of CLIST execution, explicit, modified explicit,
000008 implicit, and modified implicit. CLIST execution is made possible by
000009 the TSO command, EXEC. That command can also be abbreviated as EX.
000010 Because the command is explicitly stated in the first two modes, they
000011 are known as explicit modes. The implicit modes do not contain EX or
000012 EXEC as part of the command syntax. They also differ in their reliance
000013 upon a special file to identify which CLIST code to execute.
000014
000015 CLISTS are invoked at the TSO prompter or an interface to it. For
000016 those who have ISPF installed, this could also be OPTION 6 as well as
000017 most Productivity Development Facility (PDF) panels that have a
000018 command line. When a CLIST (or TSO command for that matter) is entered
000019 from a PDF panel it should be preceded by the word TSO. This is not
   F1=Highlite  F2=SPLIT    F3=END       F4=Redispla  F5=RFIND     F6=RCHANGE
   F7=UP        F8=DOWN     F9=SWAP      F10=LEFT     F11=RIGHT    F12=Insert
```

Figure 36.11 Alternate key display.

```
EDIT ---- TSO1234.EXAMPLE.DATA(CLIST) - 01.01 --------------- COLUMNS 001 072
COMMAND ===> keys_                                          SCROLL ===> CSR
****** ************************** TOP OF DATA **************************
000001
000002                          CLIST Execution
000003
000004
000005                      Modes Of CLIST Execution
000006
000007 There are four modes of CLIST execution, explicit, modified explicit,
000008 implicit, and modified implicit. CLIST execution is made possible by
000009 the TSO command, EXEC. That command can also be abbreviated as EX.
000010 Because the command is explicitly stated in the first two modes, they
000011 are known as explicit modes. The implicit modes do not contain EX or
000012 EXEC as part of the command syntax. They also differ in their reliance
000013 upon a special file to identify which CLIST code to execute.
000014
000015 CLISTS are invoked at the TSO prompter or an interface to it. For
000016 those who have ISPF installed, this could also be OPTION 6 as well as
000017 most Productivity Development Facility (PDF) panels that have a
000018 command line. When a CLIST (or TSO command for that matter) is entered
000019 from a PDF panel it should be preceded by the word TSO. This is not
 F1=Highlite  F2=SPLIT     F3=END      F4=Redispla  F5=RFIND     F6=RCHANGE
 F7=UP        F8=DOWN      F9=SWAP     F10=LEFT     F11=RIGHT    F12=Insert
```

Figure 36.12 Gaining access to the key settings.

```
--------------- PF KEY DEFINITIONS AND LABELS - ALTERNATE KEYS -------------
COMMAND ===>

NOTE The definitions and labels below apply only to terminals with 24 PF keys

PF1  ===>
PF2  ===> SPLIT
PF3  ===> END
PF4  ===>
PF5  ===> RFIND
PF6  ===> RCHANGE
PF7  ===> UP
PF8  ===> DOWN
PF9  ===> SWAP
PF10 ===> LEFT
PF11 ===> RIGHT
PF12 ===>

PF1  LABEL ===>          PF2  LABEL ===>          PF3  LABEL ===>
PF4  LABEL ===>          PF5  LABEL ===>          PF6  LABEL ===>
PF7  LABEL ===>          PF8  LABEL ===>          PF9  LABEL ===>
PF10 LABEL ===>          PF11 LABEL ===>          PF12 LABEL ===>    -
 F1=Highlite  F2=SPLIT   F3=END      F4=Redispla  F5=RFIND     F6=RCHANGE
 F7=UP        F8=DOWN    F9=SWAP     F10=LEFT     F11=RIGHT    F12=Insert
```

Figure 36.13 Obtaining default PF key settings.

```
EDIT ---- TSO1234.EXAMPLE.DATA(CLIST) - 01.01 -------------- COLUMNS 001 072
COMMAND ===> pfshow off_                                 SCROLL ===> CSR
****** **************************** TOP OF DATA ****************************
000001
000002                        CLIST Execution
000003
000004
000005                   Modes Of CLIST Execution
000006
000007 There are four modes of CLIST execution, explicit, modified explicit,
000008 implicit, and modified implicit. CLIST execution is made possible by
000009 the TSO command, EXEC. That command can also be abbreviated as EX.
000010 Because the command is explicitly stated in the first two modes, they
000011 are known as explicit modes. The implicit modes do not contain EX or
000012 EXEC as part of the command syntax. They also differ in their reliance
000013 upon a special file to identify which CLIST code to execute.
000014
000015 CLISTS are invoked at the TSO prompter or an interface to it. For
000016 those who have ISPF installed, this could also be OPTION 6 as well as
000017 most Productivity Development Facility (PDF) panels that have a
000018 command line. When a CLIST (or TSO command for that matter) is entered
000019 from a PDF panel it should be preceded by the word TSO. This is not
 F1=HELP       F2=SPLIT     F3=END       F4=RETURN     F5=RFIND     F6=RCHANGE
 F7=UP         F8=DOWN      F9=SWAP      F10=LEFT      F11=RIGHT    F12=RETRIEVE
```

Figure 36.14 Turning the key display off.

```
EDIT ---- TSO1234.EXAMPLE.DATA(CLIST) - 01.01 -------------- COLUMNS 001 072
COMMAND ===> _                                          SCROLL ===> CSR
****** **************************** TOP OF DATA ****************************
000001
000002                        CLIST Execution
000003
000004
000005                   Modes Of CLIST Execution
000006
000007 There are four modes of CLIST execution, explicit, modified explicit,
000008 implicit, and modified implicit. CLIST execution is made possible by
000009 the TSO command, EXEC. That command can also be abbreviated as EX.
000010 Because the command is explicitly stated in the first two modes, they
000011 are known as explicit modes. The implicit modes do not contain EX or
000012 EXEC as part of the command syntax. They also differ in their reliance
000013 upon a special file to identify which CLIST code to execute.
000014
000015 CLISTS are invoked at the TSO prompter or an interface to it. For
000016 those who have ISPF installed, this could also be OPTION 6 as well as
000017 most Productivity Development Facility (PDF) panels that have a
000018 command line. When a CLIST (or TSO command for that matter) is entered
000019 from a PDF panel it should be preceded by the word TSO. This is not
000020 required from PDF Option 6 because it was designed to accept TSO
000021 commands and CLISTS.
```

Figure 36.15 Result of turning the key display off.

corresponding key value will display in its place. In Figure 36.13 the previously altered keys and labels have been blanked out.

Using the END command returns again to the edit session that the KEYS command was entered from (Figure 36.14). The display of PF key labels shows the default values for keys 1, 4, and 12. On the same screen, the PFSHOW command is entered with the parameter OFF to remove the PF key display.

Figure 36.15 shows the same edit session after the command PFSHOW OFF has been issued. The display of PF keys 1 through 12 has been removed from the bottom of the screen. With the key display removed, two additional lines of data are visible in the edit session.

37

Log and List
Data-Set Processing

DataSet Contents

Log and list data sets are automatically maintained by ISPF. Each is used to accumulate information during an ISPF session, and each is typically printed at the end of the session. Knowing what log and list data sets are used for and how to best dispose of them will help to streamline an ISPF session.

The log list data sets is used to log ISPF events. Most users find that they don't need such a log, and they turn the logging function off. The one significant need for the log is when errors are encountered. Since this is very rare, it's advisable to leave the log off until such an error occurs. The log can then be activated and the error recreated to capture the error messages. Turning the log data set on or off will be discussed in the next section of this chapter.

The list data set is used to print information from several different sources. When one of the print options is selected, it causes the print images to be placed in the list data set rather than sending them straight to a printer. The sources for print data include the edit automatic print function, screen prints, and various utility print functions. The list data set is automatically created when the first such print function is used. At the end of an ISPF session, the list data set is either printed, deleted, or saved, potentially to be used in the next ISPF session.

Setting Log and List DataSet Defaults

Option 0.2 (shown in Figure 37.1) is used to set processing option defaults for both the log and list data sets. When the defaults are specified, it's important to choose what's appropriate most of the time. If the data sets are to be routinely printed, the

```
-------------------------- LOG AND LIST DEFAULTS --------------------------
COMMAND ===> _

LOG DATA SET DEFAULT OPTIONS            LIST DATA SET DEFAULT OPTIONS
----------------------------            ----------------------------
Process option    ===>                   Process option   ===>
SYSOUT class      ===> A                 SYSOUT class     ===> A
Local printer ID ===>                    Local printer ID ===>
Lines per page   ===> 60                 Lines per page   ===> 60
Primary pages    ===> 10                 Primary pages    ===> 100
Secondary pages  ===> 10                 Secondary pages  ===> 200


VALID PROCESS OPTIONS:
  PD - Print data set and delete       D - Delete data set (without printing)
  K  - Keep data set (append subsequent information to same data set)
  KN - Keep data set and allocate new data set

JOB STATEMENT INFORMATION:          (Required for system printer)
  ===> //TSO1234A JOB (ACCOUNT),'NAME'
  ===> //*
  ===> //*
  ===> //*
```

Figure 37.1 ISPF log and list default option.

processing option should be set for PD (to print and delete the data set), and the jobcard information should be filled in at the bottom of the screen. When either data set is printed, the JCL that's generated is added to the jobcard at the bottom of the screen.

The screen also has fields for entering the number of lines per page as well as primary and secondary pages. Together, they determine how large each data set will be. Just like any data set allocation, the primary space is obtained initially, while secondary space will be added as needed. The number of lines per page might also affect the formatting of data that's written (in terms of where page breaks occur).

Figure 37.2 shows the same screen with the processing options filled in, as well as the jobcard. (See Appendix A for a description of basic jobcard parameters.) The default processing option for the log data set was set for delete, while the default for the list data set was set for print. Either default can be overridden while exiting ISPF. The disposition of each data set can also be determined during an ISPF session using the LOG and LIST commands.

The log data set can be turned off by setting the primary and secondary page values to zero. This is shown in Figure 37.3. This is not possible with the list data set. An attempt to set the page values to zero for the list data set will result in an error. The list data set is not allocated until the first attempt is made, during an ISPF session, to write to the data set. Changes to the space allocations are typically not effective until the next session, since the data sets might have already been allocated.

In Figure 37.4, additional information has been added to the print class of the list data set. This is essentially a trick to include the FCB (Forms Control Buffer) with

```
------------------------ LOG AND LIST DEFAULTS -------------------------
COMMAND ===>

LOG DATA SET DEFAULT OPTIONS          LIST DATA SET DEFAULT OPTIONS
---------------------------           ---------------------------
Process option   ===> d               Process option   ===> p
SYSOUT class     ===> A               SYSOUT class     ===> A
Local printer ID ===>                 Local printer ID ===>
Lines per page   ===> 60              Lines per page   ===> 60
Primary pages    ===> 10              Primary pages    ===> 100
Secondary pages  ===> 20              Secondary pages  ===> 200


VALID PROCESS OPTIONS:
  PD - Print data set and delete     D - Delete data set (without printing)
  K  - Keep data set (append subsequent information to same data set)
  KN - Keep data set and allocate new data set

JOB STATEMENT INFORMATION:          (Required for system printer)
  ===> //TSO1234A JOB (tso12349999),'sample job',class=a,
  ===> //    msgclass=a,notify=tso1234_
  ===> //*
  ===> //*
```

Figure 37.2 Log and list default option supplied.

```
------------------------ LOG AND LIST DEFAULTS -------------------------
COMMAND -==>

LOG DATA SET DEFAULT OPTIONS          LIST DATA SET DEFAULT OPTIONS
---------------------------           ---------------------------
Process option   ===> D               Process option   ===> P
SYSOUT class     ===> A               SYSOUT class     ===> A
Local printer ID ===>                 Local printer ID ===>
Lines per page   ===> 60              Lines per page   ===> 60
Primary pages    ===> 0               Primary pages    ===> 100
Secondary pages  ===> 0_              Secondary pages  ===> 200


VALID PROCESS OPTIONS:
  PD - Print data set and delete     D - Delete data set (without printing)
  K  - Keep data set (append subsequent information to same data set)
  KN - Keep data set and allocate new data set

JOB STATEMENT INFORMATION:          (Required for system printer)
  ===> //TSO1234A  JOB (TSO12349999),'SAMPLE JOB',CLASS=A,
  ===> //    MSGCLASS=A,NOTIFY=TSO1234
  ===> //*
  ===> //*
```

Figure 37.3 Turning the log function off.

```
------------------------- LOG AND LIST DEFAULTS ------------------------
COMMAND ===>

LOG DATA SET DEFAULT OPTIONS          LIST DATA SET DEFAULT OPTIONS
---------------------------           ---------------------------
Process option   ===> D               Process option   ===> P
SYSOUT class     ===> A               SYSOUT class     ===> A)fcb=std3(
Local printer ID ===>                 Local printer ID ===>
Lines per page   ===> 60              Lines per page   ===> 60
Primary pages    ===> 0               Primary pages    ===> 100
Secondary pages  ===> 0               Secondary pages  ===> 200


VALID PROCESS OPTIONS:
  PD - Print data set and delete     D - Delete data set (without printing)
  K  - Keep data set (append subsequent information to same data set)
  KN - Keep data set and allocate new data set

JOB STATEMENT INFORMATION:          (Required for system printer)
  ===> //TSO1234A  JOB (TSO12349999),'SAMPLE JOB',CLASS=A,
  ===> //    MSGCLASS=A,NOTIFY=TSO1234
  ===> //*
  ===> //*
```

Figure 37.4 Changing the print characteristic.

the JCL that's created to print the data set. This relies on the standard JCL including the SYSOUT class value in parentheses and explains why they look unbalanced in the field value. Or, JES statements can be added to the jobcard to change the print destination or other print characteristics.

List Data Set Characteristics

The characteristics of the list data set can be changed in option 0.5. The current settings are displayed in Figure 37.5. The record format represents fixed records that are blocked and use ANSI carriage control. The logical record length of 121 is 1 byte greater than the line length of 120 to allow for the use of a carriage control character. Changing the characteristics of the list data set might change the layout of the data that's written to the data set.

Termination Processing

When terminating an ISPF session, implied or explicit instructions for how to process the log and list data sets are executed. The instructions are implied when using option X to terminate ISPF. Option X from the primary option menu or used as a jump function (=X) will accept the default processing options for the two data sets. This is only true if the data sets were created during the session or were maintained from a previous ISPF session. If valid defaults have not been specified, a screen will be presented that requires dispositions to be specified. That screen (shown in Figure 37.6) is also displayed when using the END command to terminate ISPF. The options dealing with the log

```
----------------------- LIST DATA SET CHARACTERISTICS --------------------
COMMAND ===> _

RECORD FORMAT            ===> FBA        (FBA VBA)

LOGICAL RECORD LENGTH  ===> 121        (Any record length for fixed)
                                       (Greater than 4 for variable)


LINE LENGTH             ===> 120        (80 - 160)
```

Figure 37.5 List dataset characteristics option.

```
-------------- SPECIFY DISPOSITION OF LOG AND LIST DATA SETS --------------
COMMAND ===>

LOG OPTIONS FOR THIS SESSION            LIST OPTIONS FOR THIS SESSION
---------------------------            ----------------------------
Process option   ===> D                 Process option   ===> D
SYSOUT class     ===> A                 SYSOUT class     ===> A
Local printer ID ===>                   Local printer ID ===>

VALID PROCESS OPTIONS:
    PD - Print data set and delete
    D  - Delete data set without printing
    K  - Keep data set (allocate same data set in next session)
    KN - Keep data set and allocate new data set in next session

 Press ENTER key to complete ISPF termination.
 Enter END command to return to the primary option menu.

JOB STATEMENT INFORMATION:  (Required for system printer)
 ===> //TSO1234A  JOB (TSO12349999),'SAMPLE JOB',CLASS=A,
 ===> //    MSGCLASS=A,NOTIFY=TSO1234
 ===> //*
 ===> //*
```

Figure 37.6 Processing log and list data sets.

data set are displayed on the left side of the screen, and those dealing with the list data set are displayed on the right. If one of the data sets has not been used, its information will not be displayed.

The different options for processing the log and list data sets are detailed in the following. The topic is approached as if the list data set were being processed, but the same type of processing is used to deal with the log data set.

Deleting the List Data Set

If the processing option default (on the right) is set to D, merely continue to exit ISPF using the ENTER key. Otherwise, set the processing option on the right side of the screen to the letter D. That value will be a one-time override of the default value. Note that use of the END key at this point will take the terminal user back into ISPF without processing the data set.

Printing the List Data Set

Option PD will print the list data set and delete it. When the option is used, a batch jobstream is created to print the data set. It will use the jobcard at the bottom of the screen in creating the JCL. The jobcard must, therefore, be valid in order to avoid a JCL error. If necessary, the jobcard can be modeled from one created for a different function. Option 7.3 (part of the dialog test function) can be used in split screen mode to scroll through a list of profile variables until one containing valid jobcard information is found. The output class field should contain a letter or number for a valid print class at a particular installation. See Appendix A for a discussion of basic jobcard parameters.

Retaining the List Data Set

There are several reasons for wanting to save the list data set. One of the most obvious is that the data to be printed is not yet complete. Saving the data at the termination of ISPF would allow it to be reused the next time ISPF is invoked. At that time, additional print material could be added to what's already there. It's also possible that the data was not placed in the list data set to be printed. Many people have used the process to capture things like data set and member lists that they will use in some other context, whether that's a separate text document or a data set containing executable CLIST code.

When the list data set is kept, it's stored under a data set name of prefix .SPFx.LIST (where x is a single numeric value). ISPF automatically increments the numeric portion of the data set name. When the list data set is saved with the K processing option, it will be reused by the next ISPF session. When the list data set is saved with the KN option, the number of the list data set is incremented, causing a new list data set to be used during the next ISPF session. The latter effect can also be obtained for a data set saved with the K processing option by renaming the data set from the ready mode. At the same time, a name that's more meaningful than prefix.SPFx.LIST can be given to the data set. ISPF will simply create a new list data set when it can't find the old one.

LIST and LOG Commands

The LIST command provides the ability to process the list data set during ISPF processing rather than while terminating the ISPF session. When the command is executed, the screen shown in Figure 37.7 is displayed. All of the options that are available while terminating ISPF are available except the keep option. Since ISPF is not terminating, a new list data set must be made available when keeping the old one. This is specified with the option KN. The name that the data will be saved in is displayed at the top of the screen.

When the ENTER key is pressed, the data set is processed, and the number suffix of the second qualifier is incremented to accommodate the next list data set. The END command can be used instead to terminate the LIST command without processing the data set.

The LOG command provides access to the log data set, just as the LIST command does for the list data set. The same options apply for specifying the disposition of the log data set. If either the log or list data set is not available at the time the relevant command is issued, a message will be issued that the particular data set is not active.

```
------------------- SPECIFY DISPOSITION OF LIST DATA SET ------------------
COMMAND ===>

   LIST DATA SET (TSO1234.SPF4.LIST) DISPOSITION:
        Process option    ===> kn_
        SYSOUT class      ===> A
        Local printer ID ===>

   VALID PROCESS OPTIONS:
        PD - Print data set and delete
        D  - Delete data set without printing
        KN - Keep existing data set and continue with new data set

   Press ENTER key to process the list data set.
   Enter END command to exit without processing the list data set.

JOB STATEMENT INFORMATION:  (Required for system printer)
   ===> //TSO1234A  JOB (TSO12349999),'SAMPLE JOB',CLASS=A,
   ===> //    MSGCLASS=A,NOTIFY=TSO1234
   ===> //*
   ===> //*
```

Figure 37.7 List data-set processing.

38

ISPF Parameter Options

The ISPF parameter options are used to set display characteristics as well as the characteristics of the log and list data sets. Other options provide access to the PF key settings and variables that control whether or not dumps are produced. Figure 38.1 shows the suboptions that are available.

Terminal Characteristics

Option 0.1 is shown in Figure 38.2. This option provides a way to specify certain terminal characteristics. These include the terminal type, the number of PF keys to be used, and the display format. Changing the display format will only be effective on terminal types that support those alternative formats.

The terminal characteristics option should also be used when it's not possible to freely insert characters into ISPF panel fields. Changing the value of the field labeled INPUT FIELD PAD to an N will cause panel fields to contain nulls rather than blanks. That will make it easier to place the terminal in insert mode and add field data in the middle or beginning of the field.

The terminal characteristics option can also be used when it's necessary to change the default value for the command-stacking character. This is the character that's used to separate commands that are chained together. A previous example showed the stacked commands X ALL;F ALL C'EXEC' assigned to a PF key. The semicolon was used to separate the first command (to exclude all lines) from the second command (that found all instances of the character string EXEC).

Log and List Data Set Characteristics

Setting log and list data-set defaults was discussed in the previous chapter. The option 0.2 screen is shown in Figure 38.3, with processing option defaults of delete for

```
------------------------- ISPF PARAMETER OPTIONS -------------------------
OPTION  ===> _

    1  TERMINAL      - Specify terminal characteristics
    2  LOG/LIST      - Specify ISPF log and list defaults
    3  PF KEYS       - Specify PF keys for 3278 terminal with 24 PF keys
    4  DISPLAY       - Specify screen display characteristics
    5  LIST          - Specify list data set characteristics
    6  GRAPHIC       - Specify GDDM graphic print parameters
    7  ENVIRON       - Specify ENVIRON command settings
    8  KEYLIST       - Modify keylist(s)
    9  DIALOG TEST   - Specify Dialog Test option
   10  COLOR         - Change ISPF default colors
   11  CUAATTR       - Change values of CUA panel elements
```

Figure 38.1 ISPF parameter options menu.

```
----------------------- TERMINAL CHARACTERISTICS -------------------------
COMMAND ===> _

TERMINAL TYPE     ===> 3278     (3277   - 3275/3277 terminal)
                                (3277A  - 3275/3277 with APL keyboard)
                                (3278   - 3276/3278/3279/3290 terminal)
                                (3278A  - 3276/3278/3279 APL keyboard)
                                (3278T  - 3276/3278/3279 TEXT keyboard)
                                (3290A  - 3290 with APL keyboard)

NUMBER OF PF KEYS ===> 24       (12 or 24)

INPUT FIELD PAD   ===> N        (N - Nulls)  (B - Blanks) (Special Character-
                                   must not be the same as COMMAND DELIMITER)

COMMAND DELIMITER ===> ;        (Special character for command stacking)

SCREEN FORMAT     ===> DATA     (Select one of the following:)
  (3278 Model 5 only)           (DATA - Format based on data width)
                                (STD  - Always format 24 lines by 80 chars)
                                (MAX  - Always format 27 lines by 132 chars)

  (3290 Only)                   (PART - Format using hardware partitions.
                                        Effective the next ISPF invocation.)
```

Figure 38.2 Terminal characteristics option.

```
   ----------------------- LOG AND LIST DEFAULTS -------------------------
   COMMAND ===> _

   LOG DATA SET DEFAULT OPTIONS         LIST DATA SET DEFAULT OPTIONS
   ---------------------------          ----------------------------
   Process option   ===> D              Process option   ===> D
   SYSOUT class     ===> A              SYSOUT class     ===> A
   Local printer ID ===>                Local printer ID ===>
   Lines per page   ===> 60             Lines per page   ===> 60
   Primary pages    ===> 0              Primary pages    ===> 100
   Secondary pages  ===> 0              Secondary pages  ===> 200


   VALID PROCESS OPTIONS:
     PD - Print data set and delete     D - Delete data set (without printing)
     K  - Keep data set (append subsequent information to same data set)
     KN - Keep data sct and allocate new data set

   JOB STATEMENT INFORMATION:          (Required for system printer)
     ===> //TSO1234A  JOB (TSO12349999),'SAMPLE JOB',CLASS=A,
     ===> //    MSGCLASS=A,NOTIFY=TSO1234
     ===> //*
     ===> //*

```

Figure 38.3 ISPF log and list defaults option.

both data sets. When exiting from ISPF with the X (exit) option, the defaults would be applied, and both data sets would be deleted. The figure also shows the log data set placed for zero primary and secondary pages to effectively turn the logging function off.

Access to PF Key Definitions

Option 0.3 provides access to PF key definitions. This is an alternative to the KEYS command and provides access only to the standard PF key settings. PF keys that are assigned to different application ids are not accessible from this option the way they are from the KEYS command. Figure 38.4 shows the primary PF key settings. Pressing the ENTER key will cause the alternate keys to display.

The alternate key settings are displayed in Figure 38.5. Just as with the KEYS command, any PF key value and its corresponding label can be changed. The label is for display purposes only, when the PFSHOW function is turned on. Default values for key and label settings can be obtained by erasing the value of a given key or label. When the ENTER key is pressed, the erased field returns to its default value.

CUA Display Characteristics

Option 0.4 allows CUA (Common User Access) display characteristics to be modified. This option is shown in Figure 38.6. It includes characteristics for whether the command line is displayed at the top or the bottom of the screen and the color and

```
---------------- PF KEY DEFINITIONS AND LABELS - PRIMARY KEYS ---------------
COMMAND ===> _

NUMBER OF PF KEYS ===> 24                              TERMINAL TYPE ===> 3278

PF13 ===> HELP
PF14 ===> SPLIT
PF15 ===> END
PF16 ===> RETURN
PF17 ===> RFIND
PF18 ===> RCHANGE
PF19 ===> UP
PF20 ===> DOWN
PF21 ===> SWAP
PF22 ===> LEFT
PF23 ===> RIGHT
PF24 ===> RETRIEVE

PF13 LABEL ===>          PF14 LABEL ===>          PF15 LABEL ===>
PF16 LABEL ===>          PF17 LABEL ===>          PF18 LABEL ===>
PF19 LABEL ===>          PF20 LABEL ===>          PF21 LABEL ===>
PF22 LABEL ===>          PF23 LABEL ===>          PF24 LABEL ===>

Press ENTER key to display alternate keys.  Enter END command to exit.
```

Figure 38.4 Primary PF key display.

```
---------------- PF KEY DEFINITIONS AND LABELS - ALTERNATE KEYS -------------
COMMAND ===> _

NOTE: The definitions and labels below apply only to 24 PF key terminals.

PF1  ===> HELP
PF2  ===> SPLIT
PF3  ===> END
PF4  ===> RETURN
PF5  ===> RFIND
PF6  ===> RCHANGE
PF7  ===> UP
PF8  ===> DOWN
PF9  ===> SWAP
PF10 ===> LEFT
PF11 ===> RIGHT
PF12 ===> RETRIEVE

PF1  LABEL ===>          PF2  LABEL ===>          PF3  LABEL ===>
PF4  LABEL ===>          PF5  LABEL ===>          PF6  LABEL ===>
PF7  LABEL ===>          PF8  LABEL ===>          PF9  LABEL ===>
PF10 LABEL ===>          PF11 LABEL ===>          PF12 LABEL ===>

Press ENTER key to display primary keys.  Enter END command to exit.
```

Figure 38.5 Alternate PF key display.

```
------------------------  DISPLAY CHARACTERISTICS  -------------------------
COMMAND ===> _

COMMAND LINE PLACEMENT ===> ASIS    (ASIS   - Display as shown
                                             in panel definition.)

                                    (BOTTOM - Display as the last
                                             line on the screen or
                                             as the last line above
                                             the split line.)


ACTIVE WINDOW FRAME

              INTENSITY ===> HIGH    (HIGH or LOW)

                  COLOR ===> YELLOW  (BLUE, RED, PINK, GREEN, TURQ,
                                      YELLOW or WHITE)

PANEL DISPLAY CUA MODE ===> YES      (YES or NO)
```

Figure 38.6　Screen display characteristics option.

intensity of the active window. At this point, few of the ISPF screens themselves are affected by the latter function. Option 0.4 can also be applied, however, to user-generated applications that use CUA panel elements. Option 0.11 goes beyond this to allow the characteristics of specific CUA panel elements to be changed.

List Data Set Characteristics

Setting the characteristics of the list data set was discussed in the previous chapter. The option 0.5 screen used to set those characteristics is shown in Figure 38.7. Based on the characteristics listed, ISPF will format print images to fit into 120-byte fixed-length records. An extra byte will be added to allow for a carriage control character.

GDDM Graphic Print Parameters

GDDM graphic print parameters are accessed from option 0.6. That option is shown in Figure 38.8. It's used to define characteristics that will apply when the PRINTG command is used to print a screen that contains GDDM graphics. The print material must be sent to a GDDM-defined printer. The installation-specific name of the printer is placed in the field labeled DEVICE NAME.

Environment Settings

Option 0.7 is used to affect environment settings. Those settings are used to enable functions that provide terminal information and allow dumps to be created.

```
------------------------ LIST DATA SET CHARACTERISTICS --------------------
COMMAND ===> _

RECORD FORMAT            ===> FBA        (FBA VBA)

LOGICAL RECORD LENGTH  ===> 121        (Any record length for fixed)
                                        (Greater than 4 for variable)

LINE LENGTH              ===> 120        (80 - 160)
```

Figure 38.7 List data set characteristics option.

```
------------------------- PRINT GRAPHICS PARAMETERS -----------------------
COMMAND ===>

FAMILY PRINTER TYPE    ===> 2           ( 2 - QUEUED PRINTER )

DEVICE NAME              ===> _           ( FOR FAMILY PRINTER TYPE 2 )

ASPECT RATIO             ===> 0           ( 0 - PRESERVE GRAPHIC ASPECT
                                          1 - PRESERVE POSITIONAL )
```

Figure 38.8 GDDM graphic print parameters option.

The information includes terminal input and output data as well as terminal characteristics. Terminal input is controlled by the TERMTRAC setting (Figure 38.9) to turn the trace function on or off. Terminal output is controlled by the TERMSTAT field. When activated, the terminal characteristics are written to the log data set.

The dump function is controlled by the ENBLDUMP field. It allows a storage dump to be taken when an abend occurs. When the dump function is enabled, it works in conjunction with the file SYSUDUMP, SYSMDUMP, or SYSABEND. One of these files should be allocated to the TSO session before the ABEND occurs.

The ENVIRON command can be used to establish the same settings. When the command is entered without any parameters, the screen shown in Figure 38.9 is displayed. As an alternative, the parameters ENBLDUMP (ON or OFF), TERMTRAC (ON, ERROR, DUMP, or OFF), or TERMSTAT (QUERY) can be used to directly affect the related diagnostic facility.

The Keylist Utility

The keylist utility (shown in Figure 38.10) is option 0.8. It can also be accessed using the KEYLIST command. The command can be entered from the primary command area of any ISPF screen. Upon returning from the keylist option, the screen that the command was issued from is displayed. The keylist utility is used to create, delete, modify, or browse a keylist.

Each keylist is a named set of PF key assignments. The list of keys can then be assigned to panels that are created with CUA attributes. That allows the PF keys to be tailored down to the level of the active panel rather than the active application id.

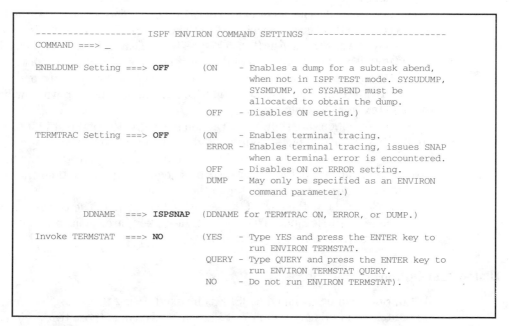

```
------------------- ISPF ENVIRON COMMAND SETTINGS ------------------------
COMMAND ===> _

ENBLDUMP Setting ===> OFF       (ON    - Enables a dump for a subtask abend,
                                         when not in ISPF TEST mode. SYSUDUMP,
                                         SYSMDUMP, or SYSABEND must be
                                         allocated to obtain the dump.
                                 OFF   - Disables ON setting.)

TERMTRAC Setting ===> OFF       (ON    - Enables terminal tracing.
                                 ERROR - Enables terminal tracing, issues SNAP
                                         when a terminal error is encountered.
                                 OFF   - Disables ON or ERROR setting.
                                 DUMP  - May only be specified as an ENVIRON
                                         command parameter.)

         DDNAME  ===> ISPSNAP   (DDNAME for TERMTRAC ON, ERROR, or DUMP.)

Invoke TERMSTAT  ===> NO        (YES   - Type YES and press the ENTER key to
                                         run ENVIRON TERMSTAT.
                                 QUERY - Type QUERY and press the ENTER key to
                                         run ENVIRON TERMSTAT QUERY.
                                 NO    - Do not run ENVIRON TERMSTAT).
```

Figure 38.9 Environment settings option.

```
------------------------- ISPF PARAMETER OPTIONS -------------------------


    Options  Change Keylists
    -----------------------------------------------------------------
                        Keylist Utility for ISR      ROW 1 TO 2 OF 2
    Command ===> _____

    Enter keylist name _____    OR

    Select one keylist name from the list below:
    Select  Keylist    T  -
    _          KEYS1      P
    _          KEYS2      P
    *********************** BOTTOM OF DATA ***********************
```

Figure 38.10 Keylist utility.

When present, multiple keylists are presented and can be selected from a scrollable list. The current list shows two keylists, both of which are private (indicated by the letter P in the next column).

The keylist utility is itself composed of CUA panels. The action bar at the top of the screen is an obvious element available to a CUA application. Another unique element is the display of windows such as that in Figure 38.11. That window displays the help text for the option, while leaving parts of the prior screen displayed in the background.

Field level help is available and is requested when the cursor is in a particular field and the HELP command is issued. Figure 38.12 shows a pop-up window displaying the help text for the keylist name field.

Two major options are shown in an action bar at the top of the keylist screen (Figure 38.13). The action bar supports pull-down windows for the suboptions attached to the selected option. In this case, five suboptions are displayed for the first option in the action bar. One of the keylists can be selected at the same time an action is selected from the action bar at the top of the screen.

Figure 38.14 shows the part of the keylist called KEYS1. The key assignments are displayed in a browse mode. The first 9 of the 24 keys are displayed. The screen can be scrolled to reveal other key assignments.

Dialog Test Option

Test options can be specified as ISPF is invoked. Using the dialog test options that are contained in primary option 7, it's possible to change those test options. Option 0.9 (shown in Figure 38.15) is used to specify what should happen to the initial test

```
------------------------- ISPF PARAMETER OPTIONS -------------------------

   Options  Change Keylists

       ┌──────────────────────────────────────────────────────┐
       │                   Help for Options                   │
       │                                                      │
       │  Press Enter to select the Options action bar choice.│
       │                                                      │
       │  If you select Options, ISPF will display a pull-down│
       │  containing choices.  These pull-down choices allow you to│
       │                                                      │
       │      Create a new keylist                            │
       │      Change an existing keylist                      │
       │      Delete a keylist                                │
       │      Browse a keylist                                │
       │      Exit the keylist utility                        │
       │                                                      │
       │                                                      │
       │                                                      │
       │                                                      │
       └──────────────────────────────────────────────────────┘
```

Figure 38.11 Keylist utility help screen.

```
------------------------- ISPF PARAMETER OPTIONS -------------------------

   ┌──────────────────────────────────────────────────────────┐
   │  Options  Change Keylists                                │
   │ -------------------------------------------------------- │
   │                   Keylist Utility for ISR    ROW 1 TO 2 OF 2│
   │ Command ===> _____ │
   │                                                          │
   │ Enter keylist name _____  OR                          │
   │                                                          │
   │ Select one keyli  ┌──────────────────────────────────┐   │
   │ Select  Keylist   │        Help for Keylist Name     │   │
   │ _       KEYS1     │                                  │   │
   │ _       KEYS2     │  Enter a keylist name.  You can select│
   │ ****************  │  from the list of keylist names on the│
   │                   │  panel, or create a new one.     │   │
   │                   │                                  │   │
   │                   │                                  │   │
   │                   │                                  │   │
   │                   └──────────────────────────────────┘   │
   │                                                          │
   └──────────────────────────────────────────────────────────┘
```

Figure 38.12 Field-level help.

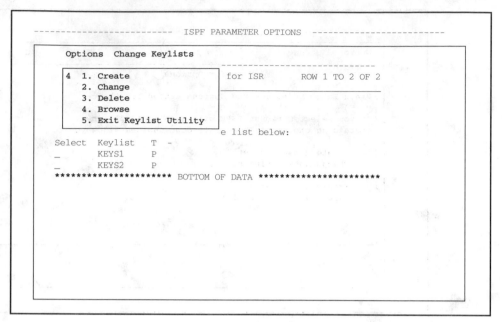

```
------------------------- ISPF PARAMETER OPTIONS -------------------------

   Options  Change Keylists
                                  -------------------------------
   4  1. Create                   for ISR      ROW 1 TO 2 OF 2
      2. Change                   -------------------------------
      3. Delete
      4. Browse
      5. Exit Keylist Utility     e list below:
  Select   Keylist    T  -
  _        KEYS1      P
  _        KEYS2      P
  ********************** BOTTOM OF DATA ***********************
```

Figure 38.13 Pull-down options.

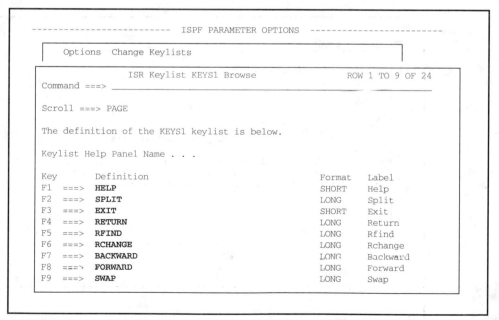

```
------------------------- ISPF PARAMETER OPTIONS -------------------------

   Options  Change Keylists

                ISR Keylist KEYS1 Browse            ROW 1 TO 9 OF 24
  Command ===> _____

  Scroll ===> PAGE

  The definition of the KEYS1 keylist is below.

  Keylist Help Panel Name . . .

  Key        Definition                        Format   Label
  F1   ===>  HELP                              SHORT    Help
  F2   ===>  SPLIT                             LONG     Split
  F3   ===>  EXIT                              SHORT    Exit
  F4   ===>  RETURN                            LONG     Return
  F5   ===>  RFIND                             LONG     Rfind
  F6   ===>  RCHANGE                           LONG     Rchange
  F7   ===>  BACKWARD                          LONG     Backward
  F8   ===>  FORWARD                           LONG     Forward
  F9   ===>  SWAP                              LONG     Swap
```

Figure 38.14 Keylist display.

```
---------------------------- DIALOG TEST OPTION -------------------------
COMMAND ===> _



RESTORE TEST/TRACE OPTIONS  ===> YES     (Yes or No)
  AT DIALOG TEST TERMINATION
```

Figure 38.15 Dialog parameter restore option.

options. When YES is specified, the initial test options (those specified when ISPF is invoked) are restored at the termination of dialog testing. When NO is specified, the test options established during dialog testing remain in effect.

Global Color Change Option

Option 0.10 is the global color change option. The option can also be invoked using the ISPF command COLOR. Option 0.10 allows any of the seven supported colors to be changed to any of the other colors. In Figure 38.16, the color green is changed to yellow. This will change the color green to yellow in all ISPF displays. This can help individuals tailor the screen displays to include colors that the terminal displays better or that people find easier to read.

The default colors can easily be reestablished. Any given color is activated by erasing the color value that was used to replace it. The CANCEL command can also be used to terminate the option without making any of the changes entered. The changed color settings are stored in the ISPF profile and so will remain set between sessions.

CUA Attribute Change Option

Option 0.11 (Figure 38.17) is similar to option 0.10, but provides even greater control. The option can also be invoked using the ISPF command CUAATTR. In option

```
-------------------------- ISPF PARAMETER OPTIONS -------------------------
O
                      GLOBAL COLOR CHANGE UTILITY
       Command ===> _____

          Globally change one or more of the ISPF default      24 PF keys
          colors and press ENTER to immediately see the
          effect.  Clearing a color field and pressing
          ENTER restores the default color.

          Enter the exit command to save changes or enter
          the CANCEL command to exit without saving.

            ISPF Default Color
               BLUE  . . . . _____
               RED . . . . . _____
               PINK  . . . . _____
               GREEN . . . . yellow _
               TURQUOISE . . _____
               YELLOW  . . . _____
               WHITE . . . . _____
```

Figure 38.16 Global color change option.

```
-------------------------- ISPF PARAMETER OPTIONS -------------------------
O
                    ISPF CUA ATTRIBUTE CHANGE UTILITY
       Command ===> _____

       Change colors, intensities, or highlights for panel attribute elements.
       Enter the exit command to save changes or enter the CANCEL command to
       exit without saving.

       Panel Element             Color           Intensity     Highlight

                                                               More:    +
       AB Selected Choice        YELLOW          LOW           REVERSE
       AB Separator Line         BLUE            LOW           NONE
       AB Unselected Choice      RED             HIGH          REVERSE
       Action Message Text       RED             HIGH          NONE
       Caution Text              YELLOW          HIGH          NONE
       Choice Entry Field        TURQ            LOW           NONE
       Column Heading            BLUE            HIGH          NONE
       Descriptive Text          GREEN           LOW           NONE
       Emphasized Text           TURQ            HIGH          NONE
       Error Emphasis            YELLOW          HIGH          REVERSE
```

Figure 38.17 CUA attribute change option.

0.11, control is extended to the individual elements that go to make up an ISPF panel. Only panels designed with CUA attributes can be modified. This would only affect a small number of the standard ISPF panels, but could also apply to numerous dialog management applications unique to a given installation. Once assigned, attributes affect all instances of the panel element.

The seven supported colors can be assigned to any of the listed elements, which start with the action bar selected choice and ends with the work area separator line. The list of elements can be scrolled up and down. The portion of the panel that says "More:" indicates whether or not more information exists. A plus sign indicates that more information lies ahead. A minus sign indicates that information can be revealed by going backwards. When both plus and minus signs are displayed, movement in either direction will reveal additional information.

Not only can the color of the panel element be controlled, but so too can the intensity and highlight characteristics of the element. The intensity can be either high or low. The highlight characteristics include no highlighting (NONE), reverse video (REVERSE), underscored (USCORE), and blinking (BLINK).

TSO Commands

39

TSO Command Processing

TSO commands are provided to allow system users to communicate with the system and with each other. These commands provide data management functions for the creation, modification, and deletion of data. They also provide for the creation and execution of load code, and optional commands are available for source language processing. TSO commands like TEST and EDIT can also be used to establish an environment from which subcommands can be issued.

TSO commands can be supplemented from other sources. These include commands that were created at a particular installation as well as commands that are shared across installations and distributed through user-group meetings. These commands can be further supplemented by CLIST and REXX EXEC code, both of which might also appear to run as a standard TSO command would. The documentation for these functions must be obtained from the installation that provides the command. Many installations have added usage instructions to the standard TSO help function. Other installations might include information on supplemental commands in the form of a standards manual or similar document.

Command Execution

Many TSO commands work from parameter input. These parameters define the processing input and output or describe options to tailor execution. Parameters are often divided into those that must be specified and those that are optional. Required information is often specified by positional parameters. Positional parameters must be specified in a particular order. If a particular parameter is not specified, the TSO command might prompt the user for the information. This is shown with the LISTDS command below. The command requires the name of a data set whose attributes are to be listed. Some validation might also be made of TSO command parameters creating the need to prompt the user to correct information entered:

```
(command)   listds
(prompt)    ENTER DATA SET NAME -
(response)  'tso1234.cntl'
```

Optional information is often supplied by keyword parameter. This information is generally characterized by a keyword and its value. The value is placed in parentheses and attached to the keyword. Unlike positional parameters, keywords can be specified in any order. Their meaning to the command is determined by the keyword name itself rather than by position. The PRINTDS command is shown in the following, with three keyword parameters (DATASET, FCB, and COPIES):

```
printds dataset('tso1234.cntl') fcb(std3) copies(2)
```

While positional parameters usually contain information that's crucial to the execution of a particular function, some processing default is usually available to make a specific keyword unnecessary during a given command execution. Validation might occur with keyword parameters as well. This includes keywords that the command might not recognize as well as parameter values that the command might check for.

Command and Parameter Abbreviation

Table 39.1 shows a list of common TSO commands. The command is listed in the left column and is followed by a brief description of the command function. The portion of the command that's in bold print indicates the only acceptable abbreviation of that command.

TABLE 39.1 Common TSO Commands

ALLOCATE	Create a data set and/or connect it to a file
CALL	Load and execute a compiled program
CANCEL	Terminate or purge a background job
COPY	Copy one data set to another
DELETE	Delete a data set or member of a PDS
EDIT	Create or modify data
EXEC	Invoke a CLIST or REXX EXEC
FREE	Deallocate a file or data set
HELP	List commands or help information on a command
LISTALC	List files and data sets allocated to the session
LISTBC	List the current broadcast message
LISTCAT	List system catalog information
LISTDS	List data set information
LOGOFF	Terminate a TSO session
LOGON	Initiate a TSO session
OUTPUT	Process held background job output

TABLE 39.1 Common TSO Commands (Continued)

PRINTDS	Print a data set
PROFILE	List or set TSO session characteristics
RECEIVE	Incorporate a transmitted data set
RENAME	Change the name of an existing data set or member
RUN	Compile, link, and execute a source program
SEND	Send a message
STATUS	Check the status of background jobs
SUBMIT	Read a background job into the system to execute
TERMINAL	List or set TSO terminal characteristics
TRANSMIT or **XMIT**	Send data or messages to connected systems

Command parameters typically show greater flexibility in how they can be abbreviated. The general rule is that command parameters can be abbreviated down to the point where they're still unique. Two parameters that are common to several TSO commands are shown in Table 39.2.

TABLE 39.2 Common Parameters for TSO Commands

DATASET	
DATASE	**DDNAME**
DATAS	**DDNAM**
DATA	**DDNA**
DAT	**DDN**
DA	**DD**

Any of the listed forms of the parameters would be acceptable. The minimum acceptable abbreviation of each parameter is two characters, since they can still be uniquely identified by those two characters. If only the single letter D were used, it would not be possible to tell which of the two parameters (or others that start with the letter D like DUMMY) should be used.

Command Environments

There are several places from which to execute a TSO command. The native mode of TSO is indicated by a READY prompt. While this is the standard environment for entering TSO commands, it's not necessarily the best. ISPF option 6 is designed specifically for executing TSO commands and CLISTs. It favors repeated execution of commands, since the initial command is retained on the screen. TSO commands can also be executed from the primary command area of ISPF screens and in background mode. The latter allows the terminal to be used for other processing. These different execution environments are discussed in the following.

READY Mode Processing

The READY prompt is a sign that TSO is ready to process a command. The command is typically typed on the line following the READY prompt and executed when the ENTER key is pressed. If necessary, the command can be continued on to subsequent lines. When command output is directed to the screen, it might be necessary to page through the output by pressing the ENTER key. The end of a page is indicated by three asterisks.

A command can be re-executed by typing over the top of a previous command. This, of course, is only possible if that previous command is still on the screen display. It's not necessary to retype the whole command. Little would be gained if this were true. It's only necessary to retype a single letter of the previous command to have the entire line executed. Adding or removing characters from a previous line displayed on the terminal can also establish it as the line to be executed. This includes computer-generated data as well as user-issued commands. When using computer-generated output to execute a command, only the portion of the line that was initially written to can be used. There are certain commands that must be entered from the ready mode. These include commands that start up the ISPF environment (ISPF and PDF), restart a TSO session (LOGON), or end a TSO session (LOGOFF).

Entering TSO Commands from ISPF

ISPF option 6 was designed solely as a place to enter TSO commands and CLISTs. The screen contains only a single field. That field is were commands are entered. The command can be continued on to subsequent lines just as if it were entered following the READY prompt. In Figure 39.1, the HELP command (abbreviated H) is issued to display help text on the SEND command.

Paging through command output is the same in option 6 as it is in the ready mode. Three asterisks mark the end of each page of output. Figure 39.2 shows the first full page of output from the HELP command. The three asterisks at the bottom of the screen mark the end of a page of output. The ENTER key can be used to page forward through the rest of the command output.

The end of the command output (shown in Figure 39.3) is also marked by three asterisks. Many make the mistake of assuming that since the terminal is no longer input inhibited, a new command can be entered. Pressing the ENTER key at that point, however, merely moves the cursor back to the command input field. Anything typed before that (while the three asterisks are present) will be ignored.

The major advantage in using option 6 to execute TSO commands is that once the command is finished, the command that was originally entered is available to be entered again or modified before it's executed. In Figure 39.4, the original command (automatically translated to uppercase characters) is displayed after all of the help text has been viewed.

The primary command area of any ISPF screen can also be used to execute a TSO command. When entered in the primary command area, the command should be preceded by the word TSO. That will identify the command and cause ISPF to pass the command on to the TSO command processor rather than treat it as an ISPF com-

```
------------------------ TSO COMMAND PROCESSOR --------------------------
ENTER TSO COMMAND, CLIST, OR REXX EXEC BELOW:

===> h send_
```

Figure 39.1 Entering TSO commands from ISPF.

```
------------------------ TSO COMMAND PROCESSOR --------------------------
ENTER TSO COMMAND, CLIST, OR REXX EXEC BELOW:

===> h send

SEND FUNCTION -
  COMMUNICATION BETWEEN USER TERMINALS, OR BETWEEN USER TERMINAL AND
  OPERATOR CONSOLE.

SYNTAX -
    SEND  ''TEXT''  USER('USERID LIST')  NOW/LOGON/SAVE  NOWAIT/WAIT
                    OR  OPERATOR('ROUTING CODE')
                    OR  CN('CONSOLE IDENTIFIER')
  REQUIRED - ''TEXT''
  DEFAULTS - OPERATOR(2), NOW, NOWAIT
  ALIAS    - SE
  NOTE     - DEFAULT OF OPERATOR(2) IS FOR MASTER CONSOLE.

OPERANDS -
  ''TEXT'' - MESSAGE TO BE SENT IN QUOTES.  IF AN APOSTROPHE IS TO BE
             PART OF THE MESSAGE, IT MUST BE ENTERED AS 2 APOSTROPHES.
  USER('USERID LIST')
           - SPECIFIES THAT THE MESSAGE IS TO BE SENT TO THE INDICATED
  *** _
```

Figure 39.2 First page of command output.

```
                        USER(S) ONLY.
           'USERID LIST'
                     - LIST OF USERIDS TO WHOM MESSAGE IS TO BE ROUTED.
                       IF '*' IS SPECIFIED INSTEAD OF A USERID, THE USERID
                       OF THE SENDER WILL BE SUBSTITUTED.
           NOW       - SPECIFIES THAT THE MESSAGE IS TO BE SENT NOW.
           LOGON     - SPECIFIES THAT THE MESSAGE IS TO BE SENT NOW (IF USER IS
                       CURRENTLY LOGGED ON) OR SAVED IN THE BROADCAST DATA SET
                       UNTIL THE SPECIFIED USER LOGS ON.
           SAVE      - SPECIFIES THAT THE MESSAGE IS TO BE SAVED IN THE
                       BROADCAST DATA SET AND NOT SENT NOW.
           OPERATOR('ROUTING CODE')
                     - SPECIFIES THE MESSAGE IS TO BE ROUTED TO THE OPERATOR.
            'ROUTING CODE'
                     - INTEGER SPECIFYING THE FUNCTIONAL CONSOLE TO WHICH MESSAGE
                       IS TO BE ROUTED USING THE INTEGER AS A ROUTING CODE.
           CN('CONSOLE IDENTIFIER')
                     - SPECIFIES THE MESSAGE IS TO BE SENT TO AN OPERATOR
                       CONSOLE.
            'CONSOLE IDENTIFIER'
                     - INTEGER OR NAME IDENTIFYING A CONSOLE.  THIS IDENTIFIER
                       IS APPENDED TO ANY MESSAGE SENT FROM AN OPERATOR CONSOLE.
       *** _
```

Figure 39.3 Last page of command output.

```
       ------------------------- TSO COMMAND PROCESSOR  ---------------------------
       ENTER TSO COMMAND, CLIST, OR REXX EXEC BELOW:

       ===> H_ SEND
```

Figure 39.4 Return to original TSO command.

```
----------------------- BROWSE - ENTRY PANEL -----------------------------
COMMAND ===> tso printds dataset('tso1234.cntl') fcb(std3) copies(2) -

ISPF LIBRARY:
   PROJECT ===>
   GROUP   ===>         ===>          ===>           ===>
   TYPE    ===>
   MEMBER  ===>                 (Blank or pattern for member selection list)

OTHER PARTITIONED OR SEQUENTIAL DATA SET:
   DATA SET NAME  ===> 'TSO1234.CNTL'
   VOLUME SERIAL  ===>          (If not cataloged)

DATA SET PASSWORD ===>          (If password protected)

MIXED MODE        ===>          (Specify YES or NO)

FORMAT NAME       ===>
```

Figure 39.5 Entering a TSO command from the primary command area.

mand. Figure 39.5 shows the previously demonstrated PRINTDS command entered
from the browse menu.

The execution of TSO commands from the primary command area can also be facilitated by setting a PF key to the word TSO. That would allow the command to be
entered in the primary command area without preceding it by TSO. After the command had been typed, the PF key set to the word TSO would be used to invoke the
typed command.

RETRIEVE and CRETRIEV Commands

Additional access is provided to previously entered commands when entering commands from option 6 or the primary command area of any other ISPF screen. The
ISPF commands RETRIEVE and CRETRIEV can be issued to step backwards
through all such commands. When the appropriate command is displayed, it can be
re-executed, or the command can be altered before it's invoked.

The RETRIEVE command will automatically position the cursor in the primary
command area and display the previous command. The CRETRIEV command is a
conditional retrieve function. It will retrieve the previous command only when the
cursor is already in the primary command field. If the cursor is anywhere else on the
screen, the CRETRIEV command will have the same initial effect as the CURSOR
command (to reposition the cursor to the primary command area).

If either the RETRIEVE or CRETRIEV command is used to gain access to previously entered commands, the retrieval command should be assigned to a PF key to

make it easier to invoke. In that way, each previous command can be brought back with a single keystroke. RETRIEVE is the standard default for PF keys 12 and 24.

Background Execution of TSO Commands

TSO commands can be executed in the background by including them in JCL that references the TSO program. Running TSO commands in a background job leaves the terminal free for interactive work. In some instances, batch execution of TSO commands is used to allow the commands to be executed when the terminal operator is not present. This might be tied to some other event like data set backups or merely late at night when data set resources are not likely to be in use.

The TSO commands to be executed are read into the file SYSTSIN. The commands can be included as instream data or placed in a data set and referenced on the SYSTSIN DD statement. CLIST and REXX code can also be executed in this way using one of the forms of the EXEC command. Reference is made to the CLIST or REXX code rather than including the CLIST or REXX statements directly in the SYSTSIN file.

Output that's normally directed to the terminal is written to the file SYSTSPRT during background execution. This file is often written to a print class, although the output can also be directed to a data set. The following is a sample jobstream that contains several DELETE commands:

```
//TSO1234A JOB (TSO12349999),'SAMPLE JOB',
// CLASS=A,MSGCLASS=H,NOTIFY=TSO1234
//STEP1 EXEC PGM=IKJEFT01
//SYSTSIN DD *
DELETE 'TSO1234.TEMP.*'
DELETE 'TSO1234.PAYROLL.REPORT1'
DELETE 'TSO1234.PAYROLL.REPORT2'
DELETE 'TSO1234.PAYROLL.REPORT3'
DELETE 'TSO1234.PAYROLL.REPORT4'
DELETE 'TSO1234.DEBUG.*'
//SYSTSPRT DD SYSOUT=H
```

40

Common TSO Commands

Before ISPF was available, tasks were run exclusively using TSO commands. In some cases, the functions that the TSO commands perform are still unique. In other cases, it could be more convenient to issue a TSO command than to execute the equivalent ISPF function. This chapter features a list of common TSO commands. Following each command is a brief summary of the command function and, in some cases, examples of how the command is used. The TSO HELP command can be used to list the complete command syntax and a description of the parameters. The commands can be executed as described in the previous chapter, or they can be executed from within CLIST or REXX EXEC code.

The ALLOCATE Command

The ALLOCATE command is used to create space for new data sets and/or dynamically connect to existing data sets. ALLOC is an acceptable abbreviation for this very useful command. When allocating data sets to a file, the file name and disposition are typically specified with the name of all of the data sets that will be allocated to the file. If, for example, a program were to be run that read data set PAYROLL.DAILY.TRANS into file TRANS01, the corresponding ALLOCATE command might be issued:

```
alloc file(trans01) dataset('payroll.daily.trans' shr reuse
```

The REUSE parameter allows the file name TRANS01 to be reused even if the file is already allocated to the TSO session. The following example shows how an ALLOCATE command can be used to create a CLIST library. In this example, many of the parameters are abbreviated:

```
alloc da(clist) sp(3 2) dir(15) tr rectm(f b) lrecl(80) blk(6160) cat
```

The command creates a cataloged data set called prefix.CLIST. The data set is allocated with three primary tracks and two secondary. The 15 directory blocks specified will make this a partitioned data set. The data set will contain fixed-length 80-byte records with a block size of 6160.

The ALTLIB Command

The ALTLIB command can be used to add up to two additional levels of libraries to the SYSPROC file search for implicitly invoked CLIST or REXX code. The additional levels of user and application libraries can be added to the existing system level.

The ATTRIB Command

The ATTRIB command can be used to define data set characteristics. Those characteristics can then be used with the ALLOCATE command when creating or referencing data sets. The command became somewhat obsolete when the ALLOCATE command was expanded to allow direct specification of data-set attributes. The command can reduce the amount of effort, however, when several data sets are allocated with the same attributes. Each of the data sets would be specified in an ALLOCATE command that made reference to the ATTRIB command result, by way of the USING parameter. ATTR is an acceptable abbreviation for the ATTRIB command.

The CALL Command

The CALL command is used to load and execute a program. The main reference is to a particular load library and member. Assumptions are made within the context of the CALL command so that all of the following examples will execute the same program:

```
call 'tso1234.load(payprog)'
call load(payprog)
call (payprog)
```

Information can also be passed to the program by way of the parm parameter, which would follow the load module data set name as a string in single quotes.

The CANCEL Command

The CANCEL command is used to cancel jobs that are executing or are waiting to execute in a background mode. When the PURGE option is used, it will also delete job SYSOUT:

```
cancel tso1234a purge
```

The command to cancel a job with a jobname that's not unique would also include the JES number:

```
cancel tso1234a(j237)
```

The COPY Command

The COPY command is an optional command and might not be installed on all systems. The command is used to copy partitioned or sequential data sets. If the "TO" data set doesn't exist, the copy command will create it. If a PDS is copied without specifying a member name, the entire PDS is copied:

```
copy 'tso1234.source.data' 'tso1234.new.data'nonum
```

The parameter NONUM keeps the COPY command from introducing line numbers.

The DELETE Command

The DELETE command is used to delete data sets. This includes removing entries from the disk VTOC and/or the system catalog for the specified data set(s):

```
delete 'tso1234.new.data'
```

Multiple data sets can be deleted with a single DELETE command. When the NO-SCRATCH option is used, the data set is only uncataloged. DEL is an acceptable abbreviation for the DELETE command.

The EDIT Command

The EDIT command provides a way to create and save data. It also allows existing data to be modified and submitted for execution. The EDIT command has an extensive set of subcommands, but is seldom used since the introduction of the ISPF editor. E is an acceptable abbreviation for the EDIT command.

The END Command

The END command can be used to terminate a command procedure. Even in that context, it's usually not required since the command procedure will end when all of the statements have finished executing. The END command can be used at other than the physical end of the command procedure, however, to provide termination at other processing points.

The EXEC Command

The EXEC command allows CLIST and REXX EXEC code to be executed. This could be done implicitly or explicitly. EX is an acceptable abbreviation for the EXEC command, which will be covered in the next chapter.

The EXECUTIL Command

The EXECUTIL command can be used to specify whether or not the SYSEXEC file is to be searched for REXX EXEC code in addition to the file SYSPROC. The next chapter explains more about REXX execution.

The FORMAT Command

The FORMAT command is an optional command and might not be installed on all systems. The command is used to format data to provide text characteristics for printing. This includes control of page characteristics and headings. Output can also be directed to a data set. FORM is an acceptable abbreviation for the FORMAT command.

The FREE Command

The FREE command deallocates resources that are provided at logon time or added with the ALLOCATE and ATTRIB commands. The resources that can be freed are:

- Attribute lists (ATTRLIST);
    ```
    free attrlist(dcb80 dcb133)
    ```
- Files (FILE or DDNAME);
    ```
    free file(sysut1 sysprint)
    ```
- Data sets (DATASET or DSNAME);
    ```
    free dataset('tso1234.source.data' 'tso1234.new.data')
    ```
- Output descriptors (OUTDES);
    ```
    free outdes(rpt1 rpt2)
    ```

Each FREE command is shown freeing two of the same objects. Additionally, different keywords can be used on the same free statement:

```
free file(sysprint) dataset('tso1234.source.data') attrlist(dcb80)
```

FREE ALL requests that all dynamically allocated files, data sets, and attribute lists be freed. None of these will be freed, however, if they're currently in use. The FREE command can also be invoked using the name, UNALLOC.

The HELP Command

The HELP command displays text explanations of the various TSO commands and their subcommands. When the HELP command is followed by a command name, it will display help text for that command. When the HELP command is issued without any parameters, it will display help text that lists the available commands. H is an acceptable abbreviation for the HELP command and is the version of the command that should be used while in ISPF. While in ISPF, HELP is interpreted as the ISPF command for help rather than the TSO command for help.

The LINK Command

The LINK command invokes the linkage editor program to convert compiler output (object code) into executable load code. It can also be used to create nonexecutable load modules and to incorporate these load modules in an executable format. The

LINK command is shown in the following with the basic elements, object code input, and load module output.

```
link 'tso1234.obj(payprog)' load('tso1234.test.load')
```

If the output data set name is omitted, the LINK command will write the load module output to a default data set name. If the output load library doesn't yet exist, the LINK command will create it. Libraries that contain subroutines that should be included in the resolved load module can be allocated to the file SYSLIB. That file will automatically be searched to resolve unresolved external references.

The LIST Command

The LIST command is an optional command and might not be installed on all systems. The command is used to display the contents of a data set at the terminal:

```
list 'tso1234.fort(payprog)'
```

The command contains parameters that can be included to specify which lines and columns will be listed. L is an acceptable abbreviation for the LIST command and is the version of the command that should be used while in ISPF. While in ISPF, LIST is interpreted as the ISPF command that provides access to the list data set rather than the TSO command to list the contents of a data set.

The LISTALC Command

The LISTALC command lists the resources that are allocated to the TSO session. The command (which is demonstrated in the next chapter) has optional parameters STATUS, HISTORY, MEMBERS, and SYSNAMES. LISTA is an acceptable abbreviation for the LISTALC command.

The LISTBC Command

The LISTBC command lists notices (including the current broadcast message) and mail. Installations will typically leave messages in a system broadcast data set that are of interest to all or most TSO users. Unless the parameter NONOTICES is used, LISTBC will access that data set and write the messages that it contains to the terminal. Messages sent specifically to a user and stored in a user log or the system broadcast data set will be listed unless the parameter NOMAIL is used. LISTB is an acceptable abbreviation for the LISTBC command.

The LISTCAT Command

The LISTCAT command lists information from the system catalog, particularly information used to locate data sets. When issued without any parameters, the command will list all of the data sets under the current prefix. Two other forms of the command are used to list individual data sets

```
listc entries('tso1234.payroll.test.data')
```

and all of the data sets with a specified set of high-level qualifiers

```
listc level(payroll.weekly)
```

The latter command example will list all of the data sets that have a first qualifier of PAYROLL and a second qualifier of WEEKLY (without regard for how many additional qualifiers the data sets might have).

By default, the data-set name taken from the catalog is listed. Optional parameters can be used to list creation and expiration dates (HISTORY), unit and volume information (VOLUME), and allocation information (ALLOCATION). The parameter ALL can be used to list all catalog fields.

LISTCAT command output can be directed to a particular file using the OUTFILE parameter. The file name would be one that had been previously allocated to a print resource or to a data set. LISTC is an acceptable abbreviation for the LISTCAT command.

The LISTDS Command

The LISTDS command is used to list data set characteristics. One or more of the data sets to be listed is specified with the command. The basic information includes volume serial number, data set organization, record format, logical record length, and blocksize:

```
TSO1234.CNTL
--RECFM-LRECL-BLKSIZE-DSORG
 FB 80 6160 PO
--VOLUMES--
 DISK1A
```

Optional command parameters can be included to list the allocation status (STATUS) and the creation and expiration dates (HISTORY). The command can also be issued with the option MEMBERS:

```
listd 'tso1234.cntl' members
```

This command lists the attributes of the data set followed by a complete list of all members stored in the PDS. LISTD is an acceptable abbreviation for the LISTDS command.

The LOADGO Command

The LOADGO command can be used to convert compiler output (object code) into executable code and then execute it. The command functions like a combination of the LINK and CALL commands, except that the executable code is not permanently retained. With parameters like the LINK command, the primary input is typically compiler-generated object code. LOAD is an acceptable abbreviation for the LOADGO command.

The LOGOFF Command

The LOGOFF command is used to terminate the TSO session. The LOGOFF command cannot be issued while in ISPF.

The LOGON Command

The LOGON command is used to start a TSO session or terminate a TSO session and begin the logon sequence for the next session. The command has parameters (ACCT, PROC, SIZE, etc.) that can be used to specify user information at installations that don't support the full-screen logon panel. The LOGON command can't be issued while in ISPF.

The MERGE Command

The MERGE command is an optional command and might not be installed on all systems. The command is used to merge one data set into another. In the following command, the content of data set TSO1234.NEW.DATA is added to data set TSO1234.MERGED.DATA:

```
merge 'tso1234.new.data' 'tso1234.merged.data' nonum nonum2
```

The NONUM parameters instruct the MERGE command to disregard line sequence numbers in both of the data sets specified. M is an acceptable abbreviation for the MERGE command.

The OUTDES Command

The OUTDES command is used to define the characteristics of a SYSOUT data set. It's used like the ATTRIB command, and like that command, can be referenced from both ALLOCATE and FREE commands. The characteristics that can be defined by the OUTDES command include output class (CLASS), printer destination (DEST), forms control buffer (FCB), and number of print copies (COPIES).

The OUTPUT Command

The OUTPUT command can be used to display held SYSOUT at the terminal

```
output tso1234a print(*)
```

or turn it into a conventional disk data set

```
output tso1234a print('tso1234.joba.outlist')
```

Where the jobname is not unique, the JES number should be added to the job-name. The command can also be used to change the output class for a job (using the keyword NEWCLASS) or delete job output (using the DELETE parameter). OUT is an acceptable abbreviation for the OUTPUT command.

The PRINTDS Command

The PRINTDS command is used to print sequential and partitioned data sets. The command can be abbreviated PR and has many parameters to control print charac-teristics. The PRINTDS command is further detailed in chapter 32.

The PROFILE Command

The PROFILE command is used to list and change certain TSO session characteris-tics for an individual. Common command parameters are:

PREFIX(prefix-name)   Used to change the prefix appended to data set names.

PROMPT/NOPROMPT   Used to enable or disable prompting from TSO commands.

MSGID/NOMSGID   Used to include or exclude message numbers with messages.

INTERCOM/NOINTERCOM   Used to enable or disable the ability to receive messages.

When the command is issued without any parameters, the TSO session characteris-tics are listed. PROF is an acceptable abbreviation for the PROFILE command.

The PROTECT Command

The PROTECT command can be used to create or change a data set password. Few installations support this type of data set protection, relying more on security pack-ages that are profile or rules driven. PROT is an acceptable abbreviation for the PRO-TECT command.

The RECEIVE Command

The RECEIVE command is used to retrieve information that has been transmitted using the TRANSMIT command. This would include both data sets and messages. The RECEIVE command will display information about each transmission to let the recipient decide whether or not to receive it. When necessary, a new data set will be created to accommodate placement of the data. The actual message or the name of the data set received can be logged in a separate log data set. At the same time, a notify function can let the sender know that the information has been received.

The RENAME Command

The RENAME command is used to change the name of a data set or a member of a data set:

```
ren 'tso1234.old.name' tso1234.new.name'
```

The RENAME command can also be used to create an alias for a PDS member. REN is an acceptable abbreviation for the RENAME command.

The RUN Command

The RUN command can be used to compile, load, and execute the source code of certain versions of selected languages. The languages include assembler, BASIC, COBOL, FORTRAN, and PL/I. The name of the source code data set is specified with the RUN command, which will also accept up to 100 bytes of parm information to be passed to the program at time of execution. R is an acceptable abbreviation for the RUN command.

The SEND Command

The SEND command is used to send messages to terminal users or operator consoles. Up to 115 bytes of text can be sent. The text is included within single quotes. Two consecutive single quotes must be used to represent a single quote within the text itself:

```
send 'Didn"t you see the earlier message?' user(tso7854)
```

If the USER parameter is omitted, the message will go to the console operator. If the parameter LOGON is added, the message will wait for a user that's not currently logged on or accepting messages. SE is an acceptable abbreviation for the SEND command.

The STATUS Command

The STATUS command is used to display the status of background jobs. The STATUS command is followed by the name of the job or jobs to be displayed:

```
status tso1234a
```

When multiple jobnames are specified, they're separated from each other using a space or comma and are enclosed in parentheses. The JES number can be included to check for specific jobs (essentially selecting from multiple jobs with the same name). When used without any parameters, the STATUS command will display all jobs, starting with the current user-id and ending with any single valid jobname character. ST is an acceptable abbreviation for the STATUS command.

The SUBMIT Command

The SUBMIT command is used to read jobstreams into the system for background execution. The command is followed by the name of the data set or data sets that contain JCL to be read into the system:

```
submit 'tso1234.cntl(compress)'
```

The SUBMIT command uses the JCL that was last saved to the specified data set or data sets as opposed to the SUBMIT command used in the ISPF editor. SUB is an acceptable abbreviation for the SUBMIT command.

The TERMINAL Command

The TERMINAL command is used to change terminal characteristics for the current TSO user. This includes defining key sequences for functions like the attention interrupt and clearing the screen. This command is seldom, if ever, required, and some of the parameters might not be supported, depending on the type of terminal they're entered from. TERM is an acceptable abbreviation for the TERMINAL command.

The TEST Command

The TEST command can be used to test or debug a program. The command is followed by the name of the load program to be tested and up to 100 bytes of parm information. The TEST command contains an extensive set of subcommands that can be executed once the TEST command is active.

The TIME Command

The TIME command will display time and date information as well as CPU time, connect time, and service units used by the current TSO session. The TIME command is executed without any additional parameters.

The TRANSMIT Command

The TRANSMIT command is used to send information. That information includes both data sets and messages. The transmission process is completed using the RECEIVE command, which will display information about each transmission to let the recipient decide whether or not to receive it. When necessary, a new data set will be created to accommodate placement of the data. The actual message or the name of the data set received can be logged in a separate log data set, and at the same time, a notify function can let the sender know that the information has been received.

The command is specified with a recipient that includes both node and user-id. Multiple users would be included within parentheses, or a distribution list can be used. The command can reference the name of a data set to be transmitted:

```
transmit node3.tso7854 dataset('tso1234.shared.data')
```

Or, the MESSAGE (MSG) parameter can be included to permit a message to be entered in a full-screen environment. Alternately, a file containing data set or message information can be referenced. Transmission logging and receipt notification are defaults, which can be turned off. The TRANSMIT command can also be abbreviated XMIT.

The WHEN Command

The WHEN command can be used in a CLIST to conditionally execute functions based on the return code of a program that immediately precedes it. The CLIST could also test the return code variable &LASTCC and use its value as the basis for conditional execution.

Access Method Services Commands

An interface exists between TSO and the control statements used with the access method services utility. This utility is more commonly known by its program name, IDCAMS. The control statements that can be accessed through TSO include ALTER, DEFINE, DIAGNOSE, EXAMINE, EXPORT, IMPORT, REPRO, and VERIFY. The interface also adheres to the standards for TSO command parameter abbreviation.

41

CLIST and REXX Execution

CLIST (Command LIST) and REXX (REstructured eXtended eXecutor) programs can be created to function much like TSO commands. Both languages feature resource control capabilities and programatic statement execution. Both run interactively and are able to use standard TSO commands. The languages are made available by the TSO product. The TSO EXEC command is the basis for their execution. In this chapter, the various forms of TSO commands will be used, with short samples of the two languages. A CLIST example will also be developed to show how private and public libraries can be combined to present a customized view of TSO and ISPF.

The EXEC Command

The EXEC command was designed to support CLIST execution and was modified slightly when REXX was made available to MVS. Two processing modes are supported, each of which has a variance. The two modes are known as *explicit* and *implicit*. They differ in appearance by whether or not the EXEC command is explicitly stated. As you might guess, the explicit mode of execution contains the command itself. The mode doesn't get its name, however, because the command is explicitly stated. It's called the explicit mode because the data set containing the code to be executed is explicitly stated. Using a CLIST example, the explicit form of execution might look like the following:

```
exec 'tso1234.clist(blksize)'
```

The CLIST can be executed from the same environments as TSO commands, since the TSO command EXEC is used to invoke it. The complete name of the data set containing the CLIST has been specified in TSO format. The single quotes around the data-set name cause the name to be taken literally. A variation of the explicit form of execution uses TSO assumptions about context and ownership to create a shorter version. The assumptions are made when the data set name is specified without quotes. Under that circumstance, the same command would look like the following, where the abbreviated form of the command (EX) is also used:

```
ex clist(blksize)
```

This latter form of command execution relies on the fact that when quotes are omitted from the data set name, TSO will automatically append the current prefix to the front of the data set name. The command can be shortened even further because CLIST is a special descriptive qualifier to TSO:

```
ex (blksize)
```

This last form of command execution relies on the context created by the EXEC command and the special significance of the descriptive qualifier CLIST in that context. All that's specified is the member name. The surrounding parentheses identify it as a member name rather than some other data set qualifier.

To make optimum use of the TSO naming assumptions just described, a CLIST library is best called userid.CLIST. This is not a requirement, nor must all CLIST code be contained in a PDS. Doing so, however, will make it easier to use the implicit form of execution. An assumption is even made when a CLIST library is referenced without a member name. In that particular instance, a member name of TEMPNAME is assumed. The member name would be placed within parentheses and added to the expanded version of the data set name. Keep that in mind while seeing how other CLIST data set names are built. (See Table 41.1.)

TABLE 41.1 CLIST Data.Set Names

Name specified in EXEC	Resultant name
'TSO1234.CLIST.TEST'	TSO1234.CLIST.TEST
TSO1234.CLIST.TEST	TSO1234.TSO1234.CLIST.TEST.CLIST
CLIST.TEST	TSO1234.CLIST.TEST.CLIST
'TSO1234.TEST.CLIST'	TSO1234.TEST.CLIST
TSO1234.TEST.CLIST	TSO1234.TSO1234.TEST.CLIST
TEST.CLIST	TSO1234.TEST.CLIST
TEST	TSO1234.TEST.CLIST

Notice that when quotes are omitted and the last qualifier is not CLIST, the last qualifier is appended. This is true even when CLIST is used elsewhere in the data-set name. Likewise, using the current prefix (in this case TSO1234) doesn't keep the prefix from being appended unless the data-set name is enclosed in single quotes.

Implicit execution relies on a special file called SYSPROC. The data sets defined to the SYSPROC file are searched for executable code. Execution is made easier because only the member name need be specified. When multiple libraries are concatenated to the SYSPROC file, they're searched in order until the member is found. It would only be necessary to specify BLKSIZE to execute the CLIST referenced earlier. Specifying parameter data (a topic covered later in this chapter) is also made easier.

A modification of the implicit mode of execution causes only the SYSPROC file to be searched. This is an efficient way to invoke REXX and CLIST code and can alleviate problems caused when such code has the same name as a TSO command. The modification is as simple as placing a percent sign in front of the member name to be executed. Specifying %BLKSIZE would cause only the data sets allocated to the SYSPROC file to be searched for the executable code. There would be no attempt to execute a TSO command called BLKSIZE, even if such a command were to exist.

SYSPROC File Allocation

Allocating libraries to the SYSPROC file is a key element of implicit execution. Generally, private or parochial data sets are added to those that are used systemwide. This maintains the base functions that are provided by the system libraries and adds to it the applications that are individually generated.

The initial consideration in adding private libraries to public libraries should be with data-set compatibility. This implies that all data sets that are connected to the SYSPROC file will have compatible physical characteristics. To help ensure that this is true, the system libraries should serve as a model in creating any private library that will be used with it. This will aid in the process known as data-set concatenation. In general terms, data-set concatenation refers to the process of reading more than one data set into a single file. With respect to the special file SYSPROC, this would be CLIST or REXX code that will be implicitly executed.

The process of concatenating data sets also applies to files that have special meaning to ISPF. These files include ISPPLIB (which contains panels), ISPMLIB (which contains messages), ISPSLIB (which contains file-tailoring skeletons), ISPTLIB (which contains tables), and ISPLLIB (which contains programs). Private libraries can be added to the public libraries allocated to these files to add functions or customize the ISPF environment.

The current system libraries can be determined using the LISTALC command (abbreviated LISTA). That command will display the data sets allocated to the current session. When used with the STATUS option, file names and dispositions will also be displayed. That will show all of the data sets allocated to a file. Figure 41.1 shows the LISTA command with the STATUS option executed from option 6. The file name is indented and appears after the first data set allocated to it. The three data sets allocated to the panel file ISPPLIB are highlighted below. Paging through the LISTA command output reveals the data set that's allocated to the SYSPROC file. This data set is highlighted in Figure 41.2.

Once the system data set names are known, they can be used in an ALLOCATE command, as in Figure 41.3. The ALLOCATE command is used to concatenate the

```
------------------------ TSO COMMAND PROCESSOR -------------------------
ENTER TSO COMMAND, CLIST, OR REXX EXEC BELOW:

===> lista st


--DDNAME---DISP--
USER.HELP
   SYSHELP   KEEP
SYS1.HELP
             KEEP
TERMFILE   SYSTSPRT
TERMFILE   SYSTSIN
USER.COMMON.PANELS
   ISPPLIB   KEEP
SYS1.ISPF.PANELS
             KEEP
SYS1.ISPV330.ISPPLIB
             KEEP
USER.COMMON.SKELS
   ISPSLIB   KEEP
SYS1.ISPF.SKELS
             KEEP
  ***  _
```

Figure 41.1 First page of LISTA output.

```
USER.COMMON.MSGS
   ISPMLIB   KEEP
SYS1.ISPF.MSGS
             KEEP
USER.COMMON.TABLES
   ISPTLIB   KEEP
SYS1.ISPF.TABLES
             KEEP
TSO1234.ISPF.PROFILE
   ISPPROF   KEEP
SYS1.CMDPROC
   SYSPROC   KEEP
  ***  _
```

Figure 41.2 Second page of LISTA output.

```
------------------------ TSO COMMAND PROCESSOR -------------------------
ENTER TSO COMMAND, CLIST, OR REXX EXEC BELOW:

===> alloc file(sysproc) dataset('tso1234.clist' 'sys1.cmdlib') shr reuse_
```

Figure 41.3 Command to concatenate CLIST libraries.

private library TSO1234.CLIST in front of the system library SYS1.CMDLIB. The private library could have also been specified without quotes, using the name CLIST. By specifying the private library first, it will be searched before the system library. That will also make it possible to execute customized versions of the code copied from the system library into the private library.

ISPF files should be reallocated outside of ISPF, since the files will be in use once ISPF is invoked. It's very common to include ALLOCATE commands for the SYSPROC and ISPF files in a CLIST or REXX EXEC. That would save typing and make it easy to execute the commands at the start of a TSO session. Private libraries could be added to system libraries before entering ISPF. Or, the LIBDEF statement could be used, from within ISPF, in a CLIST or REXX EXEC to affect ISPF libraries. LIBDEF would have no affect, however, on the SYSPROC file.

Specifying Parameter Data

Parameter data can be communicated to a CLIST or REXX program just like it would be to a TSO command. A CLIST, for example, can accommodate both positional and keyword parameters. The positional parameter data is communicated to the CLIST based upon its position relative to other data passed to the CLIST. When positional parameter data is omitted, prompts will be issued for the user to supply the data. That's because the information communicated through the positional parameters is deemed crucial to the execution of the CLIST.

A keyword is identified by the predefined (defined within the CLIST) keyword name. The keyword name is followed by any information to be communicated to the keyword variable. The information is enclosed in parentheses to separate it from the keyword name. Because the keyword name provides its identity (rather than position), keywords can be specified in any order. Keywords are generally used to communicate optional information rather than the crucial information contained in positional parameters.

Keywords might also have defined defaults within a CLIST, which is not possible for positional parameters. The assignment of default values applies where the keyword is not supplied at execution time. These defaults help to lessen the information that must be supplied during execution and are part of the reason that keywords are deemed optional. A modified keyword is one that's defined to the CLIST without any parenthetical value (even if that be a null value). Defining a keyword in this way limits its use and the value it can convey. A modified keyword can't specify a value at execution time. The keyword name can either be omitted or included on the invoking EXEC command. If a modified keyword is omitted, the corresponding CLIST variable will contain a null value. If a modified keyword is included, the corresponding CLIST variable will contain a value that's the keyword name.

A common example of a modified keyword might be the keyword DEBUG. When omitted from a CLIST that has it defined as a modified keyword, the variable DEBUG would contain a null value. When the parameter is included on the invoking EXEC command, the internal CLIST variable DEBUG would contain a value of DEBUG. This might be a signal or switch to tell the CLIST to turn its debugging or list options on.

When executing a CLIST, it's best to specify all positional parameters and keywords with the command that invokes the CLIST. That will make it easier to re-execute the CLIST, since the initial command will be restored in ISPF option 6. Another reason that all parameters should be specified at one time is that once prompting has started for missing positional parameter information, it will not be possible to specify any keyword parameters. Once the last positional parameter is supplied, execution will start.

CLIST Execution

A sample CLIST is shown in Figure 41.4. The CLIST accepts a record length as positional parameter data and calculates the optimum blocksize for a sequential data set on both a 3380 device and a 3390 device. The calculated values are then written to the screen. The first line of the CLIST defines the positional parameter (LRECL) that will be used to communicate the record length.

Figure 41.5 shows the CLIST executed with a record length value of 80. The explicit form is used, and so the positional parameter data must be enclosed in quotes. This is required of all positional and keyword parameters during explicit execution.

All of the parameters (keyword and positional) would be included within a single set of quotes. When the parameter itself contains single quotes, two consecutive single quotes would be used to show that they're embedded within the outer set:

```
ex testcopy '''tso1234.from.data'' ''tso1234.to.data'''
```

```
EDIT ---- TSO1234.CLIST(BLKSIZE) - 01.00 -------------- MEMBER BLKSIZE SAVED
COMMAND ===> _                                         SCROLL ===> CSR
****** ************************** TOP OF DATA ****************************
000001 PROC 1 LRECL
000002 SET &IBM3380 = 23476 / &LRECL * &LRECL
000003 SET &IBM3390 = 27998 / &LRECL * &LRECL
000004 WRITE THE OPTIMUM BLOCKSIZE FOR A SEQUENTIAL DATA SET
000005 WRITE ON A 3380 DEVICE IS &IBM3380
000006 WRITE THE OPTIMUM BLOCKSIZE FOR A SEQUENTIAL DATA SET
000007 WRITE ON A 3390 DEVICE IS &IBM3390
****** ************************** BOTTOM OF DATA **************************
```

Figure 41.4 Contents of the BLKSIZE CLIST.

```
------------------------- TSO COMMAND PROCESSOR ---------------------------
ENTER TSO COMMAND, CLIST, OR REXX EXEC BELOW:

===> ex (blksize) '80'


THE OPTIMUM BLOCKSIZE FOR A SEQUENTIAL DATA SET
ON A 3380 DEVICE IS 23440
THE OPTIMUM BLOCKSIZE FOR A SEQUENTIAL DATA SET
ON A 3390 DEVICE IS 27920

   ***
```

Figure 41.5 Executing the BLKSIZE CLIST.

The syntax for the same process is much simpler when the CLIST is invoked implicitly:

```
testcopy 'tso1234.from.data' 'tso1234.to.data'
```

If the positional parameter data had not been entered on the invoking EXEC command, a prompt would be issued for the information. The prompt ENTER POSITIONAL PARAMETER LRECL would have been issued for the BLKSIZE CLIST. The message ends with the name of the CLIST variable that's the object of the prompt.

REXX Execution

REXX code can be executed through the SYSPROC file when the code starts with a comment line that contains the word REXX. In that way, REXX and CLIST members can be combined in the same libraries without regard for which language they're written in. At installations that have activated the feature, REXX libraries can be allocated to and executed from the special file name SYSEXEC. The command EXECUTIL can be used to determine (on an individual user basis) whether or not the SYSEXEC file is searched for implicitly invoked REXX code. The command EXECUTIL SEARCHDD(YES) will cause the SYSEXEC file to be searched before the SYSPROC file. A value of NO will cause only the SYSPROC file to be searched, ignoring the SYSEXEC file completely.

The EXEC command also contains a parameter EXEC that identifies the code to be executed as REXX code. When that parameter is used in an explicit execution that's not fully qualified, the descriptive qualifier is expected to be EXEC. Figure 41.6 shows a REXX EXEC that's equivalent to the CLIST that was shown earlier. Notice that the first line of code has the word REXX contained in a comment. That provides the flexibility of executing the code implicitly through the SYSPROC file, implicitly through the SYSEXEC file, or explicitly with or without the EXEC parameter.

The REXX EXEC could be executed explicitly by specifying

```
ex 'tso1234.rexx.exec(blksize)' '100'
```

where the entire data set name is specified, or

```
ex rexx(blksize)' '100' exec
```

where the parameter EXEC identifies it as REXX code and will cause the descriptive qualifier EXEC to be appended automatically.

```
EDIT ---- TSO1234.REXX.EXEC(BLKSIZE) - 01.00 ----------- MEMBER BLKSIZE SAVED
COMMAND ===> _                                              SCROLL ===> CSR
****** ************************** TOP OF DATA ******************************
000001 /*  REXX  */
000002 ARG LRECL
000003 IBM3380 = 23476 % LRECL * LRECL
000004 IBM3390 = 27998 % LRECL * LRECL
000005 SAY 'THE OPTIMUM BLOCKSIZE FOR A SEQUENTIAL DATA SET',
000006     'ON A 3380 DEVICE IS' IBM3380
000007 SAY 'THE OPTIMUM BLOCKSIZE FOR A SEQUENTIAL DATA SET',
000008     'ON A 3390 DEVICE IS' IBM3390
****** ************************** BOTTOM OF DATA ***************************
```

Figure 41.6 Contents of the BLKSIZE EXEC.

Programmer Utilities

42

Background Processing of Source Code

Compile and Link Processing

This chapter covers the typical application development process, offering a description of how source code is converted into executable machine language. Additional general-information topics are covered, including basic compiler options and linkage editor options.

Most source language instructions need to be compiled or assembled before they can be executed. The source language instructions are input to a program that's unique to the source language used. That program, the compiler, produces output known as *object code*. The object code, in turn, is input to a linkage editor program that creates executable code. Both the source language instructions and the object code are typically 80-byte fixed-length records. They can come from partitioned data set members or sequential data sets. The output from the linkage editor, known as a *load module*, has very different characteristics. The load module can only be executed from a partitioned data set. The fixed record format gives way to one that's undefined. In this particular format, the record length and blocksize are equal to each other and able to vary in length.

Because the object code is an intermediate product of the translation process, it's often passed as a temporary data set from the compiler to the linkage editor. The ISPF program development utilities, however, approach the two steps separately. Because of this, the object code must be retained between the two steps. It can be deleted, however, when the process is over. The load module is kept as the executable result of program development. It can be executed any number of times without the need to recompile the program. The source code should be retained as well, in case it's necessary to recreate the load module or to modify the program function. Then too, it would also be required when attempting to correct errors that are detected after the program is placed in service.

Other data sets might be used in the language conversion process. These include source language instructions that are used to complement the source code being compiled and load code used to supplement the load module being created. Most languages support a copy or include function that retrieves external source code and places it in the program being compiled. Data set sources for these supplemental instructions are specified in "Additional Libraries" fields for the various languages. The same is true when invoking the linkage editor to create load code. Here, the reference is to libraries that contain load modules that are referenced within the program being processed. This is often indicated by program or function calls, but might also be inherent in the normal instruction set. Even stand-alone code must link in the language specific routines that support the instructions used.

A load module can be created as resolved (executable) or unresolved (nonexecutable). The latter might not seem to make sense but certainly has its place when creating a load module that's used as a component part of another. An executable load module, on the other hand, must have all of its external references resolved. The section "Linkage Editor Options" details the parameters used to create resolved and unresolved load modules.

Other information can be given to the compiler or linkage editor programs in the form of options. These options often communicate the type of output that's desired, both in the format of the basic output as well as the type of listings that should also be produced. These options vary by language and so will be discussed in general terms in the next section.

Basic Compiler Options

Compilers are typically able to write object code output to two different files. Compiler options are used to activate or deactivate those output files. The resource that's assigned to the output file then determines what form the object code output will take. The options OBJECT and NOOBJECT determine whether or not object code output will be written to the file SYSLIN. This is typically considered to be the primary form of output and is generally written to a disk data set. The options DECK and NODECK control whether or not object code is written to the file SYSPUNCH. As its name implies, the file was generally used to produce punch card output. At times, the compiler might be directed to produce no object code of any sort (with the options NOOBJECT and NODECK). This would be true when the compiler is used for syntax checking purposes only.

The SOURCE and NOSOURCE options are used to determine whether or not a complete source listing is generated with other message output. In many instances, a source listing will not be required because the source code is stored in a data set. The source listing that's generated by the compiler can be very useful, though, in resolving program problems. It might be combined with procedure and data maps (generated using other compiler options) to help isolate the statements leading to program failure. When written to a data set, the source listing can often be used in interactive debug functions to display the statements as they execute.

With some languages, compiler options can be used to specify compatibility processing modes or different levels of the compiler. Some provide options for selecting the level of generated code optimization. This is an indication of how much should be done (by the compiler) in an effort to make the code more efficient. These and other options might well be unique to the language used. The help function can be used from the ISPF option that supports a particular language to list the available compiler options. The user guide for a particular language will cover in detail the compiler options available to that language.

Linkage Editor Options

While there's a different program to compile each language (and often for different versions of the same language), there's only one linkage editor program. As a result, there's only a single set of options that can be specified. Some of the more common linkage editor options are discussed in the following.

- CALL turns on the automatic call function, facilitating the search for unresolved external references. This option is used when creating the final, resolved load module for actual execution.

- NCAL turns off the automatic call function, prohibiting the search for unresolved external references. This option is often used when creating an unresolved load module for one of the subroutines.

- AMODE specifies the address mode of the executable load module. Valid keyword values are 24, 31, and ANY.

- RMODE specifies the residence modes of the executable load module. These indicate where in virtual storage the module is loaded. Valid keyword values are 24 and ANY.

- LET causes the linkage editor to mark a load module as executable, despite some errors encountered during the link edit process.

- SIZE is a keyword that can be used to specify how much storage to give the linkage editor and how much buffer space to use. The two values can be adjusted when difficulty arises from link editing large programs.

- LIST specifies that the linkage editor control statements used are to be printed.

- MAP specifies that a map of the constituent modules is to be printed.

- XREF specifies that a cross reference table is to be printed. This output includes a module map.

- OVLY, REFR, RENT, REUS, and SCTR are used to specify load module attributes. The attributes (in the order listed) are overlay, refreshable, reenterable, reusable, and scatter format.

Background Processing Options

Background processing refers to tasks that are submitted for deferred processing. Job Control Language (JCL) statements identify the task to be executed as well as the resources to be used during processing. Option 5 of ISPF creates the JCL to provide access to background options that are largely centered around the processing of various programming languages.

The background processing options (shown in Figure 42.1) include access to compilers for COBOL, C, FORTRAN, PASCAL, and PL/I. Different versions of some languages are supported, including access to different assembler versions. The languages and versions that are available and supported will vary by installation. Source language processing is also supported by the member parts list. This option generates a list of source members connected to a main program by call, copy, or inclusion. Access to the linkage editor is provided to turn object and load code into an executable whole. A test function provides the facilities for running and debugging VS COBOL II programs. In this and the next chapter, the language processing options will be demonstrated for FORTRAN. The member parts list will also be demonstrated in the next chapter.

The field labeled SOURCE DATA PACKED indicates whether or not the source code will have to be expanded from a compressed storage format. When YES is entered in the field, the batch job is created with an extra step that will expand the source code and pass the expanded version to the compiler. Some of the options that don't support the expansion of stored data are marked with an asterisk.

The field labeled SOURCE DATA ONLINE refers to whether or not the source code is on a mounted volume. If it is, normal checks for data set presence are made. If the source data doesn't reside on a mounted volume, no check is made to ensure that the specified data set exists.

```
---------------------- BATCH SELECTION PANEL ----------------------------
OPTION ===> 3_

    1  - Assembler H              5 - PL/I optimizing compiler
    1A - Assembler XF             6 - VS PASCAL compiler
    2  - VS COBOL II compiler    *7 - Linkage editor
    2A - OS/VS COBOL compiler   *10 - VS COBOL II interactive debug
    3  - VS FORTRAN compiler     12 - Member parts list
    4  - PL/I checkout compiler *13 - C/370 compiler

                * - No packed data support

SOURCE DATA ONLINE ===> YES      (YES or NO)
SOURCE DATA PACKED ===> NO        (YES or NO)


JOB STATEMENT INFORMATION:   (Verify before proceeding)
  ===> //TSO1234B JOB (TSO12349999),'BACKGROUND SAMPLE',
  ===> //   CLASS=A,MSGCLASS=H,NOTIFY=TSO1234
  ===> //*
  ===> //*
```

Figure 42.1 Background options menu.

Background Compiling

Suboption 3 of the background options provides access to the FORTRAN compiler. Figure 42.2 shows the main screen where the data set containing the source code statements is identified. The source code data set can be specified in ISPF or TSO format.

Because the LIST ID field is not used, the compile listing will be written to the SYSOUT class specified in the field labeled SYSOUT CLASS. When a simple name is used in the LIST ID field, the compile listing will be written to a data set with the simple name as the middle qualifier. The last or descriptive qualifier of the data-set name will be the word LIST.

The TERM field option used here indicates that no terminal data set will be created during the compile. The other compile options specified here indicate that object code should be written to a data set, but that the alternate output form (written to SYSPUNCH) should not be used. Based on the name of the source code data set used here, the object code data set will be a PDS called prefix.OBJ. The SOURCE option will cause source code statements to be written with the listing output. When written to a data set, these source statements can be used within interactive debug functions to display the statements as they execute.

Additional input libraries can be specified to identify code that will be copied to the source code being processed. The libraries are searched for the objects of COPY or INCLUDE source statements for supplemental code (that will be added to existing statements).

The next screen displayed looks very much like the initial display of background options (Figure 42.3). This screen contains instructions for further processing and a message that the JCL to complete the compile process has been generated. At this point, the same or additional functions can be invoked. This includes the ability to run a link edit step to turn the object code into executable load code. The JCL for each of these other functions will be added to the step JCL just created.

When the END command is used, all generated steps will be added to the jobcard at the bottom of the screen and submitted for execution. The CANCEL command can be used instead to terminate processing without submitting the background job.

Using the END command causes the generated JCL to be submitted. Figure 42.4 shows the message (at the bottom of the screen) that indicates that the job was submitted. The message indicates both the job name and the JES number of the job that was submitted.

Background Linkage Editing

Access to the linkage editor is provided by suboption 7. The screen (shown inFigure 42.5) is very similar to that shown earlier for the FORTRAN compiler. The primary input to the linkage editor is the object code that was created during compile processing. That input is specified in either ISPF or TSO format. In the example, reference is made to the object code that was created earlier from the compile process.

When creating a fully resolved load module, the linkage editor might well have to resolve external program references. The libraries specified to SYSLIB will be

```
----------------------- BATCH VS FORTRAN COMPILE -------------------------
COMMAND ===>

ISPF LIBRARY:
   PROJECT ===>
   GROUP   ===>            ===>           ===>           ===>
   TYPE    ===>
   MEMBER  ===>                       (Blank or pattern for member selection list)

OTHER PARTITIONED OR SEQUENTIAL DATA SET:
   DATA SET NAME  ===> fort(newrate)_

LIST ID      ===>                  (Blank for hardcopy listing)
SYSOUT CLASS ===> A                (If hardcopy requested)

COMPILER OPTIONS:
 TERM   ===> NOTERM                (TERM or NOTERM)
 OTHER  ===> OBJECT,NODECK,SOURCE

ADDITIONAL INPUT LIBRARIES:
        ===>
        ===>
        ===>
```

Figure 42.2 FORTRAN compile option.

```
----------------------- BATCH SELECTION PANEL --------- JOB STEP GENERATED
OPTION  ===> _

   1  - Assembler H              5 - PL/I optimizing compiler
   1A - Assembler XF             6 - VS PASCAL compiler
   2  - VS COBOL II compiler    *7 - Linkage editor
   2A - OS/VS COBOL compiler   *10 - VS COBOL II interactive debug
   3  - VS FORTRAN compiler     12 - Member parts list
   4  - PL/I checkout compiler *13 - C/370 compiler

              * - No packed data support
INSTRUCTIONS:
   Enter option to continue generating JCL.
   Enter CANCEL command to exit without submitting job.
   Enter END command to submit job.

SOURCE DATA ONLINE ===> YES     (YES or NO)
SOURCE DATA PACKED ===> NO      (YES or NO)

JOB STATEMENT INFORMATION:
     //TSO1234B JOB (TSO12349999),'BACKGROUND SAMPLE',
     //  CLASS=A,MSGCLASS=H,NOTIFY=TSO1234
     //*
     //*
```

Figure 42.3 Generating job control statements.

```
----------------------- BATCH SELECTION PANEL  --------- JOB STEP GENERATED
OPTION  ===>

   1  - Assembler H              5  - PL/I optimizing compiler
  1A  - Assembler XF             6  - VS PASCAL compiler
   2  - VS COBOL II compiler    *7  - Linkage editor
  2A  - OS/VS COBOL compiler    *10 - VS COBOL II interactive debug
   3  - VS FORTRAN compiler      12 - Member parts list
   4  - PL/I checkout compiler  *13 - C/370 compiler

                  * - No packed data support
INSTRUCTIONS:
   Enter option to continue generating JCL.
   Enter CANCEL command to exit without submitting job.
   Enter END command to submit job.

SOURCE DATA ONLINE ===> YES      (YES or NO)
SOURCE DATA PACKED ===> NO       (YES or NO)

JOB STATEMENT INFORMATION:
     //TSO1234B JOB (TSO12349999),'BACKGROUND SAMPLE',
     //  CLASS=A,MSGCLASS=H,NOTIFY=TSO1234
JOB TSO1234B(JOB01223) SUBMITTED
***_
```

Figure 42.4 Background job submittal.

```
----------------------- BATCH LINKAGE EDIT  -------------------------------
COMMAND ===>

ISPF LIBRARY:
   PROJECT ===>
   GROUP   ===>          ===>          ===>          ===>
   TYPE    ===>
   MEMBER  ===>                  (Blank or pattern for member selection list)

OTHER PARTITIONED DATA SET:
   DATA SET NAME  ===> obj(newrate)_

LIST ID     ===>               (Blank for hardcopy listing)
SYSOUT CLASS ===> A            (If hardcopy requested)

LINKAGE EDITOR OPTIONS:
  TERM  ===>                   (TERM or Blank)
  OTHER ===>

ADDITIONAL INPUT LIBRARIES:    (LOAD libraries only)
SYSLIB ===> 'SYS1.FORTLIB'
SYSLIB ===>
SYSLIB ===>
SYSLIN ===>
```

Figure 42.5 Background link edit option.

searched to resolve those external references. The load code that's required from the libraries will be copied into the load module being constructed. In Figure 42.5, the library containing FORTRAN subroutines is entered into the first SYSLIB field. Other libraries can be referenced in the other two fields to form a concatenation of data sets allocated to the file SYSLIB.

The file SYSLIN can be used to reference a data set containing other object code and/or linkage editor control statements. This is optional input and is not specified here. It was also not necessary to specify any options to the linkage editor. When necessary, options might be specified to identify the load module's characteristics or the type of listing output that's generated.

Because the LIST ID field was not used, the link edit listing will be written to the SYSOUT class specified in the field SYSOUT CLASS. When a simple name is used in the LIST ID field, the link edit listing will be written to a data set with the simple name as the middle qualifier. The last or descriptive qualifier of the data set name will be the word LINKLIST.

As with the compile process, pressing the ENTER key causes step JCL to be generated (Figure 42.6). Other functions can be selected by option number, and they will be added as additional steps. Using the END command will cause the link edit job to be submitted, while typing CANCEL will terminate the function without submitting the job. If the job is submitted, the step JCL will be combined with the job-card information on the screen. The completed jobstream would then be entered into the system queues to wait its turn to execute.

```
----------------------- BATCH SELECTION PANEL --------- JOB STEP GENERATED
OPTION  ===> _

    1  - Assembler H              5 - PL/I optimizing compiler
   1A - Assembler XF              6 - VS PASCAL compiler
    2  - VS COBOL II compiler    *7 - Linkage editor
   2A - OS/VS COBOL compiler    *10 - VS COBOL II interactive debug
    3  - VS FORTRAN compiler     12 - Member parts list
    4  - PL/I checkout compiler  *13 - C/370 compiler

                  * - No packed data support
INSTRUCTIONS:
   Enter option to continue generating JCL.
   Enter CANCEL command to exit without submitting job.
   Enter END command to submit job.

SOURCE DATA ONLINE ===> YES     (YES or NO)
SOURCE DATA PACKED ===> NO      (YES or NO)

JOB STATEMENT INFORMATION:
     //TSO1234C JOB (TSO12349999),'BACKGROUND SAMPLE',
     //   CLASS=A,MSGCLASS=H,NOTIFY=TSO1234
     //*
     //*
```

Figure 42.6 Generation of link edit JCL.

43

Foreground Processing of Source Code

The foreground option (option 4) provides access to several compilers, the linkage editor, and some debugging programs. Figure 43.1 shows a typical foreground option menu. Note that just because an option appears on the menu, that doesn't mean the option is available. Not every installation has all the languages that the menu was designed to access. Even where the language is available, an installation can choose not to activate a particular option. Ideally, the options not available or not installed will be noted on the menu itself.

This chapter uses a small sample FORTRAN program as a representative example. The program will be compiled and link edited. In the next chapter, the same program will be run through the interactive debug program. In addition to foreground suboptions 3, and 7, the member parts list (suboption 12) will also be demonstrated.

Foreground Compiling

Figure 43.2 shows the initial option 4.3 screen that's used to compile FORTRAN source code. The primary input is a data set containing the source statements to be compiled. That data set can be identified in either TSO or ISPF format. Fields labeled ADDITIONAL INPUT LIBRARIES are available to specify copy libraries. These libraries would supply supplemental source code (identified by INCLUDE statements within the program).

The compiler option OBJECT is specified here to cause an object deck to be created. The option NOOBJECT would be used to compile for diagnostic purposes only (where no attempt will be made to translate the output into executable code). The options SOURCE and TEST are specified here for later use with the interactive debug

```
---------------------- FOREGROUND SELECTION PANEL ----------------------
OPTION  ===> _

   1  - Assembler H                *7  - Linkage editor
   1A - Assembler XF                9  - SCRIPT/VS
   2  - VS COBOL II compiler       *10  - VS COBOL II interactive debug
   2A - OS/VS COBOL compiler       *10A - COBOL Interactive debug
   3  - VS FORTRAN compiler        *11  - FORTRAN Interactive debug
   4  - PL/I checkout compiler      12  - Member parts list
   5  - PL/I optimizing compiler   *13  - C/370 compiler
   6  - VS PASCAL compiler

                  * - No packed data support

SOURCE DATA PACKED          ===>         (YES or NO)
ENTER SESSION MANAGER MODE ===>          (YES or NO)
```

Figure 43.1 Foreground options menu.

```
---------------------- FOREGROUND VS FORTRAN COMPILE ----------------------
COMMAND ===>

ISPF LIBRARY:
   PROJECT ===> TSO1234
   GROUP   ===> EXAMPLE  ===>            ===>            ===>
   TYPE    ===> FORT
   MEMBER  ===>                  (Blank or pattern for member selection list)

OTHER PARTITIONED OR SEQUENTIAL DATA SET:
   DATA SET NAME  ===> fort(newrate)_

LIST ID ===>                         PASSWORD ===>

COMPILER OPTIONS:
 OBJECT ===> OBJECT      (OBJECT or NOOBJECT)
 OTHER  ===> SOURCE,TEST,OPT(0)

ADDITIONAL INPUT LIBRARIES:
        ===>
        ===>
        ===>
```

Figure 43.2 Foreground FORTRAN compile option.

function. SOURCE will produce a listing of the source statements that can be windowed during the debugging session. TEST will create debugging hooks and might not be required, depending on the language and release of the language used. The OPT option is used here to preclude the use of any optimization of generated code.

The field labeled LIST ID can be used to specify the name under which the listing output will be written. It's not used here, and so the input member name will be used. The print output of this compile will be written to a data set name of prefix.NEWRATE.LIST. Based on the number of qualifiers in the source data set name, the object code will be written to a PDS named prefix.OBJ. It will be written to the member name NEWRATE within the PDS.

The print output generated by the compiler is shown in Figure 43.3. The first part of the output lists the options that were requested as well as those that are in effect (either because they were requested or because they were left to default). The options are followed by a listing of the source statements. The corresponding compiler-generated numbers are highlighted in the column ISN (Internal Statement Number). These numbers can be referenced in the interactive debug function.

At the end of the listing, the compiler states that no diagnostics were generated. This is equivalent to a return code of zero and indicates that no warnings (or more severe error messages) were issued.

The END command is used to exit from the compiler print output. At that point, the screen in Figure 43.4 is displayed. That screen is used to specify the disposition of the output. The output can be printed, kept, or deleted. In this instance, option K is entered to keep the data set that contains the output. That will make the source

```
BROWSE -- TSO1234.NEWRATE.LIST -------------------- LINE 00000000 COL 001 080
COMMAND ===> _                                         SCROLL ===> CSR
**************************** TOP OF DATA ********************************
LEVEL 2.4.0 (AUG  1989)       VS FORTRAN              MAR 16, 1992  10:54:21
REQUESTED OPTIONS (EXECUTE): OBJECT,SOURCE,TEST,OPT(0)
OPTIONS IN EFFECT: NOLIST NOMAP NOXREF GOSTMT NODECK SOURCE NOTERM OBJECT FIX
              SDUMP(ISN) NOSXM NOVECTOR IL(DIM) TEST NODC NOICA NODIRECT
              OPT(0) LANGLVL(77) NOFIPS   FLAG(I)   AUTODBL(NONE)  NAM
   IF DO   ISN    *....*...1.........2.........3.........4.........5.........6..
            1     100 FORMAT(F5.2)
            2         OPEN (1,FILE='BASERATE')
            3         OPEN (3,FILE='NEWRATES')
            4         READ(1,100)RATE
            5         WRITE(3,100)RATE
            6         DO 10 I=1,9
    1       7         RATE = RATE * 1.1
    1       8         WRITE(3,100)RATE
    1       9      10 CONTINUE
           10         STOP
           11         END
 *STATISTICS*   SOURCE STATEMENTS = 11, PROGRAM SIZE = 884 BYTES, PROGRAM NAME
 *STATISTICS*      NO DIAGNOSTICS GENERATED.
 **MAIN** END OF COMPILATION 1 ******
```

Figure 43.3 Output listing from foreground compile.

```
----------------------- FOREGROUND PRINT OPTIONS ------------------------
OPTION  ===> k_

  PK - Print data set and keep        K - Keep data set (without printing)
  PD - Print data set and delete      D - Delete data set (without printing)

  If END command is entered, data set is kept without printing.

DATA SET NAME: TSO1234.NEWRATE.LIST

PRINT MODE    ===> BATCH           (BATCH or LOCAL)

SYSOUT CLASS ===>
PRINTER ID   ===>                  (For 328x printer)

JOB STATEMENT INFORMATION:         (Required for system printer)
  ===> //TSO1234H JOB (ACCOUNT),'NAME'
  ===> //*
  ===> //*
  ===> //*
```

Figure 43.4 Processing the compile listing.

code that it contains available for use in an interactive debug session. At the end of the compile process, the initial option 4.3 screen is displayed (Figure 43.5). The short message indicates that the listing data set has been kept.

Foreground Linkage Editing

Foreground access to the linkage editor is provided by suboption 7 (shown in Figure 43.6). The primary input to the linkage editor is the object code that was created during compile processing. That input is specified in either ISPF or TSO format. In the example, reference is made to the object code that was created earlier from the compile process.

When creating a fully resolved load module, the linkage editor might well have to resolve external program references. The libraries specified to SYSLIB will be searched to resolve these external references. The load code that's required from the libraries will be copied into the load module being constructed. In Figure 43.6, the library containing FORTRAN system subroutines is entered into the first SYSLIB field. Other libraries can be referenced in the other two fields to form a concatenation of data sets allocated to the file SYSLIB.

The file SYSLIN can be used to reference a data set containing other object code and/or linkage editor control statements. This is optional input and is not specified here. Three options have been specified to the linkage editor. They have been coded in the field LINKAGE EDITOR OPTIONS and are separated by commas.

Upon pressing the ENTER key, the linkage editor is immediately invoked. When it's finished, the listing output is displayed in a data set. The middle qualifier is the

```
---------------------- FOREGROUND VS FORTRAN COMPILE --------- LISTING KEPT
COMMAND ===>

ISPF LIBRARY:
   PROJECT ===> TSO1234
   GROUP   ===> EXAMPLE  ===>            ===>            ===>
   TYPE    ===> FORT
   MEMBER  ===>               (Blank or pattern for member selection list)

OTHER PARTITIONED OR SEQUENTIAL DATA SET:
   DATA SET NAME  ===>_ FORT(NEWRATE)

LIST ID ===>                          PASSWORD ===>

COMPILER OPTIONS:
 OBJECT ===> OBJECT    (OBJECT or NOOBJECT)
 OTHER  ===> SOURCE,TEST,OPT(0)

ADDITIONAL INPUT LIBRARIES:
        ===>
        ===>
        ===>
```

Figure 43.5 End of compile process.

```
---------------------- FOREGROUND LINKAGE EDIT --------------------------
COMMAND ===>

ISPF LIBRARY:
   PROJECT ===>
   GROUP   ===>            ===>            ===>            ===>
   TYPE    ===>
   MEMBER  ===>                  (Blank or pattern for member selection list)

OTHER PARTITIONED DATA SET:
   DATA SET NAME  ===> obj(newrate)

LIST ID ===> newrate_                 PASSWORD ===>

LINKAGE EDITOR OPTIONS: (Options LOAD, LIB and PRINT generated automatically)
        ===> LET,LIST,MAP

ADDITIONAL INPUT LIBRARIES:
SYSLIB  ===> 'SYS1.FORTLIB'
SYSLIB  ===>
SYSLIB  ===>

SYSLIN  ===>
```

Figure 43.6 Foreground linkage editor option.

simple name that was specified in the LIST ID field. When the field is left blank, the middle qualifier is the name of the member being processed.

Figure 43.7 shows the print output from the linkage editor execution. It contains the module map that was requested in the options field. Part of the map information shows the internal module name and its hexadecimal length. The data set will also contain any error messages that might result from unsuccessful completion.

The output listing from the linkage editor is not typically as useful as that from the compiler. In Figure 43.8, the processing option D is used to delete the data set containing the listing. The data set can also be kept, and the data set can be printed whether or not it's ultimately retained. The default, if no option is specified, is to retain the data set.

Pressing the ENTER key has caused the data set containing the link edit listing to be deleted. The initial link edit screen is redisplayed (Figure 43.9) with the status of the data set in the short message area. An executable load module now exists that can be executed using the TSO CALL command or using a JCL jobstream. This sample program will be run through the interactive debug function in the next chapter.

Member Parts List

The member parts list is option 4.12. Its name is not particularly descriptive of its function, which is to display the structure of an application program. As a function, the member parts list will examine the identified source code for additional code that's called or included. Source code that's copied or included, as well as that from

```
BROWSE -- TSO1234.NEWRATE.LINKLIST --------------- LINE 00000000 COL 001 080
COMMAND ===> _                                              SCROLL ===> CSR
***************************** TOP OF DATA ********************************

MVS/DFP VERSION 3 RELEASE 2 LINKAGE EDITOR      11:16:02  MON  MAR 16, 1992
JOB TSO1234    STEP $DEF        PROCEDURE DEF
INVOCATION PARAMETERS - MAP,LIST,LET,TERM
ACTUAL SIZE=(940032,387072)
OUTPUT DATA SET TSO1234.LOAD IS ON VOLUME DISK1C

                                                    MODULE MAP

   CONTROL SECTION                  ENTRY
     NAME    ORIGIN  LENGTH           NAME    LOCATION    NAME    LOCATION
     MAIN        00     374
     AFBVINTE*  378     28C
                                      IFYVINTE    378    VFEIM#     3A2
                                      VFEIN#      3D6    VFEIL#     41C
                                      VFEE#       462    VFES#      4AC
                                      VFEP#       4E8    VFELC#     524

     AFBVIOFM*  608     22C
                                      IFYVIOFM    608    VFRSF#     636
                                      VFWSF#      660    VFCSF#     68A
                                      VFDSF#      6B4    VFESF#     6DE
```

Figure 43.7 Foreground linkage editor output listing.

```
----------------------- FOREGROUND PRINT OPTIONS -------------------------
OPTION  ===> d_

  PK - Print data set and keep        K - Keep data set (without printing)
  PD - Print data set and delete      D - Delete data set (without printing)

  If END command is entered, data set is kept without printing.

DATA SET NAME: TSO1234.NEWRATE.LINKLIST

PRINT MODE   ===> BATCH          (BATCH or LOCAL)

SYSOUT CLASS ===>
PRINTER ID   ===>               (For 328x printer)

JOB STATEMENT INFORMATION:      (Required for system printer)
  ===> //TSO1234H JOB (ACCOUNT),'NAME'
  ===> //*
  ===> //*
  ===> //*
```

Figure 43.8 Processing the link edit listing.

```
----------------------- FOREGROUND LINKAGE EDIT ---------- LISTING DELETED
COMMAND ===>

ISPF LIBRARY:
   PROJECT ===>
   GROUP   ===>          ===>          ===>          ===>
   TYPE    ===>
   MEMBER  ===>                  (Blank or pattern for member selection list)

OTHER PARTITIONED DATA SET:
   DATA SET NAME  ===> OBJ(NEWRATE)

LIST ID ===>                      PASSWORD ===>

LINKAGE EDITOR OPTIONS: (Options LOAD, LIB and PRINT generated automatically)
       ===> LET,LIST,MAP

ADDITIONAL INPUT LIBRARIES:
SYSLIB  ===> 'SYS1.FORTLIB'
SYSLIB  ===>
SYSLIB  ===>

SYSLIN  ===>
```

Figure 43.9 End of link edit process.

called subroutines, is then also examined to find other supplemental code. Eventually, a sequence or structure of the code that's used to form an application can be determined. Depending on the option selected, the member parts list will present the structure in a browse session, print the structure, or write the structure straight to a data set.

In Figure 43.10, option 1 is selected so the application structure can be browsed. The source code to be examined is identified in ISPF format as the member MAIN in data set TSO1234.TEST.FORT. Note that this is not the source code compiled previously.

The output from the member parts list execution is placed in a data set, which is then automatically displayed. That display is shown in Figure 43.11. The interpretation of the output would be as shown in Table 43.1.

TABLE 43.1 Output from Member Parts List Execution

lines 1 and 2	-	The code contained in member COMM1 is included (I) in programs MAIN, SUBPROG1, and SUBPROG2.
lines 3 and 4	-	The program MAIN itself includes code contained in members COMM1 and COMM2 as well as calls (C) to SUBPROG1 and SUBPROG2.
line 5	-	The program SUBPROG1 (which is called MAIN) includes code contained in member COMM1.
lines 6 and 7	-	The program SUBPROG2 (which is called by MAIN) includes code contained in members COMM1 and COMM2. It also calls program SUBPROG3.
line 8	-	The program SUBPROG3 (which is called by SUBPROG2) includes code contained in member COMM2.

```
---------------------- FOREGROUND MEMBER PARTS LIST  ----------------------
OPTION  ===> 1

   1 - Browse/Print member parts
   2 - Write member parts data set

ISPF LIBRARY:
   PROJECT  ===> tso1234
   GROUP    ===> test       ===>            ===>           ===>
   TYPE     ===> fort
   MEMBER   ===> main_                 (Blank for member selection list)

LANGUAGE   ===> FOR                    (Defaults to TYPE value)

GROUPS FOR PRIMARY MEMBERS ===> 1      (1, 2, 3, or 4)

OUTPUT DATA SET:                       (Option 2 only)
DATA SET NAME ===>
```

Figure 43.10 Member parts list menu.

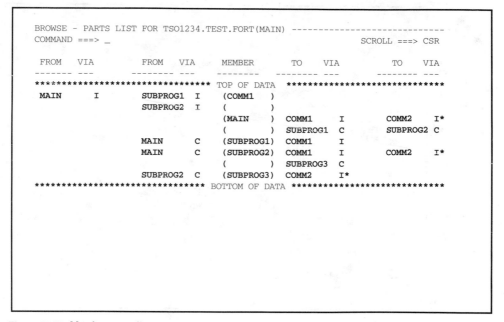

```
BROWSE - PARTS LIST FOR TSO1234.TEST.FORT(MAIN) -----------------------------
COMMAND ===> _                                            SCROLL ===> CSR

   FROM    VIA         FROM   VIA      MEMBER      TO    VIA        TO    VIA
   -------  ---        -------- ---    --------   -------- ---    -------- ---
   ****************************** TOP OF DATA ******************************
   MAIN     I          SUBPROG1  I    (COMM1   )
                       SUBPROG2  I    (        )
                                      (MAIN    )  COMM1    I       COMM2    I*
                                      (        )  SUBPROG1 C       SUBPROG2 C
                       MAIN      C    (SUBPROG1)  COMM1    I
                       MAIN      C    (SUBPROG2)  COMM1    I       COMM2    I*
                                      (        )  SUBPROG3 C
                       SUBPROG2  C    (SUBPROG3)  COMM2    I*
   ****************************** BOTTOM OF DATA ******************************
```

Figure 43.11 Member parts list output.

```
----------------------- FOREGROUND PRINT OPTIONS --------------------------
OPTION   ===> d_

  PK - Print data set and keep      K - Keep data set (without printing)
  PD - Print data set and delete    D - Delete data set (without printing)

  If END command is entered, data set is kept without printing.

DATA SET NAME: TSO1234.SPF136.OUTLIST

PRINT MODE   ===> BATCH           (BATCH or LOCAL)

SYSOUT CLASS ===>
PRINTER ID   ===>                 (For 328x printer)

JOB STATEMENT INFORMATION:        (Required for system printer)
  ===>
  ===>
  ===>
  ===>
```

Figure 43.12 Deleting member parts list output.

```
-------------------- FOREGROUND MEMBER PARTS LIST  -------- LISTING DELETED
OPTION  ===> _

   1 - Browse/Print member parts
   2 - Write member parts data set

ISPF LIBRARY:
   PROJECT  ===> TSO1234
   GROUP    ===> TEST        ===>              ===>            ===>
   TYPE     ===> FORT
   MEMBER   ===>                        (Blank for member selection list)

LANGUAGE    ===> FOR                    (Defaults to TYPE value)

GROUPS FOR PRIMARY MEMBERS ===> 1       (1, 2, 3, or 4)

OUTPUT DATA SET:                        (Option 2 only)
DATA SET NAME ===>
```

Figure 43.13 End of member parts list processing.

The member parts list function is terminated using the END command. While terminating the function, a screen is presented for dealing with the output of the function. In Figure 43.12, a processing option of D has been specified to delete the data set containing the output. If the output were printed, it would be necessary to specify a valid output class as well as jobcard information to support background job execution.

After specifying the disposition of the member parts list output, the initial 4.12 screen is displayed Figure 43.13. In the short message area of the screen is a message that the output listing has been deleted.

44

Interactive Debug

The interactive debug option can be used to resolve program problems and facilitate program testing. The option allows a program to be stopped, examined, and even changed during execution. Most languages currently have their own debug option. In the future, there will probably be fewer debug functions that are individually able to support several languages. The FORTRAN debug function (option 4.11) will be demonstrated in this chapter, using the program that was compiled and link edited in the previous chapter.

Setting Up For Program Execution

Before using the interactive debug function, the files needed for execution must be allocated. This can be done using the ALLOCATE command. The following example shows a data set TSO1234.TEST.DATA allocated to an input file called BASERATE:

```
ALLOC FILE(BASERATE) DATASET('TSO1234.TEST.DATA') SHR REUSE
```

ALLOCATE commands can be placed in a CLIST or REXX EXEC to make them easier to invoke and easier to execute in subsequent debugging sessions. The commands that would be used for this particular program are shown in the following as they would appear in a CLIST. The CLIST would be executed before starting the debugging session:

```
ALLOC F(FT05001) DA(*) REUSE
ALLOC F(FT06001) DA(*) REUSE
ALLOC F(BASERATE) DA(*) REUSE
ALLOC F(NEWRATES) DA(*) REUSE
```

In this instance, the files are directed to and from the screen to give greater visibility to the input and output processing that will take place. For programs that process significant amounts of data, this would not be a good idea. It is a good idea to make sure that the source code is available in the proper data set if it's to be displayed in the source code window. ISPF will look for the source code (that has been written out by the compiler) in a data set with the name prefix.program-name.LIST.

The Interactive Debug Option

The FORTRAN interactive debug function is accessed from option 4.11. In Figure 44.1, the load library containing the program to be executed is specified in TSO format. The option DEBUG is specified to bring the program up in a debugging mode rather than merely executing the program. Other languages might require that the program be compiled with the TEST option to provide debugging hooks.

The member name could have been omitted on the previous screen. If it had been omitted, a member list for the specified library would be displayed next. From that screen, the program to be executed would be selected using the letter S in front of the member name.

Once a program has been selected, the screen in Figure 44.2 is displayed. The screen is divided into three separate windows. Each window displays a different output type. The first window is called the monitor. It displays information that interactive debug has been asked to monitor. The second window is the source window. It displays the source code that was used to generate the load module being executed. The source code is read from a data set that contains the compile listing. The name of the data set is prefix.program-name.LIST. If the source code is not available to the interactive debug function, a warning message will be issued when this screen is first displayed. The message will not be issued if interactive debug was started with the NOSOURCE option. The third window is a log. It logs the debug commands that were entered and displays the output from them as well as from the execution of the FORTRAN program.

The Help Function

It will only be possible to demonstrate a few of the interactive debug features here. One of them, the HELP command, provides online documentation of the other features. The HELP command (abbreviated here with the letter H) is executed in Figure 44.2.

Invoking the help function causes the menu in Figure 44.3 to be displayed. Detailed help text can be displayed for everything from setting breakpoints to changing the size of the windows by selecting the corresponding number code. The END command is used to exit the help function and return to the main screen.

Entering Debug Commands

At this point, the program remains poised for execution. If the files that it uses were not already allocated, it would be still be possible to split the screen and use the second screen to prepare any required data sets as well as allocate them to the neces-

```
----------------------- FORTRAN INTERACTIVE DEBUG -----------------------
COMMAND ===>

ISPF LIBRARY:
   PROJECT ===>
   GROUP   ===>
   TYPE    ===>                 (OBJ or LOAD)
   MEMBER  ===>                 (Blank or pattern for member selection list)

SOURCE TYPE ===>

OTHER PARTITIONED OR SEQUENTIAL DATA SET:
   DATA SET NAME  ===> load(newrate)_

LIST ID ===>                         PASSWORD ===>

DEBUG OPTIONS:      (Options LIB, SOURCE, and PRINT generated automatically)
      ===> DEBUG

ADDITIONAL INPUT LIBRARIES:   (LOAD libraries only)
   ===>
   ===>
   ===>
```

Figure 44.1 The interactive debug menu.

```
IAD      Q: MAIN                         W: MAIN.2
COMMAND ===> h_                                    SCROLL ===> PAGE
MONITOR --+----1----+----2----+----3----+----4----+----5----+--- LINE: 0 OF 0
**************************** TOP OF MONITOR ****************************
**************************** BOTTOM OF MONITOR ****************************




SOURCE  0----+----1----+----2----+----3----+----4----+----5---- LINE: 1 OF 11
       1    100 FORMAT(F5.2)                                                .
       2        OPEN (1,FILE='BASERATE')                                   0
       3        OPEN (3,FILE='NEWRATES')                                   0
       4        READ(1,100)RATE                                            0
       5        WRITE(3,100)RATE                                           0
       6        DO 10 I=1,9                                                0
LOG 0----+----1----+----2----+----3----+----4----+----5----+---- LINE: 1 OF 4
**************************** TOP OF LOG ****************************
0001 VS FORTRAN VERSION 2 RELEASE 5 INTERACTIVE DEBUG
0002 5668-806 (C) COPYRIGHT IBM CORP. 1985, 1990
0003 LICENSED MATERIALS-PROPERTY OF IBM
0004 WHERE: MAIN.2
**************************** BOTTOM OF LOG ****************************
```

Figure 44.2 Interactive debug windows.

```
SELECTION ===> _                        VS FORTRAN VERSION 2 INTERACTIVE DEBUG

                            MAIN HELP MENU

Choose a topic by typing its number on the command line and pressing ENTER.
Return to this menu from any topic by typing TOP on the command line and
pressing ENTER.  Return to debugging from any topic by pressing PF3.  Toggle
between this menu and the task menu by pressing ENTER.

       1  Task Menu     16  fixup       31  next        46  right
       2  Tutorial      17  go          32  off         47  search
       3  *,"           18  halt        33  offwn       48  set
       4  annotate      19  help        34  position    49  size
       5  at            20  if          35  prevdisp    50  step
       6  autolist      21  left        36  profile     51  syscmd
       7  backspace     22  list        37  purge       52  termio
       8  close         23  listbrks    38  qualify     53  timer
       9  color         24  listfreq    39  quit        54  trace
      10  dbcs          25  listings    40  reconnect   55  up
      11  describe      26  listsamp    41  refresh     56  vecstat
      12  down          27  listsubs    42  restart     57  when
      13  enddebug      28  listtime    43  restore     58  where
      14  endfile       29  listvec     44  retrieve    59  window
      15  error         30  movecurs    45  rewind      60  zoom
```

Figure 44.3 Interactive debug help menu.

sary files. The first executable statement in the FORTRAN program is at ISN (Internal Statement Number) number two. This is the statement that will next execute when the program is started. The current position (in program MAIN at ISN 2) is shown at both the top and the bottom of Figure 44.4. In the same figure, the AUTOLIST command is issued to display two of the program's variables. Since more than one variable is requested, the variables are enclosed in parentheses.

The AUTOLIST command has caused the two variables to be displayed in the monitor window in Figure 44.5. The variable name is preceded by the program name, and the current variable values are displayed. Since the program has still not started to execute, the value of each variable is zero. Notice that the variable values are in the format specified. The variable I is expressed as a default integer value, while RATE is specified as a floating point number because of its reference to the FORMAT statement (ISN 1).

These two variables will continue to be monitored until replaced by other variables. The display will constantly be updated with the current variable value. The LIST command can be used to display the current value of variables at any given point without placing them in the monitor.

Starting Program Execution

The GO command is issued in Figure 44.5 to start program execution. More typically, breakpoints would be established to stop the program at various points so that conditions could be examined more closely. The HALT command can also be used to

```
IAD      Q: MAIN                              W: MAIN.2
COMMAND ===> autolist (i rate)_                        SCROLL ===> PAGE
MONITOR --+----1----+----2----+----3----+----4----+----5----+--- LINE: 0 OF 0
*************************** TOP OF MONITOR ***************************
*************************** BOTTOM OF MONITOR ***********************



SOURCE  0----+----1----+----2----+----3----+----4----+----5---- LINE: 1 OF 11
      1    100 FORMAT(F5.2)                                           .
      2        OPEN (1,FILE='BASERATE')                               0
      3        OPEN (3,FILE='NEWRATES')                               0
      4        READ(1,100)RATE                                        0
      5        WRITE(3,100)RATE                                       0
      6        DO 10 I=1,9                                            0
LOG 0----+----1----+----2----+----3----+----4----+----5----+--- LINE: 1 OF 4
*************************** TOP OF LOG ******************************
0001 VS FORTRAN VERSION 2 RELEASE 5 INTERACTIVE DEBUG
0002 5668-806 (C) COPYRIGHT IBM CORP. 1985, 1990
0003 LICENSED MATERIALS-PROPERTY OF IBM
0004 WHERE: MAIN.2
*************************** BOTTOM OF LOG ***************************
```

Figure 44.4 Entering a debug command.

```
IAD      Q: MAIN                              W: MAIN.2
COMMAND ===> go_                                      SCROLL ===> PAGE
MONITOR --+----1----+----2----+----3----+----4----+----5----+--- LINE: 1 OF 2
0001 MAIN.I            =        0
0002 MAIN.RATE         = 0.000000000E+00
*************************** BOTTOM OF MONITOR ***********************



SOURCE  0----+----1----+----2----+----3----+----4----+----5---- LINE: 1 OF 11
      1    100 FORMAT(F5.2)                                           .
      2        OPEN (1,FILE='BASERATE')                               0
      3        OPEN (3,FILE='NEWRATES')                               0
      4        READ(1,100)RATE                                        0
      5        WRITE(3,100)RATE                                       0
      6        DO 10 I=1,9                                            0
LOG 0----+----1----+----2----+----3----+----4----+----5----+--- LINE: 1 OF 5
*************************** TOP OF LOG ******************************
0001 VS FORTRAN VERSION 2 RELEASE 5 INTERACTIVE DEBUG
0002 5668-806 (C) COPYRIGHT IBM CORP. 1985, 1990
0003 LICENSED MATERIALS-PROPERTY OF IBM
0004 WHERE: MAIN.2
0005 * autolist (i rate)
*************************** BOTTOM OF LOG ***************************
```

Figure 44.5 Starting program execution.

stop execution when subroutines are entered or even before each statement is executed. The latter would be ideal when it's necessary to step through the program one instruction at a time. The GO command (as well as other debug commands) can be assigned to a PF key. In that way, each time the PF key is pressed, another instruction would be executed.

Because no breakpoints were set, execution was started and stopped only to read data from the screen. That's because the TSO ALLOCATE command was used earlier to assign the input file BASERATE to the terminal. The program is now ready to read from the file BASERATE, and the information must come from the terminal operator. The log message in Figure 44.6, BASERATE INPUT: PRECEDE INPUT WITH % OR ENTER IAD COMMAND, indicates that terminal input is required. Since the program has stopped, however, additional debugging commands could be issued.

Data to be read into the program is preceded with a percent sign. This distinguishes it from debugging instructions. The source language instructions that have been executed to this point have been highlighted to bring attention to the execution count at the extreme right. This count shows how many times a particular instruction has been executed, and is especially helpful when working with loop structures.

Once the program input has been supplied, there's nothing to keep this simple program from completing. The last log message in Figure 44.7 indicates that the program has terminated with a return code value of zero. At this point, debugging commands can still be issued. All or selected variables could be listed, for example, to show their values at the end of the program.

The monitor now shows the changed values for the autolist variables defined earlier in the session. The log shows a portion of the output from the NEWRATES file that was directed to the terminal. The source window shows the last portion of the source code with final statement execution counts. Where necessary, a window can be scrolled. Position in one of the windows can be established by placing the cursor there before scrolling.

Figure 44.8 shows the debug session after scrolling up in the source window. This scrolling has not changed the current execution position, which is listed at the top of the screen as ISN 10 within program MAIN. From this position in the source window, it's obvious that the start of the loop structure at statement six was executed once, while the first statement in the loop was executed nine times. Again, debugging commands can be issued because even though the program has ended, the debugging session has not.

Ending The Session

In Figure 44.9, the QUIT command is issued to terminate the debugging session. This command can also be executed before the program has terminated to preclude further execution. When the debugging session is ended, the log that was displayed as the third window is now displayed in data-set form (Figure 44.10). Command input to the debugging session is preceded with an asterisk. Since this is a normal browse function, it's possible to use all browse commands, including those to implement scrolling of the data. The END command is issued from the browse function to leave the debug log and continue session termination.

```
IAD/R    Q: MAIN                        W: MAIN.4
COMMAND ===> %37.98_                            SCROLL ===> PAGE
MONITOR --+----1----+----2----+----3----+----4----+----5----+--- LINE: 1 OF 2
0001 MAIN.I            =          0
0002 MAIN.RATE         = 0.000000000E+00
************************** BOTTOM OF MONITOR ****************************



SOURCE  0----+----1----+----2----+----3----+----4----+----5---- LINE: 1 OF 11
       1   100 FORMAT(F5.2)                                          .
       2       OPEN (1,FILE='BASERATE')                             1
       3       OPEN (3,FILE='NEWRATES')                             1
       4       READ(1,100)RATE                                      1
       5       WRITE(3,100)RATE                                     0
       6       DO 10 I=1,9                                          0
LOG 0----+----1----+----2----+----3----+----4----+----5----+---- LINE: 1 OF 7
0001 VS FORTRAN VERSION 2 RELEASE 5 INTERACTIVE DEBUG
0002 5668-806 (C) COPYRIGHT IBM CORP. 1985, 1990
0003 LICENSED MATERIALS-PROPERTY OF IBM
0004 WHERE: MAIN.2
0005 * autolist (i rate)
0006 * go
0007 BASERATE INPUT: PRECEDE INPUT WITH % OR ENTER IAD COMMAND
```

Figure 44.6 Entering instream data.

```
IAD/F    Q: MAIN                        W: MAIN.10
COMMAND ===> _                                  SCROLL ===> PAGE
MONITOR --+----1----+----2----+----3----+----4----+----5----+--- LINE: 1 OF 2
0001 MAIN.I            =         10
0002 MAIN.RATE         =  89.5550232
************************** BOTTOM OF MONITOR ****************************



SOURCE  0----+----1----+----2----+----3----+----4----+----5---- LINE: 8 OF 11
       8       WRITE(3,100)RATE                                     9
       9    10 CONTINUE                                             9
      10       STOP                                                 1
      11       END                                                  0
************************** BOTTOM OF SOURCE ****************************

LOG 0----+----1----+----2----+----3----+----4----+----5----+-- LINE: 13 OF 19
0013 NEWRATES 55.61
0014 NEWRATES 61.17
0015 NEWRATES 67.28
0016 NEWRATES 74.01
0017 NEWRATES 81.41
0018 NEWRATES 89.56
0019 PROGRAM HAS TERMINATED; RC ( 0)
```

Figure 44.7 Program termination.

```
IAD/F     Q: MAIN                              W: MAIN.10
COMMAND ===> _                                           SCROLL ===> PAGE
MONITOR --+----1----+----2----+----3----+----4----+----5----+--- LINE: 1 OF 2
0001 MAIN.I           =          10
0002 MAIN.RATE        =  89.5550232
*************************** BOTTOM OF MONITOR ***************************



SOURCE  0----+----1----+----2----+----3----+----4----+----5---- LINE: 2 OF 11
      2          OPEN (1,FILE='BASERATE')                            1
      3          OPEN (3,FILE='NEWRATES')                            1
      4          READ(1,100)RATE                                     1
      5          WRITE(3,100)RATE                                    1
      6          DO 10 I=1,9                                         1
      7          RATE = RATE * 1.1                                   9
LOG 0----+----1----+----2----+----3----+----4----+----5----+-- LINE: 13 OF 19
0013 NEWRATES 55.61
0014 NEWRATES 61.17
0015 NEWRATES 67.28
0016 NEWRATES 74.01
0017 NEWRATES 81.41
0018 NEWRATES 89.56
0019 PROGRAM HAS TERMINATED; RC ( 0)
```

Figure 44.8 Scrolling the source window.

```
IAD/F     Q: MAIN                              W: MAIN.10
COMMAND ===> quit_                                       SCROLL ===> PAGE
MONITOR --+----1----+----2----+----3----+----4----+----5----+--- LINE: 1 OF 2
0001 MAIN.I           =          10
0002 MAIN.RATE        =  89.5550232
*************************** BOTTOM OF MONITOR ***************************



SOURCE  0----+----1----+----2----+----3----+----4----+----5---- LINE: 2 OF 11
      2          OPEN (1,FILE='BASERATE')                            1
      3          OPEN (3,FILE='NEWRATES')                            1
      4          READ(1,100)RATE                                     1
      5          WRITE(3,100)RATE                                    1
      6          DO 10 I=1,9                                         1
      7          RATE = RATE * 1.1                                   9
LOG 0----+----1----+----2----+----3----+----4----+----5----+-- LINE: 13 OF 19
0013 NEWRATES 55.61
0014 NEWRATES 61.17
0015 NEWRATES 67.28
0016 NEWRATES 74.01
0017 NEWRATES 81.41
0018 NEWRATES 89.56
0019 PROGRAM HAS TERMINATED; RC ( 0)
```

Figure 44.9 Terminating the debug session.

```
BROWSE -- TSO1234.NEWRATE.LOG -------------------- LINE 00000000 COL 001 080
COMMAND ===> _                                        SCROLL ===> CSR
***************************** TOP OF DATA  **********************************
VS FORTRAN VERSION 2 RELEASE 5 INTERACTIVE DEBUG
5668-806 (C) COPYRIGHT IBM CORP. 1985, 1990
LICENSED MATERIALS-PROPERTY OF IBM
WHERE: MAIN.2
* autolist (i rate)
* go
BASERATE INPUT: PRECEDE INPUT WITH % OR ENTER IAD COMMAND
* %37.98
NEWRATES 37.98
NEWRATES 41.78
NEWRATES 45.96
NEWRATES 50.55
NEWRATES 55.61
NEWRATES 61.17
NEWRATES 67.28
NEWRATES 74.01
NEWRATES 81.41
NEWRATES 89.56
PROGRAM HAS TERMINATED; RC ( 0)
* quit
*************************** BOTTOM OF DATA **********************************
```

Figure 44.10 The debug log.

```
---------------------- FOREGROUND PRINT OPTIONS --------------------------
OPTION  ===> K_

  PK - Print data set and keep      K - Keep data set (without printing)
  PD - Print data set and delete    D - Delete data set (without printing)

  If END command is entered, data set is kept without printing.

DATA SET NAME: TSO1234.NEWRATE.LOG

PRINT MODE  ===> BATCH          (BATCH or LOCAL)

SYSOUT CLASS ===>
PRINTER ID   ===>               (For 328x printer)

JOB STATEMENT INFORMATION:      (Required for system printer)
  ===> //TSO1234A JOB (ACCOUNT),'NAME'
  ===> //*
  ===> //*
  ===> //*
```

Figure 44.11 Processing the log data set.

Processing the Debug Log

Upon leaving the debug log, the screen in Figure 44.11 is presented. It's used to specify the disposition of the log data set. The option chosen here (option K to keep the log data set without printing it) is the same disposition that's used if ending out of the screen without specifying an option. Various combinations of printing or deleting the data set are also available.

If the data set is kept, it will be reused the next time the same program is debugged (the selected program name is the middle qualifier in the data set name). ISPF will otherwise dynamically create a log data set where one doesn't already exist. After the data set disposition is specified, the initial interactive debug screen is displayed (Figure 44.12). The message in the short message area indicates that the data set was kept.

```
---------------------- FORTRAN INTERACTIVE DEBUG ---------- LISTING KEPT
COMMAND ===>  _

ISPF LIBRARY:
   PROJECT ===>
   GROUP   ===>
   TYPE    ===>              (OBJ or LOAD)
   MEMBER  ===>              (Blank or pattern for member selection list)

SOURCE TYPE ===>

OTHER PARTITIONED OR SEQUENTIAL DATA SET:
   DATA SET NAME  ===> LOAD(NEWRATE)

LIST ID ===>                         PASSWORD ===>

DEBUG OPTIONS:      (Options LIB, SOURCE, and PRINT generated automatically)
        ===> DEBUG

ADDITIONAL INPUT LIBRARIES:    (LOAD libraries only)
     ===>
     ===>
     ===>
```

Figure 44.12 The end of debug processing.

45

Dialog Management Services

The dialog manager component of ISPF allows applications to be created that contain features like those of the PDF options. The dialog manager provides facilities for screen display, table data storage, and message handling. Another feature called file tailoring allows data to make use of variable information and be selectively modified. Option 7 of ISPF provides several functions that can be used to facilitate the development of dialog management applications.

The main menu of the dialog test option is shown in Figure 45.1. It's defined as a parent menu and determines the way that dialog test options are selected. Because it's a parent menu, it will be displayed when the RETURN command is used. It will then be possible to return to the primary option menu using the END or RETURN commands. Each of the dialog test options will be examined individually, although not in menu order, since the options allow component testing long before the application is assembled.

The Panel Display Option

The panel display option (dialog test option 2) is shown in Figure 45.2. It's used to display panels outside of the normal dialog application and therefore allows component testing of panel statements. A sample panel is requested in the field labeled PANEL NAME. The panel library containing that member must already be allocated to the file ISPPLIB or connected using LIBDEF.

Before showing the actual panel display, the statements that make up the panel are shown in Figure 45.3. The variables that are used to accept input field data are highlighted (including their use in the panel processing section). Having specified

```
-------------------- DIALOG TEST PRIMARY OPTION PANEL --------------------
OPTION  ===> _

    1  FUNCTIONS        - Invoke dialog functions/selection panel
    2  PANELS           - Display panels
    3  VARIABLES        - Display/set variable information
    4  TABLES           - Display/modify table information
    5  LOG              - Browse ISPF log
    6  DIALOG SERVICES  - Invoke dialog services
    7  TRACES           - Specify trace definitions
    8  BREAKPOINTS      - Specify breakpoint definitions
    T  TUTORIAL         - Display information about Dialog Test
    X  EXIT             - Terminate dialog testing

Enter END command to terminate dialog testing.
```

Figure 45.1 Dialog test menu.

```
------------------------------ DISPLAY PANEL ------------------------------
COMMAND ===>

PANEL NAME              ===> example1_

MESSAGE ID              ===>              (Optional)

CURSOR FIELD            ===>              (Optional)

CURSOR POSITION         ===>              (Optional)



MESSAGE POP-UP FIELD ===>                 (Optional)



DISPLAY IN WINDOW    ===> NO              (Yes or No)
```

Figure 45.2 The panel display option.

```
EDIT ---- TSO1234.PANELS(EXAMPLE1) - 01.00 ----------------- COLUMNS 001 072
COMMAND ===> _                                              SCROLL ===> CSR
****** ************************** TOP OF DATA ***************************
000001                          DIALOG TEST - SAMPLE PANEL
000002 COMMAND ===>_ZCMD
000003 +
000004
000005   ENTER NAME OF DATA SET
000006   TO BE PRINTED ===>_DSN                                           +
000007
000008       PRINT CLASS ===>_C+
000009
000010       NUMBER OF COPIES ===>_N+
000011
000012       PRINTER DESTINATION ===>_DEST    +
000013
000014 ) PROC
000015   VER (&DSN,NONBLANK)
000016   VER (&DSN,DSNAME)
000017   VER (&C,NONBLANK)
000018   VER (&N,NUM)
000019 ) END
****** ************************** BOTTOM OF DATA ***************************
```

Figure 45.3 Sample panel statements.

the panel name and pressed the ENTER key, the panel is displayed as in Figure 45.4. Actual data can be placed in the panel fields to test the validation checks included in the PROC section of the panel code (lines 15 through 18 of Figure 45.3).

If the panel can't be displayed because of an error in the panel code, a full screen message will be issued, describing the error. Corrections or changes to the panel source code should be saved before attempting to display the panel again. Figure 45.5 shows a message in the short message area of the panel being displayed. The message, ENTER REQUIRED FIELD, is the result of a verify statement in the panel PROC section to ensure that a non-blank value is entered in the first data field of the panel.

After receiving the message, the value MY.DATA was typed into the first field to satisfy its requirement for data. Other facets of panel logic can be checked by using improper data classes or value ranges in the various fields. Each field test is executed in the order that it appears in the panel processing section. When data is entered that passes all field verifications, the panel remains displayed, but no message is issued. Even when it's not required for panel testing, option 7.2 can be used to bring in changed panel versions. This is possible because the option will automatically refresh the copy of the panel that's held in memory.

Variable Access

Option number 3 of the dialog test options provides access to ISPF variables. From the option, variables can be added, changed, or deleted. Figure 45.6 shows some of the variables listed by the option. The display includes a line command area, the

```
                         DIALOG TEST - SAMPLE PANEL
COMMAND ===>


  ENTER NAME OF DATA SET
  TO BE PRINTED ===> _

       PRINT CLASS ===>

       NUMBER OF COPIES ===>

       PRINTER DESTINATION ===>
```

Figure 45.4 Display of the sample panel.

```
                         DIALOG TEST - SAMPLE PANEL     ENTER REQUIRED FIELD
COMMAND ===>


  ENTER NAME OF DATA SET
  TO BE PRINTED ===> my.data_

       PRINT CLASS ===>

       NUMBER OF COPIES ===>

       PRINTER DESTINATION ===>
```

Figure 45.5 Entering required field information.

```
-------------------------------- VARIABLES ------------------- ROW 1 OF 359
COMMAND ===> _                                         SCROLL ===> PAGE

ADD/DELETE/CHANGE VARIABLES.   UNDERSCORES NEED NOT BE BLANKED.
ENTER END COMMAND TO FINALIZE CHANGES, CANCEL COMMAND TO END WITHOUT CHANGES.


        VARIABLE  P A VALUE                         APPLICATION: ISR

  '''' Z_____   S N
  '''' ZAPLCNT_   S N 0000
  '''' ZAPPLID_   S N ISR
  '''' ZCOLORS_   S N 0001
  '''' ZDATE___   S N 92/12/22
  '''' ZDATEF__   S N YY/MM/DD
  '''' ZDATEFD_   S N YY/MM/DD
  '''' ZDAY____   S N 22
  '''' ZDBCS___   S N NO
  '''' ZENVIR__   S N ISPF 3.3MVS/XA   TSO
  '''' ZHILITE_   S N NO
  '''' ZJDATE__   S N 92.356
  '''' ZLOGNAME   S N
  '''' ZLOGO___   S N YES
  '''' ZLOGON__   S N DEF
  '''' ZLSTLPP_   S N 0060
```

Figure 45.6 Initial variable display.

variable name, the variable type, the variable attribute, and the current variable
value. Variables with an S (in the column labeled P) come from the shared variable
pool. Variables with a P (in the same column) come from the profile variable pool.
Function pool variables can also be displayed; they're represented by the letters I
and V for variables that are defined implicitly or by VDEFINE.

The next column indicates the variable attribute. The letter N (non-modifiable) in
this column indicates that the variable can't be updated. This is typical for system-
generated variables. The letter T (truncated) indicates that the variable value is
longer than 58 bytes and is displayed in truncated form. A truncated variable can't
be updated from this screen.

Figure 45.7 shows the same variable list after scrolling down to the first profile
variable. The value contained in the variable can be modified by typing over (or
erasing) the current value. The line commands I and D can be used to insert new
variables and delete existing variables. Either line command can be used with a
numeric value to affect that number of lines. New variables need not be inserted
in alphanumeric sequence. The list of variables is sorted before it's initially displayed.

The LOCATE command can be used to scroll a particular variable to the top of the
list. Unlike other instances of the LOCATE command, the exact variable name must
be used (and matched to a variable in the list) before scrolling will occur.

The CANCEL command should be used to leave the variable function without making any changes. Use of the END command will cause any changes to be retained.

```
------------------------------ VARIABLES ------------------- ROW 33 OF 359
COMMAND ===> _                                           SCROLL ===> PAGE

ADD/DELETE/CHANGE VARIABLES.  UNDERSCORES NEED NOT BE BLANKED.
ENTER END COMMAND TO FINALIZE CHANGES, CANCEL COMMAND TO END WITHOUT CHANGES.

        VARIABLE  P A VALUE                    APPLICATION: ISR

 '''' AMT_____    P    PAGE
 '''' ASMT____    P    ASM
 '''' BASM____    P    LIST,NODECK,OBJECT
 '''' BASMT___    P    NOTERM
 '''' BCLA____    P    A
 '''' BCOB____    P    SOURCE,XREF
 '''' BCOBT___    P    NOTEST
 '''' BFOR____    P    LOAD,NODECK,SOURCE
 '''' BFORT___    P    NOTERM
 '''' BFOR1___    P
 '''' BFOR2___    P
 '''' BFOR3___    P
 '''' BJC1____    P    //TSO1234D JOB 'BACKGROUND SAMPLE',
 '''' BJC2____    P    //   CLASS=A,MSGCLASS=T,NOTIFY=TSO1234
 '''' BJC3____    P    //*
 '''' BJC4____    P    //*
```

Figure 45.7 Display of profile variables.

The Dialog Service Option

The dialog service option (option 7.6) allows dialog services to be invoked. The service that's demonstrated in Figure 45.8 is the TBCREATE service. It's used to create a table. In this context, the command ISPEXEC is not used. The parameters included as the TBCREATE service are invoked here as the table name (FCBTAB), the names of all key variables (FCB), and the names of all other table variables (LINES COLS LAYOUT).

Figure 45.9 shows the return code for that service just invoked. The return code value of 0 (in the short message area) indicates that the table has been successfully created. The table would also be opened automatically as a result of using TBCREATE. The dialog service option can be used as well to close the table (TBCLOSE) after it has been processed using another of the dialog test options. The dialog service option can also be used to connect data sets to various ISPF files (including table libraries) using the LIBDEF service.

Table Services

The table services are contained in option 7.4. The available table services are listed on the initial screen shown in Figure 45.10. They include the ability to display, delete, or modify existing table rows. Rows can also be added to the table at the current table position. Option 5 will display the table structure, indicating what normal and key variables have been defined to the table. Option 6 (the option selected here) is used to display the current table status.

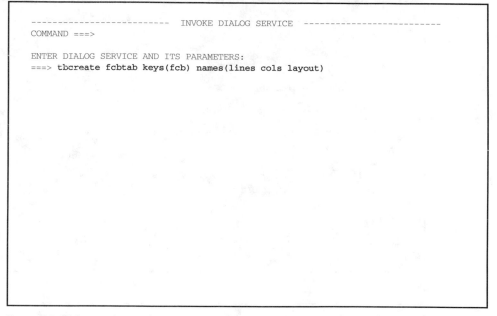

Figure 45.8 Dialog services option.

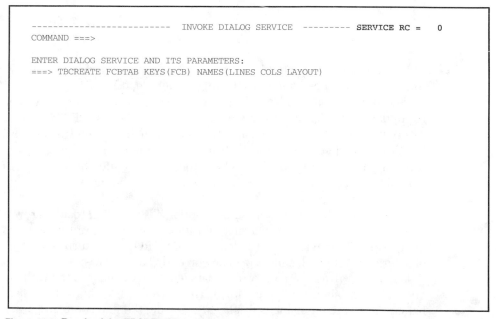

Figure 45.9 Result of the TBCREATE service.

```
------------------------------------ TABLES  ------------------------------------
OPTION  ===>  6

   1  Display row        3  Modify row       5  Display structure
   2  Delete row         4  Add row          6  Display status

TABLE NAME       ===>  fcbtab_    OPEN TABLE ===>           (NOWRITE or WRITE or
                                                            blank for no TBOPEN)
ROW IDENTIFICATION:              CURRENT ROW:    TOP

  BY ROW NUMBER ===>  *          (* = current row)

  BY VARIABLE    VALUE           (Search for row if row number blank)
  _____
  _____
  _____
  _____
  _____


DBCS COLUMN SPECIFICATION:
  _____    _____    _____    _____    _____    _____
  _____    _____    _____    _____    _____    _____
```

Figure 45.10 Displaying table status.

The table services that deal with existing tables require that the library or libraries that contain those tables be allocated to the file ISPTLIB. This can be accomplished with the command:

```
LIBDEF ISPTLIB DATASET ID(library-name)
```

That command is executed in option 7.6. The command uses the LIBDEF function to connect the named library to the table input file, ISPTLIB.

The status display in Figure 45.11 shows that the table is currently open in a write (or update) mode. This is the result of having used the TBCREATE command earlier to create the table. If necessary, the table can be opened in either WRITE or NOWRITE mode using one of the fields on the initial table screen. When opened in this way, the table services should automatically issue the proper TBCLOSE or TBEND when terminated. The statistics show that the table is currently empty and has not been updated.

Returning to the initial table screen, option 4 is specified to add a row to the table (Figure 45.12). The row is currently positioned at the top of the table, as indicated by the value TOP in the field labeled CURRENT ROW. The current row pointer value of asterisk is retained, since the table currently has no rows.

The display to add or modify table data looks very similar to the variable display of option 7.3. It's shown in Figure 45.13. The table row is displayed as a list of variable names. The variable name is displayed following the line command area. Following that is an indication of whether the variable is a named variable (N) or a key variable

```
------------------------  STATUS OF TABLE FCBTAB  --------------------------
COMMAND ===> _

   STATUS FOR THIS SCREEN   : OPEN       DATE CREATED        : 92/03/18
   OPEN OPTION              : WRITE      TIME CREATED        : 20.28.56
   TABLE ON DISK            : NO         LAST DATE MODIFIED  : NOUPDATE
   LAST TABLE SERVICE       : TBQUERY    LAST TIME MODIFIED  : NOUPDATE
   LAST SERVICE RETURN CODE: 00          LAST MODIFIED BY    : TSO1234
   CURRENT ROW POINTER      : TOP        ORIGINAL ROW COUNT  : 0
                                         CURRENT ROW COUNT   : 0
                                         MODIFIED ROW COUNT  : 0
                                         UPDATE COUNT        : 0

                                         VIRTUAL STORAGE SIZE: 224
```

Figure 45.11 Table status display.

```
----------------------------------  TABLES  --------------------------------
OPTION  ===> 4_

   1  Display row      3  Modify row     5  Display structure
   2  Delete row       4  Add row        6  Display status

TABLE NAME     ===> FCBTAB    OPEN TABLE ===>         (NOWRITE or WRITE or
                                                      blank for no TBOPEN)
ROW IDENTIFICATION:           CURRENT ROW:   TOP

  BY ROW NUMBER ===> *        (* = current row)

  BY VARIABLE    VALUE        (Search for row if row number blank)
    _____  _____
    _____  _____
    _____  _____
    _____  _____
    _____  _____

DBCS COLUMN SPECIFICATION:
    _____  _____  _____  _____  _____  _____
    _____  _____  _____  _____  _____  _____
```

Figure 45.12 Adding a table row.

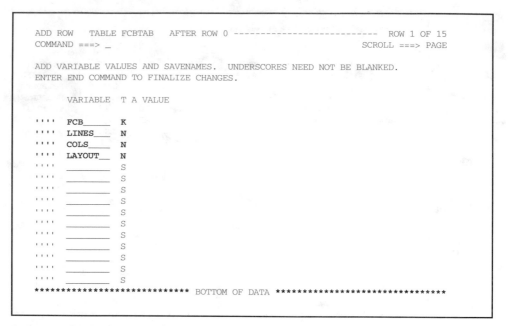

```
ADD ROW   TABLE FCBTAB   AFTER ROW 0 -------------------------- ROW 1 OF 15
COMMAND ===> _                                         SCROLL ===> PAGE

ADD VARIABLE VALUES AND SAVENAMES.  UNDERSCORES NEED NOT BE BLANKED.
ENTER END COMMAND TO FINALIZE CHANGES.

          VARIABLE   T A VALUE

''''    FCB_____    K
''''    LINES____   N
''''    COLS_____   N
''''    LAYOUT__    N
''''    _____    S
''''    _____    S
''''    _____    S
''''    _____    S
''''    _____    S
''''    _____    S
''''    _____    S
''''    _____    S
''''    _____    S
''''    _____    S
''''    _____    S
**************************** BOTTOM OF DATA ********************************
```

Figure 45.13 Blank table entry.

(K). Other variable names can be added in the blanks below. These would become extension variables that are unique to the table row that they're added to.

Actual table data is typed into the field labeled VALUE. In Figure 45.14, the table variable FCB is assigned a value of STD3, the variable LINES is assigned a value of 45, and so on. Again, the additional entries are available to add what are known as *extension variables*. A variable name must be supplied for extension variables because they're not already defined to the table. The completed table row will be placed after row zero as indicated in the screen title.

The END command is used to cause the row to be added to the table. The initial 7.4 screen is redisplayed where the short message indicates that the row has been added (Figure 45.15). The current row pointer now points to the row just added. If another row is now added, it will be placed after row one.

The fields labeled BY VARIABLE and VALUE can be used to search through existing table entries for a particular value in the specified table variable. The search is conducted from the current position in the table. An asterisk can be used at the end of the variable value to represent any string of characters.

The dialog services option (option 7.6) can be used to close the table, as in Figure 45.16. This is an important step in the process of updating a table because it causes the table to be written to disk. The appropriate table library must be allocated to file ISPTABL for the table changes to be stored.

Figure 45.17 shows that the TBCLOSE function completed with a return code of zero. The table contents would have been successfully written to the output table library. If it's not already allocated, the output table library file, ISPTABL, can still be connected here, using the LIBDEF service discussed earlier.

```
ADD ROW    TABLE FCBTAB    AFTER ROW 0 -------------------------- ROW 1 OF 15
COMMAND ===>                                            SCROLL ===> PAGE

ADD VARIABLE VALUES AND SAVENAMES.  UNDERSCORES NEED NOT BE BLANKED.
ENTER END COMMAND TO FINALIZE CHANGES.

        VARIABLE   T A VALUE

''''    FCB_____  K   std3
''''    LINES____  N   45
''''    COLS_____  N   145
''''    LAYOUT__   N   landscape_
''''    _____   S
''''    _____.  S
''''    _____   S
''''    _____   S
''''    _____   S
''''    _____   S
''''    _____   S
''''    _____   S
''''    _____   S
''''    _____   S
**************************** BOTTOM OF DATA ********************************
```

Figure 45.14 Specifying table row values.

```
---------------------------------- TABLES ---------------- ----- ROW ADDED
OPTION  ===> 4

    1  Display row       3  Modify row        5  Display structure
    2  Delete row        4  Add row           6  Display status

TABLE NAME    ===> FCBTAB    OPEN TABLE ===>        (NOWRITE or WRITE or
                                                    blank for no TBOPEN)
ROW IDENTIFICATION:          CURRENT ROW:    1

  BY ROW NUMBER ===> *       (* = current row)

  BY VARIABLE    VALUE       (Search for row if row number blank)
    _____
    _____
    _____
    _____
    _____

DBCS COLUMN SPECIFICATION:

    _____    _____    _____    _____    _____
    _____    _____    _____    _____    _____
```

Figure 45.15 Result of table row addition.

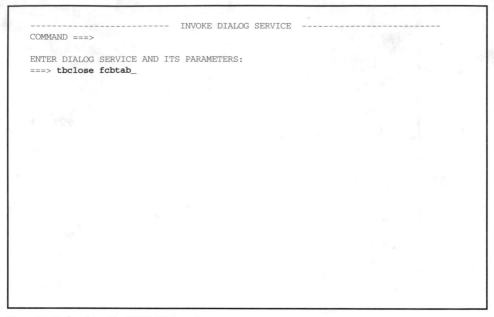

Figure 45.16 Invoking the TBCLOSE service.

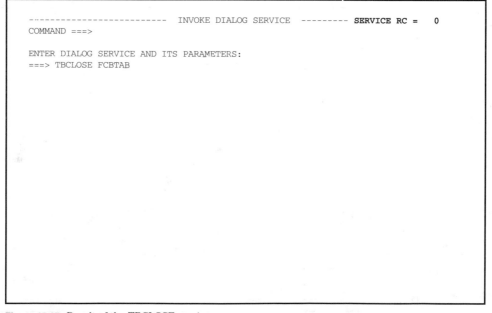

Figure 45.17 Result of the TBCLOSE service.

Function and Variable Traces

Option 7.7 provides suboptions to trace variables and dialog services. Either suboption can be selected from the menu shown in Figure 45.18. Output from any trace option selected will be written to the log data set. Option 7.5 can be used to view the log either during or after execution of the dialog being tested.

When choosing to trace dialog services, the default screen shown in Figure 45.19 is displayed. Particular functions can be specified, as well as particular dialog services within a function. Merely changing the ACTIVE column to YES would trace all dialog services within all functions.

Variable traces are specified in option 7.7. The default screen (shown in Figure 45.20) is much like that for function traces. Merely changing the ACTIVE column to YES will cause all variables to be traced. Or, specific variables can be listed and the context of the trace can be further qualified. Where further qualification is not given, all is the default.

Setting Execution Breakpoints

Breakpoints can be set before an application is run to cause the application to stop at those points. Option 7.6 is used to set breakpoints surrounding dialog services. The breakpoints can occur before, after, or both before and after a specified service. Figure 45.21 shows breakpoints being set for two dialog services, DISPLAY and TBDISPL. A separate column exists to make it easier to turn the listed breakpoints on or off.

```
--------------------------------- TRACES ----------------------------------
OPTION  ===>  _

   1  FUNCTION TRACES - Monitor dialog service calls
   2  VARIABLE TRACES - Monitor dialog variable usage
```

Figure 45.18 Dialog trace menu.

```
--------------------------- FUNCTION TRACES  --------------- ROW 1 OF 13
COMMAND ===> _                                          SCROLL ===> PAGE

ADD, DELETE, AND CHANGE TRACES.  UNDERSCORES NEED NOT BE BLANKED.
ENTER END COMMAND TO FINALIZE CHANGES.

         FUNCTION     ACTIVE       DIALOG SERVICES TO BE TRACED
         (Required)   (YES,NO)     (No entry=all)
                      (No entry=YES)  ("OR" is assumed between names)

''''  ALL_____    NO_      _____
''''  _____     ___      _____
''''  _____     ___      _____
''''  _____     ___      _____
''''  _____     ___      _____
''''  _____     ___      _____
''''  _____     ___      _____
''''  _____     ___      _____
''''  _____     ___      _____
''''  _____     ___      _____
''''  _____     ___      _____
''''  _____     ___      _____
''''  _____     ___      _____
**************************** BOTTOM OF DATA ***************************
```

Figure 45.19 Default function trace screen.

```
--------------------------- VARIABLE TRACES  ---------------- ROW 1 OF 13
COMMAND ===> _                                          SCROLL ===> PAGE

ADD, DELETE, AND CHANGE TRACES.  UNDERSCORES NEED NOT BE BLANKED.
ENTER END COMMAND TO FINALIZE CHANGES.

         VARIABLE     POOL      OPERATION     FUNCTION      ACTIVE
         (Required) (No entry=all) (GET,PUT,CHG) (No entry=all) (YES,NO)
                                  (No entry=all)              (No entry=YES)

''''  ALL_____   _____    ___       _____       NO_
''''  _____    _____    ___       _____       ___
''''  _____    _____    ___       _____       ___
''''  _____    _____    ___       _____       ___
''''  _____    _____    ___       _____       ___
''''  _____    _____    ___       _____       ___
''''  _____    _____    ___       _____       ___
''''  _____    _____    ___       _____       ___
''''  _____    _____    ___       _____       ___
''''  _____    _____    ___       _____       ___
''''  _____    _____    ___       _____       ___
''''  _____    _____    ___       _____       ___
''''  _____    _____    ___       _____       ___
**************************** BOTTOM OF DATA ***************************
```

Figure 45.20 Default variable trace screen.

```
------------------------------- BREAKPOINTS -------------------- ROW 1 OF 13
COMMAND ===> _                                             SCROLL ===> PAGE

ADD, DELETE, AND CHANGE BREAKPOINTS.  UNDERSCORES NEED NOT BE BLANKED.
ENTER END COMMAND TO FINALIZE CHANGES.

         SERVICE          WHEN           FUNCTION         ACTIVE
         (Required)   (BEFORE,AFTER,Rnn) (No entry=all)   (YES,NO)
                        (No entry=all)                    (No entry=YES)

''''  display_         _____          _____         ___
''''  tbdispl_       a_____           _____         ___
''''             _____           _____         ___
''''    _____      _____           _____         ___
''''    _____      _____           _____         ___
''''    _____      _____           _____         ___
''''    _____      _____           _____         ___
''''    _____      _____           _____         ___
''''    _____      _____           _____         ___
''''    _____      _____           _____         ___
''''    _____      _____           _____         ___
''''    _____      _____           _____         ___
''''    _____      _____           _____         ___
**************************** BOTTOM OF DATA ********************************
```

Figure 45.21 Setting execution breakpoints.

Executing a Dialog Function

Once the traces and breakpoints have been established, the dialog application can be executed in option 7.1 (shown in Figure 45.22). Separate fields exist for identifying the selection panel, foreground command, or program that's to be executed. Additional fields (unique to the type of dialog) are used to pass information to the application.

The libraries containing the function to be invoked should be connected to the proper files before the function is executed. This can be done using the ALLOCATE command or using LIBDEF within ISPF to reference the files like ISPPLIB, SYSPROC, or ISPLLIB. Figure 45.22 shows a selection panel specified in the first field. Execution of that function could then continue on to other selection menus, commands, or programs.

When a breakpoint is reached, the screen shown in Figure 45.23 is displayed. It identifies the service that created the breakpoint and provides access to other dialog test services as well as the option to continue execution (option G). The options to access variables and table entries can be used to examine the application's data. Function pool variables (whether implicitly defined or defined using VDEFINE) would be added to the display of variables shown earlier in option 7.3.

While execution is halted at a breakpoint, traces and breakpoints can be added, removed, or changed dynamically to affect the rest of the dialog test. Option 7.5 can be used to access the log data set to view error messages and trace output. When necessary, option C can be used to cancel the dialog test without running through the rest of the application.

```
------------------- INVOKE DIALOG FUNCTION/SELECTION PANEL ----------------
COMMAND ===>


INVOKE SELECTION PANEL:
         PANEL  ===> examples_            OPT   ===>

INVOKE COMMAND:
         CMD   ===>

         LANG  ===>                       (APL or blank)

         MODE  ===>                       (LINE, FSCR, or blank)

INVOKE PROGRAM:
         PGM   ===>                       PARM  ===>

         MODE  ===>                       (LINE, FSCR, or blank)

NEWAPPL       ===> NO                  ID    ===>

NEWPOOL       ===> NO                  PASSLIB  ===> NO
```

Figure 45.22 Invoking a selection panel.

```
BREAKPOINT PRIMARY OPTION PANEL - AFTER DISPLAY ----------------------------
OPTION ===>


   1  FUNCTIONS        - Invoke dialog function/selection panels
   2  PANELS           - Display panels
   3  VARIABLES        - Display/set variable information
   4  TABLES           - Display/modify table information
   5  LOG              - Browse ISPF log
   6  DIALOG SERVICES  - Invoke dialog services
   7  TRACES           - Specify trace definitions
   8  BREAKPOINTS      - Specify breakpoint definitions
   T  TUTORIAL         - Display information about Dialog Test
   G  GO               - Continue execution from breakpoint
   C  CANCEL           - Cancel dialog test


CURRENT STATUS:
  APPLICATION: ISR           FUNCTION: EXAMPLES
  BREAKPOINT : ISPEXEC  DISPLAY  PANEL(EXAMPLE1)

  RETURN CODE ===> 0
```

Figure 45.23 Dialog test options following a breakpoint.

Basic Jobcard
Parameters

Basic Syntax Rules

The typical JCL statement starts with a pair of slashes in columns one and two. In a jobcard, that's immediately followed by the jobname. The operation field on a jobcard is the word JOB. It follows the jobname and is separated from all other parameters by at least one space. All other jobcard parameters are separated from each other using a comma. The comma is used to signify continuation of the JCL statement, including when the statement is continued onto a subsequent line. A continued jobcard statement will have slashes in columns one and two, with the first parameter on the line starting in columns three through sixteen, inclusive. The end of the jobcard is indicated by a parameter followed by a space (rather than by a comma). Any information following a space is treated as a comment, including when the space follows a comma:

```
//jobname JOB parameter1,parameter2, comment
//    parameter3,parameter4 comment
```

Jobname

The jobname is formed according to the rules for a simple name, just like the qualifiers in a data set name. The jobname might, however, have certain restrictions at a given installation. Many installations impose restrictions on the jobname to make it easier to relate a particular batch job to the TSO user who submitted it. It's therefore common practice to use the TSO user-id in developing the jobname. Most restrict the TSO user-id to be less than eight characters so that any jobname can use the last available character to uniquely identify the job. In that way, a letter or number (or @, #, or $) can be added to the end of the jobname to allow up to 39 different jobnames. In many cases, when the last character is a letter or number, ISPF will automatically increment the letter or number each time the jobcard is used.

Account and Programmer Name Parameters

The jobcard has two fields that are known as positional parameters. That means that their position in the statement uniquely identifies their use, and so they must be coded in order before any other parameters. The first parameter is typically used to communicate account information and has a format that's specific to each installation. An account number that's used in many of the examples (TSO12349999) will be used here. The second positional parameter is the programmer name field. It's not typically regulated as closely as the account field, which might have to match system-defined information before the job will run. The programmer name field will typically contain the name of the person submitting the job and perhaps information that will help in contacting that person if necessary. Some installations prescribe that the 20 bytes of information be used instead to describe the job's function. If the information contains embedded spaces, single quotes should be used. The quotes don't count toward the 20 bytes of information that the field is allowed:

```
//TSO1234A JOB (TSO1234999),'SAMPLE JOBSTREAM',
//    parameter3,parameter4 comment
```

Jobcard Keyword Parameters

In addition to the two positional parameters, the jobcard is made up of keyword parameters. These parameters are usually optional either because the feature provided need not be included or because a default value will be applied if the parameter is omitted. Keyword parameters can be specified in any order since the name of the parameter is always specified and equated to some value (using an equal sign). The following common keywords are presented in order of their expected frequency of use within ISPF-generated batch jobs.

CLASS is a keyword that indicates the input class that the job is to run in. Input class assignments are installation specific, using letters and numbers to represent the different job classes. Job classes are often assigned by the amount of resource a job will consume.

MSGCLASS is a keyword that indicates the output class that certain job messages are to be written to. This is the same output class designator that's used to direct other print output. Output class assignments are also installation specific and, like the CLASS parameter, use letters and numbers to represent the different output classes.

```
//TSO1234A JOB (TSO1234999),'SAMPLE JOBSTREAM', THIS IS A COMPLETE BASIC
//    CLASS=A,MSGCLASS=H        JOBCARD FOR MOST INSTALLATIONS
```

TIME is a keyword that's used to request CPU time. The TIME keyword is only required when the default is not sufficient and at some installations where the time limit's not built into the input class. The time parameter has subparameters to account for both minutes and seconds in that order. A comma is used to separate the seconds from the minutes, as in TIME=(3,30). It's also used to indicate the absence of minutes, as in TIME=(,30). Parentheses are not required when only minutes are specified, as in TIME=3.

REGION is a keyword that's used to request memory. The keyword is only required when the system default is not sufficient. Memory is requested as a numeric value in kilobytes (K) or megabytes (M). The parameters REGION=2048K and RE-GION=2M both ask for the same amount of storage.

NOTIFY is a keyword that requests notification at job termination. NOTIFY=TSO1234 requests that a message be sent to userid TSO1234 when the job terminates. JCL errors and ABENDS encountered during execution might also be noted in the text sent:

```
//TSO1234A JOB (TSO1234999),'SAMPLE JOBSTREAM', THIS JOBCARD HAS KEYWORDS
//       CLASS=A,MSGCLASS=H,              ADDED FOR TIME MEMORY AND
//       TIME=(1,30),REGION=2048K,NOTIFY=TSO1234 END OF JOB NOTIFICATION
```

Comment Lines

Comment lines are started with the characters //* in columns one through three. In this case, the entire line is treated as a comment (rather than just the end of the line, as in previous examples). Many of the jobcard fields on ISPF screens will be marked in this way until the line is used for valid jobcard information. This should not be confused with lines that start with /* to designate a JES (Job Entry Subsystem) statement. JES statements can be added after normal jobcard lines to determine things like job and print routing as well as print characteristics. In most cases, it's also possible to leave the last lines of the jobcard fields (on ISPF screens) blank. ISPF will not include those blank lines, which would otherwise cause a JCL error.

Sample Edit Macro

Edit macros use a special element of the ISPF dialog management language that provides access to editor primary and line command functions. These can then be assembled in programmatic fashion with other statements from the host language (like CLIST or REXX). The result can be used to automate edit command sequences or, as in the example presented here, create functions that are not currently available to the ISPF editor.

The following is a CLIST edit macro called SCRATCH that can be used from an edit session to delete the member currently being edited. The edit macro captures the name of the member and data set being edited and then uses library management facilities to delete the member. The appropriate message is set depending upon whether or not the process was successful. Cancel is used to end the macro so the member is not written back to disk:

```
ISREDIT MACRO
CONTROL END(ENDO)
ISPEXEC CONTROL ERRORS RETURN
ISREDIT (MEMBER) = MEMBER
IF &LENGTH(&MEMBER) = 0 THEN +
  DO
    SET &ZERRHM = ISR00000
    SET &ZERRSM = SCRATCH NOT ALLOWED
    SET &ZERRLM = SCRATCH CAN ONLY BE USED FROM WITHIN A PDS
    ISPEXEC SETMSG MSG(ISRZ002)
    EXIT
  ENDO
ISREDIT (DSN) = DATASET
ISPEXEC LMINIT DATAID(PDSNAME) DATASET('&DSN') ENQ(SHRW)
ISPEXEC LMOPEN DATAID(&PDSNAME) OPTION(OUTPUT)
ISPEXEC LMMDEL DATAID(&PDSNAME) MEMBER(&MEMBER)
IF &LASTCC > 0 THEN SET &NOT = NOT
SET &ZERRHM = ISR00000
```

```
SET &ZERRSM = MEMBER &NOT DELETED
SET &ZERRLM = MEMBER &MEMBER WAS &NOT DELETED FROM DATA SET &DSN
ISPEXEC SETMSG MSG(ISRZ002)
ISPEXEC LMCLOSE DATAID(&PDSNAME)
ISPEXEC LMFREE DATAID(&PDSNAME)
ISREDIT CAN
```

The data set containing the edit macro member called SCRATCH should be allocated to the file SYSPROC as described in chapter 42. The edit macro would be invoked from the primary command area as shown in Figure B.1. The macro is only designed to delete the active member. It can't be used to delete a sequential data set.

After the edit macro is executed, the member has been deleted and the previous screen is displayed (Figure B.2). The message set from within the macro is displayed in the short message area of the screen.

```
EDIT ---- TSO1234.EXAMPLE.DATA(BLKSIZE) - 01.04 ------------- COLUMNS 001 072
COMMAND ===> scratch_                                        SCROLL ===> CSR
****** *************************** TOP OF DATA ***************************
000001 -----------------------------------------------------------------
000002                        Block Size Chart              |
000003                                                      |
000004 -------------------------------------------------------------------
000005       | 3380           | Device             | 3390
000006       |                | Blocks Per         |
000007       | Min.|   Max.   |   Track            | Min.  |  Max.
000008       |_____|_____|_____|_____|_____
000009 | 23477 |  47476   |     1          | 27999 |  56664
000010 | 15477 |  23476   |     2          | 18453 |  27998
000011 | 11477 |  15476   |     3          | 13683 |  18452
000012 |  9077 |  11476   |     4          | 10797 |  13682
000013 |  7477 |   9076   |     5          |  8907 |  10796
000014 |  6357 |   7476   |     6          |  7549 |   8906
000015 |  5493 |   6356   |     7          |  6519 |   7548
000016 |  4821 |   5492   |     8          |  5727 |   6518
000017 |  4277 |   4820   |     9          |  5065 |   5726
000018 |  3861 |   4276   |    10          |  4567 |   5064
000019 |  3477 |   3860   |    11          |  4137 |   4566
000020 |  3189 |   3476   |    12          |  3769 |   4136
000021 |  2933 |   3188   |    13          |  3441 |   3768
```

Figure B.1 Invoking the SCRATCH edit macro.

```
------------------------ EDIT - ENTRY PANEL  ------- MEMBER BLKSIZE DELETED
COMMAND ===>

ISPF LIBRARY:
   PROJECT ===> TSO1234
   GROUP   ===> EXAMPLE  ===>            ===>            ===>
   TYPE    ===> BLKSIZE
   MEMBER  ===> _             (Blank or pattern for member selection list)

OTHER PARTITIONED OR SEQUENTIAL DATA SET:
   DATA SET NAME   ===>
   VOLUME SERIAL   ===>          (If not cataloged)

DATA SET PASSWORD ===>           (If password protected)

PROFILE NAME      ===>           (Blank defaults to data set type)

INITIAL MACRO     ===>           LMF LOCK   ===> YES   (YES, NO or NEVER)

FORMAT NAME       ===>           MIXED MODE ===> NO    (YES or NO)
```

Figure B.2 Result of the SCRATCH edit macro.

Index

ABOUT THE AUTHOR

Kurt Bosler has held a number of training and technical support positions for the past 15 years. His experience includes presenting detailed training sessions in TSO/ISPF. He is the author of CLIST PROGRAMMING (McGraw-Hill, 1990).